Modern
Augustinian
Confession

To Rob & Lori,
Happy New Year &
all the Best.
Peace & love
Neighbor Jim
Giest

Modern Augustinian Confession

Memoir of an Urban Pedagogue, Minister and Activist from Allentown Pennsylvania.

JAMES CURTIS GEIST

To order additional copies of this book, contact:
Xlibris
1-888-795-4274
www.Xlibris.com
Orders@Xlibris.com
747587

#967973137

Dedicated to those persecuted for their religious beliefs,
the twenty-seven million enslaved, those fighting for
fairness in the workplace, and those in recovery.

**What matters most is that I still have, after
all that has preceded, poems left.**
—Charles Bukowski

Life is not a problem to be solved but a mystery to be lived.
—M. Scott Peck, *The Different Drum*

Geist – ghost, spirit
Heilige Geist – Holy Spirit
Poltergeist – mischievous spirit
Zeitgeist – "spirit" of the times

CONTENTS

AGES 30-35 1996-2,000
Part III: There Are No Absolute Answers

AGE 36-45 2001-2011
Part IV. Midlife Crisis: Entering The Cave

AGE 46-50 2012-2016
Mid-Life Crisis Resolution – The Best Years

Part VI: Mellowing (Friends And Privacy Important)

ACKNOWLEDGMENTS

Thanks to Ginny Ann (Mom) and William Thomas (Dad) Geist; my sister, Jody Lynn Geist; the Short and Geist families; and Uncle Tom and Aunt Adele Meyers for sharing family stories with me.

Thanks to Pastor Mike Brogna, the public teachers who loved me, my Sunday school teachers from the Lutheran Congregational, Methodist, and Christian and Missionary Alliance traditions; Nyack College Vice President David Jennings; Dr. John Ellenberger and Dr. Tite Tienou of the Alliance Seminary; and Dr. Edward Nanno.

Thanks also to Rev. David Dyson, the National Labor Committee, Rev. John Hiemstra of the NYC Council of Churches, Sam Hirsh of the New York Labor-Religion Coalition (RIP), Beth Gilinski, WABC radio host Steve Malzberg, A. M. Rosenthal (RIP), Nina Shea, Andy Anderson (RIP) of WMCA radio, Ann Noonan of the Laogai Foundation, Maria Sliwa of AASG, Steven Haas of the International Day of Prayer for the Persecuted Church Nat Hentoff of the *Village Voice*, and David Gonzalez of the *New York Times*.

Special thanks to *mi esposa*, Helen Pagaduan Geist; my sponsor Paul R. J. (Recovery Jesus); my enemies, who helped me look into my own dark well; the angel sent in my life to crush my heart for the many life lessons I needed to learn, to Saint Augustine and to the Trinity.

INTRODUCTION:
WHY WRITE A MEMOIR?

September 2016: My name is James Curtis Geist. James Curtis Short is my grandfather on my maternal side, and Dale "James" Geist is my youngest uncle. I was born on Uncle Dale's birthday on March 2. I was born in 1966 and my sister was born on March 1 four years later in 1970. We were not Catholic, but somehow, my parents must be employing the "rhythm method."

I never met Pappy "Fred" Geist; he passed when my father, William, was sixteen. Grandpa Short wrote a ten-page memoir and reflected, "Why would anyone commit to writing the story of his life? This autobiography may be of some interest to some future relative who may be curious about the life and times of a particular ancestor." Grandpa Short's father did not write a minihistory; thus James Curtis Short spent years going to libraries and archives looking up genealogical studies for information with "less than satisfactory results."

<u>First</u>, I write this autobiography while I have my mental faculties. Country singer Glen Campbell has Alzheimer's and completes his last tour. Seeing him in the movie *True Grit* (1969), it is hard to imagine him becoming sick and frail.

In the last year of her life, while Nana Short was in the Moravian Home Square in Nazareth, Pennsylvania, her roommate was a book author. When I asked the roommate the name of her book, she said, "I don't know."

As I started this book in April 2016, comedian Robin Williams has taken his own life. It came out that his brain was showing the beginnings of Parkinson's and Alzheimer's. I loved Williams for the characters he chose to play in life: Patch Adams, a compassionate doctor; the teacher he played in *Dead Poets Society*, where he aroused the curiosity of students; the doctor who helped patients who have been in coma for years to come out of them in *Awakenings*; and the caring psychologist in the movie *Good Will Hunting*. I miss him already.

Second, I have had at least a dozen students over the years who suggested that I write a book. I have also met authors who have written books, and many did not impress me to have extra intellect or to have lived an exciting life. Fifty years aboveground has given me a few stories, and at age fifty, my inner ding has told me to listen to my students' urging to write my opus.

I have no grandiose idea of myself, but I do believe in the greatness God has planted inside me, and I am willing to write about it. As Marianne Williamson says in *Return to Love,*

> Our deepest fear is not that we are inadequate. Our deepest fear is we are powerful beyond measure . . . You are a child of God and playing small does not serve the world . . . As we let our light shine, we unconsciously give other people permission to do the same. As we are liberated from our fear, our presence automatically liberates other people.

The title of J. D. Salinger's book _The Catcher in the Rye_ came from a Robert Burns poem. My favorite poet is Charles Bukowski, who died in 1994 I was going to use the title "The Sound of My Life," a poem by Bukowski, but Modern Augustinian Confession is the correct title for this book.

As a seminary student, I took a few anthropology, missiology, and sociology classes; and it was clear humans wore cultural eye glasses when viewing life. I am a Pennsylvania Dutch (47.5 percent German, 47.5 percent English, and 5.0 percent Scots-Irish). My cultural eye glasses came from growing up in a blue-collar, Democratic, and prounion family; and I became an evangelical Christian at age fourteen, grew up in an Anglo family on the northeast of the United States, and later in life realized I am also a Democratic Socialist.

If I have to pay taxes, I want those paid taxes coming back to me and other taxpayers in the form of universal health care and universal state college education for those who qualify. I am tired of tax money being used by the welfare queens like the military industrial complex and corporations for subsidies. If you study a breakdown by percentages of where your tax money goes to for government services and see 57 percent of your money going to the military, you will be shocked and then angered and demand changes. If you want taxes cut by one-third, take it back from the military and corporate welfare (John Cort, _Christian Socialism_, Orbis Press).

The truth is history and culture have affected my views of life brought out to me by Richard Niebuhr's (brother of Reinhold) _Christ and Culture_. As Father Richard Rohr points out, in Japan, a non-Christian country, you may place your camera outside the Hiroshima Museum, and it will be there when you get out. In the "Christian" country of America, the camera will not be there if you leave it in front of your Red, White, and Blue Museum.

I have found much in my subconsciouswilling to come out, when I took the time to sit with thoughts and feelings while writing the memoir. Of course, the key to good writing is to write, edit, and then reedit what you have written, according to William Zinsser's _On Writing Well_. In the seminary, Dr. William Crockett requires his homiletics (preaching) class to read the book because "most of you as preachers will be boring, so please keep the sermons short."

Third, I write this for my niece Madison and nephew Jordan, for my family, for future generations, interested former students, and those who attend my funeral and think, _I wish I knew James' story better._ Socrates said, "The unexamined life is not worth living." This book called out to me shortly after I hit the age fifty, and the process has been a labor of love. They say most people are not most afraid of death but of getting near death and realizing they have not lived a well-lived life.

Confessions was written by St. Augustine of Hippo (Algeria) in 354. Most pictures showe him as white even though he was African and must be brown or black. His book outlined his sinful youth and his conversion to Christianity. It was widely seen as the first Western autobiography ever written. The young Augustine struggled along his spiritual path, and the older Augustine looked back and found a direction he was unable to recognize at the time. It carried the dual message of guilt and praise. He talked about his sexuality, being a "slave to lust," and being affected by a heartbreak. Sex and Love Addicts Anonymous was also called The Augustinian Fellowship, which taught skills to have healthy relationships with others, the self, and God (or your higher power). Augustine helped set the moral doctrine of the Christian church.

I apologize if you find any spelling errors or grammar mistakes. Feel free to inform me of any errors you may find along with the page number. I did hire an editor, but it is a long book. Should the book become a popular seller, I am sure the next publisher will go through the book with a fine-tooth comb. It is all about progress, not perfection. I have included historical and cultural events from the different decades to help you get a feel for the different time periods, and I hope cultural and historical events bring up positive memories from your lifetime.

To err, to make mistakes, to sin, to soar is what makes us human. I will try to share without purposely or intentionally hurting others and will maintain anonymity for those necessary.

James Geist
You may reach me at jcgAugustine@gmail.com

AGES 1-19 1966-1985

Part I: Who Am I?

<u>Hometown, Family, Schooling, Sports, Hunting, and Mack Trucks</u>

CHAPTER 1

Growing Up in Allentown, Pennsylvania, 1966–71 (Ages 1–5)

MARCH 2, 1966: The average home was $3,840, the average price of cars was $2,650, and gasoline was 32¢ a gallon. The U.S. population was 195 million. The miniskirt was taking off; and on the radio, you would hear the Rolling Stones' "Under My Thumb," "Yesterday" and "Revolver" by the Beatles, and "Pet Sounds" by the Beach Boys. In the month of March, two hundred thousand protests took place around the world against the Vietnam War, Ronald Reagan was elected governor of California, and the Black Panthers have formed in Oakland. The Space Race was on between the United States and the USSR as to who would get to the moon first. The country was still healing from the assassination of JFK—the smart, young, and hopeful president. Then an ex-marine killed fourteen and injured thirty-one at the University of Texas, cigarette packages now had warning labels on them, and the Supreme Court upheld the Miranda rights. And on March 2, 1966, James Curtis Geist was born in Allentown, Pennsylvania, to Virginia Ann Short-Geist and William Thomas Geist. His sister, Jody, was born four years later in 1970.

EIGHTH STREET APARTMENT, DOWNTOWN ALLENTOWN, PENNSYLVANIA: The apartment was on Eighth Street between Allen and Tilghman Streets. Dad was gone most of the day working, and sometimes Mom watched me, or Nana Short watched me, or some nice ladies at some local church watched me. Dad came home in his blue jeans and blue-collar shirt. Bill and Ginny had me right out of high school, nineteen-year-old kids trying to make ends meet. Dad worked at Mack Trucks until the layoff. He worked two jobs; one was at Bethlehem Steel, from where he came home, and Mom would have a bagged lunch for him to run off to his other job at Laneco Food Store, where he worked at the deli until he got called back to Mack's. He also was a driver for a vending company, which treated him well. He also used to be a deliveryman for Anchor Lumber, but the greedy boss would always take out a half hour every day on his paycheck even though he ate his brown-bag lunch while driving.

Dad met Mom at Allen High School. She worked at Mary Ann Donuts for a few months. Dad worked at Sewards, where he made burgers and steak sandwiches. When they met, Ginny was shy, but Bill figured after some time how to get the shy girlfriend to come out of her shell. Dad drove to Congress Street to pick up Ginny for school for a while, until he got her to school late a few times. Ginny was an excellent student and did well academically. Bill was a "good-time Charlie," who would rather play sports and work to make money for clothing and other goods than keep his head in the books. They dated for a while, and Mom ended up in the family way, and they married in the summer of 1965. In Ginny's parents new home at 1950 Linden Street in Whitehall was a picture of Dad in his graduation gown and cap, holding his diploma over a grill, cooking burgers and hot dogs.

Sometimes Mom would take me to the Laneco Food Store Deli to see Dad. We would see Dad slinging potato salad, cutting ham, and cutting the cheese (ha!). He would give me a slice of ham, a slice of cheese, and a little plastic fish hanging in a fishnet for decoration; and he would give me a little marlin or tuna as a toy. Whenever he was laid off, he would race to the unemployment office to get ahead of everyone; and whatever job openings they had open, he would claim to have experience in it. He would say, "If they needed a brain surgery assistant, I would have said, 'Of course, I have brain surgery experience.'" Dad had a 1952 light blue Plymouth, which he bought for $10 and had bad brakes. When he would park the car, he would hit the wall at Sears to come to a complete stop.

FLUFFY: The Eighth Street landlady was Flo. She was nice, and she gave me cookies. She must not have baked much because she kept her boxed cookies stored in the oven. When I visited her twenty years later and wheeled her around in her wheelchair, she said I was the best and safest wheel driver she has ever had.

During those years, I used to have a yellow security blanket that was named "Fluffy." I loved Fluffy and took it everywhere, like Linus from Peanuts. I would drag it around, and it would get quite filthy. From the wear, my 3' × 3' blanket in the end became the size of a facecloth. Mom took Fluffy to put in the wash, and it was four or five days later when I asked for Fluffy. Mom told me Fluffy had been thrown away. It was my first lesson in "letting go," a concept I would finally embrace thirty-eight years later.

CHIRPS: Around the corner from us on Tilghman Street lived the Galiano family: John, Connie, Gina, Johnny, and Greg. John and Dad became best buds. They both graduated from Allen High School, were young dads, played high school football, and loved hunting, fishing, and playing softball. They both came from immigrant backgrounds, one German and the other Italian. They both worked for Mack Trucks and, through the United Auto Workers (UAW), were also union brothers.

My parents and the Galianos went fishing together. Connie kept saying I caught a "chirp," but what she meant to say was perch. I like chirp better. John's dad owned a car wash in town, and when the "connected" came to town for a visit, they used his business.

U.S. History, 1960s

1960:   Movements: Antiwar, counterculture, civil rights, Hispanic and Chicano, gay rights

- Election of John F. Kennedy

1963:   MLK's "I Have a Dream" speech, March on Washington DC

- Assassination of President Kennedy

- VP Lyndon Baines Johnson became president.

- The Great Society and the War on Poverty

1964:   Beatles came to America, known as the British Invasion.

1966:   The United States sent five hundred thousand troops to Vietnam.

1968:   Democratic National Convention antiwar protest in Chicago

- VP of Eisenhower elected, Richard Nixon (defeated Humphrey and Wallace)

- MLK and Bobby Kennedy assassinated

1969:   Moon landing

- Woodstock Festival (four hundred thousand showed up, New York State Thruway closed)

Inventions of the 1960s

1961:   Valium, nondairy creamer

1962:   Audio cassette, Spacewar! computer video game

1963:   Video disk

1964:   Permanent-press fabric

1965:   Astroturf, soft contact lenses, compact disk, Kevlar

1966:   Car fuel injectors

1967:   Handheld calculator

1968:   Computer mouse, RAM (random-access memory)

1969:   Arpanet (first Internet), artificial heart, ATM,

Cars of the 1960s

1960:   Ford Falcon, Ford Valiant, Dodge Dart

1962:   Mercury Comet

1963:   Chevy Corvair Testudo

1964:   Oldsmobile F-28 Deluxe, Rambler Classic 770, Mustang

1966:   Pontiac GTO

1967:   Shelby GT500, Camaro Convertible

1968:   Mercury Cougar, Toyota Corolla

Music of the1960s

1965

Petula Clark: "Downtown"

Righteous Brothers: "You've Lost That Lovin' Feeling"

The Temptations: "My Girl"

The Beatles: "Ticket to Ride"

Beach Boys: "Help Me, Rhonda"

Four Tops: "I Can't Help Myself"

Rolling Stones: "(I Can't Get No) Satisfaction"

Sonny and Cher: "I Got You Babe"

Barry McGuire: "Eve of Destruction"

The Byrds: "Turn! Turn! Turn!"

Comedy: Smothers Brothers

1966

Nancy Sinatra: "These Boots Are Made for Walkin'"

Barry Sadler: "Ballad of the Green Berets"

Young Rascals: "Good Lovin'"

The Mamas and the Papas: "Monday, Monday"

Percy Sledge: "When a Man Loves a Woman"

Comedy: Jonathan Winters

1967

Aretha Franklin: "Respect"

The Doors: "Light My Fire"

Box Tops: "The Letter"

Comedy: Lenny Bruce

1968

The Lemon Pipers: "Green Tambourine"

Otis Redding: "(Sittin' On) The Dock of the Bay"

Herb Alpert: "This Guy's in Love with You"

Comedy: Woody Allen

1969

The Rascals:	"People Got to Be Free"
Zager and Evans:	"In the Year 2525"
The Archies:	"Sugar, Sugar"
Elvis Presley:	"Suspicious Minds"
The 5th Dimension:	"Wedding Bell Blues"
Peter, Paul, and Mary:	"Leaving on a Jet Plane"
Comedy:	Dick Gregory, David Steinberg

Television Shows in the 1950s

Candid Camera (1948–2004)	*American Bandstand* (1952–1989)
Gumby Show (1955–1968)	*The Twilight Zone* (1959–1964)
Wonderful World of Disney (1954–2008)	*The Jack LaLanne Show* (1956–1970)
The Ed Sullivan Show (1948–1971)	*Meet the Press* (1947–present)

Television Shows in the 1960s

60 Minutes (1968–present)

Batman (1966–68)

The Brady Bunch (1969–1974)

Rowan & Martin's Laugh-In (1969–1973)

Sábado Gigante (1962–2016)

Sesame Street (1969–present)

The Smothers Brothers Comedy Hour (1967–69)

Star Trek (1966–69)

That Girl (1966–1971)

The Tonight Show Starring Johnny Carson

Get Smart (1965–70)

H. R. Pufnstuf (1969–71)

Hawaii Five-0 (1968–1980)

Hogan's Heroes (1965–1971)

Jeopardy! (1964–present)

Jonny Quest (1964–65)

The Carol Burnett Show (1967–78)

The Courtship of Eddie's Father (1969–1972)

The Dating Game (1965–1999)

The Dean Martin Show (1965–1974)

Davey and Goliath (1960–1975)

The Dick Cavett Show (1968–1975)

Dragnet (1967–1970)

The Lawrence Welk Show (1951–1982)

Lost in Space (1965–68)

The Mike Douglas Show (1961–1982)

Mission: Impossible (1966–1973)

The Mod Squad (1968–1973)

The Newlywed Game (1966–1980)

Games of the 1960s

Rock 'Em Sock 'Em Robots	Sketch-o-Matic	Boggle
Let's Make a Deal	Life	Battleship

Hands Down   Clue   Parcheesi

Spirograph   Bowling Pins   Booby-Trap

Girls' Baton Set   Risk   Barrel of Monkeys

Super Balls   Trouble   Twister

Concentration   Ker Plunk   Candy Land

Wham-O Frisbee   Hula-Hoop   Operation

Old Maid Cards

Candies of the 1960s

Atomic Fire Balls   Bit-o-Honey   Bubble Gum Cigar

Candy Buttons on   Candy Cigarettes Caramel Creams
Tape

Chiclets   Clark Bar   Good & Plenty

Junior Mints   Taffy   Planters Peanut Bar

Pez   Root Beer Barrels Milk Duds

Necco Wafers   Tootsie Pops   Tootsie Rolls

Passing of Family and Friends

Fred Howard Geist	b: 1-10-01	d: 1-22-63 (62)
Barry Short	b: 1955	d: 1968 (13)
George William Rippel	b: 6-14-29	d: 5-19-1981 (51)
Norman Geist	b: 1932	d: 12-21-82 (50)
Ruby M. Rippel	b: 2-8-1902	d: 2-9-84 (81)
Earl F. Geist	b: 9-26-21	d: 3-25-90 (68)
Kyle Thomas Wertz	b: 4-8-82	d: 4-9-90 (8)
Edith F. Geist	b: 7-22-12	d: 7-3-90 (78)

Peter Radocha	b. 1973	d: 1992 (19)
John Gainer	b: 1972	d: 4-3-93 (25)
Mary Grace	b: 1908	d: 4-21-94 (86)
Steve Guthorsmen	b: 1964?	d: 12-25-94 (30)

CHAPTER 2

Elementary School, 1971–77 (Ages 5–11)

MOON LANDING, 1969: I have a few memories of living on Union Street in Allentown. I was two to three at the time, and we lived literally from up the hill from Nana Geist's home. Dad called me over to the TV in 1969, when the United States has landed on the moon. Dad said, "Come over here! This is history! Humans landing on the moon!"

"Okay, first, what does history mean? Second, what is the big deal, Dad? Have you not seen the *Jetsons*, or *Lost in Space*? They have rockets all the time and land on all kinds of moons and planets." The next time the Millers—Nana Geist's neighbors—babysat me, I used their telescope to see if I could find the lunar capsule and see the astronauts playing on the moon but to no avail.

Dad was doing sit-ups and challenged me to do so. I could not do a sit-up. I pointed my fingers and tried to push myself up but could not do it. I think I would be asked to do this when Mom and Dad needed a laugh. Mom watched on TV this guy in a tight skinsuit who sat on chairs, did exercises, and always was smiling and doing jumping jacks and that sort of thing. His name was Jack LaLanne. "You are what you eat," he said. Mr. Health died at age seventy-five from a flu, which could have been treated at a hospital, but he did not realize he was deathly ill.

Dad bought Jody and me a summer ice cream cone from the ice cream truck. From thereon in, anytime I would hear the Mr. Frosty theme song coming up the street, I would start salivating like a Pavlovian Lab dog.

MAGIC CAR: I liked it when Dad would take me with him on errands. He had a 1966 beige Mustang. When driving, he would say abracadabra, and the washer fluid would turn on. I was *astounded* by this! When we would come to a stop sign in a T in the road, he would say, "Mustang, which way should we go?" and the blinker would tell us to make a right or a left. I thought we had a magic car that was able to take voice commands.

When Mom did nighttime driving with Jody and me, the moon followed us. I asked why the moon did this, and she said it was not really following us; it just looked like it was. Dad would have had a better answer. He probably would have said, "Of course the moon follows us. We are important folks!"

A few years later, when he had the Scout, Dad would drive down the hill on Walnut Street. And just before the stone bridge by the Union Terrace (UT) Pond, the Scout would go in the air and create a roller-coaster, empty-stomach feeling. Jody would say, "Do it again!" Dad would do it again.

1148½ UNION STREET: Our brick home had a door and window trims of hunter green and was an eighth of a mile north of Nana Geist's home. The neighbor kid was named Brian. He had no father because his father was killed working in Bethlehem Steel. Their alleyway was next to our row homes, which led to some woods between our home and Nana's place. My family's friendly neighbors were Nana and the Millers. Their split house was the only home across from Fountain Park.

I played in the woods by myself or with my neighborhood buddy Butch. We built forts and made formations out of rocks and sometimes dug out plants and rearrange them as settlers of the Union and Lawrence Streets woods. Buddy Butch and I rolled rocks down the hill, and a big one accidently slid to the right, and it banged into the back of Nana Geist's home. Nana came out and yelled, "What the heck are you kids doing up there! If you roll another rock into my home, I will call the police on you!" I was pretty sure she did not know it was me, but I would have felt embarrassed for having to go to jail for any damage I may have caused to my own Grandmothere's house.

I had a tricycle and a wagon, and on garbage days, I liked to pretend I was a garbageman and move people's garbage to different homes. When I found any gems, I hid them in the fort in the woods. In the alleyway down to the woods from the apartment, I saw small white quartz crystals. On TV, I saw actresses wearing stunning sequined dresses and decided one day I would make a sequined dress for my Mom using the white quartz crystals, of course not realizing, if I succeeded at this, the dress would weigh over eighty pounds when completed.

CORNER STORE RUNS: Mom and Dad sometimes sent me up to the deli up the hill to buy milk. Sometimes I would buy gum, an ice cream bar, or Super Bang strip caps with little pockets of gunpowder that made a snapping pop when hit with a small rock. Next to the deli was a two-story property with a garage on the bottom and a storage on the second floor. It was owned by my grandmother's neighbor Lynford Miller, who was a carpenter and roofer. Inside of it, he had two pinball machines, which he let me play for free. Mom would get upset when I would leave the store forgetting to bring home the change. Luckily, the store owner would give me my change when I went back.

SUPERMAN: One day, I thought I would play Superman by swinging from the third floor window like a monkey. Luckily, Nana Ruby checked in on me before there were any broken limbs. When she asked me what I was doing, I told her I was being Superman.

I lived on the third floor, and I loved the view from my window. I had a nice view of the row homes up the street to the deli. In the summer, Dad would put a metal fan in my window. Butch came over one day, and we had a contest as to who could put their finger in between the metal protection bars until Butch lost. The light aluminum fans could really cut a finger pretty good, and that was when the game was over.

DRUM SET: Uncle Norm bought me a drum set for my birthday. When I visited Nana's, Uncle Norm asked me how the drumming was going and told me to play them as hard as I could. Dad set it up in the basement, and I loved "beating the skins" as we called them in the drumming circles. My drum set lasted for about three weeks before I had put a hole in the tom-toms and bass, and then they were thrown away. For the three weeks that I played, I drummed in my head to the songs of Creedence Clearwater Revival, the Stones, and the Doors. I tapped into my inner Ringo Starr, Keith Moon of the Who, and John Bonham of Led Zeppelin, not even knowing the names of the bands or the members thereof. Uncle Norm gave me the gift to torture his brother Bill because brothers did that sometimes. The other gift was a cowboy hat with cap guns and a holster for the guns. Like Glen Campbell, "I was a Rhinestone Cowboy" without the rhinestones.

KNEE GETS STITCHES: I loved jumping off the basement steps at the six- to eight-foot spot. One day, I jumped with such gusto that I flew about eight to ten feet in the air, and my left knee landed on something lying against the cold gray concrete wall. What I landed on turned out to be a ninety-degree angle of a metal bed frame. When I got up, I felt my knee pulsating. It was not an outstanding pain; it was just that I could "feel" my knee. The left knee area of my pants had a slight rip in it. I took my right index finger and stuck it in the hole, only to bring out my finger covered up to the knuckle in blood.

I ran upstairs to my mother and father, who were sitting at the kitchen table, and one of them said, "We have to take him to the hospital for stitches." Hospital? Stitches? They wrapped my knee with a towel and tape. On the way to the hospital, Dad told me if I was brave and did not cry, he would treat me to McDonalds.

I couldn't remember if Dad took me to Dr. Baush's office or the hospital emergency room, where they gave me a local shot of anesthesia. The doctor stitched my knee with a U hook and a thread. I did not think I was deserving of going to McDonalds, and I was pretty sure I cried, but Dad said my bravery deserved a cheeseburger, fries, and soda.

President Johnson (1963–68)
Domestic

Civil Rights Acts of 1964 and 1968	Voting Rights Act of 1965
Elementary and Secondary Education Act	Higher Education Act
Head Start, Work-Study, food stamps	Medicare, Medicaid
Presided over manned flight to the moon	National Endowment for the Arts

Foreign
Liberalized immigration policy
Escalated U.S. troops from 16,000 to 550,000

DIRTY TRICKS: In August of 1964, the Vietnamese supposedly shot nine underwater torpedoes at a U.S. destroyer; and the next day, three Vietnamese PT boats charged a U.S. ship. Captain Herrick said, supposedly, the torpedoes happened in the dark of night with a really freak weather and an overeager sonarman. The next day, James Stockdale, a navy pilot and Ross Perot's VP candidate, flew around and said, "There were no PT boats. The destroyers were shooting at phantom targets."

Daniel Ellsberg, who published the <u>Pentagon Papers</u> in August of 1971, showed that the presidents from Truman on down knew it was best to negotiate, but the determination to not suffer political consequences outweighed the human costs of continuing. Both Johnson and Nixon did not want to be the first president to lose a war. Fifty-eight thousand Americans and millions of Vietnamese lost their lives. President McKinley did the same thing, getting the United States into the Spanish American War for the blown-up USS *Maine*, which turned out to be a U.S. boiler blowing up on the Uninted States ship.

SUNDAYS: Every Sunday, all the Geists would gather at Nana Geist's on Lawrence Street after church (if your family went to church). The Geists were up on the poor side of town, not far from the Negroes. They grew up across from Fountain Park, where they played baseball and football, swung on the swings, and hung from the monkey bars. Dad had seven siblings, and he played at the park every day till Mom Geist called out "Billlleeeeeeee!" with the emphasis on the second consonant. He hated that. Billy was the second youngest of the Geists, so he usually had his younger brother, Dale, in tow. Talk about being embarrassed or hoping that no one saw you doing or saying anything embarrassing.

POTPIE VS. PYE-PYE: I loved pye-pye, but I was trying to say potpie. I went from pronouncing it from pye-pye to pop eye and eventually to potpie. It took me a while to learn the difference and that potpie was not called pye-pye or pop pie. Sheesh. I also used to call Popeye the Sailor Man Pye-Pye.

Another word that gave me trouble was "whale." Dad tried to teach me proper pronunciation but laughed and laughed and laughed when I said, "Waaaaa-ale." Another time, I was taken to volunteer at a fire company the day after they had a clambake, and it smelled, well, clammy or of bad clams, and I said, "Something in here *shwinks*." I know, *stinks*; I was a little kid. Thirty-five years later, in a Washington Heights, NYC, school, I would have a student, Lucy, calling me "Missss-ter!" She could say "mis," and she could say "ter," but she could not say Mister; it always came out "Missss-ter." I could identify with Lucy.

Growing up, many TV shows were in black and white, and others were in color. I thought that people born before the 1950s lived in a black and white world, and I wondered what event caused the world to suddenly have color. I asked my mom when the world began to have color and saw the look in her face. Was it during the airing of the *Wizard of Oz*, when the movie changed from black and white to color? I was sure Mom thought, *What is wrong with my kid?* My question would one day become a delightful movie called *Pleasantville*.

DAD'S MUSTANG AT NANA RUBY'S: We visited Nana Ruby, my great-grandmother or my mother's grandmother. She lived on the east side of Allentown on a hill and near the state hospital and a huge blue water tower. On the ride home, as we drove down the hill, we saw a nice view of the other side of Allentown. Nana Ruby lived in an apartment complex. Her apartment was a small living room with a kitchen on the side and two bedrooms, one she slept in and the other she used as a sewing room. Mom used to bring Jody and me over to visit fairly frequently. Mom also used to walk down the concrete steps to the freezer in the basement to get different items for Nana to transfer to her refrigerator in the apartment.

There was a parking lot surrounding Nana Ruby's apartment, and lots of trees provided shade for the parked vehicles. I must be three or four at the time, and as the "adults" were inside talking about dull adult stuff, I ran around the complex and eventually started playing with the smooth river stones on both sides of sidewalk. "I wonder how high I can throw this rock in the air." I threw the stone fifteen to twenty feet in the air, and it looked so pretty as the white stone glistened in the air and hit its apex before descending. The two seconds of enthrallment ended with a crackle of the front window of the Dad's 1966 Mustang. Oh boy. Dad was upset when he saw the window, but the look of disappointment in his face made me feel terrible. I had 154 pennies in my piggy bank. I hoped that covered the cost of the new window.

DIERUFF HUSKIES AND THE ROCK (DWAYNE JOHNSON): Nana Ruby lived in enemy territory, the home of the Dieruff Huskies. Dad and Mom went to Allen High School on the west side of town, and our mascot was a canary. Why a canary? Our rivals used to be the Bethlehem Liberty Hurricanes, and the only bird that could fly through a hurricane was a canary. One of the most famous alumni of the Liberty is Dwayne "The Rock" Johnson, who played college ball for Miami, became a famous wrestler in the WWE, became a famous action hero actor, and is an all-around excellent human being.

Grandpa Ripple passed before I was born. He was a pressman, working on newspaper presses. He worked for a newspaper in Kansas City, Missouri, and used to work with John Cameron Swayze. I only knew John Cameron Swayze from a Timex commercial, where his line was "Timex watches take a licking but keep on ticking." Mr. Swayze sent a Christmas card to Nana Ruby even after Grandpa Ripple passed. Grandpa Ripple also worked in Washington DC for the U.S. Printing Office as a proofreader, looking over bills and making grammar corrections in the evening so the congressmen, senators, and committees would have the documents in the morning. Grandpa Ripple's office used to be that of the Tennessee senator Davy Crockett. There was a famous painting of a U.S. flag hanging on a pole, and somehow I ended up with Davy Crockett's famous American flag print in my bedroom.

Nana Ruby was an excellent cook, and she made awesome fried chicken. She stood in the kitchen for hours with her fork, turning over the individual pieces of chicken over and over. There was a great movie called *Soul Food* about the importance of food in the African American community. It was called "soul food" because of the amount of time it would take to cook and the love that was infused into the food for the family. That movie reminded me of Nana Ruby's cooking. She lived in Virginia outside of Washington DC, so she was influenced by Southern cooking. Nana Ruby must love the state because she named her daughter and granddaughter Virginia, or Ginny. Virginia Short is Grandma, and Virginia Geist is Mom.

NANA RUBY: Nana Ruby used to babysit Jody and me frequently. Jody and I fought like cats and dogs. One time, I said, "I hate my sister!" Nana Ruby said, "Jimmy! You don't ever hate anyone, especially your sister! You may not like a person or their behavior, but don't ever hate!" Nana was kind and spiritual. She went to church when someone would take her, but her favorite show was *The 700 Club* with Pat Robertson. She also used to read her Bible and have prayer time daily. I knew she prayed for Jody and me and the rest of her family. Some of the shows she watched with Jody and me at home on College Drive were *Little House on the Prairie* and *M*A*S*H**, which was about a medical unit in Korea during the Korean War. I was sure part of her connection with the show was the fact her son Bill served there.

Nana used to watch a program called *Sha Na Na*, which was a half-hour comedy with an old 1950s doo-wop band. One of the more colorful band members was named Bauzer, and he had a huge mouth. Nana used to say, "I would like to stuff a box of tissues in his mouth." There was another show called *Star Search*, a competition show. It would have singers, dancers, and sometimes comedians competing against each other; and at the end of the year, they would choose the best of the best in each category. *Star Search* was hosted by Ed McMahon, the famous sidekick of the late-night show host Johnny Carson, who used to open the show with "Heeerrrreee's Johnny!" Sister Jody would laugh when she remembered Nana sitting in her yellow comfort chair, watching *Star Search*, moving her head, and banging the armrest with her fist to the rhythm of the music.

When Nana Ruby passed, Mom was with her. Nana was home in bed, and Mom was there for her last breath. It was a peaceful passing, and how fortunate to have a loved one with you when it happened. I am grateful Nana Ruby was in my life and that I am a part of her legacy. When the stuff was moved from her apartment, I ended up getting two bookshelves, which I still have to this day and still remind me of Nana Ruby when I look at them. I will never sell them or give them away.

THE DAY NANA SHORT CRIED HARDER THAN JIMMY: Nana and Grandpa Short were babysitting me at their home on Linden Lane in Whitehall Pennsylvania. They had a porch area with a concrete floor with a connected area of slate and white stone in the back of their home. Half of the porch was covered by a proper roof, and the other half was covered with a canopy with green and white stripes. There was a swinging chair under the porch with several tables to sit and sip the Shorts' famous summer tea with mint leaves in it. Short was an English name; thus they were Methodist and loved to drink tea. I was three or four at the time and playing outside. The metal screen door was heavy, and as Nana walked from the porch to the inside of my house, I had my left pointer finger next to the crease of the door; and as it closed, it sliced a quarter inch of my index finger. It hurt, and I was crying. Whenever that story came up, Nana Short would say, "I cried more than Jimmy that day. I felt so terrible about what happened."

CHRISTMAS AT THE MEYERS: We were at Uncle Tom and Aunt Adele's. It was a Christmas party, and the Carpenters' Christmas show was airing. The Meyers had a lovely Lehigh Valley home on top of a hill across from the Little Lehigh River. As the party was in full swing, the men were congregated downstairs by the bar, drinking, playing billiards, some smoking cigarettes or cigars. The Meyers had two German shepherds in the car garage—Heidi, the mommy, and Baron, the huge son. The ladies were upstairs by the kitchen or sitting in a circle in the living room in front of the TV. I enjoyed drinking root beer and eating candy, pretzels, and bologna. Cousin Lori had posters in her room of Donny Osmond, cousin Tommy had a drum set in his bedroom, and cousin Mike had a nice red Camaro. Mike crashed it through the brick wall in the garage one night. Uncle Tom took the view. "It's time to fix the wall."

BREASTS VS. THE OTHER WORD: I was five or six, sitting on Aunt Adele's lap in front of all the ladies, and I grabbed one of her Christmas cards with a picture of an old lady on it with droopy breasts and said, "Look at those funny tits!" My aunt gasped and said, "No, Jimmy, that is a word you should not say in front of company." I felt terrible and confused and wondered why this word was used by some adult men and by boys at school. I slowly snuck away downstairs and thought, *There is much to learn about social norms.*

GOATS, HORSES, AND DOGS: Cousin Laurie wanted a goat, and she got one. It often liked to stand on top of the Volkswagen's roof. On the side of the house was a tire hanging from a tree you could swing on, and next to the swing was a fenced-in area for Laurie's horse. Laurie said the horse wouldn't get up to let her ride it. Uncle Tom went out to use some horse psychology on it, and when it refused to get up, he punched the horse in the nose, and it jumped right up. Ten years later, when he visited the horse in a barn, it was lying down; but when it saw Uncle Tom, it jumped right up.

Another time, the boys Tommy and Mike told Uncle Tom they thought the big dog Barron has swallowed a golf ball. Uncle Tom took his arm and reached down the dog's mouth and throat. Nope, no golf ball.

FRIDAY, APRIL 10, 1970, THE BEATLES: Most people equate February 3, 1959, as "the day the music died," when Buddy Holly, Richie Valens, the Big Bopper, two rockabilly musicians, and a famous DJ died in an airplane crash. Many say the Beatles are instrumental in introducing a new style of rock music to the world, and many fans are heartbroken on April 10, 1970, when the Beatles announced to the world their breakup.

LINCOLN SCHOOL: I attended Lincoln Elementary School for six months before we moved to the west end of Allentown. My kindergarten teacher's name was Ms. Frey. Aunt Arlene, Uncle Jack, and my three cousins Sandy, Donna, and Brenda lived next to the school playground. For years, Brenda was my "girlfriend," and we were kissing cousins in our early years. I also had a crush on a girl named Lisa, who had long reddish hair, and I held her hand by the kindergarten room next to the school library. Nana's neighbor Carol Miller served as a school aide there. I moved to a new part of the world to Union Terrace about three miles away.

AFRAID OF HEIGHTS: For my parents, it must have been nice to have a driveway to park in. At the Union Street row home, there was a parking spot behind a retaining wall of about twenty feet high on a dirt road on the side of a hill. Dad tried to get me to jump off it into his arms, but I was afraid to jump because I did not have wings and did not want to break a leg or crack my skull. Down the street was a small open pit next to a car garage where an old lady had fallen into and actually did die from a fractured skull. I saw the bloodstains as a kid at age five. There also was a warehouse down from us that caught on fire, and Uncle Fritz's picture was in the *Morning Call* newspaper, next to a person in an ambulance cart covered in a blanket at the fire in Neuweiler Brewery, next to Nana Geist's home.

COUSIN BRYAN; *QUINCY M.E.*; AND TROPICAL FISH: Catty-corner to the school on Fifteenth Street lived Uncle Fritz, Aunt Rita, and cousins Bryan and Sherry. They all had red hair, so I had a close connection with my ginger family members. My hair was not flaming red and has lightened with time. I guess I am more a strawberry blond today. I used to sleep over at Bryan's. We watched *Quincy, M.E.* when it was on; it was Bryan's favorite TV show.

Mom and Dad had a ten-gallon fish tank. In time, I was responsible for cleaning the tank twice a year. I also bought new fish when they died. I loved angelfish, kuhli loaches, and neon tetras. Cousin Bryan was into fish tanks, and we swapped fishy-fishy tank ideas.

Sometimes Bryan and I would sit on his front concrete porch steps by the corner traffic light at Union Street and Fifteenth Street. As goofs, just before the red light changed green, Bryan and I would stand up and point at the sky like we saw a UFO, and people would start looking up at the sky to see what they thought we were seeing. Another time, their neighbors had moved, and the landlord hired Bryan and me to help clean up the apartment. I made $20 for four hours of work. I also found two autographs by the great Philadelphia Flyers hockey winger Reggie Leach, known as the Rifle.

LUMPY'S BAR: Across the street from Bryan's was a small bar on Fifteenth Street called Lumpy Lou's Bar and Grill, where Dad sometimes went after work with some Mack coworkers. One of them lived in our neighborhood, and sometimes they would race home to see who could get home first. Dad would shake his head as he said, "We are lucky we never were pulled over by the cops, speeding and with alcohol on our breaths."

UNION TERRACE ELEMENTARY GYMNASIUM: For me, the U.T.Elementary School is fun.. I feel blessed to have been able to go to school with many mates for seven years, some for ten years, and some for thirteen years. In total, 186 days × 13 years mean living with someone for 6.5 years full time. I find most of the teachers there to be loving and encouraging. It has been fun working on projects together, eating lunch together, taking gym classes together, and playing kickball, wiffle ball, football, dodgeball, track meets, etc.

PRINCIPAL WAGNER: We had special programs, and we had to greet the principal in unison. She would say hello to us children. "Heelllllloooooo, Miiiisssssss Waaaaaggggggnnnnnerrrrrr," would be the annoyed six-second response from "the children." We would have to repeat this exercise three to four times until we could say it with appropriate enthusiasm.

Every year, the "animal guy," like Marlin Perkins and sidekick Jim Fowler from *Mutual of Omaha's Wild Kingdom*, came to show off small wildcats, opossums, sloths, snakes, etc. We had plays we attended, and I was pretty good at spelling games, reading, and bingo games. Once, a mime came to our gym who was trained by Marcel Marceau, and the show was entertaining yet annoying. I should have made crying mime faces and the thumbs-down signs as he preformed.

NOTE TO PROPERTY TAXPAYERS OF ALLENTOWN, 1970–1984: *Thank you for paying your taxes so I can receive a lovely education.* I do think schools should be paid for based on income tax versus property tax. No old person should ever be kicked out of their home because they can no longer pay their property taxes. If public education were paid for by income taxes, retired people would get a break from paying school taxes as they should. For more information, google www.PTCC.us or the Pennsylvania Taxpayers Cyber Coalition and their support of the Property Tax Independence Act (HB/SB76).

KINDERGARTEN: Our class did a play about William Allen, founder of Allentown, Pennsylvania, and his home was called Trout Hall. I was to play a father, and they wanted me to wear pajamas in front of the school. My pajamas were Charlie Brown, and I purposely left them at home because I did not want to wear pajamas. What if my little willy poked out or my tie pants fell down? There was also a bag of items traded between William Allen, played by me, and the Native Americans of the area at the time. I thought I had to pull out the items in order as they were sung in the song by my classmates. It was a terrible experience for me. A little directing advice not to worry about the order of items would have relieved much of my stress.

UNCLE FRITZ AND U.T. POND: It has been a fun day at Union Terrace Elementary. The fire department came with their shiny red trucks, ladders, and hoses; and the firemen told us about how to keep safe if there was a fire.

I was quite proud of my Buster Brown shoes made of light and dark brown leather. The weekend before, I wore them to Uncle Dale and Aunt Sandy's wedding. At the ceremony, I was told by some of my family I was dancing so hard that there was smoke coming off my shoe soles.

School was let out. For some reason, I was one of the last to leave that day. On the way home (a 2.2-mile walk), I walked along the edge of UT Pond. Wet mud and hard shoe sole plastic met, and it was like the pond had a Buster Brown shoe magnet in the lake. In asecond, I was in the pond; but with the grace of a tightrope walker, I did not fall in face first. I kept myself in a standing position. Wow, that was a close one. Well, I was in the pond, and water was just below my knees, so I might as well enjoy it and then walk in it to the end of the pond.,I am having the time of my life when I hear, "Hi, Jimmy!"

As I squinted through the 3:30 p.m. sun, I saw my Uncle Fritz sitting in a yellow Allentown City pickup truck. Uncle Fritz was a kidder and a talker. Darn, darn, darn! The whole Geist family would be informed on the Sunday gathering about the story. "Jimmy, what the heck are you doing?" I answered, "I am washing my bedamn shoes!" And I heard this story every Christmas at our annual party. That was okay because I later learned Uncle Fritz used to sleepwalk to the kitchen in the Lawrence Street home, open the tin trash can with his foot, and pee in it.

UNION TERRACE ELEMENTARY POLEMIC CLUB: I loved debating with classmates about who had traveled to the best places over the summer, which sports teams were the best, or which of Charlie's Angels was the cutest. If you had to marry someone, would it be the art or gym teacher? If you live near Philadelphia, why would you not root for the Phillies, Flyers, Eagles, or 76ers? Some rooted for the Pittsburgh Steelers; okay, at least the team was in Pennsylvania. Some rooted for the Miami Dolphins, some for the Dallas Cowboys, etc. It was fun to talk about music and argue over which rock band was better. It was fun to compare lunch boxes at the beginning of the year. *Planet of the Apes* was pretty big back in first and second grades. Another topic of hot debate was the music of the times, which groups and songs were the best.

Taking class pictures was always a break from ordinary classwork or teacher lecturing. For several of my pictures, my hippie hair was not always well-groomed. One of my favorite pictures was from 1978, at age twelve, where half my front tooth was missing.

UT LIBRARY PORN: Another favorite thing to do was to go to the library and look at the *Sports Illustrated* pictures of all the latest sporting events and the *National Geographic Magazine* photos of boobies of the more primitive or natural or even healthier areas of the world.

The librarian snuck over one day and caught several of us and said, "I knew it!" I wish I had said, "Hey, lady, the school puts these magazines in the library, and I am trying to get an education here, so let's cut down on the judgment please."

MY HAIR BROTHER: Next to Union Terrace Elementary School was a candy store owned by Mayor Joe Daddona's family. They had these great homemade lollipops, assorted goodies, Swedish fish candy and a pinball machine in the back of the store. For many years it was the Ted Nugent pinball machine.

One day, one of my family members said, "We saw Jimmy walking with a cute blondie." This did not happen, although I had no problem walking home with cute girls, but they must have seen Alan Mills, who was my height and also had red hair. The day he came into my class as a new student, as he told me, I walked over to him and said, "My name is Jim Geist! And don't you forget that!" We became friends and to this day call each other hair brothers.

EGG SANDWICH STORY: For many years, I brought in lunch. Sometimes I walked the 2.5 miles home, and sometimes I took the bus for 25¢. Twenty-Fourth Street was a busy intersection and was the halfway point back home. There was a crossing guard there, and I think she was there for all of my elementary through high school years. She always gave us candy on Halloween and at the end of the year.

On this particular day, Mom had made me an egg salad sandwich. On the way home, my tummy started to feel strange. At Twenty-Fourth Street, I knew I had to make it home, or I was going to crap my pants. I made it all the way to Hamilton Park by the CMA church. I started walking down Flexer Street. Just two more blocks. And just as I got to the one block marker on Elm Street, I felt the warmness of the egg salad sandwich's remnant fill up my underwear. I walked in a very funny way for the last ninety-seven steps to my home. It was a fun walk that could have made Monty Python's Silly Walk Institute Hall of Fame. No one was home, so I was able to change and discard the underwear without anyone ever knowing.

U.S. History, 1970s

1970:   U.S. movements included antiwar, women's, environmental, and conservative backlash.

- Bhola cyclone killed five hundred thousand in Bangladesh.

1971:   *NY Times* printed the Pentagon Papers from Daniel Ellsberg.

1972:   Richard Nixon reelected, defeated George McGovern (Jaime Story)

1973:   Oil crisis

1974:   Watergate scandal: President Nixon resigned, and Vice President Ford became president.

1975:   Saigon fell, end of the Vietnam War

1976:   Jimmy Carter elected president

1978:   Camp David Accords: President Carter, Israeli prime minister, and Egyptian president shook hands.

1979:   Shah was ousted in the Iranian Revolution, and Ayatollah Khomeini reigned (52 U.S. hostages, 444 days).

- Disco has peaked.

Inventions of the 1970s

1970: Jumbo Jet, lead-free petrol, Intel semiconductor memory chip

1971: Floppy disk, Intel microprocessor

1972: Video games on screens, stunt kites

1973: Genetically modified organisms, disposable lighters

1974: Post-it notes, Rubik's Cube, liposuction

1975: First supercomputer, first personal computer (Gates and Allen), digital camera

1976: Gore-Tex, Apple computer (Jobs), ink-jet printer

1977: MRI: see anatomy without surgery or X-ray

1978: Space Invaders, computer spreadsheets

1979: Sony Walkman, telecommunications satellites into orbit

Cars of the 1970s

1970: Plymouth Duster

1971: Ford Pinto, Buick Riviera, Chevrolet Nova SS

1972: Camaro, Ford Granada, AMC Gremlin, Lincoln Continental, Volkswagen van

1973: Chevy Monte Carlo

1975: AMC Pacer, Chevy Corvette, Chrysler Cordoba, VW Rabbit/Golf, Datsun, Range Rover

1976: Oldsmobile Cutlass

1977: Chevy Impala, International Scouts

Music of the 1970s

<u>1970</u>

Simon and Garfunkel:	"Bridge over Troubled Water"
The Guess Who:	"American Woman"
Jackson 5:	"ABC"
The Beatles:	"Let It Be"
The Carpenters:	"(They Long to Be) Close to You"
Edwin Starr:	"War"
Van Morrison:	"I Shall Sing"
B. J. Thomas:	"Raindrops Keep Falling on My Head"
Comedy:	Flip Wilson

**Beatles breakup

<u>1971</u>

Three Dog Night:	"Joy to the World"
Bee Gees:	"How Can You Mend a Broken Heart?"
Donny Osmond:	"Go Away, Little Girl"
The Temptations:	"Just My Imagination"
John Denver:	"Take Me Home, Country Roads"
Rod Stewart:	"Maggie May"
Tony Orlando and Dawn:	"Knock Three Times"
Comedy:	Monty Python

<u>1972</u>

Don McLean:	"American Pie"
Al Green:	"Let's Stay Together"

Bill Withers:	"Lean on Me"
Looking Glass:	"Brandy"
Roberta Flack:	"The First Time Ever I Saw Your Face"
Comedy:	Lily Tomlin, George Carlin, *National Lampoon*

1973

Tony Orlando and Dawn:	"Tie a Yellow Ribbon Round the Ole Oak Tree"
Jim Croce:	"Bad, Bad, Leroy Brown"
Elton John:	"Crocodile Rock"
Marvin Gaye:	"Let's Get It On"
Helen Reddy:	"Delta Dawn"
Diana Ross:	"Touch Me in the Morning"
Comedy:	Martin Mull, Albert Brooks

1974

John Denver:	"Sunshine on My Shoulder"
Mac Davis:	"Stop and Smell the Roses"
Gregg Allman:	"Midnight Rider"
Ray Stevens:	"The Streak"
Grand Funk Railroad:	"The Loco-Motion"
Billy Joel:	"Piano Man"
Ringo Starr:	"Oh My My"
America:	"Tin Man"
Joni Mitchell:	"Help Me"
Harry Chapin:	"Cat's in the Cradle"

Bachman-Turner Overdrive: "Takin' Care of Business"

Comedy: Cheech and Chong

1975

Doobie Brothers: "Black Water"

Bee Gees: "Jive Talkin'"

KC and the Sunshine Band: "That's the Way (I Like It)"

Linda Ronstadt: "You're No Good"

Elton John: "Philadelphia Freedom"

Glen Campbell: "Rhinestone Cowboy"

Barry Manilow: "Mandy"

Sweet: "The Ballroom Blitz"

Leon Russell: "Lady Blue"

Neil Sedaka: "Bad Blood"

Pure Prairie League: "Amie"

John Lennon: "Stand by Me"

Roger Whittaker: "The Last Farewell"

Abba: "SOS"

Comedy: Richard Pryor

1976

Wings: "Silly Love Songs"

The Who: "Squeeze Box"

Diana Ross: "Love Hangover"

Fleetwood Mac: "Rhiannon"

Paul Simon: "Fifty Ways to Leave Your Lover"

Boston:	"More Than a Feeling"
Carpenters:	"There's a Kind of Hush"
James Taylor:	"Shower the People"
Bay City Rollers:	"Saturday Night"
Kiss:	"Beth"
Blue Öyster Cult:	"(Don't Fear) The Reaper"
Firefall:	"You Are the Woman"
John Sebastian:	"Welcome Back"
Nazareth:	"Love Hurts"
Seals and Croft:	"Summer Breeze"
Roxy Music:	"Love Is the Drug"
Baretta's Theme Song:	"Keep Your Eye on the Sparrow"
Paul Simon:	"Still Crazy After All These Years"
Comedy:	*SNL* Album

1977

Eagles: "Hotel California"

Lynyrd Skynyrd: "Free Bird"

CSN: "Just a Song before I Go"

Van Morrison: "Moondance"

Steve Miller Band: "Fly Like an Eagle"

Jimmy Buffett: "Margaritaville"

Kansas: "Carry on Wayward Son"

Atlanta Rhythm Section: "So Into You"

10cc: "The Things We Do for Love"

Ted Nugent: "Cat Scratch Fever"

Peter Frampton: "I'm in You"

Supertramp: "Give a Little Bit"

Firefall: "Just Remember I Love You"

Al Stewart: "Year of the Cat"

Little River Band: "Help Is on Its Way"

Rush: "Fly by Night"

Electric Light Orchestra: "Telephone Line"

Aerosmith: "Back in the Saddle"

Outlaws: "Hurry Sundown"

Comedy: Steve Martin

1978

Bee Gees: "Stayin' Alive"

Andy Gibb: "Shadow Dancing"

A Taste of Honey: "Boogie Oogie Oogie"

Player: "Baby Come Back"

The Blues Brothers Album

John Travolta and Olivia Newton John: "You're the One that I Want"

Comedy: Steve Martin

1979

The Knack: "My Sharona"

Chic: "Le Freak"

Rod Stewart: "Da Ya Think I'm Sexy?"

Donna Summer: "Bad Girls"

Village People: "YMCA"

Gloria Gaynor: "I Will Survive"

Television Shows of the 1970s

Zoom (1972–1978)	*Monday Night Football* (1970–present)
The New Zoo Revue (1972–77)	*Kolchak: The Night Stalker* (1974–75)
All in the Family (1971–79)	*The Odd Couple* (1970–75)
The Rookies (1972–1976)	*The Partridge Family* (1970–74)
The Andy Williams Show (1976–77)	*Rhoda* (1974–78)
Battlestar Galactica (1978–79)	*The Bob Newhart Show* (1972–78)
PBS NewsHour (1975–present)	*The Phil Donahue Show*
Project UFO (1978–79)	*Quincy, M.E.* (1976–1983)
The Six Million Dollar Man (1974–1978)	*The Bionic Woman* (1976–1978)
Starsky & Hutch (1975–79)	*The Streets of San Francisco* (1972–77)
SWAT (1975–76)	*Taxi* (1978–1983)
Three's Company (1977–1984)	*The Tim Conway Show* (1970)
That's Incredible!	*The Flip Wilson Show* (1970–74)
The Gong Show (1976–1989)	*Good Morning America* (1975–present)
Happy Days (1974–1984)	*Welcome Back, Kotter* (1975–79)
What's Happening!! (1976–79)	*WKRP in Cincinnati* (1978–1979)
Wonder Woman (1975–79)	*The Waltons* (1972–1981)

In Search Of . . . (1976–1982)

The Incredible Hulk
(1977–1982)

James at Fifteen (1977–78)

Kojak (1973–78)

Land of the Lost (1974–76)

Chico and the Man (1974–78)

CHiPs (1977–1983)

Dallas (1978–1991)

Dance Fever (1979–1987)

Diff'rent Strokes (1978–1986)

Dinah! (1974–1980)

Donny & Marie (1976–79)

The Dukes of Hazzard
(1979–1985)

Eight Is Enough (1977–1981)

Emergency (1972–1977)

Family Feud (1976–present)

Fantasy Island (1978–1984)

Fat Albert and the Cosby Kids
(1972–1985)

Little House on the Prairie
(1974–1982)

Mary Hartman, Mary Hartman
(1976–77)

The Mary Tyler Moore Show
(1970–76)

M*A*S*H* (1972–1983)

Maude (1972–1983)

The Jeffersons (1975–85)

Good Times (1974–79)

The Muppet Show (1976–1981)

Sanford and Son (1972–1977)

Kung Fu (1972–1975)

The Life and Times of Grizzly Adams (1977–78)

Movies of the 1970s

4-1970 (Prenursery school):	*The Aristocats* (cartoon) *MASH, Patton, Love Story, Woodstock*
5-1971 (Nursery school):	*Fiddler on the Roof, Willy Wonka & the Chocolate Factory*

6-1972 (Kindergarten):	*The Godfather, Deliverance, The Cowboys, The Candidate*
7-1973 (First grade):	*American Graffiti, The Exorcist, The Sting, The Wicker Man, Papillon, Serpico*
8-1974 (Second grade):	*Young Frankenstein, The Godfather Part II, Blazing Saddles*
9-1975 (Third grade):	*Jaws, The Rocky Horror Picture Show, One Flew over the Cuckoo's Nest, Dog Day Afternoon, Monty Python and the Holy Grail*
10-1976 (Fourth grade):	*Network, Rocky, Taxi Driver, The Omen, All the President's Men,*
11-1977 (Fifth grade):	*Star Wars, Close Encounters of the Third Kind, Annie Hall, Smokey and the Bandit*
12-1978 (Sixth grade):	*Superman, Grease, The Deer Hunter, Animal House, Halloween*
13-1979 (Seventh grade):	*Alien, The Warriors, 10, Mad Max, Apocalypse Now, Norma Rae, The China Syndrome*

Games of the 1970s

Pay Day	Jaws	Evel Knievel Stunt Cycle
Connect Four	Rebound	Stratego
Perfection	General Hospital	Tank Battle

Dungeons & Dragons	Crossfire	Electronic Football
Atari Pong	Rook Cards	Big Wheel
Coleco Electronic Quarterback		

Pinball Games of the 1970s

Evel Knievel	The Hulk	Captain Fantastic
Charlie's Angels	Nugent	Six Million Dollar Man
Saturday Night Fever	Kiss	Dolly Parton
Playboy	Elvira	James Bond
Star Trek	Elvis	Addams Family

Candies of the 1970s

100 Grand Bar	Blow Pops	Candy Necklace
Dubble Bubble	Fruit Stripe	Hershey's Special Dark Bar
Kit Kat	Lemonheads	Jawbreakers
Rolo	Red Hots	Sugar Daddy
Swedish Fish	Wax Lips	York Peppermint Patties

1970 - BABY JODY: My sister Jody was born on 1970. I was not sure how to feel about this. I guess it was okay even though considering the attention given to me would be cut in half.. She sure got a lot of attention from Mom, the grandparents, and other family members. She had blond hair and cried loudly. Everyone asked if I was happy to have a sister, and I gave an obligatory yes, but time would tell. We fought like cats and dogs for our elementary school years, but from college on, we have become best friends, and I am grateful to have her in my life.

When my folks pass into eternity, she will be my connection to the family memories.

MY FIRST DAY AT UT (1971): There were two kindergarten teachers, and kindergarten class was a half-day long; I was in the afternoon session. I was enrolled in the middle of the year. Mom would drive me there, and there was a long U-shaped driveway complete with the U.S. flag in the front grass yard. The orange brick school had rows and rows of doors in front. In the front was the kindergarten and the first and second grades. The building was in the shape of a square, and as you walked clockwise, the grades went up grade by grade upt to sixth grade.. Above the front stairs with a stone roof was the entryway. As you entered, the inside stairs led down to the gym, the music room, a few more basement classrooms, and eventually the cafeteria.

KINDERGARTEN—OCEAN AND CIRCUS: I don't remember my kindergarten teacher's name, but she was the younger of the two kindergarten teachers. Ms. Magilicutty (fake name) asked us to bring "smocks" to class. We students asked our fathers for an old shirt they could do without, and we covered our smocks in watercolors and paint. Smock was my favorite character on *Star Trek*. It was not until years later I realized it was pronounced Spock.

One of my favorite projects was about the ocean. We had paper, pencils, markers, crayons, paints, scissors, and the bottled glue that Drew and Albert enjoyed eating. Ewe, My poster had all kinds of ocean fish in it. Our class had a beach day once, and we dressed up in our swimming gear, and we brought different kinds of food to the event—tuna, crab, crackers, pretzels, and chips.

On a New Jersey Shore trip with Mom and Dad, we ate at a seafood place by the water; and as I was eating my flounder and scallops, I wondered if their brothers and sisters were swimming nearby. I kept looking at the water, waiting for Flipper, the dolphin, to pop his head out and say, "Eee-eeee! Eeee-eee!"

Another project we worked on was the circus. We studied up on it and had a circus day. Each of us was to do an act that was used in the circus. I was to be a juggler. Quite surely, I was not juggling three balls, but I did juggle two, not bad for someone aged five.

Mike Bodner had a birthday party up the street from the school, and I got a kick out of lifting up the girls' skirts by sneaking up from behind and loved having them chase me.

PUPPY LOVE: One day in the middle of class, a young lady was brought into the room and introduced by the teacher. She had long black hair, and was she cute! I was in love, puppy love anyway. We were sitting in a circle, and she introduced herself, "My name is Elizabeth Silon," and I was smitten. She was a Russian Scottish mix, I would find out twenty years later. She sat down, and I got up from my crossed-leg sitting position, moved over to where she was sitting, pushed the boy sitting by her, and sat right next to her. Long story short, I had a crush on this young lady from kindergarten all the way through high school and never asked her out. I was bashful around girls. In fifth grade, Liz took one of her school pictures, tore it up, and threw it in the garbage. I waited till lunch and picked up all the pieces, and when I got home, I taped them up and saved the picture until I gave it back to her two decades later.

There was a young Asian American girl in class, and one day, the teacher informed us she has been in a car accident and was hurt. We made up a big card, and all signed it. I couldn't remember if she came back or transferred. I was very upset to learn a classmate was in the hospital; it was unnerving and sad, especially since I never saw her again.

SCHOOL LUNCH: On the radio daily was the Galloping Gourmet, who read the school lunch menu in a slowed-down voice. I loved listening to him on the way to school, reading the Allentown lunch menu for the day. Favorites of mine were pizza, Salisbury steak, steak sandwiches, barbecue sandwiches, and tater tots. Most of the food was cooked from scratch, and they were excellent.

After lunch, we would go on the swings or shoot hoops or run around like maniacs or play hopscotch or bouncy ball. Next to the school gym on the outside was a small macadam hill. We would bounce a volleyball off the hill, and whoever caught it would become the next "bouncer" of the ball. I could really bounce the ball a good distance. We had annual marble tournaments, and I never placed, but I took pride in my bag of shiny colorful marbles.

MOVING ON UP: When I was a baby, we lived on Eighth Street before moving to Union Street. The 1148½ Union Street had row homes and was on the east side of town by Fountain Park. I attended Lincoln Elementary for kindergarten for half a year, and Ms. Fry was my teacher. We then moved to the west side of Allentown by Hamilton Park, about 1.5 miles away from Dorney Park. On Saturday nights, I had trouble falling asleep hearing the derbies at the car track. My parents moved here so my sister and I could attend this fairly progressive elementary school called Union Terrace. Half a mile down the road was Cedar Crest College, and 1.5 miles from us was Muhlenberg College.

DAD, CARVEL, AND FOUR NEIGHBORHOOD KIDS: We moved to 512 College Drive in 1972. In our first summer there, Dad put in a walkway next to the driveway. He bought railroad ties, gray walkway pallets, and small white decorative stones. He took out poles with string to mark off the area. He took out the shovel and dug down eight to ten inches, put down some plastic, and then laid the concrete walkers before filling the rest of the area with white stone. For lunch, he treated me to Carvel and bought a banana split for him and me. Carvel was half a mile away. When we came back, as Dad was working, four kids from the neighborhood walked over to watch Dad work. He spoke with them and then asked them if they wanted some ice cream. We all drove to Carvel together, and Dad bought them ice cream cones of their choosing: vanilla, chocolate, or the twist. Surely, it made an impression on those kids; for years, they probably talked about the guy on College Drive who bought them ice cream cones in the summer. I knew it made an impression on me.

COLD BEDROOM: I liked the new home. It had grass in the front of the house and a backyard with a tree in one corner and a tree counter in another with a rail fence around it. It was a ranch home with a kitchen, living room, bathroom, attic, and three bedrooms. We would each get our own rooms. Downstairs had a washroom with a concrete floor, a bathroom but with no shower or tub, a spare room, a workroom for Dad for his tools and camping and hunting stuff, and a TV room with a bar in it. The one thing I did not like about my room was it got cold in the wintertime. With enough blankets, I kept warm, but I hated climbing out of the bed into a cold room. After I graduated from college, Dad said, "I had the heating furnace service guy come over to clean up the system. He fixed it, and he said the vent to your room was closed, which is why you did not get heat in your room."

DJ JAZZY JIM: I had a bunch of 45 rpm records of single songs, many of which came from my parents. I would go to Hess's Department Store in downtown Allentwon to buy the latest hits. I loved pretending I was a DJ in a radio station. The record player was made of white plastic with two speakers and a black rubber on the turntable so the record would stay in place as it spun. For the 45s, you set the player at 45. Most of the 45s came from my parents. For the albums, it was set at 33. Of course, I always changed the speed because it was the wrong thing to do and sounded funny.

My favorite albums are of Tony Orlando and Dawn, the greatest hits of Bob Dylan, and Three Dog Night. "Shambala" is my favorite song. I would meet Tony Orlando's sister-n-law who works as a secretary for the West Milford Township. She goes to the Tony Orlando Christmas show every year at the Sands Casino Concert Hall in Bethlehem Pennsylvania.

FRED ASTAIRE: I had some Walt Disney movie albums as well, which I tap-danced to. I must have been inspired by watching Sammy Davis Jr. on *The Dean Martin Show*. I may look more like Gene Gene the Dancing Machine on *The Gong Show*. I had aspirations to be a tap dancer for about four to five weeks. I sweated up storm and even had the white towel around my neck like the dancers in *All That Jazz* or the show *Fame*, which was about a high school of music and arts in NYC. I think there was even some smoke coming off the soles of my shoes a few times as I "hoofed" to the song "Mr. Bojangles."

HOBBYIST OR HOARDER?: I loved my room. It had four windows on the front of the home and a large one on the side. I had my own bed, desk, and dressing drawer to put stuff away. My closet had clothing, my binoculars, my coin set, my stamp set, and my beer can collection. My grandfather started me on the coin and stamps. I lost interest in the coins and focused on stamps. I ordered them from places found in the back of *World* magazine. After losing interest in stamps, I started collecting beer cans. I must have collected over 250 of them. One of the more famous beers was Billy Beer. It was the beer started by President Jimmy Carter's brother, Billy. When Mother Carter would be asked if she was proud of her son, she would say, "Which one?" Before leaving for college, I wanted to get rid of my beer can collection. In the end, I could not even get a nickel deposit for each of the cans because most of them were not made out of aluminum. I had a large green Genesee inflatable beer can about four feet high hanging in my room. I ended up going to a Christian college and took it with me on my junior year as a spoof.

FLEXER PARK: Up the street from College Drive was Flexer Park, where Flexer Avenue and Mosser Street met. It had swings and a half basketball court. There was a kid named Matt who lived next to the park, and he was a year ahead of me, and we frequently shot hoops together. His neighbor was Suzy, and I wished she would shoot hoops with me.

One day, I brought my walkie-talkies with Scott Van Horn. Some kids asked if they could borrow them, and I said no. They said I could hold on to their slingshot as collateral, and when they came back, they would give me the walkie-talkies back. I had my doubts but gave them my property. When the older kids came back and we exchanged our items, as I closed the antennae back into the slot, it broke. The older kids had taken a knife and slit the aluminum antennae so it would break. I should have listened to my gut instincts.

CUB SCOUTS AND VOTING: I joined the local Cub Scouts down at St. Timothy's Lutheran Church on 140 Ott Street. I liked the blue uniform, the Cub Scout book, getting badges, and going to special events. At one event, we made macaroni necklaces, painted them, and handed them out. I did not get a badge, but I should have.

Mom and Dad went to vote for the primary and general elections. Dad took me one time, and I saw the sign-up tables, the voting booths, and a police officer. Some activists were handing out literature in the church parking lot to influence voters. I heard some Mack workers say they liked to wear a big "Vote Democratic" button on their shirt or hat to piss off any Republicans working at the polls. I thought, *What is a Democrat, and what is a Republican?*

1971 - BRIAN PICCOLO MOVIE: In 1970, Chicago Bears running back Gale Sayers wrote a book, _I Am Third_. It was made a movie in 1971. It was the story of him and fullback Brian Piccolo, a white football player, who were bunked together during the summer practice sessions. Piccolo was played by actor James Caan, and Sayers was played by actor Billie Dee Williams. Piccolo made the team as a free agent in 1966. It was about his decline, the discovery of cancer, and the battle he put on after having the tumor removed. He died of embryonal cell carcinoma on June 16, 1970. The movie moved me because it was about sports, friendship, family, race relations, illness, and death. There are more important things than games.

1972 - FIRST GRADE: Ms. Sotak was my first- and second-grade teacher. I liked her because she was a happy person, and I learned much from her, and I made her laugh. I won the jump rope contest in my class, held on the front lawn by the flag pole. In fourth grade, I almost won the Halloween costume contest. I wore a ballerina's outfit with a creepy fleshlike mask. Before the contest, I snuck into a bathroom at the other end of the school so none of my classmates saw me. You should have seen the custodian's face when he saw a young boy dressing into a ballerina's outfit. It came down to two finalists, myself and another. Unfortunately, it was John B.'s chance to guess who was in the outfit, and he recognized my blue sneakers with mustard yellow stripes. Darn, darn, darn! I was sooooo close to winning. I also liked the days when we could bring in something of a certain color and then give a presentation to class. We were allowed to bring in 45 rpm records at the end of the school year, and I brought in "One" by Three Dog Night. One is the loneliest number.

MUSIC CLASS: In first grade (1972), I had just seen a military movie, and all the soldiers were answering their commanders, "Yes, sir!" As usual, I was in the back row of Ms. Becker's music class, not paying attention or fooling around, and she commanded me to listen. Wanting to practice what I learned over the weekend, I said, "Yes, sir!"

With that, her playing of "Jimmy Crack Corn" or "John Jacob Jingleheimer Schmidt" or "Swing Low, Sweet Chariot" stopped, and Ms. Becker—a tall woman with dark hair and in her early fifties—got up from her synthesizer organ and promptly walked back to my seat and grabbed me by the back curls of my hair. She lifted me up and said, "What did you say?"

I said, "Yes, sir?"

"When you speak to a woman, you use the term *ma'am*!" Got it. Ouucch!

ITCHY AND SCRATCHY: About the third hour of school, I noticed my groin area was itchy. I was itching and itching and about to lose my mind over this. It was like having scabies and the crabs at the same time (based on the testimony of a future roommate). I asked permission to go to the school nurse. I told Nurse Ratchet about my problem, and she asked me if my mother had washed curtains with the clothing. The nurse said that the fiberglass in the curtains could get in the clothing and make a person itchy. I said I don't know, but when I got home and asked Mom, she said, "Yes, I did wash the curtains with the clothing." The school nurse was wise probably because she tortured her family by washing their clothes with fiberglass curtains.

1972 SUMMER OLYMPICS: In Munich, Germany, Marc Spitz won seven gold medals as a swimmer. Dan Gable won a gold in wrestling, and Frank Short won the marathon. Olga Korbut from the USSR was a standout in gymnastics. The Winter Olympics was held in Japan, with the United States not standing out in any category. I was seven years old, and my family was driving to Nana and Grandpa Short. The 1972 Summer Olympics was in full swing. On the radio, they announced that the Israeli team had been taken hostage by some guerillas. I thought, *Why would African mountain gorillas want to kidnap Olympic athletes and hold them hostage?* It was confusing to me. Did the gorillas communicate via hand signals? How could they communicate by phone?

1972 WINTER OLYMPICS: The U.S. hockey team won the silver. The gold winners were Barbara Cochran (alpine skiing) and Anne Henning and Dianne Holum (speed skating).

HEART DISEASE: One of the Geist family traditions I loved the most was meeting at Nana Geist's house on Sunday mornings. Having eight pairs of aunts and uncles led to having many cousins. I never knew Pap, my father's father. Fred Howard Geist passed from heart disease when my father was sixteen and three years before I was born. The last time he went to the hospital, the doctor told him, "You have a sick heart and have two months to live."

What is it like for a person to know they have only one to two months to live? What is it like for the family members? I guess it must be a time of fear and sadness and perhaps some anger. If heart stents had been around back then, it probably would have saved Fred Geist's life. Imagine asking God to save your father's life, and your father passes. How will that impact your faith?

Many of the Geists had heart disease, including Nana and Uncle Norm. Stents saved the lives of many in the future, including Uncle Fritz, Bart, and my father.

FOUNTAIN PARK: The Geists grew up on Lawrence Street, on the poor side of town across from Fountain Park and Allentown Water Works. The park had swings, monkey bars, a volleyball court, a basketball court, and a large pavilion with a silver tin roof. As kids, we had to be especially careful crossing Lawrence Street; the cars drove way too fast here. While I was on second grade, someone was hit on the street, whose sneakers flew off fifty feet from the body, and the pedestrian was killed on contact. I was at Nana's the evening it happened and remembered all the sirens and red flashing lights on the police cars and ambulance. I knew the person was hurt badly or killed. It was creepy to cross the street from thereon in knowing a body once lay dead there.

At the other end of Fountain Park were the soccer fields, and further down toward the Eighth Street Bridge were the free pool and two baseball-softball fields. The park was surrounded by a twelve-foot-high cement wall with the Little Lehigh River behind it and the Mack Trucks factory plant on the other side of the river.

UNCLE TOM WORKS ON THE RAILS: Uncle Tom said he used to walk to work and pass all the black row homes back and forth. He liked the way black people talked to each other and even saw a knife fight between two of them. He was never bothered by them. At age fifteen, he got a job working for the railroad. He was supposed to be at least sixteen but pulled it off by looking older. To save himself from walking an extra three miles to get to the job, he packed work clothes in a plastic bag and swam across the Big Lehigh River, changed, and then went to work. Doing this twice a day kept him from walking an extra 6 miles a day, or 30 miles a week, or 120 to 150 miles during the summer.

SNOW DAY IN THE SUMMER: I liked sitting on Nana's elevated porch and on the Millers' porch. I enjoyed sitting and watching people playing basketball, volleyball, soccer, or baseball in the park. I liked the change of the seasons, watching the leaves fall, looking at the snow-covered park, and enjoying the sunset of the spring and summer by the Eighth Street Bridge.

The Millers had two daughters, Dianne and Suzy. They are ten years older than I was. In the babysitting years, Dianne got into kung fu, and Suzy took art classes and made incredible sketches, cartoons, and paintings. One day, in the middle of the summer, Grandpa Geist was sitting on his metal glider seat, and a very young neighbor girl, Dianne, was sitting next to him. He looked at the sky and said, "Uh-oh, it's going to snow. You better get your boots on." Dianne ran next door and came back with a winter hat, jacket, and boots on an eighty-degree day.

BUMS AND RATS: Dad said, when he was younger, he used to hang out with the bums behind the wall because they had always had great stories to tell. He used to go to the dump with his BB gun and his buddy Joe P. to shoot mice and rats. Joe and Bill also used to run around the woods and shoot sparrows and would mark the wooden stock of their guns with a small round indentation to keep track of their kills. Dad used to play baseball, football, and basketball at Fountain Park, usually with his younger brother, Dale, in tow. He knew it was time to come home when Edith called from the front steps, "Bill-eeeeeee! Bill-eeeee!" He hated that.

To get to Nana's house, you had to walk up a flight of cement steps. On the right side of the wall by the steps was a black cement jockey that held a light. On the front porch of the house, which had a metal fence, there was a metal gliding bench and two metal chairs. Upon entering the home, one would see the stairs to the second floor, the television was to the right, and the first floor had a TV room, living room, and kitchen.

LAWN JOCKEY JOCKO GRAVES: Next to the stairs was a lawn jockey, a small statue of a black man in jockey clothes holding a lantern. Originally, they were used in front yards as hitching posts for horses. There were two versions of it, the "Jocko" and the "cavalier spirit." The Jocko version was shorter and clearly a black man. The cavalier version was taller and nondescript or whiter looking. Today the 21 Club in Manhattan and the Santa Anita Park Clubhouse in LA have the cavalier jockeys prominently displayed. Jocko Graves was supposedly the youth who faithfully served General Washington and whose job it was to wait on the Pennsylvania side of the Delaware River and tend to the troop horses and keep a lantern so Washington's troops could find their way back after attacking the British in Trenton. Jocko was so faithful that he stayed the whole night with the horses and lantern and ended up freezing to death. In honor of the young boy, Washington had a Jocko statue made to honor him at his Mount Vernon estate.

At age twelve, my dad bought the Jocko light as a gift for his mother. He grew up playing with white and black kids in Fountain Park all the time, never knowing that this gift would be the cause of controversy twenty-five years later, to be written about in the Allentown *Morning Call* newspaper. It was also said the statues were used to help point the way to freedom for escaped slaves. That account has not been corroborated by historical records. Some people today find the lawn jockeys racially offensive. I find in the story that it represents and honors people of color who have served the country.

In 1992, Lawrence Street was renamed Martin Luther King Drive. Shortly thereafter, someone took a bat and hit the lawn jockey. The lawn jockey was fixed and repainted from black to white. My cousin Bryan spoke to the homeowner who bought Nana's home and was able to obtain it to keep in the family. To me, the lawn jockeys were a Rorschach (inkblot) test that revealed how a person felt about race in this country.

RACE OR ETHNICITIES?: Actually, I hate the word *race*. Humans are not from different races. We are one race, the human race. Now if you want to talk about ethnicities, then we come from different ethnicities. As humans, as communities, we are like a beehive, with each of us playing different roles, but we all have roles that hopefully contribute to the good of the hive, or locally, and of world community. I blame the *encomienda system* for racism brought over to the New World by the Spanish conquistadors. Sometimes I see my Dominican students comparing skin color. "Oh, you are way darker than I am." I wonder where it comes from until I teach a lesson about the economic system of the Spanish.

An encomienda, a royal charter, was a land grant that established an agricultural system based on the feudal system. The upper class had the landed wealth and recruited cheap or free labor to work the land. Those born in Spain were the *peninsulares*. The children of the *peninsulares* born in the New World were called *creoles*. These two were at the top of the encomienda pyramid. The children of the Spanish and Native Americans were called *mestizos*, and the children of the Spanish and African slaves were called *mulattoes*. These two groups were in the middle of the pyramid. At the next level were the *Native Americans*, and at the lowest level were the *slaves*.

As you can see, the lower you go down the pyramid, the darker the skin; and the higher you go up, the lighter the skin. Lighter skin means you are worth more economically. You can judge a person's class and wealth by his or her skin color. Where did racism start in the Americas?

DR. JOHN: The summer counselor at Fountain Park was John Canzano. John ended up becoming Dr. John to thousands, as he became a dentist with a great sense of humor. He called me Baby Jimmy every time I had an office appointment, even into my twenties. He was an excellent basketball player at Allen. Whenever he worked on me, he would ask me questions that I could not answer with cotton, gauze, and tubes in my mouth. I always thought of Robert Klein's bit about visiting the dentist when I would go there. Across the street from Dr. John was Dr. Kistler, the eye doctor. He looked at my eyes and said, "When you turn thirty-five, you will need reading glasses." I turned thirty-five and indeed needed reading glasses.

WATERWORKS AND THE CREEP: In between Fountain Park and the waterworks used to be a large pool of water about the size of a football field, with a fifteen-foot drop and an iron fence around it. If you fell in, there was no ladder for you to climb out. It had goldfish and/or carp, and Susie Miller, our babysitter, would sometimes take Jody and me there to feed the fish. Suzie was an excellent artist and could make a succulent tuna fish sandwich. One day, as Susie Jody, and I were walking under the pavilion on our way to the waterworks to feed the fish, Jody ran ahead of us, and hiding in the corner was an old man who started walking toward her. He did not see Susie and me, but when Susie yelled at him, he jumped and quickly slunk away in a creepy way. Susie saved Jody from a potential pedophile or worse.

ALLENTOWN FAIR: Each year, there is a fair at the Allentown Fairgrounds the week before Labor Day. It has rides, food, and an agricultural area where you can see chickens, cows, horses, and goats. In Agricultural Hall, they have all kinds of booths set up with all different kinds of supplies and contests for the best pies, honey, milk, vegetables, and that sort of thing. They have drag racing there and a demolition derby and a donkey that jumps twenty feet into a swimming pool. They also have carnival barkers with all kind of games where you throw darts at balloons, shoot water into a tube to make your racehorse move, or shoot basketballs into a hoop. There is also the strong man contest, where you swing a sledgehammer and hit a block of wood and see if you can make the small weight hit the bell.

Susie was walking me around the fairgrounds, and I was loving the smells of sausage cooking, funnel cakes being fried, and french fries crisping.

SHE'S A BEAUTY: We walked by a tractor-trailer where there was a freak show going on, and on the trailer was a 10' × 10' painted picture of the "most beautiful woman in the world" that had perky breasts prominently displayed. I could not stop looking at the magenta-colored nipples of her baby milk delivery devices. I was fixated, and Suzy tried to cover my eyes as we were walking, and it angered my animal nature, something I was feeling for the first time. Suzy dutifully pulled me along, laughing, until I was able to fixate on other non-titalating things.

LYNFORD MILLER: Lynford collected antiques, and he had a metal detector. It looked like a golf club with a box and meter on top and a wire to connect to headphones with a plastic saucer on the bottom, which made a "weerrr" noise when it went over metal. You would take the pole, swing it slowly back and forth, and walk in a straight line.

On the boardwalk in New Jersey, there were guys who walked the beach with their metal detectors. It was not about becoming rich; it was about having a hobby, where you may come across something valuable. Lynford would go to Fountain Park across the street and to the areas where people congregated to watch soccer games or the swing area. He would find coins, sometimes rings, sometimes jewelry, or small old metal toys similar to matchbox toys after bending over with a small shovel and digging up whatever the machine had detected. If you would look up metal detectors' best finds in history, you would be amazed at some of them.

Cousin Mike Meyers said Lynford Miller did not age. At age forty-five, he stopped aging. Why, even at age eighty, Lynford could bend over and touch his toes. Lynford was a carpenter and roofer. Dad sometimes worked with Lynford, and for lunch, they sometimes stopped by the bar for a drink or two.

NEW YEAR'S EVE: Every year, Carol and Lynford Miller used to babysit Jody and me for New Year's Eve. They had shrimp every year, and we would watch the New Year's special with Dick Clark and watch the ball come down in Times Square on TV. They had a piano that took rolls, and when you would pump the floor pedals, the piano would play songs. "Downtown" was my favorite. The Millers had this married coupe who came over, and one day we were all around the piano singing the song "She's Too Fat for Me." The Lady was a big lady, and as we sang, I pointed to the big lady and before anyone could see me, Susie smacked my hand, because kids need that sometimes.

I am grateful for Carol, Lynford, Susiey, and Dianne. Susie was a great artist, always drawing and painting. Dianne was into Kung Fu. I did not now many people into marial arts, but especially for a young lady to do so, it impressed me. I am sure she was a fan of the great Bruce Lee. To me, they are family in my growing up years. I still like to stop by when I can. Their home, with all the antiques, makes me feel like I am a kid in the 1970s again.

When they watched Jody and me, some of the shows they watched were *Emergency*, *Star Trek*, *Hogan's Heroes*, and *The Wild Wild West*. We sometimes played the board game Life, and they sometimes would buy Jody and me a McDonald's cheeseburger and fries or treat us to a Carvel hot fudge ice cream. They were always laughing and a pleasant family to hang around with.

TICKLING OR NO COOKIE: At Nana Geist's, the kids hung out in the TV room, and the adults were in the kitchen, drinking coffee or sharing gossip about the family, politics, what was happening at Mack Trucks, or news in Allentown. Nana was a chain-smoker, so there was the smell of coffee and cigarettes in the air. There were always plates of candy and cookies or cake on the round table, with thick wooden chairs surrounding it. I was the only redhead, and if I wanted to get a cookie, candy, or a soda, I had to enter the kitchen to do so. As a little one, Uncle Fritz or Uncle Norm would grab me and tickle me. It was torture for me. I was sure it was their way of showing love, but for me, it was torture to lose my breath. I had to be really hungry or thirsty to enter the kitchen, and I always tried to enter quietly and sneakily and run out as quickly as possible before being grabbed.

WHO COULD SHOW UP AT NANA GEIST'S ON SUNDAYS

- Uncle Lee, Aunt Barb, Barry, Bruce, and Debby from Arizona
- Uncle Earl, Aunt Dixie, and Suzie
- Aunt Arlene, Uncle Jack, Sandy, Donna, and Brenda
- Uncle Norm, Aunt Lucille, Karen, and Denise
- Aunt Adele, Uncle Tom, Tommy, Mike, and Lori
- Uncle Fritz, Aunt Rita, Bryan, and Sherry
- Aunt Carol, Uncle Bill, Cheryl, Timmy, Alan, and Cindy
- Dad (Bill), Mom (Ginny), Jimmy (me), and Jody
- Uncle Dale, Aunt Sandy, Jessie, and Danielle

This meant that if everyone showed up, minus the relatives in Phoenix, Arizona, you could have up to seventeen adults and nineteen kids or thirty-five people. And if the Arizona branch showed up with all three kids, that would make a total of forty-one people, and that was before cousins have gotten married and had their own children and grandchildren.

THE SIWY-BRADY BUNCH: Aunt Carol has Cheryl, Timmy, Alan, and Cindy. The family of Aunt Carol and her second husband, Bill, reminds me of *The Brady Bunch*. It must be nice to have brothers,

One summer, the Geists went to Bill Furlongs place in Easton on the Delaware River. Bill was the step father to the Siwys. They had a boat and went waterskiing. Timmy bottomed out the boat, and it needed repairs. The boat scimmed over some rocks in the low water. The Siwys are a handsome family; Cheryl looked like Cheryl Tiegs, Timmy like Matt Damon, Alan like Patrick Swayze, and Cindy like her beautiful self.

As an aside, actress Christine Taylor, who played Marcia Brady in the 1995 *The Brady Bunch Movie*, was from Allentown, Pennsylvania, and was born in 1971. She married actor Ben Stiller in 2000 and has been in the movies *Dodgeball*, *Zoolander*, and *The Wedding Singer*. Christine (class of '89) and her brother graduated from Central High School.

As cousins, the Siwy kids and I liked to share scary stories, but they loved the movie *Trilogy of Terror*, with actress Karen Black and the little Zuni warrior doll that came to life. They would run around and chase each other, saying, "Za, za, za!" I never saw it as a kid, but I did not need to. They also saw the movie *The Exorcist* and told me stories about it and scared the bejesus out of me. That movie helped me convert to Christ, plus the song by Kansas entitled "Dust in the Wind" got me thinking about eternity and where we came from as humans and individuals.

MY FAMOUS COUSIN CHERYL: Cheryl looked like model Cheryl Tiegs and ended up doing modeling work on the side and has been in dozens of movies as an extra. I saw her play a woman who got murdered on *Forensic Files*, and she was a movie extra in *The Village*, *Hancock*, and *Spider-Man 2*, to name a few. She has also written a book called <u>*Welken's Angel*</u>.

GORILLA STORY: Jody woke up crying. When I asked what was wrong, she said she had a dream that a gorilla spanked her. Sometimes, to get her in trouble, I would bang on the wall between us and then shout, "Jody, stop pounding on the wall!" Mom was in her room one day when I pulled this and got in trouble. We played the games in the car, saying, "Stop looking at me!" and "Don't touch me!" Ay-yi-yi.

JIM THORPE, PENNSYLVANIA: Uncle Fritz and Aunt Rita took me with their family for a drive on the Pennsylvania Turnpike, and as we drove through a mountain tunnel, it made me want to sing the John Henry song. On the way to Jim Thorpe, an Elvis song came on, and Uncle Fritz always teared up when he heard it. As we crossed a bridge, Uncle Fritz asked me if I wanted to stop to wash my "bedamn" shoes. The song "Sherry" came on by Frankie Valli, and we all sang in falsetto. He told some stories about Nana and Grandpa Geist, family members, and being in the military, and I liked hearing about our history. In the town of Jim Thorpe, we stopped to take a look at the grave of the greatest athlete of the twentieth century.

OLYMPIC ATHLETE JIM THORPE (1887–1953): He was born in Oklahoma and died in Lomita, California. He stood 6'1" and weighed 201 pounds and was a member of the Sac and Fox nation. James Francis Thorpe was the first Native American to win Olympic medals for the United States. He won gold medals in 1912 in the pentathlon and the decathlon. He lost his medals when it was found he was paid to play semiprofessional baseball before the Olympics. He also played in professional football, basketball, and baseball leagues. In 1920–21, he was the president of the American Professional Football League, which became the NFL in 1922. He played professional sports until age forty-one. He struggled to make a living after that, living in poverty and suffering from alcoholism. ABC Sports conducted a poll, and Jim Thorpe was voted the Greatest Athlete of the Twentieth Century, among the likes of Ali, Babe Ruth, Jesse Owens, Wayne Gretzky, Jack Nicklaus, and Michael Jordan.

JIM THORPE, PENNSYLVANIA: "Mauch Chunk" was derived from the Indian term *Mawsch Unk* (Bear Place) in the language of the Munsee-Lenape, Delaware, people. Following the 1953 death of Olympic medal winner Jim Thorpe, his third wife and widow, Patricia, was angry when the government of Oklahoma would not erect a memorial to honor him. When she heard Mauch Chunk and East Mauch Chunk were willing to rename the town and erect a monument, she had the remains sent to what is now known as Jim Thorpe. He had been a student at the Carlisle Indian Industrial School in Carlisle, Pennsylvania. His family tried to get the remains back to Oklahoma in a 2010 case, but the U.S. court of appeals ruled in favor of the township in 2014. The Supreme Court refused to hear the appeal.

THE MOLLY MAGUIRES: Mauch Chunk is the location of the trials of the Molly Maguires in 1877–78, a secret society of Irish miners who fought against the injustices and exploitation of the coal mining company against coal miners. The coal region includes the counties of Lackawanna, Luzerne, Columbia, Schuylkill, Carbon, and Northumberland.

The Molly Maguires was a union before unions were protected under the constitution. The company hired Pinkerton detectives to out the Molly Maguires, and four ended up being pronounced guilty and hanged in the courthouse. Alexander Campbell put his hand in the mud, made a handprint in the prison cell wall, and said, "This handprint will remain as proof of my innocence." The handprint can still be seen on the wall today even though it has been washed and painted over numerous times.

1970 - THE MOVIE: The movie *The Molly Maguires* was filmed in Eckley, Pennsylvania, in 1969 and came out in 1970. It starred Richard Harris and Sean Connery. The Irish had a self-help organization called the Ancient Order of Hibernians (AOH), but the Molly Maguires was a secret society. The accused were arrested by the Coal and Iron Police, and they were tried by private detectives, private police, and private attorneys. Historians felt the trial was a surrender of state sovereignty of the Commonwealth of Pennsylvania and that several of these men were falsely accused of murder.

I love the funeral scene in the movie when Sean Connery's character walks to the coffin with the old man and says, "Don't just lie there. Say something! You were always silent! What's the point of living if you are not heard, if you do not speak out for right!" I know my grandfather Fred Geist; my father, William Geist; and my uncle Tom Meyers did this for the workers of Mack Trucks.

VENISON IN THE FREEZER: At Nana Geist's home, I knew exactly where the coffeemaker was because a few years earlier, I took my finger and stuck it in the open socket where the coffeepot was plugged into. Next to the kitchen was the mudroom that has an old-time washer in it and a huge freezer, which, for over thirty years it was around, held tons of venison from the Geist hunting trips or duck, chicken, or rabbit meat that the family raised to supplement meals. In the basement was a huge wooden box where my aunts and uncles stored potatoes they gleaned from the farmer's field on full moon nights to help them make it through winter. They would go out to the fields with Pap in his car and, on the way home, lay on top of the pile of potatoes, which filled up the inside of the old Pontiac as heavy as a tank. Before the gleaning, the backseat of the car was taken out to fill it with potatoes.

JIM AND JODY IN THE PAPER: My family liked to laugh and tease and had a bunch of jokesters in it. My sister and I fought like cats and dogs. I heard my uncle Norm say, "Did anyone read in the paper about Jimmy and Jody still fighting?" Other uncles would say, "It is so embarrassing because the guys at work keep asking if I am related to them." While my uncles may have been joking, I was horrified to hear this. I felt such shame because the last thing I would EVER want to do is bring shame to the family.

MY AUNTS AND UNCLES AS KIDS: For Halloween, my aunts and uncles as kids ended up taking turns wearing certain outfits, such as the scarecrow, the bum, the clown, and the cowboy. For Easter, Uncle Tom took some of the rabbits and painted polka dots on them. For Christmas, the Geist kids didn't get much but appreciated what they got. Pencils, oranges, and one gift you took care of with your life.

Fred Geist set up a Christmas putz, an electric train set with a village and mountains.

One afternoon, when Fred Geist came home, Edith said, "I could not make dinner. There is no food in the fridge." Fred took his gun and went down to the river. It was wintertime and Fred waited for the black birds to wash themselves. For approximately one minute, the birds could not fly, until the water that has frozen on their wings unfroze from the body temperature. In that minute, Fred shot several black birds, and they had some meat for shepherd's pie that night.

Yogi Berra, catcher of the N.Y. Yankees was once asked, "Would you feel nervous if you were in the seventh game of the World Series, and you were the batter in the bottom of the ninth inning and your team was losing?" Berra responded, "When you have a house full of kids, and you have just been given a pink slip from your employer, that is called pressure."

The family fished, and the boys went deer hunting to help supplement the food supply. The family used dogs for small game hunting, and if the dog did not hunt or chased deer, it was sent off to doggy heaven. The Geists had a garden and raised chickens, rabbits, and ducks. In the fall, after the potato harvest, Fred would take the kids out on a full moon night, and they would glean the fields for potatoes after the farmer has picked them with his machines. The kids filled up the car, where the backseat has been removed, and lay on top of the pile of potatoes on the way home.

JOYRIDING: When Bill was fifteen, he would take his dad's car out for a joyride. He and his buddy took the car to the gas station to put in 23¢ of gas so the gas tank register would not show the car has been driven. At the gas station, as Dad tried to pull out, the car went in reverse and knocked over an orderly pyramid stack of oil cans. The gas attendant yelled at Bill, the fifteen-year-old kid, and his buddy, and they peeled out like robbers, running from the Keystone Cops until they parked the car back on Lawrence Street.

BULL'S-EYE!: There was an atomic clock in Fred and Edith's bedroom. It was a regular clock, except the hands of the clock have been painted with nuclear material that makes the hands glow. Dale took the BB gun and, with precise aim, shot off the hands of the clock.

Another time, they went out in the woods, and Dale was about to tattle on Dad about something and started running to the house. Dad said, "Well, I have to shoot him." Taking the gun, Bill aimed toward the back of Dale's head and watched the BB leave the muzzle of the barrel. With arched trajectory, it hit Dale smack in the middle of the head. Dad thought, *I am going to catch hell for this one*, and he did!

RUNAWAY CAR: Uncle Fritz had a hot date and asked his father, Fred Howard Geist, if he could borrow his car. Fred said yes to Fritz, who washed the car, which had a gearshift on the steering wheel. Everyone was in the house except for Billy, who was in the yard and saw the family car begin moving with no driver in it. The car made a right turn across Lawrence Street and jumped the curb. It went between a fountain and a tree and straight toward the metal maypole in the park. Billy ran in the house, yelling, "The car is moving! The car is moving!" Fred, Fritz, and Billy watched the car veer around the pole like there was an invisible driver in it. The car picked up speed and hit a tree instead of the large concrete wall two hundred yards away at the end of the park. The car got scratched, but luckily, Fritz worked with an uncle at an auto body shop and was able to fix all the car boo-boos.

There is a reason they are called accidents, and it happens to all of us.

RACIST JOKES: Sometimes racist jokes were used, including "n" word. One joke I heard was "How do they keep the Puerto Rican population down? They told the blacks the Puerto Ricans taste like chicken."

One day, I was sitting on Nana's porch by myself, and a middle-aged black man was walking across the street, and I said the "n" word under my breath, but he heard me. He gave me a look, and it was more a look of hurt than anger. I would never forget it. I felt sick and dirty inside and knew I had done a wrong.

I hope my life has been a living amends in trying to be part of the melting pot and showing love and kindness based on the humanity of another. I have tried to treat all as equals—male, female, and all ethnicities.

In the 1980s, Allentown's demographics changed as many Puerto Ricans moved in from NYC. It caused tension with the older Pennsylvania Dutch, who were private and quiet and considered cleanliness next to godliness. It was a cultural clash that you could read about in an *NY Times Magazine* article called "The Latinization of Allentown, Pa."

BLACK TEENAGER HELPS ME: One day, I went to the park, and a bunch of African American kids were there, and I asked if they wanted to play kickball. They said yes, so I ran to Nana's and grabbed a red rubber ball. We played on the basketball court and had a great time. The biggest kid on the other team came up for his turn to kick. When he did, the ball came screaming right at me, nailed me in the stomach, and took my wind. I went down, gasping for air, and this was the end of the game. The black teen walked me up the stairs to Nana's and explained what happened. He was a true sportsman and gentleman.

1973 - SECOND GRADE: Mrs. Sotak gave a project to write a story as if for a TV show. I worked with Danny Arkey. Danny looked like the singer John Denver to me. Danny was smart and funny. I enjoyed sitting and brainstorming on ideas with him, but when push came to shove, Danny did most of the work and wrote out the story. I felt guilty for the rest of the year for getting a high grade on a project that I did not put little work into. I guess the lesson for me was that I would get out of something only what I put into it. Danny never made me feel guilty about it.

For Christmas, our class went to Symphony Hall to watch *The Nutcracker Suite.* I liked the music, and when my sister Jody and I put tinsel on the Christmas tree at home, we put on *The Nutcracker Suite,* danced around, and threw the tinsel on the tree.

I think this was the age when Mom read a book to me about the birds and the bees. It showed how babies were made with pictures. "Ew, really?" I thought it was gross, and I would never want to do "that." Dad said, "One day, you will be asking your sister for her friends' phone numbers." Okay, Dad, that would be the day. But he was right.

HALLOWEEN: I loved Halloween and the Charlie Brown Halloween special with Linus waiting for the Great Pumpkin. I even stood in front of the Laneco Food Store and collected money for UNICEF for two years. I liked going door to door collecting candy in my neighborhood. I took the dog, put a tutu on it, and got double the candy.

For school, I wanted to win the class Halloween contest. I dressed as a ballerina, with my fleshy plastic mask, and I stayed under the radar. I dressed in the bathroom downstairs so none of my classmates would see me change, but the custodian walked in and gave me a strange look. As the contest went on, I made the final two. I was going to win. John Bukis said, "I know who the ballerina is! It is Jim Geist." He knew because he recognized my blue sneakers with yellow stripes. Dang! So close to winning.

THE BARBER OF SEVILLE: Dad used to take me to Beaky's to get my haircut. Dad knew Paul Beaky from high school, and he was a funny guy who liked to play tennis. He asked me what I wanted to do for a living, and I said, "Cut hair." Paul told me he had an extra chair for me and that I could work with him. Paul died in a bad car accident not far from our home. I missed going to his place for the barbershop conversations.

SISTER PIPPI LONGSTOCKING: Down the street from me was Teresa. She was in my grade and had red hair. She was a cute version of Pippi Longstocking. Many in the school believed we were brother and sister. I would go to her house, and we played. At Christmas, her home looked like the set for *The Bing Crosby Show*'s Christmas episode. We made up our own Christmas show.

In the summer, we were playing outside when some older kids invited us to play. We joined them, and they took us to an outside stairwell that led to the basement and decided to make us hostages. I did not like the hostage game. The two bigger boys sat at the top of the stairs. Teresa started crying, so they let her go. They kept me for a half hour to forty-five minutes, but it felt like all day to me. I wanted to hurt those guys, but they were bigger, and there were two of them.

The last time I went to Teresa's, we were downstairs, and she asked me to turn around. I did. She said, "Okay, you can turn the other way," and there she was with her pants pulled down. There was no hair there, and her hoo-ha looked like an albino sucker to me. I ran out of the house. Her sister was arrested eight years later for prostitution.

MS. JANE PITTMAN'S STORY: On television was the story of a black woman who grew up in the South in the 1850s and lived into the 1960s to see the civil rights movement. I have never heard of slavery, so when I watched this movie about slavery, whippings, raping of women, the Ku Klux Klan, lynching, voter discrimination, and segregation, I was disturbed. I asked Mom if our family owned slaves, and I was relieved to find out we did not. I could not understand what Africans did to be treated this way in the United States. The following year, the

TV series *Roots* came out, but I was not allowed to watch it because of some of the horrid scenes, like whipping, lynching, and rape.

LEARNING TO RIDE THE BIKE: I have been riding a red bike with training wheels. Dad took them off and took me to Hamilton Park. I rode while he held the backseat. As I started riding from the East Texas Boulevard side of the park toward the Flexer Avenue side on a slight downward slope, I said, "We are moving now, Dad! Dad? Dad?" I looked back and saw Dad standing with his hand on his hips and a smile on his face two hundred yards behind me. He was not holding the backseat of the bicycle anymore. My front handlebars started veering back and forth as I lost my confidence, and I wiped out just before the slide; otherwise, the bottom of the slide would have decapitated me or knocked me out.

THE BANANA BIKE: I later got a yellow bike with a banana seat and loved riding around the neighborhood. One day, I was riding down Flexer when I veered left to get on the sidewalk in front of the Kotran home. My front wheel made it, but my back wheel caught the ramp's flared curbing, throwing the back of my bike in the air. I was driving on the front wheel like a clown in a circus or Evel Knievel for twelve feet when I flipped over the front handlebars luckily into the grass. No one saw me, but if they had, they would have been impressed by the show.

COLLEGE DRIVE NEIGHBORHOOD FRIENDS: Growing up, I watched way too much television. What did I do to keep entertained? I kept busy doing homework, listening to music, and hanging out with neighborhood friends, mostly Mike Brogna. When I first moved to 512 College Drive, I became known as the hippie kid. Perhaps my hair was long, and I wore bell-bottom jeans. I did not really understand at the time.

JEFF: I became friends with the neighbor boy across the street, Jeff Ruth. He was a year older than I was, and he was an excellent baseball player, a pitcher. We used to throw the football and the baseball together. He had a younger brother, David, who was three years younger than I was; a sister, Mary, who was a year older than Jeff; and a sheepdog named Daisy.

One summer day, we went to Cedar Beach in their family car. Mrs. Ruth was driving, Jeff was on one side of me, and Lori was on the other. I was looking at the *Tarzan* book next to me. Lori was cute, but when she talked to me, her breath was so bad. I thought I was going to pass out. Perhaps she had not brushed and gargled that morning, and/or she had eaten a doody sandwich for breakfast. She seemed a little less cute the rest of the trip to the pool.

OLÉ!: Grandpa Short came back from Spain for Fuller Company. He was an engineer, and when there was a problem somewhere, they sent him to fix it. He got to travel the world. He actually had two patents, and one was for a device that moved wet concrete from the ship to the concrete silos on land. In Spain, he caught a bullfighting show, which he did not fully enjoy, and he bought me a big black velvet sombrero with ornate golden thread and beads. On the Ruth driveway, with a dozen kids there, I walked over with my hat on. I took the sombrero, threw it on the ground, and started dancing around it like a Mexican jumping bean. I had some moves that would have made Michael Jackson jealous. The neighborhood kids loved the show and laughed.

SNAKE CHARMER: At home, in our basement TV room were two upside-down barrels, each about three feet high. Jeff and Dave came over to hang out, and I told them I had a cobra under each of the barrels. The best part was they really believed me. I asked if they wanted to see one, and they looked like they were ready to crap their pants. I walked over to the barrel, and Jeff begged me not to do it. I lifted the barrel, and they ran out of the room like bats out of hell. Really, who keeps a cobra as a pet?

BUFFALO BILLY KICKER: Up on Saxon Street was Billy Kicker. He had an elder brother and sister. They had a Saint Bernard puppy that was fun to play with, but it always had a funny odor to me. They had an aboveground pool in the backyard we played in. We ran around, making a whirlpool. Their TV room had a fireplace, shag carpet, and couch in it, and we watched the "after-school specials" sometimes. Billy and I loved the shows *The Rookies*, *SWAT*, *Sierra Madre*, and *Baretta*. Billy and I would play and act like we were the characters in those shows, and it was a blast. The mother and daughter loved the show *I Love Lucy* and watched the reruns every day. We played football in the front yard with my Eagles helmet and his Buffalo Bills helmet.

1973 - O. J. HITS TWO THOUSAND YARDS!: O. J. Simpson was worshipped in the Kicker family. O. J. reached the two-thousand-yard rushing record in 1973 for one season and did so on his last game of the season against the New York Jets. I watched that game; it was exciting to watch a historic event. He was ballet dancer Baryshnikov on the football field, moving faster going sideways than many could run forward. He ran like the devil was chasing him or the police when they were trying to arrest him for murder.

OH MY . . . GOODNESS!: The Kickers have the famous velvet picture of the dogs sitting around a table playing cards. His parents had seen *West Side Story* in NYC and had the album. I listened to this album with Billy many times, never really understanding this Sharks and Jets conflict.

Sometimes Ms. Kicker and my mom took turns with driving us to school. One day, when we were driving, I said, "Oh my god!" Ms. K turned around, looked at me, and said, "Don't take the Lord's name in vain!" Oops. I felt terrible. I had never heard that before, but I never said that around her again. She was a devout Catholic.

NEW KID: A new kid named Jimmy moved two homes away from Billy, and they started hanging out. I was hurt and jealous but was surprised when on my birthday they both came over with a present. It was a stuffed yellow happy face; the wrapping paper was from the newspaper comics but it was the idea that counted.

SCOTT V. H.: Another new kid moved in named Scott Van Horn. "Van Horn, honk, honk, honk!" He hated that. We played street hockey, listened to records, shot hoops, and even set up a lemonade stand. He liked Sweet, Paul McCartney, the Wings, and the Beach Boys.

HITTING PORN LOTTO: Scott had a sandbox, a big green plastic turtle with a shell covering the back, that I used to hide some pornography for a few weeks. I had gone to Nana Geist's second floor and looked through some of the toys. One was an erector set of long metal pieces that you could build, similar to Legos but clumsier. In the box were some ripped-out pages from a *Playboy* magazine with some nudes of actress Joey Heatherton. Who put them there? It was probably one of my uncles when they were younger. It was like hitting pay dirt, "oil, black gold" as they used to say in *The Beverly Hillbillies* TV show. I ended up getting rid of the pics out of guilt and concern for getting caught.

THE JONES: On the other side of Jeff's were the Jones. They had two daughters and a son, Chris, Jill, and David. They were Phillies fans. Mr. J. was strange. He never said hi, even when you said hello to him, but his wife was lovely. Jill was my age. We played kickball, wiffle ball, and kick the can at the Jones' as well. Chris was a year ahead of me, and I got wind that her cute friend Sally was interested in me. I was too shy to pursue anything—my loss. Why couldn't I overcome this shyness with girls? I liked Mrs. Jones. She used to sing to the birds when she hung up the laundry. It was sad when she died from cancer in her early fifties.

BB GUN WAR: Down on College Drive were the Ackermans. They were a few boys and girls. Dad used to say, "Don't ever point a BB gun at anyone. You could shoot an eye out." One day, while playing army in the neighborhood with BB guns, the eldest Ackerman boy was hit in the eye. It turned blue and cloudy looking until it was replaced with a glass eye.

INCREDIBLE HULK: Brothers Billy and Steve Notter were a year apart and lived next to Jeff. I hung out with them after Jeff "betrayed" me. The Notter boys and I watched the *Incredible Hulk*, *The Six Million Dollar Man*, and *Wonder Woman* together. Downstairs in the basement was their father's workroom, with trains, a rock polisher, rocks, a washing machine and dryer, and a seven-foot Frankenstein, which used to creep me out. One day, we were playing with walkie-talkies, and someone started talking to us. It turned out to be Mr. Notter messing with us.

The Notters bought a collie puppy, which was cute. I didn't know what the dog ate, but one day, as we were throwing the football, the dog ran out to go number two, and it shot out like a hose. I laughed so hard that I buckled over, and Steve yelled at me to stop laughing, but Steve was wrong, there some things you laugh at.

As a sidenote, thirty-five years later, on the subway platform at Fifty-Ninth Street, waiting for the A train, I saw the Hulk, Lou Ferrigno. He was still in good shape and was carrying a gym bag.

Next to the Notter family were the Butlers—Billy, Ellen, Ken, and Timmy. Ken was a year ahead of me, and Timmy was a year younger. They had a divorced mom, who worked for AT&T as a phone operator. They were Catholic, and I was told she kept a missile next to her bed. I was not sure why she needed military equipment in her bedroom, but I later learned it was a Catholic prayer book. Ken and Tim went to St. Thomas Moore, which was the Catholic school up the street, and I later learned that the Butlers had Irish blood. St. Thomas Moore held a summer festival in its huge parking lot. I remember winning one of the contests and taking home a cake as a prize. I also played some basketball and soccer in their gymnasium in the winter, it was a break from the winter blues.

EMERSON STREET CREW: Two houses down from Ken's home was Sean Steigerwalt. He was a funny guy and athletic, an excellent football player. We played together at Alton Park. Sean told me about how his breast muscles seem to get bigger during a make-out session. He was a year ahead of me on the Alton Park football years.

Around the block on Elm Street was a horseshoe-shaped street connected to College Drive. On that street was the Medernoch family of Christine, Constance, John, and some younger kids. There were also Frank, Peter, and Gina R.; another house with Mary K.; and someone who was three years older than I was named Mike Palanski. Mike got involved with the volunteer fire company and was probably headed to becoming a police officer. He lived directly behind Jeff's home.

KUNG FU FIGHTING: One summer, we held a competition in front of Christine's yard. It was Lisa Kotran vs. Christine M. in ballet dancing, and I and some other kid who was a bit spastic competed in the karate competition. The summer Olympics were going on, so the neighborhood competition had to happen. We gave scores between five and ten to each other, but mostly, it was fun. I was sure the TV show *Kung Fu* inspired this grasshopper. There was such a craze over martial arts that there was a cartoon of a martial arts dog called *Hong Kong Phooey* and a song that came out called "Kung Fu Fighting"— "Everybody was kung fu fighting. Hah!" At least I was part of it in the early '70s.

NORTH POLE INJUSTICE: As kids, we would play football and wiffle ball on College Drive where Saxon Street intersected with it.

We also played kick the can and cops and robbers, chasing each other around with our bicycles. Mike P. was fast!

One Christmas season, I was invited over to Jeff's for a party to meet Santa Claus. For some reason, Jeff and David got new bicycles, and I received a pack of cards. I was angry at Santa for showing such favoritism. These guys were this much better than I was this year?

BEATDOWN CITY: I was not sure why there was a falling out between Jeff and me, but I could tell you when it happened. I was in Jeff's backyard, and the kids there just started razzing me and were starting to get physical. I got out of there ASAP.

Someone knocked on my door, and there was a card for a party at the Ruths. Mom said, "You have to go to this." I had a *bad feeling* about this. At the appointed time, I showed up to the yard, and six to eight kids surrounded me and started to beat the crap out of me. I was on the ground, and kids kicked me, and Jeff got on top of me and hit me with his right and left hands. I looked to the left at the kitchen window, and there was Mr. R. with a pipe in his mouth, laughing. I suspected this whole thing came about because Mr. R. never really liked me. I felt such a feeling of betrayal, confusion, and sadness.

KENNY: My next bestie from College Drive was Kenny Butler. I did not really know his elder brother and sister, for the brother went off to college, and his sister lived at Villanova with her handsome track star husband, who looked like a model. We played Little League baseball together for Penner's Sunoco and won the championship when I was thirteen.

PENNER'S SUNOCO 1976 CHAMPS: Kenny played second baseman, and I played third baseman. We actually set a little altar in my basement, like the Buddhists and the Catholic Church did, putting two baseball bats on the table with a baseball, a Bible, and some candles and praying to win the championship. Did we win because of prayer or because we were the better team, were in better condition, and had more confidence? I was sure there were Christians on the other team in the championship game who prayed to God as well. I was sure God was more concerned about the Russian invasion of Afghanistan, the taking of the fifty-two American hostages by Iran, people starving in some country, or those suffering from AIDS. It felt good to win and to get a trophy.

Kenny and I hung out, watched the Phillies, ordered Domino's Pizza, and played Las Vegas board games. We even built a baseball dugout with plywood and field in his backyard for wiffle ball games. I called it called Butler Stadium.

Kenny had two albums that stuck out to me, *2112* by Rush and the first album by Queen. The Bay City Rollers had come out with "Saturday Night" at that time—"S-A-T-U-R-D-A-Y night!"

Ken had an evergreen pine tree that grew next to his house, and we climbed it up to the second-floor window, looked at the stars, and had all kinds of conversations. We used to look for UFOs since there was a TV program on at the time based on *Project Blue Book*. We were believers way before the TV show *The X-Files*.

The Butlers had a dog named Benji, and it looked like the little dog in the movie *Benji*.

SAXON HILL SLEDDING: In the winter, when it snowed, we used sandpaper to sand the rust off the blades of our sleds, and we took candles or wax paper to wax them up. We sled down Saxon Hill, about 8.5 properties long. The police put up wooden barriers at the top and bottom of the hill. We would place one sled on top of the other in an airplane formation and ride down the hill or roll over and crash, but with snow gear on, it rarely hurt. Down the street from us was a huge and steep hill behind the Cedar Crest College Library. You could ride your sled almost to Cedar Creek about 200 feet from the bottom of the sledding hill.

There was a family that lived on Saxon and College Drive, and the mother wrote a cooking book. I read it in the *Morning Call* and thought to myself, *I could never write a book. What could I ever be an expert on? It also sounds like hard work. Whoever can write a book must be very smart and disciplined.*

TIME? WINE O'CLOCK: Many summer nights, I ended up playing kick the can or cops and robbers with the neighborhood kids. One night, I ran in the house thirsty, and Dad was on the phone. I said, "I am thirsty." As he was talking, he pointed to his glass of red fruit juice, and I took it from him and drank it. He said to whoever he was talking to, "My crazy kid just took my glass of wine and drank it all!" I ran out of the house to continue kick the can with a little glow on.

LAWN BUSINESS LESSON: New neighbors moved in across from us. They were a married couple with a son and daughter younger than Jody and I were. Our families became friendly, and Mr. Leo Furlong, the homeowner, asked me to mow his lawn while they were on vacation. I said of course. They came back from vacation, and I have not mowed it, and Mr. Furlong was upset. He said to me, "We made a deal, and you did not keep your end of it, Jim." I mowed the lawn the next day, and the grass was really high. I was mumbling and upset at Mr. Furlong, but the truth was I made a deal, welched on it, and suffered the consequences. If I had mowed the lawn on day seven of their vacation, it would have been an easy job. I waited until the grass was doubly high, and it took me twice as long to do it. I learned a valuable lesson that day: do the job when it is to be done, or the job will be tougher later on. I was really mad at myself but projected it on the wrong person.

JODY KNIEVEL: Dad built a swing set in the backyard. When my sister, Jody, was three years old, I heard her screaming. I ran out, and she was hanging from the top bar, begging me to grab her so she wouldn't fall. I said, "Hold on a little longer! A little longer!" She fell to the ground and cried. I felt terrible.

Another time, Jody was sitting on her tricycle on the front stairs made of concrete. She took one cycle of pedaling, and the tricycle tumbled over with Jody on it. She cried loudly.

One morning, I heard her crying, and I ran in the room. "Are you okay?" She replied, "No! I had a dream a gorilla hit me!"

One another occasion,, I was banging on the wall between her room and my room, saying, "Jody, stop banging on the wall!" Mom walked in Jody's room and caught me in my unsuccessful "spy vs. spy" games. I was foiled, and I was also punished, as I should have been.

One of my favorite toys ever was the wind-up Evel Knievel doll on a motorcycle. It had a strong red plastic winder on which you place the cycle and wound up the back wheel until it flew off and jumped off the homemade ramp one would make. Evel Knievel's crashes and broken bones were relived and reinacted all across this great land of ours with young boys and their Evel K. dolls.

ABC'S WIDE WORLD OF SPORTS: Every Saturday afternoon, for a few hours, there was a sports program that ran from 1961 to January of 1998. The host who made it most famous was the commentator Jim McKay, whose line at the running of the show promo was *"ABC's Wide World of Sports.* The thrill of victory and the agony of defeat!" While saying "the agony of defeat," they ran the video of a Slovenian alpine jump skier wiping out a little over 1,924 times over 37 years.

YARD SALE: I organized a yard sale to get rid of some of my stuff, and Mom donated some. Dad put up the tent, and I put on a dog show with Mandy. There were three showtimes, and I put on one show for Lisa Kotran, two years older than I was. Hubba-hubba! It was 25¢ for the show to see Mandy speak, sit, lie down, and roll over. Just before closing the yard sale, Steve Notter looked around and, just as he left, grabbed a handful of money from my shoe box cash register. Steve was faster than I was, but I was so angry that the adrenaline rush helped me tackle him on the neighbor's grass before he could cross the street to his home. I was able to wrestle the money out of his hand, and he cried that I hurt him, just like the burglar suing the homeowner for falling through a roof window and breaking his leg. Wah!

1974 - THIRD GRADE: I had Ms. Ott for teacher. She had blond hair, blue eyes, and glasses. She could be moody at times and could yell loudly. John B. sat next to me. One day, I looked at him, and he looked green. I never saw a person look green before, and before I could finish the thought, he puked all over his desk, with some on mine. Now this was where I thought, *What the hell is the teacher thinking?* Ms. Ott said, "Jim, would you please clean up the mess?" And because she was the teacher, an authority figure, I did. I gagged a few times and was surprised at the warmness of it. I did wash my hands very well after that. Why did the teacher not call in the school custodian?

Another strange incident I remember was when I heard someone behind me crying. It was Michelle Farmer; she was the only African American in our class at the time. There was a huge puddle of yellow around her, and her body was just heaving up and down, I assumed from embarrassment. Tommy laughed his ass off, and I thought, *How terrible to laugh at the misfortune of another.*

IS SANTA REAL?: Third grade was also the absolute last year you could believe there was a Santa Claus because the non-believers embarrassed you so badly that you had no choice but to accept the reality of the truth. A Jewish kid told me his family did not celebrate Christmas. I felt sorry for him, *until* I learned that he celebrated Hanukkah (whatever that was) and received presents for eight nights in a row. When students busted me for believing in Santa Claus, when

I went home, I confronted Mom in the bathroom. "Mom? Mom? Moooooom! Is there a Santa Claus? I want to know the real, real truth because so many students are making fun of me!" After a ten-second pause, she said no. And that was when the trust for parents began to happen. The truth could be painful sometimes. No Santa, no Easter Bunny, no tooth fairy. What else have the big people lied to me about?

In Ms. Ott's class, we had to write a report on an animal. I chose the northeastern rattlesnake. I took out a small book from the library and copied it word for word. I received an A+ for it. The teacher even used my report as an example as to how to write a report. 'Glad she did not check my resources. When people asked me how to write an excellent report, I said, "It takes time, research, effort, and good sources."

HAPPY FEET: For some reason, the shoes Jody wore made her feet break out in red and white blotches. Mom and Dad put her on the bed, put extra lights out like professional photographers, propped her feet on pillows, and took pictures for the doctor. I think she had to wear leather shoes, and that took care of the problem. It was not easy having a sister with freakish feet.

However, there was a time we went to the beach, I had an ingrown toenail, and my right big toe was hurting terribly. Jody stepped on my foot by accident as we are walking along the edge of the waves, and I pushed her hard and yelled at her. Dad said, "Jim, if you don't take care of your toe, we will have to take you to the doctor!" YouTube had not been invented yet, so I had to learn how to do this myself. The day I finally I dug out the "ingrown" part of my nail causing the pain, I was a happy camper knowing I avoided the doctor's poking, pulling, prodding, and cutting into my big toe. It was pure joy feeling the release of non-stop pain after my self-surgery. As a sidenote, a characteristic of being a Geist was having large, big toes.

NOT A CROOK: It was a Thursday evening on August 8, 1974, and the TV stations kept saying there was going to be an important announcement by President Nixon. I didn't know much about Nixon. I knew my grandparents liked him, and my parents didn't. It made me a little sad my grandparents and parents didn't agree on everything. I was hearing much about this Watergate issue, and I did not understand it. At least the mountain jungle guerillas who kidnapped the Israelis at the 1972 Olympics in Munich had not kidnapped our president. I watched the announcement by myself in the downstairs TV room.

The next day, I watched the news as they showed Nixon giving a speech, saying, "When you hate the others, you lose." He walked up the helicopter stairs, turned around with his wife, and gave his famous victory salute with both hands. Vice President Ford was inaugurated as president, and even though he was a football college athlete, *Saturday Night Live* made fun of him all the time. We now had a new president, President Ford.

President Nixon (1969–1974)

Domestic

Initiative to fight cancer	Establishing the Environmental
Affirmative action in hiring women	Protection Agency and the Occupational Safety and
Title IX for tax money for women's college sports	Health Administration
	The shuttle missions

Welfare reform to get money to the poor

Foreign

Signed agreements on nuclear controls	Initiated detent with the Soviet Union
Diplomatic relations with China	Supported Israel in the Yom Kippur War

DIRTY TRICKS

1. **Nixon committed treason by undercutting President Johnson and the American public and soldiers by prolonging the Vietnam War** (Smithsonian.com): In 1967, Nixon sent an aide to tell the South Vietnamese to withdraw from peace talks because if he was elected, they would get a better deal. Once in office, he escalated the war into Laos and Cambodia, with the loss of an extra twenty-two thousand Americans until the peace agreement in 1973.

2. **The War on Drugs** (CNNpolitics.com): The Nixon campaign of 1968 had two enemies, the antiwar left and black people, according to Nixon's policy chief John Ehrlichman. The War on Drugs was a way to win the White House and to disrupt those communities, arrest leaders, and vilify them night after night on the news, according to an article from *Harper's Magazine*.

3. **Supporting a military coup to overthrow a democratically elected Chilean president**: President Allende, democratically elected, was kicked out with CIA help and replaced by a puppet dictator Pinochet, who committed terrible human rights abuses. Why would the United States go against a democracy to place in a dictator? To benefit U.S. business, of course.

4. **Watergate**: Nixon supported the break-in of the Democratic National Committee in the Watergate Hotel to place "bugs" in order to listen in on their meetings.

ASSASSINATIONS OF THE 1960S: Pres. John F. Kennedy, Rev. Dr. Martin Luther King Jr., and Robert Kennedy all were assassinated (TheNation.com, 11-22-13). President Kennedy had a plan to withdraw U.S. forces from Vietnam beginning on the first of December 1963. It was the actual policy on the day he died. Had he lived, it would have remained the policy. Of course, MLK spoke out against the war, and RFK—when he ran—was going to end the war, and they all were killed. MLK was also organizing the Poor People's Campaign, and that probably also contributed to him being killed. President Eisenhower, the five-star general who led the Allies on D-day, said, "In the councils of government, we must guard against the acquisition of unwarranted influence . . . by the military industrial complex [defense contractors and the military]. The potential for . . . misplaced power exists and will persist." Former secretary of defense Robert Gates said it was difficult to cut military spending, "to make tough choices that will displease powerful people inside and out of the Pentagon."

1975 - THE VELODROME, VALLEY PREFERRED CYCLING CENTER: The velodrome was built in Breinigsville, Pennsylvania, just outside of Allentown. It was built by Robert Rodale, publisher and Olympian himself. The first bicycle races took place in October of 1975 and had since produced over 140 national champions. We went frequently over the years to watch the cycling contests, of course always waiting for the wipeouts. I was able to watch speed skating Olympic medal winners from the 1980 Lake Placid, New York, Winter Olympics—Eric Heiden (five golds) and sister Beth Heiden (bronze medal)—biking there. Their thighs looked like tree trunks.

SNOW DAYS AND THE BROAD STREET BULLIES: Getting days off due to inclement weather was the best. It was a chance to make money shoveling snow, to go sledding, to watch TV, or to hang around with friends. My favorite memory was staying up with my family to watch the Philadelphia Flyers win in a play-off game in 1974 and then getting the announcement on the news that school would be closed the next day because of snow. That was one of my best days ever. What I loved about it was, as a family, we were watching and rooting for our team together and would jump up and down as our Flyers would score a goal.

The Flyers won the Stanley Cup in 1974 and 1975. Gene Hart was the voice of the Flyers on TV, and a famous singer from the WWII era, Kate Smith, was brought out to sing "God Bless America" when the patriotic feelings of the country were at a low with the quagmire of Vietnam and when the people was feeling betrayed by the president with the Watergate scandal. Coach Fred Shero told the team before the Stanley Cup victory, "We walk in together today. If we win today, we walk together forever!"

The centers on the team were Bobby Clarke, Rick MacLeish, Orest Kindrachuk, Bill Clement, and Terry Crisp. The wingers were Dave Schultz, Bill Barber, Bob Kelly, Don Saleski, Gary Dornhoefer, Ross Lonsberry, and Reggie Leach. The defensemen were Ed Van Impe, Tom Bladon, Barry Ashbee, Andre Dupont, and Joe and Jimmy Watson. The goaltenders were Bernie Parent, Bobby Taylor, and Wayne Stephenson.

1976 - FLYERS VS. RED ARMY GAME: On January 11, 1976, the USSR Red Army team faced off with the Flyers. Up to now, the Russians were undefeated against the NFL teams on their tour in the United States and Canada. The Goodwill Games was filled with tension. Commentator Gene Hart taught the Flyers owner Ed Snider a phrase to say in Russian to reach out at the beginning of the game, but when Snider saw the Russians' cold faces, he could not say it because he "hated those sons of bitches."

In the first period, the defenseman Ed Van Impe put a clean check on one of the Russians who lay on the ice for a minute. The Russian coach called his team off the ice and refused to continue the game. Snider sent word to the Communists that if they did not finish the game, they would not get paid. Getting a taste of capitalism, the team came back out. The Flyers beat the undefeated Russians, 4–1, outshooting the Russians, 49–13. The Russian coach called the Flyers "a bunch of animals," and the Philly fans took it as a compliment.

QUARTERBACK PHIL SIMMS: It was 2004, and I was walking out of ShopRite in Ramsey, New Jersey, with my groceries in a cart. As I neared my car, I saw to my right the former Giants quarterback with his wife walking toward the store. I was wearing a *Flyers* jersey. He saw me looking at him and probably thought, *I hope this is not an annoying fan*, and looked at my jersey. I just nodded at him, and he smiled back in appreciation of me respecting his privacy. Phil knew how crazy Philly fans could get.

NEW YORK AND NEW JERSEY HOCKEY TEAMS: The New York Islanders won the Stanley Cup four years in a row, 1980–1983. I was living in Queens when the New York Rangers won the cup in 1994. There were some people driving around with Ranger flags, but that was about it. I thought there would have been more celebration. Interestingly, Brazil won the World Cup in 1994, and there was more celebration in my neighborhood over that than the Rangers winning the cup. On Thirty-Fourth Avenue, next to Forty-First Street, they closed down the street and had a band playing Brazilian music on a tractor-trailer, and people were drinking and dancing. I was not even sure if I was living in the United States, and it was quite the celebration. The hockey giant of the 1980s was the Edmonton Oilers, winning four

Stanley Cups in 1984–88 with the Great One, Wayne Gretzky, the leader of the Oilers from 1979 to 1988. When I went to see the Flyers play Edmonton, Gretzky was on the injured list, so I never saw him play in person. The New Jersey Devils won the Stanley Cup in 2000 and 2003. Teresa worked for Couch Braunsdorf Insurance, and they had season tickets to the Devils, so I was able to watch them play the Flyers from very good seats.

UNCLE BOB'S CEMENT TRUCK: A large cement truck pulled up in front of 512 College Drive. Uncle Bob came in to talk with Mom and me and said, "Do you want to help me pour some concrete? I have a job in your neighborhood." I said of course and got to ride in a huge green and yellow cement truck driven by my uncle. I was sitting five to six feet above car roofs, and I loved the view and watched Uncle Bob work the gears as the truck vibrated along. The job was a pool job, and I got to work the switch allowing the cement to slide down the shute into the summer workers' wheelbarrows. When the job was done, Uncle Bob paid me $5. Wow, he paid me. Later in the day, I went to Gino's and bought some KFC chicken. If Burger King had been built at the time on Hamilton Street, I would have bought a fish sandwich.

Uncle Bob delivered concrete all over the Northeast and often had to go to NYC. One day, as he was getting off a bridge, there was a broken-down car on the side of the road. The NYC traffic cop told Uncle Bob to keep the truck moving. Uncle Bob said, "I will hit that car if I keep moving." The cops said, "Don't worry about it. Keep moving. We can't have a traffic jam here and now." Screeeeeechhhhhhh! He drove ahead, and the broken-down car would need major body work.

Another challenge Uncle Bob had as a cement truck driver was when he got the truck with the transmission put on backward. When he drove, he had to do the complete opposite for reverse and the first to fourth gears.

FOURTH GRADE (1975): I had Ms. Yazefski as a teacher. She was cute and had a curvy body. I used to get on her nerves but probably for a good reason. Anyone who was a professional and took time to plan lessons or to think about things for the class to do would be. Sometimes I would make the "I don't want to do that" face, or I would roll my eyes. She would get upset when she caught me doing this.

The one day that stuck out in my mind that year was Valentine's Day. I made real effort that year in signing my cards, addressing them, and writing comments to certain people. I also took pride in the Valentine's box I made for myself, the pink paper, and the tape job.

A new student joined our classroom, Gregory Paxamatus. He was tan and had curly black hair. He was from Greece, spoke with a bit of an accent, and told me he has swum with the dolphins in the waters off the Greek coast. I looked at Gregory and told him I think he was full of baloney, but he could have in a country of many islands in the sea.

GERMAN HERITAGE CHALLENGED: This was the year a Jewish student said to me, "You know, your people killed my people."

"What are you talking about?" I said.

He said, "Your name is Geist. Are you not German?"

"Ahhhh, I have German heritage, but I know not what you speak of." It made me feel angry that someone would make such a statement to me. It also made me feel like I came from a line of bullies. Later, Mom explained to me about the Holocaust as best she could, and I felt better, knowing none of my direct relatives were involved in such an atrocity.

PENNSYLVANIA GERMAN SOCIETY: The Pennsylvania Dutch came over in 1683. The German immigrants had moved to Pennsylvania 234 years before WWI, and 258 years before WWII, fascism and genocide took place. The German Society of Pennsylvania said that one out of three Americans was German or had German heritage. While studying up on the Germans who came over to

Pennsylvania, they subsisted on agriculture, went to church on Sundays, and made pies out of everything; and the fathers ran the home with a stern discipline and were not to be questioned. Well, that explained much for me. I joined the German society in 2015 for $60, and they sent me books, magazines, and DVDs explaining about Pennsylvania Dutch culture for any who were interested in that kind of thing.

RED ROBIN'S THERAPIST: In 2014, I was sitting at the bar, eating lunch at Red Robin in Allentown, just before I went to see the movie *Flight* with Denzel Washington. I got talking to a guy next to me, who turned out to be a family therapist. He told me, "Half my cases in the Lehigh Valley are the angry blue-collar fathers and the depressed homemaker mothers." I wondered how many of my classmates grew up in a home like this.

PIGEON TOES: I couldn't remember Dad going to parent-teacher conferences; usually, Mom went. For the most part, my grades were fine; but in fourth and fifth grades, my attitude and/or behavior was brought up as a possible issue. It was strange to see kids still in school after dinner when it was dark out. I saw Billy G., who people said had a pigeon-toed walk but could run like the wind. When I pointed this out, Mom, she whispered, "Don't say that out loud in public."

BOBBLEHEAD DAD: When Dad came home from work, he would sit on the gold-colored couch and read the newspaper until dinner was put on the table. Many times, he was so tired that he would fall asleep holding the paper, and then his head would begin to bob forward, and he would sway back and forth several times and then open his eyes. When he did this, I would get Jody or vice versa, and we would watch and laugh. When Dad caught us, he would slink away to the bedroom to avoid the gaze of his kids, who had no idea about how tough and tiring earning a living on an assembly line was.

SATURDAY NIGHT LIVE: My parents, being the first of their high school cohort, bought a home, and this equated to many of their friends coming over to visit a lot. I liked it. They put on cool rock albums with the latest hits and sat around and smoked their homemade cigarettes, and most of the friends were funny, and they talked about work, books, movies, who was getting married, who was buying a home, and what was going on in the world, politics, religion, and the music world. I sat there and took it in.

One night, Dale and Sandy were over, along with a few other people, and we watched this show called *Saturday Night Live*. I laughed my butt off after the monologue because they played a fake commercial called the Bass-o-matic. The humor was avant-garde, and for some reason, it resonated with me. *Saturday Night Live*, *Laugh-In*, the Smothers Brothers, Flip Wilson, and some of the variety shows with Johnny Cash, Dean Martin, and Mac Davis—I loved all that stuff. When I first saw Monty Python and then Benny Hill, I was in comedy heaven.

It does not cost anything to be nice or to smile or to make someone laugh. The act of muscles moving when you laugh releases endorphins. Some are junk food junkies; I am an endorphin junkie. Actually, I am both.

There were some funny kids at school, and those were the ones I sought and enjoyed hanging out with. Some of the funny ones to me were Darryl Lorenzo, John O'Keefe, Danny Arkey, Eric Ebert, Kenny Steward, Harry Nicholson, and so many others I have not listed.

I WILL PEE IN YOUR BED!: Jody was in my room, sitting on the bed. I was telling her jokes when she said, "You have to stop, or I am going to pee on your bed." I thought she was bluffing. I told her a few more, and Jody kept laughing and laughing and laughing, and I was wondering what she was laughing at, so I asked. She said, "I peed in your bed! I told you so."

THE **MESSIEST ROOM I HAVE EVER SEEN:** Uncle Tom stopped by and looked in Jody's room. "That is the messiest room I have ever seen." Years later, Uncle Tom said, "My daughter used to be messy, but now that she has her own place, she has one of the cleanest houses around. Your sister will do the same when she gets her own place."

THE WHITE (BLUE) STATION WAGON: Regarding the white (Dad said it was blue) station wagon, Dad could control its back window with a power window switch. When he would move the switch up to close the window, Jody and I would have a competition of pointing our fingers in and out until the window closed. The last time we played, Jody got her finger smashed by the closing window. She screamed, and Dad screamed. and I won by not getting my finger crushed.

FIFTH GRADE (1976): I had Ms. Davis for homeroom. She had curly dark hair, blue eyes, and cat-eye glasses. For some reason, I tested this poor woman, who only wanted the best for me. As a person who has had the chance of teaching sixth graders from Newark, New Jersey, I think I have gotten my just karma for my time with her. She was nice enough, but I was an immature fifth grader.

I became friends with Dave, who used to live by the shore, had a surfer hairstyle, and the kind of bracelets people from the shore wore, and he looked older than a fifth grader. He used to work in a deli, and when I heard about the money he made, I too wanted to work in one. I did get a weekly allowance for taking out the trash and for doing the dishes.

For a Ms. Davis class project, John Christenson and I made a representation of the Jamestown Fort in Virginia. To make up grass, we ground up twenty pencils in the sharpener, dyed them green for the grass, and glued them to the cardboard bottom. It was messy, wasteful, and fun.

MICHAEL DISCO DUCK: My dad was buddies with Skeeter as kids. They used to chum and go fishing together. Skeeter's father took them fishing in the kind of place where you paid for the fish and then took them out to eat. Dad, growing up poor, never forgot that. Skeeter used to have a gray Datsun, and he took a lot of guff from his coworkers for owning a foreign vehicle when he was a union worker at Mack Trucks. "Buy union! Buy American!"

DAD'S FROZEN TWENTY-ONE-INCH TROUT: Skeeter's son Michael was the same age as I was, and we became buddies. We used to fish together on the Little Lehigh River on the first day of fishing and on the annual contest days. If you caught a trout with a tag on it or a large trout, you might win a prize. Dad caught a twenty-one-inch trout one year, and he wrapped it up in tin foil, and it stayed in our fridge for five years. Every time the conversation turned to fishing, the twenty-one-incher was bound to be pulled out of the freezer. He won second prize for that trout and a nice trophy to go with it. On one sad day, he unwrapped it and buried it with honors.

BIG RED MACHINE - 1970–76: Mike loved the Cincinnati Reds, who beat the Boston Red Sox in 1975 to become the world champions. The team was Johnny Bench (C), Tony Perez (1B), Joe Morgan (2B), Dave Concepcion (SS), Pete Rose (3B), George Foster (LF), Cesar Geronimo (CF), and Ken Griffey (RF), with pitching from Gary Nolan, Don Gullett, and Rawly Eastwick. At some point, Mike began also cheering for the Oakland A's when Billy Martin became its manager, and their style of play was called Billy Ball. In 2002 and 2003, the Oakland A's got to the playoffs on a $44 million budget vs. the Yankees' $125 million a year budget based on sabermetrics developed by Billy Beane.

EMMAUS HALLOWEEN PARADE: Skeeter hooked up a wagon to his John Deere mower and pulled Mike and me through the

Emmaus, Pennsylvania, Halloween parade with hay and blankets in the wagon. We threw candy at people, and it was a blast. When I was in the Cub Scouts andwe marched in the Allentown Halloween parade. Dad made a candle outfit by taking a heavy cardboard barrel, probably from Mack Trucks, that he spray-painted red; cutting out holes for my arms; and putting a flame on top connected to a flashlight. He put in fireman hosing for the shoulder straps, but by the end of the parade, I was in tears from the pain of the straps digging into my shoulder. The barrel was pretty heavy.I did not enjoy that parade. It was like the short story "Cruel Shoes" by Steve Martin, but it was "cruel straps." Still, it was a cool-looking costume. The price of being pretty is painful sometimes.

PAPPY AT TIDABOCK'S CAMP IN PIKE COUNTY: Mike's grandfather had a nice log cabin in Pike County, which I was able to visit a few times. It had a loft on the second floor with a TV room downstairs and a kitchen, dining room, and fireplace. There was a lake nearby, and they went hunting in the woods behind the camp. Mike, Jody, and I went out exploring, looking for orange newts, and climbed up on one of the deer stands. When we came home for lunch, a doe and a big buck ran in front of all of us on the path back. Mike said that was "Pappy the Buck."

ON GOLDEN POND: Mike, Jody, and I and our folks walked to the lake. A small water snake was swimming across the lake twenty yards away. Mike threw a rock at it, and the snake turned and made beeline right at Mike, who ran away. I went back later with my fishing pole and caught a fifteen-inch pike off a boat dock. I felt like Norman in the movie *On Golden Pond* when he hooked into Walter the Trout. I also loved the smell of the ferns up at his grandfather's property when a breeze blew down the mountain and through the woods.

ROLLER-SKATING AND SKIING: There was a skating rink in Emmaus, and Mike went there every Saturday from age twelve to sixteen. He was an excellent skater and quite the ladies' man. I could get myself around the rink, even skate backward, but I could not do spins or kicks like Mike could. I liked the smell of the rink. They always did the "Hokey Pokey" in the middle of the skating time, and they also would have races for different age groups. The song "Disco Duck" was played weekly in 1976. I also went skiing on Doe Mountain in Emmaus with Mike. Craig Blose started calling me J. C. Killy, (pronounced Kee-lee) the 1968 downhill skiing Olympic gold champion, because my initials are JC, and I skied. I screwed my boots in too tightly, and when I fell, I twisted my ankle badly on the mountain.

FROM SKEETER TO NEIL TO BLOSE: Mike's mom, Linda and Skeeter broke up in the late 1970s, and she ended up dating another guy named Craig Blose. Linda was pretty and had long dark hair like Cher. Linda was related to Doug Cope and Stacey Cope, whom I went to high school with. Stacey ended up becoming a cheerleader for the Philadelphia Eagles. She also picked up Johnny Galiano to drive him to school every day.

Skeeter and Blose, or Bips, played on the Roach softball team with Dad and were able to maintain a relationship as friends. Craig lived on a mountain road and over the years had Labrador retrievers, black, chocolate, and yellow. Craig took us fishing a few times, and I watched the movie *10* at his place starring the beauty Bo Derek and funnyman Dudley Moore. Craig used to make this noise when he was expressing frustration: "It's like . . . it's like, aaauuuuuhhhhh!" I laughed every time.

Craig stopped by our home on a Saturday, and he and Dad were talking. The song "Abraham, Martin, and John" sung by Dion started to play. Blose said, "This song makes me tear up every time I hear it. This world would be different had they not assassinated JFK." Dad said, "The song bums me out as well." Sidenote: Blose passed in November of

2016. I found out he had served in Vietnam, but I never knew it because he never talked about it. At Skeeter's funeral, I thanked Craig for all the fun and love he showed me as a kid growing up.

MINIBIKE WIPEOUT: Mike had a minibike. We rode that thing up and down the mountain road. He let me drive it myself. I was pulling into the stone driveway with it, and before I could stop it, I wiped out, with the minibike on top of me. Mike ran down the driveway, saying, "Oh my gosh! Oh my gosh!" It was good to know I had a friend who cared about my welfare. When he got up to me, he pulled the bike off and me and started checking it out for scratches, saying, "Oh my gosh!"

DAVID LETTERMAN: There was this crazy guy on TV in the mornings from ten thirty to eleven thirty every day. His name was David Letterman, and he was a bit odd and very sarcastic. Whenever Mike slept over at my place, we would watch Letterman in the morning. "Stupid Pet Tricks" was always good. He once wore an outfit of Alka-Seltzer pills and dove into a kiddie pool that turned into a raging volcanic fuzz, foaming all over. Another time, he put on a Velcro suit and jumped off a minitrampoline and into a wall covered with Velcro and immediately stuck to it. He was a guy with an odd sense of humor and was not a corporate suck-up and would go down as one of the best late-night-show entertainers.

My favorite episode was in November of 1987, when Cher came on and was extremely chilly toward Dave. When he asked why, she said, "I think you are an a———hole!" After the commercial, he asked her if she would ever perform with Sonny again. As she was thinking about it, the band started playing, "I Got You Babe," and Sonny walked out to the stage, and Cher graciously walked over to him. They hugged and sang the song together. A few years later, Sonny died in a freak skiing accident hitting a tree head on.

ROACH PICNIC, 1982: After junior high school, we saw less and less of each other, except maybe at the Roaches summer picnic at Uncle Dale and Aunt Sandy's farm property. One year, the old chicken coops had been cleaned up and painted; and the fridge, drinks, and food were there.

In 1982, the song "Abracadabra" by Steve Miller came on, and Skeeter laughed as Miller sang, "Abracadabra, I want to reach out and grab you!" With the famous Skeeter laugh, he chuckled, saying, "I love that song!"

Whenever you walked in and out of the small building, you would get insulted by the one foot tall plactic gnome with motion detector, and it could scare you if you forgot it was there.

Skeeter used to have a girlfriend named Juanita, who was a dancer. I liked her; Mike did not. He then had a girlfriend named Kathy, and when a party ran out of beer, she wanted to find the next party that had some. He was a member of a nudist camp, and I think it was awesome that someone could be so comfortable with his body image. Kathy had a son also named Michael. He was a nice kid, but I think Michael Tidabock was not happy about it.

THE BICENTENNIAL, 1976: The bicentennial of the birth of our country, and 6th grade takes a t to Philadelphia. Students compared lunches; some had sub sandwiches, while others had peanut butter and jelly. Some brought bags of chips and pretzels and shared. It was fun to ride on such a nice bus with plush seats, which were blue with spirogyra graphics. We visited Constitution Hall and saw the Liberty Bell.

HOMELESS AND HUNGRY: We ate lunch in the park across the street, sat on benches, and fed the bold squirrels and pigeons. I was horrified to watch some old men in skanky, worn-out clothes going up the garbage cans and picking through our thrown-out lunches to eat any of our leftover morsels. I have never seen hungry, homeless people before. This had more of an impression on me than the bus ride, the cute girls in our class, and anything of historical significance that day. It was a reality enigma for this ten-year-old.

ROCKY AND PHILADELPHIA FREEDOM: I found 1976 (sixth grade) to be an exciting year. The movie *Rocky* came out and was filmed in Philadelphia. It turned out to be a very good movie, funny and inspiring with the Italian Stallion, Rocky Balboa, taking on Apollo Creed and winning. I saw the movie with Mom. Elton John also came out with the song "Philadelphia Freedom," and it brought more pride. My family watched a television series called *1776* about the creation of the Declaration of Independence, and our family cheered as delegates from the different colonies voted to secede from the country of England.

1976 SUMMER OLYMPICS: At Montreal, Bruce Jenner won the decathlon, Sugar Ray Leonard won the gold in boxing, and the United States got thirty-four gold medals, thirty-five silvers, and thirty-five bronzes for a total of ninety-four medals. The United States came in third behind the USSR and East Germany. It also was the summer of fourteen-year-old Romanian gymnast Nadia Comaneci, who won the gold and got a perfect 10 on the uneven bars. A theme song was even written for her called "Nadia's Theme Song." My uncle Dale and aunt Sandy went to Montreal for the Summer Olympics and brought home an autograph of Sugar Ray Leonard for me.

THE 1976 WINTER OLYMPICS: In Innsbruck, Austria, Dorothy Hamill won the gold in freestyle skating, Franz Klammer of Austria won the downhill event, and Ingemar Stenmark of Finland won the alpine jump.

SIXTH GRADE - 1976: I had Ms. Wessnor as teacher. She was young and tough, and she never really liked me but tolerated my presence. I went into class early from lunch, and I sat at my desk, and as she entered the room, I pointed my finger at her and pretended to shoot. She went nuts! "Geist! Don't you ever do that again! I hate guns! That is really inappropriate!"

In sixth grade, we used to switch classes—English, math, and science. I had Mr. Hutchison for science, Ms. Aries for English, and Ms. Wessnor for math. If you chewed gum in Ms. Aries's class, she took the gum, put it in your ear, and made you chew it again. A friend of Mr. Hutchison brought in a live rattlesnake one time. I stood on a desk in case it got loose. It was creepy. Cousin Bryan loved Ms. Aries, but not as much as the show *Quincy M.E.*, the precursor to all the future hospital and CSI programs of the 1990s and 2000s.

ART, MUSIC, AND GYM: The boys always talked about which of the three they would marry: Ms. Gatos, the art teacher; Ms. Becker, the music teacher; or Ms. Carol, the gym teacher. I always said I would marry Ms. Gatos.

For music class, we had the chance to do something creative. My group came up with the idea of singing a song by Kansas, complete with fake guitars. I had to do a report on the song "Lonely People" by the Beatles. I could tell by the melody it was a sad song, but as a young kid, I had times of feeling lonely but not the existential loneliness adults might experience.

For gym class, floor hockey was my favorite. In school, you were not to raise your stick in the air after you scored, or you lost the point. I played so much street hockey at the time, it wa second nature to me. I would gander half my U.T. goals were un-done by my automatic stick raising habit. The gym teacher Ms. Carol taught us to dance the hustle - "Do the hustle!"In fifth grade, we had a marbles and the hopscotch contest. I learned to play hopscotch as a way to hang with the ladies.

NYC SCHOOL TRIP: In 1977, the sixth grade class took a trip to NYC. I sat on the stairs of the Metropolitan Museum with fellow students and gawked at all the people walking up and down the street in front of us. There were some street performers, and we also took a subway ride to the Twin Towers. There was a 1977 version of *King Kong* with actress Jessica Lange (ooh la la), where Kong climbed up the towers instead of the Empire State Building in the original movie. It was amazing to be looking at towers 110 stories high and that I had just seen in the movies.

JAMES AT 15: I hung out with my buddy Mike Brogna, and as our class walked into one of the towers, Mike and I turned around to look at the elevators just in time to see actor Lance Kerwin, who was in a TV series called *James at 15*. Lance's eyes grew bigger as if thinking, *I hope these elevator doors close before these kids chase me down!* I loved that show, and seeing the actor helped make my 1977 trip to NYC all the more memorable. I loved the NYC museums but hated NYC—the traffic, the homeless, the fear of crime and being mugged, the smell of garbage and urine in the streets, and home of the Yankees. Ugh!

UT PLAYGROUND FOOTBALL FIGHT: It was a glorious fall Saturday afternoon, with leaves falling to the ground, when a group of sixth-grade guys played tackle football. It was six on six, and we played in front of Union Terrace Elementary. It was a perfect field, sidewalk on one side and playground macadam on the other, which gave us our parameters. On the opposing side was Scott Schleicher, also called Scooter, a very good running back and was to become a Pennsylvania State champion in wrestling in five years. It was a competitive game, and on defense, I was imagining I was Eagles linebacker Bill Bergey or Steelers linebacker Jack Ham or Jack Lambert. There was some trash talk going on, and Scott came to the middle of the field for a short pass to the middle when I put on a solid tackle on him. Scott jumped up and started pushing me.

Like singer Michael Jackson, I was a lover, not a fighter, but something in me snapped on the second or third push on the fateful day. I pushed him back so hard that he fell on the ground, and I jumped on top of him and started hitting him with my right fist and then my left fist, and I hit him five to six times before I was pulled off him. He said something like "You got lucky!" and walked away. The game ended, and I walked away with some street cred and my peers shaking their heads, saying, "It was a clean tackle." I was Muhammad Ali and Sugar Ray Leonard for the rest of the day.

WEDDING RECEPTIONS: I enjoyed going to Aunt Sandy, John and Liz, and Uncle Bob and Aunt Davy. I was in the wedding party for Uncle Bob and Aunt Davy. I must have been four or five. I had on my tux. When we went to the Rose Garden in Allentown, Pennsylvania, for the wedding pictures, I slid down the grass hill on my butt with another young guy in the wedding party. At Dale and Sandy's wedding, I was very distraught when I heard the bride had been kidnapped and held for ransom. The best parts of the receptions for me were the food, having live music bands, running around with other kids, and dancing. I was scared when I first saw a drunk person. A woman was trying to get her husband to the car, and he had lost his senses. *Why would a person want to get drunk?* I thought.

"LITTLE MONSTER": In the winter of 1977, I was in sixth grade, and President Jimmy Carter gave the schoolkids two days off to help conserve on oil because of the energy crisis. It was the days of odd and even, when you could only get gas depending on the last number on your license plate, whether it was odd or even. After a few sledders went down the hill, I said to Kenny, "Did you see that guy with the camera and the other person with the pad of paper? I think that is a reporter" from the *Evening Chronicle*. The next time we slid down, the reporter asked us if we wanted to be interviewed. We said, "Of course!" They wanted to know what we thought about President Carter closing down the schools for two days. I said, "It is awesome, but my mother wishes 'we monsters' were back in school!" The monster reference was to my sister, four years younger, and me, who fought like cats and dogs. Mother was horrified that the Pennsylvania Child Services was going to pay a visit to our house. I liked the picture in the paper because half of my front tooth was missing from the summer before, and the caption under the picture of me, with a big smile and my parka hoodie fur surrounding my face, said, "Jimmy Geist, Happy Monster."

President Jimmy Carter (1976–80)

Domestic

Created the Department of Energy	Created the Superfund
Created the Department of Education	
Signed the Alaska National Lands Conservation Act	<u>Deregulated airlines, trucking, and rail</u>
Created a national energy policy	<u>Deregulated communications and finance industries</u>
Pushed for new energy technologies	

Foreign

Panama Canal Treaty	Boycotted the 1980 Olympics (USSR in Afghanistan)
Camp David Accords	Iran hostage crisis

AUTOGRAPHS: Kenny and I both were into collecting autographs. I sent probably a hundred letters to various sports players from 1974 to 1978. It was always exciting to get a package that came from Veterans Stadium, the Spectrum, or Three Rivers Stadium. I had family and friends collect them for me as well and gave them to me. Listed below are the autographs I have collected over the years.

Jim Geist's Autograph Book (1975–1985)

<u>Boxing</u>

Muhammad Ali

Sugar Ray Leonard (1976 Olympics, Montreal)

Larry Holmes (Easton Assassin)

Danny Musico (middleweight champion)

<u>Tennis</u>

Jimmy Connors

<u>Five Topps Large Cards</u>

Garvey, Palmer, Schmidt, Jackson, Carew

<u>Philadelphia Eagles</u>

Bill Bergey (linebacker, 3 autographs)

Vince Papale (movie *Invincible* based on his life, with Mark Walberg)

Dennis Harrison (defensive end)

Drew Mahalic (linebacker, 2 autographs)

Harold Carmichael (1979, great wide receiver)

Ken Payne

Guy Morriss

Cleveland Franklin

Richard Osborne

Tom Luken

Ray Phillips

Matt Bahr (Penn State University [PSU], kicker)

Lem Burnham

<u>Dorothy Hamill Card</u>

Ice Capades (Hershey, Pennsylvania)

Softball

Eddie Feigner

The King and His Court

Philadelphia Phillies

Steve Carlton (pitcher)

Tim McCarver (Carlton's catcher and baseball commentator)

Tommy Hutton (first baseman)

Randy Lerch (pitcher)

Philadelphia 76ers

George McGinnis (2 autographs)

Andrew Toney

Philadelphia Flyers

Reggie Leach (winger, a.k.a. "the Rifle," 2 autographs)

Pantomimist

Jon Harvey (studied under Marcel Marceau)

Celebrities

David Hartman (*Good Morning America*)

Cheryl Tiegs (1978, at Ali's training camp)

Leonard Nimoy (Spock of *Star Trek*)

1910 Mecca Cigarette Baseball Card

James Dygert

J. B. Seymour

Baseball

Steve Garvey (first baseman, LA Dodgers)

Bill Robinson (Pirates, deceased)

Ed Ott (catcher for the World Series champs Pirates, on two baseball cards)

Dave Winfield (NY Spankees—I mean, Yankees)

Chris Cichocki (Detroit Red Wings)

Terry Bradshaw (quarterback for the Steelers, football TV commentator, and movie actor)

Ray Nitschke (NFL's meanest linebacker)

Mike Singletary (linebacker for the Chicago Bears)

Bruce Harper (NY Jets)

Hockey

Soccer

Jeff Tipping (Pennsylvania Stoners)

Football

Jack Ham (linebacker for the Steelers)

Robert Newhouse (running back, Dallas Cowboys)

Matt Millen (linebacker for Penn State/Oakland Raiders)

Keith Dorney (all-American for Penn State, 1978)

Olympics

Millard Hampton

- silver in 200 meters

- gold in 4 × 100 meters

THE AM-FM RADIO PRIZES: I had an audio cassette recorder and listened to the radio all the time. Sometimes I would sit at night while I was doing homework or a project and listen to the radio. Every time a song or a commercial would end, I would get ready to hit the record button to make a tape of the latest songs. It was so cool to be able to record things without having to pay for the songs. Sometimes my tape would not catch the beginning of the song, or the DJ would talk over the music, or the commercial would start before it was finish.

When there were contests, I called in. I won tickets to see Dorothy Hamill, ice-skating Olympic gold winner in the Ice Capades in Hershey, Pennsylvania. I went with Mom, Nana Short, and Jody. Another time, I was the twenty-fifth caller and won the album *Damn the Torpedoes* by Tom Petty on WAEB.

I loved the Walkman radio. I could listen to cassette tapes as I delivered my newspapers until the cassette started running slow from the drained batteries.

HALLOWEEN TICKTACKING: I went into the cornfield next to Flexer Park with one of my paper bags and filled it with hard corn. We used to peel the corn and then went "ticktacking," the Halloween tradition where you took a handful of corn and threw it against a home's window, and then you would run like hell. Many times, sitting at home, when the corn hit our window, it made me jump. I hated the kids who did that.

FAMILY TRIPS: In third grade, we took a trip to NYC. I was happy to get a day off. Sister Jody was dropped off at Nana and Grandpa's. It was a rainy and foggy day, and we took the Lincoln Tunnel into the NYC. As we came out of the tunnel, I saw the Empire State Building. One thing about my parents and trips was they would get stressed and then snippy. I got it, driving to and in NYC was stressful, especially if you were used to country driving. We parked the car in a parking lot, and we walked over to the Museum of Natural History. There were showcases of the animal life, the cavemen scenes, the asteroids, the dinosaur bones, the mummies in the Egyptian section, and the huge blue whale hanging from the ceiling in the middle of the museum. It was a large and cool museum.

For local trips, we went to the Trexler Game Preserve. The drive to the park entrance was pretty, with the Jordan River in the valley and the covered red bridge before the park. With the drive through the park, there was a section where you "ford" through the Jordan River. There was a concrete driveway in the river to drive over, but it always felt to me like we were going to be swept away in the river. As you drove past the river, you could see white-tailed deer and then a section with the elk with huge antlers. As you drove around the long curve up the mountain and started heading down into a valley full of bison (buffalo-cattle mix). It was sad that groups of hunters used to ride the trains and shoot herds of them to let them die and rot in the sun as a way to help take away the life of certain Native American Central Plains groups.

One of my favorite trips was to Great Adventure. Before going to the section of the park with rides, we went through the safari section first. After seeing all the African animals, we enjoyed a day of going on rides. We went at least twice, and on one of the trips, *The Mike Douglas Show* filmed an episode there, and we were able to watch it get filmed in the rodeo arena. It amazed me that an event could be broadcast all across the nation as I watched it live. On one ride, the Flume, there was someone in line who I thought was singer Lionel Richie.

We tried to get to a place called Jungle Habitat, a drive-through safari in Northern New Jersey, but we ended up getting lost and never made it there. It turned out to be in West Milford, New Jersey, a place I would move to thirty-five years later. Jungle Habitat is now abandoned, and it was said some of the animals were just let loose from the cages when the park closed. Black panthers had been sighted in the Palisades area of Rockland County in March of 2009 by several people. My current neighbor Richie, who works at FedEx, is not a bull shyster, and he said he and a coworker spotted a large cat with a long tail that was black and huge. A television show called *MonsterQuest* even did a show about panthers in East New York.

The most memorable trip Mom and Dad took my sister and me on was to Walt Disney World in Orlando, Florida. I believe I was a seventh grader at the time, and I usually brought in the mail. I went home at three thirty, and Dad usually got home at about four fifteen. Mom was not home, and I called Jody over. "Hey, Mom and Dad got a letter from Walt Disney World. Should we open it?" I opened it, and it said, "Congratulations, you will be coming to our park on such and such date." I felt bad that I stole the surprise from Mom and Dad, and he was bummed out, but then he said, "Hey, we are going to Disney World!" We had much of it on an 88 mm film, and I was grateful for the recorded memory. We took an airline called People Express. When our plane landed, the pilot announced, "Ladies and gentlemen, welcome to Orlando, Florida!" The passengers broke out into an enthusiastic applause. The workers and their families were going to have some fun!

TRIP TO PHILADELPHIA: On my first family trip to Philadelphia, we went to the Franklin Institute and the Philadelphia Zoo. A fellow Mack worker and his family came with us one time, and we stopped by a McDonald's in Philadelphia. Most of the workers were black. This would have been in the early 1970s, and as a young kid, I was not really aware of racism and the tensions in Philly at this time. Frank Rizzo was the mayor of Philly at the time, and he was a hard-nosed pro-police leader. Apparently, we were given bad service, and a black worker placed a booger in between my chocolate shake cup and the cup cover. It made me sick to my stomach. On the way out of the parking lot, the family friend took our bags of leftover food and garbage and threw it in the parking, and Dad's buddy yelled, "You can pick up our white trash!" I have never heard that saying before.

On the Schuylkill Parkway, people were driving like maniacs. Mom and Dad got so nervous on road trips, especially if they missed the exit. This was before GPS, so when you got lost, it was easy to get really lost. I understood why it was called "the Sure Kill Parkway. I couldn't remember anything about the zoo, except feeling sad for the tiger that kept pacing back and forth in his little cage, and it made me wish he was back in the jungle.

THE THIN BLUE LIE: Frank Rizzo was the police chief of Philadelphia before becoming mayor. He tried to change the city charter so he could run for a third term. Jonathan Neumann, a reporter for the *Philadelphia Inquirer*, broke the story about the deaths of thirty-eight people at the American Legion convention in Philly that became known as Legionnaires' disease. Neumann won a Pulitzer Prize in 1977 for opening the lid on the police department's framing of innocent people, routine torture of suspects, and murder of troublesome witnesses. Neumann's journalism resulted in federal indictments of Rizzo and others on civil rights abuses.

THE MOVE TRIAL IN PHILLY: A family friend was called in jury duty review for a group in Philadelphia called MOVE. Dad's friend told the judge, "One, I would never go against a police officer. Two, especially when a *n———er* is involved." He was told by the judge he would not be serving on the jury.

MOVE was started in 1972 by John Africa and was preceded by a group called Christian Life Movement. It was about black power, communalism, and anarcho-primitivism. Founder John Africa opposed machines, electricity, heat, and soap. They ate fruits, vegetables, and nuts and fed the babies raw meat. The children were not sent to school, and they were kind to all animals, including bugs and rats, with fifty to sixty unvaccinated dogs living with them. The children wore little clothing, so their skin was tainted. In 1975, neighbors started to complain about garbage, fecal odor, rats, unvaccinated dogs, clear health code violations, and concerns of child neglect. The members built a bunker on the roof of their home and shouted obscenities from a bullhorn late into the night. In 1978, the Philadelphia Police and MOVE had a stand-off regarding police brutality, and an officer got shot and killed.

In 1985, there was a standoff again with the police under Philadelphia's first black mayor, Wilson Goode. A Pennsylvania State Police helicopter came in and dropped an arsenal on the MOVE commune, and the fire spread and destroyed sixty-five homes, and eleven were killed, five of whom were children. When the fire started, the police chief Leo Brooks said, "Let the fire burn." Philadelphia spent $42 million to the families as a settlement.

JERSEY SHORE TRIPS: Dad built a plywood box with suction cups and straps to hold it down and spray-painted the U.S. flag on it to be put on the Mustang's roof. This way, Mom and Dad could fit all the camping stuff—tents, pillows, sleeping bags, etc.—in addition to the trunk of the car. We used to have a ten-person tent with red, white, and blue stripes on the canvas ceiling, feeling like a circus tent.

We visited many of the spots on the Jersey Shore and seemed to keep moving further and further south. In New Jersey, we hit Atlantic City and Sea Isle City and eventually made it to Wildwood and Cape May. We stayed in Rehoboth Beach in Delaware and Ocean City in Maryland and eventually went to Virginia. One thing my family noticed was the further south you went, the nicer the beaches and the fewer crabs you stepped on. *Jaws* had come out in 1976 and forever ruined it for me to enjoy a carefree wading in the ocean waves the rest of my days. I could only swim in a pool or lake after that movie. Thanks Speilberg!.

ALLENTOWN, LEE IACOCCA, AND THE MUSTANG: The Mustang automobile was created by Lee Iacocca, one of the famous sons of Allentown, Pennsylvania. He was given credit for helping save Chrysler from demise. I went to school with Jim Iacocca, nephew of Lee. The Iacocca family started the Yocco's Hot Dogs in Allentown. It was called Yocco's because people had trouble pronouncing Iacocca.

ICE CREAM, SPRINKLES, AND CIGARETTES: We camped with the Tidabocks and Tokars one time: Skeeter, Linda, Michael (who was my age), and Mike and Corrine and their daughter Melissa, who was Jody's age. We went to the boardwalk at night, and it was fun to see the rides at the amusement park and all the flashing lights, boardwalk entertainers, and people walking around. We visited the Planters Peanut Shop to meet Mr. Peanut and to buy some taffy.

At the ice cream shop, Dad had a cigarette in his hand. The hallway in the ice cream store was tight and full of customers. Someone walked by with a sundae, and Dad looked at his hand and saw that his cigarette was gone. Someone found a cigarette in his/her sundae.

When we got back, I heard the adults laughing and figured out I was entertaining them by making hand shadow puppets against the tent canopy via the light from the campfire. I could make a good hand rabbit and wolf face.

JODY KNOWS WHO SHE IS: One of my favorite parts of camping was having campfires. Jody and I would go out and search for wood along the campground woods' edges. This campground had a store where you could buy penny candy, ice, and supplies. It also had a playground, and they hosted concerts every few weeks. My sister went to the store to buy something. Someone from our camping party asked Jody to find out if there was a concert on Saturday and who was playing.

The campers were joking, "Hope it is Elton John or David Bowie." As she came back to camp, I asked, "Who is it?" as in who was playing on Saturday night. Jody, with a quizzical look on her face, said, "It's me, Jody!"

PLAYGROUND RESCUE: I went to the playground one late afternoon before dinner, and there were two younger kids, probably brothers. The one kid was at the top of the slide, and the other kid said, "You can make it down." He replied, "No, I can't. I am afraid of the slide, and I am afraid to look down on the stairs." The kid on the ground looked at me and said, "Can you save my brother?" I kicked up my *Rookies, SWAT, Emergency, Adam-12* mode and climbed the stairs and talked the kid down. I moved his hands and feet one step at a time and told him to look straight ahead. I got him down the stairs, and he looked me in the eye and said, "Mister, you saved my life." Yes, I did.

SHAKE YOUR BOOTY: Our family has upgraded to a hitch camper approximately six by twelve feet. When pulled out, it had beds on each side and a small table with a kitchen in it. Our family this weekend had camped up in Potter County. We were in a Pennsylvania state park that was beautiful.

I woke up in the middle of the night at about three or four. I was not sure why, but then I fell back asleep. At the time I delivered papers, I used to get up five thirty every morning; thus I had no problem falling asleep when I had the chance to do so. After breakfast, my sister sat next to me with her wrinkled up nose and said, "I can't believe Mom and Dad!"

"What?"

"Mom and Dad!"

"What happened?"

"Did you hear them?"

"No."

"Did you not feel the camper moving last night?"

"What?" I giggled and giggled.

"Yeah! Mom and Dad had nooky last night, and I heard it all and felt the camper moving up and down."

"I guess that is how you and I came into the world." I laughed. My sister later had two kids of her own; she understood, I was sure.

GRAND CANYON OF PENNSYLVANIA: Uncle Dale and Aunt Sandy took a canoeing trip down the "Grand Canyon of Pennsylvania." She ended up writing a very nice piece in the *Morning Call* newspaper about her experience.

On one camping trip, Skeeter took a can of baked beans and placed it by a campfire. Ten minutes later, as people were sitting by the fire, a bomb went off. When baking beans by the fire, one should poke some holes in the can for steam to escape; otherwise, the can would explode. Those sitting around the campfire were covered in baked beans.

Another time, Jim Swartz was sitting in a lawn chair by the campfire when he screamed and fell back. He said, "I thought I was falling into the fire." On another trip down the canyon, a big rock rolled down the cliffs, just missing one of the canoes. On another day, a black bear swam across the river right in front of Dad's canoe.

CHINCOTEAGUE AND ASSATEAGUE, VIRGINIA: These were the islands where the wild ponies swam away from a Spanish ship when it crashed unto the islands. The volunteer fireman moved the horses every end of July from Assateague across the bay to Chincoteague, actually ran down the main street of Chincoteague for a mile, and then they were put in a corral. The horses would have their hooves trimmed and their health checked, and the firemen volunteers sold off a certain amount so the horses could keep surviving. A few days later, they would swim back to Assateague. There was a famous book called *Misty of Chincoteague* about one of those horses.

Our family traveled in Chincoteague in 1977 (sixth grade), for this was the year *Star Wars* came out, and we saw the movie there. That was a highlight for me on that trip. Of course, it was perfect for my sister, being the horse lover that she was. Tenting was fun, going out to eat was fun, renting a boat to go fishing was fun, crabbing was fun, and going the beach was okay for me. Having red hair and fair skin made it easy for me to get sunburned. Our modus operendi was to get up, eat breakfast, pack up the beach stuff, go to the beach, and stay on there from 10:00 a.m. to 4:00 p.m. For me, this was an eternity, but my parents loved the beach—wading in the water, getting sun, sleeping, reading, and sometimes fishing. Dad had a four-wheel-drive Scout. He would let some air out of the tires, and we could drive on the beach sand.

In 1978 (seventh grade), we went back to Chincoteague but with Uncle Tom's and Uncle Fritz's families. It was fun having cousins at the camp. Mosquitoes could be bad at the campground at times. The campground had a truck driving through the campground every night to spray for mosquitoes. I went down with Uncle Fritz's family. Mom and Dad showed up a few days later. Dad had an eight-track player in his Scout. He had bought Heart's latest album that had "Magic Man" and the new Foreigner eight-track. I had such hip parents who love rock 'n' roll.

SHARK SOUP: We went fishing, crabbing, and sunbathing at the beach. The night we ate the crabs we caught, the mosquitoes were terrible. Everyone ran into their tents, but Aunt Rita just sat out there, eating her crabs. Either they did not bite her or she just did not care. It was a sight to see.

The next day, we went to the beach. Uncle Tom is strong and a good swimmer. He went out swimming. We were sitting on the beach when someone said, "Is that a fin out there?" Sure enough, as Uncle

Tom was swimming, a fin that was not a dolphin fin was circling him. The family started screaming for him to come into shore, but the ocean was so loud that he just waved back to us. It was a scary thing, and he made it in one piece.

Our family went out clamming one day. We brought our little rakes and a raft with a basket in it to throw the clams in. It was Dad, Uncle Fritz, Uncle Tom, and myself. We were clamming near a canal where there was a bridge and you could watch traffic going by. Two older African American men said, "Don't go over there to go clamming. We saw a fin over there." My uncles thought they were bluffing to keep us from a hot clamming area, but it turned out they were right, and there were two fins, not one. That was the end of our clamming, and we moved as fast as one could when they were in waist-high water. We later cleaned the clams and had a wonderful feast of them after.

1979 - THE NASA ROCKET SCIENTIST: Mom and Dad went solo down the Kitty Hawk region of North Carolina to check it out. Let's face it, part of family time was having alone time without the kids. On their trip, they got a flat tire. A car pulled over, and a gentleman got out to see if he could help. As they got talking, he said he worked at NASA, and he helped work on something called the space shuttle. He told my folks he could mail some space shuttle artist renditions to them if they were interested. Three weeks later, I got a large yellow envelope; and when I opened it, there were eight 12" × 16" paintings of the space shuttle *Columbia*. I immediately taped the pictures all around my room. The first space shuttle, *Columbia*, took off in 1981. In 1986, the *Challenger* exploded in flight for all the world to see.

KITTY HAWK, NORTH CAROLINA: From 1979 on, we began to go camping in the summer at the outer banks in North Carolina. The campground was very clean, and so were the showering facilities. The campground was up against a bay and had a boat dock and a teen center where you could buy candy and soda and that had some pinball machines.

One morning, as we were eating breakfast, I saw a kid ride his bike by, and he looked like David Stauffer from my Union Terrace Little League baseball team. I told my parents, and they laughed at me. I jumped on my bike and slowly perused all the campsites to find this young man. As I turned one corner, I saw Dave and his elder brother playing wiffle ball, and I asked if I could play. They were surprised to see me, and I had two guy buddies the rest of the week at the campground. It was especially fun because I could make them laugh easily. *National Lampoon* had an album about, and I would always do the bit on "save the whales before they blast themselves into extinction." I also would do the bits from the McKenzie brothers album *The Great White North*, "Okay, eh!"

There were Benjamin Franklin Grocery stores down in North Carolina, and the one day Dad and I were standing by the doors when a guy looking like Fran Tarkenton, quarterback for the Minnesota Vikings walked out. He even had surgery marks on the knee he just had surgery one. I was too shy to ask it it was him, but I am 90% sure it was.

GOATS AND SWIMMING TRUNKS: In the center of the campground was a gated area with goats. Jody wanted to borrow the camera to take some pictures, and take some pictures she did—forty pictures worth. We went fishing one day on the bay, and when we went out to eat for dinner, as I was sitting on a solid bench, it felt like I was still on the boat. I was sitting still, but the restaurant felt like it was moving, like I was still on the boat. Mom and Dad dropped me off in a water park the next day and went shopping with Jody. I did not bring my swimming trunks; I was wearing a pair of blue gym shorts. As I came down the slide, Mom and Dad called me over and told me that my boys, my junk, my testes were flying around without the fine netting of swimming trunks for all the world to see, coming down the waterslide. Lesson learned.

OREGON INLET, NORTH CAROLINA: There was a long bridge next to Oregon Inlet, where fishermen chartered boats and fished for wahoo, tuna, and marlin. It was fun to go there in the late afternoon to see what people have caught. The second mates were cutting up the fish for the fishermen and throwing over the leftovers in the dock waters for the seagulls to fight over. Outside the marina headquarters was a hanging stuffed shark that was caught there at one time. Many people went out on the bridge, which was twenty-five to thirty feet above the water. Some had special nets you lowered by rope that allowed you to pull the fish up without it getting away. The fish they were mostly going after was the striped bass or the croaker, a fish with a black spot behind the gills and which made a "croak, croak" noise like a frog. We ended up fishing there and had luck. One day, I looked down and saw three large fish swim by. The three fish looked like thee had ram's horns, but they were hammerhead sharks.

SIR WALTER RALEIGH: Next to the campground was a playhouse where they ran "the Lost Colony." In the late sixteenth century (late 1500s), Queen Elizabeth I sent Sir Walter Raleigh and one hundred colonists to set up an English colony in the New World, but they disappeared. It was believed the people were killed by Native Americans or may have ended up intermarrying into the tribes to survive. We went clamming right behind where the colony used to be, and I imagined Indians and colonists with fishing nets and clamming for survival.

As we sat at our campsite, we cleaned the 250 clams we have dug up. Scrub, scrub, scrubby scrub, scrub for hours. Dad told Jody and me that if anyone asked where we got those, we should tell them we didn't know. A passerby asked where we got our clams, and Jody said, "Dad says we are not supposed to tell anyone!"

Twenty years later, England sent three ships with 114 people to start a colony in Jamestown, Virginia, which our family also visited on a vacation. Jamestown learned it could make money growing the cash crop tobacco by using slave labor. *The Lost Colony play* was good, but I liked the play *Pippin* better, about the king who tried to make everyone happy but realized it was an impossible thing to do. *Pippin* was first shown in New York in 1973. It was a show about existentialism, what is life about, and left me with an empty feeling at the end of it. Both plays asked questions but did not give you any answers, which was very unsatisfying. Both plays were examples of existentialism, about the "nothingness" of life sometimes.

I ended up getting sunburned badly. As Mom was putting the Noxzema lotion on my back in the tent in the evening, I sang "Hurts So Good" by John Cougar Mellencamp, and Mom laughed. What was not funny was I ended up with second-degree burns on the top of my feet. I looked like a cooked lobster.

VIVE LA FRANCE: As we were on the beach, Jody and Mom were in the waves. Dad and I were lying on the towel, and two couples walked up about twenty feet away from us. They laid down their towels and were wearing shorts. The two ladies took their shorts and shirts off and changed into their bikinis in front of us. They changed into their bottoms and tops in ten seconds, but Dad and I looked at each other like, "Did, we just see that?" Yup. They spoke with accents, and I think they came from France, where many of their beaches were topless. And I was always grateful to France for helping the English colonies overthrow their English masters in the Revolutionary War.

KUDOS TO MOM AND DAD FOR CAMPING TRIPS: After camping for so many summers, Mom and Dad created a list to follow for future trips. This way, they could start organizing weeks ahead of time. The list consisted of making sure the truck was in running order, camping supplies, amount of food needed, medical stuff, bathroom toiletries, beach stuff, fishing stuff, and clothing, in addition to planning where to go and making reservations in advance. They could be tent camping consultants. When Dad bought a camping trailer, we went from poor camping to middle-class camping.

MOM VS. ROCKY: We had a ten-person tent, and then Mom and Dad bought a screen tent to put around the picnic table. One day, before leaving for the beach, Mom said, "I need to get something from the cooler," and walked into the screen tent. Dad, Jody, and I were in the truck when we heard "Ahhh! Aaaaahhhhhh! Aaaahhhhh!" There was a squirrel in the screen tent, and it started charging Mom. Monty Python had its killer rabbit, and Mom had her killer squirrel. In the cartoon *The Rocky and Bullwinkle Show*, Bullwinkle was the moose, and Rocky was the intelligent squirrel, who wore a leather pilot's helmet.

MUHAMMAD ALI AND DENNIS "YOGI" YOUNG: My dad and Uncle Tom loved boxing. There was a time when boxing used to be part of gym class in high school. There was a time when high schools had .22-caliber rifle teams. Kids used to carry rifles to and from school, and they used to box in school. Dad liked Ali, and so I grew up watching about two-thirds of Ali's fights; making Ali feel like he was family. Ali's training camp was in Deer Lake, Pennsylvania, just forty miles from Allentown. My high school philosophy teacher said he worked at Howard Johnson's when Ali came in and ordered some ice cream. He was joking around with people, and Ali lost his next fight to Ken Norton. My dad's buddy from Mack's Dennis Young used to drive out to the Deer Lake camp and had the chance to hang out with Ali many times. Dad said he could have gone to Ali's camp one hundred times, but because he was working on the line and as a committeeman for the UAW, he did not have time to go with the other Mack workers like he would have.

DATE OF MUHAMMAD ALI FIGHTS

Total record: 61 fights, 57 wins, 4 losses

12-11-81	L	Trevor Berbick	Bahamas
10-2-80	L	Larry Holmes	Las Vegas
9-15-78	W	Leon Spinks	New Orleans
2-15-78	L	Leon Spinks	Las Vegas
9-29-77	W	Earnie Shavers	New York
5-16-77	W	Alfredo Evangelista	Landover, Maryland
9-28-76	W	Ken Norton	Bronx
5-24-76	W	Richard Dunn	Munich
2-20-76	W	Jean-Pierre Coopman	Puerto Rico
10-1-75	W	Joe Frazier	Philippines
6-30-75	W	Joe Bugner	Malaysia
5-16-75	W	Ron Lyle	Las Vegas
3-24-75	W	Chuck Wepner	Richfield, Ohio
10-30-74	W	George Foreman	Zaire
1-28-74	W	Joe Frazier	New York
10-20-73	W	Rudie Lubbers	Indonesia
9-10-73	W	Ken Norton	Inglewood, California
3-31-73	L	Ken Norton	San Diego, California
2-14-73	W	Joe Bugner	Las Vegas
11-21-72	W	Bob Foster	Stateline, Nevada
9-20-72	W	Floyd Patterson	New York

7-19-72	W	Alvin Lewis	Dublin
6-27-72	W	Jerry Quarry	Las Vegas
5-1-72	W	George Chuvalo	Vancouver
4-1-72	W	Mac Foster	Tokyo
12-26-71	W	Jurgen Blin	Zurich
11-17-71	W	Buster Mathis	Houston
7-26-71	W	Jimmy Ellis	Houston
3-8-71	L	Joe Frazier	New York
12-7-70	W	Oscar Bonavena	New York
10-26-70	W	Jerry Quarry Atlanta	

SUSPENSION: March 1967–October 1970 (3½ years) for refusing to fight in Vietnam

1960–1967: 29 wins, 0 losses

Ali dies on Saturday June 5th, 2016, 8 months after I send the letter below to the Muhammad Ali Center and two days after I type up Ali's boxing record for this book.

JIM'S LETTER TO THE ALI CENTER IN LOUISVILLE, KENTUCKY:

October 8, 2015

Dear Muhammad Ali Center,

I grew up in Allentown, Pennsylvania, about one hour away from Ali's Deer Lake training camp. My father worked at Mack Trucks and used to tell me about his buddy who used to "hang out" with Ali all the time. I was born in 1966 and grew up watching the Ali fights on TV. In 1978, just before the Leon Spinks fight, my dad took me up with his buddy Dennis "Yogi" Young (who looked like the Philadelphia Eagles linebacker Bill Bergey, no. 66) to watch Ali train in his camp.

I was able to walk around his camp, watch him jump rope and do some sparring, and later meet "the Greatest" and get his autograph. He shook my hand and handed me the autograph. I was twelve, and I was in sixth grade. I was also able to meet David Hartman of *Good Morning America* and supermodel Cheryl Tiegs, who were there to interview him, and got their autographs. During the sparring, I was sitting in row two. When his partner hit Ali, his sweat landed on my left leg. I had the greatest sweat of the world on my person. LOL.

I served as a pastor for five years in Queens (near Corona), where Malcolm X's house was firebombed. I now have been a high school history teacher for fifteen years. My last seven, I have taught in Washington Heights on Audubon Avenue, just a mile up from where Malcolm X was killed.

I am a fan of Muhammad Ali because he was the people's champ. He treated everyone equally regardless of class or ethnicity (I hate the word *race* because we are all of the human race, and all have black in us since our ancestors originated from Africa). As a history teacher, I have respect that he used his boxing as a springboard to speak out for civil rights, against the Vietnam War, and for respect for all people by having fights in the Philippines, Africa, and even Bangor, Maine. And now his advocacy is in fighting for a cure for Parkinson's and for being part of the movement that believes "black is beautiful."

I write this letter to say thank you to Muhammad Ali for his advocacy, his humor, and his love of justice. I write this letter because of the friendship he had with Dennis "Yogi" Young. When Sugar Ray Leonard fought in Allentown, Pennsylvania, my dad said to Yogi, "Hey, Ali just walked in." Yogi waved at Ali, whose eyes widened, and he smiled and nodded in recognition of Yogi.

Dennis "Yogi" Young is a salt-of-the-earth blue-collar worker who visited Ali frequently. Ali had the chef cook for him, let his kids play with his pinball machines, took Yogi into the barn to see his horses (would not all Howard Cosell in that day), allowed Yogi to come into his personal cabin (which he did not allow anyone to do), allowed Yogi to take pictures of his wife and kids, and hung out with a bunch of Mack Truck workers (all white), joked around with them, let them take pictures, and even put on a Mack Truck shirt (which he was reluctant to do at first but did) for the workers to see. Ali would hit the bag, which would swing three to five feet. He told Yogi, "Go ahead and hit it." Yogi was a big guy and almost broke his wrist, and it moved only a few inches, and Ali laughed. In Ali's cabin, the talk was about religion, the Bible, politics, boxing, life, etc. If you go to the Facebook site of Mr. Dennis "Yogi" Young, you may find some incredible pictures that you may want for the sake of history or posterity.

As an aside, I was the NYC director of the American Anti-Slavery Group for five years (www.iAbolish.org), speaking out against modern-day slavery and genocide in Sudan. I also spoke out against child labor and sweatshops. I was voted Teacher of the Year in 2012 at my school. I suggested we name the High School for Health Careers and Sciences to the Harry Belafonte High School because he graduated from George Washington High School but to no avail.

Thanks for your consideration,
Jim Geist
Northern New Jersey

DOGS: Grandpa Short always liked dogs. The name of the Shorts' dog was Queeny. When the neighborhood bully picked on Grandpa, he took his childhood dog with him the next day. When he saw the bully approach him, Grandpa pointed at the bully and said to his dog, "Sic." And after some biting, pulling, and tugging by the dog, the bully stopped messing with Grandpa as a young man.

BEOWOLF: When we were young, my parents gave Jody and me a dog named Beowolf. It used to belong to Andy and Barbara, but they lived in a small apartment. Andy and Barb were a fun couple, hippies, and always laughing. Andy took me to the movies, and Barb climbed the tree behind our home and had she had blue eyes and long hair. I didn't know what breed Beowolf was. It may have been a mix and was hyper, did not listen well, and bit me on the hand one day. It also jumped up on the new golden-colored couch Mom and Dad bought one day and took a huge steaming dog crap on it. I couldn't remember who said it, but what I heard was "That's it! That dog is gone!" And that was how the tale of the Beowolf ended.

MANDY: My folks took Jody and me out to the country to some farmhouse in a white station wagon. Jody and I thought it was white, but Dad always said, "It's blue!" We approached a barn, and an English setter puppy came out, which would be our new dog named Mandy. The Barry Manilow song "Mandy" was a hit around this time and probably had something to do with the dog's name. It had on a pink bow when we picked it up. We were given the "if you want a dog, you must walk it and clean up after it." Yeah, yeah, yeah.

It took a while, but Mandy became house-trained. She was a female, so when she went in heat, she left blood marks in the home. She was a good dog, but she loved to run. She was a hunting dog, meant to run the fields looking for birds; the breeding and bloodline demanded it. To take her out, we would attach the dog leash to her collar and then hook her up to the wire in the backyard. Dad would put in a metal pole with a line attached to it. We would attach the line to Mandy's collar and let her go until she was done with her business.

Mandy was a medium-sized dog. We went over to visit some friends of Dad and Mom, Frank and Kathy. Frank was a mellow guy, and I liked his smile. Kathy was an English teacher at Whitehall High School, pretty, and always happy. Frank and Kathy had the larger version of an English setter. The dog's name was Timmy. When we got out of the car, I was holding the dog chain to Mandy. I could feel her tugging, tugging, and tugging to get over to Timmy. My sister, four years younger, said, "I want to hold Mandy." I said to my parents, "I don't think that is a good idea." Dad said, "Give your sister the leash." I did, and my sister flew into the air about four feet and hit the ground, being dragged like a dogsled bouncing up and down on the grass. I thought it was horrifying and funny. I said to the folks, "I told you so." Jody cried.

Kathy was a teacher in Whitehall Pa, and died in her early sixties. I was told Frankie, who worked at Mack Trucks, was lost without her, and he followed her by dying of a broken heart. They were good to me as a kid, and I wish they were still around.

SWAG AND BO: We visited Dale and Sandy, who had an English setter named Swag and an Irish setter named Bo. When we brought Mandy, all three dogs ran around the property. Mandy was a happy dog when she got to run on Dale and Sandy's farm. It was funny to watch her run full speed with the dogs chasing her, and then she just stopped as they ran by, and she ran the opposite way.

BUCKY: Nana had a beagle with black, brown, and white coloring named Bucky, who lived in a doghouse with a cage surrounding it. The dog cage area reeked, especially in the summer. When Dale and Sandy moved to their country home out in Northampton, they took Bucky with them.

One weekend, when I slept over at Dale and Sandy's, I went to pet Bucky, and he snapped at me. Bucky turned out to be a chicken killer. The neighbors next to Dale and Sandy kept having chickens killed, and they figured out it was Bucky doing the killing. An old farmwives' tale said that if you took a dead chicken and wired it to the dog's neck, it would take the killer instinct out of the dog. Bucky ran around swinging the chicken around its neck like it was a game, sporting the chicken necklace like it was an Olympic gold medal.

MY SISTER AND CHORES: Jody is excellent at art, is a good volleyball player, has many friends, and loves horses. We have a bond of the same parents, lived in the same home, shared vacations, shared memories of family events at the place of our grandparents and other family members, and went to the same schools and even college, and had mutual neighborhood and school friends.

For our chores, I had to collect the trash weekly, clean up the dog poo, and wash dishes nightly. We had a dishwasher, but Mom and Dad had Jody and me, and you could save some money on electricity by using the kids. My philosophy was "Let's get this done as soon as possible." My sister really hated doing them; thus I chose to wash the dishes so I did not have to sit around waiting for her to finish washing. We did many dishes, and doing dishes was a sign of being blessed and much better than not doing dishes and going to bed hungry.

POO ON THE SHOE: As I was in the backyard cleaning up dog poo, Jody came and started chanting, "Jim cleans the dog poo! Jim cleans the dog poo!"

I said, "Jody, you better stop, or I will take the dog poo on this shovel and fling it at you."

She said, "No, you won't!"

I said "Yes, I will!"

She laughed. "No, you won't!" I took the shovel and flung the poo toward her, not intending to hit her but to send the message "Be glad you don't have to clean up the poo, and leave me alone." The flying pile of poo smacked her on the left cheek, and Jody screamed bloody murder. It was a great day!

GRANDPA SHORT AND THE CONGRESSMAN: Grandpa Short worked for Fuller Company. He often went abroad around the world, representing Fuller and helping solve problems. He was asked to meet with the local congressman at the time in Washington DC. Our local airport was the ABE or Allentown-Bethlehem-Easton Airport. As he was sitting there in the waiting area to leave for DC, it was announced the flight was overbooked, and if one passenger waited for the next flight, he/she would get a free ticket to fly anywhere in the continental United States. A man raised his hand and said, "I'll take that deal."

At DC, my grandfather got out of the taxi in front of the Capitol Building and went to the congressman's office. The secretary said, "Sorry, the congressman has been delayed." Two hours later, the congressman walked in and shook Grandpa Short's hand; he was the man who volunteered to take a free ticket.

CHAPTER 3

Raub Junior High School, 1978–80 (Ages 12–14)

<u>JUNIOR HIGH AND SENIOR HIGH FRIENDS</u>

TIMMY: Kenny and I had a falling out, and I was not sure why. Today I realize that people come into my life for a day, season, or a lifetime. For me, I would be very sad when losing a friendship. Ken must have started a new job or hung out with other friends from school, so his brother, Timmy, became my new buddy, and he was funny. We spent a lot of time on the basketball court. It was here I met Frank Radocha. Frank lived on Elm Street. We would meet at Hamilton Park and play basketball. Rich Baker showed up, and he went to St. Thomas More Catholic School like Timmy. There was another Ken, Mike Sabler, whose father was the basketball coach of the Allen High School Lady Canaries. There also was another guy a year ahead of me who had blond hair named Lee. We often would have two-on-two, three-on-three, four-on-four, or—if others showed up—full-court basketball games. Between walking to and from school, riding bikes, having a paper route, and playing basketball, I was in the best shape of my life.

FRANK: It was much fun to be able to hang with friends, blast the stereo, go to movies, and go to Friendly's for the famous Reese's Pieces sundaes or Yocco's for hot dogs or the Brass Rail for steak sandwiches. When I got my driver's license at age seventeen, Frank would come with me for Sunday deliveries, and I would give him $10 for helping out. And then we would go to Dunkin' Donuts, pick up a coffee and doughnut, and drive around the Lehigh Valley, listening to the radio or audiotapes. Frank always made me laugh because he had a dry and boring way of saying, "That's grrreeaaatttt," if anyone thought they had something exciting to share. On icy days, Frank laughed when I hit an icy spot and took a dive. Frank loved that I accepted it and went limp instead of tightening up and getting tense before the hitting of the groud, those who tense up usually break bones when hitting the ground. I also had on a big pudgy winter jacket, boots, gloves and a winter hat that served as protection.

BLUEBERRY PIE: Frank had a younger brother, Pete, and a sister, Gina. Frank's dad was from the coal area and used to be an excellent basketball player in his high school days. Frank's mom was very nice. The family, except for the dad, attended St. Thomas More Catholic Church.

One day, as we were watching MTV before heading up to the park to shoot hoops, Mrs. R. gave us a piece of her blueberry pie. She made the best pie ever. I also remembered the day she bought a new brown Honda car. She loved it!

During the summer, we spent many nights sitting in Frank's carport with his record player, listening to various Bill Cosby records. Cosby was a master storyteller, and we used to use Cosby phrases on each other as the years went by. It was fun to sit under the carport roof when it was raining or when it was a clear night, and we could see the stars and the moon. We always laughed at the God-Noah bit. "You want me to build an ark? Riiiiggghhhhttt! You want me to measure in cubits? What's a cubit? You want two of every animal? Riiiigggghhhhttt!"

EAST TEXAS BOULEVARD SIRENS: On East Texas Boulevard lived a family with four sisters: Lisa, Laurie, Sherri, and the new baby. The father was a state police officer, and the mom was a homemaker. In year sixteen or seventeen, another rooster joined the crew. His name was Roger, and his father gave him a red sports car. I was unaware at the time that Frank was competing with me for Laurie's attention.

NUTS ABOUT PISTACHIOS: Laurie mentioned that she liked pistachios. I walked all the way downtown one day to the Nut Hut to purchase half a pound for her. When I gave them to Ms. H., her attitude was like, "Whatever." One day, when I was able to take her to Friendly's alone, the waitress came up to me and asked if I was Jim because I had a call. When I answered the phone, it turned out to be a crank call. I knew who did it. Tim took Frank's side on this, and when I saw Frank's bike at Timmy's place, I became so angry I saw red, grabbed a utility knife, and slashed his one tire. In time, I admitted to it and bought Frank a new inner tube. Mrs. R., when she found out, said to me, "Jimmy, I am so disappointed." I heard her, and I too was disappointed in my vengeful response. . Roger ended up dating you-know-who. How could anyone compete with a guy who has a red Firebird when the rest of us did not own their own car?

TRAGIC DAY: Gina was Jody's age, so they used to pal around together. They both liked to play volleyball and were good at it. Peter was good at every sport but especially at baseball and basketball. His dad used to say, "Pete will end up either as president or in jail."

One day, Pete drove down College Drive to the stop sign on Hamilton Boulevard. This boulevard was four lanes wide, and when pulling out by the National Bank, especially if you were making a left turn or going straight to Cedar Crest College, you had to make sure no one was coming or had to give it gas to make sure you did not get hit. There was a small hill on the left, and by the time you get visibility of an oncoming car, it could be too late if the vehicle was speeding.

On this day, a dump truck came down Hamilton Street, hitting Pete's car pulling out of College Drive next to National Bank, killing Pete, and severely injuring his girlfriend. It was a dangerous intersection with four lanes of traffic, and the east lane was a hill, giving a limited view. It was a tragedy, and nothing more could be said. As in all passing, I always prayed to God to give strength, courage, and grace for family members and friends to sit with the grief until they were able to function again, although maybe never the same.

THE NEW KID ON 512 COLLEGE DRIVE: One day, a new kid showed up with the College Drive crew of kids. He must have been visiting an aunt or uncle for a few weeks that summer because I never saw him again after that. I couldn't remember his name, but we were playing wiffle ball in front of the Ruths. The new kid was "new," so he should have kept his mouth shut and learned the pecking order before opening his mouth. He started bossing me around, telling me what to do, and calling me names. I ran into the house and told Dad. Dad looked at me and said, "Here's what you do. Go outside, walk up to the kid, and punch him in the nose." I said, "What? Really?" Dad nodded. As I walked out into the cooling of the late afternoon summer sunset, I walked up to new kid bully; and as he was about to make some smart-ass comment, I smacked him right in the nose. He grabbed his nose with both hands and said, "What the hell is wrong with you?" He started tearing up and ran to his home (wherever that was). He was not in the neighborhood very long, and he never bothered me after that. I was sure the other kids must have gotten a kick out of seeing me sock him in the schnoz.

TENNIS PLAYERS OF THE 1970s: A tennis craze started in the United States in 1972. We had Jimmy Connors, John McEnroe, Chris Evert, and Billie Jean King. In 1973, Bobby Riggs, who was fifty-five, played Margaret Court and beat her in May of 1973 but then played Billie Jean King on September 20, 1973, at the Astrodome. He made fun of women's tennis, and the matches were called the "Battle of the Sexes." He was paid $50,000 to wear a yellow Sugar Daddy candy jacket, and he lost to Billie Jean King. Riggs owed some gambling debts and betted against himself and won. He said he had "underestimated" Billie Jean, and she deserved to be the victor.

1972 TENNIS CRAZE HITS THE GEISTS: For a couple of summers, Mom, Dad, Jody, and I went to the courts to hit the tennis ball in around 1978–80. We used to play at Lindbergh Park and a few times at Alton Park courts. We had wooden rackets and were not very good, but it was a fun memory. Grandpa Short used to be a good player, winning the Allentown City Championship before going to Kings Point. He also played on the Penn State tennis team when he came back from working for the merchant marines shipping goods, ammunition, armaments, and troops back and forth from the States and the battle theater.

It was always funny to hear Mom go "umph" or make a frustrated "hurrumph" when she hit the ball into the net or outside the line. It was always a good workout, and many times, the balls flew over the metal fencing like Hank Aaron cranking out a home run. When I played with fellow friends, one of our main goals was to hit the ball as hard as we could when someone was near the net to hit them in the balls.

Throughout the years, as I lived in Queens (1996–2002), I got the chance to attend the U.S. Open on a half dozen occasions. The tennis stadiums were next to Shea Stadium, and the game was a fun event for me to attend. I was able to watch Andre Agassi, Roger Federer, Michael Chang, and Pete Sampras.

<u>Greatest Male Tennis Players</u>
    1960s: Rod Laver
    1970s: Bjorn Borg, Arthur Ashe, Jimmy Connors, John McEnroe
    1980s: Boris Becker
    1990s: Jim Courier, Andre Agassi, Michael Chang, Pete Sampras
    2000s: Juan Carlos Ferrero, Roger Federer, Rafael Nadal

<u>Great Female Tennis Players</u>
    1960s: Margaret Court
    1970s: Evonne Goolagong, Billie Jean King, Chris Evert
    1980s: Martina Navratilova, Steffi Graf
    1990s: Monica Seles
    2000s: Justine Henin, Venus Williams, Serena Williams

ZELLER TENNIS TOURNAMENT: I was friends with Teddy Zeller. He lived on Union Street near Twenty-Fourth Street. His house was big and in the middle of a street block, and one side was a tennis court with a ten-foot fence around it, and on the other side of the house was a large wad of grass we played tackle or touch football on. Teddy had a younger sister, Emily, and they both had blond hair. Their father died from cancer, so the mother set up a tennis tournament every year to raise money to fight cancer. I think it cost $5 to enter the tournament, and that was where I first learned that when you served the ball, it had to fall into the right or left service court, depending on which side you were serving from. I also stayed around and served as a ball boy for a few other games. All the tennis playing would come in handy later in life, when I had the chance to play with mates in college on the Nyack courts and with significant others, such as Joy, Sarne, and Tiffany.

ZELLER FOOTBALL AND WINTER HOCKEY: We played many football games at the Zellers from fifth grade through eighth grade. I considered Teddy to be my "rich" friend. In the wintertime, we made a hockey rink out of his tennis court. I made two nets out of two-by-fours. When it was freezing out, we would hose the court down, and it would freeze nicely. When it snowed, we would shovel the snow on the street side against the green fencing; on the opposite side, we just piled up the snow, and we ended up with a nice-sized rink. I did not have hockey skates; I had ice-skater skates. It was so much fun to check each other into the snowbanks. Tony Germano, Bob Duncan, Drew Whitner, Alan Mills, Mike Watson, John Christianson, and whoever else showed up would join us. I took a slap shot, and it hit Drew Whitner in the mouth and chipped his front tooth. He was pissed at me. I did not do it purposely, but at least he did not look like Bobby Clarke with all his missing front teeth, and I had my tooth knocked in half during baseball and did not cry about it or blame anyone. The tennis courts had night-lights, so we could also play hockey at night. This was one of my favorite childhood memories.

TED NUGENT IN ALLENTOWN: It was 1975, and Mike Watson was standing outside his home, next to the Youell's Oyster House at 2249 Walnut Street, when a bus pulled up. Just half a mile down the road was Mayor Daddona's little store next to UT that had a Ted Nugent "Cat Scratch Fever" pinball machine, which I have played many times. The bus door opened in front of Watson, and a guy in blue jeans and crazy long hair said, "Hi, kid! I am Ted Nugent. Do you want to see what our tour bus looks like?" So Mike Watson was Allentown's ambassador for welcoming Ted Nugent before his 1975 show at Agricultural Hall.

ALTON PARK FOOTBALL (1975–1979): When I started playing Little League football in sixth grade, I started out with the Alton Park Comets B team (80 lbs.) in 1975, the A team (85 lbs.) in 1976, and the 100 lb. team in 1978 and 1979.

MIKE "HERSCHEL WALKER": I told Dad I was interested in playing football, so he took me up to Alton Park, where we sat on a grass hill to watch the different teams practicing. As we were watching, the running back, after getting tackled next to us, ran over, waved, and said, "Hi, Mr. Geist! Hi, Jim!" He had on a football helmet, so I could not tell who he was. It was not until later I realized it was Mike Brogna. Dad spoke to the coaches, and I went there the next day early, where I was suited up for practice and started my short-lived Little League football career playing right tackle and, in my final year, linebacker on the practice squad, which was a different kind of fun.

I was given a play list and told to memorize the plays. After a few days of practice, it was determined that I would play offensive line, right tackle. I liked the system that was in place for the team. We met for practice and formed a circle, and the coach gave a little pep talk. We would run around the field for warm-up and get back in a circle, and the captain and co-captain would lead us through different exercises. We had different things we practiced on different days of the week. Sometimes we broke up the linemen from the running backs and quarterbacks.

Mike Brogna always loved Herschel Walker, running back of Georgia Bulldogs. He also loved no. 34, Walter Payton, also called "Sweetness," the running back for the Chicago Bears. When asked what he loved most about football, Payton used to say "contact." When could you remember a running back saying contact was their favorite part of football?

ALTON PARK PRACTICE: We used to practice the tipping exercise, where the quarterback threw the ball, a person would tip it by hitting the bottom tip of the ball with their hand, and the person behind him would catch it. We did the monkey drill, where three people lined up; the person in the center jumped down and rolled to the left, the person on the right jumped over the center person and roll to the right, and then the person on the right jumped over the left person— over and over again. Another drill was having several lines of us facing each other and tossing a football in the center like a fumble to practice grabbing loose balls. There was another exercise called powder puff, where you were put in the middle of all the circled players and had to do all you could to get out while the players chanted, "Powder puff!"

Our practice outfits were white pants. We were given shoulder pads, football pants, and a light blue helmet with a white stripe down the middle and dark navy stripes next to the white one. We had to buy our own cleats and jockstrap. The game outfit was nice. The pants were light blue with matching stripes of the helmet, and we had nice shirts with our number on it. We looked sharp. They also gave us a clear plastic mouthpiece we put in boiling water, wait for twenty seconds after pulling it out, bite down into for ten seconds, and then put in cold water. It was important to use the toothbrush and toothpaste on it nightly, or weekly anyway.

We run plays, offense against defense, to practice running actual plays. That was the fun part, but then came the hard part of conditioning at the end of practice. It could be doing the crab walk up the hills next to the football field. It might be running around the field for several times, or it might be wind sprints, where you ran to the five-yard line and back and then the ten-yard and back and then the fifteen and back and so on. We would be dragging by the end of practice, but we had excellent coaches, who knew that if two equal teams played each other, the better conditioned team was more likely to win.

My coaches in 1975 for the 80 lb. team were <u>Head Coach Williams and Assistant Coaches Ernie Fenstemaker, Lou Ortelli, and B. Cronaure</u>. On the team were Mike Brogna, myself, Mike Schuler, Bill Cohen, Dale Miller, Brendan Sherman, Mark Lanzone, John Pope, and John Dini, in addition to the many people listed. In 1976, I played with Troy Fenstemaker, John Donmoyer, Sean Steigerwalt, Eddie Barnett, Sammy Brehem, Tony Capobianco, Tony Dellacroce, Scott Kern, Mike Kozar, Tom Levy, Cory Mest, Mike Rosten, Mark Roth, Barry Ruth, Scott Schleicher, Robert Sletvold, Scott Steffie, Craig Stevens, Matt Stevens, and Steve Whippel. As a sidenote, in 1976, Mike Wolf, who played for the 120 team, went on to play lineman for the Penn State but had a knee injury and became a workout coach for the Eagles. His brother, Joe, was on the 100 lb. team and played at Boston University and then for the Arizona Cardinals. Bill Robinson died in July of 2007 and was not the same Bill "Bojangles" Robinson, the famous dancer.

1976 AIR FORCE BOWL AT EMMAUS HIGH SCHOOL STADIUM: On Sunday, November 21, in the eighty-five-pound game, Alton Park, trailing 7–6, scored on an eighty-five-yard pass from Troy Fenstemaker to John Dini with two seconds in the game to eke out a 12–7 victory over Catasauqua. The four outstanding players for the Alton Park Comets were Mike Brogna, John Dini, Scott Schleicher, Andy Hart, and Scott Steffie. All the winners and outstanding players were handed awards by Pittsburgh Pirates star (and Phillies player) Bill Robinson. Robinson died in July of 2007 and was not to be confused with Bill "Bojangles" Robinson, the tap dancer. We also were the league champs with thirteen wins, zero losses, and two ties.

100 LB. CHAMPS IN '77 AND '78: In <u>1977,</u> I played with Eddie Barnett, Sammy Brehem, Tony Capobianco, Tony Dellacroce,

Scott Kern, Mike Kozar, Mark Lanzone, Tom Levy, Cory Mest, Mike Rosten, Mark Roth, Barry Ruth, Scott Schleicher, Robert Sletvold, Scott Steffie, Craig Stevens, and Matt Stevens. The coaches for the one-hundred-pound-pound team in 1978 were Head Coach Gary Fisher and Assistant Coaches Dick Rivera, Bill Mest Jr., and Steve and Mike Klegarth. Mr. Rivera always brought oranges to the games, and we all consumed half oranges for energy for the second half.

The person across from me for most of the time that I was at Alton Park was Tim Dempsey. He was the left defensive tackle. I was the right offensive tackle. Most of my time was practicing blocking to make room for the running backs. I was not really focused on being a tackler. I think we helped make each other better players. In my last year there, a new kid came along, and he was

NFL FOLLIES: One of the fun memories I had of being on the team was the night we met for a pizza party at the Alton Park clubhouse and watched some NFL funniest moments films. We ate and ate pizza and laughed and laughed. The other thing the Alton Park League wanted was to get night-lights for night football. The four years I was connected with the Comets, I sold many raffle tickets and brooms. The lights were finally put up the year after I finished playing football with the Comets. Anytime I was back in Allentown and I passed Alton Park, I filled up with some pride and said, "I helped pay for those lights."

Alton Park also had a cheerleading program at each level, so it was fun at our games to play and have family and friends there—cheerleaders, referees, and the blue truck that sold drinks and hot dogs. It was quite the event. Mom was the assistant coach of the Pom-Pom Girls in 1978 and sister Jody was a Pom-Pom girl. Some of the cuties on the cheerleading squad were Kristina Brogna (B team); Susan Fainer, Michelle Lang, Michelle Maron, and Susan Laudenslager (100 lb. team); and Lisa Dellacroce and Jane Laudenslager (125 lb. team). Hubba-hubba – they made my loins burn.

SOUL FOOD AND THE MILLVILLE, NEW JERSEY, GAME: We drove to Millville to play a team in New Jersey. We drove down on a Saturday night and stayed over at the Millville players' homes. Our game was on a Sunday. There was one black kid on the Millville team who was the running back. His name was Lamont, and somehow, the coaches picked me to stay with his family. Driving back to Lamont's trailer home, his father looked at me and said, "Have you ever had soul food before, Jim?" By my look, he laughed. We had a nice meal of chicken bucket meal from Kentucky Fried Chicken, just like what my white family enjoyed and ate frequently. As we hung out in the trailer, talked, and watched TV, Lamont and his dad brought out a lotion and started rubbing it on themselves. His dad said, "Black people have to use lotion, or they will shrivel away." Lamont was a quiet and mild kid, but when the quarterback put the football in his hands, he ran like the devil was chasing him. Millville beat us the next day. All the Alton Park kids wanted to know what it was like staying with a black family. I told them about soul food and lotion and having many laughs together.

ALTON PARK CIRCA 2016: I am fifty and try to get to my parents' home every six to eight weeks, which is two hours away from my home. In the room where I sleep is a cut-out news article, "Comets Reunion Sparks Memories," by Keith Groller of the *Morning Call* paper (August, 8, 2016). Alton Park football has ended because of a lack of number of people in Allentown willing to put in the time to help the community's kids.

Coach Mike Klegarth who used to play as a Comet and later coached said, "Over the years, we taught things like dedication, perseverance and discipline. Alton Park helped to develop bankers, builders, doctors and lawyers, people who went on to make an impact in the community."

The program produced NFL players like Keith Dorney, Mike Lush, and Kevin White and others who were excellent college players and some who went on to coach at the high school and college level. Bill Mest, another coach of mine, said, "It was an unselfish, caring community where everyone pulled together. We raised our own money, and many nights stayed in the clubhouse until 3:00 a.m. making hoagies, and everyone in the neighborhood bought them." There used to be a roach coach that sold hot dogs, chips, soda, and coffee to help keep the program going during game times. The Comets would live in the hearts of all who participated in that stellar program of volunteerism.

UNCLE BILL RIPPLE: The name of Nana Ruby' son was Bill. I knew Uncle Bill from all the Thanksgiving and Christmas meals we celebrated together or on a birthday celebration of some relative. Bill used to wear a necklace with a tiger's claw. It supposedly was to keep tigers away, and I honestly could say I never saw any tigers around in Pennsylvania when he was around. He had a handsome big flop of dark hair and a big businessman's smile and always had a joke or two to tell.

When Uncle Bill was a boy, he used to love magic. He gave me his magic book, and there was a time when I dabbled in it and enjoyed seeing people's look of amazement when a trick was done. Uncle Bill had practiced his craft and had some friends come over for a show. Nana Ruby was to be the curtain person, and at one point, when she was not paying attention during the show, Bill scolded her by saying loudly, "Mom, the curtain!" Nana Ruby always gave a hearty laugh when she shared that story.

Uncle Bill served in the Korean War. Nana Ruby had a spiritual-emotional connection with Bill, and when he was in trouble, she could sense it in her spirit. One day, she said, "Bill is in trouble!" She prayed and prayed and prayed, and sure enough, because of all the carnage and death Uncle Bill witnessed in the war, he ended up in an asylum, a place easy for any sane, peace-loving, and spiritual person could end up with such a constant barrage of images of death and war wounds. Today it would be called PTSD. It was at the asylum hospital where he would meet a nurse named Ida, and they later would marry. When he was released, he served. It was my first or second year as a newspaperboy (ages thirteen to fourteen) that Mom called me into the living room to tell me the horrible news that Uncle Bill had taken his life. I was in shock and saddened that this happened. I went to the viewing, funeral, and the reception afterward. I used to get up at 5:30 a.m. to deliver papers, and at the reception, I started falling asleep at the table. When Aunt Ida walked by and saw me, she smiled because she knew I got up early to deliver papers.

At one point, Grandpa Short was out on his back porch while smoking a pipe, under the green and white canvas covering, and said to a family member, "Why? I don't understand." Grandpa had served in World War II, but I didn't think he saw what Uncle Bill saw. Maybe Grandpa was angry he lost a brother-in-law or maybe because it was just a sad loss of life. I did not judge; I felt empathy for a person who saw so much in a war and ended up taking medication, and if he did not take it, he may have become suicidal.

And who does not think about being suicidal? Many therapists say there is a difference about contemplating suicide and actually planning to do so and that the mere contemplation of it often brings relief to whatever it is that is causing pain in a person's life. I have also learned that many who seriously consider suicide do so to get out of the emotional pain he or she is in and are in such desperate state that any idea that it can get better seems impossible.

CHRISTMAS: Christmas is a fun time for me. I don't know about those who have to cook, clean, shop, and wrap gifts on the q.t.

On the Geist side, we would visit two homes a night and over two to three days at a stretch. There was food, storytelling, laughter, and watching some funny antics of drunk family members. One year, Uncle Fritz gave our English setter, Mandy, some beer, and she became real loopy. Another time, when Uncle Fritz got drunk, he got hold of a bra and wore it for a third of the party. Uncle Tom, Uncle Fritz, Earl, Dale, Dad, and my aunts had a good sense of humor. In Christmas 1976 at Uncle Fritz and Aunt Rita's place, I brought a ten-page play of *A Christmas Carol*; and Timmy, Allen, Bryan, and I played all the characters and recorded it on a cassette recorder. When we finished, we brought it down for the adults to listen to. I wish I still had that tape!

On Mom's side of the family, the requests for Christmas gifts were put in at Thanksgiving. My funny memory about that was cousin Becky saying to my mom, "I want a, b, c, and x, y, z. But that is all I want from you, Aunt Ginny!" Ha. Smart kid, if she could weasel out five to six toys per family, she could end up with eighteen to twenty-five gifts instead of the usual one gift per aunt and uncle and grandparents. I walked in on Mom wrapping gifts one day and said, "Who is that gift going to?" She said, "To one of your cousins." I got upset because it was a toy I wanted. Surprisingly, I ended up getting that toy. Way to be quick on your toes, Mom!

The way it worked for Ginny, Bill, Jody, and me for Christmas was we would go to Nana and Grandpa Shorts and the extended Short family on Christmas Eve. We would meet at six in the evening for a dinner, which was usually beef soup with sandwiches and "special" eggnog for the adults. After dinner, the kids (cousins) went for a car ride to look at Christmas lights; and often, we would spot Rudolph the reindeer's nose in the sky. Oula! When we arrived home, Santa would have stopped by to drop off the gifts at the tree. Once, I wanted to stay home to watch this miraculous event but was informed Santa could not use his magic when children were around the tree. Afterward, Uncle Bob and Aunt Davy's kids—Chrissy, Becky, and Jason—and myself and Jody would be "ripping and tearing" at the wrappers of the presents. When I got older and knew there was no Santa, I whined, "Do I have to go look at the lights this year?" Nana laughed.

On Christmas Day, we would wake up to cookie crumbs and a note from Santa thanking us for the cookies. Jody and I would wake up Mom and Dad, eat a nice breakfast, and then go downstairs for part two of the Christmas tradition. It was better to give than receive, they would say, but I loved receiving! Our dog Mandy would get gifts as well, and we laughed when she would rip off pieces of the wrapping with her little doggy teeth and spit it out. Hilarious!

After opening our presents on College Drive, part three of our annual tradition began by going to Nana Geist's to hang out there for a few hours. I didn't know how Nana Geist did it, but she used to give all her grandkids and great-grandkids $5 in cards. I knew some of her sons and daughters used to beg her not to do this since Nana was a pensioner and did not get much from social security.

SANTA SCARES THE BEJESUS OUT OF JIM AND JODY: Saying "scared the bejesus out of me" was a favorite of Nana Geist. It was the holiday, and Jody and I were doing the dishes when someone in a red hat and white beard stuck up his face in the kitchen window. My sister and I screamed. It turned out to be a visit from Santa Claus via Uncle Fritz. He got us good. My parents used to warn my sister and me that if we kept fighting, Santa would put coal in our Christmas stocking because we had been bad. One Christmas morning, we went downstairs to find coal in our stocking. I went into shock. Sister Jody and I looked at each other in disbelief. Oh, the horror, the agony, the shame of being on the naughty list! "Wait a minute, Jody, it could be candy coal!" I took the big piece of coal and took a bite, and a piece came off; it did not taste sugary. It was real coal!

THE NUTCRACKER SUITE: When decorating the tree with tinsel, my sister and I would put on the album *The Nutcracker Suite*, dance around like ballerinas, and throw the tinsel on the tree. Jody would laugh so hard. We used to put small candy canes on the tree as well. Any that were put within reach of the dog would end up getting pointed ends like a match projector from the dog licking them. It was actually impressive Mandy could lick the candy canes without knocking them off the tree.

ALCOHOL BRINGS OUT TRUTH (WAR STORIES); Many of the guys shared deer hunting stories, since buck season always opened on the Monday after Thanksgiving. Many of the men worked at Mack Trucks, so we heard many Mack Truck factory stories as well. Uncle Tom sang "Silver Bells" and did a nice job. Some of the family served in the military, so we heard those stories as well. Uncle Earl was the eldest, and he had served in WWII and was in the third picture after the original picture of the flag raising on Mount Sarabachi in Iwo Jima. He is on the left side of the picture and the only one with a cigarette in his hand. Uncle Fritz served in the Army, and Uncle Norm had served in Korea. Sometimes Earl got to telling war stories after getting a few drinks in him. At one point, Earl broke down crying. It would not be until decades later when I watched the movies *Flags of Our Fathers* that I understood how much carnage Uncle Earl had seen. The HBO series *Band of Brothers*, also showed the many conundrums that happen in the midst of war. What should a soldier do when the commander is clearly insane and not thinking clearly?

FAVORITE CHRISTMAS TOYS FROM THE PAST:

1. Air hockey: this game brought many, many hours of fun and entertainment. We would place the game on a table so it was at waist height, like if you went to the arcade.
2. Coleco handheld quarterback game: This game was battery operated, and as quarterback, you could move to the left for right based on the arrows you picked and release the ball. You could also run the ball, and when you scored, it made a "daaaa-da-da-daa-da-da" sound.
3. DMX racing track game: This game was cool because you had two tracks your car could pass on, but the joystick you held had a button that when you hit it, the cars switched tracks, meaning you could pass your opponent.

Those are my three favorite toys. The worst toy was my large piece of coal.

COUSIN BABY JESSIE NEEDS PRAYER: Dale and Sandy had Jessica Geist on December 23, 1977. When I got the news, I was told she was a premature baby, a "preemie" they called them. I prayed and prayed and prayed and prayed for her. I believe I even made a deal with God that I would do all I could for his kingdom if he helped her live. I believe the promise I made was like the scene in the movie *The End*. When it became clear that cousin Jessie was going to make it, I was sure my promise became less serious as her health continued to improve.

***THE END*:** In the movie *The End*, the Burt Reynolds character tries to take his life several times. In one attempt, he goes out unto a beach and begins swimming out into the ocean. His goal is to swim out far enough so, should he change his mind, he will end up drowning. In this attempt at his life, he realizes that he wants to live; and as he starts swimming to the shore, he begins making promises to God of what he will do with his life if he lives. He says, "I will not cheat, I will not kill, I will not commit adultery. I will . . . I will . . . I will learn all the commandments if I survive. I promise to keep most of the commandments if I survive." As he is crawling out of the water onto the dry sand, he says to God, "Ahhhh, forget it."

JANUARY 1, 1979 MOVIE *THE CHINA SYNDROME*: A movie came out showing the potential danger of using nuclear power and what could happen if there would be a meltdown in a reactor. Michael Douglas and Jane Fonda starred in the movie. March 28, 1979

THREE MILE ISLAND (TMI) IN MIDDLETOWN, PENNSYLVANIA: I got in Aunt Arlene's car for the ride home, and she had the radio on. It was talking about a possible meltdown in a nuclear reactor in Middletown Pennsylvania, next to Harrisburg, just ninety miles from Allentown, or 1.5 hours away by car. What if nuclear steam got out into the atmosphere, and the wind carried it to our area? Did we have to move away until the crisis was resolved? Would our area be contaminated and we have to relocate? TMI was blamed mostly on human error, and a catastrophe was averted, but how strange the movie *The China Syndrome* came out just three months before, predicting what could possibly happen? Have we studied the lessons from 1979? Yes. Have some positive changes been made as a result? Yes. Has the government and nuclear plants done everything they could do to avert future meltdowns? Sadly, no.

PRE-SEVENTH-GRADE BUG COLLECTING SUMMER: In our last year of elementary school, we were told we needed to find an x amount of insects for our seventh-grade biology class. There were many days spent running around fields with a butterfly net and pinning insects in our insect boxes over the summer. I took a shoe box, covered it in aluminum foil, and put a Styrofoam in the bottom of the box for my insect collection. I think I got an A for my project, but there were many others who had handed in much better works of dead bug art.

RAUB JUNIOR HIGH SCHOOL: For homeroom, I had the following teachers: Mr. Henits, English teacher, seventh grade; Mr. Wescoe, French teacher, eighth grade; and Ms. Sandt, the German teacher, ninth grade. I was given the certificate of outstanding performance with stickers for first, second, third, and fourth marking periods in seventh and eighth grades. I was in honors classes for English, social studies, and science. After seventh grade, I asked to be taken out of honors for math. My GPA was usually a B, with three As, two Bs, and one C. In my ninth-grade year, I received an honor certificate for the fourth marking period. The only Ds I ever received were in my German lab classes. In my ninth-grade year, Mr. Doran became our principal, and he was on my paper route. I liked him.

Mr. Henits loved literature. Next to him was the English teacher Mr. Lutz. Mr. Lutz had my father as a student when he went to Raub. He also had my sister in class after me. Mr. Lutz, for his weekly vocabulary, played a video cassette saying the words students must spell correctly and give definitions for. Mr. Henits liked to make fun of cheerleaders and those who played certain sports. He was sarcastic and could be mean at times, but he never went after me. He made me laugh. One time, he said, "Being a teacher is like being a swineherder. I am the shepherd." If he is a swine herder, what does that make the students?"

RAUB JUNIOR HIGH SCHOOL AND SANDY'S ROADSTER (1978–80): I used to get home by 6:30 a.m. from my paper route, and I would shower, have breakfast, and get picked up by seven ten to get a ride to Raub or Allen High School by my cousin Sandy, who worked downtown for the DA's office. She always got to see all the gruesome pictures. She drove an orange and red Roadster that had a roadrunner emblem on the side. She had a cool-looking car, and I loved getting out of it in front of school. It was like getting dropped off at the red carpet of a Hollywood event, as students would look at me and shake their heads in approval. Sandy also was a Philadelphia Eagles fanatic. Every Monday during the football season, our moods were influenced whether the Eagles won or lost. When the Eagles lost the Super Bowl in 1980, it was a rough three weeks commuting because of our Eagle-induced depression.

Sandy's younger sister, Brenda, and I were the same age and went to school together in Raub and Allen. Brenda was involved with the flag team. She was very good at swinging it around and looked quite graceful and regal when she danced in parades during the Raub and Allen football games. In high school, she used to hang out with cousin Cindy. Cindy had blond hair and developed early. One day, in the cafeteria, Watson said, "Look at that body on her. What I would like to do—" I hit him in the arm and told him, "That's my cousin you are salivating over, numb nuts!"

U.S. BOYCOTTS THE 1980 SUMMER OLYMPICS (USSR): Unfortunately, Pres. Jimmy Carter announced that the United States would be boycotting the Olympics because of the Soviets' invasion of Afghanistan. I was disappointed, as the athletes who have trained for years and years were denied the opportunity to shine, and the idea of the Olympic was to help build world unity through sports. This would have been the year that the great diver Greg Louganis would have shown his star to the world.

1980 WINTER OLYMPICS (LAKE PLACID, NEW YORK): Beth Heiden won the bronze in speed skating, and her brother Eric Heiden won five gold medals in speed skating. This was the year of "the miracle" when the U.S. skating team won the gold medal against the Soviets only a year after the supposedly invincible USSR invaded Afghanistan.

I LOVE YOU TO DEATH: In 1983, in a quaint home on Walnut Street, where Reading Road intersected and crossed Twenty-Fourth Street in Allentown, Ms. Frances Toto tried poisoning her husband and then later shot her philandering pizza restaurant owner husband Joey Toto in the head with a .22-caliber handgun while he was sleeping, and he lived. She chose to kill him because she refused to get a divorce. The day after the shooting, we passed the house on the way to Raub, and it was surreal to hear of a murder attempt in Allentown. Frances was prosecuted and went to jail from 1984 to 1988. A black comedy movie was made in 1990 called *I Love You to Death*. Joey was played by Kevin Kline, Frances by Tracey Ullman, and the hit men played by William Hurt and Keanu Reeves. The ironic thing was when Frances got out of jail, they got back together. By law, Frances could not make money from the crime; but since her husband was the victim, he could collect. I drove by the home in 1990 after the movie was made, and it still felt surreal. School friend Patty Heller lived a couple of houses away, and I wondered if her family was friendly with the Totos.

LUNCH LADY CONNECTIONS: At Raub, Aunt Lucille Geist was a lunch lady. Interestingly, I always used to get a little extra food on my plate. Some of my classmates caught on, and when they called her out on it, they would get a little extra as well. Aunt Arlene, Sandy and Brenda's mom, was also a lunch lady at my high school. I used to get the special treatment there as well.

SEVENTH GRADE - ROADSIDE AMERICA AND FOSSIL HUNTING: One trip, we went to see Roadside America, which was a large building that had the world's largest miniature village in model form, complete with mountains, valleys, rivers, tunnels, and trains running all around it. I think Uncle Bob would love this since he was a Lionel Train model buff during his youth. We then went to an area with rocks to look for fossils. Someone brought a bag with them and caught a snake that was a copperhead. The teacher, Mr. Hahn, who used to wear clogs, thought it was the greatest thing ever. Imagine if the kid got bit. "Where's Billy?" "In the hospital, convalescing from a copper head snake bite!" It was actually fun to be running around outside, looking for trilobite fossils on the rocks.

RAUB DANCES: I went to my first dance in 1978. There was a DJ setup in the front of the cafeteria, with lights and a mirror ball. There were refreshments.

Todd Cocivera took two packs of Bubble Yum and stuffed all the gum pieces in his mouth. What came out looked like a pink brain of a small monkey. When it was all in his mouth, he was struggling to get the air in and out, with a bit of saliva dripping out.

I went out on the floor to cut up some rug and had no problem with the free style of dancing. I even asked my heartthrob to dance with me, and I snapped my fingers so hard while I was dancing that I developed blisters on my thumbs. I also slow-danced with her to the Led Zeppelin song "Stairway to Heaven." The problem with this song was (1) it was a long song, five minutes long, and (2) at about the three-quarter mark of the song, it sped up for thirty seconds, and the slow dancing turned into a quasi-awkward freestyle that transitioned back into a slow song. Many broke up their slow dancing in the middle of the song because of the length of it. I came, I saw, I danced like my life depended on it. At least I was not a wallflower standing on the side, helping hold up the walls.

RAUB - JOHN LENNON DIES: Sometimes Mom drove me to school. On December 8, 1980, John Lennon was shot and killed in NYC. The next day, as Mom was driving me to Raub in my ninth-grade year, WZZO was playing Lennon songs and asking people to wear black bandannas on their arms and to put on the headlights of their car. I asked Mom to put on the headlights, which she did. December 9 at school was a very sad day, and in Downtown Allentown was a memorial march for him on Hamilton Street, where people made posters and carried candles.

RAUB SKI CLUB: I joined the ski club my last two years. We went to Wind Gap Lodge to ski. Today it is called Blue Mountain and between Palmerton and Danielsville. We took the bus there on Fridays, left at 3:30 p.m., and got back at around 9:00 p.m. The trips were fun, sitting with the Raub snow bunnies or joking around with the guys. I liked riding on the ski lift wearing my ski pants and toque. It was not competitive, except we had to try to not fall down. I started out doing the V-shaped snowplowing and eventually got to the place where I made turns on the edges of my skis. Feeling the wind and the swoosh of the skis on the snow, watching natural snow falling or the man-made snow flying up into the night-lights was a beautiful sight. Being on top of the mountain and watching people weave back and forth down the slope felt like a human fish tank or a living, real snow globe. I love the ski club. I was able to go down the toughest slopes there but never got to the black diamond slopes of Hunter Mountain in New York.

1980 - RAUB FOOTBALL WITH COACH ROSCH: The team philosophy was "Playing sports is a privilege, and with privilege goes responsibility. We expect you as a member of the Raub football family to handle responsibility and do nothing to embarrass or disappoint our school, team, or parents." The club priorities were to (1) do everything we could to keep injury-free, (2) develop into "good people," and (3) win games.

In the summer, we had double sessions. Our assistant coach was Mr. Kessler, who was the head coach for wrestling. We were in the suburban league and won the championship with a record of 6–1. Outstanding players were Mike Brogna, Ernie Brown, Eric Small, Tony Collins, John Thompson, Tony Harris, and John Brown. Ernie Brown scored forty-six points, and Mike Brogna scored forty-four points, according to team statistician Todd Cocivera and a *Warrior* paper reporter.

Mr. Rosch gave us a talk during summer training, he did not want to hear any cursing on the team. We then ran drills, and I was asked to be the stand in quarterback, but when the defense broke through the offensive line, Big Dave Irvine charged me as I was standing there and rammed his thigh into my jewels and tackled me hard to the ground. I pushed Dave off, yelling, "What the f—— is wrong with you? Did you not hear the f——ing directions by the coach? What is wrong with you, SOB!" I was told Coach Rosch stood there with arms crossed, smiled, shook his head, and said nothing to me except to sit on the side until the pain on my smashed privates slowly became manageable to participate in practice again.

Every Friday, we would wear our football jerseys to school. Ms. McGuiren, our algebra teacher, was a huge Raub football fan. Every week, Mr. Rosch gave us a report of what to look for with other team plays and what our team needed to focus on. At the end of the year, he gave each player a personal handwritten letter telling us what he appreciated about us in our contribution to becoming champions. The final junior high football game was played on Saturday, October 25, 1980, between the Raub Indians and the Harrison Morton Minutemen.

I was not a starter and only got to play in a few games at the end, but here was what the coach wrote to me. "I think one day you would make a good coach. You're witty, intelligent and tough and have charisma . . .We needed someone like you to liven things up and to maintain us with humor . . . Even though you did not play much, you contribute more than you realize . . . I appreciated your efforts and you are as much a champion, maybe more so, than the guys who started . . . Good luck in the future and come back and visit us. Mr. Rosch (1980)." What a classy guy he was.

FAST FORWARD TEN YEARS: I liked Joey L. on the football team. I enjoyed hanging out with him during lunch. I went to visit the testicle crusher Dave Irvine, who now lives in a McMansion in Hunter County, New Jersey. Dave was always a great artist and became a graphic designer. He worked for BMG Music and for *Playboy* magazine. Dave's father was a pastor before he passed, and his mom was a teacher and ended up serving on the Allentown City Council. While we were playing billiards in the basement, Dave told me that Joey was in jail. All I could say was "What?"

SWIMS WITH THE FISHES: Joey was at a bar in the Poconos and got into a scuffle with one of the pub clients. A fight ensued, and Joey grabbed a fire hydrant and hit the guy in the head. The guy hit the floor, and Joey grabbed the dead body and threw him in his car trunk. As Joey was driving on the Pennsylvania Turnpike, thinking of a place to dump the body, the red and white flashing lights of a Pennsylvania State Police vehicle pulled him over. The officer walked up to the window, and Joeys said to the officer, "The body is in the trunk." Luckily, the fellow bar mate whom Joey battered was still alive. He did ten years in the big house.

1980 - RAUB BASEBALL: Mr. Bill Snyder was the baseball coach, and we won the championship with an 8–2 record. I was designated the locker room coach by Coach Snyder, the best tobacco chewer who the best attitude on the team. I again was not a starter, but he put in me the Troxell game at second base for three innings, and the Troxell team hit the ball to me eight times out of nine, and I was given the game ball by Coach Snyder.

The starting team was Brogna, Barnett, Kucharczuk, Pope, Parker, Lanzone, Pinnock, Neikam, Boyer, and Kerrigan. I did have a good time on the bench sitting with Tommy Barnes, Bryan Sibbach, Tony Dzema, and Dennis Fritchman when he was not pitching. We had a very cute managing squad of Sue Laudenslager, Chris Duser, and Lisa Oswald. *Chicas.*

RAUB JUNIOR HIGH PROM: I decided to go to the prom and talk with the guys to find out which ladies have not been asked. Someone said, "Carol G. has not been asked." Carol G. looked like teenage heartthrob Robby Benson's younger sister. To me, she looked like a younger version of Barbie Benson. I built up the courage to ask her. I did play football and baseball that year, and I was a year older. She said yes, but then some of the other players and haters would be the twenty-first-century word for the jealous types, and a week before the prom, she told me she did not want to go. I found out she was going with Chad B., the backup quarterback of the football team and fellow baseball player. At the prom banquet, it was reported to me that he sat back on his chair and acted cockily and ungentlemanly, including burping loudly. I think it could not happen to a nicer girl.

CEDAR CREEK HOOLIGAN FISHING CAMP: In ninth grade, the week before fishing season, I was part of the cool group setting up a camp in the woods by Cedar Creek behind the Popes, just down from Union Terrace. We gathered firewood and set up two tents, and there was supposed to be beer the evening before the first day of fishing. There were John and Mark Pope, Mark Gabler, Carlos Fox, Jill Newman, and a few other people. I was sitting in a tent with Carlos who was holding a BB gun pistol, and he pointed it at my face just five feet away. I said, "Put the gun down. You don't ever point a gun at anyone, even if it is not loaded." Ping! He fired the gun, and I felt a sting in my right palm. If my hand had not been there, I would have lost my right eye.

Later, when I went to bed in the other tent, Mark Pope got up at mid-nightand I said, "Mark, what are you doing?" He unzipped his zipper and began peeing all over me. I got up, took my shirt off, and sat by the fire to dry my shirt out. Of course, in the morning, he did not remember this happening. It was a mostly fun night.

MARTIN LUTHER'S INFLUENCE ON MY FAMILY: Martin Luther, German reformer, may have been anti-Semitic, blaming the Jews for killing our Christian savior, but as Kinky Friedman of the country band the Texas Jewboys sang, they think it was Santa Claus who killed Christ. Well, despite his anti-Semitism, Luther played a great influence on the German thinking theologically and politically by challenging the divine right of kings theory, meaning, if you were king, crazy or not, God placed you there, and what you said happened. Here is a brief outline of Luther's influence—and I believe a large influence—on the Geist family, some consciously, most unconsciously.

REFORMER MARTIN LUTHER

I.   German monk posted *Ninety-Five Theses* in Wittenberg.

    1.   He criticized the practices of the Catholic Church.

        a.   Sale of <u>indulgences</u> (donation for forgiveness)

        b.   <u>Nepotism</u>: clergy appointing unqualified family members

        c.   Salvation by works

    2.   Luther's plan for reform

        a.   Salvation is attained by faith, not by works.

          - Works is the "evidence" of faith.

        b.   The Bible is the only guide to salvation.

        c.   All Christians (not just clergy) should

          i)   read the Bible,

          ii)   interpret it on their own.

    3.   In 1521, Luther was ex-communicated from the church.

         - His followers were called Protestants (protesters).

I. How did Luther's ideas influence the church?

    1. Luther continued to preach his ideas.

        a. He translated the Latin Bible into German.

        b. His *Ninety-Five Theses* was printed and distributed.

    2. Civil War broke out in Germany (Catholics and Protestants).

        a. Many German princes wanted to break from Rome's control.

            a) 1555 Peace of Augsburg treaty

                - Princes were given the right to choose their own faith.

Sidenote: As a teacher, many of my students in Global II get Martin Luther confused with Martin Luther King, whom I covered in U.S. History II.

INFLUENCE OF WALTER REUTHER AND THE UAW ON THE GEISTS: Walter Reuther was born in Wheeling, West Virginia, in 1907. His father was a Socialist brewery worker who emigrated from Germany. The Reuthers, like the Geist family, came from the Swabian tribe of Germany. In 1936, he became the president of the United Auto Workers in Detroit, representing one hundred thousand workers. He was a union organizer who survived two assassination attempts. He and his wife, May, died in 1970 when the Learjet crashed on the way to UAW's Black Lake, a family and educational center.

He had two brothers, Victor and Roy. Victor wrote a book entitled <u>The Brothers Reuther and the Story of the UAW</u> in 1976. Roy said, "Our lives may provide a more sure path for those who pick up the torch and run in the next heat." The brothers' grandfather Jacob said, "The church pays too much attention to the afterlife of its parishioners and too little to their plights on earth" (1). Their grandfather hated all injustice. Their father Jacob's politics were Christian Socialist. When he could find no local church leadership empathetic to the workers with low pay and cold homes with meager heat, he held church in his own home. The family sang hymns, had prayers, and read the Bible together. Pappy Fred Geist would eventually become a charter member of the UAW Local 677 in Allentown, Pennsylvania. To the Geists who worked at Mack Trucks, Walter Reuther was a saint.

SLEEPING OVER AT NANA'S AND GRANDPA SHORTS (BATMAN): I sometimes would sleepover at Nana and Grandpa Shorts in Whitehall, Pennsylvania. On the garage side of the house was a kid my age named Jeff. On the other side of my grandparents' were the twins. They twins had a property that had a pool and was surrounded by a chain-link fence, and they always had sheepdogs. I liked hanging out with Jeff; he was okay. When we were at his home, we used his little sister as a prop as he and I played the paramedics of the show *Emergency*. We also used to watch *Batman* and *Superman* together. One time, we played superheroes with the twins. We had our guardians take diaper pins to tie towels around our necks. Twin 1 was Batman, Twin 2 was Robin, Jeff played Superman, and I wanted to be Spider-Man, but the only way I could play with them was for them to call me Supergirl. I wanted to run around the neighborhood with them with my magic towel on. Every time they called me Supergirl, I would loudly correct them, saying Spider-Man or Ultraman. Kids can be pricks sometimes.

Across the street from Nana and Grandpa Short were parents who had two sons, Eric and Wesley. Wesley was older and taller. Sometimes the neighborhood kids would play tag or capture the flag on their property. Wesley ended up playing for the basketball team for Whitehall High School. When I ran into their mother at my grandfather's funeral service in March of 2007, I asked her how the boys were, and she said Eric was doing well; and with tears in her eyes, she added, "We lost Wesley to throat cancer four years ago." I wished I had not asked because I could see the pain and the tears well up in her eyes at my question.

PARTY AT JIM, THE PLUMBER: One day, the family packed up into the station wagon near the Nineteenth Street Theater neighborhood to attend a party. The family hosting the party was the Urichs. Jim was a plumber, and we pulled up to a back alley, where there were cars parked everywhere, and people were sitting all over the property in lawn chairs, and inside the open garage were tables full of food and a cooler full of soda and another with beer. *Wow*, I thought. This family was okay, providing food, drinks, games, and other kids to play with all afternoon. I figured they had to be a rich family, and I was happy Mom and Dad had some "rich" friends.

One day, Jim stopped by our home with his little Austin-Healey and let me drive it with my driver's permit. He was telling me to turn left and turn right, and on Colorado Avenue, he told me to make a right, and I almost hit a fire hydrant. He should have given me directions a little earlier on that one. Dad had another friend named Eddie Greenawalt, and he lived in Macungie and had a river behind his home, and I remember he did the same thing. Eddie worked as a driver or Pepsi and my football coach in the future at Raub would tell me he remembered Eddie G. playing football at Raub. Ed had a pumpkin head, and they needed to special order a helmet for him, and his smoking of cigarettes impeded his ability in athletics by stealing air from his lungs.

SLEEPING AT NANA GEIST'S (TIMMY, ALAN, BRYAN, AND JIM): Timmy, Alan, Bryan, and I stayed at Nana Geist's one night, and we ate together, probably cooked chicken, and sat around and shared stories. It was fun to hear stories about our fathers or mothers and aunts and uncles and to learn more about Pappy Geist. Alan told the story about when playing bucking broncos and he was riding Timmy's back, Alan's tooth stuck in Tim's head. With a couple of tugs, he pulled his tooth out, and blood spurted out of Timmy's head like hitting an oil gusher.

It was dark out, and as we talked about Pappy Geist, a squirrel scratched at the screen window. We believed it was Pappy stopping by to say hi to his grandsons and Nana. It was not so much creepy as reassuring and a welcomed thing. As we were watching TV, someone passed gas, and Nana broke out the air freshener and started chasing us around and spraying us with it.

The next morning, we did some yard work for her, and we were filthy. Nana brought out the garden hose and said, "Strip down to your underwear," and she hosed the dirt off us. We hooked up the hose to the sprinkler and jumped back and forth over the spray of water going back and forth. We laughed and laughed and laughed for those two days. The only thing questionable with my cousins was they were Dallas Cowboys fans. When I inquired if they were born in Dallas or in Texas, they said no. How did one in Eagles country become a Dallas fan?

NANA GEIST AND THE SECOND AMENDMENT: In the morning, I had to use the bathroom, and there was Nana, fully dressed, sitting on the end of the tub with a .22-caliber rifle pointed at the garden at a groundhog. She said, "Shhhh," and slowly pulled the trigger, and the gun made a popping "crack" noise and exterminated the furry garden thief.

Years earlier, I stayed at Timmy and Alan's house. It was winter, and we played outside. A car drove by, and I threw a snowball at it. When I got home, my parents confronted me. All I could think was I couldn't believe cousin Timmy ratted me out. Timmy became a military police officer and, as a career man, got voted Military Man of the Year. Colin Powell recruited him to become a personal security guard for him. He could tell me more, but then he would have to kill me.

Timmy came up to hunting camp one time, and Camp Captain Chas asked if Timmy could cook breakfast. Dad laughed and said, "Tim is a career military man. Tim can juggle three grenades and make eggs over easy without breaking one! I am pretty sure he can make breakfast."

GEIST PARTY AT DALE AND SANDY'S: Dale and Sandy had a beautiful property with a farmhouse, a barn, a screen building that used to be a chicken coop, a springhouse on the lower property, and a pond. They had horses, chickens, pigs, and dogs. The Geist family gathered there for a picnic. With all the eating, volleyball, horseshoes, and festivities, Bill Furler, Aunt Carol's husband who played guitar and looked like a country singer, got on the pony to go for a ride, and the pony took off and began bucking. It bucked Bill off its back, and luckily, he was not hurt.

I was wandering around with cousin Brenda and sister Jody. We were walking by the house when a sixteen-foot aluminum ladder fell and hit Jody in the head. Brenda and I asked if she was okay, and Jody nodded yes and said, "I am okay." She took her hand to the top of her head, saw blood on her hand, and began crying.

Uncle Dale was the fireworks guy and broke them out as the sun started setting, and the party finished with a wonderful summertime fireworks show. The Geist crowd was pleased with it.

RATTLESNAKE HUNTING: Uncle Tom bought a trailer near Weatherly off Route 80. Behind it was a power line, and his woods trailer was a great place to go deer hunting or to have summer picnics. The Geists met up at the trailer one summer for a family picnic, and they got talking about rattlesnakes. Uncle Tom used to go hunting for black snakes when he was a kid, and they would go up like a cobra, even though they were not poisonous. The black snakes were good because they ate a lot of mice and rodents. Dad and he put on pistols and decided to look for rattlesnakes. When they came back to the party, they both looked like they saw a ghost. When they were walking by the railroad tracks, they kicked up a black racer. On the way back, Uncle Tom stepped right over a rattlesnake without even seeing it. Ka-bloom! Dad got it. That was the end of the hunt.

ALPINE SLIDE: Someone mentioned there was an alpine slide up at Camelback ski resort. We all packed into cars and drove up there. The adults imbibed a few drinks at the bottom of the mountain at the ski lodge before getting to the lifts. We took the ski lift to the top of the mountain, and they had a track that looked like a bubble cut in half on which a little cart rode that you controlled with a stick with a brake on it. There was no steering involved, but you had control of the speed. It was a fun ride, unless someone rammed into you before you got off the cart at the end, like what happened to poor cousin Cheryl. Nana Geist came along and rode, and it was always wonderful to hear Nana's wheezy laugh.

1978 - STEVE MARTIN: I saw Steve Martin in his Wild and Crazy Tour at the Allentown Fairgrounds. He took out his binoculars and said, "Look, the mayor, with some hookers." I went to buy tickets and took Mom and Dad to the show. "Do you mind if I smoke? No. Do you mind if I fart?" Martin tapped into a void of America wanting absolute silliness after the country found out about the president lying about Watergate and the lies getting us into Vietnam.

HAMILTON PARK BASEBALL: I was lying in an ambulance gurney, looking up at the white ceiling, strapped down in a bed as my shoulder throbbed, when I heard the sound of the siren. *How awesome is this!* I was put into an ambulance in front of a crowd at Hamilton Park, and all my baseball teammates would be wondering what happened to me. We will get to this story later in the separated shoulder section.

I was thirteen, playing third base, or the hot corner as they called it. This game was a source of pride for me and an esteem builder. I had a strong arm, had a good glove, and an excellent batting average. It ranged from 300 to 350 at most times. I was not a power hitter, but I often got on base with singles and doubles. I had the circle one time with a single, double, triple, and home run. I was pretty sure I had the highest number of runs batted in and was proud to often get the team revved up in cheering each other on for rallies.

GOLD GLOVE MIKE SCHMIDT: I usually batted first, second, third because I had a good batting average and on-base average. I knew we were always taught to look at the first pitch, but I soon learned that pitchers knew that as well. I knew the first pitch was usually coming right down the center of the plate unless it was a wild pitch or bad pitch. This was one of the reasons I was attributed to be a good hitter. "Swing batter, batter!" I sure did. I went to Laneco and picked out a size 34 ounce bat. I took it home, and I spray-painted the bottom of the bat red so I could identity it among the other bats. Kids used to call me Rusty or Schmidty (for Phillies third baseman Mike Schmidt) or Geister Brau, like the Meister Brau beer.

WONDER BOY BAT: In the movie *The Natural*, Robert Redford named his bat Wonder Boy. I did not have a name for my bat; I called it "Jim's bat" or no. 34. At game time, buddy Mike Brogna asked me if he could use the bat; he really liked it. What I should have said was "I love you Mike, like a brother, but if the bat breaks, it should be me who breaks it." Mike went to the plate and swung the bat, and as the ball met the bat, "Crack!" Mike hung his head, looked at me, and said sorry. I never got to use my bat, but maybe in the future, I could spit some chewing tobacco on Mike's white disco pants as payback.

The Phillies were having a great season that year, and my teammates used to call me Mike Schmidt or Rusty because there was a commercial with some red-haired guy named Rusty. One mean kid called me the Duck, because he thought I waddled when I ran. I probably did, but the Los Angeles Dodgers third baseman Ron Cey at the time used to waddle as well when he ran and played in the major leagues. I thought the Roaches 2nd baseman Don Strohl ran like Cey.

ED MCCAFFREY: I played third base, Mike Brogna played second, and Ed McCaffrey played shortstop. Ed used to be very hard on himself, so I told him to lighten up and to enjoy the game more. Of course, he became a professional ball player, and I did not. He was an excellent athlete in baseball, basketball, and football. He went to Stanford and then was drafted by the New York Giants in 1991. He played with the Giants for four years, San Francisco for one year, and the Denver Broncos for nine years. He has three Super Bowl rings (SF in 1994 and Denver in 1997 and 1998). His brother Billy played basketball at Duke, and his sister Monica played basketball at Georgetown.

When he came to New York in 1991, I called the Giants and left a message for him that if he wanted to meet for lunch or dinner, I was available. I never heard from him. When I went to Phoenix, I called the Phoenix Cardinals and left a message for Joe Wolf. Joe called me back, and we had lunch together. That was nice of Joe, and it was good to see him. Dad played football at Allen with punter Larry Seiple, who became a kicker for the Miami Dolphins and won two Super Bowl rings with them.

PHILLIES, 1980: The Phillies have lost in the National League play-offs over the last several years. It was painful and frustrating to be a Phillies fan. The Phillies were able to get Pete Rose, "Charlie Hustle," to become a Philly. The Phillies ended the season with a 91–71, ahead of the Montreal Expos. The Phillies defeated the Houston Astros to become National League champs and played the Kansas City Royals in the World Series. The Phillies were called "the Cardiac Kids" because of so many games they have almost blown.

The players were Pete Rose (1B), Manny Trillo (2B), Larry Bowa (SS), Mike Schmidt (3B), Greg "the Bull" Luzinski (LF), Garry Maddox (CF), and Bake McBride (RF); and they are coached by Dallas Green. The pitchers were Steve Carlton, Larry Christenson, Randy Lerch, Ron Reed, Bob Walk, and Tug McGraw.

It was a glorious day for Philadelphia, the Lehigh Valley, and Eastern Pennsylvania, as the Phillies finally won a World Series after a long drought since 1950 when the Whiz Kids lost to the New York Yankees in 1950. As a sidenote, the Phillies were the last team to integrate; it took ten years after Jackie Robinson joined major league baseball.

SEPARATED SHOULDER: It was a perfect spring day with a blue sky, and the sun was beginning to set. The opposing team's batter hit the ball up high along the third base at about three feet aboveground, four feet foul of the base along the visitors' bench. I dived for the ball with my outstretched glove connected to my left arm and landed on my shoulder. When I hit the ground, I felt something, and it was not good. "Is this what a broken bone feels like?" As I lay there, my two coaches ran over. "I think he has a separated shoulder." This was before cell phones, so I didn't know who made the call or where it was made; there was no public phone at Hamilton Park.

When I got up, they put a jacket over me because they felt I was in shock. I sat on the bench until the ambulance showed up. My uniform was covered in brown baseball infield dust. The ambulance attendants wheeled me into the emergency room. My parents showed up. The doctor took his finger and began pressing. "Does this hurt?" No. "Does this hurt?" No. On the third "Does this hurt?" my scream revealed the the point of separation. They gave me an arm sling and aspirin. It eventually healed on its own.

FRONT TOOTH BROKEN: During our spring training, as we were warming up by throwing pitches to each other, the coach called my name. I turned my head to the coach and back to my throwing partner, only to have a baseball hit me in the kisser. Getting hit so forcefully by a small hardball kind of put me in shock, and I felt a sharp pain go up my tooth, like it was breathing in air. I could feel with my tooth; half of my front tooth was gone.

For some reason, I feel embarrassed to admit to the coach that half my tooth had been knocked out. I waited until after practice to inform my parents of what happened. My official school picture with my half tooth was taken before my dentist, Dr. Canzano, was able to put a cap on it.

Little League baseball was not the only sport I played at Hamilton Park. I spent probably way too many hours on the court of playground basketball. Ironically, most of my injuries happened playing baseball, not football. I ended up getting sprained ankles and fingers, a separated shoulder, and a broken tooth in baseball but nothing serious in football.

PAPERBOY STORIES: I started my paper route in late 1978, just in time for "the snow blizzard of the century" in the Lehigh Valley when I was thirteen years old. The snow was up to my waist, and what normally took fifty-five minutes to do took me two and a half hours. The *Morning Call* newspaper gave all the paper delivery people a light blue shirt with the words "I survived the storm of 1978!"

I obtained Route 276 from Dustin Hoffman, an older boy down the street from me. When I started, I used to pick up my papers on Flexer Avenue in front of the Kotrans' home. Steve was three years older than I was, and he delivered papers. Jeff Ruth used to deliver papers as well, and when he went off to college, he gave his route to his brother, David. Steve's dad was a state trooper, and Steve had a cute sister, Lisa, who was two years ahead of me.

I liked delivering papers when it was not raining or below twenty degrees. I loved all the seasons except for the winter. What I really did not like was collecting the money every two weeks. What I found interesting about collecting money was that homes had different smells. Some were neutral, some had a pleasant smell, and some I did not like. Each person had a manila card with all the weeks on it, and when they paid, I would clip the weeks they paid for with my paper clipper. There was one house that had a dog, and one day, I accidently dropped the paper clipper on its head. From thereon in, it would sit and growl at me whenever I came over for collection. The dog unfortunately had a good memory.

I used to get up at 5:30 a.m. to deliver the papers, seventy-five on my route, and then get home by 6:30 a.m. Then I would shower and get picked up by cousin Sandy in her red Roadster with orange highlighting. There was a time where young boys were disappearing in Chicago and down in Atlanta, and it creeped me out and made it a little scary when passing large bushes in the early morning darkness. Thank god they captured John Wayne Gacy, the children's clown, and Wayne Williams.

For most days, I needed just two of the green *Morning Call* paper bags, which had fluorescent, padded orange strap. I put one on my left shoulder and the other on my right. I would go across the street to pick up my papers, which were bundled with a plastic strap that had a pull away to open it up. After placing the paper in the bags, I jumped on my bike and rode up College Drive to East Texas Boulevard, made a right on Ott Street, and parked the bike at College Lane for twelve drops, Colorado Drive for ten drops, Emerson Street for sixteen drops, Ott Street for seventeen drops, and Green Acres Drive for twenty-two drops. I would then race up Green Acres Drive to Emerson to College Lane through East Texas Boulevard and down to College Drive to my abode at 512 College Drive. The largest papers were on Thursday, and Sunday, with Sunday being the heaviest paper. I had a metal cart I hooked up to my bike for those days.

One day, I was riding fast toward home; and as I made a left-hand turn unto the driveway, I wiped out with the bike on top of me. My sister could verify this story because I saw her face looking out her window to witness the post-crash commotion. She had a big smile on her face, like Damien in the movie the Omen when he saw suffering.

I had the paper route for 5½ years, and when I got my driver's license, delivering the Sunday papers became a cinch. Frank was a car buff and began helping me deliver papers on Sundays, and then we would drive around town in Dad's light blue Scout and stop by Dunkin' Donuts for some coffee and doughnuts with our huge bag of cassette tapes, listening to rock 'n' roll.

SNEAKERS, PAPER ROUTES, AND PRAYERS: Our family was about to leave for vacation this day when I came back from my paper route. I was asked to get a pair of sneakers for fishing, crabbing, the beach, etc. As I drove up to my route, I prayed because I needed a pair of sneakers. I delivered my papers and drove home and had one leftover. I got home, got a call from the person I missed, drove past East Texas Boulevard, and dropped off the paper. And as I drove toward East Texas Boulevard, I saw what looked like a McDonald's bag in the center of the five intersecting streets, but it turned out to be a pair of sneakers. I picked them up; they were not new, and they had some paint drops on them, but they were in good shape. I looked at the shoe size, and it was a size 9, my exact size. I said, "Thank you, God" and had my sneakers for vacation fishing and clamming.

1980 - FOUR PHILLY TEAMS MAKE IT TO THE FINALS!: The Flyers, 76ers, Eagles, and Phillies made it to the championship games. The Flyers lost the Stanley Cup to the Islanders, the 76ers lost the championship to the Lakers, and the Eagles lost the Super Bowl to the Oakland Raiders, but the Phillies won the World Series against the Kansas City Royals!

The Eagles were slotted to play the Oakland Raiders in the Super Bowl in January of 1980. It was exciting times. All over the place, people put up Eagles paraphernalia in support of the team. I went to Hess's and saw they had a nice Eagles key chain. I shoplifted it. No one was around, and I wanted it. Years later, I wrote to Hess's and sent them a $10 check to make amends for what I had done. They sent me a response letter thanking me for my honesty and an invitation to visit the store again anytime.

1980 PHILADELPHIA EAGLES

OFFENSE
> Q: Ron Jaworski
> RBs: Leroy Harris, Wilbert Montgomery
> WRs: Harold Carmichael, Scott Fitzkee, Rodney Parker
> TEs: Lewis Gilbert, John Spagnola
> Center: Guy Morriss
> Guards: Petey Perot, Ron Baker
> Tackles: Jerry Sisemore, Stan Walters

DEFENSE
Kicker: Tony Franklin
> DB: Herman Edwards, Randy Logan
> LB: Bill Bergey, Frank LeMaster, Jerry Robinson
> DL: Dennis Harrison, Claude Humphrey, Charlie Johnson

Three of the four Philadelphia teams lost the championship, but the Flyers gave us victories in 1974 and 1975. However, ten months later, with the help of new Philadelphia Philly Pete Rose, the Philadelphia fans would get something to celebrate!

Buddy Mike Brogna's father bought season tickets every year for the Eagles. Mike went to all the home games in good years and in bad, in good weather and in bad weather, and often with fights in the stands nearby. If anyone knew the Eagles better than anyone, it was him. He used to go the Philadelphia Eagle camps for Little League football players and was able to meet most of the Eagles players. I was sure Mike has stories to tell. I believe if the Philadelphia Eagles management had hired Mike to be the coach, the Eagles would have won a Super Bowl by now, maybe even two.

EAGLES RUNNING BACK DUCE STALEY AND DAD HANG OUT (2014): Dad's Mack Truck buddy was working on Duce Staley's motorcycle and invited Dad over for the day. Staley, as of 2016, has been the running back coach for the Eagles and has a career 5,785 yards with then averaging 4.1 yards a carry. His reception average is 8.9 yards. Dad said he was a nice guy, and when Dad patted Staley on the back, it was like hitting a rock.

SUMMERTIME AT HAMILTON PARK: In the summer, we had a park counselor, Greg Muhr. We had him in the summer of 1978 and 1979, the years he played guard for the Allen High Canaries basketball team. We made crafts; played volleyball, kickball, wiffle ball, softball, and basketball; and hung out and talk, sitting under the pavilion or under the shade of the trees. Hamilton Park won the city championship for the slow-pitch softball tournament (thirteen and under) with me as pitcher. The scandal was I was really fourteen at the time. I guess the records department needed to give the second place team the championship, if they still had it on record somewhere or if anyone really cared. Greg dated Gina Galiano, Johnny Galiano's cheerleading sister.

BLOODY NOSE: One day, we played wiffle ball, and a young kid, Mark, who was on my paper route, ran back to catch a fly. He was running full speed, and his head was the exact height of the highest seat on the bleachers he was running toward, and boom, he smashed his nose. I took his shirt covered in blood, held it to his nose, and walked him home. It was a real gusher.

ALLEN BASKETBALL - EASTERN CHAMPS, 1979 AND 1980: The Canaries took the eastern championship (PIAA Class AAA) in those years with Billy Dreisbach, Tony Semler, Sean Ward, Jeff Lucien, Scott Foiweiler, Greg Muhr, and Bob Erie. The Canaries lost the state championship to Valley in 1979 and to Erie Prep in 1980. Dad and I went to see them play in Hershey in both years. It was fun rooting for the local team and "agony" to watch the team lose in both years in states. Coach John Donmoyer had a record of 423–226 and passed away in August of 2014. Of the 1979 team, he said, "I have never coached a harder-working team." Whitehall won the state championship in 1982 with Scott Covall. Every time we would visit Uncle Dale and Aunt Sandy's farmhouse, we would pass the park that has his name on it.

HOOSIERS: The movie is based on the small school Milan High in Indiana. The coach, played by Gene Hackman, says, "Five players function as a unit—team, team, team." He goes on, "My practices are not designed for your enjoyment." Before the championship, one of the townsfolk says, "Win this game for all the small schools!" At the end of the movie, it shows a kid shooting ball in the gym years after the state championship victory, the camera pans on the picture of the championship team and slowly closes in, and the coach's voice from the past says, "If you put effort and concentration into playing to your potential and play your best, I don't care what the scoreboard says at the end of the game. In my book, you are all champions!" There is a pause, and the voice says, "I love you, guys."

BASKETBALL AT HAMILTON PARK: I spent much time up at Hamilton Park on Ott Street, between Flexer Avenue and East Texas Boulevard. The court was on the East Texas Boulevard side, complete with small bleachers and a water fountain. It was a decent court. Allentown repaved it and put up new boards, and it went from a 7 court to a 10 court. If no one was there, I would practice free throws, run up and down the court to improve my dribbling skills, and just shoot around. If there was another person, we could play one on one, shoot around, or play around the world. If there were three people, we could play a fun game of 21.

Our team point guards were usually Rich Baker and Timmy Butler. If we played two on two or three on three, Frank Radocha and I would play centers. The forwards were anyone else who showed up. Mike Sabler, son of the girls' basketball coach at Allen High School. There was another teenager named Ken, who was a nice guy and very quick. There was another guy, and I think his name was Mike; he was a year ahead of us, and his shoulders reminded me of Frankenstein. He had dirty blond hair and a strange "ha" laugh, but he was a decent player. Sometimes Mike Brogna would show up. Mike was a great football running back and strong, and sometimes he would clothesline you as you came in for a layup; he would stick out his arm around your neck and knock you over. Jimmy S. used to play every now and then, was a lefty, and had a strange jump shot; and he was an excellent tennis player. Another good player, who was a year younger than I was and went to Salisbury High School, was Danny Reichenbacher. Danny had a great outside shot. He was intense and an excellent guard as well. He was a hair too cocky for me, but he could back up the bravado.

When Frank and I played against each other, I would give a fake move like I was going to shoot, and get Frank to jump, and then I would move around him or just stand there and take my open shot. I used to sing Steve Miller's song "Fly Like an Eagle" when he did this, and it would really piss him off. Frank's father, Mr. R., and Frank's younger brother, Pete, would come up and shoot hoops sometimes. Mr. R. used to be a good basketball player in high school up in the coal area. He always wore an old baseball hat somewhat pulled down, so it was hard to see his eyes sometimes. Mr. R. used to say of Peter, "Pete will end up either president of the United States or in prison." Sadly, Peter would end up in a cemetery just five years after I heard his dad made the Peter prediction.

Sometimes we played full court if another crew would show up to the court. It was a summer day in 1984, and the usual suspects were shooting around when two cars pulled up, one a convertible with some kids in it. It was blasting the song "Money for Nothing" by Dire Straits. It was a crew from Alton Park. I used to play Little League football, so I knew several of the players, one being Craig S., who was tall and had a vulturelike hunchback. The other player was one of my former assistant football coaches, named Mike. He was short and husky and looked like a linebacker.

Rich Baker was the point guard, Timmy the shooting guard, Frank the center, the other Kenny played forward, and I the power forward. Larry Bird was one of my favorite players. Bird used to say he got as much enjoyment from getting an assist as scoring a point. I loved setting picks to open up an outside shot for our better shooters. I would set pick for a forward or center to be able to take it inside for a layup or a short shot.

The game between Hamilton Park and Alton Park was a close one, and it was starting to get physical under the net. Craig S. from Alton Park was covering Frank and pushed him. He cursed at him and threw a punch at Frank. I saw red. I was half a court away when I took off and was to tackle Craig. Just as I was about to take Craig down, I felt a perfect linebacker tackle take me down by Coach Mike. "Whoa, whoa, whoa, calm down there, Geisty!" Frank was not really a fighter, nor was I for that matter, and Craig was puffing his cocky feathers because he had "homeys" there to protect his butt. Alton Park did beat us, but not because of intimidation, they were better than us. They beat us by three points. It was strange to be competing against my football teammates on the basketball court.

Sometimes I would go out and shoot in a light rain. I liked the solitude. I liked shooting hoops until the sun set. Sometimes Roger would pull up with his red Firebird and blast the music from his speakers, or someone would bring their boom box, and we would shoot hoops with music.

BIRD AND WALTON: At different times in my life, I was called "Walton," for redheaded center Bill Walton; "Bird," for my passing and picks and rebounding; or "Big Man." I liked those names. Larry Bird was a Hoosier from Indiana. He was drafted by the Boston Celtics. Larry Bird had blond hair and was not especially athletic looking, but he was the key guy to go to for the buzzer shot or the guy to get the team going on a rally. He liked to set picks, he loved to rebound, he loved to make passes and to get assists, and he liked to score. He was not flashy, did not like the media, and kept to himself. Magic Johnson came from Michigan State University and was drafted by the LA Lakers. Magic Johnson had a big smile, liked to talk, loved the press, liked Larry Bird, and liked to make passes, to get assists, and to score.

PHILADELPHIA 76ERS: They both were competitors. To get to the NBA championship, the 76ers had to play and beat the Boston Celtics in order to face, usually, the Los Angeles Lakers. The 76ers had only won one championship, in 1983, and that was because they acquired Moses

Malone for center, who predicted, "Four, four, four," meaning the 76ers would win the semifinals, the finals, and then the NBA championship. They did. Thanks to him! There were so many good years in the 1980s when Dr. J. faced Larry Bird, or Dr. J. faced Jamaal Wilkes. It was 76ers centers Caldwell Jones or Darryl Dawkins, Moses Malone, and Bob McAdoo taking on the Celtics centers Bill Walton, Dave Cowens, or "the Chief," Robert Parish. Or in a championship game, it could be 76ers' Caldwell or Malone taking on the Lakers' Kareem Abdul-Jabbar.

The 76er guards in the early '80s were Henry Bibby, Doug Collins, and Lionel Hollins. In the mid-'80s, the guards were Maurice Cheeks and World B. Free. The 76er forwards were Charles Barkley in 1984 and guard World B. Free in 1986. What an awesome name to have. If I were to have children, I would give the first name of General, Pastor, or Doctor because these are interesting first names; the kid would get respect, and it would mean a lot of money to not send them to college.

THE PHILADELPHIA 76ERS CHAMPIONSHIP TEAM: In 1983, there were Maurice Cheeks, Andrew Toney, Bobby Jones, Julius Erving, and Moses Malone, coached by Billy Cunningham. The championship team of the Celtics, coached by Bill Fitch, was made up of guards Tiny Archibald, Danny Ainge, Pete Maravich, and Dennis Johnson. The Celtic forwards were Larry Bird, M. L. Carr, and Kevin McHale. The Celtic centers were Bill Walton, Dave Cowens and Robert Parish. The championship team of the Lakers, coached by Pat Riley, was made up of guards Magic Johnson, Norm Nixon, and Michael Cooper. The Laker forwards were Jamaal Wilkes, Spencer Haywood, Kurt Rambis, and James Worthy. The Laker centers were Kareem Abdul-Jabbar, Bob McAdoo, Mark Landsberger, and Earl Jones.

MAGIC AND BIRD: Magic and Bird had a special relationship. They both were great competitors and helped take their teams to the championship. As competitors, they had great respect for each other's abilities. Magic was a flashy point guard, and the Lakers had the West Coast fast-paced court-to-court games. The Celtics were into setting up for the shot, making calls and plays to get the best shot. Bird was not flashy, was not a talker, and let his play do his talking. Magic loved the cameras and loved to talk. As different as they were, Converse sneakers had them do a commercial together; and from thereon in, they were friends. When Magic found out he had HIV, the first person he called was Larry Bird. One of the reasons I loved Larry Bird was his blue-collar work ethic. When asked what Bird would be doing had he not made it into the NBA, he responded, "I would probably be the supervisor of the sanitation department in Deer Lick, Indiana."

Allen High School won the state championship in basketball back in 1935. Dad took me to Hershey, Pennsylvania, to watch the Whitehall High School win the state championship back in 1982, when I was a sophomore at Allen. Some of the great basketball players to come from our area were Billy McCaffrey, who ended up playing basketball for Duke and with sixteen points was the star in helping them beat Kansas for the championship in 1991 and then for Vanderbilt in 1993 after a year off; Gerry McNamara from Scranton, Pennsylvania, who played as point guard for Syracuse University from 2002 to 2006; and Central's Michelle Marciniak, who played for Notre Dame and transferred to Tennessee with Coach Pat Summitt to win the national championship against the Connecticut Huskies in 1996.

I taught at Park West High School and had the chance to watch Ramel Bradley play point guard in 2001 and 2002. He was a gentleman and an athlete. He went to Pendleton School in Florida in his senior year and was drafted by the University of Kentucky (UK) by Coach Tubby Smith and played for them from 2004 to 2008.The UK won a national championship in 1996, 1998, and 2012; but Bradley played for them in the final-four drought.

PHILADELPHIA SPORTS TEAMS'
CHAMPIONSHIP HISTORY
since 1974

*1974:   *Flyers win Stanley Cup* against the Boston Bruins, with Coach Shero.

*1975:   *Flyers win Stanley Cup* against the Buffalo Sabres, with Coach Shero.

1976:   Flyers lost in the <u>Stanley Cup</u> finals to the Montreal Canadiens.
Phillies lost the NL championship to the Cincinnati Reds.
*Movie *Rocky* came out (with boxer from Philly).

1977:   Phillies lost the NL championship to the LA Dodgers.
The 76ers lost the <u>NBA Finals</u> to the Portland Trail Blazers.

1978:   Phillies lost the NL championship to the LA Dodgers.
The 76ers lost the East Conference Finals to the Washington Bullets.

1979:   *William Allen High School Boys Team won the Eastern Championship Title II AAA.*
- Billy Dreisbach, Tony Semler, Greg Muhr, Jeff Lucien, Sean Ward, Bob Erie (30–6 record)

- Coach Donmoyer: "Hardest-working team I have ever coached!"

- Coach Donmoyer died on August 16, 2014, with a record of 423 wins and 226 losses.

*1980:   Flyers lost in the <u>Stanley Cup</u> Finals to the NY Islanders.

<u>*Eagles* lost the Super Bowl to Oakland.</u>

*Movie *Invincible* (Mark Wahlberg playing Vince Papale)

Phillies won the World Series against the Kansas City Royals (Pete Rose).

The 76ers lost in the <u>NBA Finals</u> to the LA Lakers.

William Allen High School Boys Team won the eastern championship.

1981:   The 76ers lost in the East Conference Finals to the Celtics.

1982:   The 76ers lost in the <u>NBA Finals</u> to the LA Lakers (who beat the Celtics).

Penn State Nittany Lions became national champions!

Whitehall High School Boys Basketball won the Pennsylvania state championship!

1983:   Phillies lost the <u>World Series</u> to the Baltimore Orioles.

- Dad and I were at the game in Philly when the Orioles won.

The 76ers won the NBA Finals against the LA Lakers (Moses Malone), who beat Celtics.

1985:   Flyers lost in the <u>Stanley Cup</u> Finals to the Edmonton Oilers.

The 76ers lost in the East Conference Finals against the Celtics.

Villanova beat Georgetown for college basketball championship.

1986:   *Penn State Nittany Lions* became the national champions!
- "Why is the sky blue and white? Because God loves PSU."

1987:   Flyers lost in the <u>Stanley Cup</u> Finals to the Edmonton Oilers.

1989:   Flyers lost in the NHL Conference Finals to the Montreal Canadiens.

1993:   Phillies lost the <u>World Series</u> to the Toronto Blue Jays.

1995:   Flyers lost in the NHL Conference Finals to the New Jersey Devils.

1997:   Flyers lost in the <u>Stanley Cup</u> Finals to the Detroit Red Wings.

2000:   Flyers lost in the NHL Conference Finals to the New Jersey Devils.

2001:   Eagles lost the conference championship to St. Louis Rams.

           The 76ers lost in the <u>NBA Finals</u> to the LA Lakers (Iverson vs. Kobe).

2002:   Eagles lost the conference championship to Tampa Bay Buccaneers.

2003:   Eagles lost the conference championship to Carolina Panthers.

2004:   <u>*Eagles* lost the Super Bowl to New England Patriots.</u>

           Flyers lost in the NHL Conference Finals to the Tampa Bay Lightning.

2008:   Eagles lost the championship to the Arizona Cardinals.

           Flyers lost in the NHL Conference Finals to the Pittsburgh Penguins.

           Phillies won the World Series against the Tampa Bay Rays.

2009:   Phillies lost the <u>World Series</u> to the New York Yankees.

2010:   Flyers lost in the <u>Stanley Cup</u> Finals to the Chicago Blackhawks.

           Pre-1960: Eagles won three championships and lost one.

PENN STATE RECORD YEARS AND BOWLS: As of 2015, Penn State football has had three "perfect seasons," in 1973, 1986, and 1994. They were the national champions in 1982 and in 1986, one of their perfect seasons. Regarding bowl games, PSU has been invited to forty-six bowl games and had a record of 28–16–2 (63% winning record); and in major bowls, PSU had a 14–6–1 or a 69%t winning record. My guess was the reason PSU switched from the Big East league to the Big Ten league was they were tired of getting passed over for national championship opportunities, even when they had perfect record seasons, because those who cast ballots for rankings thought the Big East was an easier schedule than the teams in the Big Ten. As far as college football went, Mom and Dad and the Shorts were Penn State Nittany Lion fans. Why did God make the sky blue and white? Because He loves Penn State.

On my mother's side of the family, Grandpa Short and Uncle Bob went to Penn State. Grandpa studied engineering, and Uncle Bob was a business major from 1967 to 1971. Aunt Davy joined him in 1970, and he worked in his senior year. He was able to go to the Gator Bowl in 1968 and the Orange Bowl in 1969 and 1970. Joe Paterno became coach of the football team in 1966, the year of our Lord and the year I was born, until I was forty-five in 2011.

Cousin Cheryl was a few years ahead of me on the Geist side of the family and was the first to graduate from college. Cheryl's brother Alan graduated from Penn State and often went to the game in the family camper to become part of the parking lot party before PSU football games. In their corner of the parking lot, Alan was known as "the Mayor."

UNCLE BOB AND PSU NITTANY LION MARCHING BAND: Growing up, one of the topics of conversation at Nana and Grandpa Short's place was about the PSU football team. Uncle Bob played French horn in the college band. He was able to travel to away games and play in the PSU stadium. What an awesome experience that must be to hear the roar of the crowd when touchdowns were scored and to play the PSU theme song. His senior year, his wife moved in with him, who started working as a nurse. Uncle Bob got to see linebacker great Jack Ham and running backs Franco Harris, Lydell Mitchell, and John Cappelletti.

1977 - SOMETHING FOR JOEY: In 1977, at age eleven, a movie came called *Something for Joey* about John Cappelletti, who was the running back for PSU. He had a ten-year-old brother, Joey, who was very sick with leukemia. When John asked Joey what he wanted for his eleventh birthday, he said, "I want you to score three—no, four touchdowns against the West Virginia Mountaineers." John ran three touchdowns in the first quarter, and Coach Paterno took him out because he did not like running up scores on opposing teams. What a classy gentleman! Cappelletti sat on the bench and kept his mouth quiet; he did not tell him about Joey's request. After the second half, one of the players went up to the coach and told him about Joey's request. Coach Paterno yelled, "Number 22, get in the game!" And the rest was history.

UNCLE BARRY'S PASSING - 1968 (AGE THIRTEEN): The movie's story had meaning for me because, first, I was the same age as Joey when it came out, and it was at age eleven when he died. Second, my Uncle Barry died of leukemia at age thirteen. And third, Uncle Bob played in the PSU band; and in his senior year, John Cappelletti played PSU football. I could vaguely remember my Uncle Barry and loved the picture of him playing with me on the floor as a baby. He liked baseball, and I had no real memory of his passing, just that he was not around anymore until I could understand what happened.

When Barry was in the hospital bed, he asked everyone to leave. Mom felt he knew he was about to pass and wanted to be alone when it happened. A few years later, at age five, on our weekly visit to Nana Geist, I was told cousin Barry was going to be there. I became so excited that I thought I was never going to see him again. When we got to Nana Geist's, I crossed the street to play in the park. I could still see it in my mind's eye. I was sitting on the highest part of the monkey bars when I heard my name called; this meant Barry was there. I climbed down the bars as fast as I could, ran to the street, looked both ways, ran up the concrete stairs, opened the door, and ran into the kitchen.

Dad called me over and said, "This is your cousin Barry."

I looked and said, "What?"

"Well, say hello to your cousin!" I said hello to him and went upstairs to a bedroom and lay in one of the beds very sad and upset. It was cousin Barry Geist from Arizona, from my dad's side of the family; it was not my uncle Barry Short, who would have been sixteen at the time. The idea of death separation was such a tough pill to swallow for a five-year-old.

2012 - NEPHEW JORDAN AS A PSU NITTANY LION: My nephew Jordan started going to Penn State in 2012 and worked on the football team as an equipment manager. He went to the practices and worked hard, making sure the team had all it needed. One day, he took Mom and Dad on a tour of the facilities and took them to the lockers and workout area under the stadium. He said hi to the team secretary, and when he came back out of the office, he brought the PSU coach to meet Mom and Dad. This made my parents' year. Working with the team, he was able to go to school for free for a fifth year. I was sure Jordan would be able to write a book about his experience with the PSU football team for the five years he worked as the equipment manager.

Thanks to Jordan, I get to see the Nittany Lions play Temple in Happy Valley and P.S.U. play Rutgers in New Jersey in 2016.

CARL, THE BUM: Walking home from Raub past Union Terrace Elementary School, past Union Terrace Pond, and over the Cedar Creek Bridge was a young bum, Carl, who lived under there for approximately two summers. Next to the park was a restroom, which was perfect if you were a bum. On the weekends, the underage students gave Carl money to buy them beer and gave him extra payment for doing so.

When we walked home from school, we would call out Carl's name, and he would walk out and say, "Hey, what's up?" The bridge was only eighteen to twenty feet above him, and we would drop our change down to him. The rumor was he was the son of a judge in Allentown, Pennsylvania, who became a burnout from drugs. The Roaches had a softball game at the UT fields one time, and as they were cooking burgers and hot dogs, I told Dad about Carl, and the guys said, "Bring him over." I invited Carl over, and they fed him hot dogs, burgers, and beer. They even asked him questions about what it was like living under the bridge. Bud said, "I would have a tough time living under a bridge. Hearing the river run all the time would make we want to pee all the time." Dad gave me $5, and I went over to Yocco's Hot Dogs and played Asteroids for an hour before coming back. Carl seemed like a nice guy, and I wondered what it felt like to plummet from the Eighth Street Bridge, 250 feet high, to the macadam below just before his death, just a quarter of a mile down from Nana Geist's.

SUMMER OF 1980 - SPEEDY'S RECORDS AND THE COOL GANG: It was my summer of eighth grade, and I was bored and wanted something to do. It was time for me to update my album collection. I walked three miles from my home to Speedy's Records on Hamilton Street in Downtown Allentown. It had music playing, was full of posters, and had all the latest albums and 45 rpms for sale. After perusing the store, I walked out with *Moving Pictures* by Rush, the *Greatest Hits* of the Steve Miller Band, and the latest album by the Police entitled *Zenyatta Mondatta*. With the albums in a bag, I walked down to Lawrence Street, walked under the Eighth Street Bridge, stopped by Nana's to say hi, nabbed some cookies, and got a glass of water.

As I walked under the Fifteenth Street Bridge past the YMCA, along the Little Lehigh River on the train tracks back to the neighborhood, on the bridge trestle, I saw four youths in shorts jumping into the deepness of the river. It turned out to be the "cool gang" of Raub Junior High School: John Pope, Mark Gabler, and Carlos Fox. "Hey, look, it's Geist! What do you have there? Ohhhh, cool records. Nice choice, Jim! Why don't you join us?" I took off my shirt and shoes and began jumping off the trestle, about a ten-foot drop into the Little Lehigh. I was able to swim and jump in the river with the cool guys and sit in the grass and take in the sun as we talked about the upcoming school year and about the attractive girls we would be seeing in about a month. Wow, talk about serendipity. It was this event that would let me hang out on the edges of almost being cool in school for my ninth-grade year. It was the best day of my summer in 1980. My inner Fonzie of the *Happy Days* was saying, "Aaaaaaaa!"

GEISTS ARE LUTHERANS AND CONGREGATIONALISTS: The Geist family was Congregationalist (which came from German Lutheranism) and attended St. James Church on Fifteenth Street and West Maple Street. The church was a beautiful stone structure. I had vague memories of going to Sunday school. Uncle Dale and Aunt Sandy got married there, as well as cousin Sandy and the Strohls.

My mother's side was Methodist. The original Asbury United Methodist Church burned down, and members had to meet in a church in Midtown Allentown until the new church was completed. The new church was built in Salisbury, Pennsylvania, and was a modern and white brick one. Grandpa Geist served as an usher there, Uncle Bob played French horn, and Aunt Davie was part of the bell choir.

1981: GINNY NORMA RAE GEIST: Mom was an LPN, licensed practical nurse. She worked at Cedarbrook Nursing Home, next to Dorney Park and Route 78. It did not have a union, and she and some of the other nurses worked to organize the 1199 Union. It would improve working conditions and wages for the nurses. She worked really hard at this, and 1199 lost by a few votes. Mom was really upset, but I was so proud of her. She was generally very quiet, but I saw her inner Mama Grizzly Bear come out. A few years later, she graduated from Northampton County College with her RN (registered nurse) diploma.

Mom is smart, has a good memory and is one of the most diligent students I have ever seen. I am proud of her.

HAMILTON PARK CHURCH AND MRS. VANSKIKE: There was a church up the street from my home next to Hamilton Park on Ott Street and Flexer Avenue, the Hamilton Park Christian and Missionary Alliance (CMA) Church. During one summer, when I was in fourth grade (age ten), as I was evening cruising on my yellow bicycle with a big black banana seat by the church, they were showing a movie up on the side. The smell of popcorn and butter drew me in. I sat down, watched the movie, and met Sunday school teacher Ms. Vanskike.

I attended Sunday school here and there, and Ms. Vanskike would pay us 50¢ if we memorized our Bible verse for the week. We were supposed to bring our Bible to class. I thought what I brought was a Bible, but it turned out to be a large book of Bible stories for kids. She really loved us and sometimes even called to see how I was doing and hoped to see me show up for Sunday school. It sometimes made me feel guilty.

JESUS VISITS ALLENTOWN: I grew up in Allentown, and many of the towns around us have biblical names, such as Bethlehem,

Egypt, Nazareth, and Emmaus. In Sunday school, I asked, "Ms. Vanskike, Allentown, Pennsylvania, is so much nicer than Bethlehem, Pennsylvania. Why didn't Jesus ever come to Allentown?" It is not until I attended the Alliance Seminary in Nyack, New York, that I learned about the Moravians setting up mission colonies to reach the Delaware and Lenape American Indians and gave the towns the biblical names.

In seventh, eighth, and ninth grades, I went fairly infrequently to Sunday school until I hit age fourteen, just as I was beginning to tap into my inner party animal, wanting to drink, smoke pot, and get laid. I was just starting to get in with the cool crowd of John P., Mark G., Carlos Fox, and Scott P. I was the fifth wheel. They always went to parties, and I wanted to go to the parties. I knew the way to heaven, but I wanted to sow some wild oats before getting serious and committing to Christ. It was as St. Augustine said in his book *Confessions,* "I want to serve you Lord, just not yet." I identified.

GOLFING WITH GRANDPA SHORT: Grandpa went golfing every Thursday with his buddies. He took me miniature golfing and then to a driving range. I expressed interest in golfing, and he gave me an old golfing bag with clubs. He gave me a paper telling me approximately how far each club would take a golf ball. For driving a ball, Grandpa taught me to put my left foot just ahead of the teed ball on the ground. The key was to keep the eye on the ball and to not kill the drive but to put all my power in my left arm when I swing down, to follow through with the swing, and to let your golfing buddies tell you where the ball went.

DORNEYVILLE CHIP AND PUTT: Down the road from my home was the chip and putt. It had miniature golf, a driving range, and the par three chip and putt where you would only bring a nine-iron and a putter. It was a great way to practice to play on a real golf course. I had free time in the summer and got pretty good at my drives, chipping and putting. Grandpa took me out to the Twin Lakes Club to play. On the driving range, a teen summer worker drove the mower that pulled a ball-catching contraption. The mower had a metal cage around it, and you were not supposed to aim at the mower when driving golf balls, but we did, and we got our jollies when we hit the caged mower with a drive. We did that because kids often did stupid things.

TWIN LAKES GOLFING: Grandpa and I went golfing with another pair of guys. I did okay. It was a bit nerve-racking trying to hit a drive with three people watching. Grandpa rented a golf cart. I was used to carrying my bags or using a bag carrier with wheels. At one tee, I took out a ball with a red stripe. Grandpa said, "No, no, no, put that away." I learned the ball was a ball from a golf range, and I must have found it at Hamilton Park when I was practicing chipping there. After the eighteen holes, Grandpa bought me a hot dog and soda. It was a nice memory with my Grandpa Short.

GOLFING WITH NEIGHBOR DAVID R.: I went golfing at the Allentown Municipal Course with Dave Ruth. It was nice to get some exercise, walk, compete with the self and another, and enjoy the sunshine and breeze. Dave introduced me to the mulligan, meaning when you hit a bad shot, you got one do-over. I think Dave really practiced multiple multimulligans per game. On one drive, I had a nice long shot, and neighbor Dave stepped on my ball so it dug into the ground. We had a lot of laughs and fun golfing, if we didn't get too crazy about getting a high score.

THE ROACHES SOFTBALL TEAM: My father played for the coolest Mack Truck Softball League team called "The Roaches." It was not for cockroaches but for the little tool used to hold marijuana blunts to get the most out of a joint. Kids at my high school knew about this team. I used to attend the Roach games during the week. It was so much fun for me. The Roaches improved year by year, and with a little belief in themselves, they were no worse than any other team, but they might actually be better than the other teams and won the championship one year. I loved to watch them play. Dad was the team pitcher, and Uncle Dale, a lefty, played first base.

ROACH PLAYERS AND POSITIONS:

Catcher: Skip R.

Pitcher: Dad

First base: Dale

Second base: Don S.

Shortstop: Jim S.

Third base: Bart B.

In the outfield were four players, either John G., Bud, Skeeter T., Dale S., John Y., Doug C., or Craig B.; and there were five to six others. Robbie Stevens, who was a few years ahead of me in school, got a job at Mack's and became a Roach. He ended up buying and running his own bar one day.

One Roach aftergame party was at Canal Park. Craig Blose had a black Lab named Tar. I had a tennis ball and could throw it over the canal into high grass, and the dog jumped into the canal and would find the ball every time. Skip was a big man with a baby face and the catcher for the team. He could really hit the ball far. His nickname was Boom-Boom, and usually, the song "Boom, Boom, Boom (Out Go the Lights)" played at every party. Dougie fell asleep on one of the benches that night and was picked up by the police to be taken to the tank.

At another game where it had rained, some of the guys poured lighter fluid and gasoline on the playing field to try to dry it out. Jody and I were sitting on the bench as the fire was burning when, out of the blue, Skip ran through the fire, and the whole crowd went crazy.

The shortstop had a quick temper, and he and our second baseman had words for each other. Jim went over and cracked the second baseman right on the jaw. It went to court and cost him $1,000. Jim later owned a bar called the Stop Light, after Mack Trucks moved to Winnsboro, South Carolina. The night I was there, he said, "If I knew it would only cost me another $1,000, I would hit him again."

After one game, Dougie said to Dad, "Let's go to the Allentown Fair." It was dark out at this time, but Doug pulled up in his convertible and said to security, "I have to get my car to my stand." The security said, "Go ahead," and my dad and Dougie drove through the fairgrounds in his car with them both laughing their heads off. I went to school with Dougie's niece Stacey, who one year became an Eagles cheerleader with a successful try out.

ROACHES AND THE BUS TRIP TO PHILLY: The Roaches chartered a bus to a Philadelphia Phillies game. As we were driving down, the cannabis smoke began to fill the bus. The bus driver said that if they didn't stop, he would pull the bus over. Ten minutes later, he pulled the bus over and said, "I am not driving anymore!" Without a beat, one of the Mack workers said, "I'll drive the bus then!" The official bus pulled steered the bus back on the road again.

Skeeter was walking around the bus with pills, saying that the red pill did this, the blue pill did that, etc. One of the wives said she had to pee, but there was not a bathroom on the bus. Three people held up blankets so she could pee. Just before she finished, someone yelled, "It's a boy!" The whole bus of riders lost it with laughter.

The Roach charter finally made it to the game. As the game proceeded, one of the Roaches, Craig B., got pushed or kicked by some guys behind him, and he rolled down three aisles of seats and ended up in the sitting position. He shook his head and kept watching the game like nothing happened. I couldn't remember if the Phillies won, but I would never forget the trip. Before we left, we were missing a person, Jim. Jim Swartz was a big buy with brown hair, brown eyes, and a brown beard. We found him an hour later in the parking lot and finally could head home. What a trip!

1980 - TOUGHMAN CONTEST: In August of 1980, something called the Toughman Contest came to the Lehigh Valley. It came out of Detroit, and it included boxing matches between novice amateur fighters, with three one-minute rounds and forty-five-second rests. For those who were unemployed or just wanted extra money, it was a chance to get $1,000 for first place and $500 for second place. Of the thirty-two people who signed up for the Toughman Contest, included were workers at Bethlehem Steel and Mack Trucks, truck drivers, and general laborers. There were a tree surgeon, a counselor, and a minister who joined the matches.

Jim Swartz from the Roaches softball team entered, and it was held at Stabler Arena on Lehigh University. I made a sign with blue and red markers, and it said, "The Roach Assassin!" He had at least eight to ten family and friends there rooting for him. In the first round, he walked around the ring throwing few punches; but once he got hit in the face, his eyes opened up wide, and he started punching wildly. He won his fight in the first round and ended up losing in the second round. My hat was off to Jim for having the courage to enter the ring. After the match, his wife, Sue, asked if they could have the poster for a keepsake. I gladly gave it to them.

1980 SUMMER OLYMPICS: We had no summer Olympics, as President Carter wanted the United States to protest the Soviet Union's invasion of Afghanistan (along with sixty-five other countries). Greg Louganis was in his prime for diving, as many other American athletes, and would be robbed of the chance of competing. This was one area I wish we would always remain neutral in for the sacrifices of athletes and their families. Louganis never got the chance to be on a Wheaties box after his future gold medals, for America was not ready for gay athletes to be fully accepted yet.

1980 WINTER OLYMPICS: Eric Heiden won five golds in speed skating, and his sister, Beth Heiden, took a silver (speed skating). The U.S. hockey team won the gold. It took twenty hockey players to win one gold but only one speed skater to win five.

THE MIRACLE ON ICE: The Russians have won gold in hockey every year since 1960. Dave Anderson of the *New York Times* wrote, "Unless the ice melts or the U.S. Team performs a miracle, the Russians are expected to win gold again." The Soviets hockey players were all active duty military and worked out in world-class training facilities. The U.S. head coach Brooks held tryouts in Colorado Springs with college and amateurs in the summer of 1970 to choose his twenty players. Brooks trained them for one year and taught them how to play a European style of hockey. He set up an exhibition game with the Soviets in the Madison Square Garden three days before the Olympics, and the Soviets crushed the United States, 10–3. On February 22, the United States played the Soviets; and at the end of the second period, the USSR was winning, 3–2. The United States went on to score two goals in the third period, and as the game wound down to ten seconds, Al Michaels announced, "Do you believe in miracles?" The United States went on to defeat Finland, 4–2, and won the gold medal.

DELAWARE RIVER CANOE TRIP: The Roaches even went on an overnight camping trip down the Delaware River. As we were loading up the canoes, Donny Strohl went to lower his daughter Jennifer (aged three) into the canoe with her life vest on, and she slipped out of his hands and took a dunk into the water that was four to five feet high. Her eyes got as big as silver dollars. She was fine.

There must have been seven to ten canoes full of people. We floated down the river and found a nice spot on the left side to set up camp. We sent up tents and started up a campfire. Before sundown, another daughter of a Roach girlfriend started wading out into the river. Her name was Tara. Before you knew it, she was halfway in the middle of the river. Tara's mother was screaming bloody murder. Everyone in the camping area ran from the tents and lounge chairs to the river. I event tried to get out a bit, even though I myself was not a strong swimmer.

Several people were trying to get out to her. The boyfriend, Skip, was a monster of a man. I never saw anyone hit softball as far as he could. "Boom, boom, boom, out go the lights," they used to sing after he would hit a home run. Tara went under one time, now two times. Skip grabbed her, and she was fighting so desperately. She started to push him under to keep her breath. He had to throw her away from him so he did not drown. Just as she was going down for number three, a stranger pulled up with his canoe, and she grabbed unto the side, where he canoed her over to land safely.

It took some time for things to settle down. I grabbed Dad's ax to cut up some wood for the campfire. I grabbed several pieces and began chopping. Chop, chop, chop! Darn! The ax bounced of the one piece of wood knickng he right side of my right ankle and left a nice cut above by the ankle bone.. It was not a huge cut, but what little it got was deep and bleeding quite well. I hoped Dad would not flip out. The cut was taped up, and I was grateful the ax did not end up in my foot or shin. That was a trip I would never forget.

Curt, who was not a Roach, came on this trip. He was a karate master and teacher and a Mack worker. If you wanted to learn how to kill a man, Curt could have shown you a dozen ways. Curt, in my eyes, was very cool—Steve McQueen cool. I would like to be like him one day. Even his girlfriend (maybe even wife at the time) was very pretty.

Curt was not an official Roach, but he was always welcome to come to the games and to party with the crew afterward.

ROACH ROOFING COMPANY: Dad needed a roof put on the house. He recruited six to eight Roaches to help out. They helped take off the roof, put down the felt rolls, and then measure out where the shingles were to be nailed in. The starter row went on backward before laying the roof down. At one point, Dad noticed something was wrong. Someone was putting the shingles on backward, and that was quickly fixed. Mom provided drinks and pizza for the guys, and before dark, the Roaches have helped Dad put on a new roof, just like an Amish barn raising; it was a Roach roofing job. Those Mack United Auto Workers knew how to work hard! What a group of great guys!

I SAW THE LIGHT!: The tree in the backyard needed to be trimmed. Dad climbed the tree and began cutting and sawing away. There was a power line that ran in the backyard, and it was starting to get dark out. Dad put his saw on a branch, and it looked like it was glowing. He did this one more time, and when he saw the glow again, he quickly climbed down the tree, called the Pennsylvania Power and Light (PP&L), and asked them when they could trim the tree for him. Now there was a guy who loved his life.

BUDDY MIKE BROGNA: My best friend from elementary all the way through high school was Michael B. He was funny, athletic, artistic, and a scholar. He had a younger brother, Carmine, who was a year younger, and a sister, Chrissie, who was four years younger, the same age as my sister Jody. We really bonded after playing Little League baseball together for Hamilton Park and Little League football for Alton Park. Mike's family had a pool table, a piano, and a large record collection. The basement had pennants of all the NFL teams and a map of Italy that had the blue, red, and white bars in it. We used to hang around in the basement, listening to music and playing billiards. Mike's dad was Italian and a plumber. His mom was short, had dark hair, and used to be Lutheran before getting married and then became Catholic; she was a homemaker and later became a nursing assistant. His mother was an excellent cook.

At one of Mike's birthday sleepovers, they had pizza and goodies and so much food. Mrs. B. came downstairs and asked if we needed anything else. Jokingly, I said, "I could go for a steak." And she said, "Coming right up!" I had to stop her because she ran up the stairs and was going to make me a steak. She was one of the best cooks—bakers—I ever knew.

Mike told Dave he did not like his present, and Dave cried. Later, while we were running around, Mike started choking on a pretzel; luckily, he threw up, and the pretzel came out, opening his airway.

One time, I went to Mike's, and I put on a McDonald's hat, the kind the workers wore at the time. I thought Mike or Carmine would open the door, but Mr. B. did, and I said, "How can I help you? What would you like? Big Mac, Chicken McNuggets, fries, shake?" Mr. Brogna started laughing, and we went back and forth on his order for a few minutes. Such a crazy kid.

Mr. Brogna liked to paint and had his works throughout the house. He was also an Eagles fan and, for many years, had season tickets. I was quite jealous of this. Mike also used to attend the Eagles training camp for Little League and had the chance to meet many of the Eagles and to play football with them. Mike's dad also had a stash of *Playboy* magazines behind the bar, and many times, we caught a peak. The Brogna family were dog people. They loved boxers. The first was Spartacus, the next was Buster, and the last was Nia.

Mr. Brogna had his own plumbing business, and when he got a contract to work at the Lehigh County Jail to lay some piping, he had his sons, Mike and Carmine, help him do the work. I think the young men were scared straight and never forgot their experience. Sadly, Mr. Brogna passed on October 13, 1997. I drove from NYC for the service and felt such sadness for the Brogna family losing their father. He was a good man with a good sense of humor.

1981 - ALLEN HIGH PRINTING TEAM: In February of 1981, the Secret Service of the United States was called to Allentown, Pennsylvania, to find out where fuzzy $1 and $5 bills were coming from. They had been found in change machines at the arcades, at the local pizza places, and even by one of the town prostitutes. It turned out a seventeen-year-old student from Allen had printed out $11,000 worth of $1 and $5 bills in the print shop. This story even made it to Johnny Carson's late-night show in the form of a joke. The following year, students walked around with yellow T-shirts with "Varsity Printing Team" on the front and a picture of a $5 bill on the back.

1983 - CARVEL: I went to Carvel with some friends, and the high school girl serving us looked just like the Hess's model I saw in the *Morning Call* paper the day before. I asked her if she modeled, and she gave me a goofy look and said, "That is a terrible pickup line." I went home, grabbed the paper, and brought it back. Her two fellow ice cream slingers looked at it and said, "He is right! The model does look like you."

1981 - HUNTING AT THE TALL PINES CAMP: Having grown up with the Geist family that hunted, I too looked forward to when I could go hunting with my dad and uncles. I took my Pennsylvania hunter safety course and passed with a score of 97.5 percent. I used to get *Outdoor Life* magazine, the *Outdoorsmen*, and the *Pennsylvania Game News*. I especially liked the section of the *Pennsylvania Game News* called "Field Notes" from Pennsylvania conservations officers. The stories were only two to three paragraphs long and usually were funny stories.

Dad and John Galiano took Johnny and me up to the Tall Pines Camp in Clinton County in 1980 to get a feel of the roads and how the camp worked. We scouted some areas for wildlife and went up to an area for target shooting. Much of my time in the study hall in high school was for reading articles about hunting and fishing and daydreaming of being out in the woods.

FDR'S TREE ARMY: Our camp was off Coon Run Road, and if you looked at a Chuck Keiper Trail map, it was where it said "State Camp." The cabin was built in the early 1930s as a Civilian Conservation Corps (CCC) camp. In 1933, to help fight the Depression, Pres. Franklin D. Roosevelt put thousands of men to work on projects with environmental benefits. The program was open to unemployed, unmarried male citizens between the ages of eighteen and twenty-six and was also called "Roosevelt's Tree Army." Participants were paid $30 a month with a minimum enrollment of six months. The work was physical, and the men planted trees, cleared and maintained access roads, reseeded grazing lands, fought forest fires, and implemented soil erosion controls, wildlife shelters, and water storage basins. While administrators would tell you the program did not practice segregation, blacks were placed in de facto segregated camps.

COMPANY 1330, S-76, RENOVO, PENNSYLVANIA: It was organized in June of 1033 in Renovo and was told to be a white company, but by the company picture, it was composed of Negro employees. The men contributed 879 days of heroic firefighting under the guidance of fire wardens and contributed flood relief work, most outstanding during the disaster of March 17, 1936. The Works Progress Administration (WPA) office was located in Lock Haven, Pennsylvania, and two qualified instructors from Penn State University offered classes via correspondence in agriculture and home economics without tuition.

THE CHUCK KEIPER TRAIL: The trail was over fifty miles long and ran through Centre and Clinton Counties through the Sproul State Forest. It was named for a district game protector for Western Clinton County from 1951 to 1973. The trail ran behind the Tall Pines Camp. The rail was rugged and ran through Fish Dam Wild Area, the Burns Run Wild Area, the East Branch Wild Area, and the Cranberry Swamp Natural Area. The trail was made possible by the federal Title X program of 1976. Parts of the trail had already been blazed by the old CCC camps of Middle Branch, State Camp, and Panther Camp. Unfortunately, there were several areas of clear-cuts as the result of the oak leaf roller (a caterpillar) from 1968 to 1972. In some places, 50 percent to 100 percent of the trees had to be cut down.

WEATHERLY, PENNSYLVANIA -HUNTING: The Geists used to hunt in Weatherly, Pennsylvania, forty-two miles from Allentown. Weatherly was twenty-seven miles away from Mount Pocono. They sometimes stayed at an aunt's home, or they would get up early at three, stop by the diner in town, get the coffee and bacon smell in their hunting pants that a deer can smell a mile away, and then drive to their spot in Weatherly. And when they got cold, they crawled into the car to warm up or to take a nap. And at the end of the day, they drove an hour home and in the morning do it all over again. Some of the uncles had talked about buying a cabin together that they could all hunt out of, but it never happened. Uncle Tom bought his own place in White Haven, Pennsylvania, and Dad joined up with John Galiano to become a co-owner at the Tall Pines Camp in Clinton County. How serious was buck hunting in Pennsylvania? Mack Trucks closed down for "shutdown" during that week because they employed so many hunters.

COUSIN TOMMY, MIKE, AND LAURIE MEYERS: Cousin Mike picked me up on a Friday night to go to Uncle Tom's trailer. It was snowing, and when we got off the Pennsylvania Turnpike on the local roads, it was quiet, and no one was out. As Mike was driving, he turned his wheel, and the car started doing doughnuts (car circles) on the quiet empty road.What a crazy cousin. Cousin Tommy, Mike's elder brother, came up to camp, and you could identify his tree by all the cigarette butts underneath it. Laurie and I made a $5 bet that whoever got a deer first would win. Later in the year, in January, I got my first deer, and Laurie paid up and congratulated me. She is a person of her word.

1981 - SHOOTING MY FIRST DEER: Dad bought me a Thompson .54-caliber muzzle-loader, the kind used in the Revolutionary War. You took the gun; put gunpowder in it, a round thin cloth patch, and then the pumpkin ball; and push it down with a ramrod. Then you put in powder in the chamber, so when the flint hit the lock, the sparks lit up, and there was a quarter second before the gun went off. The flash of the pan powder could make you flinch, and it also had set many hunters' beards on fire.

I practiced shooting the gun, and I harvested my first deer, a big doe. It was a cold January day, and Dad put me up in a tree stand and put on a silent drive. He walked a mile away from me and then, with snow on the ground, found three sets of tracks and slowly and silently pushed them my way. Shooting at a target and shooting at a live thing were very different. Many Olympic archers and gun shooters were good at target practice but could miss when killing an animal. When we get to Allentown, Dad pulled into the Quik Mart next to Yocco's on Hamilton Street, and Gary Sampson was there and went crazy over the deer. He looked at me and said, "You shot this? That is a big ass doe! Congratulations!" .

MYTHOLOGY OF ANCIENT HUNTERS: From the cavemen to the Native Americans, there was always a prayer of thanks to the animal or the great spirit for the sacrifice of an animal's life so the hunters' family could go on living, according to Joseph Campbell, the writer on the importance of myth and the consultant in the making of the *Star Wars* movies.

I have had some students or church friends get upset when they found out I hunt deer and turkey. If I then find out they are not vegetarians, I educate them about the others who kill their meat that they purchase wrapped in cellophane clean and neatly packed, with no blood showing. For those who are vegans or vegetarians, at least I can respect your consistency. For me, hunting helps keep me connected with life, where my food comes from. And by being a hunter and paying for hunting licenses, I help conserve wildlife and wildlife areas for others who may use it for hiking, scenic driving, or fishing. I support sport hunting, not meat hunting. My license pays for conservation officers and scientists who keep track of wildlife and the forest and to help keep nature protected to be passed unto future generations. Licensed hunters and fishermen and women are the first to complain when there is pollution affecting land, rivers, game, or fish for the rest of the state's nonpaying population to enjoy. How much does PETA contribute to purchasing land to create game preserves for wild life?

DECEMBER 1982 - HUNTING AT UNCLE TOM'S: Originally, Uncle Tom had a hunting trailer in White Haven, Pennsylvania. He stopped by my home to pick me up. I didn't really know Uncle Tom well at this point. I loaded up all my hunting stuff in the back of this truck and sat in the front seat with him, wearing my Woolrich hunting outfit. With the heat running in the truck, I started sweating, and Uncle Tom started laughing and pulled over so I could take off my jacket.

In the morning, Uncle Tom took me to a tree to hunt out of. We left at five fifteen in the morning while it was dark out, and with our flashlights, we made it to my pine tree, which I climbed. I sat up there for what felt to be five to six hours. I was getting thirsty, so I climbed down the tree and walked back to the cabin in the snow. As I got five hundred feet from the cabin, I heard a "shhup" noise. I looked up, and it was my uncle up in a tree, and he said, "Jimmy, what are you doing? It is 8:00 a.m., and this is prime time when the deer are moving." I said, "Oh, I thought it was noontime. I am going in for a Pepsi." My shoes were a size 10, but wearing boots, they looked like a size 12. Uncle Tom gave the path from the cabin to my pine tree, the "Pepsi trail." There was a commercial out called "The Pepsi Generation," and Uncle Tom always liked to sing it or hum it whenever he could to remind me of my first year hunting.

THE 3:00 P.M. OPOSSUM: For those two days I hunted at Uncle Tom's, at 2:55 p.m., I heard something walking in the woods. I hoped it was a buck approaching. It turned out to be an opossum that walked underneath my tree. The next day, at 2:55 p.m., again, I heard something walking in the woods toward my tree, and it turned out to be the same opossum.

BEAR SCAT UNDER MY TREE: On the second day of hunting, when I came back to my pine tree, there was a pile of poo under it. I did not see it when I climbed the tree and accidently stepped on it on my way up. I noticed my left foot kept slipping as I was trying to climb the tree, and that was not a comfortable position when you were climbing with a high-powered deer rifle. As I walked back to camp, I ran into Uncle Tom, and I told him about the bear crap. He said, "Let's go back to your tree and take a look, young man." We got to the tree, and Uncle Tom said, "Jimmy, did you step in that pile of shit?" I said, "Yeah." Uncle Tom started laughing and said, "Were you slipping your way up the tree?" I said, "Yeah." Then he really started laughing and said, "I don't think that is bear scat, Jamesy, unless your bear uses toilet paper." Every time this story came up, Uncle Tom laughs so hard that tears came down his face.

THE STOMACH STUFFER: If you have ever done anything outside in cold weather for a long time, even just sitting or standing for six to eight hours, the heat your body created would develop a strong appetite to eat when you got back home. I was hungry when we got back home. The older men drank beer, whiskey, and water and ate pretzels, chips, and bologna. Uncle Tom said, "Let's get a pizza!" There was a place called the Stomach Stuffer that made pizza. He called them up to order a pie. Before a couple of guys went over to pick up the pie, Uncle Tom said, "The problem with the Stomach Stuffer is the chef has long stringy hair, and sometimes it gets in the food. If you go to the Stuffer for breakfast, you need to bring a razor with you to shave your fried eggs." The pizza got home, and when the box was opened, there was a long black hair in the middle of the pizza. I was starving at this point, but the hair so grossed me out that I just went to bed and decided I would have to wait until breakfast to eat.

1982 - UNCLE NORM LEAVES CAMP EARLY: Uncle Norm and Uncle Tom were buddies. They worked together, went to family events together, and used to house paint together to make extra money. Norm had an account with the Sherwin-Williams store in Allentown. They used to gamble and hunt together. Uncle Norm stayed overnight at the trailer. Dad, John Galiano, and Johnny came up to go hunting as well. On Monday, Uncle Norm left for home after lunch. He left a note saying he was not feeling well, like he had the flu. Long story short, Uncle Norm had suffered a heart attack. He went to the Lehigh Valley Hospital and was there for a week and ended up dying there on December 21, 1982. Uncle Norm had a great sense of humor, and it was sad to lose him, and I had hoped to get to know him better by getting time with him at hunting camp.

TURKEY HUNTING WITH DAD: The nice thing about spring gobbler season is spring. The ferns are coming out, there are buds on the trees, and as the sun comes up, you can reach temperatures in the sixties or seventies; in other words, you are not sitting on top of a tree in the middle of winter, freezing your butt off. You have to be out of the woods by noon, and then after lunch, it is an afternoon of trout fishing. It is a nice switch and makes the day more interesting, splitting time between being on the mountain and spending time in the river.

During the spring, it is mating season. A hen will lay one egg a day but needs a gobbler to fertilize the egg. There is a lot of turkey sex going on in the woods at this time. Hens will give out clucks and purrs to call in a gobbler. A gobbler may respond with gobble, double gobble, or a triple gobble or may sneak in without even calling. The idea is to locate a gobbler. Go out in the late afternoon or early evening, and use a crow call or an owl call. If you get a gobble back, that is the area you want to hunt the next day. If you find no gobble, look for a turkey sign or for an area that looks like a turkey country.

TURKEY HUSSY: Dad and I hunted an area and had no luck. After a few hours, we walked along the mountain ridge, and Dad made some calls. We got a gobble down the valley. We moved quickly down the mountain, about a third of the way, and set up. Dad called again, and the gobbler responded, and he was closer, meaning he was moving in. This went on for ten minutes, and just as we thought we would be getting a shot at our first gobbler, some whore hen cut in between us and led the gobbler away from us. The gobbler had no idea how this sneaky hen whore has saved his life.

YEA!, TURKEY HUNTING!: We had a good crew of guys for turkey hunting. In addition to Dad and me, there were John Sr. and John Jr. Galiano, Captain Chas and his nephew who worked in the post office out in Long Island, Bart Barthal and his step grandson Brandon, and Ed Wertz and cousin Mike Meyers. We got up very early to go hunting, and on the first morning, there was much excitement. After a day of turkey hunting, fishing in the afternoon, and staying up late to bat the breeze and play cards, it took a toll on us day after day. On morning one, Ed said, "Let's get a turkey!" On morning two, Ed said, "Today we will get a turkey!" On morning three, Ed said in a tired and unenthusiastic voice, "F——ing turkeys." After our dinner meal, Mike put on a turkey decoy on his head and pranced back and forth behind the couch, putting on a turkey dance show for the crew.

DEER? TURKEY? COYOTE? BEAR? BOBCAT?: The night before the hunt, I was reading an article in *Outdoor Life* about turkey hunting. When making hen calls, you could call in a bobcat or even a coyote; and in this story, a hunter had a bobcat jump on his back. Just what I needed to read before going out hunting. I shared the story with the crew, and Johnny talked about when he was archery hunting, an owl came in and attacked his boots, thinking it was some kind of prey.

In the morning, I was sitting against a tree trunk and making calls. I heard movement in the leaves behind me. I was guessing at fifty yards. I thought, *Great, I am calling in a gobbler*, but I got thinking about the article I read the night before. Now I thought, *This could be a turkey . . . or a deer. . . or a bear. . . or a bobcat.* I was sitting on the ground, not twenty feet up in a tree, and this thing on the ground is sneaking up behing me liteally getting closer. Just when the living creature is behind me, something grabbed my shoulder, and I jumped to the high heavens, screaming. It turned out to be common gray squirrel that jumped on my shoulder I hate squirrels sometimes.

FISHING THE KETTLE CREEK: In the afternoon, we went to Kettle Creek to go trout fishing. Dad used salmon eggs when he went bait fishing, but over the last fifteen years, he seemed to prefer fly-fishing. I have never learned to fly-fish, but I loved the movie about two brothers and a minister father in Montana who loved fly-fishing, *A River Runs Through It*. Brad Pitt played the one brother, and the movie ended by showing the other brother as an old man reminiscing about life as he was fishing and closing with "The river haunts me," haunting him with happy and sad memories from the past, as the river was a metaphor for living in the present.

BILL, THE MASTER FISHERMAN: Dad taught me how to fish with salmon eggs. You threw the bait upstream, and he taught me a few tricks I was not allowed to share with the public. When the brothers were fishing in *A River Runs Through It*, one asked the other what fly the fish were taking, and the successful fisherman kept saying "What? The river is too loud to hear you." Dad said, "When you learn how to master this technique, you can come up to a fishing hole with another person across from you, and you will whip the fish out if it's in front of him, and he will be amazed, and maybe a little upset, with your fishing skills." I was able to do this several times in my fishing career, and it was funny to watch the other person's reaction. He said if the fish were not biting, spit on the bait. I was not sure if he was pulling my leg, but I did hook into some fish after spitting on the bait.

ALMOST KILLED IN FREAKY INCIDENT WHILE FISHING: Dad was fishing with a buddy, who said, "Bill, go upstream seventy-five feet. There is a nice fishing hole there!" Dad immediately reeled in and walked the seventy-five feet upstream when a huge tree fell across the stream, right on the spot where Dad was fishing a minute earlier. Dad's buddy and the deep fishing hole saved his life. He would have been flatter than a silver-dollar pancake.

WHAT THE HELL IS IT? On this day, I was fishing by a metal bridge. I threw in my line and let the bait bounce down the river. With a worm, it took two to three nibbles before you set the hook; but with a salmon egg, when you felt a hit, you set the hook immediately. Dad was above me, and his pole was bent all the way over. He looked at me and said, "I am not sure if I am stuck or if I have something on the line. It feels like a catfish maybe." As I watched, the pole kept bending up and down. "Yup, I definitely have something on the line." A minute later, he called me over. "Jim, Jim, get over here!" It was the type of call you knew you had to move immediately. I walked upstream in my waders, and in the shallows of the clear, cold water where the rock bottom was visible in three inches of water was a three-foot creature on his line.

Dad looked at me and said, "What the hell is that?" I nodded and said,

"I don't know." This thing looked like a giant prehistoric salamander with a large round flat head, snake eyes, wrinkled light brown leathery skin, four legs, and a long tail. It must weigh four to six pounds easily. It was a hellbender, found in rivers in the Northeast, and settlers thought the creature came from the pit of hell. Other names for the hellbender were snot otter, devil dog, and mud devil. As ugly looking as it was, they were harmless and part of the salamander family. I figured hellbender was a good name for it, since most anglers that hooked into it probably said, "What the hell is that?"

YOU SHOULD HAVE SEEN THE ONE I MISSED: On the Pine Creek, we were fishing next to a stone bridge. I threw in my bait, and immediately, I got a hit. I set the hook and felt a fish on it. It did not fight with the usual gusto of a mountain fish. The fish you would catch in the Lehigh Parkway that came from the fish hatchery would fight, but up in Central Pennsylvania, in the big waters with much more current, they felt like pulling in a marlin and often jumped out of the water, trying to spit out the hook. This one I felt move to the bottom of the pole, and the pole was moving up and down. I thought, *Oh no, I hope I did not just hook into a hellbender like Dad did last year.* I had this lunker on for two minutes, but to me, it felt like ten minutes. I was thinking it was a hellbender, and then I felt the tension in the line releasing a bit, so I reeled in, keeping the line taut. It was then I saw a enormous fish tail come out of the water, and I realized I have hooked into the biggest trout in my life; it could be my trout of a lifetime.

During turkey hunting, we had two trophies, one for the biggest turkey and one for the biggest trout. If I pulled in this fish, I would be the winner for sure. I saw the tail one more time, and I got an empty, sick feeling in my stomach. I did not want to lose this fish. I had to wait until it tired out before reeling it in. Dad saw me fighting the fish, laughed, and said, "You have a nice one on?" I was so nervous that I could barely speak because it felt like I had a green olive in my throat, and with that, I felt my pole tip shoot upup in the air, as the pressure on the fishing line was went limp. The fish was so big with such a strong current that the hook pulled off my line, even though I had it double tied the hook. My heart sank to my stomach, and I still have dreams of that tail coming out of the deep fishing hole on Pine Creek next to the stone bridge.

THE LOCOMOTIVE AND TWISTER (NOT THE DANCE): After lunch, our crew took two separate vehicles to go fishing on the Kettle Creek. An amazing thing about the mountains was it could rain on one side but be sunny on the other side. You could have a sunny day in the winter and on the other side have a blizzard. We all drove up a mountain road that was paved but not very big. One crew of guys drove five miles down the river to fish, and Dad and I pulled over to fish our spot. We ate our lunch in the Scout. It was sunny out but looked like some rain clouds were moving in. We were in a valley with mountains on either side of us, and the river ran on close to the bottom of one mountain, and on the other side of the river was approximately 150 years of a grass field. Dad said, "I am going downstream a ways." I said, "Okay, we will meet when we meet."

Fifteen minutes passed, and it was starting to get darker out. The wind began to pick up, and two to three bolts of lightning hit the field behind me. I realized I was standing in water up to my knees with lightning striking. I got out of the water, and it began to hail. The wind picked up so much that my poncho was starting to fly over my head. On the top of the mountain behind me, I heard what sounded like a locomotive engine and train was coming my way. I thought, *Wind, hail, train coming. Ahhhhh, that could be a tornado.* There was a strange electric-like feeling in the air and I looked down the river where Dad walked, but I did not see him, plus I could not really help him anyway, each man for himself in this situation. They said you should not sit in a car in a tornado.I couldn't stand in the river for fear of electrocution. I went over to some trees where at least I could hang on to and hoped my trees were not hit by lightning. It felt to me as my air was being pulled out of my lungs, and this was one of the scariest situations I have ever been in. I hoped to not see a twister come down the mountain into the valley.

This whole thing happened in five minutes, but it felt like a half hour to me. The train sound stopped, and ten minutes later, Dad came upstream, and we drove down to to rendezvous with the other party. We talked about what happened and believed a tornado hit the mountain, and the other crew looked at us like we drank a gallon of moonshine and made this up. We drove up the mountain, and as we started descending, there were trees knocked down in the woods, branches and leaves all over the roadway, and some trees twisted up like a gorilla twisting straws. The road was closed ahead of us, as the volunteer fire department was on the road with chain saws, cutting up some trees that were lying across the road. One of the nonbelievers asked the old-timer fireman what happened, and he said, "A twister came across the mountain."

BORN TO BE WILD: Dad, John, and some of their buddies, before becoming members of the Tall Pines Camp in the early 1970s, took up an RV for deer hunting. They drove it down Hicks Run and parked it off on a logging road. On another trip, Dad and John took a four-wheel drive and drove through an open field, not considering the consequences of hitting a large hidden rock or large hidden tree stump. They pulled over to look over a valley, and John jumped up on a hollowed-out tree stump for a better view. Standing there, he kept hearing a buzzing noise that sounded like a bee's nest. When he looked down, he was standing over a snake den full of baby rattlesnakes making the lovely "buzzing noise" with their cute little rattler tails.

SMART BUCK: There was snow out, and Bill and John went out to the clearing. They saw a buck. They knew the deer would probably circle them, so they moved to an area where they would see the deer, but the deer would not see them. They waited and waited and could not figure out what happened. They went back to the spot where they first saw the deer to follow the tracks. It was as if the buck disappeared. After scratching their heads, one of them looked at the ground and said, "Look at our boot tracks. There are deer prints inside our boot tracks." That buck did not walk in a circle but walked back the way we walked in, in our boot prints, so we would not be able to track it. Smart buck!

MY FIRST BUCK: In 2001, I went hunting in Upstate New York at the property of a friend's uncle. I saw nothing in the morning and went in for lunch. I was so tired that I said, "Strap me into my chair so I don't fall into my soup!" I went back out to my spot and immediately fell asleep, and I was awakened by the sound of something moving through the brush. I woke up, but by the time I saw the buck, I missed the chance to get a good clean shot. The next day, when I went back to my spot, I came across the buck, and it was lying dead. Here laid a five pointer someone shot, but lost track of. If I had no fallen asleep the in the afternoon the day before, I could have harvested this deer, which was now lay wasted.

On the third day, I went hunting. It was foggy out, and it is 3:30 p.m. I had maybe forty-five minutes of daylight before it got too dark out. I was on the edge of a field, and like a ghost, I saw a doe pop out of the fog. Two minutes later, very warily, a six-point buck was following her. I raised the rifle, and my scope was fogged up. I moved in closer to the scope to put the crosshairs just behind the front shoulder where the heart and lungs were. Boom! I felt like I was just hit by Joe Frazier or Tommy Hearns! The buck went up in the air with its two hooves like a bucking bronco and went down. I gave him fifteen minutes, and I finally had my first buck. I also had blood coming down my face, a headache, and a crescent moon mark on my forehead just above my right eye from the scope pounding into my skull from the high-powered rifle shot recoil. I still have the mark to this day, but I am doing better than my first buck.

PTSD AT CAMP: One of our guys was a Vietnam vet and served as an assassin. The helicopter would drop off our camp friend and his partner into enemy territory near an enemy camp with the picture of the leader they wanted killed. They could be there from three to ten days until the mission was completed. At night, they slept back to back; and if one had to go to the bathroom, you woke the other up because if you woke up and your partner was missing, you assumed "Charlie" had kidnapped him. Our friend woke up, and his partner was missing, and he began to think the worst. His partner broke protocol by going away to do his business without waking his partner..

When the eneym target was shot with a sniper rifle, you ran like hell to your rendezvous point to be picked up. Our friend used to call out his partner's name, "Rod, Rod, Rod!" in the night during hunting camp, and Dad used to say, "Buddy, it's okay. We are just at hunting camp." Our Vietnam vet friend would say, "Oh, okay, sorry," and went back to sleep. I found out later in the week that, when our friend was in

Nam, sitting on a log with his partner, his partner was shot and killed by the enemy. War was hell, and many suffered from post-traumatic stress disorder. PBS ran a series called *This Emotional Life* over three nights, and there was treatment that would help vets let go of past memories and to be able to sleep through the night. Our one football coach at Allen High School fought in Vietnam, and whenever a helicopter flew by, he would stop and give it the "1,000 yard stare" until the helicopter was clear from view.

COYOTES: When I first started hunting, the Pennsylvania Game Commission's position was they were not sure if there were coyotes in the woods of Pennsylvania. Many hunters were claiming to see coyotes or coydogs, a mix of a coyote and a German shepherd. In time, the commission admitted there were coyotes in the Pennsylvania woods. John Sr. was hiking one day, and he could hear coyotes calling in three different spots around him, and they were getting closer, triangulating him with their coyote GPS senses. He got back to his truck as quickly as possible. One night, it was dark out, and Dad and Dougie Cope pulled the Jeep up to the shed to start the generator to the cabin. As they got out of the Jeep, the coyote calls were so close that they felt as though they were going to get nipped in the heels. Dad started the generator, and the loud gas-powered engine scared the coyotes away.

TED NUGENT WANTS TO HUNT COYOTES AT THE TALL PINES: John Galiano Sr. was at the Allentown Sportsman Show in Agricultural Hall in approximately 1990, and someone from Ted Nugent's *Archery* magazine was speaking. He said, "If anyone is familiar with the Fish Dam Wild Area in Pennsylvania, please raise your hand." After the program, the speaker called John over and said, "Ted Nugent wants to go coyote hunting out of your cabin." Unfortunately, this never happened because some local from Renovo, Pennsylvania, on a night when there was a snowstorm, drove around where we hunted and burned down seven cabins. The rumor was it probably was a kid of someone in the fire department. The cabin was rebuilt in the early 1990s, but Ted never got to hunt with Tall Pines owners, Bill, John, Chas, and Jimmy.

MOUNTAIN LIONS: One day, we ran into a fellow camp person just down the road during the flintlock season. He had a beard and came over after dinner to join Dad and me for coffee. He told us he worked for the U.S. Forest Service and was a fire jumper. They flew him into fire zones to fight fires. The test to stay with the firefighters was to step up and down a bench about two feet high for three minutes. If you could do that, you kept your credentials for the next year.

We got talking about deer hunting and coyotes, and then the word *cougar* was brought up. This gentleman told us that the year before when he was walking down a trail during turkey season, way in front of him, he saw a large cat that was yellow in color and had a long tail. As it was walking down the path, he could see the shoulder blades behind its neck moving up and down, and it would take three to four steps, lift its head over the ferns slowly, put its head down, and do it all over again in its search for turkeys or any food source for that matter. The Pennsylvania Game Commission said they did not believe there were any cougars, pumas, mountain lions, or Nittany lions in Pennsylvania, but they said the same thing about coyotes just a decade earlier and were wrong. In a 1993 edition of the *Pennsylvania Sportsman* magazine, they encouraged hunters to report any cougars they saw to the East Coast Puma Society. Some said the East Coast puma was extinct, but after a five-year study by the U.S. Fish and Wildlife in their 2011 report, they had 573 reports from the East Coast with 270 or half of them coming from Pennsylvania.

2002 - PENNSYLVANIA SPORTSMEN'S SHOW, HARRISBURG: I went with Dad to the sportsmen's show in Harrisburg in Pennsylvania. In Clinton County, when Dad started hunting, he said there used to be herds of deer. When I started hunting in 1982, there were some deer; but if you wanted to get a kid into deer hunting, they had to see deer. We came across the booth of the Pennsylvania Game Commission. At the booth was the commission's executive director Vernon Ross. Dad talked about how deer had plenty of food around farmland, but in the forest, the oak leaf roller killed off the acorns, and some parasitic fungus killed off the American chestnut trees, so the deer also lost this food source. What was the commission going to do? He talked about how deer hurt the farmers' fields and how they damaged cars, and Dad and I said, "Do you work for farmers and the insurance companies? Who pays for your salary? The hunters of Pennsylvania pay for hunting licenses that, in turn, pay you. Do you get paid by farmers and by insurance companies? Never forget you work for and represent hunters!" The executive director then said, "Have you ever gone squirrel hunting? Squirrel hunting is fun, and there are a lot out there." Wow, talk about a "squirrelly" answer for a mismanaged deer herd.

1999 - GARY ALT DEER MANAGEMENT PROGRAM: Gary Alt started working for the Pennsylvania Game Commission in 1977 to work with the bear management program. In 1999, he was asked to head up the deer management program. Hunters were complaining about not seeing deer and bucks with nice antlers. Alt came up with the "points program" that you could only shoot a buck if one of the antlers had three points on it. In 2002, in Eastern Pennsylvania, where 90 percent of the bucks used to be harvested, 50 percent survived to contribute to the gene pool. Forty thousand bucks that would have become venison in Pennsylvania made it through the whitetail season. Gary Alt went through some trying times for five years, but in the end, 80 percent of hunters ended up agreeing to the program, according to *Outdoor Life*. Seventy thousand antlerless deer were harvested in 2002, accomplishing the mission of reducing the deer herd while improving the trophy potential of its buck population. I didn't agree with the deer herd reduction aspect of its mission. I wanted to see more deer and have a better chance of harvesting one.

THE LONG WALK HOME: : Dad and I found a spot and did our turkey hunting. We moved to several other spots, walking down the mountain and up the valley. It was time for us to start heading back, and we came across a dirt road. Dad said, "Left or right?" I said, "Left." He said, "I think right." We went right and came across a woman on a John Deere tractor, mowing her lawn. We flagged her down, and she said, "You boys look lost. Where are you trying to get to?" Dad mentioned the camp we were at, and she said, "Oh, you want to keep going this way for about five miles. It's a really nice walk." In other words, she was not driving us there. The next morning, Skip Ritter, catcher of the Roaches, was with us and said, "I keep hearing something chewing on something under my van. I got up with the flashlight, and it was a porcupine chewing on my muffler pipe."

WORST TURKEY CALLING WE EVER HEARD: Dad and I were hunting on Uncle Tom's property, and at the end of the hunt, as we were walking back on a railroad bed, we heard a cluck here and one there. They sounded raspy, and they were like hunters making the calls. We laughed, and Dad said, "That is the worst calling I have ever heard." Three birds flew by us into the next swamp of evergreen trees.

CHESCATHE DOG, GETS LOST: Dad was up at camp and took Chesca, short for Francesca, the dog my sister adopted in Virginia when she went to an equestrian school She brought the dog home. My parents were upset at first but ended up loving the dog and keeping her. Chesca was a black Lab and border collie mix. She was mostly black with a white stripe down her nose and white socks on her feet. She was very smart, and when you went for a walk, she would stay within fifteen feet of you. In her last few years, she had lost her hearing. Dad took her for a walk up at Tall Pines Camp on a logging road full of ferns and mountain laurel. She took off. It was starting to get dark out, and she has disappeared. Dad started to hear coyotes calling, and he yelled as loudly as he could. He stayed out for an extra hour to find her, knowing if the coyotes found her first, she would be their dinner. Unknown to Dad or the family at the time, Chesca's hearing was almost gone. This would not be found out until a later time. Just as Dad gave up on finding the family dog,, he saw her running down the road toward him. It was a happy reunion for both.

PAPPY GEIST'S TRICK: My father's father went small game hunting with his beagle. When the beagle got on a trail sent, it was gone. I saw a beagle in my backyard once with his nose to the ground and did this all the way over the mountain without ever looking at me when I called out to him. At the end of the hunt, if the dogs were not around, he would lay down his hunting jacket on the ground and in the evening, when he went back, the dog would be sleeping on the jacket. Uncle Norm, when he went small game hunting, kept his pickup truck door open so the dog could jump in when it got tired. If the dogs chased deer or did not hunt, they were sent to doggie heaven.

LAVA OUT MY MUZZLE-LOADER BARREL: I was hunting with Uncle Tom and some of his buddies. His nephew Tom was hunting with us. As we stood where the power line was and looked out at the view of the mountains of Pennsylvania, the nephew had his gun pointed in the direction of my crotch. I spoke to Uncle Tom about my concern of never pointing a gun in the direction of another person, and he straightened out his nephew. At the end of the hunting day, if you had a flintlock, it was best to fire the gun and reload in the morning to avoid the chance of the powder in your barrel chamber getting wet and not firing. When I shot my gun, it looked like some lava just shot out of my barrel. I looked at Uncle Tom and said, "What the heck happened there?" Tom's buddy and old-timer said, "Well, I'll be. I have never seen a gun take a piss before."

1992 - TALL PINES CABIN, A VICTIM OF ARSON: I was not sure of the year, but I would guess the cabin of Chas Gingrich, Jimmy Miller, John Galiano, and William Geist was set on fire in the winter of 1991. Rumor had it in the town of Renovo, Pennsylvania, that the fire chief's kid allegedly drove up the mountain on a snowy night, went on a rampage, and burned down ten cabins. The camp had insurance but just enough to cover materials, not the rebuilding of it. The owners had to go up every weekend and, with the help of family and friends, rebuilt the Tall Pines from the foundation up to the roof. I was in the seminary at the time, and my contribution was bringing up my buddy, future Dr. Edward Nanno, with me to stain the cabin.

We drove out the cabin via Route 80 and took Route 144 to Hicks Road to get to camp. At the exit to 144, we stopped by a local store and bought two large hoagies for our dinner. We also brought cereals, milk, peanut butter and jelly, and some bread to sustain us for the weekend. The cabin was built, and the porch was to be put on later. It was a glorious two days in the '70s, and we stained away, making the sandy wood color of the T-11 wood a dark brown color. We brought the radio and blasted away tunes. About three hours into our project, a red Austin-Healey pulled into the camp. It was the owner of the store we bought our hoagies. He said he forgot to put in the oil and vinegar for our subs and wanted to make sure we got them. How about that for service?

1993 - STARRY, STARRY, COLD NIGHT: I believe it was April when we stained the cabin. The camp had no electricity. It had spring water and propane for cooking. The camp, at this point, was not fully built, but it was ready to be stained. There was a small opening along the top of the wall and the roof. In the evening, we sat around with our lantern and played cards. We thought we were on spring break, and it got very cold in the evening. We did not bring enough warm clothing. Until we went to bed, we wore underwear on our heads to keep warm and put painting drop clothes over our sleeping bags, and we are alive to tell the tale today. We woke up at three in the morning to a strange howling, and it was a pack of coyotes. It was a creepy, eerie sound. I am grateful to Edward for contributing his time and labor to the camp.

CAMPING AND FISHING IN CANADA: Uncle Tom, Tommy, Norm, and Dad took a tent up to Canada to go fishing. On the trip, they took the boat unto an island, and one of the guys jumped on the island and right back into the boat. In April through May, it was mating season for water snakes and garter snakes, and thousands of snakes swam unto the islands. They also experienced a hurricane when they were up in Canada, and Tommy slept so well that they could see his body on the cot covered by the tent canvas. Also on this trip, someone hooked Uncle Tom in the forearm. He had to push the hook barb through the skin and cut the barb off with pliers to get it out.

RATTLESNAKES EVERYWHERE IN TOWN: In Central Pennsylvania, I believe near Lock Haven or Snow Shoe, I read in the *Morning Call* newspaper about the construction of a FedEx warehouse when the construction workers dug up a rattlesnake den. (I could not find the town or date, approximately in the late 2000s.) As a result, snakes ended up all over the town by the site, just like the movie *Snakes on an Airplane.*

They say the rattlesnake population in Pennsylvania is getting smaller due to pipeline building, development, and ATV trails. In Pennsylvania, it is illegal to kill a rattlesnake under forty-two inches. You may take one snake over that size once a year with a proper permit. In all my years of hunting and fishing, I have not come across a Pennsylvania timber rattler; and for that, I am grateful. I am not a snake fan but understand they have an important role in the ecosystem. Yuck!

ALMOST LOST IN THE WOODS FOR A NIGHT: Up at Uncle Tom's camp, I walked up the mountain and crossed over the power line clearing after lunch. It got dark at about four thirty at this time of year. I kept walking away from the camp, doing some still hunting. I walked twenty to forty yards and stood for ten minutes and so on. Then I looked for spots that looked good for deer hunting, and before I knew it, I was not sure which way to go. I didn't have matches on me, so I wouldn't be able to make a fire if I had to stay in the woods overnight. I had a compass, so I just kept walking westward, hoping to find a road. Eventually, I ran into a dirt road, and I started walking in the downhill direction. A pickup truck drove by with an old-timer, and he asked where I was headed. I gave him the street name that Uncle Tom's place was on, and he said, "Oh, you are lost. I will give you a ride there." He drove me over to the house, and I said, "You can drop me off here at the crossroad, I will walk the rest of the way," but the old-timer drove up the driveway, and Uncle Tom came out. "Jamesy, what happened?" The old-timer said, "I picked him up at the Eckley Miners area." Uncle Tom laughed and said, "Jesus Christ, you were ten miles away!" I was glad the old-timer picked me up. It was one of the best dinners I ever consumed in my life, and I appreciated my comfortable warm bed with the soft fluffy comforter blanket that night as well.

JODY'S WILE E. COYOTE: After college, Jody had a job on College Drive where she got home late. She got home at about 1:00 a.m., got out of the car, and saw what looked like a dog in the Ruths' yard across the street; but when she really looked at it, it was a coyote with a fuzzy tail. She told Dad, and he thought she was seeing things. The following week, Dad took Chesca for a walk by Cedar Creek behind Cedar College. As they came near the path that veered to the right before Cedar Creek Boulevard, to the Rose Garden side of the creek, he saw a dog sitting by the edge of the woods. As Dad was able to get a closer, the raggedy-looking dog was really a coyote. Jody's sighting was confirmed.

BILL "JIM FIXX" GEIST: Dad was a runner. He went jogging three to four times a week. He said that the nice thing about running was you could eat whatever you wanted and not gain weight. Mom ran sometimes but did a lot of walking and took Mandy, the dog, with her when she did so. Jim Fixx was a famous runner and wrote a book called _The Complete Book of Running_. Mom and Dad had the book. Fixx died from a heart attack at age fifty-two.

BILL "LARRY BOWA" GEIST: Dad took me to see the Phillies play the Dodgers. I got all-star first baseman Steve Garvey's autograph. Dad did not care for Garvey 'cause he acted like his poo did not stink, and his hair was always perfect, like Coach Jimmy Johnson of Miami University. The Philly seating assistant took us to our seats and said, "May I ask you a question? Are you Larry Bowa?" Bowa was the shortstop for the Phillies at the time and was known for being a hothead. After a bad call, he took a baseball bat and smashed up a toilet in the locker room. Dad said, "Yeah, but let's keep it quiet. I have off tonight."

2003 - DAD'S TROPHY BUCK: In 2003, Dad and Mike Vaka went out to Fulton County, Illinois, to a 1,600-acre farm called "Strictly Bowhunting." The story was written in the October 2005 magazine called _North American Whitetail_ entitled "Double Trouble in Illinois" by Ron Willmore. Dad's buck was 181 4/8, nontypical, taken on November 11, 2003, at 2:30 p.m. Vaka took his eleven-point buck, scoring 171, two hours later. Both hunters agreed to shoot nothing less than 150 points, and they hunted a quarter mile from each other. On one day, Dad saw a ten-pointer and four other bucks the day before. It was a three-page article and ended by saying, "For these two close friends, every opportunity to bow hunt is a gift. Every once in a while, you get the buck of your dreams."

ANGEL STORY: I had an older family member who told me a story of being with his grandmother when she passed. Before she passed, this person, as a young child, saw two people with wings standing next to his grandma. The mother looked at the child and said, "What do you see?" This person told her and, to this day, swore that was what they saw, and nothing would ever change his/her mind. He/she was the last person you would ever think this happened to, but this person swore on it.

CHAPTER 4

William Allen High School, 1981–84, (Ages 15–17)

U.S. History in the 1980s

1980: MTV (Music Television) started.

- *Ronald Reagan* elected president (defeated Dukakis)

- Age of Reaganomics and the New Right

1981: Space shuttle *Columbia*

- Personal computers introduced

1985: Live Aid (helped in the Ethiopian famine)

1986: Chernobyl, Ukraine, nuclear reactor disaster

- Iraq-Iran War ended (one million killed).

1988: *George Herbert Walker Bush* elected president (defeated Michael Dukakis)

1989: Fall of the Berlin Wall

Inventions of the 1980s

1980:   Hepatitis B vaccine

1981:   MS-DOS, scanning tunneling microscope

1982:   Human growth hormones

1983:   Soft bifocal contact lenses, Cabbage Patch Kids, virtual reality

1984:   CD-ROM invented, Apple's Macintosh

1985:   Windows program by Microsoft

1986:   Superconductor, synthetic skin, disposable camera

1987:   3-D video games

1988:   Digital cellular phones, abortion pill, Doppler radar, Prozac, first patent for a genetically engineered animal at Harvard

1989:   High-definition televisions

Cars of the 1980s

Jeep Wrangler, Jeep Wagoneer, Pontiac Firebird, Chevy El Camino, Ford Series F pickup trucks, Ford Explorer, Ford Thunderbird, Chrysler minivan, Ford Escort, Ford Fiesta, Chevy Camaro, Dodge Aries (K-cars), Audi 5000, Nissan Maxima, BMW 3-Series, Mazda RX-7, Honda Civic

Music of the 1980s

<u>1980</u>

Pink Floyd: "Another Brick in the Wall"

Blondie: "Call Me"

Queen: "Another One Bites the Dust"

Rolling Stones: "Emotional Rescue"

Devo: "Whip It"

Pat Benatar: "Hit Me with Your Best Shot"

John Lennon: "Starting Over"

Kansas: "Hold On"

Gary Numan: "Cars"

Ozzy Osbourne: "Crazy Train"

Journey: "Any Way You Want It"

Romantics: "What I Like about You"

Vapors: "Turning Japanese"

Firefall: "Headed for a Fall"

Billy Joel: "It's Still Rock 'n' Roll to Me"

Christopher Cross: "Sailing"

Comedy: Redd Foxx, Rodney Dangerfield

1981

Rush: "Tom Sawyer"

Foreigner: "Waiting for a Girl Like You"

The Who: "You Better You Bet"

Journey: "Don't Stop Believin'"

38 Special: "Hold on Loosely"

Joe Walsh: "Life of Illusion"

Blue Öyster Cult: "Burnin' for You"

Outlaws: "(Ghost) Riders in the Sky"

Jefferson Starship: "Find Your Way Back"

Squeeze: "Tempted"

Little River Band: "The Night Owls"

Molly Hatchet: "The Rambler"

Kool & the Gang: "Celebration"

REO Speedwagon: "Keep on Loving You"

Rick Springfield: "Jessie's Girl"

Comedy: "Great White North," McKenzie brothers

1982

Human League: "Don't You Want Me"

Toto: "Rosanna"

Tommy Tutone: "867-5309/ Jenny"

Go-Go's: "We Got the Beat"

Alan Parsons Project: "Eye in the Sky"

J. Geils Band: "Freeze Frame"

Willie Nelson: "Always on My Mind"

CSN: "Southern Cross"

Rick James: "Super Freak"

A Flock of Seagulls: "I Ran"

Missing Persons: "Destination Unknown"

Kim Wilde: "Kids in America"

Bob & Doug McKenzie w/ Geddy Lee: "Take Off"

Joan Jett: "I Love Rock 'n' Roll"

Steve Miller Band: "Abracadabra"

John Mellencamp: "Jack and Diane"

Men at Work: "Who Can It Be Now?"

Hall & Oates: "Maneater"

1983

Def Leppard: "Photograph"

Animotion: "Obsession"

Quiet Riot: "Cum on Feel the Noize"

Talking Heads: "Once in a Lifetime"

U2: "New Year's Day"

Don Henley: "Dirty Laundry"

Golden Earring: "Twilight Zone"

Scandal: "Goodbye to You"

Asia: "The Smile Has Left Your Eyes"

Greg Kihn Band: "Love Never Fails"

The Kinks: "Come Dancing"

David Bowie: "Let's Dance"

The Fixx: "One Thing Leads to Another"

ZZ Top: "Sharp Dressed Man"

Police: "Every Breath You Take"

Stray Cats: "(She's) Sexy + 17"

Loverboy: "Hot Girls in Love"

Duran Duran: "Hungry Like the Wolf"

The Who: "Eminence Front"

Rainbow: "Street of Dreams"

Michael Jackson: "Billie Jean"

Comedy: Eddie Murphy, David Brenner

1984

Yes: "Owner of a Lonely Heart"

U2: "Pride"

Genesis: "Illegal Alien"

Rush: "Distant Early Warning"

Van Halen: "Jump"

Pretenders: "Middle of the Road"

The Police: "Wrapped around Your Finger"

Robert Plant: "In the Mood"

Cyndi Lauper: "Time after Time"

Duran Duran: "The Reflex"

Tina Turner: "What's Love Got to Do with It?"

Prince: "When Doves Cry"

John Waite: "Missing You"

Wham: "Wake Me Up before You Go-Go"

Huey Lewis and the News: "I Want a New Drug"

Billy Squier: "The Stroke"

Rod Stewart: "Infatuation"   Comedy: Weird Al Yankovic

Kenny Loggins: "Footloose"

1985

Starship: "We Built This City"   Power Station: "Some Like It Hot"

Honeydrippers: "Sea of Love"   John Cafferty & the Beaver Brown Band: "Tender Years"

Bryan Adams: "Run to You"

John Fogerty: "Centerfield"   Foreigner: "I Want to Know What Love Is"

Sting: "If you Love Somebody, Set Them Free"   Simple Minds: "Don't You (Forget about Me)"

Dire Straits: "Money for Nothing"   Tears for Fears: "Everybody Wants to Rule the World"

Miami Vice Theme Song

Mr. Mister: "Broken Wings"   Comedy: Steven Wright

1986

Robert Palmer: "Addicted to Love"   Eddie Money: "Take Me Home Tonight"

John Mellencamp: "Rain on the Scarecrow"   INXS: "What You Need"

Kenny Loggins: "Danger Zone"   Outfield: "Your Love"

Moody Blues: "Your Wildest Dreams"   Sting: "Russians"

Steve Winwood: "Higher Love"

Bananarama: "Venus"

Patti LaBelle: "On My Own"

Bruce Hornsby: "The Way It Is"

Peter Gabriel: "Sledgehammer"

Comedy: Robin Williams, Sam Kinison

1987

Gregg Allman: "I'm No Angel"

Whitney Houston: "Didn't We Almost Have It All?"

Bon Jovi: "Wanted Dead or Alive"

Aerosmith: "Dude (Looks Like a Lady)"

U2: "With or Without You"

Europe: "The Final Countdown"

U2: "I Still Haven't Found What I'm Looking For"

Paul Simon: "You Can Call Me Al"

Billy Idol: "Mony Mony"

Comedy: Judy Tenuta

1988

Guns N' Roses: "Welcome to the Jungle"

U2: "Desire"

Traveling Wilburys: "Handle with Care"

Scorpions: "Rhythm of Love"

Fabulous Thunderbirds: "Powerful Stuff"

INXS: "Need You Tonight"

Guns N' Roses: "Sweet Child O' Mine"

Bobby McFerrin: "Don't Worry, Be Happy"

Richard Marx: "Hold on to the Nights"

Rick Astley: "Never Gonna Give You Up"

Debbie Gibson: "Foolish Beat"

Comedy: Dennis Miller, Roseanne Barr

1989

Don Henley: "End of Innocence"

Living Colour: "Cult of Personality"

Mike + the Mechanics: "The Living Years"

Bangles: "Eternal Flame"

Bette Midler: "Wind Beneath My Wings"

Fine Young Cannibals: "She Drives Me Crazy"

Comedy: Sandra Bernhard, Rita Rudner

Television Shows of the 1980s

Hill Street Blues (1981–87)	*L.A. Law* (1986–1994)
America's Most Wanted (1988–present)	*The Oprah Winfrey Show* (1986–2011)
The People's Court (1981–present)	*Roseanne* (1988–1997)
Seinfeld (1989–1998)	*Simon & Simon* (1981–1989)
The Simpsons (December 1989–present)	*Tales from the Crypt* (1989–1996)
Frontline (1983–present)	*The Greatest American Hero* (1981–1983)
Unsolved Mysteries (1987–1999)	*The Wonder Years* (1988–1993)

It's Garry Shandling's Show (1986–1990)

Cheers (1982–1992)

China Beach (1988–1991)

The Cosby Show (1984–1992)

Cops (1989–present)

Fame (1982–1987)

Family Ties (1982–1989)

The David Letterman Show (1982–2015)

Magnum, P.I. (1980–1988)

The McLaughlin Group (1982–present)

Miami Vice (1984–1990)

Moonlighting (1985–1989)

Murder, She Wrote (1984–1996)

Murphy Brown (1988–1998)

Movies of the 1980s

14-1980 (eighth grade): *The Shining, Airplane!, The Blues Brothers, The Elephant Man*

15-1981 (ninth grade): *Raiders of the Lost Ark, An American Werewolf in London, Arthur, Chariots of Fire, On Golden Pond*

16-1982 (tenth grade): *Fast Times at Ridgemont High, Poltergeist, E.T.,*

17-1983 (eleventh grade): *National Lampoon's Vacation, Scarface, Beverly Hills Cop, A Christmas Story*

18-1984 (twelfth grade): *Purple Rain, Amadeus, The Terminator, The Karate Kid*

19-1985 (frosh at Nyack College): *Back to the Future, Mask, Pee-Wee's Adventure, The Killing Fields*

20-1986 (sophomore at NC): *Platoon, Ferris Bueller's Day Off, Top Gun, Stand by Me, The Mission*

21-1987 (junior at NC): *Full Metal Jacket, The Princess Bride, Predator, Wall Street*

22-1988 (senior at NC): *Die Hard, Big, A Fish Called Wanda, Rain Man, Coming to America, Romero*

23-1989 (youth pastor): *Dead Poets Society, Look Who's Talking, Born on the Fourth of July, When Harry Met Sally . . .*

Games of the 1980s

Trivial Pursuit	Sorry!	Simon
Scrabble	Pictionary	*Asteroids
Hungry, Hungry Hippos	Trump: The Game	*Pac Man
Teenage Mutant Ninja Turtles	*Space Invaders	*Donkey Kong
Uno Cards		

Candy of the 1980s

Airheads	Appleheads	Bubble Tape
Bubblicious Bubble Gum	Gobstoppers	Pixy Stix
Mike and Ike	Nerds	Sour Patch Kids
Starburst	Reese's Pieces	Hot Tamales

MACK TRUCKS: On November 15, 1940, the workers of Mack Trucks voted for the United Auto Workers to represent them. My grandfather Fred Geist was a charter member of the UAW Local 677 in Allentown, Pennsylvania. My grandfather, Uncle Tom, Uncle Norm, Dad, Uncle Dale, and Uncle Jack worked there. Uncle Tom said when he started working there, most guys could not read. When the payroll person came around with cash, the workers put an *x* next to their names to know they received their pay. He said they may not have been educated, but they knew to the penny what they were owed, most were good Democrats, many knew their contractual rights, and all of them took pride in Mack Trucks. As the saying went, "Built like a Mack Truck."

CINDERELLA MAN: My grandfather remembered when guys would stand at the factory gate, and bosses would pick who was working for the day, like the similar scene in the movie *Cinderella Man* with Russell Crowe. The workers who had bribed bosses with money, liquor, or pies were picked over the other workers. Imagine if you had yourself, a wife, and eight kids, or ten stomachs to fill every night. This was a huge reason why Pappy Fred Geist became a charter member of the UAW Local 677—for equality, justice, and representation, to have a say in the workplace, in addition to seniority. Unionism was seniority.

I have heard several stories about Mack Trucks, since I had family and family friends who worked there. I am sure there is a great book to be written about what Mack Trucks was like from the workers' perspective, but it needs to be done soon before we lose another generation of workers and their stories.

COMMITTEEMAN: Henry Ford introduced the assembly line and forever would change the way cars and trucks would be built. Imagine trying to put parts on a moving truck as it is shaking while moving down the line. As anything else, it becomes second nature the more you practice, but working at Mack's is a tough job. You are battling time, bosses, machinery, heat, and any personal stuff that may be going on at home.

I wanted to work at Mack's. My grandfather did, my father did, three uncles did, and many family friends did. Dad said to me, "No, go to school. The way the world is going today, the Mack job may not be there for you for the rest of your life." Uncle Tom loved working there.

Uncle Tom became a committeeman for the United Auto Workers Local 677, and Dad ran and became the vice president of the local. When there was a problem in an area, the shop steward would call the committeeman to try to bring resolution between the worker or union and the company. When Uncle Tom needed to talk to the workers, he shut the line down and called them together to inform them of the latest union news. This was when the UAW had power.

BOSS STORIES: The bosses used to have their offices in truck trailers that were bolted along the edge of the factory walls. By contract, union workers could be anywhere on plant property. One day, Uncle Tom and Dad went to talk to a boss about an issue. The boss said, "I don't want to talk to you guys!" and walked out of the office. Dad looked at Vice President Meyers and said, "What do we do now?" Uncle Tom said, "Take a seat on the couch over there. Let's see what is in the desk here. Oh look, cigars!" Dad and Uncle Tom sat in the boss's office, smoking the boss's cigars.

There was a boss who used to go around and bring a little notebook with him and would write down stuff about the workers in his area. One day, when the boss was on break, a worker named Mike the Honkie opened the desk to see the famous little notepad where the boss used to snitch on to his bosses to look good. Mike took a large bottle of industrial glue and dumped it in the drawer with the snitch-snitch pad and, when it dried, became a permanent part of the desk.

There was a meeting when Dad and Uncle Tom met with a boss, and when Uncle Tom went to make a point, he took his fist, banged it on the table, and accidently hit the huge ashtray on the desk, and all the cigarette and cigar butts and ashes went flying in the air like an African sandstorm. The boss ended up agreeing with Dad and Uncle Tom, and they walked out of the room, table and carpet full of ashes.

For the most part, in Uncle Tom's area, the bosses left the workers alone. The bosses knew that the workers worked and usually met whatever number the work order was. When the company needed some extra work done, the UAW workers were able to meet the quota. One time, Uncle Tom accidently scratched the red paint job of a fire engine. The boss started yelling, "Who did this?" Uncle Tom said, "I did! It was an accident." They got together, and the boss said, "Do you think you can get this fixed by tomorrow?" Tom said, "Of course, we can!" And they did.

Dad used to work in an area where the guys built their own fort out of cardboard and plywood. They had a little Crock-Pot and coffeemaker to enjoy their lunch period. They had a little window with curtains, so if a boss came over during their lunch, they would tell him not to bother them because they were on lunch break.

One of the guys they worked with was an alcoholic, and the other guys had to work extra hard to cover for their friend. They did not want to see him get fired. One of the buddies took some cardboard boxes and used a utility knife to cut out holes and put them on the drunk guy, and he ended up looking like a walking robot. This person eventually entered rehab and got sober to keep his job. Thanks to the UAW Local 677.

THE 5C PLANT: Mack Trucks was going three shifts a day. They closed down for two weeks in the summer so that the machinery could be cleaned up and maintained to keep up the assembly line work. The majority of workers took pride in the product they built. The saying was, "Built like a Mack Truck!" When a company, person, or government bought a truck with a bulldog on the front hood, they have bought the best. One reason why Mack Trucks was doing well was because Iran, through the shah, was buying many Mack Trucks.

They made all kinds of vehicles there, including Daycabs or cabs with sleepers that pulled trailers. They made dump trucks, fire engines, and garbage trucks. Any truck that you wanted, they would build it. Many of the workers were not college educated but, as tool and die makers, could design anything. Whenever a boss gave any grief about a product, Uncle Tom would ask the boss how to design a piece that they should do. Often, the college-educated engineers were not able to design and build what the "hooftie" tool and die workers were able to do.

SOME OF THE WORKERS: Uncle Tom said he liked to work. He enjoyed making things, the camaraderie of the workers, union negotiations, and working with the company in finding win-win resolutions.

Uncle Jack used to work in race car driver Mario Andretti's pit team when he started out at the racetrack in Nazareth, Pennsylvania. There was Muskie Marv, a worker so committed to fishing for muskies that his nickname had a fish in it. There was Ty Stofflet, the world's fastest left underarm throwing pitcher. One worker known as John S. liked to wear dresses to work. The contract did not say he could not wear a dress. He also kept a fish tank next to the assembly line with a picture of a cat's face on both sides. He also kept a large hanging plastic milk bottle next to his work area so he could urinate there instead of having to walk to the bathroom. He also used to have a word of the day. He announced the word of the day on the speaker systems, and if you told him the word, he gave you a quarter. He died in 2005 and was a member of the Baptist Slovak Catholic Church and known for his unique sense of humor and having a kind word and compliment for all. When you served in the 101st Airborne (1958–60), you have earned the freedom to wear a dress to work.

Uncle Dale worked in a machine that installed the tires. He said it was like the metal suit Sigourney Weaver wore in the movie *Aliens* when working in the spaceship and when she got into a battle with one of the giant aliens. One time, Dad's job was to drive the trucks off the assembly line. The trucks rolled off every two minutes. He got into a conversation with one of the workers when the worker said, "Hey, Bill, isn't that your truck rolling off the line without a driver?" The truck rolled off the line and hit the padded wall without injuring anyone.

Yogi was a big guy with a beard, and he looked like Bill Bergey, no. 66 linebacker of the Philadelphia Eagles. Bill Bergey came to Mack Trucks for a tour one day and met Yogi. Bergey said to Yogi, "You look like me." Yogi said, "No, Bergey, you look like me!"

Another big guy was named Pinky. How awesome was that? He grew up an orphan and lived in the Hershey's orphanage, next to where they built Hersheypark. He was a Mack worker, and he did not have a good heart. He told his buddies all the time, "I just want to be able to live to walk my daughter down the wedding aisle." The day came for his daughter to get married, and Pinky proudly walked his daughter down the aisle and was filled with joy that his wish has come to fruition. Pinky's daughter and son-in-law flew to Hawaii after the wedding reception, and as soon as they got to the hotel, they were told to call home. She called home to find out that her father has died of a heart attack as they were in the air to Hawaii. They flew back the next day for her father's funeral.

One worker talked about how he lived in a haunted home. Another worker talked about how, when he was driving home one night, a UFO flew over his car and spun his car 180 degrees in the other direction. I wish a book was written about the Mack Truck workers! One worker was stealing fellow worker desserts, so a wife put Ex-Lax in the frosting of a chocolate cake, and the suspect was found out when he ran to and from the bathroom a dozen times.

GOODWILL BETWEEN THE COMPANY AND THE UNION: One worker lost it one night. He got pushed over the edge by who knew what, but life could do that sometimes. He went in the work bathroom and tore out the sink and some hanging pipes, and busted up a toilet. Dad got called in to meet with the bosses. The company agreed that if the other workers were able to get the bathroom in working order by morning, then the upset worker could keep his job. The UAW workers fixed the bathroom and helped save the job of a fellow brother.

ARBITRATION: Dad had to represent people to the company and sometimes in arbitration. The sign of a good union representative is to do your best in fighting for a person, even if you may have disagreed with what they may have done. This is where contract language is very important. The arbitrator listens to the understanding of language and then makes a decision. In many ways, it is being an attorney representing a client to the best of your ability. It can be about drug or alcohol use, it can be about allegedly stealing something, it can be about chronic lateness or missed work days, and it can be because someone had a gun in their glove compartment. What most arbitration comes down to is who the arbitrator believes, meaning there have been guilty parties who are good liars and have won and honest people who should have won their cases but lost because the arbitrator do not find them credible. When you go to arbitration, you put your future in the hands of another.

There were times when Dad would do everything to get a meeting set up for an addict or a drunk, the struggling person would promise to show up the next day, and they left Dad sitting there with the company men. That was not on Dad; that was called the disease of alcoholism or drug addiction.

UAW SUMMER PICNICS: Every year, the UAW threw a picnic for the members of the Mack Truck union workers and their families at Dorney Park. We received free passes to go on the rides, and the excellent food was served in the picnic area—burgers, hot dogs, fried fish, soda, and beer. If you ever said to my dad, "I am going to the Mack picnic," he would correct you and say, "The company did not pay for this, the UAW Local 677 did!"

MACK PARKING LOT: The union also had Mack Trucks have two separate parking areas, one for workers who owned American vehicles and another for the workers who owned foreign vehicles. How interesting that Mack workers who lived in America would buy a vehicle from the competitors. Did they not have solidarity with other union brothers and sisters in the country? Did they not understand that a middle-class economy depended on union workers buying products from other union workers?

CONTRACT NEGOTIATIONS: Dad sat in one meeting, and as the negotiations went on in the morning, Dad was taking notes on his legal pad. After lunch, when the Local 677 reps and the company met for afternoon negotiations, one of the bosses began to contradict what the company was saying. Dad pointed out via the notes he has taken that what he was saying was different than what was being said in the morning. The company negotiator, not liking that he was being called out for lying, got up, took off his tie in an aggressive manner, and then started pacing back and forth. I was not sure what that was to accomplish, besides being a weak intimidation technique or lively entertainment, but it did not impress the union negotiators. Uncle Tom used to be on the negotiating committee for the workers.

In a UAW video from the 1980s, a negotiator in Detroit said, "I just told the company we had $1 million in our strike fund, and our members were ready for the long haul." The company took the bait. He said, "I don't have a dollar in my pocket, nor do we have a strike fund." Wow, what a good bull shitter!

<u>FUN ON THE JOB</u>: This was the heyday of unionism. The company was making money, and the workers had protection and representation and could even have some fun at work. The forklift drivers at Mack Trucks were so proficient at working their machines that they occasionally ran a forklift rodeo. That was something I would love to see. I was sure it was something that would go viral if it was posted on YouTube.

<u>UAW CONVENTIONS (EVERY FOUR YEARS)</u>: Uncle Tom would grab Dad by the sleeve and say, "Let's go up to the stage and talk to our leaders." It was there they told UAW leader Bill Casstevens that the UAW needed to take the lead in fighting for single-payer universal health care in the early 1980s. They were way ahead of President Clinton and President Obama. With the moving of half the Allentown Mack Trucks to Winnsboro, South Carolina, Dad told Casstevens that, first, the UAW International needed to fight for higher wages for the workers who transferred, as $7.50 was not going to cut it. Second, the UAW needed to buy some land so the workers had a place to build homes. South Carolina hated unions and would make it tough for those who transferred to find shelter. They did both for the Mack UAW 677 transfers. The union threw in an extra $2.50 an hour for the workers who transferred, and the land and homes for the workers was called Sands Springs Estates.

<u>AFFIRMATIVE ACTION</u>: In the 1980s was a push for affirmative action. The only thing that was asked of the ladies was, "If you can't do the heavy lifting, you don't deserve the union pay. If you can, you deserve it." For the African Americans who were hired, some would complain that they wanted certain jobs, but the whole point of unions was seniority. You gave the easier jobs to the guys who have worked in the plant for twenty years or more. No one got an "easier job" when they first started, no matter the color of their skin or gender.

President Reagan (1981–88)

Domestic

Reauthorized the 1965 Voting Act by twenty-five years

Civil Liberties Act, compensating Japanese Americans in WWII

Appointed Sandra Day O'Connor to the SC

Fired 11,345 striking air traffic controllers

Foreign

Substantial arms reduction with USSR

Provided arms to mujahideen and contras

Negotiated the Intermediate-Range Nuclear Forces Treaty reducing nuclear weapons

Supported anti-Communism in Angola, Cambodia, Nicaragua, and elsewhere

POOR POLICY AND DIRTY TRICKS:

1. **Sabotaged President Carter's deal with Iran to free the hostages (treason?):** Behind Carter's back, to screw the Carter campaign, the Reagan campaign met with Khomeini to keep the hostages captive until after the election. Iran released the captives the exact moment Reagan was sworn into office.

2. **Iran-contra deal** (HuffingtonPost.com/RickRoss): Iran and Iraq had a war from 1980 to 1990. Reagan sold arms to Iran to free an American hostage and to get money to fund the CIA-backed contras. Senator Kerry and his investigators found the contra war was permeated with drug traffickers who gave the contras money, weapons, and equipment in exchange for help in smuggling cocaine into the United States. The U.S. government agencies turned a blind eye to this (Salon.com). San Jose *Mercury* reporter Gary Webb wrote "Dark Alliance"

in 1996 reporting about this. He killed himself four years later because of the backlash of his report and its impact on his career. The CIA said they were not part of a conspiracy, but nonpaid assets who ferried supplies to the contras did not have to follow CIA policy regarding smuggling drugs into the United States.

2b. **School of the Americas**: On March 24, 1980, Bishop Oscar Romero was shot while performing mass; and on December 10, 1980, four nuns were kidnapped, raped, and murdered by members of death squads trained in the United States at the School of the Americas. The school started in 1946 at Fort Benning in Georgia and, in 1961, changed its goals to anti-Communist and counterinsurgency training. Who were the counterinsurgents? Priests, nuns, community organizers, and union organizers—leaders trying to improve the lives of the poor. Death squads killed seventy thousand in El Salvador, one hundred thousand in Guatemala, and thirty thousand in Nicaragua. Jose Efrain Rios Montt, dictator of Guatemala, was a favorite of *700 Club* televangelist Pat Robertson and the Moral Majority's Jerry Falwell. Rios Montt was charged with genocide by the Latin American court. Amnesty International noted many of the killings of the native people used shooting, burning alive, hacking, disembowelment, drowning, and beheadings. Small children were smashed against rocks.

3. **Escalated the War on Drugs and mandatory minimum sentences** (Drug Policy Alliance): We have spent over $1 trillion on the War on Drugs since 1971, coming to an average of $51 billion a year. More than half of our 2.3 million incarcerated were there for drug law violations. We spent $30,000 a year for a prisoner and $11,665 for a public school student. The

Cato Institute said legalizing drugs (like Portugal) would save the United States $41 billion a year using treatment instead of criminal penalties.

4. **Increased the national debt by Reaganomics:** This was through cutting taxes and increasing military spending.

UAW LOCAL 677 STRIKE OF MACK TRUCKS: The Mack workers went on strike, and the Allentown police showed up. Dad knew the assistant chief and talked with him, and the police left to let the workers have their legal picket. Had the police not left, I was sure the blue-collar assembly line union workers would have worked over the police with comments such as "Don't we have a constitutional right to strike and picket?" "Hey Officers, aren't you guys part of a union? Why are you here harassing your fellow union brothers?" "Hey, don't we pay your salaries with taxes? If we don't work, we can't pay taxes so you can get your salaries!" "Isn't it time for a doughnut break?" "Shouldn't you guys be out there solving murders, rapes, and cold cases? Shouldn't you be arresting drug dealers? Why are you harassing working people?"

MACK TRUCKS MOVING PLANT TO WINNSBORO, SOUTH CAROLINA: On July 1987, Mack Trucks wanted to move the plant and give the workers a July 15 deadline. On August 3, 1987, the Winnsboro plant opened. Mack Trucks closed the 5C plant in Allentown, and 1,800 workers were laid off. Mack Trucks' goal was to bust the UAW by doing this. They wanted to hire all new workers from South Carolina, but they would not find the same work ethic there as they had with the Pennsylvania Dutchmen. The company went after Dad, using vans with one-way windows and helicopter to get him fired. They used ex-FBI agents with a Pinkerton guard outfit, like the coal company did to the Molly Maguires. They claimed to have something on Dad and told him he could keep his job if he stepped down from the

UAW position. If it went to arbitration and he lost, he would not be able to support the family and pay the mortgage. I was a junior in college, so they knew they had him in a catch-22. No wildcat strike was called by Local 677. Only a few workers walked out. Herbie Herbacheck was a good friend to Dad during this tough time.

Mack Trucks leadership waited until Uncle Tom Meyers retired in 1987 to do this because they knew Uncle Tom would have shut down the line and called a wildcat strike. I think back to all what Dad sacrificed for the workers for many years, and when Dad needed them most, they were so frightened about keeping their own jobs that they forgot about the importance of union "solidarity" as Lech Walesa did for the electricians and shipbuilders in Poland to help bring down the collapse of the Soviet Union by taking a stand.

MACUNGIE PLANT - MANDATORY OVERTIME: Dad said he has done about everything there was to build a Mack Truck, from putting on cabs to putting on wheels to sanding the hoods to dashboards to working in the spray painting area of the Macungie Plant after the 5C closing. In the new plant, there were no more forklift rodeos, but there was "mandatory overtime."

DAD GETS A NOTE FROM THE DOCTOR: For Dad, according to the contract, when it came to mandatory overtime, the bosses had to ask him if his back was able to do the mandatory time work. He never took the overtime, and a new boss came along and chose not to ask him to do the overtime. Dad went to the boss and said, "Why don't you ever ask me if my back is okay to do overtime?" The boss said, "'Cause you never take it." Dad took it to arbitration and got paid overtime for every day the boss did not ask him to work.

Dad's buddy went to the Fiesta Bowl in Florida in 1987 to watch Penn State play. He told his buddy, "Do me a favor. Send a card to my work department at Mack's, and write on it, 'Having a great time in

Florida and also going to the PSU game,' and sign my name on it. I will be on vacation that week, but the boss does not know where I will be." The week of the game, a card went to the department, and it was a card with women in bathing suits on a Florida beach, and it said, "Hi, guys, Mack Trucks gave me some extra money last month, so I am going to Florida and to the Fiesta Bowl to root on PSU." During lunch, Dad's coworkers saw the boss go to the board and take the card off to read. When he finished reading it, he slammed the card on the table. Dad's buddies laughed.

DEMOCRACY IN THE WORKPLACE: When I think of America, I think of the democratic process. Our form of government is not a "direct democracy" where every member votes. You can do that in Athens, where you have 200 men voting, but not in a country of 220 million people. We have a "republic," or a representative government; we elect people to vote for our area. Interestingly, Michael Moore, the blue-collar bishop of the working class, says, "When you enter the workplace, democracy ends."

At the Macungie Plant of Mack's, when the company demanded overtime, the foremen went around and announced it to the workers. Remember, you thought maybe you were going to take a nap when you left work, go fishing, watch your kid's Little League game, or go to visit someone in the hospital. No, you were going to continue working on the assembly line in Macungie, Pennsylvania, in the greatest country in the world, the United States of America, like a Chinese worker in a Communist plant or in a prison system somewhere.

1980 - CONFIRMATION CLASSES: Mom asked me how I felt about going to church. I was in ninth grade, and I said, "I don't want to go to church." Mom said, "Well, I am your mom, and you are going to church until you move out." We started attending Asbury United Methodist Church, where my grandparents went. They offered confirmation classes, so I signed up. The pastor leading the classes was Pastor John Peters. He was young, wore glasses, and had tan hair and a beard. He was married and had children.

We were given a United Methodist confirmation book and met weekly from September to May. In my class was Bev, David, Lynn, Mark, Erin, Ann, Chris, Janet, Joanne, Beth Ann, the other Beth, Jennifer, Julie, and Steven. I went because we have five to six cute girls attending, and the guys were pretty cool. I also liked discussing issues of life and spirituality. During the year, I began attending a Bible study and really enjoyed it. I read the Gospels and the Pauline letters, and my faith really grew. We visited a Catholic church, and I saw people kneeling when they prayed, and I learned this was called genuflecting. At the Calvary Temple Pentecostal Church, someone spoke out in tongues, and we didn't know what was being said. The Calvary pastor told us it was the language of angels, and there was usually interpretation to edify the body.

Pastor Peters told us that he would visit all of us during the year to get to know us better. When he visited me, I asked how a person entered heaven. He told me all people would eventually go to heaven. God is a god of Mercy." I asked, "What about Hitler, Stalin, Charles Manson?" He responded, "We all get in." I retorted, "Then why did Christ even have to die on the cross if we all get in?" I was disappointed by this conversation. I went on. "Then why even go to church or live the godly life if everyone is going to heaven?" After this, for me, I wanted to attend another church.

At the end of our time together, we attended a retreat weekend. It was nice. We played games and had a time for debriefing and for accepting our confirmation, and our time was over. We closed with a nonformal communion service as the boys drank their orange and root beer soda we had stolen from the kitchen.

PASTOR TIM BUCK TWO: After a discussion with my mother, we started visiting churches to find a home church that proclaimed the Gospel. We visited a Fundamentalist Baptist church in Emmaus, Pennsylvania, pastored by Pastor Tim Buck. He came over to visit our home later in the week. He told us he had a son who was named Tim as well, and they called him Tim Buck Two (har, har). Listening to this man was like getting a grilling from an inquisitor about our faith. He was so insensitive and judgmental in his presentation, that he made my mother cry.

Jody, Mom, and I ended up attending an evangelical church on Route 222 in Trexlertown, Pennsylvania. It was a good church that preached the Scriptures, and I helped volunteer to help out with the summer vacation Bible school. My one memory of the vacation Bible school was riding with the bus with a student from Allen one year ahead of me named Dutch, and while sitting in the back of the bus, he kept singing the song, "Lucky Man" by Emerson, Lake & Palmer. "Ohhhh, what a lucky man, he was!" I was not sure how it happened, but one day, Mom, Jody, and I decided to visit the Hamilton Park CMA Church, and that became our church.

1981 - ALLEN HIGH SCHOOL (AHS): William Allen High School is a mixture of junior high students from Raub, South Mountain Trexler. The juniors and seniors look bigger and older. There are more buildings at AHS than my junior high school. There are more students, teachers, and more activities and more clubs. We have a nice football stadium, and we have a gymnasium that can hold three full court basketball games at one time. We have an Olympic-sized pool with a diving area on the other side. I like my high school experience, but I like my Raub experience just a bit more.

ETHNIC MIX AT SCHOOL: My homeroom teacher was a home economics teacher, pleasant and always laughing. In my homeroom sophomore year, it was Dianne Rodriguez. The first words I learned in Spanish were "Aye Dio" and "Ay, chihuahua!" She was Puerto Rican with a lovely face, nice cheekbones, tan skin, large brown eyes, and long black Native American hair. She was one of the prettiest ladies I have ever seen in my fifteen years of life.

Puerto Ricans and Dominicans have Taino blood, the native people who lived on the islands before the Spanish conquered them and renamed them Puerto Rico and Hispaniola. The Puerto Ricans are a mixture of Taino Indian and Spanish. The Dominicans are usually a little to a lot darker because, in addition to the Taino and Spanish blood, there is also African blood from the slaves brought over. My rough guess is that 92 percent of the population is Anglo, 5 percent is African American, and the other 3 percent is Latino in 1984–88.

Uncle Tom was part of the class of 1956, and they contributed the bushes in front of the school. Whenever he drives by today, he yells at any kids messing with his bushes.

AHS SOPHOMORE - SMOKING IN MR. EVANS'S CLASS: Early in my tenth grade, before my conversion, I had a social studies class with an older teacher, Mr. Evans, who used to be a wrestling coach and was out of his mind. He was a person who should not have been teaching, but maybe he did not have enough time in for his pension. I had some weed, a small amount, and sitting in the back row of the classroom. As we were working on a class assignment, I put up my book, took out a pipe, and tried lighting up the pipe packed with cannabis. What the heck was I thinking? Lighting up in the classroom? Even an unconscious teacher would be able to smell the smoke. Luckily, the pipe did not light up, but my left eyebrow did, as I burned off a third of it, trying to smoke pot in class.

TURKEY CALL IN HOMEROOM: My eleventh-grade homeroom teacher was Mr. Holenda. He was a bodybuilder. Johnny

Galiano was in my class. One day, I brought in a turkey call and made purrs and quiet clucks with it. Johnny was rolling on the ground. Mr. Holenda got up in the middle of homeroom, quietly walked over to me, and in my ear said, "If I hear that thing one more time, I will make you swallow it!" I stopped; he made me a believer. He was generally a laid-back guy who let his muscles do the talking.

WILLLIAN ALLEN HIGH SCHOOL - PHILOSOPHY CLASS: In my junior year, I had a philosophy class with Mr. Steckle. He was a handsome man with brown hair and a mustache. He looked like the Anglo version of Geraldo Rivera, the reporter who became famous from helping uncover the terrible conditions of Willowbrook, a facility that took care of the mentally challenged. He also had the *Miami Vice–Magnum, P.I.* thing going on. He was smart, cool, and funny and used to stop by the court several times to join us in some games. What I remembered from his class was the book _The Prince_ by Machiavelli, about how a leader must act like a politician, switching political beliefs depending on the times to stay in office, about being a sellout whore to keep the income coming in.

He also was a teacher in my study hall where I used to pass out Jack Chick tracts or minicomics on how one entered heaven. Many were entertaining, and I swear on my life, in one class, I had all twenty students reading them, including the teacher. When they finished one, they passed it on to get a new one. I used to purchase them from Hackman's Bible Bookstore on MacArthur Road across from the Jordan Bowling Alley and by an awesome steakhouse that had excellent Texas toast. Mr. Steckle asked what it was, took one, read it, and laughed when he saw the 9¢ price tag. "So, Mr. Geist, for you, 9¢ is a reasonable price to pay for the salvation of a soul." I replied, "Of course, Philosopher Steckle. I think Machiavelli would be proud of my actions!"

FLYING THE FRIENDLY SKIES: Scott Kern lived on my paper route on Ott Street, and we played football together at Alton Park, and we went to high school together. Scott volunteered with EMS, and he also was working on accruing hours for his pilot's license. He rented a plane out of Queen City Airport, and it cost him $40 to fly for an hour. He said I could fly with him if I paid $20 to pay for half the gas. I thought that was a good deal, to fly around and see Allentown from the sky.

This would be the second time I flew with him. We got to the runway, and as we took off, the plane went higher and higher. It was like magic when the plane hit lift speed. We cruised around and flew over the Alton Park football field, we flew over the Lehigh Parkway, we flew over parts of the city, and then it was time for the landing. In the air, it was easy to fly the plane. He even let me steer the plane in the air. "I am flying a plane! Look at me!" What makes a true pilot is being able to take off and land.

As we began descending toward Queen City Airport, we were approaching the fields of Alton Park again and would be flying over Route 22 to land. The wind began to pick up, the pilot side wing lifted up, and the passenger wing lowered. Student Pilot Scott Kern was going "Ahhhh! Ahhhhhhhh! Aaaaahhhhhhh!" A hundred feet before we land, he straightened the wings out, and it was a fairly soft landing. That was the last time I helped him earn flying hours. I also stained my underwear. Hearing a pilot go "Ahhh! Ahhhh! Ahhhhh!" was like hearing the surgeon who was working on you say, "Oops!" Scott now is a pilot for the U.S. Airways and still an EMS worker.

1983 PHILLIES: The 1983 Phillies made it to the World Series against the Baltimore Orioles. They beat the Dodgers to win the pennant, and that made Dad happy because he could not stand the righteous all-American look Dodger Steve Garvey was always giving.

The Phillies were called "the Whiz Kids" because they had so many veteran players on the team, like Pete Rose (1B), Joe Morgan (2B), Mike Schmidt (3B), Garry Maddox (CF), and Gary Matthews (LF). The younger players were Bo Diaz (C), Ivan DeJesus (SS), and Von Hayes (RF). Dad scored tickets for October 16, 1983, at Veterans Stadium, and I could say I have been to a World Series game and watched the Orioles win the World Series that night. It was painful at first, but the Philadelphia fans were gracious and began to cheer the Orioles for their World Series win.

Note: Whoever is the Phillie Phanatic is a creative, athletic, and funny guy!

1982 - PARTY LIKE IT'S 1999: I was aged sixteen when Prince's song "1999" came out in 1982. In 1982, I was a sophomore, meaning 1999 was seventeen years away. "We are going to party like it's 1999." I would be aged thirty-three by then. What would I be doing? Since I was planning on becoming a man of the cloth, I figured I would be eighteen when I graduated high school, twenty-two after college, and twenty-five to twenty-six after grad school; so by age thirty-three, I would be a pastor of a small CMA church, be married, and have two to three kids in 1999.

PRINCE DIES: Seventeen years before 1999, when the song came out, I was sixteen. Seventeen years after "1999," I would be aged thirty-three. In 2016, seventeen years after the song "1999," I would be fifty, when Prince died from a prescription drug overdose in Minneapolis in his home. Prince was only fifty-seven and was reported to play 127 instruments and was an advocate of having music programs in all schools. I could play the radio, the kazoo, and some chords on my guitar. I never was a fan of Prince's music. Prince was a Jehovah's Witness and thus not supposed to expose their good works. I am not a

Jehovah's Witness and will do some healthy sharing of my life successes and failures as Augustine did in *Confessions*.

1983 - THE DAY AFTER (A NUCLEAR ATTACK): On Sunday. November 20, 1983, a program aired on TV called *The Day After*. It was about what life would be like after nuclear attacks by the superpowers. On WZZO Radio, they were calling Saturday, November 19, "<u>the Day Before</u>." People were asked to call in and share what their day would look like if they knew Saturday was their last day. It must have been a warm pre-Thanksgiving weekend because I was up at Hamilton Park with my boom box, playing WZZO and listening to music while shooting hoops and sitting down on the benches to listen to listeners' responses.

It was aneerie day, being cloudy and unseasonably warm November day. I was thinking about Thanksgiving coming up, what to be thankful for, and what it would feel like if the planet were to end via of nuclear weapons. It brought up fear and sadness for me. One listener's response was "I would spend the day with family and friends." Some said they would engage in sports to try to keep their minds busy from the oncoming doom. Another caller asked, "If today is the day before, and tomorrow is the day after, when is the actual day?" Some said they would spend the day in bed with their lover. My favorite answer was the guy who said, "I would strip naked, smear myself with peanut butter, and run around screaming all day!"

It reminded me of a *The Simpsons* episode when an asteroid was on its way to destroy the town, and with the local bridge broken down, there was no escape for the dwellers of Springfield. With the Simpson family sitting on the roof, Homer said, "It is at times like this I wish I was a religious man." The next scene was Reverend Lovejoy, with his white robe and purple vestments, running down the street screaming, "We haven't got a chance!"

PREACHING IN THE AHS PSYCHOLOGY CLASS: I was in the new football coach's psychology class. His name was Mr. Lewis. We had to come up with a psychological test and present the results to the class. My topic was about biases and preconceived ideas people have about the Bible without having read it themselves. I had questions like "What does the Bible say about hunger, poverty, abortion, homosexuality, and salvation?" The teacher gave me the okay. I wrote up a survey, and the day came for me to present my information.

The psychology room was in the shape of a college room with seats on rows of elevated seating. I read the questions, gave the percentages of the yes or no questions, read passages from the Bible on the issues, and then gave a presentation in class about what the Gospels say about entering heaven. As I looked at the class and the teacher, many had their mouths open. I felt nervous when I started, but at the presentation went on, it flowed smoothly. As they said, things that wouldn't get you into heaven were good works, baptism, church, religion, Sunday school, charity, money, mass, communion, parents, political affiliation, denomination, friends, positive thinking, and just being a good person. The thing that would get you into heaven was Jesus. Chrissy Zimmerman said to me, "You are a unique person, and I respect the courage you have in sharing your faith publicly." From my junior year on, I was called Pastor Geist.

SPANISH CLASS: I had Ms. Bennett for social studies. Ms. Bennett said she would rather have another baby than have a tooth pulled. This was one of the most amazing statements I have ever heard. One time, she gave me a Spanish word to interpret in front of the class, and I said, "To come," as in "Come here, Fido." The whole class lost it, and her face turned beet red. Such dirty minds my classmates had.

There were three pretty ladies in class, and we all liked the band Judas Priest. I brought my Bible to school one day, and three ladies in class made fun of me—Alison, Andrea, and Joy. They said, "Is that a

Bible? That book is gay! You have dry-looking hair that your hair dryer has turned your hair into hay!" In 2011, Andrea passed at age forty-five, and Joy died in 2010 after a four-year struggle with breast cancer. I have reconnected with Alison via Facebook, and we now have an amicable Internet relationship.

1982 - PIRATES CATCHER ED OTT MOVES INTO THE HOOD: Ed Ott was the retired catcher of the 1979 world champions Pittsburgh Pirates. The Pirates were Willie Stargell (1B), Rennie Stennett (2B), Frank Taveras (SS), Phil Garner (3B), Bill Robinson (LF), Omar Moreno (CF), Dave Parker (RF), and Ed Ott as the catcher. His home was on East Texas Boulevard, and whenever I knew I would be riding my bike by his home, I put two of his baseball cards in my back pocket with a pen. As I rode by, he was mowing his lawn, and I walked over, and he graciously signed the cards and showed me his huge World Series ring. The song "We are Family" by Sister Sledge was the theme song of the 1979 team. Ed Ott became coach of the Allentown Ambassadors semiprofessional farm team for the Phillies, which went out of business but then came out of the ashes as the new Allentown IronPigs team, which has helped mold and create several Phillies.

1982 DRIVER'S LICENSE: I got my driver's license at age seventeen. When I came back from my freshman year of college, I found out all my younger buddies I hung around with have moved on. I felt hurt and used. Where they just hanging out with me for rides to the mall, the movies, and Friendly's for Reese's Pieces sundaes? I learned that some came in my life for a day, a season, or a lifetime. I had my first and only accident ever at age seventeen, a fender bender by Cedar Crest College on Cedar Crest Road. The person slammed on the brake, and I hit her car from behind.

One accident × 33 years × 365¼ days divided by 1 is my average in accidents. That is 1 in 12,053 days.

1983 - ANDRE THE GIANT: I was not really a WWF fan, but I ended up going to a match at the grandstands of the Allentown Fairgrounds and got to see Andre the Giant, the Iron Sheik, and Superfly Jimmy Snuka in 1983. In 1983, Snuka was charged with killing his girlfriend in Allentown, and I thought, *Did I see Snuka just before or after he killed his woman?* In 2016, Snuka was charged mentally incompetent to stand trial. Dwayne "the Rock" Johnson graduated from Bethlehem Freedom High School in 1990. The future "Rock" would have been seven years old in 1983, and I wondered if he was at the same Fairgrounds Wrestling Match I went to as a seventeen-year-old.

FOXCATCHER'S **DAVE SCHULTZ**: There was a big debate if wrestling was fake or not, if it was a true sport or just entertainment. WWE wrestler Dave Schultz got charged with battery when reporter John Stossel of ABC's *20/20* asked him if wrestling was fake. Schultz slapped Stossel in the ear and head several times. This was not the Flyers hockey player but the wrestler and brother of Mark Schultz, the Olympic champion murdered by multimillionaire John du Pont, portrayed in the movie *Foxcatcher*. While pro wrestlers may be athletic, the courts ruled that pro wrestling was entertainment. Dave was a survivor of dyslexia.

Fellow Allen student Christina Seneca worked the food concessions at the fairgrounds grandstands and got to see all the shows for free. She got a backstage pass to see Def Leppard and the groupie skanks tried to steal her backstage pass. She said, "Back away, skanks!" One of the members propositioned her, and she said, "Naaahhh, I don't think so."

HAMILTON PARK CHURCH (1981–84) - GETTING SERIOUS WITH GOD: Hamilton Park was what the majority of churches in America were, about seventy to seventy-five people. They sang hymns, had a prayer time and a good scripture-based sermon, and gave frequent invitations to receive Christ as savior. The church was almost too small for a youth group. It essentially was the pastor's son Elliot and sister Karen and Doug S. I went fishing with Doug a few times; we would get together, play board games, and listen to Christian rock or "contemporary" music. We went floating on the Delaware River of Floats and attended something called the Creation Fest 1983, which was held in Central Pennsylvania and the Christian equivalent of a Woodstock Festival. My first was in the summer of 1983, the year before I graduated from high school. There was a large stage for the shows and dozens of tents for smaller venues of seminars, speakers, music, books, and food.

MEMORIES OF HAMILTON PARK CHURCH: These memories included Doug and Duane Steckle Handsome Jim Walborn, Elliot, and Karen Vanskike; rafting down the Delaware River; Bob Jenkins leading us with Sunday evening sing-alongs; Wednesday night Bible studies with Terry; going to Mahaffey Camp and Nyack College with Duane Steckel; going to Great Adventure and the Allentown Fair; my buddy Mike Brogna going to church with me; seeing the church every morning when I delivered papers; Elliot's wit; and Karen playing field hockey for Emmaus. One funny memory was when the morning music leader Mr. Barker said, "I would like to welcome everyone here on Easter. Why, it's not Easter. It's Mother's Day!" We sat in the back row and could not stop laughing for the rest of the service. The night before going to Nyack peeling corn with the Walborn family, the church throwing a spaghetti fund-raiser dinner to help me to Mali, West Africa ($700 raised, and Nana Geist went!), Karen and Jon Bouw's wedding.

CREATION FEST 1983: We brought tents and food. It started on Friday at noon; they had music sessions in midmorning, in the afternoon, and in the evening. If you were a fan of Christian contemporary music, it was truly an event to not miss. In between the bands, they would have speakers give messages; one of my favorites was Dr. Tony Campolo of Eastern University. One of his famous sermons was "It's Friday, but Sunday is coming!" He was also to become part of a group called Evangelicals for Social Action, which I would join in the future. Karen brought a stuffed monkey named Boo with her that she always slept with. I hid it, and when she cried, I felt terrible, especially since I had a WWJD (what would Jesus do?) bracelet and that made it all the worse.

1984 SUMMER OLYMPICS GOLD WINNERS: Carl Lewis, Edwin Moses (hurdles), Evelyn Ashford, men's basketball team, Tyrell Biggs (boxing), Greg Louganis (diving), Bart Conner (parallel bars), Mary Lou Retton (individual all-around gymnastics), men's volleyball team, Bobby Weaver, brothers Dave and Mark Schultz (wrestling), Tiffany Cohen, Mary Meagher, and Tracy Caulkins (swimming)

1984 WINTER OLYMPICS GOLD WINNERS: Bill Johnson, Phil Mahre and Debbie Armstrong (alpine skiing), and Scott Hamilton (figure skating)

1986 CHURCH CHRISTMAS PLAY: Mrs. Vanskike ran the annual Christmas play. When I came back from college, I had just finished my finals and all my reading and was thinking and writing papers. As Ecclesiastes said, "Study makes the body weary." I just wanted to come home, sleep, relax, and have no responsibilities. Mrs. Vanskike called me and told me to show up for play practice. I let her know I was not interested, and she said, "This will be your last year doing this." I got my lines as the father of Mahalia, and I had a good number of them to learn. Jody played my daughter. The night of the play came, and it went by without a hitch. Then came the last line of the play, where I was supposed to say, "I am so proud of you, my little Mahalia!" I said, "I am so proud of you." I repeated the line, hoping the name would pop in my head—nothing. I tried a third time and said, "I am so proud of you . . . what is your name again?" Well, the crowd loved it, and that was the last time I had to be in a play for Mrs. Vanskike.

FEBRUARY 2003 - THELMA VANSKIKE'S PASSING: The last time I saw Mrs. Vanskike was over Christmas in 2003. I knew she was fighting cancer. She came over to me and gave me a hug, and with her characteristic laugh, she asked me, "Am I glowing? I had my radiation treatment this week." She passed on February 12 at age seventy-one. Thank you, Thelma, for reaching out to me, loving me, and sharing your Christian faith with me.

CHRISTIAN BANDS: I was a fan of Randy Stonehill, Petra, Mylon LeFevre, Sandi Patty, and the guy who used to be in Santana. When it was time for Amy Grant to play, the electricity went out. To be able to hear her, they hooked up a speaker to a car battery, and everyone in the audience who had a flashlight put it on the stage. It actually was an experience to remember. I would never forget it. I would also not forget how sick I got when I got home. I mean, the night I got home, I ran into the bathroom, and it came out both ends. What I thought might be a Satanic attack for having such a great time in the Lord turned out to be that the Creation Fest organizers forgot to run chlorine through the copper pipes, and many got sick because of bacteria that had not been sanitized beforehand. I heard it on the radio the next day.

BIBLE QUIZZING TEAMS: There were three to four CMA churches in the area, and they had Bible quizzing teams. We would memorize certain passages, and we would meet at a church on a Wednesday evening. There were three contestants on each side. The host would start reading a scripture reference, and the person who hit the clicker first would be given the chance to recite the verses. It was competitive and fun, and most importantly, we learned verses.

BIBLE STUDY WITH CAROLYN H.: Mom attended a Bible study led by a godly woman named Caroline Holmberg. The study moved from home to home, and when it was held in our home, I overheard some of their conversations about the book of Revelation, talking of the "End Times," the Antichrist, a false prophet, and the second coming of Christ. What? I needed to learn more about this! I started attending. I started reading Revelation, Daniel, and the Gospels.

GOOD LIFE ADVICE FROM DAD (TENTH GRADE): Dad asked me, "What do you want to do with your life, Jim? How will you make a living?" I said I was not sure. My dad, who was a nonbeliever at this point, said, "I see you read the Bible a lot. Maybe you should consider ministry. You have to work a long time until you retire, so choose a profession you enjoy doing. There is nothing worse than getting up in the morning and on the way to work saying, 'I really hate my job!'" It was at this point I considered becoming a pastor, and the more I thought about it, the more it made sense to me.

HORIZONTAL VS. DIAGONAL LAWN MOWING: In addition to washing dishes with my sister, taking out the trash, and cleaning up the dog doodoo, I mowed the lawn weekly. It did not take that long, and the yard did look good after a mowing. Dad told me to mow the grass diagonally. Diagonally? So I adjusted the mower so that the right side of the mower was three clicks higher than the left side. Why Dad wanted the rows of grass to have Gumby-like hairdo look was beyond me, but sometimes you wouldn't question Dad.

When he came home from work, he asked why I had not mowed the lawn diagonally. When I explained to him what I had done, he just shook his head. He then showed me he wanted me to make the rows from corner to corner to create a diagonal look, and I understood. He said, "Mow the lawn in straight lines one week, and then do it diagonally the next. It was good for the grass." One week, I mowed diagonally from the east to west. I started from the opposite corners. And then on week three, I mowed horizontally. Apparently, this gave the grass a good workout, and it also looked like Fenway Park outfield when finished.

CALL FROM GOD: One Saturday afternoon, as I was mowing the lawn, I thought I heard someone say Jim. Mom, Dad, and Jody were not home; so I thought I was hearing things. I kept mowing the lawn, and again, I heard "Jim" at a little higher volume. I looked around, and no one was in my neighbors' yards to the west, north, or east. I must be hearing things or losing my mind. Wait a minute, could it be God? As I kept mowing, for a third and definite third time, I heard "Jim!" I said, "Yes, Lord, it is I. What do you want?" And I heard laugher coming from the corner of my neighbors' window, but I could not see anyone because he was behind the screen, and there was a shadow over that side of his home this time of day. Mr. McCormick said, "Jimmy, you made my day! You thought God was calling you, and it was just me. Har, har, har." Mr. McCormick was a good man. He was a good Catholic who attended St. Thomas More and often served as usher.

HIGH SCHOOL BIBLE STUDY: My senior year, I hosted a Bible study at my home. The following students attended: Mike Brogna, Micky Wise, Angie Treese, and several others. Mike attended the Hamilton Park Alliance Church with me one evening when there was a special speaker named Robin DeMaggio. As he is praying, Pastor DeMaggio said, "I am getting a message that there is a person in our midst who will be used to bring thousands to God." He pointed to Mike and asked if he would come up front. He laid his hands on Mike's head and said a prayer.

MIKE "BILLY GRAHAM" BROGNA: As Mike attended the University of Arizona, he got involved with Campus Crusade for Christ. He ended up working at Berkeley University for several years. He has worked as a pastor, and he has worked as a college professor teaching Bible classes.

I am pretty sure he has reached thousands with his ministry work. He is a good friend, husband, father, and minister of the Gospel. He is an excellent athlete, artist, dog lover, a funnyman, and a decent human being.

PREACHING TO THE BASKETBALL BLEACHERS: It was summertime., 11:00 a.m., and we have just finished playing hours of basketball. There were ten to twelve guys sitting on the basketball bleachers at Hamilton Park, and I felt the urge, the prompting, a burning desire to share my story. Included in the unsuspecting audience was Mr. Gary Sampson, a student who frequently got in trouble with the school administration. I said, "Guys, I want to share something with you." They looked at me like they were thinking, *Whhhaatttt?* I told them how I have been searching for meaning in life and how the Bible and Christ have brought much fulfillment to me, and said I hope that they would give it a shot if this day ever happened to them. "In the Old Testament, God says, 'If you seek me with your whole heart, I will make myself real to you.'" The stands were quiet for ten seconds as if in shock, and Gary Sampson said, "Wow, I truly respect that. *That* took a lot of courage to stand in front of some guys and give a share like that! Thank you." How about that? Gary Sampson who some thought of as a trouble maker in school, complemented me on my first deer kill, and now complementing me on speaking my truth to a bunch of sweaty basketball players.

1983–1986: MUHLENBERG SUMMER STUDENTS PAINTING: The church service ended and fellow parishioner Lou LaBasi came up to me to ask me what I was going to do for my tenth-grade summer (aged sixteen) and if I was interested in a summer painting job at Muhlenberg College. The school hired a certain number of college students and high school students to help paint dorm rooms. It was minimum wage, and it was money I could start putting away for college. It was one of America's best premed schools and was home of the famous "Muhlen-burger" at the campus café.

The campus was a pretty campus, and many of the students were premed students. There were many cars there that had New Jersey licenses. The Buildings and Grounds Building had tools and machinery for metal and woodworking on the first floor. The small basement was the painting supplies area. The boss and assistant had work desks, and there were shelves and shelves of all types of paint (oil based, latex or water based, flat, egg shell, and semigloss) and all the colors of the rainbow.

THE JERKY RIGHT TURN: My workday started with me getting picked up by Lou. He had an old-fashioned station wagon that was light blue. In the car were Lou and Elliot and Karen Vanskike, who were in the youth group of the Hamilton Park Church. Lou picked them up before getting me. I was about two miles from the college, and we would drive down a long street that ran by Cedar Beach Pool to the right and the Rose Garden on the left. There was a light at the bottom of the hill and a second light halfway up the other side of the hill. A funny thing about Lou was he only steered with one hand, so when we made the right turn, we would start moving right; and then he let go of the steering wheel to grab it at the bottom to complete the right-hand turn, causing the young workers in the back to all jerk to the left in the process, squeezing the person sitting next to the door behind the driver's seat (usually me since I was the last one picked up).

We would take our punch cards and punch in, and on the nice weather days, we would sit on the concrete steps on the east side of the B&G Building, until Larry, the supervisor, would come up and give the painting assignments for the day. We usually worked in teams and were allowed to pick our painting partners. Most of the workers there were Pennsylvania Dutch and were "Dutchified," meaning they spoke with an accent. I liked it. It was a combination dialect of German and English. Many of my uncles could speak it or phrases of it. I did not.

I enjoyed the house painting. One year, they hired a full-time painter named Timmy. He had glasses and a hippie beard and loved rock music. I liked working with him. He was quiet, was a good worker, and laughed easily. Most of our work was inside work, but I got the chance to work with him in "staining" T-11 wood on some of the campus housing by the tennis courts. Stain was like working with water, and you used different brushes. I actually liked working with it, although my painting clothes looked like they have been sprayed with a water sprinkler filled with rainbow-colored paint afterward.

CARPENTRY: I was recruited by one of the carpenters for a two-week project. His name was John B., and his parents lived near the church on Ott Street. He thought it would be nice for a painter to get a break from painting. I would have preferred to keep painting, but it was an opportunity for me to learn something about carpentry. He liked to bust on the other two carpenters and the electrician. He said the election would let an extension cord set for a minute to make all the electricity was out. The senior carpenter was a Dutchie and a perfectionist and took his time. John used to say it would take him a day to make a bookshelf, as way to a mild work time. The other carpenter had a huge beer belly and seemed to get workman's compensation every year. John said he probably hit himself in the knee with his own hammer to get the time off.

One of the student painters was named Phil; he was the quarterback for the football team, and he was planning on becoming a minister. When I asked him how to get to heaven, it was not the evangelical answer. There was another tall painter who played center for the basketball team and was from the Netherlands, Hans. I thought he looked a bit like the singer George Michael. He did not believe in God and was sarcastic, and I liked him. He liked to taunt Phil and me; I just told him to invest in an asbestos suit to wear in his coffin when he passed. Dougie was the college preppy, who spoke with an air of superiority, although he may not have been that way in real life. There was Steve and Alice who worked together and, within three weeks, were involved in a summer romance and I am sure they think of when they hear the Motels sing "Suddenly, last summer," or the song "Those summer nights" in the Grease soundtrack.

DREAMING OF WORKING: My first year painting, I still had my paper route. I would get up at 5:30 a.m., and we would get to Muhlenberg at 7:45 a.m. There were times I was tired. One day, I was working with Neil; he was the frat boy who liked to have fun. In the dorm rooms, bed frames were often made from plywood, and some rooms had bunk beds in perpendicular positions. We had lunch, and with all the blood flowing to my tummy and it being a hot and humid day, working with all the heat that floated up to the third floor, Neil said, "Go ahead, take a five- to ten-minute catnap. I will keep an eye open for Boss Bud or Supervisor Larry." I felt extremely guilty, but my body was on the verge of shutting down. No sooner did I put my head down when the boss walked in and clapped his hands. "C'mon, get up! Time to work!" and he walked out. *Well I am sure today is my last day.* I was not called in, and nothing was ever said to me. I could tell you, after that, I was wide awake!

For lunch, I packed a brown bag, but there were days I liked to eat at the college café. The specials of the day were affordable and decent to eat. It was a place to see professors, campus workers, and summer students as well. The campus had a nice library and arts center. Campbell's Soup used the stairway of the administrative building to film a commercial of dancers to get you to eat more cream of celery, tomato, or chicken soup or something like that.

During lunch one day, Larry called Preppy Dougie to follow him. They began walking toward Doug's car. As they walked away, someone said, "I told Doug to ask permission." With that, we watched him open his car trunk and carry back two gallons of paint. He was fired on the spot. The sad part of this saga was if he had asked if he could have some paint for free, they would have given it to him.

Larry was a big man who had slicked-back black hair and a Godfather mustache. The supervisor had trouble pronouncing his *v*'s. He used the *w* sound for *v*'s. He also owned a Volkswagen, and I always liked to ask him what kind of car he had to hear "Wolks-wagon." He never caught on. He and his wife could not have kids, so when the adoption came through, he was a very happy man. We would hear about his "bub" for years. The boss, the supervisor, and Timmy liked me; so in the idle of the summer, I was given a full-time job opportunity to work as a painter at Muhlenberg College. I would have received pay, benefits, free college education for my children if they attended Muhlenberg College, and apparently free paint if I asked the boss for some. I said, "Wow, thanks, guys. It is a real honor of you to ask me to stay on full time, and I truly appreciate the offer, but I feel the call to go into ministry, and I will be going to Nyack College in September."

1986 - ROAD TRIP TO THE UNIVERSITY OF ARIZONA (TUCSON): Seals and Croft sang, "We shall never pass this way again," and that was how I felt after graduating from high school. I have spent three to thirteen years of my life with seven hundred of the graduating seniors from Allen High School. I ended up driving with my best friend Mike Brogna to Tucson, Arizona, and it was like a high school reunion talking about our growing up years from elementary school, Raub and Allen High, the Little League baseball and football, and what our college experiences have been like up to now.

It took us four days to get to Arizona. We stayed overnight in Indianapolis; Tulsa, Oklahoma; and Albuquerque, New Mexico. In Indianapolis, windows were blown out of high-rise and business buildings from a twister that has hit before we arrived there. While in Tulsa, there was a tornado warning given, which was not fun. The best McD's Quarter Pounder I ever ate was in Missouri.

When we drove through the panhandle of Texas and pulled over for gas, the gas attendant had gold-plated teeth with a cowboy hat and boots. As we pulled out, sage brush blew across the road, and so did a long rattlesnake. We agreed to split any speeding tickets, and Mike ended up getting one; the cop took his driver's license and said, "You will get it back when you pay the fine." They could do that? The last memory before Arizona was driving through the mountains of New Mexico in late June, and it snowed! I loved the University of Arizona campus, and the Sonoran Desert area, full of cactus, rattlesnakes, and scorpions.

Passing: Family and Friends

Linda Anderson	b: 7-11-63	d: 6-30-95	(32)
William P. Brogna	b: 1943	d: 10-13-97	(54)
Lisa Petulla	b: 1981?	d. 2003	(22)
Thelma J. Vanskike	b: 1935	d: 2-12-06	(71)
James Curtis Short	b: 1924	d: 2007	(83)
Lee Geist	b: 2-21-28	d: 3-20-07	(79)
Patrick Joseph McCormick	b: 6-27-17	d: 10-15-07	(90)
Jack Lohrman	b: 1935	d: 1-16-09	(74)
Thomas Aquinas Shea	b: 4-5-44	d: 10-16-09	(65)
Bruce Geist	b: 4-13-52	d: 1-20-11	(58)

Ron J. Beyer   b: 9-18-50   d: 2-24-12   (62)

Dale Geist   b: 3-2-51   d: 9-20-12   (61)

Frank "Razz" Radocha   b: 1937   d: 4-3-14   (77)

Coach Bill Snyder   b: 1942   d: 12-11-14   (72)

Virginia Short   b: 1925   d: 2-11-15   (90)

Ms. Sandy McGurrin   b: 1959   d: 8-11-15   (56)

Mr. Robert Kotran   b: 1955   d: 8-10-15   (60)

VEHICLES JIM HAS OWNED

'73 Chevy Caprice – green   '98 VW Gulf – red

'79 Oldsmobile – light blue   Toyota pickup – gray

Gremlin – brown   Dodge Aries K-car – green

1996 Jeep Cherokee Sport – green   2007 Ford Focus – white

DAD'S VEHICLES

Jeep Grand Prix   1966 Mustang – beige

Ford Hybrid – gray   Station wagon – blue and white

3 International Scouts

FAMOUS PEOPLE I HAVE SEEN IN NYC

Grandpa   John C. Reilly
Munster

Alec Baldwin   Sarah
                 Silverman

FAMOUS PEOPLE I HAVE MET

Ali   Dennis
                 Boutsikaris

Cheryl Tiegs   Deborah
                 Hedwall

Howard Stern	George Takei	David Hartman	Jackie Martling
Katie Holmes	Jon Lovitz	Bill Murray's dog	Phil Donahue
Natalie Portman	Gene Hackman	Ricki Lake	Fred Norris
Joe Franklin	Michael McKean	William Forsythe	Michael Moore
Laura Linney	Sylvia Miles	Eric Idle	Isaac Hayes
Tim Robbins	Angelina Jolie		
Don Imus	Actors of *The Sopranos*		

POLITICIANS I HAVE MET   PRESIDENTS I HAVE SEEN

Senator Wellstone	Senator Schumer	Pres. Barack Obama
Senator Specter	Mayor Koch	Pres. Bill Clinton
NYC Council Speaker	Peter Vallone	
Cong. Charlie Rangel		

AGES 21-29 1886-1995

Part II: Climbing The Career Ladder

<u>College, Grad School, Move to NYC, Ministry</u>

CHAPTER 5

Nyack College and Mali, Africa, 1984–1988 (Ages 19–22)

GRANDPA SHORT – "WHAT IF I CHOSE A DIFFERENT PATH?": "What if I had stayed? How would my life be different?" It reminded me of the scene in *Good Will Hunting* where Ben Affleck said to Matt Damon, playing Will, his best friend with a genius intellect, "Don't get me wrong, I would love for you to stay and we go to our kids' little league games and we celebrate holidays in South Boston, but, pal, you have a gift. If you don't ever leave this stink hole, I will kill you. We want you to succeed. I need you to succeed." My grandfather, after serving in WWII and finishing his Penn State studies with his engineering degree, went to an interview at Fuller Company. He sat there for fifteen minutes and said to himself, *If I have to sit here another five minutes, I am leaving.* The boss came out three minutes later and called him in for an interview. Grandpa used to say, "What would I have done for a living if I had not been hired by Fuller Company?"

MATT DAMON AND HOWARD ZINN: When Matt Damon grew up, he grew up next to Howard Zinn, the author of the book *A People's History of the United States*. Zinn accepted a professor's position in Boston University and taught there from 1964 on. Damon's mother was a public school teacher, and Zinn lived next to the Damons, so Matt used to see Professor Zinn at night through the window correcting papers, thinking, and writing books. Damon paid homage to Zinn by telling the psychologist played by Robin Williams, "If you want to read something that blows your socks off, read Zinn's *A People's History*." Dad thought my cousin Timmy looked like Matt Damon with dark hair. I was told my former Hamilton Park first baseman player was roommates with Damon up at Harvard.

If I had stayed in Allentown I would have probably married a Pennsylvania Dutch woman, had two to four kids, worked as a painter, attended church and family functions, gone to the fairgrounds in August and the farmers' market on Saturdays, attended my kids' sporting events and plays, thrown birthday parties, joined a gym and shot hoops at Hamilton Park, attended Allentown Flyers hockey games and IronPigs baseball games, maybe even volunteered with the youth group, went deer and turkey hunting and trout fishing, went to Dorney Park, and bought a nice home somewhere in Allentown or the outskirts of Allentown, and it would be a great, satisfying, and eventful life, but God had other things in store for me.

FALL of 1984 - NYACK COLLEGE: I attended Nyack College from 1984 to 1988 and Alliance Theological Seminary from 1990 to 1993. From Allentown, Pennsylvania, Nyack is a two-hour drive via Route 78 West to 287 North to the Garden State Parkway North to the New York Thruway East to the Tappan Zee Bridge. Nyack College was called the Mount of Prayer and Blessing, founded by A. B. Simpson, a visionary from the mid-1800s who wanted to send missionaries to lands untouched by the Gospel to usher in the second coming of Christ.

ALBERT BENJAMIN (A. B.) SIMPSON: If you went to our church for at least two to three months, you would hear about his college called Nyack College. It was the "official college" of the Christian and Missionary Alliance (CMA). He had a heart for evangelization and mission work; thus the middle name of CMA is "Missionary." It was based on Jesus's great commission statement to "go into all the world and make disciples of all nations." By *all nations*, the Greek told us it really meant "ethnicities or people groups."

ONWARD HO TO NYACK COLLEGE: My number one choice was Nyack College. I wanted to go to an evangelical school. I wanted to supplement my education with some biblical classes. I was worried about the financial impact this would have on my parents, and when I said I would be willing to go into the military for two years to help pay for school, Dad said, "No, get into school and finish your studies."

The summer of 1984 went quickly. I painted at Muhlenberg College as a summer painter, and it was my last year as a paperboy. The week before departure, I started packing up my stuff. On departure day, we loaded my stuff into the Ford Ranger pickup truck. We left at about 9:00 a.m. to get to the college in time for the freshman orientation after taking up all my stuff to the dorm room.

HELP!: As Dad and I left 512 College Drive and entered Route 22 East.Just before Easton, on 22 East are a series of S turns, the Ranger started conking out. The engine stopped running, and Dad found an area to pull over the brown pickup packed to the gills with stuff for my college dorm. We got out to look at the engine, and Dad said, "Damnation." This ise the age of cell phones, so we couldn't just call AAA. I walked away and said a prayer. "Please, God, help." Ten minutes later, a car pulled over, and it turned out to be the Vanskikes from church, taking their daughter Karen to Nyack College. Long story short, the Vanskikes drove Dad to a garage, he got the Ford towed and fixed, and we made it to Nyack just before dinnertime.

ROOMMATES: My roommate in my freshman year was to be Phong Tran, but Phong moved in with Tron. Doug Anthony became my freshman roommate. He was a music major who played the euphonium and was hypoglycemic. When he had sugar, it made him slur. One morning, as he tried talking and slurred at me, I thought it was time to call an exorcist. He was clean and friendly. My sophomore roommate was Fred Manning. Fred Bud was messy, frugal, and from the South and considered French kissing to be oral sex, until he got his first girlfriend and changed his views. I had to draw a line in the middle of the room because he had a way of throwing clothes everywhere.

SEPTEMBER 16, 1985 – AMERICA BECOMES A DEBTOR NATION: "Before the 1914, the U.S. had been a developing country, dependent on outside investment . . . in 1914, New York replaced London as the world's financial capital in the world . . . On September 16th, 1985, when the Commerce Department announced the United States had become a debtor nation, the American Empire died. In 1992, our debt reached 4 trillion . . . The money power shifted from New York to Tokyo, the end of our Empire . . . we the white race have become the yellow man's burden. Let us hope he will treat us more kindly than we treated him" (*The Decline and Fall of the American Empire*, Gore Vidal, 1992, pp. 7, 10).

My junior roommate was Scott Kang, who was one of the best students I have ever met. He had trouble waking up in the morning, unless it was a phone call from his girlfriend Sarah; right away, he jumped out of bed. My senior year roommate was Dan Kerrigan. Dan was from Buffalo, had played quarterback in his high school, and was clean and organized, keeping all his shirt hangers two-thirds of an inch from each other and ironing all his shirts. Dan would eventually introduce me to Jaime Arnita from Rockland Painting.

1987 - KISSY FACE: I ran down the Moseley Dorm's stairs to meet some friends outside. On the first floor, Dan was sitting with his girlfriend Melanie, a gorgeous Puerto Rican girl. She played on the basketball team with her twin sister. Dan introduced us and said, "Go ahead, kiss my girlfriend!" I looked at him and her and laughed. He said, "No, I want you to kiss her!" I looked at him again, perplexed. He said, "Listen, you are my roommate, and I want you to kiss her." I bent over, grabbed her, and planted one on her lips. They both looked at me stunned, but when you asked me to kiss a beautiful woman, especially three times, don't be surprised when it happenes.

THE BEST LEADERS ARE USUALLY CODEPENDENT: A. B. Simpson worked with a church in NYC. He turned his attention to creating a college to develop missionaries, to usher in the second coming of Christ.

Of course, one problem of ministry, working and having your own business, working in the corporate world, or a workaholic in general is you can spend so much time in your job that you can sacrifice your family in the process. Sometimes pastors and missionaries can be so busy that they don't have the time they should for spouses and/ or their children. This can cause internal conflict and guilt, for to be a good Christian, you are to make time with God, your family, and your ministry. With so much need and evils in the world to confront, a good person in ministry (or social work) can work so much that they can burn themselves out. It is also my conjecture that most people in ministry (or any job that helps people, such as nurses, counselors, teachers, ministers, etc.) tend to be codependent. In other words, a big part of their identity comes from helping others. Often, codependents cannot tell you how they are feeling, but they can tell you what others are feeling. Many codependents have trouble saying no or feel guilty about it and can feel guilty when they have free time or feel they should rarely, if ever, have fun and always play the martyr. An ironic thing about being codependent is they usually do the most work and die thinking they have not done enough.

FRESHMAN DORM NEIGHBOR DAVE JENNINGS: Dave came from McKeesport, Pennsylvania, a suburb of Pittsburgh. He was a music major playing euphonium, like my roommate Doug Anthony. Dave loved to play hoops and ended up getting a job working at Dave Wallach's, a small shop at the back side of Main Street that did woodworking for Rolls-Royce. I took partial credit for helping Dave get his college degree. On the day of the finals for Western Civilization with Professor Eldred, Dave was not in class. I ran from the room just as the finals started to Boon Center and up to the fourth floor of Moseley Hall and banged on Dave's door. I yelled, "Dave, you are missing the finals!" He said, "Yeah, I am on my way." When Dave entered the class, the students gave him a round of applause.

Dave kept talking about his fiancée Cindy. Dave married Cindy that summer, and I drove them home in the summer of 1985 back to Nyack in my dad's Scout. On the way home, we stopped by my parents' place, and Dad had some bear stew cooking.

We both also served on the Queens gospel team, and he is one of the most honest people I know. As of now, Dave has served as a vice president of the Nyack College for at least a decade. I also will serve with Dave as a copastor down in Queens at New Life Fellowship Church for five years. He has one of the best business minds of anyone I know. He also has started a health clinic down at the Elks to help minister to the poor.

1984 SUMMER OLYMPICS – GOLD: Carl Lewis, Evelyn Ashford (running), Florence Griffith Joyner (long jump), Greg Louganis (diving), Matt Biondi and Janet Evans (swimming), Zina Garrison and Pam Shriver (doubles tennis), and the men's volleyball team

1984 WINTER OLYMPICS-GOLD: Brian Boitano (figure skating) and Bonnie Blair (speed skating)

GUMBY: One of my favorite people in life is Pete Weisgerber. He was a senior at Nyack College when I was a freshman. He was from Long Island and from a German heritage and did not suffer fools well. He came across as a cocky New Yorker with a Long Island accent but also had a heart of gold. Pete was committed to Christ and was involved with Long Island Youth for Christ. In college, he was a history major, played the trumpet, and was going to become a teacher.

He was the opposite of my roommate Doug Anthony, for Pete was hyperglycemic. If he had too much sugar, he would fly off the roof; Doug would become sleepy. Pete was smart and very funny. He also was a gifted guitar player. For the Alliance Youth Corps, he went to the Bahamas and worked with a pastor there for six weeks. Seeing so much poverty had an impact on his worldview and gave him extra compassion for the poor and oppressed.

Pete was engaged to Judy. He could not wait to graduate and get married. He was very excited about starting carnal relations with his fiancée. Pete had a small pickup truck. One of the freshmen, Johnny S., got hold of Pete's car key and made a copy. For one week, Johnny would take Pete's car and move it to different parking spots. Pete thought Judy was playing games with him, and it almost caused a rift in their relationship. When it came out that it was a trick played on him, Pete guffawed loudly and said, "Good one, good one. You guys got me good! That is a funny joke! Thank god you told me! I thought I was losing my mind!"

Of all the seniors, Pete gravitated to me the most. Pete had a small trumpet he kept hanging in his room, and he told the freshmen of the fourth floor on Moseley Hall he was going to pass the trumpet on to one of us and that when we became seniors, we were to do the same to another. The trumpet was passed on to me. The reason he did so was because he felt I was a "real" person. I did not put on airs. What you saw was what you got, and he was impressed with my walk with Christ at the time.

Pete worked with a Christian school in Bayside, Queens, for a few years, teaching history, and then moved down to Maryland to work with a Christian school there. He ended up working as a teacher for nineteen years but quit with all the changes that were happening to education in the country starting in the 1990s, doing away with teacher-centered teaching and moving to group work and blended learning, class control being taken away from teachers, and hounding assistant principals using "gotcha" tactics instead of setting goals and working with the teacher in a positive and nurturing way to help achieve them. He ended up becoming a chef at a Vermont summer camp and working at various restaurants. He really got joy from creating spicy and tasteful dishes that bring satisfaction to customers. He also worked at Killington Ski Resort on Pico Peak. As chef, he earned the nickname Pico Pete.

FEELING CLEAN, REFRESHED, AND ON FIRE: Pete ended up getting a divorce from Judy, but they stayed in contact because they shared a twenty-six-year-old daughter and still are friends. I found that amazing and refreshing. I went up to visit him in Vermont, and I used his restroom. Next to his toilet were what looked like clean wipes. I have never used one before, and I have heard they could be quite refreshing. When I used it, I set my sphincter hiney muscle on fire. It was not clean wipes but a Clorox Bleach Wipes for disinfecting bathroom counters and toilets.

DROPPING WATER BALLOONS ON THE 280ZX: We had someone who lived on our floor in my freshman year. He had a pretty girlfriend he married, and he frequently made sexual remarks. We were sexual beings, and God, not the devil, created sex, I get that. I was not sure about how committed he was to God, but he ended up making decent money with a tech company he helped start in Manhattan. He had a Datsun 280ZX, and Gumby and I dropped a water balloon on his car, and it caved in his roof. He was upset but was able to push the dent out. In the late 2000s, he was arrested for child molestation and spent a few years in jail.

BUTT SLIDING: Moseley Hall was about the length of a football field. Something stupid and fun we did was we would fill up buckets with water, fill the hallway up with water and dish detergent, and then run and slide on our butts the rest of the way to the closet door (prayer room). Students put towels in front of their doors to revent water from getting in their roosm. It was a lot of fun. Robin Swope, from Erie, Pennsylvania, was a big guy; and when he went to jump to his bum for the slide, he slipped, and his head bounced off the floor. He looked like an unconscious sea manatee floating down the hallway, bouncing from wall to wall like a pinball. Rev. Swope is now known as the "Paranormal Pastor." You can google it.

One time, a Mosely 4 Northman went started the ignition of his slide when crazy Dan Gwin poured two lines of dry washing machine detergent like two huge lines of cocaine. When Mitch Fodor's naked rump hit the two dry detergent lines, you could hear two screeching noises, like car tires going over speed bumps. It was funny to hear the screeching sound, but the sting of the detergent on the strawberry-like abrasions was like dumping rubbing alcohol on an open wound. It sounded something like "sssssssssssssss-erk-ssss-erk." Poor Mitch got up and started screeching like a mutt that just dug up a hornet's nest or a self-improvement fan who has just burned the bottom of his or her feet at a Tony Robbins hot coal walking event in Hawaii.

JON SCHUERHOLZ: QUEENS GOSPEL TEAM: I became buddies with Jon in my freshman year. We were both part of the

Queens Gospel Team (QGT). Nyack College had Gospel teams that went into NYC every Friday to start and work with kids' clubs or to go witnessing on the streets. There was one in Queens, Brooklyn, and Manhattan. We worked in coordination with churches to guide people for discipleship if they wanted to grow in his/her faith. I used to go to the mall on Queens Boulevard or on the streets in the fall or spring when the weather was nice to talk to people about faith. Four times out of five, it was a positive experience.

The one day I was with Dave Jennings, a lady called him to come upstairs. When he did, a man in the home has been stabbed. Dave got someone to call an ambulance. The man could not speak but kept looking at Dave, who said it was something he would never be able to get out of his mind.

1984 - BROKEN-DOWN CAR SETUP: As the QGT van was driving down the Harlem River Drive, we noticed a car on the side of the road. We pulled over; and Jon, Dave Porter, and I got out. I asked the guy what was wrong with the car, and he pulled out the dipstick and just looked at it. John Porter said, "This is a setup. Look across the road." Two other guys were getting ready to run across the highway to mug us, to get all the money we had on us, but we all jumped in the van and took off. I learned from another Gospel team they pulled over to help someone who robbed them at knifepoint. How terrible of thugs to take advantage of the good of human nature.

1986 - SPRING BREAK QGT TOUR: I was part of the QGT for four years. To raise money, some Gospel teams went on tour during spring break to put on presentations to churches. It was mostly skits and then a message and an offering. We would stay in parishioners' homes and move on to the next town in a college van. Much camaraderie was created when you traveled with the same group of people for five days or more. Joe Kissel was the QGT president and did an excellent job coordinating the whole tour.

2001 - NEPHEW JORDAN'S CELL PHONE GETS SWIPED: Jordan was in NYC in 2001–02 and had his phone out. A black kid grabbed it and ran away. Jordan chased the kid, caught him, and grabbed his phone back. Wow.

QGT-NLF CONNECTION VIA PRAYER: In 1984, the QGT met behind the Elks Lodge on Queens Boulevard. Dave Jennings said, "Let's pray." It was about 8:30 p.m., dark outside, and he said, "God, please use us to bring the Gospel message to those who are hungry for it. Please help plant a church here in the heart of Queens to help build disciples for the kingdom." In 1987, Pete and Gerry Scazzero started a church plant in Corona, Queens. In September of 1993, nine years later after Dave Jennings's prayer, New Life Fellowship moved into the Elks Lodge in Elmhurst, Queens.

1985 - CHRISTMAS IN NYC WITH LARRY BIRD: My roommate Doug Anthony, Jon Schuerholz, and Dave Jennings decided to go into NYC to see the Rockefeller Christmas tree. As we drove down Broadway, we saw the Knicks were playing the Boston Celtics. Dave said, "I have never seen Larry Bird in person. Let's try to get tickets!" Jon found a place to park his car. We ran up to the garden, and the ticket guy told us the game just finished the second quarter. "Hey, at least we get to see Bird for half a game!" Dave and Doug bought tickets off a scalper and took off ahead of Jon and me. Jon started hemming and hawing, saying, "I am not comfortable buying tickets from a scalper." The scalper showed the tickets for the Celtics and Knicks. He wanted $20 for a ticket. I said, "Hey, the game is half over, $10 a ticket." The scalper, who was African American said okay, and he disappeared very quickly. We ran up to the ticket guy, and he said, "Did you buy this off a scalper?" I said, "I will not lie. We did." The ticket guys said, "That's too bad. This ticket is for yesterday's game." So much to learn about city life.

URBANA, 1985: Every three years, InterVarsity Christian Fellowship holds an event to encourage college students to get involved in mission work. It is held on the Urbana Campus of the Illinois University after Christmas and before the New Year. They have incredible speakers, seminars, and a plenary session every morning and evening with worship and a message.

The singing at this event was just out of this world. Billy Graham came every year to give a message. As the president of Christian service for the student government, I was asked to give a briefing of the event in January of 1986. I used humor and my experience, and it went well. I knew so because from thereon in, women would sit at my table during lunch and dinner in the cafeteria.

MIRACLE METS - OCTOBER 25, 1986: On the first floor of the room was a TV room with a vending machine in it and a few ratty coaches. This was the time before cable TV, and there were twenty guys stuffed in this little room watching the World Series. It was game six, bottom of the tenth inning, and the Red Sox were beating the Mets, 5–3. Mets Wally Backman flew out to the left. Keith Hernandez few out to the center. With this, Mets fan Jon Schuerholz said, "I can't watch this," and left the room, only to miss the miracle. The Red Sox were one out away from winning their first World Series. Gary Carter got a base hit. Kevin Mitchell got a hit, Carter scored, and the game was now Red Sox 5, Mets 4. Ray Knight got a hit. Mookie Wilson came to bat. It was now a 2–2 count on seven pitches. On the eighth pitch, Sox pitcher Bob Stanley threw a wild pitch, with Mookie falling to the ground and Mitchell scoring. The score was now tied, 5–5! The count was 3–2, and on the tenth pitch, Mookie hit a dribble up the first base. Vin Scully of NBC called the game, saying, "There are two outs, a roller up the first base, behind the bag. It gets behind Buckner! Here comes Knight! The Mets win!"

NYACK COLLEGE BASKETBALL (1984–88): For a small school, we had some excellent basketball players, including Mr. Dan Bailey, who was a guard and an excellent shooter, and Greg Bender, who was one of the best rebounders I have ever seen. At the beginning of the school year was a tryout basketball practice. Coach Jerry Slocum asked me to play. At one point, when there was a loose ball, I went for it the same time as Dan Bailey; he stepped on my foot and ended up breaking his leg. Great, I was the guy whom the Nyack's all-time scorer broke his leg on. Before the season, Coach Jerry Slocum asked me if I would like to be the team scorekeeper. Between classes, the QGT, student government, dating, and working, I was afraid it would hurt my academics. Tim Maloney, who played basketball for Manhattanville and graduated in 1982, used to come up and shoot hoops with Dan Bailey. Those guys were such great shooters and dribblers and competitors. I loved to watch them play one on one. They both exemplified positive attitudes and had a great sense of humor and a Christlike spirit.

CAPTAIN KITCHEN: We had a new guy come into the kitchen in 1987. He seemed the nice quiet type. When basketball season started, he walked onto the court just before the men's game dressed in all white, with a white cape, a white mask like the Lone Ranger, and a white captain's hat. He ran around the gym, was able to get the audience to do the wave, and danced around the cheerleaders. This guy was a hit. He was the Phillie Phanatic for Nyack basketball for the season in 1987 and 1988.

1985 - TV STAR: In October of 1985, Greg Bender, Nyack College basketball player, who looked a little like Chevy Chase, only more handsome and with curly dark hair, became a TV star. The name of the CBS program was called *Hometown*. He answered a call for basketball players at a tryout in an NYC elementary school and was eventually chosen to be in the playground basketball scene with two other hoopsters from Fordham and Seton Hall. The name of the episode was "Fade-Away Jumper." It was of students who played for "Whitley College." The scene took two days to shoot, from 7:00 a.m. to 4:30 p.m. each day. Greg said he never really worried about it because he felt comfortable being on the court. It was exciting to see a friend on national TV during prime time.

BANDICOOTS BASKETBALL: I was part of an intermural team that consisted of Dave Jennings; Dr. Ricke, my English professor; Steve Nanfelt; John Schuerholz; Ed Nanno, and a few others. We named ourselves the Bandicoots, which was the name of an Asian rat. We ended up becoming the champs of the intermural league, and it was a blast to play with that team. Steve Nanfelt had more energy than anyone I ever met. He could play a full game of soccer for the college team and then go and play full-court basketball games. He always had a quizzical look on his face and laughed easily.

CREATION FESTIVAL, 1986, WITH JON: Jon Schuerholz and I drove up to the Christian Woodstock Festival called Creation Fest in 1986. I brought a tent, and we brought food in a cooler. Jon and I were like Oscar and Felix from *The Odd Couple*. I was on the clean and perfectionist side, and Jon was into living life and being in the moment and not the neatest guy. I freaked out when he took a hot dog and dipped it into the mustard after taking a bite. I was horrified; his attitude was "whatever." We had a good time listening to bands and speakers and interacting with people at the event, but we learned we loved each other as friends but could not be roommates, so the trip also gave us insight. On our way back, on the turnpike, as we approached the tollbooths, I stuffed my mouth with pretzels and pretended to blow my cookies at the horrified look of passing cars. Jon was laughing so hard that he begged me to stop. I too had tears in my eyes. Oh, the sophomoric humor.

We served on the student government together for two years. In our senior year, I was in Jon's car and was making some criticism of him when he hit me in the arm hard. I was not aware of it, but I was unaware of my codependency, focusing on the lives of others, offering unsolicited advice without really focusing on my life. At the time, I was upset he hit me; but today, as I looked back, I realized he was right. I should have stayed in my business. I only should have commented if he asked me for advice or if I asked him permission to share my thoughts.

I went to Jon's home one evening and before dinner; his parents reached out their hands, and we all held hands and had a Quaker moment of silence before eating. Jon's brother was an activist in Washington DC, working for SANE/Freeze. His father was an artist, cartoonist, painter, and sculptor. He worked as a special ed teacher for a living. Mrs. Schuerholz worked at the YMCA in Nyack. I liked his parents. They were funny and smart. Mr. Schuerholz said sex was like a sneeze. "Ah . . . ahhhh . . . ahhhhhhchoo!" There was a build up until the sneeze. We watched the rockumentary *This Is Spinal Tap*, which was a comedy about a heavy metal band on tour.

TIMBER: It has rained for over three days straight. I was standing behind Schuman Hall, the library, looking at the woods behind the building. As I was standing there, Dr. Joe Ricke walked out and stood next to me. Dr. Ricke was our English professor and played basketball for Nyack when he was a college lad. He had blond hair, boyish looks, and blue eyes and was from Texas. He was the all-American boy who looked like actor Jon Voight when he was in the movie *Deliverance*. Dr. Ricke was a good ole boy from Texas, played guitar, and made a recording of songs on audio cassette called "In a World without

Synthesizers," which was excellent. I understand he still plays in a club near Taylor University in Indiana, where he teaches in 2016.

I played intermural basketball with Dr. Ricke, who was known to have a temper when he played. He made a comment once to me. "I have never seen a person have such intensity in getting a rebound or trying to score inside like you, Mr. Geist." I took that as a high compliment coming from someone who was recognized as an excellent hoopster.

We stood behind Schuman Hall, the college Library for thirty seconds when this noise slowly began to build. It was an "eeeeerrrrrr" noise and then crash with a bouncing noise involved and it turned out to be a huge oak tree whose roots could no longer hold the giant in the moist dirt. There was crackling as the huge tree hit the other branches of its brothers and sisters still standing and then a huge thud as the monster hit the ground. I turned and said to Dr. Ricke, "If a tree falls in the woods and no one hears it, does it make a noise?" The doctor shook his head in disbelief as to what we just witnessed this rare and beautiful oddity.

STUDENT GOVERNMENT ASSOCIATION (SGA) PRESIDENT, 1986–88: I served as SGA president for two years. I enjoyed the act of democracy and meeting weekly the presidents of the freshman, sophomore, junior, and senior classes and the secretary, treasurer, the vice president, and the Christian Service Council president. Our advisors were Dr. Collier and history professor Eldred. We had our own office, where students could meet with us to discuss concerns. We had the opportunity to meet with the president of the college to discuss those concerns as well. I learned how to run meetings, how to work as a diplomat, and how to try to get things done. We helped organize the annual blood drive and brought in concerts and movies, and my contribution to college life was by having a "short out" so we could wear "appropriate shorts" in September and in May when the weather was warm. In 1988, about seventy-five students wore shorts to lunch, with sweatpants over them. I took the microphone and announced what many students were requesting, and then we took our sweatpants off. Nothing happened. There was no drama. It was my understanding, the year after I graduated in 1988, the shorts policy was changed.

SITTING ON THE DOCK OF THE BAY: I took Teresa down to the Hudson River behind Simpson Hall on Piermont Avenue. We walked to a dock and sat there to watch the sunset and the traffic crossing the Tappan Zee Bridge and had view of the GM plant over in Tappan, New York. Ducks and geese were swimming around. With our feet dangling over the dock, she said, "Do geese bite?" I said, "Of course not." As soon as I finished talking, a goose bit her foot, and she screamed. We got up, and I leaned against a fence so she could lean into me, for some kissy face action. As we were oscillating, I felt something pulling on my shoelace. I looked, and there were two big raccoons by our feet, looking at us. I said, "Teresa, turn around slowly, don't scream, and walk away calmly." She turned around slowly, saw the raccoons, and started making a muffled, high-pitched noise under her breath. I talked to the raccoons calmly. I said, "Hello. I am going to walk away slowly," and I did. They stayed in place and watched me walk away. Teresa was already at the top of the hill, ready to jump in the car. I was glad I was not bitten and did not need a rabies shot.

1987 - PAINTING WITH IRISH DAVE AND HARRY: My girlfriend Teresa Haggerty was roommates with Amy. Amy was seeing a guy named Thomas, who had a rap sheet. Thomas lived in Nyack and ran a painting business in the Bronx. Tom did some time for stealing some boats from a dock, but now he is living the clean life. He was handsome and cocky and did not like the Christian faith. He had two undocumented workers from Ireland, named Dave and Harry. Dave was short and had an Elvis-like haircut, with long sideburns, and Harry was tall and frumpy with messy sandy-colored hair and a good sense of humor. Dave was more serious and liked to use the phrase "I could give a rat's ass!" They were Catholic, and they asked me questions, and I told them about a Bible study held on the Nyack campus during the summer. Dave said, "I was born Catholic, and I will die Catholic." I said, "You can stay Catholic. This is about learning what the scriptures teach." They were intrigued and came to the Bible studies, and their faith grew. Mom and Dad graciously allowed me to bring them home for Thanksgiving, and they enjoyed a nice meal with my grandparents, and my parents loved asking them questions about Ireland, life, and living in NYC.

IRISH EYES ARE CRYING: A year later, I called the guys to see how they were doing. They told me they have started attending a church called Disciples of Christ. The church believed you must be baptized after conversion by water immersion to be saved. After we caught up, Dave and Harry began quizzing me about the theology of baptism and the kingdom of God. They sent me some papers and told me that Billy Graham did not preach the full Gospel. We ended up parting ways because I did not want to argue theology. It was sad to me that two people who came into my life now considered me a messenger of the Anti-Christ or Devil. Years later, I was on the radio program on WABC *Religion on the Line* with Steve Malzberg, and the guys heard me talking about the day of prayer for the persecuted church in 1997.

I got a phone call, and it was Harry. "Is this Jim Geist?"

"Yes."

"The Jim Geist who used to work with Dave and Harry in the Bronx?"

"Yes?"

"The Jim Geist we heard on WABC radio talking about helping persecuted Christians in Communist and Islamic countries?"

"Yes."

"How are you?" I told him how hurt I was when they treated me like I was a cult leader leading them to hell with bad theology. Harry said, "Yeah, our views have changed over the years. I am sorry how I spoke to you back then. It was out of line. You were kind to Dave and me. Good to talk with you." We are now connected by LinkedIn.

JIM GEIST DOLL: In my sophomore year, a freshman from North Carolina named Karen took a shine to me. She hung out with her roommate who had a "gothic thing" going. She gave me this doll made from a Bert doll of Ernie and Bert from *Sesame Street*. The hair was made of orange yarn, the mouth had braces made of tin foil, and it had a long black trench and a small camo hat and a Mack Truck bulldog pin on it. It looked like me. Once every semester was an open dorm night until ten thirty, and the ladies could visit the men's dorm and vice versa.

Every day, we went to the chapel; and on the way there, on Christie Hall, hanging on string was the underwear of a dozen guys from Moseley Hall. The underwear was dyed pink with the names written with permanent blue marker: Schuerholz, Geist, Kunzelman, Fodor, James, Spazchek, etc. It was creative and funny. I wish I had taken a picture.

In addition to missing a pair of underwear, I noticed the doll had been kidnapped. I was informed that if I said anything, something bad would happen. I asked several times to get it back, and they kept playing with me. I went to the dean's office and asked them to speak to Karen and the roommate. That night, I received the doll back with its head cut off. Luckily, they had made an extra doll to do this, and I received the original back. I loved the Jim Geist doll and still have it to this day. I am grateful for the time, energy, and creativeness put into it.

JIM GEIST BLUES: Pete Weisgerber, Bob Talbot, and Rick Bush all played guitar. On any given night, one or a combo of these guys would play together, and it was fun to watch and listen. Bob Talbot was a huge fan of blues guitarist Stevie Ray Vaughan. Bob's dad was a vice president at IBM, and the family lived in France for a spell. The American school was next to a French school, and the students used to exchange barbs at one another at the metal chain fence separating them. The ultimate comeback for the Americans was always "If it was not for the United States, you Frenchies would be speaking German and eating sauerkraut." Of course, France did help us defeat England in the Revolutionary War.

Rick Bush, before he graduated, kindly sat in the stairwell of Moseley and, with his guitar sang the song "Aime" by the Pure Prairie League, broke into a blues song, and made the Jim Geist blues. The song closed with "Look at that mustache. Don't you wish you had one too?" I still have that tape and will never forget the night. It is said to lean forward and let the guitar touch your chest when playing, for the poetry of music comes from the heart.

CAR KEY STORY NO. 1: In my sophomore year, I asked Amy Feather, a year younger than I was, to the sophomore banquet. I did not have a car, so her father, a bigwig in the Alliance, said I could use his. I met Amy, and she gave me the car keys at lunch. I was to pick her up at 6:00 p.m. I went to the car, a white Buick, in the lower parking lot of the college, and the key would not open the door.. That was strange. I could not get in the car. I was flustered. I called Amy, and she walked down from Simpson Hall to meet me at the car. When I showed her the key did not work, she said, "Maybe it is the white Buick next to this one." What were the odds of two exact cars parking next to each other on a college campus the night of a banquet?

CAR KEY STORY NO. 2: My Bronx painting boss Thomas, allowed me to borrow his van home and told me to drive to the jobsite the next day. I parked the car, locked the doors, and then realized I have locked the van keys in the van. It was a Thursday night, and I taught Bible study at a family's home, the Noonans, in Pearl River, New York. My friend drove me to the Bible study. I did a quick lesson on "faith." I then said, "Now we are going to put our faith into action." I told the four to five people there, four guys and a young lady, we were going to my place, and we were going to get the keys out of my boss's van. We pulled up to the van and got out. One of the guys said, "This van is a Ford. My car is a Ford. Let me try my car key." I looked at him and laughed. I said, "You really think your key is going to work?" He said, "Let's try, ye of little faith!" He tried the driver's door—no luck. He tried opening the passenger's side door—no luck. He went to the back door of the van and put the key in and turned it, and the van door opened, letting me get my boss's keys in the ignition. The student taught the teacher.

GEISTETTES: In 1986, Heidi Turner asked me to go out on a date. I was flattered that a pretty young lady was willing to ask me out. That night, as I was in my dorm room working on a paper, Johnny Spaz came in, looked at me, laughed, and walked out of the room. He did this two more times, and on the fourth time, he said to me, "Jim, I have to tell you something I overheard at dinner tonight in the cafeteria. Heidi and Holly and Amy and Connie are going to pull a stunt on you! They are each going to ask you out over the next two days to see how you respond, and then on the appointed night, they are all going to show up to the dorm." Wow. This was great. I had a heads-up on the Heidi game.

The next day, one asked me out in class, another at lunch, and another at dinner; but they all asked me out for the upcoming Saturday night. My response to them was "I am so honored and flattered you would ask me out, but let me get back to you. I may not be able to meet you." I found out later they got together in the evenings to debrief on how I responded. In the end, I told Heidi I planned to meet with her. I also found out later that, had I not picked Heidi, the caper would have been canceled!

The appointed date night came, and I waited for the ladies to pick me up. The fourth-floor hall phone rang, and Heidi told me she was ready. When I walked out the door, there were the four beautiful ladies dressed to the hilt, and all of them said, "Hiiiiii, Jim!" With that, Doug Rowse, Johnny Spaz, and a few other guys walked out the first-floor door and said, "Our dates!" The ladies' eyes grew big and could not believe their plan had been found out. They all surrounded me, hugged me, and said, "Sorry, guys, this is Jim's night, and we are all his dates!" The ladies took me out to a restaurant, and we had a lovely time. During dinner, they dubbed themselves as the "Geistettes." Thanks, Heidi (and the Geistettes) for the great college memory!

GEIST WEAR: From freshman year on, I began wearing ties to class. I figured if being a college student was my job, then I should dress for it. What happened was students would start bringing ties to me that their fathers were throwing out, and I would wear them. I loved going to the thrift store to find dress jackets, hats, and ties. In my junior year, there was even a contest for the best "Geist wear" outfit. I was a big fish in a small pond—SGA president, my own clothing line, and several ladies I could call the Geistettes.

I am so grateful to Nyack for my education, the opportunity to develop leadership and speaking skills, opportunities for ministry and developing friendships, and so many great memories.

ROAD TRIP TO ALLENTOWN – SIXTH STREET HOOKERS: During spring break in 1985, the following went to Allentown to my folks' place: roommate Doug Anthony, Dave Jennings, and Fred Manning. Fred had a blue Volkswagen with "Fred Bud" on his license plate. Our first night, after Mom and Dad made us a nice barbecue dinner, we did some "cruising" in the downtown area. We drove in Dad's Scout, and I drove the boys down Sixth Street, notorious as the streetwalkers' lane. As we were at the light, someone said, "Look at the chicks to the right." I looked over, and I heard, "Hi, Jim!" There was my cousin Brenda driving with two of her friends. My friends hitting on my cousin on Sixth Street—such scandal! We then drove to Chuck E. Cheese's and crawled around the floors to find quarters to play the games they had there.

On Saturday afternoon, we paid a visit to the local thrift store and came home with jackets, ties, and coats. On Sunday morning, we got a picture of Fred out cold in his sleeping bag, put a number of Billy Beer cans from my beer can collection around him, and took some funny pics. That was a fun weekend.

FAVORITE COLLEGE CLASSES: My favorite classes at Nyack College were Old Testament, New Testament, World Religions, History to Christianity, Christology, History of Christianity, Biblical Apologetics, Cross Cultural Adjustment, Parables, and History of Political and Social Thought. I graduated with a 2.67 grade average, which according to the GPA equivalencies for universities is an 81.7. All these years, I thought I was an "average" student in college, but I was really "barely above average."

1988 - LAMB'S CHURCH AND THEATER: In NYC at 130 West 44th Street was the Lamb's Theater. I have gone there to watch the play *Godspell*. I went to visit an acquaintance, Janelle Hartman, who was three years older than I was and has graduated from the Alliance Seminary. She had a heart for the poor and was a fan of John M. Perkins and ended up getting an internship at the Lamb's Church, working as a counselor with the poor. I was a senior at Nyack, and for one of my classes, I needed to visit several places and write papers about it. I met with Janelle, and we went out for lunch. On the way back, as we were entering the Lamb's Theater, where her office was, we bumped into a woman of about age eighteen with dark hair and who was a bit pudgy. Janelle recognized this person and said, "Aren't you Ricki Lake from the movie *Hairspray*?" The woman said, "Yes, I am. It is so nice to meet you, Janelle." Janelle started singing a song, which I later learned was called "Mashed Potato Time," and the two sang a duet there in the doorway and then hugged each other. I had a moment with actress Ricki Lake, who starred in the 1987 movie *Hairspray*. She went on to get her own television talk show. Good for her.

11-26-88 - NYACK, NEW YORK, EARTHQUAKE: In my room, I slept in a bunk bed. I woke up at roughly six in the morning, thinking someone was shaking my bed. It felt to last three to four seconds, and I was not sure if I was dreaming or not. I later heard on the news that there was a minor earthquake in the Northeast, and it was felt in Nyack, New York. I was not dreaming.

There was another time when I woke up because my bunk bed was shaking, and I thought it could be another earthquake, but it turned out one of my roommates' guest was waxing his carrot. I said in an annoyed voice, "Stop, shaking the bed!" One of my Moseley friends while in the Air Force caught a guy masturbating in a bathroom stall next to him. He told the spunky fellow to buy him a case of beer to keep quiet about the incident. Dennis got the case of beer, called over his fellow Air Force buddies, and immediately told them how they were able to get a free case of beer.

1996 RED AND TAN BUS ROUTE 9W TO NYC: I walked to Downtown Nyack to take the bus to NYC. The bus was packed, and there was only one open seat on it. On the way to the city, I was seated next to a short, bald, and fat man named Piaggio. I was reading a book, and it looked to me like he was trying to touch my left thigh with his right pinky. He touched my leg, and I said, "Piaggio, if you don't want me to break your pinky finger, don't touch me again." He sat with his closed hands for the rest of the trip.

HE TOUCHED ME: For one of my classes, I had to go to NYC to visit a church. I went to a Pentecostal church with Doug Rowse and Denley Ederton. The pastor was a black woman, and at the end of the service, a whole bunch of people went up front. She began touching them on the foreheads, and the happy parishioners fell down. The she-pastor said, "I am getting a word that one of you needs to come forward." She pointed at me. *Great*, I thought. I was not really Pentecostal in this way. I went forward, and she started praying for me, and then she touched my head, but then she started pushing, and I pushed back. She pushed harder, and I pushed back harder. She then gave me a pro wrestler Jesse Ventura arm push, and "the Spirit" took me down. The congregation started yelling, "Amen! Hallelujah!" I was on the floor, looking at the spinning fan on the ceiling, thinking, *She pushed me.* I walked back Doug and Denley, who were wide eyed, and Denley said, "Did you feel the power?" Yeah, the spirit of a strong black lady's arm, not the gentleness of the Holy Spirit. When we got in the car, I told them she pushed me. There was a lovely song called "He Touched Me," but we sang, "She pushed me," all the way back to Nyack College.

RIGHT TO LIFE MARCH - JANUARY 22, 1987–88: I went on the bus trip from Nyack College to Washington DC in 1987 and 1988. We took a huge Grim Reaper that had been created by Robin DeMaggio, an evangelist for the CMA who prayed over my buddy Mike Brogna in 1983. As a result, there was a picture of me in several national magazines (*Time* [July 13, 1987] with Mitch Fodor and Fred Manning over Reagan's appointment of Judge Bork, the life constitution issue, and *U.S. News and World Report* [February 4, 1985]), standing in the crowd in front of the Supreme Court with the Grim Reaper. Someone claiming to be from the Smithsonian said they would like to have the

Reaper to display it. First, it was not mine to give away. Second, I did not know if this person really worked for the Smithsonian. We brought it back to Nyack.

PRIVATE FIRST CLASS DAVE'S WAKE: Dave was in the National Guard, grew up in Germany in a military family, and was one of the nicest guys you could ever meet. I believe he was planning on becoming a chaplain in the military. He volunteered many times and in many ways for many organizations on campus. He had volunteered for SGA to help us set up a movie night under the stars. We were juniors, and he had a brown Volkswagen van. While he was helping with the movie, two seniors, Craig Morris and Bryan McKnight, thought it would be funny to steal the seats from Dave's van. They all knew others from the volleyball team. When Dave told me what happened, I found out who did it. It made me angry because Dave was worn-out and had to get to church the next day and had some other commitments on Sunday. He had no energy to find out who did this, and he looked so defeated by this sophomoric act.

The senior roommates got in late and went to bed. I began pounding on their door to ask where they put the seats. At first, they played stupid, but then they fessed up, saying, "We hung up his chairs from the flagpole in front of the school library." I said, "You need to get up, go to the library, get the chairs, and put them in Dave's van." They laughed and said, "No, it's too late to do that."

I recruited fellow classmate Dan Gwin, or "Gwinny," and we found Steve's car. We took his four wheels and placed it on concrete blocks. We hid the tires behind the B&G Building, and man, where they upset when they had no vehicle to pick up their girlfriends to go to church. What was good for the goose was good for the gander. If they only put Dave's seats back. They were very upset by this and did not find out where the tires were until after the Sunday lunch meal. For these pranksters who enjoyed pulling pranks, I thought they would have appreciated being played pranks upon, but they did not. I found the volleyball-playing seniors to be inconsistent. How funny it was wrong of Gwinny and I do such a thing, but the blinders to stealing Dave's car seats was "funny."

SUMMER 1987 - MALI, AFRICA: In 1986, with the Alliance Youth Corp, I sent out a fund-raising letter for the $2,000 I needed to go to West Africa for six weeks to do some mission work. I went with another gentleman and two ladies. Two were from Toccoa Falls, a sister CMA college, and the other from a CMA college up in Canada. The Hamilton Park church threw a spaghetti dinner fund-raiser for me and raised $700 for my trip. I had many family and friends donate to the cost and paid 80 percent of my trip. I would be forever grateful to all who donated.

What stuck out from my mind from this trip was seeing poverty, the sacrifices first-world missionaries made materially by moving here, and the generosity of the West African people. We stayed with six different mission families over six weeks. During the day, we would do volunteer work for the local churches or missionaries; and at night, we would go to churches, missionary hospitals, or villages and put on a show with singing and with sharing our testimonies, which would be translated by Pastor Tangora, an African pastor who traveled with us. If we went to a village, the missionaries would show the *Jesus* film. It was interesting to witness how the Malians reacted to the different scenes. Much of Mali was Islamic, but one tribe was Christian because they raised pigs for a living and would lose their income if they became Muslims.

Living with the missionaries showed me that most were not superspiritual but sinners saved by grace, human beings who loved Jesus and were willing to love people in another country and, through service and humility, lead people to the Jesus road. Interestingly, most missionary family had a cook, a house cleaner, and a gardener. These were jobs many Africans were all happy to have. The one family had a very nice pool. It was clear one couple we stayed with was having marital difficulties. He even confided to me and said, "I think you see my marriage is having its challenges."

MY INDIANA JONES HAT: I brought a hat with me that looked like the hat Indiana Jones wore in the movie *Raiders of the Lost Ark*. The hat was given to me by a graduate student from the Alliance Seminary named Andy. Later, Andy went to work in Africa and while rounding a corner on his minibike got hit by a large truck and was severely injured. Students asked, "Why did this happen? How could God allow this?" Theology professor Dr. Tite Tienou from West Africa said, "It happened because when Andy was rounding the corner, he did not see a truck coming."

GOING TO THE MARKET: Going to the market in Mali was an amazing thing. There were many colors and many smells. There were monkeys, donkeys, and people walking around carrying amazing amounts of items balanced brilliantly on their heads. There were stands selling food items with beans of all types of foodstuff and plants; stands with amazing cloth designs; stands selling beads and masks; stands with woven baskets or clay pots; stands with simple farming equipment; stands with dried fish; stands with animal bones of crocodiles, birds, and lizards and python skins; stands selling audio cassettes; and stands with hanging goats that got skinned and cut up when you order one.

CULTURAL DIFFERENCES: In Africa, you could see men walking down the street holding hands. This did not mean they were gay; it was a sign of friendship. One day, we were walking in a village when Pastor Tangora grabbed my hand, and I could feel my shoulders go up with discomfort, so I kept repeating to myself, *This is a sign of friendship. This is a sign of friendship.*

You had to be careful when taking pictures. Some Africans felt you were stealing a bit of their soul when you did that. Dogs were not really seen as pets; they were just animals. When you greeted someone, it must be with the right hand. Many did not have toilet paper, so the left hand was the "dirty hand." When eating food, many did not use utensils; so when eating, you ate with your right hand. I played the CD "You Can Call Me Al" by Paul Simon for Pastor Tangora since it had many South Africans singing on it with an African flair. He did not care for it.

EVENT ORIENTED VS. TIME ORIENTED: An American missionary might tell a village that the service will start at 11:00 a.m. By eleven thirty, some will show up; by noon, more will show up; and by twelve thirty, there may be enough people to start the service. That is called African time. Americans may say the Africans are always late, and the Africans will say Americans are controlled by the clock. If you are to ask an African if you can speak with him/her, they will answer, "I have all the time in the world." Africans will also say Americans are more concerned about doing things than spending time with people. Some say Africans are lax, and others say Americans are pushy. Which one is right? Well, maybe it is not about right or wrong but about differences. And this is why presidents and politicians have advisors or counselors who make them aware of cultural differences so they do not pull off a major mistake by not understanding or respecting another's culture.

GOING TOPLESS: Another difference I have noticed in Africa is that sexual sex is not a seen as a major sin, but greed is a major sin..Many of the Malian woman did not wear tops to cover their breasts. Malians viewed women's breasts are seen as feeding instruments for children, not a sexual thing. There are Malina girls aged thirteen to fifteen who have developed breasts, and when they walk by me, I try not to stare at them. Like the cartoon character Homer Simpson, boobies can hypnotize me.

There used to be a TV show called *The Man Show* with Adam Carolla and Jimmy Kimmel, and the audience could ask questions at the end of the show. The one question was "Why do men love looking at boobs?" Jimmy Kimmel responded, "Why do men like to breathe?"

DANCING FOR CHRIST: Why are most churches against premarital sex? It might lead to dancing.

I grew up and loved dancing at wedding receptions or a party or sometimes going to a boat called the *Binghamton* in Hoboken, New Jersey. It was a transport ferry across the Hudson River from 1905 to 1967 and became a restaurant and dance club from 1975 to 2007. I really enjoyed going there, three times anyway, when I was in college.

In the mid-1800s, mission work not only proclaimed the Gospel but also tried to westernize peoples they were trying to convert to Christ. What eventually happened was that mission agencies began to separate "westernization" from the Gospel. How would we respect another's culture and allow others to worship within their cultures? In Africa, dancing became part of worship services. Often, as the village musicians played their instruments, some would come out and do the "African shuffle," which was circling around a fire or lantern and dancing to show their love of life and God.

I am glad missionary work does not equate "westernizing" as part of the mission anymore. Authentic mission work is getting to the place where indigenous leadership is raised and turned over to the local population. Letting go of power is never an easy thing.

THE AFRICAN SHUFFLE: While you could get in trouble at Nyack College for dancing at a club, dancing was frequently part of the African Christian experience. I asked the missionaries if it would be okay for me to join when a shuffle dance broke out during worship, and they said, "Absolutely, you should." During the one worship session outside under the stars, a shuffle dance broke out around the lantern on a tree trunk, and I joined in. I later found out two people accepted Christ because they had never seen a white person dance with the Africans.

MANY MOSQUES: In Mali is the Niger River, the famous city of Timbuktu is there, and Bamako is the capital. We visited Bamako, Sanekuy, Tominian, Koutiala, Baramba, Yorosso, Sikasso, Farakala, Sevare, Sangha, Ntorresso, and Katiena. The general things I remembered about the trip was there was a mosque in every city. This was something that came from Saudi Arabia and all their oil money. No matter how poor an area was, it would have a mosque. I heard the calls for prayer over there several times a day. I also noticed that football or soccer as the Americans called it, was played all around Africa. Great game for the poor, not much equipment needed, only a ball.

THE KIDS: I liked the kids; they loved to sit by me and touch my arm to see if the white came off. I brought over candy, and they loved the candy as all kids do. I also did some juggling and taught them how to make the farting noise with a hand on your armpit by moving your arm up and down, like baseball player Joe Morgan used to do, moving his bended arem up and down when up to bat. I was amazed at the one village when Pastor Tangora was speaking to the children. There were over two hundred kids sitting in the mud building with a tin roof overhead. All of them sat on the ground, legs folded and their hand in their laps, with full attention. No one was playing around, not listening, or being disrespectful. I think it would be easier to teach one hundred African kids than teaching twenty students from Newark, New Jersey.

On our way to a village, the missionary ended up getting lost. This was before cars had GPS systems. . We were driving on a road that had fields on either side of us. A kid, probably six to seven, was bent over with a hand hoe, digging away, and Dennis spoke to the kid in some native tongue. The kid stood up and looked at five white people in a truck, and his eyes got as big as cup saucers. He dropped the hand hoe and took off like a bat out of hell. We all got a laugh out of that. The kid probably ran to his family to tell them five boogey people scared him to death. You'd never know; he may never have seen an Anglo up to that point. We might as well walkedout of a spaceship.

IMPACT OF COLONIZATION: Africa was divided up by the European countries for colonizing in what was called the Berlin Conference of 1884–85. Whenever we went into a village, they would give us the best seats. Whenever we went to a village, no matter how poor, when we showed up, they would slaughter chickens, guinea hens, a goat, or a pig. Hospitality was very important in Mali. I sometimes felt guilty for how well they treated us. The Malians treated us like rock stars.

While in Africa, I also read a book by David Lamb called *The Africans*, which talked about a phrase called *WAWA*, meaning "West Africa wins again." Why don't Africans fight to make things better? Lamb chronicles how many times it gets worse when there is a revolution and new leadership is brought in. So instead of trying to change leaders, many West Africans accept life and political leaders as they are, for it can always get worse.

AFRICAN WOMEN ARE THE WORKERS: The men may work the fields, but there is an ebb and flow of being a farmer based on the seasons. Imagine having no washing machines and no microwaves and working from sunup to sundown. It is fun to watch the women when they were pounding millet. They take the seed and put it in a pot, and three ladies with what look like oversized wooden baseball bats each take a turn at pounding the millet in a synchronized way—lady one first, then lady two, and finally lady three doing it all over again. They sometimes throw the millet bat up in the air and clap their hand before grabbing it again. They sometimes sing while doing this, and you never see an African man doing this. They put it in a big bowl and shake it up in the air, where the wind pushes away the shells from the millet seeds.

I joined in three ladies doing this, and they looked at me in disbelief when I did the clapping maneuver that they were doing. They stopped beating the millet because they started laughing so hard. As they say, "Too-baboo-fato" or crazy white man.

DOGON CLIFFS: The highlight of my trip was going to the Dogon cliffs. It was made up of rock cliffs, and the missionary McKinley took us through rock caverns, up rock steps, and up to an area that was an ancient burial place. In the cliffs were seven to eight cylinder-shaped mud structures that had human bones in them. All types of bones with human skulls scattered over them. From the burial site was a small lake at the bottom, and on the opposite side was a stone plateau that went on for over a mile, with a few scattered bushes. I am glad I have pictures from my 1987 adventure.

HOW AFRICA CHANGED ME: Today I appreciate electricity. In the capital city of Bamako, the electricity is shared. Half the city gets electricity one night; the other half gets it the following night.

I learned to appreciate paved roads, electricity, hot water, medical facilities, modern buildings for work and school, access to telecommunications, and my family. When I got back to the States, I wanted to kiss the ground. It also taught me about hospitality, taking time to listen to others, the sin of greed, and the fact that you would not need material wealth to be happy. In fact, the happiest people I had ever seen up to this point in my life came from Mali. Thank you, Nyack College professor Jim Bollback, CMA Alliance Youth Corp director Don Young, all those who gave me financial support, the missionary families, all the Malian church leaders, and the people of Mali, for showing me what is really important in life.

1988 - MOVE TO 156 PIERMONT AVENUE: I attended Nyack (Missionary) College from 1984 to 1988. I took a year off between college and grad school to give my mind a break. I took on an internship at Baldwin United Methodist Church from September of 1988 through May of 1989. I wanted to get some practical experience under my belt before starting seminary. I moved into an eighty-year-old woman's home in Nyack for the summer of 1988 before I moved to Long Island in September. Fellow Nyack grad Robin Swope would move in and live at the home the nine months while I was away.

NYACK LANDLADY MARY GRACE AND MONICA: Mary is a lovely person who loves the arts, poetry, and reading. Mary had a garden in the backyard that I used to tend or work on to keep the weeds out. The driveway was connected to the two-car garage next to the backyard and garden. Behind the home was the back entryway into the home, and above the entryway was the second-floor bathroom for the northern side rooms. Mary's master bedroom had its own bathroom.

As I was pulling out weeds from Mary's flower garden,, I looked up and happened to glance at Monica getting out the shower through the open venetian blinds. I could see her rose-colored areolaes and her shapely body. I looked for three seconds, put my head down, and continued weeding. I was actually proud of myself that I did not ogle for more than three seconds, and I would have loved to. She lived there for one month until some busybody at the college found out and reported it to the dean. Perhaps they were afraid I was going to ravage her one night or that her boyfriend might do the same thing.

When Monica Mendez moved out, Mr. Ed. N. moved in. I had the chance to live with Robin S., Monica M., and now Ed Nanno. The understanding was that when I married my love, Teresa Joy, Ed would move out. By that time, Ed was already on his way to Yale University and then unto Edinburgh. My father said, "Ed was the most congenial guy I ever met. That is why I call him Mr. Congeniality."

1988 SUMMER OLYMPICS GOLD WINNERS: Carl Lewis, Florence Griffith Joyner, Jackie Joyner-Kersee (running), Greg Louganis (diving), Matt Biondi, Janet Evans (swimming), Zina Garriso, and Pam Shriver (tennis doubles)

1988 WINTER OLYMPICS GOLD WINNERS: Brian Boitano (figure skating) and Bonnie Blair (speed skating)

PAINTING THE NYACK POLICE BARRACKS: The Nyack Police hired Rockland Painting, and I got the job of painting the police locker room. It was an ugly gray. I went to the store and bought a new gallon of ugly gray paint. I moved stuff around the barracks and laid down the drop cloths. I found one police boot, but I was not able to find the other boot. I painted the barracks and packed up the stuff in the car, and on my way out, I noticed that the guy working dispatch only had one leg. I found the other boot. Another Nyack officer said, "There are so many colors in the world, and you picked the same ugly gray to paint our locker room with?" I said yup.

1-ADAM-12 - RABID RACCOON: It was midday, and I noticed a raccoon walking around the yard at one, and it looked like it was drunk. Uh-oh, this thing had rabies. I called the cops, and an officer showed up. He called dispatch to say he was firing a shot. Boom! He shot and killed the suffering animal. It reminded me of Old Yeller. It was so sad they had to kill the dog after it got rabies.

Plays, Shows, Concerts, and Sporting Events I Have Attended

TV SHOWS

The Phil Donahue Show: 1-29-92

Late Show with David Letterman: 9-7-93, 3-1-94*, 4-4-94, 9-1-94

Cosby: 2-11-99

PLAYS AND THEATER ACTS I HAVE SEEN

Godspell (Lambs Theater): 6-25-88

A Christmas Carol: 12-9-95

Anything Goes (London)

Miss Saigon: 10-19-96

Cats: 5-30-89

Sunset Boulevard: 1-9-97

Les Miserables: 2-20-91

Bring in 'Da Noise, Bring in 'Da Funk: 3-28-98

*Sight Unseen (Dennis B. and Deborah H.): 5-19-92

Blue Man Group: 2-2-02 (Howard Stern)

Guys and Dolls: 7-23-93

Penn and Teller: 6-7-00

An Inspector Calls: 10-6-94

Vanya and Sonia and Masha and Spike: 8-23-13

Crazy for You: 3-1-94*

Damn Yankees: 6-3-95

Wild (movie): 12-25-14

CONCERTS

Creation Festival (1983,1986)

Almost Heaven: Songs of John Denver (2-10-08)

Phil Keaggy, Nyack College (1985, 1986)

U2, Giants Stadium (*Joshua Tree* Tour) (9-14-87)

Mylon LeFevre (9-24-1987)

James Taylor, Hershey (10-11-86)

James Taylor, Stabler (9-27-87)

Whitecross (3-3-89)

Yes (MSG) (7-15-91)

101.1 Music '60s and '70s (1991)

Corzine and President Clinton (2009)

Jethro Tull, Paramount (11-11-91)

Rush (12-7-91) (Ed and Monica)

John MacArthur, Nyack (3-7-92)

Bonnie Raitt (Radio City) (8-4-94)

R&R Reunion Concert, Paramount (3-24-95)

Corzine and President Obama (11-1-09)

Huey Lewis and the News, Mahwah (7-21-01)

Crosby, Stills & Nash (10-22-12)

Bob Dylan and Leon Russell (8-12-11)

Rush Angels Tour (10-20-12)

Ringo Starr and His All-Starr Band (6-16-12)

Elton John (12-3-13)

Rodriguez (10-10-13)

Chris Isaak (12-20-14)

Rockin' the '70s (Al Stewart, Firefall, Orleans, and Atlantic Rhythm Section) (1-17-15)

Foreigner (2-17-15)

David Crosby Acoustic (6-19-15)

Chicago (9-1-15)

Foreigner Acoustic (2-14-16)

John Denver Tribute (12-6-15)

America (11-8-15)

Bill Maher (Beacon)

Diana Ross (3-31-16)

Justin Hayward (of the Moody Blues) (5-14-16)

SPORTING EVENTS

76ers vs. San Antonio, 2-17-78 (George McGinnis and Dr. J dunked from the foul line.)

Phillies vs. Pirates (doubleheader)

Flyers vs. Edmonton (Gretzky hurt)

Flyers vs. Montreal Canadiens, 9-23-82

Flyers vs. Winnipeg, 3-2-82 (JG's birthday)

Flyers vs. Colorado, 3-11-82

Mets game (President Clinton)

Phillies vs. Orioles, Oct. 1983 (Baltimore, world champions)

Eagles vs. Redskins, 1991 (with Mike Brogna)

Knicks vs. Celtics, 12-1986 (scalped tickets from the night before with Jon, Dave, and Doug)

Yankees vs. Chicago White Sox, 7-17-88

Phils vs. Mets (Shea), 6-19-88

Nets vs. Indiana Pacers, 11-13-89 (Nyack girls played before the NBA game)

Hofstra vs. Lafayette 2-27-89, (Andy Wescoe)

Yankees vs. Brewers, 7-1-89 (Dan K.)

Flyers vs. Islanders, 1989, (Baldwin Church)

Yankees vs. Rangers, 8-27-91

Islanders vs. Indiana, 1989 (Baldwin Church)

Cowboys vs. Arizona, 10-14-90 (J. Wolf)

Arizona vs. UCLA (Rose Bowl), 10-6-90 (Mike Brogna)

U.S. Open, 9-8-92

PSU vs. West Virginia, 10-26-91

Yale vs. Cornell, 11-7-92 (Yale Bowl, Ed)

PSU vs. Maryland, 9-26-92

Yankees vs. Tigers, 6-30-93

Nets vs. Portland, 4-3-94

Phillies vs. the Mets, 9-15-95 (Clinton there)

NY Rangers vs. LA Kings, 12-10-96

St. John vs. Miami, 2-2-03 (MSG) KAP

IronPigs, 4-11-15

PSU vs. Pitt, (1982–84?)

MUSEUMS

LBJ Library

Guggenheim (Watercolors), 2-5-94

Guggenheim (Frank Lloyd Wright), 5-23-09

George Takei (*Star Trek*)

Philadelphia Museum of Art, 7-5-08

JFK Presidential Library, 8-4-09

Most NYC museums, 1993–2000

Newseum, 12-31-15

SUMMER OF 1989 - JAIME ARNITA PAINTING: My roommate Dan Kerrigan got a house-painting job with a guy named Jaime. Dan got me work with Jaime during the year. He was skinny; had long hair, a great sense of humor, and a good heart; and was a hell of a painter. He paid fairly, and he bought us Gatorade and sometimes lunch. Jaime was married and had two babies. He said the crows ripped open his garbage every day because they loved to eat baby crap. Ew. Jaime loved the New York Mets, and during lunch every day, he read the sports section of the *New York Post* and *Daily News*. We called ourselves the "rock 'n' roll painters" because we blasted the music when we worked.

What is the most important instrument when it comes to painting? The radio.

TURNING JAPANESE: We were painting in New City, New York, at a condo complex on a ninety-degree-plus day. I was working from a forty-foot ladder to paint a chimney, with the ladder leaning on cedar shakes. To reach the end of the chimney, I must stand on my left leg, with my right leg at a ninety-degree angle, my right hand holding unto the ladder rung, and my left hand holding the paintbrush as far as I humanly could to get the spot I needed to reach. Just as I got in the position, a yellow jacket wasp came out from under a shake, just six inches from my face. It jumped on my forehead in between my eyes, so I dropped my brush to whack it off, and just as my hand hit it, I felt the sting of venom go into my forehead. This happened at about 1:00 p.m. I put some mud on the bite and finished out the day.

I helped John Schuerholz with his youth group in Old Tappan, and at about seven thirty, I started to feel dizzy and sick to my stomach. I told John I had to leave. I went home, went to bed, and woke up at 5:00 a.m. When I got up, my face felt tight. It was a strange sensation. I went to the bathroom and put the light on, and I saw that my forehead was blown up, and my eyes were starting to shut. I looked like I had Japanese eyes.

I went to Nyack Hospital's emergency room, and the woman behind the window on the computer keyboard asked me what was wrong. I said, "Well, either my head is going to blow up or I am turning Japanese." She looked up with a bored look, and when she saw me, she went "Ooooohhhhh my! Let me get a doctor for you." I looked like Rocky Dennis from the 1985 movie *Mask* with his condition called lionitis. Cher was in that movie and did a great acting job of being Rocky's mother.

CURSING OUT A U.S. PRESIDENT: Jaime had a blue van full of painting equipment and had ladders on top of it. He was painting in the Bears Nest Village in Saddle River, home to the rich and professional athletes. Jaime left his van door open, and when he walked outside, he saw some guy looking in his van. Jaime yelled, "Get the f——k away from my van!" When the gentleman turned around, with two security agents standing near him, it turned out to be Pres. Richard Milhous Nixon. For every one Democrat in Saddle River, there were four Republicans. They loved having Nixon and called him "the Sage of Saddle River." Jaime said," Ah . . . ahh . . . I am sorry for cursing at you, Mr. President." Nixon looked at Jaime, laughed, and said, "Don't worry about it." It was not often that you got to yell profanities to the face of an American president.

THE PHIL DONAHUE SHOW: I got tickets for *The Phil Donahue Show*. I got to go twice—once in November of 1991 because I was hoping they would have Clinton, Perot, or Bush on for an interview. I had my questions prepared. The show started in Chicago and moved to NYC in Rockefeller Center. The other show I attended was in the spring of 1992, and I brought my fiancée at the time, Teresa Joy. The show was about relationships, and the two ladies on were advocating for getting married later in life. Donahue was a Catholic and a divorcee and remarried Marlo Thomas of *That Girl* TV show. During the breaks, he walked around the audience and chummed around with people. He stood next to me and put his hand on my shoulder. In the last segment, I raised my hand with a question. Donahue ran over, and I said I had a couple things to say. He interrupted me and said in a very curt way, "One question!" I said, "If it takes forty years to find the right person, good for you." Then I looked at Donahue and said, "Second, I am going to marry this fine lady in June." The show was being shown live, and he said, "You are getting married? Stand have to stand up, miss!" The audience clapped, and Donahue said, "Congratulations."

The next day, I went to Turiello's Pizza in Nyackand the guy behind the counter stuck his finger at me and said, "You, you! I saw you on *Donahue*." Yup. Funny the power of the being on TV yet not powerful enough to get a free slice of the pizza pie.

CHAPTER 6

Youth Pastoring at Baldwin United Methodist Church, 1989 (Age 23)

1989: BALDWIN UNITED METHODIST CHURCH: I finished college and needed a break from studies—thirteen years from kindergarten through grade twelve and four years of college. I did not want to read another book, sit in another class for a lecture, take any more notes, write any more papers, or eat any more ramen noodles. I became a coffee addict in college out of necessity, in order to stay awake after dinner when I went to the library to finish studies and late at night when I was reading, doing research, or writing papers.

My plan was to attend the Alliance Theological Seminary (ATS) and to get a degree one had to do to complete a minimum of a six-month internship. On the ATS, next to the 2nd floor student lounge was a community board. I found a United Methodist church in Baldwin, Long Island, that was looking for a youth pastor from September up to May. Baldwin was about a half hour from the Whitestone Bridge on the lower section of Sunrise Highway. The previous youth pastor had come from ATS, and the church was happy with his service.

I did some house painting that summer to make money. I moved to the church the Tuesday after Labor Day. The pastor of the church was named Rev. Derek Moon. He was English, and I loved his accent. He and his wife had been at the church for five years. In his second year at the church, his son got into a terrible car accident and became a paraplegic; and while he had communication skills, it came out slowly. His name was Leslie, and when I first met him, he said, "So this is the baby minister." Funny and true.

On the west side of the church sanctuary was a parlor room, and on the north side was a gymnasium-kitchen-stage area, where any special dinners or events were usually held. On the east side was a two-floor structure with rooms for Sunday school and for choir, and on the second floor at the end was a small apartment with two rooms.

SCARY TRUE STORY: The car was unloaded, and my stuff was all moved into the church apartment. I sat in my office room and said a prayer of dedication. I prayed that God may use me to reach kids for Christ and to help those under my care. In the evening, I woke up in the middle of the night in the dark room and heard, "You are no good! Who do you think you are! You will never make it in ministry!" I was scared to death. I lost my breath and wondered if I was hearing audible voices or if this was just in my head. I mustered some faith in spite of my fearful state and said out loud, "If this is demonic in any way, I command you to stop in the name of Christ!" SILENCE. I lay there for thirty seconds, contemplating what just happened. I then said out loud, "God, please protect me and fill this room with your angels." With that, I felt the peace of God and went back to sleep with no fear. I became aware that I was involved in a spiritual battle.

WHERE AM I?: I went to bed early; it was a Saturday night. Next to my bed was one of the old-time heavy metal phone, and it rang almost as loud as the bells of Notre Dame, as I was in a deep sleep. I picked up the phone scared out of my wits and said, "Who is this?" It was my girlfriend Teresa. I then shouted, "Where am I?" She said I was in Baldwin, Long Island, and that I lived in a church apartment. It was a strange thing.

ANOTHER EVENING VISIT?: It was March 2, and I came home from the Hermanns, who have thrown me a birthday party complete with some balloons. I went to bed and woke up in the middle of the night. I saw something in the corner, and it was moving up and down in a floating manner and began "levitating" toward me. As the figure moved closer and got bigger, it looked like a ghost, and then I realized a slight breeze has blown the balloon I brought home the evening before toward my bed. My birthday balloon almost sent me to the hospital with "the big one," like what the actor Redd Foxx playing Sanford, the junkman, of the TV show *Sanford and Son* used to have, clutching his chest and talking to his passed wife, saying, "Elizabeth, I am coming home to join ya!"

INTERN DUTIES: My duties were Sunday school every week, a Bible study during the week, a sermon once a month, youth group on Sunday evenings, and special events with the youth group or trips. Some of the trips consisted of apple picking, organizing a Halloween night for the younger kids, seeing a Hofstra University basketball game, watching a Nyack College basketball game to see my future fiancée play, going to the coliseum for an Islander game and to see the Ringling Brothers Circus, etc. One of the advantages of being in Baldwin was having an active Long Island Youth for Christ chapter organized by the energetic and positive Mr. Jack Crabtree. I also had my college mentor, Mr. Pete Gumby, who was a senior when I was a freshman and passed on the torch (the famous small trumpet) to me.

One of the great things about the youth group is the opportunity to be creative in coming up with fun games, fun skits, and fun songs and in trying to have fun lessons for Sunday school. There are great books out there for youth group skits and games. With my last sermon, they made a large sign and hung it from the banners that said, "Nice honkin' sermon!"

PEOPLE OF NEW YORK VS. JAMES GEIST (OPERATION RESCUE): On January 13, 1989, I was arrested with 176 other people for blocking the entrance of an abortion clinic in NYC. Over 1,000 people showed up to protest. We were told to bring four subway tokens, no ID, and a pen or pencil; to dress in layers; and to have a newspaper to sit on for insulation. The spokesperson for the Operation Rescue was Randall Terry.

My arrest number was 116 or John Doe 116. The New York District Attorney's Office said my case would be dismissed if I was not arrested again in the next six months. When arrested, we were carried into buses and shipped off to a prison, where we lay on mats in the gymnasium. They gave us water and bologna sandwiches for dinner. As the evening approached, we walked into a courtroom to be represented by an attorney.

Why is abortion so controversial? Like all controversial issues, there are good arguments on each side. My views over the years have changed. I believe giving up the baby for adoption is best, but God also allows for people to make mistakes. We are sinners saved by grace or sinners not aware of the grace given. I take the view of Gov. Andrew Cuomo. I do not support abortion, but women should be given the dignity to choose.

In 1995, I found out Randall Terry was against birth control. I sent him a letter on November 1, 1995, to express my disappointment with this. I told him that studies showed birth control lowered the amount of abortions that took place.

ISLANDERS HOCKEY RECORD: I was in Long Island in 1989, and the Islanders were a powerhouse team, winning the Stanley

Cup in 1980, 1981, 1982, and 1983. The Nassau Coliseum was only one exit away via the Southern Parkway to the Meadowbrook Parkway and seventeen minutes away.

YOUTH GROUP FLOOR HOCKEY: The youth group consisted of twenty students, of whom ten to twelve showed up consistently for weekly events. One of the favorite events back in 1985 was playing floor hockey. The youth group loved playing it in the church gym, and one night, I found some guys drinking in the alleyway between the church and the building next to us. It turned out to be a group of fifteen to sixteen guys I called the Fred Roach gang. They used to come over on Friday nights, with permission from the church governing committee. During the halftime of every game, I would give a minilesson and a Gospel presentation. I must say most of the nonchurch kids were respectful of the church property.

THE HERMANN FAMILY: One family, Leslie and Buzz Hermann adopted me. Leslie worked with the nursery school at the church, and their son, Chris, was in the youth group. They also had a cabin in Ellenville, New York, and allowed the youth group to use it. We stayed there for a hockey tournament at Sunshine Acres Christian Camp and went up again in the spring for a retreat. I have gone up a couple of times since, and they graciously let me use their boat to go fishing. I went up with Ed Nanno one time, and we smoked cigars as we fished. Across from the Hermann camp was a place for kids with special needs, so you could hear screaming a couple of times a day.

CHEEZ WHIZ WHIPPED CREAM PIE: The youth group got a kick out of a highway sign called Lake Homowack and pulled over to take a picture. On the Saturday night of the retreat, the kids, who never wanted to sing, said, "We want to sing some campfire songs!" I walked out wearily, and as I got near the fire, three kids grabbed me and took a plate of whipped cream and Cheez Whiz, and I got "pied in the face." The group howled in laughter like a pack of wolves in heat. I went in the cabin to clean up. I could smell the Cheez Whiz for three days, which permeated deep into my pores.

JONES BEACH: The youth group went to the Jones Beach several times. It was a nice beach and had a concert hall area that hosted big-time banks for shows. There were stone bridges on the way out to Long Island on the parkways, purposely designed this way by Abraham Moses to prevent buses from bringing people of color from NYC to live on Long Island. Shortly after I moved away, dead bodies were found in the high beach grass every few months, and the search was on for a serial killer.

JOEY AND AMY: While I served as an intern in Baldwin, Long Island, one mile down from the church on Merrick Road, seventeen-year-old Amy Fisher kept visiting auto repair shop mechanic Joey Battafuoco, thirty-five, and had an affair with him. In 1992, Fisher shot Mary Jo, Joey's wife, in the face. Joey did time for statutory rape, and Amy did time for attempted murder. Joey and Mary Jo divorced in 2003.

HOFSTRA UNIVERSITY VS. LAFAYETTE: I went to the Hofstra to watch a basketball game. I grew up knowing Andy Wesco, and he ended up playing basketball for Lafayette College in Easton. I went to the game, and as I walked by the Lafayette bench, I saw Andy and tapped him on the shoulder. He turned around with an annoyed look until he saw it was me, and I got a big smile. I did not get to see Andy play guard because he had a twisted ankle.

CHRIS HERMANN TEN YEARS LATER: Father Buzz has told me several times that I played an important role in influencing Chris when I was a youth pastor. Chris ended up becoming a leader in the youth group at a Baptist church he started attending and eventually earned a doctorate at John Jay in NYC in criminal studies. Way to go,

Professor Christopher Hermann! He married Maria from Haverstraw, New York, and they had two beautiful children.

BILLY GRAHAM SCHOOL OF EVANGELISM (SYRACUSE, NEW YORK - APRIL 24–28, 1989): I spent four days in Syracuse and, during the day, attended the School of Evangelism and the Crusades at 7:30 p.m. in the Syracuse dome. It was a great opportunity to hear the best minds in Evangelicalism, with the chance to attend three different seminars a day, one after breakfast and two after lunch. There was plenty of time to process what was learned since there were two coffee breaks and time to talk with other delegates at the meal times. I got to hear Millie Dienert, Paul Cedar, Ron Hutchcraft, Art Erickson, and James Kennedy.

OTHER CRUSADES: I attended the Long Island Crusade announcement on May 13, 1989, where the strategy was explained for the September 23–30 event to be held at the Nassau Coliseum. At the event, Jack Crabtree from Long Island Youth for Christ spoke about the history of Youth for Christ in Long Island. He was a smart, funny, and down-to-earth guy I got to know better by living in Long Island.

The other event I attended was in September 22, 1991, while I was in the seminary at Central Park. My sister joined Teresa and me at the event, where 250,000 people showed up. More showed up than for the concert of Simon and Garfunkel and of Dianna Ross in Central Park. Mayor Dinkins welcomed Graham, Johnny Cash and June Carter Cash, Sandi Patty and the Brooklyn Tabernacle Choir, and a Korean choir. The Salvation Army played Beethoven's *Ode to Joy*.

Billy Graham has appeared in 84 countries and preached the Gospel to 110 million people as of 1991. I have respect for his integrity, and he often is voted in the top 10 respected people in the world every year. My favorite story he tells is about a guest preacher who is invited to speak for 45 minutes, but he goes on and on, and the host pastor gets so upset that he throws a hymnal at the guest speaker, only to hit an old lady parishioner. He runs over to apologize, and the old lady says, "Hit me again. I can still hear him speaking!"

Pres. George H. Bush (1989–92)
Domestic

Signed the Americans with Disabilities Act	Radiation Compensation Act	Exposure
Reauthorized the Clean Air Act	Raised taxes to lower the deficit	

Foreign

Gulf War, got Iraq out of Kuwait

Invaded Panama to oust Noriega

Spearheaded negotiations for North American Free Trade Agreement

Signed the U.S.-Russian strategic plan with Gorbachev <u>after the dissolution of the Soviet Union</u>.

JULY 3, 1990 - NANA GEIST PASSES: Nana passed at age seventy-seven. I was age twenty-four, and it was my first year in the seminary. The tradition used to be to go to church, and afterward, we would go to Nana Geist's to visit with the Geist family members. When Nana died in July of 1990, the tradition stopped. There was a hole in the Geist soul. When church was over, the thought was *What do we do now?* Nana was the glue who held the Geist family together. In time, the Geists started the family tradition of holding a summer picnic and then a Christmas party that was held at a veteran's hall, was catered, and had a visit from Santa Claus. I was always asked to open the event with a prayer when I was present, which I think is a great tradition.

1990–93 - ATS AND LIVING OFF CAMPUS: My friend Doug Rowse had moved to a home off campus in his senior year. It was with an eighty-three-year-old woman named Mary, who lived on Piermont Avenue in Nyack, New York, right behind Simpson church, the official CMA church of Nyack, Nyack College, and the Alliance Seminary. I knew Doug was moving out in June or July of 1988, so I wanted to take advantage of this great opportunity. Ms. Grace did not want any rent money. She just wanted someone in the house to feel safe, to have some noise in her home, and to sometimes be taken to the store or the train station. She had an infirmed husband and also needed help with him from time to time. I grabbed Doug early in 1988 and said, "Doug, I want in on the home on Piermont Avenue." He told Mary, and her son, Dan Menaker, who was a writer for the *New Yorker* at the time, and an interview with me was set up. Mary and Dan liked me, and I was hired to become the free graduate tenant at 156 Piermont Avenue in Nyack, New Yeah. Yay, me!

I moved into the house for one summer before heading to Baldwin. Robin Swope, a friend of mine from Nyack College and ATS, moved into the home with me. He stayed in the home from September through June or July till he married Melissa. He moved to Western Pennsylvania, with his new bride. At this time, Monica M., a mutual friend of mine through Ed Nanno, was looking for a way to save money. I suggested she move into Mary's home with me. It was a big home with a kitchen and two large rooms on the first floor and four bedrooms upstairs.

12-5-93 - JORDAN TAYLOR SMITH IS BORN: In May of 1993, I received a phone call from my mother. She said, "Jody wants to talk with you about something." I said, "Oh, okay." I thought, *Why is my mother announcing my sister to me? If Jody wanted to talk with me, Jody would just call me.* Jody got on the phone, and she was crying and unable to talk. I was now concerned because I was afraid she was going to tell me she had a life-threatening disease. "Jody, what is it?" I kept asking. Mom got back on the phone and said, "You are going to be an uncle." I said, "I don't understand." Mom said, "Jody is pregnant." I knew Jody wanted to try out for the U.S. Olympic equestrian dressage team, but as they said, "Man makes plans, and life happens." She would now be donning the mommy hat. She was afraid I would condemn her, but I told her I loved her and would support her any way I could.

9-23-95 - JODY MARRIES: I was a pastor at New Life Fellowship, and Jody asked me to officiate the wedding. It was my impression that the rehearsal and wedding were just a formality. Jody and Kevin met while playing volleyball down at Cedar Beach. Mom wanted to give away Jody with Dad, but Kevin objected, saying it was not tradition. Mom was furious, and Jody said nothing. Mom did not talk to Kevin at all during the rehearsal; she occupied herself playing with Jordan. The night before the wedding, Jody reminisced with Teresa Joy and me about brother and sister stories and about Nana Ruby. The wedding went well in the Rose Garden the next day. I officiated the wedding. Kevin was going to become a Pennsylvania State trooper. Mom and Dad took in Jody and Jordan the six months Kevin was in Hershey, Pennsylvania, for his cadet training. Dad was happy because now Jody and Jordan would get health coverage under Kevin's health plan paid for by the Pennsylvania taxpayers.

1996: JIM HELPS JODY AND KEVIN PAINT A NEW HOME: Jody and Kevin had a home built on Elm Road in Danielsville Pennsylvania, and it needed some indoor painting. I went from Queens to help my sister and brother-in-law. I brought equipment, and I did most of the edging while Jody and Dad rolled. For lunch, I mentioned my back was hurting, and Dad gave me a pill. He has been having serious back problems and had some OxyContin pills. I took one, and in five minutes the pain was gone, and I was painting like a madman. I asked Kevin if he was going to help, and he said, "I don't paint." When he said this, I edged out the last two rooms and said, "I am leaving now." He expected me to paint his house without out him contributing some sweat equity, especially when I had a four-hour commute, plus gas and tolls. I really did it for Jody, Jordan, and baby Madison on the way.

JULY 31, 1996: MADISON TANNER SMITH ENTERS THE WORLD: She and Jordan are really amazing human beings. She is smart, pretty, funny, and a hard worker and can be in the moment. In 2016, she is a sophomore at Michigan State as a Spartan. Her brother is a senior at PSU, and they like to razz each other about school sports but love each other. They also call Nana and Pap Geist weekly, and that really makes my parents' week. I am grateful I can be a small part in their lives and vice versa.

2000: RAFTING DOWN CEDAR CREEK: I had three inflatable tires and took my nephew Jordan (ages seven) and niece Madison (aged four) rafting down Cedar Creek. It was a fun memory of rafting, sunshine, willow trees, and laughter with such cute kids. My niece and nephew were so cute, the little "toe heads" with blond hair. It was worth it to see them smile when the intertubes went through the rapids. It was good to make memories with family.

WRESTLING, FOOTBALL, ARCHERY, AND CHEERLEADING: It was tough for me to get back to Pennsylvania with my ministry duties in NYC, but over the years, I was able to witness Jordan play in some Little League football games and some wrestling matches and to watch Madison cheerlead to compete in archery competitions. They grew up so fast.

1990–95 - UNCLE TOM AND SOLE II VS. TRI-COUNTY LANDFILL: Tri-County Landfill proposed a fifty-five-acre landfill in Foster Township in Luzerne County, Pennsylvania. The Save Our Local Environment II (SOLE II) hired Atty. John Childe to represent them. The plaintiffs in the case were Tom Meyers Seniro, Lawrence P., Lind Korpalski, Charles Wessel, and Kenneth Powley. SOLE II's concern was leachate, runoff, raw sewage from the landfill seeping into the Mauch Chunk Aquifer, the drinking water for Carbon County, and into the Lehigh River, threatening the drinking water for Allentown, Northampton, Whitehall, and Walnutport. The white-water rafting on the Big Lehigh also was a tourist attraction, and in 1989, Governor Casey allocated $3.3 million for the construction of aquatic bypasses or fish ladders to lure the shad upstream on the Lehigh. The DER also said the mine subsidence may cause leaks in the landfill liner and contaminate water and vegetation in the area. SOLE II won its case and prevented Pagnotti Industries and Beltrami Enterprises from building the landfill and helped protect our water. Thank you, SOLE II!

KITTY VI (SHORT FOR VIOLET): Mary had a tabby cat named Violet. I was not a big cat fan, but she would sit next to me when I watched TV. I stroked my palm on her head and began to give her a vibrating shake of the head, and the cat loved it. She moved her head toward me, and I gave Kitty Vi the headshake. She was not a big cat. Robin was a jokester and saw a tabby in Mary's yard, and it was twice as big as Violet, and he let the kitty monster into the house. Mary walked in the kitchen, saw this cat at the food dish, and said, "Hi, Vi! Oh my, that's not Vi!" The clay character Mr. Bill from *Saturday Night Live* could not have done it better.

CHAPTER 7

Alliance Theological Seminary in Nyack, New York, 1990–93 (Ages 24–27)

HOW SEMINARY WAS DIFFERENT THAN COLLEGE: From speaking to seminarians who used to lunch at the college cafeteria, it was clear there were many more papers to be written in graduate school than in college. In college, I struggled with every paper I wrote. I did it in my own hand writing and then would have to pay a female student $1 a page to get it typed. How was I going to afford paying for my graduation papers? What I learned was to trust my writing more. I used to write and then rewrite my college papers and receive so-so grades. In the seminary, I had more papers to write; and because I did not have as much time, I had to learn to trust my instincts more, and my writing became better. I also received higher grades in graduate school.

1990 - LEARNING TO TYPE AGAIN: I had taken a typing class in high school but did not take it seriously. I learned the basics, such as how to sit properly and where the different lettered keys were, but when it came to being tested for typing, I would think of the song by the Who called "Eminence Front" and would type to the rhythm of the song. What to do now? I went to the Nyack Public Library in mid to late

July, took out a book on typing, and practiced twenty to thirty minutes a day for a month. I also bought a rebuilt computer (word processor). I bought it from a guy who worked at IBM and came up with the idea of communicating by computers via underwater insulated wires vs. using a regular phone, which saved companies millions until e-mail was invented. It was not hooked up to the Internet. I was not even sure there was an Internet yet in 1990. I did not begin experimenting with the e-mail until 1993, when I moved to Queens, New York, to work at New Life Fellowship.

1988: JOHN AND ROXANNE GAINER: Roxanne grew up in McKeesport, Pennsylvania, and grew up knowing Dave and Cindy Jennings. John was a one-thousand-point scorer for the basketball team. He grew up in Ohio and was captain of the basketball team in 1992. John's father was a barber, and John gave me two pairs of hair scissors and said they would never go dull. I lost one pair, but here it is today in 2016, twenty-eight years later, and the scissors are still sharp.

Teresa and I went out with John and Roxanne into NYC in May on a Saturday night to a Mexican restaurant in Lower Manhattan. There was a tequila girl trying to get people to drink shots. We had a nice time. John was a funny guy with a good heart. John and Roxanne were planning to move to Ohio after John graduated and then married

In April of 1993, John was a well-liked middle school teacher. He was sitting in a La-Z-Boy chair, holding a joystick, and playing a Nintendo video game. Roxanne called him to bed. He said, "I will be right there." She fell asleep. When she woke, John was not in bed. She walked into the living room and saw John holding the joystick. Thinking he has fallen asleep, she tried to awaken John, only to find a brain aneurysm has taken his life. Several vans from Nyack College holding over sixty people attended the funeral, showing how much John was loved by so many.

1989 - THE CMA MOVES TO COLORADO SPRINGS: ATS used to be right next to the college, but when the CMA headquarters moved from Nyack to Colorado Springs in the year 1989, ATS bought the old CMA headquarters in Nyack. Many Christian organizations were moving to Colorado Springs, and many of them said they were moving because God was directing them to do so. I respected the organizations that said we were moving because we got a better tax rate living there.

1990 ROAD TRIP AND HORSE GAS: My sister went to an "equestrian school" in Virginia in 1989 and 1990. She later went to Nyack in 1991 and 1992. My girlfriend Teresa Haggerty, two years younger than I was, had a basketball player roommate living down in Maryland, Amy. Amy was pretty, conservative, and a good basketball forward. Teresa played point guard for the team and became a Hall of Famer at Nyack College. Teresa and I visited Amy and decided to take a road trip to see where Jody went to equestrian school in Virginia. Of course, horses had a smell, and so did horse manure. Amy put on the girly girl act and kept complaining about the smells of the country farm. For me, it was good to see Jody and where she was getting her horsey education in "dressage," a certain type of style in showing horses. As all four of us were standing in the barn next to a stall where a horse's back end was next to us, it let out a horse fart in Amy's face, and she was contaminated all the way back to her abode in Maryland.

AMY TWENTY YEARS LATER: It was July of 2010, and I was watching the NBC six-thirty *Nightly News*. A woman named Mrs. Velez filed a suit in 2004 against Novartis, a Switzerland-based drug company in the United States. Mrs. Velez and four other women filed for discrimination over pay and promotion and pregnancy. The case was called *Velez vs. Novartis Corporation* in the U.S. District Court of New York in Manhattan. Of the $152 million sex bias settlement, the twelve women would split $3.4 million jury award and 250 in punitive damages. Sixty million dollars would go to the back pay of 5,600 female employees, $40 million for attorney fees, $22 million to improve Novartis personal policies over three years, and $3.4 million to the twelve ladies. I watched the piece and thought, *Good for this woman standing up for her right, just like Erin Brockovich.*

In 2014, I received a Facebook message from Amy, only her married last name was Velez. She wrote to tell me she was sorry for the injustice I have experienced as an educator in NYC and in Newark. When I watched the piece in 2010 on the news, I did not realize it was the Amy I went to college with. I thought, *Wow, the owner of the farting horse is lucky Amy did not take her to court.* She was now blackballed in the pharmaceutical industry and, after taxes, really only won enough money to live on for two years with her boys. Life was not easy for whistle-blowers. We all knew what happened to all the Old Testament prophets. Who knew she was a Norma Rae–Erin Brockovich type? Good for you, ladies of the Velez-Novartis sex bias case. Salute!

1992 SUMMER OLYMPICS GOLD WINNERS: Carl Lewis (long jump), Jennifer Capriati (tennis singles), and the men's basketball team

1992 WINTER OLYMPICS WINNERS: Kristi Yamaguchi (figure skating), Cathy Turner and Bonnie Blair (speed skating), and Donna Weinbrecht (freestyle skiing) from West Milford, New Jersey!

1992 - ATS: CLINTON SIGN ON MY CAR: While in college, I took much heat for being a Democrat. The key issue for most Nyack College Republicans was abortion. At this time, I was a pro-life Democrat and have done more for the cause than 95 percent of the students. It was 1990, and with changes in the economy and with facts showing that the economy and the deficit went down under Democratic presidents, I put a blue Clinton sign on top of my car. Whenever I drove around the ATS campus, people stopped and looked and must think, Who *is this crazy person?* Someone took yellow spray paint and sprayed an X on my sign. Some got into heated discussions with me, and I would ask this question,, "When you become a pastor, will you have Democrats go to your church? How will you speak to them? I hope not like you are speaking to me." It was an opportunity to challenge some thinking of my brothers and sisters.

1992 - CLINTON-BUSH ELECTION: The pro-life movement Operation Rescue put out a pamphlet in 1992 entitled "To Vote for Bill Clinton Is Sin against God." It said the predominate reason Christians may be tempted to vote for Bill Clinton was for the economy, in other words *money*! "If Bill Clinton is elected, he will help destroy three centuries of Christianity in America!" The main focus of the pamphlet was on the abortion issue; it did not address any other moral or ethical issues. I was upset by this propaganda, so I created my own pamphlet entitled "To Vote for George Bush Is to Sin against God!" My points were as follows:

1. Bush does not submit to governmental authority (trading arms for hostages).
2. He does not care about human rights (China trading status, denied fleeing Haitians asylum, quiet about Lithuanian demonstrators gunned down).
3. Bush does not care for the homeless.
4. Bush coddles the rich!
5. He lied (about tax raise).
6. He gives evangelicals lip service to pro-life movement.
7. He is not the environmental president he promised to be.

I had fun with this, and it showed how movements exploited the evangelicals to vote for Republicans.

IS UNEMPLOYMENT AN ISSUE EVANGELICALS SHOULD BE CONCERNED ABOUT? *The Billy Graham Christian Worker's Handbook* (p. 63) says

With every 1 percent rise in unemployment:

4.3 percent more men & 2.3 percent of women go to the mental hospital.

4.1 percent more people commit suicide.

4.7 percent more people are murdered.

4 percent more people go to prison.

1.9 percent more people die of heart disease and stress related ailments.

Child abuse and spousal abuse increases.

1991–1993 AFRICAN INLAND MISSION: My wife at the time, Teresa Joy, was working for the African Inland Mission in Pearl River, New Jersey. She worked there for three years, and the people over there were really nice. They had one to two banquets a year, and I always enjoyed attending them. While working there, she had the opportunity to go visit Kenya for a week.

1988: ROAD TRIP TO HOULTON MAINE: My girlfriend Teresa lived in Houlton, Maine. It was a ten-hour drive from Nyack, New York, and you would take Route 95 North. It took five hours to get to Maine and another five hours to get to Houlton after passing Portland, Augusta, and then Bangor. From Bangor on, all you would see are pine trees for two hours until you got to Houlton. As her father, Larry, liked to say, "Bangor is not the end of the world, but you can see it from there." We went to visit the family, and we took turns driving. I thought, *How cool would it be for me to drive into Houlton, pull into the driveway as Teresa is sleeping, and then tap her on the shoulder and say, "Your turn to drive!"* only for her to see she was home.

It did not work because I fell asleep at the wheel before that could happen. Route 95 was separated by trees in the center lane during the last two hours up to Houlton. I was driving and started feeling sleepy. What I should have done was wake up Teresa to switch driving duties. No, I wanted to surprise her. My head bobbed two times, and the next thing I knew, I heard the "thump, thump" of the wheels driving over the rumble strip of Route 95 North unto the shoulder of the road, and we were headed toward trees on the grassy area approximately fifty feet away. When I saw this, I was immediately awakened.. I was saying, "Sh——t, sh——t, sh——t!" under my breath and turned the car. Amazingly, I kept the car parallel in between the shoulder of the road, and there was no rumble of the tires on the highway but a beautiful quiet swishing sound of the gliding tireson the grass, which I could not appreciate untilyears after the incident.

Halfway in the midst of the car sliding on the grass embankment of the Maine highway, Teresa woke up and grabbed the front dashboard; and as the car stopped eight feet in front of a tree, she got out of the car and yelled, "What happened?" A pulled-over truck driver was walking down the hill, laughing, and he answered her, "He fell asleep." I was in shock and full of embarrassment over me not pulling over when I felt sleepy. Did I surprise her? Yup! There was not much conversation during the last hour of the trip to Houlton.

HAGGERTY FAMILY: I always enjoyed going up to Houlton, Maine. Her father, Larry, was a man's man and loved to go hunting and fishing. Teresa had three brothers and three sisters. The mother was the least athletic of the family, and she was the traditional mom, who was a great cook and made awesome pies of all kinds. Larry had a canoe, two motorcycles, two quads, a pickup truck, and a trailer. Most of the family members were good singers and talented athletes. I liked Greg, the youngest son. He went to school in Houghton and was studying engineering. He worked with a construction crew in the summer, digging ditches. His workmate gave him dating advice and said, "Date fat chicks! They appreciate you giving them attention, and when they give you sex, they give it like they will never get it again." Who said you can't get good relationship advice from a ditch-digger?

BASKETBALL HOULTON-STYLE: The high school and sports played an important role there. Teresa played basketball, and Houlton won the championship with her two years in a row. The first year they played in Bangor, they were losing the game, and you could hear Teresa, who played point guard, scolding the center of the team to get a hustle on, and they slowly caught up and ended up winning. Whenever Houlton had an away game, the school bus would have a line of town cars behind it, following the team to root them on, just like in the movie *Hoosiers.*

BASS, SALMON, AND EAGLES: A half hour south of Houlton is the Penobscot River. It has bald eagles flying around and has great bass for fishing. It will have salmon run up the river, and there is always the chance of hooking into one.

Larry took me out on his canoe one day with a motor on it. We sailed up the river and were hammering the bass. By law, you could keep one salmon a year if you caught it. I threw my lure out and, wham, felt a hit. I said, "Larry, I have a nice fish here!" Out of the water jumped a two-foot salmon at the end of my line. He shouted, "You have a salmon." I battled the salmon, kept the line tight, and got the salmon within three feet of the boat. Larry reached out to grab the line. I scolded him, "Don't grab the line!" Anyone with a little experience knew that if you grabbed the line, frequently, the fish would be able to get off the hook. I said, "Grab the net!" Larry grabbed the line to pull the salmon in, and "kaplunk," there it fell into the river. He looked at me like, "Duh." To this day, I think he did it purposely. It would have taken away from his salmon story from the year before.

MAINE POTATOES: Houlton is part of a farming community. The area grows potatoes. During the WWII, German prisoners of war were brought into Houlton to help pick potatoes. After the war, they resorted to child labor, and many of the kids—many of Irish descent—would go into the fields to do the back-breaking work of picking potatoes for a few weeks to make extra money. You were never to throw small potatoes at another for fear of hitting someone in the eye, and every season, someone would get hit and walk around with a black-and-blue eye.

BROOK FISHING WITH LARRY: I went quad riding with Bill (husband of Dianne), Larry, and Teresa on the back roads of Houlton in the woods. When we got back after lunch, I went brook trout fishing with Larry and Ron Walbor, husband of Wanda. To fish, they would wear hip waders and walk downstream. The fish were faced upstream and wouldn't see you walking up, and if you threw the bait in front of them, they would take it. The river was not big. So on team one was Larry and Bill, and on team two, behind them, was Jim and Ron.

The fish were not very big, but the way Carol fried them up, they were delicious. Larry let me borrow one of his rods and reels. He said to me, "They don't make those reels anymore, so be real careful with it." On the front of the reel was a device called drag adjuster, and it controlled how much pull you gave to a fish when it took your line. If the drag was too tight, the fish could break the line. I went to loosen the drag adjuster, and the piece fell into the river. Great, this guy was not gonna let me marry his daughter if I lost this piece. I told the guys I had to pee in the woods. When Larry and Bill turned the corner, I told Ron what happened. I was praying and reaching around the water with my hand. I went on the edge of the riverbank and reached my hand as far as it would go under to where the water met the wall of the ground cavern, and I found the piece. Maybe it would have been better for my future had I not found it.

HOULTON, FOURTH OF JULY: It was a small town in the USA, and many showed up for the parade. Before the parade was a five-mile run, and I joined and felt good about completing it. Later at the parade were many farming tractors, the school band, the town band, fire department trucks with red lights flashing, and local businesses with their floats. Some threw out candy to the parade watchers. The Ice Cream Store drove its truck down the street, and ten volunteers were handing out small ice cream cones to the parade watchers. The local store had a float, and they were cutting up watermelon and handing it out to the parade goers. I have never seen such a thing. We later went to the Houlton Festival and, in the evening, enjoyed the fireworks. Larry got a kick that the town gay guy sat next to me on the bleachers. One of the funny things about my future father-in-law was that he saw no problem using the "ni——er" word but found it upsetting when I talked about getting pissed off about something. The Haggerty family had many who worked as missionaries in Africa or worked in ministry in the United States.

1998 - MY LAST GAME OF GOLF: I went golfing with Larry, Greg, Bob, and Ron at the course in Houlton, Maine. It was a good time with the guys, and Larry liked to stick his club up your crotch just before you swing on your drive. I had a terrible game. I had been living in NYC for years and just didn't get out much to play. On the last hole, I was so frustrated that I took my putter and hit my golf bag next to the green. When I got home, I realized I have bent two of my club shafts. My bag has been collecting dust in my shed for eighteen years as of 2016.

ALLIANCE THEOLOGICAL SEMINARY: I moved back to Nyack to Mary Grace's home on 156 Piermont Avenue after doing my nine months as an intern in Baldwin, Long Island. When I moved back, Robin has married Melissa, and Ed Nanno moved in the house with me in 1990 and 1991. Ed graduated in 1991 and moved to New Haven, Connecticut, to attend Yale Divinity School with the likes of professors of hermeneutics and theology Nicholas Fry, Nicholas Wolterstorff, Hans Frei, and Brevard Childs. Ed was brilliant. For one test, I studied all afternoon and all night. Ed came home from the seminary and studied for an hour. Ed went out and played basketball and after dinner, he hung out with his girl friend. I spent seven hours preparing for the test, Ed studied for one hour; Ed received and "A" and I received a "B." Life is so much easier for intelligent and handsome people.

1990 TRIP TO ARIZONA AND CALIFORNIA: I have been in school for most of my life up to age twenty-six. I felt I needed a break before my last year of studies. I took off a semester to do some traveling. I took a plane ride from San Fran to Arizona to visit my family who lived there—Uncle Lee, Aunt Barb, and cousins Debby and Barry. Uncle Lee worked for America West, which became U.S. Airways in 2006. I flew into Phoenix, and he picked me up. I was really tired when I got there, and I was hungry as well. My uncle Lee was a talker. I didn't know him real well except for our talks at the Geist Christmas parties in Allentown. I was grateful he got me, but in addition to being hungry, I also had a headache. He was talking and talking and talking. I finally said, "I am sorry, I am not listening well because I am tired and hungry and have a headache." He took me to a fast-food place, and when I got to his place, I took a nap. Lee always talked about Debby and Barry. It was if Bruce was invisible, but some parents have trouble accepting having a gay son or daughter.

After my nap, I was in a better condition to do some listening. It was nice to hear his stories about growing up in Allentown. I enjoyed learning about my family history. While I was in Phoenix, I was able to have lunch with Joe Wolf, whom I knew from William High School and who was now playing guard for the NFL Phoenix Cardinals. I went see him play the Dallas Cowboys that Sunday. He was a big boy.

I flew to the Grand Canyon, brought a backpack, and took a pup tent. On the flight there, it got bumpy flying on a small plane. The fat lady sitting across from me had to use her puke bag. I got to the canyon campground by 3:00 p.m. They told you it would take twice as long to walk out of the canyon as it did to walk into it. The guide who gave the donkey tours was asked, "Has anyone ever fallen off a donkey into the canyon?" He said, "People hold on so darn tight to the reins with their hands, and with their legs around the donkey's ribs, we have never lost a person in the canyon yet."

There was hardly anyone there in September. I set up the tent and hiked into the canyon. I made it down to the Bright Angel Trail to the Phantom Ranch, which was 10.3 miles and a four- to six-hour hike, depending on how fast you hoofed it. I wanted to scream out for Bobby Brady, remembering how he got lost there on a *Brady Bunch* episode. I hustled to make it back up to the top of the canyon before dark and drank all my water from my canteen by the time I got close to the top. It was beautiful watching the colors of the rocks changing as the sun moved toward sunset.

I made a shortcut through some bushes up to my site and came across three Native Americans sitting in a circle in their green national park outfits, with their cowboy hats and boots on, drinking beer. At this time, I was a teetotaler for the most part. They called me over and said, "Sit down. Have a drink." I thought, *I have never hanged out with Native Americans before*, and I had a beer with them. It has never happened since, and I am glad I took the opportunity the universe gave me that late afternoon.

When I got back to camp, with no one around, someone put their tent right up to mine. I guess that was okay, but the two couples were enjoying food and drink and never invited me over for some conversation. I would have enjoyed that. That night was cold. The dessert temperature in the summer would reach 74 to 103 degrees. On the North Rim, it would reach 44 to 74 degrees. It felt colder than 44 degrees to me. I did some reading, journaling, and praying before going to bed. The next day, I took the bus and train to the airport in Phoenix; and the following day, I flew up to San Francisco.

JULY 1992 - LEE AND BARB TO NYACK, NEW YORK: Uncle Lee and Aunt Barbara visited me in Nyack, New York. We took a road trip up to West Point, New York, and walked around West Point. West Point was established by Thomas Jefferson in 1802. It was approximately sixteen thousand acres in Highlands, New York. It was a fortified site during the Revolutionary War. A great iron chain was laid across the Hudson River at this point in order to impede British Navy vessels but was never tested by the British. Gen. Benedict Arnold attempted to turn the site over to the British for twenty thousand pounds (or $1.3 million in 2009 dollars), but the attempt failed. West Point Academy was established in 1802 and was the nation's oldest service academy. I walked around with Lee and Barb across the Bear Mountain Bridge over the Hudson River. Inside the West Point Museum was a large piece of the Berlin Wall, which was knocked down on November 9, 1989.

RICE-A-RONI - THE SAN FRANCISCO TREAT: I was picked up by my best friend, Mike Brogna, who was working with Campus Crusade for Christ at University of California in Berkeley. I flew into San Francisco, and he picked me up. The nice thing about the area was

I could take a subway from Berkeley into San Francisco to do some exploring. The Golden Gate Bridge was glorious with the backdrop of San Fran and the bay.

Next to Mike's apartment building was an empty car, and there was a crazy guy who lived there. When the homeless guy had his shouting outbursts, Mike went out and talked with him. The "houseless" guy's name was Jackson. He dropped out of society in the 1960s. He liked to argue with talk radio loudly in his car. Mike invited Jackson up to watch the 49ers football game, and Jackson pushed Mike over. No more invites to Jackson into the apartment.

Mike has a roommate named Ray, who was Chinese American. In a conversation, I asked him if he was oriental. He said to me, "The proper term is Asian American. Oriental is the name of a rug." Point well taken.

My first night in Berkeley, I woke up at 2:00 a.m., and there were helicopters flying around, shining their powerful light beams around the campus area. I thought, *What the heck is going on here in Berkeley? I guess I will find out tomorrow.* The next day, I asked a student what happened. He told me students were taken hostage by an Iranian man at the Hotel Durant, and one student was killed and the gunman too. I saw a newspaper dispenser, and I purchased one. The picture on the front page was of the Hotel Durant on Durant Street with all types of police surrounding it. As I put the paper down, I realized I was standing in the spot the photographer took the picture. I held the newspaper picture up and down, up and down. There was the living picture in front of me.

9-27-90 - BERKELEY HOSTAGES AND SHOOTING: Seventy-five people were in the bar area, some for a birthday party, when an Iranian man suffering from schizophrenia took out some guns and held people hostage. He held twenty people hostage, shot and injured eight, and killed one. At 7:00 a.m., the SWAT team rushed into the room and shot the hostage taker, who was dead by the time he got to the hospital. What a way to start my trip in Berkeley.

By the famous Berkeley gates, student groups set up tables to recruit students to their clubs. Walk two hundred feet, and you would get to the Student Union Hall. Next to it, you would get people giving speeches on religion and politics. For anyone who preached, there was a guy called the "Hate Man," who liked to mimic the preacher and make opposite comments. He dressed up as a bum with opposite colors for his socks and shoes and vest.

I stayed at Berkeley for three weeks with Mike. I attended a weekend retreat with his Campus Crusade people. It was a lovely retreat in a dessert area that had a pool. It was a trip where I got to travel, read, think, talk with people, and attend Bible studies with Mike with his Campus Crusade students. At the one Bible study, the California college girls were dressed like they were going to the beach, and it was tough for me to keep my focus just on the Scripture study for that lesson.. There were places on campus I recognized from the movie *The Graduate* with Dustin Hoffman, Anne Bancroft, and Katharine Ross.

10-17-90 - ANNIVERSARY OF THE 1989 EARTHQUAKE SERIES: It was the anniversary of the 1989 World Series earthquake. It was all over the news on TV and on the radio. People on campus were talking about it. It was an earthquake that shook for fifteen seconds, reached 6.9 on the Richter scale, and was the largest since the San Francisco earthquake of 1906. A piece of the upper deck of the Bay Bridge crumbled to the lower level on Interstate 880, and it cost $6 billion of damage, killing 63 people and injuring 3,757. People mostly remembered getting ready to watch game three at Candlestick Park between the Oakland A's and the San Francisco Giants of the World Series when ABC announcer Al Michaels cut off Tim McCarver, talking about whether Dave Parker was safe, by saying, "I'll tell you what, we are having an earthquake." The game was postponed and played ten days later, and the A's won the series, 4–0.

In the center of the Berkeley campus was a large clock tower, 307 feet tall, called the Sather Tower Carillon. You could take an elevator to the top. As I stood at the top, looking over the campus, the San Francisco Bay, and San Francisco, I felt the tower begin to shake. There was a cage around the walkway, which I presumed to prevent jumpers, and I grabbed unto the bars, thinking, *Oh, dear God, not an earthquake on the anniversary of the big one!* I had visions of the tower falling over, whether I would survive the fall or not over a football field high, what the newspapers would say about the guy who died in the tower, how much this was going to hurt, and if I wanted to live as a cripple or if it was better to die. The elevator door opened, and the tower stopped shaking and the elevator operatorand dryly said, "The tower shakes when the elevator moves up or down. It is not an earthquake."

YOSEMITE PARK: Mike and I took some time to go visit Yosemite National Park and walk through a forest of redwoods. It was a beautiful state. We even went to a football game at the Rose Bowl and watched UC Berkeley play a game. I was so proud to have a best friend who has given his heart to Christ and loved being a minister and teaching from the Gospels and the New Testament.

At Pikes Peak, there was a rock climber dangling two hundred feet in the air, and he looked like he needed help. I turned to Mike and said, "That guy needs help." The woman at the bottom of Pikes Peak said, "Honey, help is coming." I was definitely having a better day than Mr. Dangles right now.

JIM'S MENTORS: I was not the smartest guy, but I was a hard worker and persistent. The person who helped me at Nyack College was Jon Schuerholz. When we had classes together and I had trouble understanding something, Jon had a way of finding analogies to help me. When I was in the seminary, Ed Nanno was the person who did this for me. These brothers helped me and modeled for me how to help students I would work with in the future who struggled with concepts.

We think in pictures, not in words or letters. If I say bird, you do not think b-i-r-d but probably picture an animal with legs, wings, a beak, and certain colorings. Using images, analogies, and stories is a crucial tool in teaching, just as the master teacher Jesus did.

FISHING FOR STRIPERS: It was 1991, late March. Ed ran into my room as I was working on some paper. He said, "You have to come with me. You have to see the fish they are catching now in the Hudson. They are beautiful fish called stripers!" I jumped and said, "Let's go!" We drove to Piermont and Clinton Streets and made a left on Clinton all the way down to the Hudson River and the park. There were two black guys fishing, and we watched. We started talking to the fellows, and they shared everything they knew about striper fishing.

The Hudson River is considered brackish waters, a place where freshwater and salt water meet. You do not need a fishing license to fish the ocean or brackish waters. The stripers run up the Hudson to lay eggs, just as salmon do. The best time to hook into one is when the tides change. We use bloodworms, and when you feel a hit, you wait until the second hit to set the hook. That is what a striper hit feels like. If you feel your line go out slowly, and it is a "tug, tug, tug" feeling, then you have a channel catfish on.

It was relaxing to sit on the sand and rocks by the Hudson and fish. Even if you got nothing, the view was beautiful to take in. It was nice to connect with nature. Timmy Maloney, the awesome basketball player, told me he loved fishing. I told him about the spot, and he joined me several times to go fishing. He was a smart and funny guy, and he looked like one of the Kennedy kids to me. The fishing time was even better when you hooked into one. You were allowed to eat one per week. A pregnant woman may eat one a month.

TAPPAN ZEE BRIDGE BEING REBUILT: In the *New Yorker* magazine was a story why a new bridge needed to be built. The Hudson used to be very polluted. The GE plant had dumped many PCBs into the river, but thanks to the Superfund site monies, it was cleaned up. The Hudson became alive again. The mooring of the Tappan Zee Bridge was made of wood. Since the river has been cleaned up, there was microscopic life that was eating away at the wooden moorings. As a result, new moorings had to be put in that they could not eat away at. Construction started in 2015 and would be completed in 2017. It was amazing to see the ship involved in making this happen and the progress the engineers and bridge builders were making. It actually made me swell with pride that America could still build things in our country.

MIDDLE BLUE AT UPS: I worked at United Parcel Service in 1993 for a semester in Spring Valley, New York. It was the only job around where you could get full medical benefits working full time. If you were a married student with kids, it was a perfect job. I was a loader, the middle blue cage. Cages ran in a circle—blue, yellow, red, green, orange—timed perfectly so when you loaded the brown truck, there was the next blue cage. It paid $15 an hour, but if you maintained a B average or higher, you received a bonus, so it was really like making $25 an hour.

The guy next to me, Gus, never talked to me. The song "Wicked Game" had just come out by Chris Isaak, and he would sing the "Uh-ahhhhhhhhh" part every time. I was studying Hebrew at the time. I had Hebrew vocabulary cards and my UPS route number cards, and I was trying to learn both at the same time. My shift was from 3:30 a.m. until 7:30 a.m., and my classes started at 8:00 a.m. I would go to the seminary in my jeans and sweatshirts covered in dust and with messy hair. For the first time in my life, I understood the song "Welcome to the Machine" by Pink Floyd.

1992- ATS DEAN DAVID HARTZFELD STEPS DOWN: At the Alliance Theological Seminary, we had student mailboxes; and in February, we got a note from Pres. Paul Bubna that Dean Hartzfeld would no longer be our dean. Fellow student Dan Gettman and I went to visit the dean at his home, and he was distraught. "I never saw this coming." Dan and I sit next to him, and I said, "I don't know what to say." Hartzfeld said back, "You don't have to say anything. Your visit and concern is enough." Dan and I spoke with some professors to get the skinny, and we wrote a half sheet asking students to ask if the dean was let go based on a review and to send them to Peter Nanfelt, who was a trustee at the time. As students were entering the chapel, we handed them out. Afterward, an administrator came up to me and said, "President Bubna has heart problems. Are you trying to put him in his grave?" No, I liked President Bubna, and I also liked Dean Hartzfeld.

AUTO ALMOST SMASHES THE GARAGE DOOR: I was invited to the Seminary's Presidents' home for a dinner, and his wife drove me from the seminary to their home. As she parked the car in front of her garage, she got out to open unlock the front door of the house,, but she had left the car in drive and had not put it in park. The car began to move, so I jumped over and put my foot on the brake and stopped the car before it rammed into the closed wooden garage door. I put it in park and turned off the car. I explained later to Mr. President what happened. From when I met her, she always seemed aloof, and I suspected she may be suffering from Alzheimer's, something I would never wish on anybody.

1988 - BILL MURRAY AND LINDBERG PAINTING: I saw on the Moseley Hall bulletin board that a painter named Tom Lindberg was looking to hire. Tom went to Nyack College but lost his faith.

He used Nyack College students because they were trustworthy and hardworking. I called him and found out he was working on a home in Palisades called Sneden's Landing. We worked at the home that used to belong to the Isley Brothers, but they did not pay their taxes. Bill Murray ended up buying the mansion of six acres for $6 million. That was $1 million an acre, plus a free mansion. The mansion was in bad shape, and there were construction guys there. I did some painting there but never got to meet Murray. The crew said he was a nice and funny guy. I met his Golden retriever named Bark. I was asked if I wanted to work over Thanksgiving, but I said I wanted to go home. I later learned that Steve Martin came over the Thanksgiving weekend, but he was not nice to the workers. Perhaps he was grumpy from wearing cruel shoes.

Tom got another job at the former home that Margot Kidder, the actress who played Lois to the Christopher Reeve's *Superman* in 1980. In the home, I found empty liquor bottles in closets and in other places. Before Ms. Kidder, Ethan Hawke and Uma Thurman lived in the supposedly haunted home. We painted the rooms in this old home with a beautiful view of the Hudson River. As I was painting in the living room, a man walked in the room, and it turned out to be actor Gene Hackman, who was in a play with Richard Dreyfuss called *Death and the Maiden*. He looked at me, and he was not very friendly. He had an Asian woman with him, I assumed his wife or girlfriend.

CONTACTING THE NEW YORK LABOR DEPARTMENT:
Tom told me he had to let me go because of lack of work. He asked me if he could pay me the following week. I said sure. The next week, he did not stop by and pay me. I called him, and he asked if he could pay the following week. He did not show. After the third week he did this, I contacted the New York State Labor Department and filed a complaint. Three days later, Lindberg called me and said, "Why did you

file a complaint? That goes on my record!" I said, "Get the money to me by today, and I will withdraw the complaint." He paid me that day.

1990 - ROCKLAND PAINTING: Jaime Arnita hooked up with his old high school buddy Perry to work with Rockland Painting. They both used to work with Bryan's Painting, but both ended up quitting because they thought Bryan was an ass. Bryan was a bodybuilder, and Jaime was skinny. Bryan grabbed the bottom of Jaime's ladder and carried him around, with Jaime screaming his head off. One time, one worker took a gallon of paint and dumped it over Bryan's head. I worked. I worked with Rockland Painting for two summers and then went on my own.

There was an interesting cast that worked there. They listened to Howard Stern in the morning and then the rock 'n' roll in the afternoon. The three brothers—Anthony, Rocko, and Frankie—were funny. Rocko "slipped" at a Mobil station, hurt his back, and sued Mobil. He ended up getting $10,000 to settle because they did not want to spend the extra money going to court. There was Mitchie; he was related to Perry and did crack. He was a nice guy and funny but an addict. There was Mike in a twelve-step program; he was funny. He said AA coffee was the best. He used to ask me all kinds of theological questions because he believed in a higher power. There was another Mike, who never paid for lunch; he used to say, "Put it on my tab!" At one lunch place, the kid who worked behind the counter did not have to write anything down. He could take eight orders and get it all right. He had an amazing level of memory.

My last year working for Rockland was not as fun as it used to be. The boss and the foreman started doing cocaine, and the easygoing guys with a good sense of humor turned into impatient, nasty, and condescending bosses. I knew it was time for me to go out on my own and start my own summer painting business the following summer, which I did.

I HAVE BEEN TO ALLENTOWN TOO!: Chris was a foreman at Rockland Painting and he also was in the twelve-step program. Back in his drinking days, he would have blackouts. One day, when he was drunk, he jumped into a lake in a quarry and broke his back. They helicoptered him to the Lehigh Valley Hospital in Allentown, just two miles where I grew up. He said, "Yup, I have been to Allentown. I don't remember much about it, except being in a hospital with a broken back."

SOUTHERN CARPETBAGGERS: In 1989, Hurricane Hugo hit Rockland County. Fellow students Ed Nanno, Dan Kerrigan, and I worked for Rockland Painting. Two guys in a pickup truck with a camper on the back hooked up with Perry and worked on the crew. They both had mustaches, one with dark hair, the other with brown hair. The one with brown hair said, "I don't work on ladders." Perry still hired this guy. They stayed at a campground, liked to drink, and worked with us during the day. After the Civil War, many from the North packed up and went South with carpetbag suitcases to make money in the rebuilding of the South. These guys came from the South to do the same thing after Hugo's devastation up North.

They told us a funny story about working at a lady's home, painting her room the yellow she picked. And then she said she wanted the room repainted. They told her they would lighten up the paint and repaint the room. They locked the door, took a two-hour nap, opened the door, and asked the lady if she liked it. She said, "I love it!" Of course, the color on a wall would change according to the time of day and the amount of sun it was getting. They charged her double for the job. Talk about Southern hospitality. We always thought they were homosexuals, but that was their business.

ALBANY HOOKER STORY: Perry got a job in Albany. It would be a three-day job, and we would sleep there for two nights. We stayed in some cheap hotel up there. We went to the bar the first night we got there. The business owner who hired Perry met with us, and he was gay. He told me I could sleep at his place, and I declined. We left the bar in two cars. When we got to our room, I saw a big girl getting out of the car, and two of the guys were talking about how much they were willing to pay for oral sex. I was studying to go into ministry and told the boss, "If you don't take her back to the bar, you can take me to the train station." He took the hooker back to the bar. One of the guys asked her, "If you stayed over, how would you have gotten home?" She said, "My mother would have come over to the hotel to pick me up."

1991 NYC - RUN INTO AN OLD FRIEND: It was the summer of 1990, and my summer painting boss has landed a job in NYC painting the offices of Calvin Klein near Central Park on Fifty-Third by Fifth Avenue. We would be painting there for four to five days, making the commute from Nanuet, New York, from Paley's to NYC. The hostess of the offices was was named and she was beautiful. At this time, I was planning on going into ministry. For lunch, we walked around the corner and sat on the fountain walls on the Avenue of the Americas. It was fashion week in NYC, which happened on a quarterly basis, and there were beautiful women walking around everywhere. As I was sitting with the painting crew, the guys were ogling the women and making lewd comments when someone said to me, "Hey, Jim, would you like to have sex with any of these women?" Because of my evangelical commitment, I would not have sex until I married at age twenty-six. I said to the guys, "You know, you can look at a woman and appreciate her beauty without thinking you have to jump her bones."

I was sitting on the cool alabaster wall with traditional white painting shorts and white shirt with multicolor drops of paint all over my outfit. I saw a woman walking towards us and thought to myself, *I know her*. I said to my friends, "I know that woman over there." They looked at me, laughed, and said, "Bulls——t!" I walked over the tall woman with long black hair, and she stopped in her tracks. I said, "Hi, Liz!" She said, "Hi, Jimmy Geist!" and gave me a hug. It turned out to be the young lady I crushed on from kindergarten all the way through high school. We exchanged numbers, and I ended up meeting her at a diner in the near future for dinner. It turned out she graduated from Syracuse University, studied acting, and was working as an actor in NYC. I saw one of her Off-Broadway plays, and she was very good. It turned out she lived on Fifty-First Street by Tenth Avenue, just a block away from the high school I would start working at in 1999. Small world.

ATS 1992 VERSION OF FACEBOOK: It was clear I was part of the 1 percent at Nyack College and the Alliance Theological Seminary who was a Democrat. Most evangelicals were Republican, most of whom were watching TV preachers who were likewise, such as Pat Robertson of *The 700 Club*, Rev. Jerry Falwell of the Moral Majority, and the psychologist and pastor James Dobson of Focus on the Family. They all talked about family values and being pro-life (antiabortion), but they never took any prolabor or prounion positions. If anything, if you took a prolabor position, you could be branded a Socialist or a Communist. Many of these churches were also mostly white, and many did not support the civil rights movement in the 1960s.

This was exactly what the father of United Auto Worker founder Walter Reuther talked about; he did not want to be part of any church that did not help improve the life of people while they were alive. Muhammad Ali said one reason he became a Muslim was he did not just want a mansion in the sky when he died; he wanted some pie while he was alive on earth, and he saw many churches not speaking out against injustices for the poor or people of color. I was always amazed how most of my classmates were concerned about abortion but did not see unemployment as a moral issue.

I used to write letters to the editor of the Nyack College newspaper, and I always stirred things up with my Progressive Democratic views of the Gospels. We did not have such a paper at the Alliance Seminary. I was able to get permission from the administration to start a board in the student lounge where students could write letters on various issues, and people could have the chance to respond. It was an opportunity for me to work on responses to issues politically or on church polity and to get my conservative friends to perhaps change their views on some issues. I started the primitive version of Facebook at ATS in 1992, twelve years before the 2004 launching of Facebook via the Internet.

FAVORITE SEMINARY CLASSES: My favorite classes were New Testament Exegesis, American Religions, Person in Ministry, Church in the Modern World, Contextual Theology, Systematic Theology, Ethic in Culture and Society, Church and the Urban Poor, the book of Amos, and Current Theologies. My GPA at ATS was 3.16, which according to the GPA equivalencies for universities was an 86.6. My grades were definitely above average in the seminary.

AMNESTY INTERNATIONAL: In 1992, I tried to start an Amnesty International, a human rights group that spoke out against those unjustly jailed and those being tortured in prison. The founder of Amnesty, Peter Benenson, said, "The candle burns not for us, but for those whom we failed to rescue from prison, who were shot on the way to prison, who were tortured, who were kidnapped, who disappeared. That's what the candle is for." Isaiah 1:17 said, "Learn to do right, seek justice and encourage the oppressed." The purpose of the group was to send letters to governments to inform them we knew what they were doing to do the right thing. The Alliance Seminary "Urgent Action

Network" of letter writers died out in a month from lack of interest. The hole in the evangelical mind was boggling me.

PARSON PAINTING: In 1993, I went into business with fellow seminarian Steve Harper. We painted two homes on Laveta Place in Nyack. Rosie O'Donnell had just moved into Helen Hayes's home on Broadway and the corner of Laveta. We were making decent money. We got our stuff from the hardware store in Nyack, but the owner, Lenny, was a slick one. We did not get monthly statements showing everything we have bought. He just gave us receipts, but they were confusing to read. If I could do it over, it would have been best to use a credit card instead of paying cash. He called us "deadbeats," but I called him crooked.

***THE DREAM TEAM* MOVIE**: I did some inside work for a couple on Laveta Place; both were musicians. The house next to them definitely needed a paint job. I asked if they knew their neighbors, and they said they both were actors and were currently in a play in NYC called *Sight Unseen*. Dennis, one of them, has been in several movies. I went over and introduced myself to Dennis Boutsikaris and Deborah Hedwall. He told me to give an estimate. I got Steve, and we walked around and came up with the number $5,000, but since they make good money, I said, "Let's make it $6,000." When I gave Dennis the number, he said, "Is this not a little high?" I said, "No, no, no. That is the going price for a professional job." He said, "Take off $1,000, and you have a job."

Dennis has been in the 1987 movie *Batteries Not Included*, produced by Spielberg, and in 1989 was in the movie *The Dream Team* with Michael Keaton, Christopher Lloyd, Peter Boyle, and Lorraine Bracco. They needed some carpentry work done, and I called Dave Sirois. Dennis said, "Please don't tell him we are actors," and I didn't. When

Dave got there, he pointed his finger at Dennis and said, "Hey, were you in *The Dream Team*?"

We started doing work for Dennis and Deborah, who married in 1982. They were starring in a show called *Sight Unseen* with actress Laura Linney. They both won Obie Awards for their performances. The couple found out I was engaged to get married and gave me a pair of tickets to see the show. The show was good, and Teresa and I headed home because I had painting work the next day for Dennis and Deborah. Dennis came out and said, "Where were you?" I said, "In the seats the ticket numbers had." He said, "What I mean is when you are given tickets by an actor, you go out to dinner with them afterward. We would have treated you two." I said, "Thanks so much. I was not aware of this tradition. I was never part of drama before."

TOM (ARNOLD) SHOW: Dennis had a role on the TV show *The Jackie Thomas Show* with Tom Arnold in 1992 on ABC. Tom Arnold then got a show with CBS called *Tom* for the 1993 season. It was July, and I was painting an outside window. It had a screen and was open, and the phone rang. Dennis picked up and said, "Uh-huh, uh-huh. I will take it." He said, "Jim, you are the first to know. I have been hired by Tom Arnold to star in his next show called *Tom*." I said congratulations. A few weeks later, we were sitting in the back at the picnic table, and I said, "So, Dennis, if you don't mind me asking, what do you get paid per episode?" He said, "I will tell you, Jim. I will get $50,000 per episode, and I am guaranteed payment for five shows even if it gets canceled." I watched the first episode the next fall, and it was terrible. They canceled it after the first show. I think Dennis got a quarter million for five weeks of work and couldn't throw Steve and I a $1,000 bone to help pay for our graduate school bills. Maybe I was in the wrong business.

CREDITS: They divorced in 2002. Deborah Hedwall had an acting studio for twenty-five years as a coach. She starred in *You Don't Know Jack* on HBO with Al Pacino about Jack Kevorkian. She had roles in *The West Wing, Law & Order*, and *The Big C*. She played the mother in the Emmy Award–winning series *I'll Fly Away* with Regina Taylor. Dennis has been in *Crocodile Dundee II, The Bourne Legacy, Money Monster,* and Oliver Stone's *W* as Paul Wolfowitz. He has been on the shows *ER, Law & Order, The West Wing, Shameless,* and *Better Call Saul.*

MCGRUFF THE CRIME DOG PAINTING: Steve moved to Ohio in mid-July with his wife and knew Parson Painting was made up of Ed and myself. Ed lived with the Kyles, who lived on River Road in Piermont, New York, by the Tappan Zee Bridge. Piermont Avenue in Nyack and River Road were the same road with different names. Jack Kyle was the creator and voice of McGruff the Crime Dog. I have graduated from ATS, and I was about to become a pastor in NYC. We painted, and then we drank some beers and watched this stupid show on MTV called *Beavis and Butt-Head*. They were both airheaded teenagers. One loved fire and said, "Fire, fire, fire!" excitedly, and the other liked to use the word "Cornholio." It made us laugh.

Ed invited me over for dinner with pasta and spaghetti sauce. He said, "The more times you cook spaghetti sauce, the better it gets!" I took a bite, and it was so acidic that I could not taste it. I said, "Ed, this is so acidic that you could pour this in a car battery that was dead, and it would be a new battery!"

KERRIGAN VS. HARDING: On January 6, 1994, Nancy Kerrigan was attacked by a metal-baton-wielding assailant as she left her practice in Detroit. The assault accomplice caved in and confessed to the FBI that it was the idea of Harding's ex-husband to get Kerrigan out of the way. The attack on Kerrigan's knee was not as bad as the crush of tabloid media coverage in the next few weeks. Kerrigan recovered to enter the 1994 Olympics, and the media called the competition the second battle of Wounded Knee. Kerrigan headed into the finals and lost by the slimmest of margins to Oksana Baiul of the Ukraine in a 5–4 split by the judges.

1994 WINTER OLYMPICS: Tommy Moe and Diann Roffe (alpine skiing), Cathy Turner (short track speed skating), and Dan Jansen and Bonnie Blair (speed skating) got golds. It was silver for Nancy Kerrigan (figure skating).

GETTING WINDOWS REPLACED: A friend of mine hired a contractor to put in new windows in her home. After he finished, she called him back to fix up two to three of the windows she was not happy with. He came over to fix them up. Two days later, she opened up the paper, and there was a picture of a murderer the police caught, and it was the guy who replaced her windows.

Whenever Dad got a phone call from a window replacement company, he would say, "Guess what I do for a living? I replace windows! Please take my name off your list." They always did.

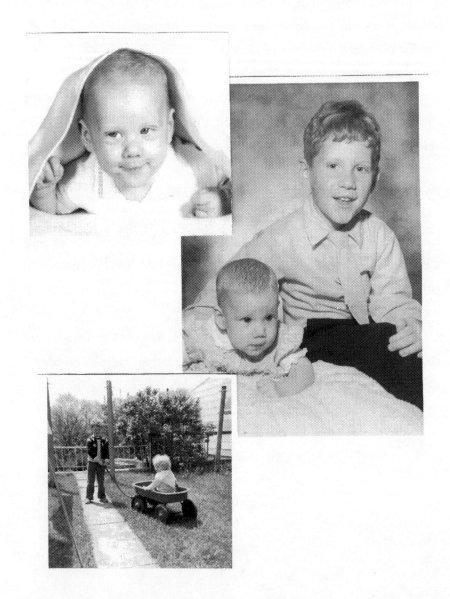

a) Jim 3 ½ months 1966 b) Jim 4 yrs. – Jody 3 ½ months 1970 c) Jim
    5- Jody 1 ½ 1971

Captions: a) 2nd Grade Class (73) b) Alton Park Football Team pic (75)

1980

1980-81

a) Hamilton Park Baseball Team (80), b) Golfing (1976-age10) c) Raub J.H. Baseball (81)

a) 12-28-81 – First deer – Clinton County Pa w Dad b) missed deer
(98) Capt. Chas cuts shirt tail

Captions: a) Family Pic (1986) Ginny (39), Bill (39), Jim (20), Jody (16).

Captions: a) Asbury Unite Methodist Church Allentown Pa
Confirmation Class (1981 – 15)

Captions: a) Union Terrace Basketball Team pic (81), b) Fishing Kettle
  Creek – Dad- 1998

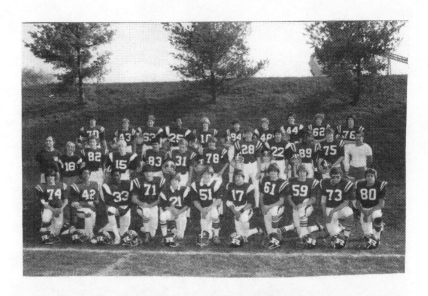

Captions: a) Raub Junior High Football & Baseball Teams (1980-81).

Captions: a) Tall Pines Camp (Clinton County Pa) Feb. 1992. b) burned down March 92, c) New Tall Pines Camp

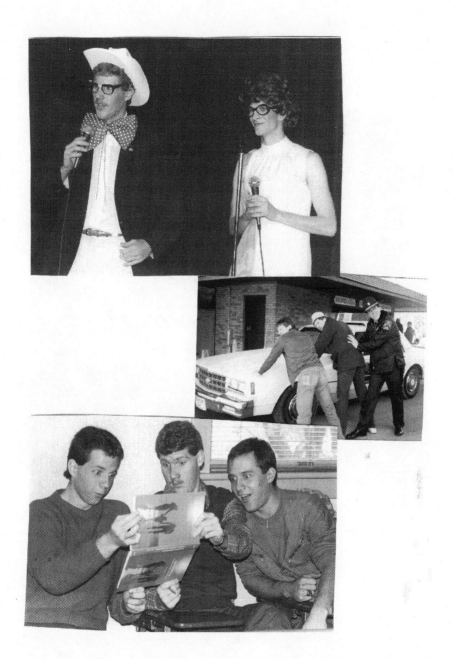

Caption: a) Church buddies Karen & brother Elliott, Nyack Spring Break 1986 in Allentown Pa – Room-mate Doug, myself, Dave, Fred-bud, Jon after Thrift Store spree, c) Greek Finals –Doug, Jim, Fred.

Caption: a) Jim & Dwayne K. Spring Fling M.C. @ Nyack College, b) Dennis & Jim with Cleveland OH Officer during Nyack College Missions Review Spring Break (88). c) Doug, Jim & Dan in Family Class.

Caption: a) Fred & Edith (Law) Geist (paternal grandparents) b) James & Virgina (Rippel) Short (maternal G.P.s)

Caption: a) Geist Siblings (1976) [back] Bill, Fred, Dale, Norm, Lee [m] Arlene, Adele, Carol, Earl, [front] Nana Geist b) 1989 Annual Geist Christmas Party Reunion

Caption: a) Uncle Bill gets the kiddies to sing Jingle Bells for Santa (89),
b) Bill, Dale, Fred, Adele, Carol, Arlene

Caption: a) Cousin Jason, Uncle Bob (Mom's brother), Aunt Davina Short, b) FDR Club, Uncle Tom, Jim, CarlLa, Mom & Dad.

Caption: a) Mandy – English Setter, b) Chesca – Border Collie –Lab mix: smart, great temperament, funny, c) Nephew Jordan, d) Niece Madison

Caption: a) Jim & Jody at Renaissance Fair in Tuxedo NY (90) b) Seminary Gradation (93) c) Dad, myself, Mom, Jody, d) Mary Grace (age 79) my Landlady – free rent

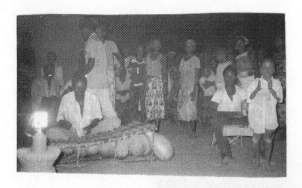

Caption: a) Nyack College London Winterum (87) Tea with Janine, Valerie & Mitch, b) Stonehedge, c) Painting Summers (91), d) Painting buddies Dan & Jaime (2008?) in Hewitt NJ.

Caption: a) Alliance Youth Corp – Mali West Africa (1987) a) Music,
   b) African Shuffle, c) Dancing with the Tuaregs –or Berbers-of
   Arab Descent.

Caption: a, b, c: Dogan Cliffs in Mali

Caption: c) Welcomed back at JFK by Dave (bowl on head), Robin (drum) and Jon. Robin went to Burkina Faso and Jon went to Mali the year before me.

Caption: a) Fishing the Kettle River – Chas, Bart, Brandon Bruce & Dad, b) Dad's Turkey c) Dad's Illinois Buck was ½ a point away from a World Record (2003).

Caption: a) Donnie, Howard H. & Uncle Dale in Weatherly Pa (1990), b) Hang Glider- Hyner Mountain (93) c) Helicopter coming in to re-fuel to kill Gypsy Moths @ Fish Dam in Pa (93).

Caption: a) Jim Buck Hunting in NY in after ice storm (2002), b) Tornado aftermath, c) Work Camp (2002) [f] Bruce, Chas, John Sr., Johnny Jr. [b] ???, Jimmy, myself

Caption: a) Buck Camp- 1998: [f] John Sr., John Jr., John S., Ed, [m] Chas, [b] ???, Jimmy, Fred, Bill Geist. b) Buck Camp Dinner (yr 1997?) [l] John G., Godfather Joe, me, Soley Brothers, [m] Chas, [r] John S. ???, Jimmy, Jim.

Captions: Homes painted by Jim, Steve H. & Edward N. in Nyack
    NY 1994

Caption: Baldwin NY (Long Island) Youth Group a) Christmas (89), b) Apple Picking (89) c) Hockey Tournament @ Sunshine Acres in Ellenville NY (1990)

Caption: When Youth Groups attack Youth Pastors with Cheese Wiz & Cream Whip (90).

Caption: a) Berkeley U in Ca. Famous Gate, b) Red Wood in Yosemite, c) Hate Man in Berkeley, d) Mike & Jim sitting at Yosemite Park (Ca. -1990).

Caption: a. 1996 Colorado Springs, b) Red Rocks in Boulder Co., CMA symbol @ CMA Headquarters – Christ the Savior, Sanctifier, Healer & King (1996), d) Grand Canyon (1990).

Caption: a. Riding donkeys in the Grand Canyon, b) Mom getting her
LPN license at graduation – 1983? - Northampton Pa, c) Riding
on Killington Mountain Vermont d) Camping up in Lake George
NY & in Vermont (1994).

Caption: a) Small water plane in Alaska (92), b) Dog Sledding in Minnesota (95), Vermont (94).

Caption: a) Hudson River Valley Rockland County (91), b) Mary Grace's Kitty Vi (Violet), c) Sister Jody serving the Volleyball for Nyack College (1991).

Bear Mt. Bridge

West Point NY

Uncle Lee & Aunt Barb
visit Jim in Nyack NY;
July 1992.

Part of the fallen
Berlin Wall.

Caption: Visiting West Point with Uncle Lee & Aunt Barb from
Phoenix (July 1992).

Caption: a) New Life Fellowship @ the Elks Lodge on Queens Blvd in Elmhurst NY b) NLF Team to do missions work in the Philippines, c) Retreat @ Sunshine Acres – Ellenville

Caption: a) John F., Judy & George Reitz (CMA NYC Metro Ministry) -2001, b) Dr. John M. Perkins (94) in my Long Island City Queens apt., c) 1999 Trip to Germany, Austria, France, Check Rep. w Joy.

Caption: a) Judy & "Gumby," or Pete in 2003 New Hampshire, b) Pete Baldwin Long Island (1990), c) Dad, Mom, myself & Jody (1992) d) Mike, Jon, Dad, Edward & myself in center (92).

Caption: New Life Fellowship Retreat @ Sunshine Acres in Ellenville NY with N.W. Queens District (1998).

Caption: a) Bull McCabe's Bar (49 St. & 9th Ave. Hells Kitchen) with Park West UFT brothers & sisters - 2004 b) NYC Councilman Miguel Martinez before being arrested for fraud in 2009 c) Jim teaching @ Park West High School - 2006

Caption: a) Where D.R. is, b) Hanging with the P.W. H.S. crew at Druids Bar (50th St. & 10th Ave.) 2001 c) Halloween Party @ my apt @ 34-09 41 St. #3C in Long Island City. -2,000

Caption: a) Protesting @ MLK "I have a Dream Speech" 30th Year Anniversary against NAFTA (1993) b) Having a teach about Disney Sweatshops @ the Disney Store in Forest Hills Queens (1997). c) Mark Torres and I handing out info in front of Starbucks about GMO products in Astoria Queens (approximately1998). Mr. Torres is now a labor lawyer.

Caption: a) Rally in front of the Egyptian Consulate in NYC with the Interfaith Alliance for Christian Human Rights with the American Coptic Union from Jersey City NJ. c) Persecuted Christian Concern started by Brother Stuart Willet of Jamaica Queens picked up the ball on the persecution of Christian issues with Maria Sliwa as I was burning out in 1999-2,000 and trying to salvage my marriage. Common issue among human rights folks.

Caption: a) Curtis Sliwa, founder of the Guardian Angels, brother of
Maria Sliwa speaking at one of our rallies in front of the United
Nations against the persecution of Christians in Communist and
Islamic fundamentalist countries. b) myself with Francis Bok,
escaped slave, and author of <u>Escape from Slavery.</u>

Caption: Candidate Sign – 2006

Caption: Turkeys in Back Yard - 2013

Caption: 7-2-12 16' Albino Burmese Python

Caption: 7-5-12 10' Caramel Burmese Python

Caption: 99% Rally NYC Oct. 2011 (2)

Caption: 99% Sign in Zucotti Park

Caption: 99% Zucotti Park NYC Ground 0.

Caption: 2012 TEACHER OF THE YEAR

Caption: Alien Wife Loves U.S. - Green Card please!

Caption: Aunt Sandy helps Helen land in Lunker. -2015

Caption: Bear in Back Yard -2011

Caption: Biking in Wildwood NJ 2015

Caption: Bill's Honey 2015

Caption: Candidate Sign – 2006

Caption: Council Candidate 2006

Caption: Donahue & Jim 4-10

Caption: Easton Pa - Jody & Jim

Caption: Easton Pa

Caption: Halloween 2015 (2)

Caption: Halloween 2015 (2)

Caption: Hanging in the Hammock 2015

Caption: Helen - Covered Bridge

Caption: Helen's B-Day - June 27th

Caption: Jan. 11, 2016

Caption: March 1st - Jody & March 2nd, - Jim – 2013

Caption: Mike & Jim 2015

Caption: Neigbor #1 Kenny

Caption: Pastor Geist & Pastor Pete Scazzero of NLF – 1998

Caption: Pat Battles NBC News July 2012

Caption: Uncle Earl Geist - 3rd from the left with cigarette in hand circa 2-23-45, the day Mount Suribachi was taken by the Marines in the Battle of Iwo Jima in WWII. The first two pictures were of six Marines famous Flag raising, memorialized in Washington D.C. statue honoring the Marine Corps. Uncle Earl is in the third picture with 17 other Marines taken by A.P. Photagrapher Joe Rosenthal, who won a Pulitzer Prize for the historic pictures.

Caption: a) Jim at 3 ½ months (1966) b) Jim (9) & Jody (5) -1975, c) Nyack Graduation 1988 – Doug, Dave, Jon, me. d) Bull's eye shooting with the Muzzle Loader – 1992

Caption: Pastor Jim Geist with the Riverside Church in NYC behind him - 1998

AGES 30-35 1996-2,000

Part III: There Are No Absolute Answers

Pastor, Advocacy, Teaching, 9/11 Experience

CHAPTER 8

Pastor at New Life Fellowship in NYC 1993–1996 (30–32)

U.S. History 1990s

1990:   Hubble Space Telescope

-World Wide Web and CDs became more popular than cassettes

-Nelson Mandela released from prison

1991:   August coup - USSR disbanded

1991:   Gulf War (Kuwait)

1992:   **Bill Clinton** elected president (over Herbert Bush and Ross Perot)

-U.S. basketball team won Olympic gold

1993:   Oslo Peace Accord (Israel-Palestine)

1994:   Genocide in Rwanda

-Nelson Mandela elected president of S. Africa; apartheid ended

1996:   President Clinton reelected (defeated Bush and Ross Perot)

1997:   Dolly the sheep cloned; Princess Dianna died in a car crash

1998:   Kosovo War and the Good Friday Agreement - N. Ireland
and England

1999:   Columbine gun shooting (thirteen killed)

-thirty-one school shooting incidents up to 2012 Sandy
Hook incident

Inventions of the 1990s

1990:   World Wide Web (http)

1991:   The digital answering machine

1992:   The smart pill

1993:   Pentium processor

1994:   HIV protease inhibitor

1995:   Java computer language, DVDs (digital video discs)

1996:   Web TV

1997:   Gas-powered fuel cell

1998:   Viagra boner pill

1999:   Flash drives, Tekno Bubbles

Cars of the 1990s

Ford Focus, Ford Fusion, Ford Taurus, Olds Aurora, Dodge Viper,
Dodge Caravan, Chevy Impala SS, Chevy Silverado trucks, Hummer
H1, Saab 900, Jaguar XJ6, Toyota Camry, Lexus LS 400, Honda
Accord

Music of the 1990s

Tom Petty: "Free Fallin'"	Black Crowes: "Hard to Handle"
Faith No More: "Epic"	Aerosmith: "Janie's Got a Gun"
Tesla: "Signs"	Midnight Oil: "Blue Sky Mine"
Madonna: "Vogue"	Vanilla Ice: "Ice Ice Baby"
	Comedy: "Andrew Dice Clay"

1991

Metallica: "Enter the Sandman"	Nirvana: "Smells like Teen Spirit"
Chris Isaak: "Wicked Games"	R.E.M: "Losing My Religion"
Red Hot Chili Peppers: "Giving It Away"	Black Crowes: "She Talks to Angels"
Jesus Jones: "Right Here, Right Now"	Aldo Nova: "Monkey on Your Back"
Marc Cohn: "Walking Memphis"	C&C Factory: "Gonna Make You Sweat"
EMF: "Unbelievable"	Extreme: "More Than Words"

1992

Eric Clapton: "Tears in My Eyes"	R.E.M.: "Drive"
Sir Mix-a-Lot: "Baby Got Back"	Vanessa Williams: "Save the Best for Last
U2: "One, Even Better Than the Real Thing"	Comedy: Janeane Garofalo

1993

Stone Temple Pilots: "Plush"

Radiohead: "Creep"

Pearl Jam: "Daughter"

Boy George: "The Crying Game"

10,000 Maniacs: "These Are the Days"

Cranberries: "Dreams"

UB40: "Can't Help Falling in Love"

Mariah Carey: "Can't Help Falling in Love"

Comedy: Tracey Ullman

1994

Collective Soul: "Shine"

Smashing Pumpkins: "Landslide"

Sheryl Crow: "All I Wanna Do"

Peter Frampton: "Day in the Sun"

Celine Dion: "The Power of Love"

Comedy: Margaret Cho

Comedy: Carl Reiner and Mel Brooks

1995

Goo Goo Dolls: "Name"

TLC: "Creep"

Seal: "Kiss of a Rose"

Comedy: Sarah Silverman

1996

Counting Crows: "A Long December"

Alice in Chains: "Heaven Beside You"

Soundgarden: "Blow Up the Outside World"

Sublime: "Santeria"

Los Del Rio: "Macarena"

Toni Braxton: "Unbreak My Heart"

Comedy: Ellen DeGeneres

1997

Third Eye Blind: "Semi-Charmed Life"

Bush: "Cold Contagious"

Wallflowers: "The Difference "

Hanson: "MMMBop"

Comedy: Al Franken, Brian Regan, Bill Hicks

1998

Godsmack: "Serenity"

Everclear: "Father of Mine"

Marilyn Mason: "The Dope Show"

Barenaked Ladies: "One Week"

Will Smith: "Get Jiggy with It"

1999

Santana: "Smooth"

Foo Fighters: "Learn to Fly"

Creed: "Higher"

Comedy: Chris Rock and Mitch Hedberg

Television Shows of the 1990s

Ally McBeal (1997–2002)	*Beavis and Butt-Head* (1993–1997)
MTV's *Behind the Music* (1997–2006)	*Sex and the City* (1998–2004)

South Park 1997–present)

Talk Soup (1991–2002)

Touched by an Angel (1994–2003)

Twin Peaks (1990–1991)

The X-Files (1993–2002)

In Living Color (1990–1994)

Larry Sanders Show (1992–1998)

The Crocodile Hunter (1997–2004)

The Drew Carey Show (1995–2004)

The Conan O'Brien Show (1993–2009)

The Louie Show (1996)

Mad TV (1995–2009)

Martin (1992–1997)

The Nanny (1993–1999)

SpongeBob SquarePants (1999–present)

That '70's Show (1998–2006)

Fresh Prince (1990–1996)

Who Wants to Be a Millionaire? (1999–2014)

Home Improvement (1991–1999)

Judge Judy (1996–present)

Chicago Hope (1994–2000)

Dennis Miller Live (1994–2002)

ER (1994–2009)

Law & Order (199–2010)

Mad About You (1992–1999)

The Man Show (1999–2004)

The Martin Short Show (1994–1995)

NYPD Blue (1993–2005)

Movies of the 1990s

24-1990:   (ATS) *Dances with Wolves, Goodfellas, Awakenings, My Left Foot*

25-1991:   (ATS) *The Silence of the Lambs, Regarding Henry, Soap Dish, Last of the Mohicans*

Movies of the 1990s

26-1992:   (ATS) *A League of Their Own, A River Runs Through It, Malcolm X, Hoffa*

27-1993:   (Ca, Az., ATS) *Dazed and Confused, Schindler's List, Jurassic Park, The Fugitive, Fire in the Sky*

28-1994:   (NLF) *The Shawshank Redemption, Pulp Fiction, Forrest Gump, The Lion King, Ace Ventura: Pet Detective*

29-1995:   (NLF) *Se7en, Braveheart, Toy Story, Apollo 13, The American President*

30-1996:   (NLF) *Independence Day, Fargo, Kingpin*

31-1997:   (AASG-painting) *Starship Troopers, Men in Black, Good Will Hunting*

32-1998:   (AASG-painting) *Big Lebowski, Saving Private Ryan, Patch Adams, Rushmore*

33-1999:   (PWHS) *Fight Club, The Matrix, American Beauty, The Green Mile*

Board Games of the 1990s

Nintendo handheld video games   Mario Brothers

Candies of the 1990s

Jolly Ranchers	Laffy Taffy	Skittles
M&M Crispy	Red Hots	Starbursts

I WILL SERVE YOU BUT NOT IN NYC: They say you should never tell God what not to do. I ended up taking on a ministry in NYC. If it were up to me, I would have been happy taking on a small CMA church of seventy-five people somewhere in Pennsylvania; but I was married, and my wife, Teresa, had the bug to move to a big city. I had taken a class called church in the modern world, and I read the book *Urban Christian* by Ray Bakke, whom I had heard speak at Urbana back in 1983. He talked about if Jesus calls us fishers of men, then we need to go where the fish are. The other benefit is people from all over the world come to cities and know the culture and language of their own people and then send Americans abroad to preach the gospel.

1993 - NEW LIFE FELLOWSHIP CHURCH QUEENS: The church was started by Pastor Pete Scarrero and his wife, Geri. He graduated from college and worked with InterVarsity, a Christian ministry to college students at Rutgers University. He then went to Princeton Theological Seminary and Gordon-Conwell Theological Seminary. In 1984, he married and then went to Costa Rica for a year to learn Spanish. In 1987, they started New Life Fellowship in Corona, Queens. You can read about the church today at www. NewLifeFellowship.org.

ELMHURST, NY: This is the most ethnically diverse area in the United States. I love that our church consisted of Asians, Africans, African Americans, Caribbean Americans, Latinos, and Anglos. The church is a place of different genders, generations, and ethnicities. Through this area runs the number 7 "elevated" train that will take you to Shea Stadium or to the U.S. Open Tennis Tournament. In 1999, Atlanta Braves pitcher, John Rocker, said, "Riding the #7 train to Shea is depressing because it is like riding through Beirut next to some kid with purple hair next to some queer with AIDS next to someone who just got out of jail next to a 20 year old Mom with four kids." In 2012, Rocker said, "I still hate NY and New Yorkers." Ha.

1988 - COMING TO AMERICA: It was the summer of 1988, and I went to the theater to take in the movie *Coming to America* starring Eddie Murphy and Arsenio Hall. It is about an African prince moving to Queens, NY, to find his queen wife. In the movie, he works at Mac Donald's, a rip-off restaurant of McDonald's franchise. Where it is filmed is really in the Wendy's restaurant on Queens Boulevard across the Elks Lodge that New Life Fellowship now owns and worships out of. When I was watching the movie, I realized this, and it reminded me of all the great memories I have had working with the Queens Gospel Team, praying with Dave Jennings and the others whom God would plant a church in the heart of Queens.

I identify with the prince character in the movie. The world is my oyster. I have been recruited from the Alliance Theological Seminary by the Rev. Pete Scazzero of New Life Fellowship. I will get the chance to work at a church with buddy David Jennings and my wife, Teresa, and be part of a cell group church and one of the cutting-edge churches in the Christian and Missionary Alliance. I will be in an urban center working with all types of people, using all the education I have accrued from Nyack College, the Alliance Seminary, and my experience as a student government president, my experience teaching at Simpson Church and the Korean church at St. Paul's in Nyack that paid me $300 a month to teach, and my experience with the Queens Gospel Team and as a youth pastor at the UM Church in Baldwin, NY.

What will life in ministry be like?

What will life in NYC be like?

I am ready, willing, and able to serve. Bring it on, God!

Sometimes you have to live in a cave like David did before you are prepared to lead. Sometimes you need to have some spears thrown at you to learn leadership lessons. To be a leader God wants you to be, you will go to the schooling of brokenness and sometimes have to live in a cave. If I only knew what I was really asking for.

CELL GROUP CHURCH: New Life Fellowship is a cell group church based on the Jethro model in Exodus 18:13–27. The district pastor takes care of 250–500, the zone pastor takes care of 25–75, and the cell servant takes care of 6–16. The purpose is to make sure all get pastoral care. The cell groups (Bible studies really) are to be the place of learning and where "real church" is supposed to happen, and when everyone meets on Sunday, it is when the whole body gets together to worship.

SUMMARY OF MY EXPERIENCE: For me, I believe I will still be in the ministry had I gone to a small church in Pennsylvania. I had four years of college, an internship, and three years of seminary training; and I wanted to teach. New Life was not a traditional church, and Sunday school was not a big part of their system, and I really wanted to teach. I started working at New Life in September of 1996 with nine other interns. I had to raise $10,000 in support to work there. Grandpa Short said it was the silliest thing he ever heard. The long story short is many people ended up getting burned out at New Life, lay leadership and professional leadership. I was frustrated I was not able to teach as much as I would like. They finally allowed me to start teaching Sunday school classes. I ended up teaching a new beginners' class, a baptism class, a course on spiritual gifts, and the book of Acts and led a Passover celebration at my home.

MENTOR A FILIPINO: I also worked with Mike Ortiz, a parishioner who wanted to become a Sunday school teacher. Mike is a Filipino, but thanks to the Spanish colonization via Ferdinand Magellan, mixing with the Filipino people, many have Spanish surnames now. Mike used to say "Filipinos must have rice every day. Otherwise, they begin to shrink away." Thanks to the Spanish spreading their seed all around the world, we have many beautiful-looking brown people. In my first few years, I ended up working as an usher in the church instead of teaching Sunday school. I worked with an old-timer from the Bronx, and in time, we figured out he had been stealing money from the plate for a long time.

LEADER WITH VISION: Pastor Pete was a leader who was charismatic and was often casting "vision" for individuals or the church. We had weekly staff meetings, and I would take notes. After two months, I had about thirty things written down God wanted us to do, and I asked which top 5 we should focus on. It was a struggle for me to work in a place where I made my own schedule. Sometimes I could have a morning free or an afternoon free or an evening free if I was not leading a cell group. I guess teaching worked better for me because I had set hours and had a clearer job description than pastoring. For me, God speaks to me in a still, quiet voice from within; and dealing with the Pentecostal types was frustrating because they had words every week, so the ministry focus was changing all the time. About halfway in the internship, I took my list of fifty to seventy-five "words from God" and said, "Which three should I be focusing on?"

Our staff took a retreat in 1995; and in the midst of our quiet time, prayer time, and confessional time, Pastor Scazzero said, "I am so ashamed of our past." I am very proud of Pastor Pedro for getting counseling, learning how to love himself, and for learning to let go more in regard to the direction of the church. He, in brutal honesty, chronicles his struggles, the lessons he had learned, and how dealing with his past and keeping current with his emotions is an important role in keeping his life healthy. His books and conferences will help promote much healing for many by dealing with family of origin issues and working through the necessary pain and emotions involved instead of running from them by keeping busy doing Kingdom work. I was doing this on an unconscious level; but when I hit my own wall, I too was forced to enter the cave, the very thing I feared the most.

THE EMOTIONALLY HEALTHY CHURCH: Pastor Pete wrote a book in 2003 entitled *The Emotionally Healthy Church*. The importance of this book is, I believe, about how the evangelical church for the most part has ignored the emotions God has given us. What is the purpose of emotions, what do they tell us, and what is the proper response to live a life of emotional health? What if you do not feel your feelings? What if you cannot identify them? I will say this: for me, I was not able to identify my feelings for forty-two years. For me, it took getting into the twelve-step program Codependents Anonymous to be able to identify my feelings, and to be able to sit with them without feeling uncomfortable, and to be able to process them. This program saved my life. I had connection with God but not with myself. I will talk more about it later in my recovery section.

EMOTIONALLY HEALTHY SPIRITUALITY: In 2006, Pastor Pete wrote a book called *Emotionally Healthy Spirituality*. On pages 70–74, he talks about Fr. Richard Rohr's work on the *true self* vs. the false self. The book talks about how God feels feelings, especially feelings of sadness frequently. It talks about how Jesus is not selfless; He does not lose Himself in His relationship with others. While Jesus is not selfless, He also is not selfish. Jesus knows who He is, and He knows who He is not. I would not be able to feel my feelings, have the boundaries I have today, have the power to say no without guilt, and have the ability to sit with myself and enjoy my own company if it were not for the twelve-step program Codependents Anonymous.

PATRON OF THE CHURCH - FORMER JCPENNEY, CEO: DON SEIBERT: One person who helped support the church financially was Donald V. Seibert, the former CEO of JCPenney. He started out as a shoe salesman in Bradford, Pennsylvania, in 1946; became the store manager in 1953; and moved to NYC as the director of planning and research in 1963 to a vice president in 1967. In 1974, he was elected chairman of the company at a time when the country was in a recession. In 1982, he called for a realignment of merchandise that focused on apparel and soft home furnishings. He was a passionate believer in teamwork and was a jazz musician, and when he died in August of 2000, memorial gifts were requested to be sent to the New Life Community Development Association. He was a good man, and I had the chance to speak with him about my concern about the use of sweatshops and child labor being used to make apparel for the American economy. I figured he had some influence over JCPenney even though he was retired, but he was tepid about meeting with the National Labor Committee or speaking out on the issue of sweatshop and child labor.

CORONA, QUEENS - LOUIS ARMSTRONG AND MALCOLM X: Our church offices used to be in Corona, Queens, by the number 7 train just half a mile from Shea Stadium. We eventually moved the offices to Elmhurst after the church bought the Elks Lodge. One of my favorite songs is "What a Wonderful World" by Louis Armstrong, and he grew up in Corona, Queens. Malcolm X also used to live in Corona, and it was where his home was bombed out. I have much respect for Malcolm X after reading his autobiography. After going to prison, he became a reader and used his mind, humor, and preaching in Harlem as a way to fight racism in America and to help energize people to stand up for their rights. One book I enjoy is _Malcolm and Martin_ written by James Cone from Union Seminary. They both wanted to have their dignity, freedom, and political rights but approached it from different strategies.

MIKE, MONICA, AND RAMI: Teresa and I had a cell group meeting in our home on Wednesday nights. John Peck brought a person he met in Astoria named Rami. Rami is an Egyptian, and he boxed in the Olympics for Egypt. After our Bible study, Rami told us how he met a lovely couple named Mike and Monica when he was in Romania. They were Americans, and they had shared the gospel with him and then moved back to the States. Rami asked if we knew these people. I laughed and said, "No, I don't know them. There are ten million people in NYC, and I have not come across them." The following week, Rami was not there; but a couple named Mike and Monica came to our Bible study, and they shared they attended Times Square Church in Manhattan and had done some missionary work in Romania. They also told us about a boxer from Egypt they had met but lost contact with. I gave them the number of Rami, and they called him up, and they were able to reconnect again. How do people reconnect after having lived in Romania and then moved to America and, within a week, by God's grace, are able to reconnect with one another before the invention of the Internet?

NEED A CAR: My grandparents gave me a light-blue Buick when I was in the seminary. Baby Blue was on its last legs. Teresa and I were sitting at the dinner table, and we discussed what we were going to do. After we paid all our bills, we didn't have much left over, let alone now adding a monthly bill of purchasing a new car. I said, "Let's pray. God, we are in NYC to serve you. Thank you for meeting our needs. We really need a car, and we ask you provide one to us so we can use it in getting around for the ministry." The next day, Teresa got a call from one of our old classmates, Dennis. Dennis Kunzelman used to be called the Moocher because he had the reputation of borrowing stuff and then not returning it. I loaned him a copy of my cassette *Cat Stevens Greatest Hits* and never saw it again. Dennis, who works as a youth pastor in Virginia near Washington DC, said, "Amy and I just bought a new car and have a 1987 Volkswagen Gulf. It is not the cleanest car, but it runs, and for some reason, God put you and Jim on our minds." Talk about miracles, God not only put a burden on their heart for us, but we also got a free car from "the Moocher." I would say that was a good trade for an audiocassette.

KAUFMAN-ASTORIA STUDIOS: 34-09 41 ST. APT. 3C: The apartment I moved into was on the border of Astoria and Long Island City. We lived one block away from the Steinway subway stop, two blocks from the Astoria Sports Complex gym, and three blocks from the Kaufman Astoria Studios, where they filmed *Sesame Street* and *The Cosby Show* and movies, such as *Apollo 13*. The *Don Imus Radio Show* was also broadcast from there. In my third year in Queens, they began filming *The Sopranos* around the corner from me at a restaurant; and I was able to see James Gandolfini, Lorraine Bracco, and Michael Imperioli. I had not seen the show because I did not get cable until 2001, so I only recognized Lorraine Bracco from the movie *Good Fellows.*

CRACKHEAD STORIES: There was a man who came to our church and was brought by his sister. He apparently was unemployed and good at working on cars, so I asked him to do something on the car. I paid him, and it was not until a few days later that I realized my toolbox was missing. He had stolen my toolbox and sold it for crack. I did not get repaid, and I did not get my toolbox back. My other crackhead story took place at the Saint John the Divine Church in Harlem. It is a beautiful cathedral that is still under construction. I went there with Teresa and some friends to take a tour. Outside was a sweaty black man who wanted a dollar. When I asked him why, he said, "Because I am hungry." I then told him I would take him to the pizza place and buy him a slice of pizza. Then the sweaty, shaky man with a razor haircut said, "No, man, I need the money for a haircut." I said, "I can't help you."

MY NEIGHBORS CRACKHEAD GIRLFRIEND: I had a neighbor below my apartment who was an alcoholic. For the most part, he kept to himself, but Saturday evenings were always a problem. As a pastor, Sunday is a work day for me, and I need good sleep in order to be my best self. My neighbors girlfriend was a crackhead, and the arguing, and yelling and sometimes thrown pans began from 11pm until mid-night. This happened for a three to four month period when I could no longer take it.

On this particular Saturday night, she climbed out of his window and up the fire escape to my living room window and began pounding on the windows screaming, "He is going to kill me! Let me in!" I called 911 and called in burglary in progress. If you call the NYC police over a domestic squabble, it could take an hour for them to show up. If you call in burglary in progress, they show up right away. Within three minutes there are police cars with red lights flagshing and with spot lights on my apartment building, and people coming out unto the strees to see the show. Long story short, she swings at the commanding officer, and ends up going to jail for six months. All I knew after that day, was I did not see her for a long time.

One Saturday as I am about to walk up my apartment stairs, I see my neighbors girlfriend sitting on the stairs. I say hello and and she say hi back. I ask what happened to her and she tells me she spent 6 months in prison. I tell her that I am the one who called the police. I was not sure what her response would be, but she said, "Thank you for calling the police. I was so out of my mind on crack, if I had not been sent away, I would be dead right now." I hope she has been able to get clean and sober and to stay that way.

BIBLE AND *NY TIMES*: I was the highest educated usher at New Life Fellowship who felt stunted because I was not being given the opportunity to preach (maybe once a year). I wanted to be able to think and grapple with the Scripture and modern life. As Reinhold Niebuhr said, "As Christians, we should have a Bible in one hand and the *NY Times* in the other." I was leading three Bible studies (they were called cell groups) and sometimes a Sunday school class as well. Reinhold Niebuhr also wrote the "Serenity Prayer": "God grant me the serenity to accept the things I cannot change, the courage to change the things I can, and the wisdom to know the difference." Reinhold was a writer, theologian, and professor and had a brother, Richard, who did the same. Reinhold felt before anyone could be a minister. They should minister in an urban center for three to five years to gain real-life experience. I agree with him.

APRIL 24–26, 1998 - OVERSEAS MINISTRY STUDY CENTER AT YALE: I was invited to attend a discussion and study on the worldwide "Persecution of Christians: Assessment of a Worldwide Tragedy." Some of the speakers included were Paul Marshall, Steve Haas, Nina Shea, and Gary Haugen. We recessed for lunch at the Yale Divinity School. I ran into Dr. John Ellenberger from the Alliance Seminary and Dr. Tite Tienou from ATS, who is not teaching at Trinity Seminary in Deerfield, Illinois. Part of the discussions was about the impact of the senate stripping the trade sanctions clause of the Religious Persecution Bill, about why Billy Graham and the Dalai Lama did not support sanctions, and about the lobbying group called USA Engage, which corporate interests and money comes and compromises or alternatives in addressing the persecution of Christians in foreign lands.

WIFE'S FAMILY COMES TO VISIT: Dad did not want me to go to Africa to do missions work. He was afraid the family would never see me. You do go away for four-year terms, and on your sabbatical back, do have to speak to churches to help raise money for missions. I moved to NYC, but Dad hates NYC, and the only thing worse he hates is driving through NYC. In the eight years I lived there, my parents came once to visit me. I think if I went to Africa, they would have visited me more than once. Teresa's sister Wanda and her husband, Ron Walborn, who is the nephew of my former Pastor Walborn in Allentown, Pennsylvania. Ron's dad and my pastor are brothers. Ron's dad one time hired a prostitute to go into his brother's room to freak him out, and it did! The Walborns' pastor out in Redding, California, and came to visit our apartment in NYC. Before our grand NYC tour, Teresa and I threw a chili together to slow cook in the Crock-Pot while we play the tour guide's role. We took them on a tour of the city, taking the subway to midtown and to Central Park and a ride on the Staten Island Ferry and a trip to the top of the Twin Towers. We ate dinner, sat around and talked, and went to bed. Their youngest daughter, Kylie, crawled up next to me to cuddle. Ron and Wanda looked at each other and said, "We have never seen Kylie do this before. You must have a special gift."

Ron had just finished a dissertation and told us how he had all of it on his laptop and had not saved any of it on any disks. He and Wanda went food shopping one day and left the family dog in the car with his laptop and dissertation on it. When they got back to the car, the dog was missing. Someone stole the dog. Pastor Ron looked for his laptop, and there it was on the passenger seat. The thieves only wanted the dog. Had they taken the laptop as well, he would have lost all the time and energy he had spent on his dissertation.

The next morning, when the Walborn family left, I asked the kids what their favorite part of NYC was. I expected to hear the subway ride, the boat ride, or the view of the city from the towers; and all three chimed in at one time, "The chili!"

THAT SPECIAL GIFT: Kylie Walborn, when she was about two, cuddled up with me. "She does not do that with many people," I was told. When I went to visit my parents in Danielsville, their dog, Chesca, slept in the room with me. Dad said, "She only does that with you." When I went to visit a therapist, a dachshund (hot dog-looking dog) jumped on the couch and fell asleep next to my leg. The therapist said, "He never does that with other patients." I visited another therapist with a beagle. The Beagle did the same thing, and the other therapist said the same thing. Well, I have a special gift. Whatever it is, I am not sure. The Dog Whisperer, Cesar Millan, says dogs can read human emotions, so that must mean I give off trustworthy vibes most of the time.

Not all appreciated this gift, for one morning while I was lying in bed, Teresa woke up and hit me in the arm with Mike Tyson enthusiasm. "Ough! What the heck is wrong with you?" Teresa said, "I am mad at you! You were mean to me in my dream."

JODY AND KEVIN COME TO NYC: One thing I appreciate about Kevin is his ability to organize trips and make them happen. If he says I want to go to place *XYZ*, he usually does. It is more impressive to me that Jody and Kevin do this with two little kids. They came to visit Teresa Joy and I in NYC. We took the subway, went to Central Park and Astoria Sculpture Park; went for a ride on the Staten Island Ferry, and ate out. On the subway, Jordan, who must be five or six years old, stared at a pretty Dominican lady. She just smiled. I said my nephew did not get to see many pretty Latinas living in the farmlands of Pennsylvania. Jordan ran around with his hands up, making siren noises, as he loved the program *Cops*. "Bad boys, bad boys, what you gonna do when they come for you?" Madison is a screamer when she cries; she is loud! We watched *SpongeBob SquarePants*, and it is an entertaining off-beat and funny cartoon.

MY TRUTH ABOUT NYC (FOR ME): I have a love-hate relationship with NYC. There were many benefits in living there. I was able to make friends of all ethnicities; there was always something going on in the city whether it was a sporting event or concert, or show, or museum to visit; and transportation via subway can get you to any place at a reasonable price. I did not like the congestion, the noise, and the pollution; and I felt stifled in the ministry at New Life Fellowship. I did not feel I was able to use all my gifts and talents that I would have been able to use had I worked with a smaller church. I agree with theologian Reinhold Niebuhr's suggestion that all pastors should live in a major city for a time before moving on to another pastorate. I learned much, it was part of my journey, and I am grateful for the lessons and memories. Teresa loved living in the city; I did not. The one thing I realized that I was missing was having my own home and property to work with and to work on. This is one of the things I will love when I move to West Milford, New Jersey, in the summer of 2002.

SUMMER OF 1993 - SAN FRANCISCO, CALIFORNIA: Teresa and I went to San Francisco to witness her sister Linda marry Bob H., who is an attorney and had the opportunity to depose Rush Limbaugh on a case over cigars and wine. Some of Bob's male friends and neighbors came over and watched the movie *The Cowboys*, and we drank Dewar's top-shelf whiskey, which is like drinking liquid smoke. My favorite line in the movie is when John Wayne tells the young boys who are the "cowboys" of this particular doggie drive, "Let's get moving. The sun is a-burning!" Bob and Linda took us to a party, but they forgot to tell us it was a gay costume party. It was just like the gay party scene in the movie *Philadelphia* with Tom Hanks and Denzel Washington. It was clear I was one of the straight guys there, but all attendees were polite and welcoming to us.

The day before the wedding is an annual run called the Bay to Breakers. It is a five-mile run, and what I remember is a group of over a two dozen people with giant hats that look like salmon, and they run the opposite way of the race, and it really looks like salmon going up a stream to breed. The wedding was held at a resort in a tree grove with redwoods, and it was a fun wedding reception. Linda's father is not a dancer, but I told him, "You only get one chance to dance with a daughter at her wedding," and he was able to overcome his religious beliefs to connect in an act of love for daughter Linda.

STREETS PAVED WITH GOLD: Teresa and I have friends, Lou and Joy Riconda, who invited us over several times a year for dinner. Lou grew up near the Corona Ice King and, twice a year, went on forty-day fasts. Often, when he fasts, he cooks meals and invites people over to eat. On our way over, I was driving; and we were three blocks away when I saw a pile of something in the street, some type of garbage I think. As I passed, I screeched my breaks and said to Teresa, "That is a pile of money!" Before I can back up, a car pulled up, and two guys got out and said, "*That is our money.*" There is also a park nearby called Spaghetti Park that has a bocchi court set up and is a Mafia meeting place.

Where did the money come from? Did it fall out of a Brinks truck? It was not *Candid Camera*. Someone else claimed it. What if I had grabbed all the money and threw it in my trunk? Would my faith have had me take it to the police or put it under the bed mattress? That would have been a test of faith. In the movie *American Gangster*, when Essex county detective Richie Roberts finds over $1 million of drug money in the trunk of a car in New Jersey and turns it over, none of the cops trust him. It is the same thing that happened to Det. Frank Serpico of NYC when he refused to accept bribes from bookies and drug dealers.

JACKSON HEIGHTS HOOKER STORY: I have just finished teaching a Bible study cell group in Jackson Heights, Queens, when I noticed a woman on the corner, looking distraught. She was walking around and looking at the ground, obviously having dropped something. I pulled over and asked, "Is everything okay?" She answered, "No, I had a $5 bill, and now I can't find it. I just walked over here from the food store, and I think I dropped it." She asked if I can help her. She got in the car, and I asked her what she does for a living. She said she is a hairdresser. She was unkempt; her hair was messy, and her breath was terrible. It was clear she is a hooker. I drove her across the street to the food store, and I helped her retrace her steps. We walked over to the produce aisle, and I started thinking, *She did not lose $5. She needs $5 and is hoping I give her $5.* I prayed, asking for guidance; and right where I was looking, under the raised metal floorboard, I saw a crinkled green paper rolled up. I grabbed it, opened it, and voilà, it was a $5 bill. I said, "Ma'am, is this what you were looking for?"

LONG ISLAND CITY HOOKER STORY: I used to go to Astoria Park three to four times a week to go jogging. Teresa and I also had a permit to play tennis there. One early morning, at six thirty, I was on my way to the Astoria Park in my car; and an Asian woman was on the corner. My window was down, and she walked over and asked where I was going. I told her, and she said, "I live there. May I have a ride?" I said sure, and she said, "I really appreciate the ride." I said, "You are welcome," and then she said, "I would be willing to do anything to thank you." I thought, *Hmmm, I am not sure what she means by this.* Then she made a sexual remark, and I said, "Miss, I am going to take you near Astoria Park, and that is it." She then said, "Make a left here." I pulled the car over and said, "I am not a taxi service. I am dropping you off here. You will close the door and then say thanks for giving me a ride for over a mile to my place." She slammed the door and said, "F—— you!" When I got to the church office for our weekly meeting, I told them how I picked up a hooker by mistake. One of the pastors said, "You are lucky she did not scratch your face and start yelling rape. Your picture would have been on the front page of the *NY Daily News* and *NY Post*." Wow, that was a close one. This is what can happen when you try to "help someone."

1993 - MARY GRACE PASSES: I got word Mary, my former landlady, had passed. She was more grandmotherly to me than just a landlady. After Mary died, Dan said my wife and I could have any piece of furniture in the house as a show of appreciation. We chose the Chippendale wooden secretary to take to Queens with us. The day we took it home and began to get it organized with our papers and records, I put the radio on; and the song by Jimmy Hendrix, "The Wind Cries Mary," was playing. Mary also had a famous picture from the Depression. Only a hundred copies have been made called Migrant Mother or Mother of Seven taken by famous Depression Era photographer Dorothea Lange, which I was also interested in, but the dresser won out.

MARY'S MEMORIAL SERVICE: I attended Mary's Grace's memorial service in the Piermont Community Center on the Hudson River. My wife, Teresa, was with me. No other room mates were there—Monica, or Robin, or Ed—but I was there. People were given the chance to share, and I got up and shared. I broke down crying because Mary was like a grandmother to me. Her son, Danny Menaker, wrote for *The New Yorker* magazine; and with his hands in a clapping position moved them together, signaling to shorten what I was saying. I finished it up to respect his wishes.

I was distraught, and Teresa and I stopped by the Nyack Park on the Hudson River and sat on a park bench under a tree about 3:00 p.m., looking at the Tappan Zee Bridge. We both cried and cried and cried. When we got our composure, we started to drive back to Queens. As we got on the Tappan Zee Bridge, I put on the radio, and the song "The Wind Cries Mary" by Jimmy Hendrix was playing, and I started crying again.

BOOK: <u>MY MISTAKE</u>: Daniel Menaker, son of Mary and writer for *The New Yorker* magazine, wrote about the memorial service in his

2013 book *My Mistake*, page 147–148. He did not use my real name; he used the name Greg. When I read what he wrote about my share at the memorial, I was saddened and angered. I sent Dan a two-page e-mail, reminding him of all the things I did for her was out of love. He thanked me for my e-mail and promised to add a sentence to his paperback coming out in 2014. The sentence he added was "Later I recall how generous he was with his time and attention Greg (Jim) had been with my mother, not only because of doctrine, but also because of love." He is a man of his word; he did add a line. Had Mary's memorial service been today, I would have shortened it. As to my crying during the share, I am not responsible for others feeling uncomfortable with making my sadness a visible thing.

1993 - PHILLIES LOSE THE WORLD SERIES TO THE TORONTO BLUE JAYS: John Kruk said the Phillies were "24 morons and one Mormon." The team was referred to as shaggy, unkempt, and dirty. They ended the season with a 97–65 record and defeated the Atlanta Braves to win the National Pennant. The team was made up of Darren Dalton C, John Kruk 1B, Mickey Morandini 2B, Kevin Stocker SS, Dave Hollins 3B, Milt Thompson LF, Lenny "Nails" Dystra CF, and Jim Eisenreich RF. The pitchers were Curt Shilling, Tommy Green, Terry Mulholland, and Mitch "Wild Thing" Green.

6-1-93 - THE O. J. SIMPSON CRIMINAL TRIAL: It began on June 13, 1994, and ended on October 3, 1995. Most blacks said he was innocent; most whites said he was guilty. The jury declared him innocent. In the civil trial, he was found guilty and was to pay thirty-three million in compensation. ESPN did a five-part series in 2016 called *Made in America* about Simpson's life. There were two of Simpson's closest friends, A. C. Cowling and Ron Shipp, a black LAPD officer, who said Simpson killed Nicole Simpson and Ronald Goldman. Even after the trial, he still had the celebrity "O. J." effect on the general public and kept his celebrity status with his charm. In 2008, he was charged with armed robbery and kidnapping where he tried to recover supposedly personal items a collector was selling in Las Vegas. He got a thirty-three-year sentence. It was reported Simpson had accepted a gay lifestyle in prison.

In 2015, Dr. Bennent Omalu, the doctor who discovered CTE (chronic traumatic encephalopathy), believed O. J. Simpson suffered from chronic traumatic encephalopathy based on Simpson's irrationality, his impulsivity, his sexual improprieties, his violent tendencies, and his domestic violence history. Omalu estimated 90 percent of all NFL players have CTE, a disease that can only be diagnosed after death.

NLF RETREATS: To recreate means to recreate, to take time to get refreshed, and to make new. I organized a few retreats to Sunshine Acres in Ellenville, NY; and it was always good to get away from the city, to the woods, and to play games and take time for study, prayer, and sharing. On one retreat, November 4, 1995, I became sad to the point of tears when I heard about the assassination of Israeli leader Yitzhak Rabin. He won a Nobel Peace Prize for negotiations with Palestinian leader Yasser Arafat. Even with Israel willing to give 90 percent of what Arafat wanted, he would not accept it. This is the best chance, I think, the Palestinians had to getting the best deal they ever could have gotten from the Israeli government.

It snowed that weekend, and we played football and floor hockey and made a snowman and had a snowball fight. I always find God showing up in a strong way at retreats.

QUEENS JOURNAL ENTRIES

January 10, 1995: On January 7, my wife and I watched *Shadowlands*, a movie about C. S. Lewis losing his wife to cancer. In the movie,

Lewis said, "The boy chooses safety, the man chooses pain," and "We read to know we are not alone." The movie closes with him saying, " In the end, the pain and suffering becomes part of our joy and happiness, that's the deal."

February 8, 1995: Why do I feel so unhappy? It makes me feel guilty I do not feel happy when I have connection with the Almighty God. Should not my connectedness be enough?

March 12, 1995: Dietrich Bonhoffer said, "Christ bids us to follow him and die." (*No cheap grace*). Bonhoeffer left Germany pre-WWII, attended Union Seminary in NYC, and attended Abyssinian Church in Harlem and learned about racism and justice. He left NYC to go back to Germany to denounce the Nazi movement. He was hanged by the Nazis on the day before WWII ended.

April 15, 1995: Henry Nouwen said, "Christ calls us to downward mobility. To love people in the name of Jesus is not relevant in the world's eyes."

May 22, 1995: M. Scott Peck said, "Life is difficult . . . Discipline helps us live life . . . True Spirituality is caring about the spiritual development of others."

June 10, 1995: Eugene Peterson said, "Stay where you are: This is St. Benedicts Vow of stability. Jonah wanted to go to Tarshis, (a far off and idealized port city) but every congregation is a congregation of sinners. Jonah was a prophet that did not pray. Prayer shapes our vocations, we lose our grip on job descriptions and ease ourselves into God's work."

June 25, 1995: In *Disappointment with God*, Philip Yancey said in chapter 26, "Is God Silent?" "There is no neat formula . . . There is no better way to love God than by experiencing fidelity faith." This is having faith when we are not hearing his voice.

George McDonald wrote, "Everything difficult in life indicates something more than our theory of life, yet embraces it."

VACATIONS

1990: Arizona: Phoenix, Grand Canyon

1990: California: San Francisco, Berkley, Yosemite (Centennial)

6-92: Alaska

7-93: Europe: Germany, France, Austria, Check Republic

4-94: San Antonio (Alamo) and Austin, Texas - LBJ Library

1994: Lake George, NY; Lake Bomoseen, Vermont

3-95: Lake Schroon, Adirondacks, NY; Duluth, Minnesota (dogsledding)

1996: Denver and Colorado Springs

4-97: Washington DC

1998: Lake George, Upstate NY

1999: Newfoundland (famous UFO sighting - Canadian Navy)

4-01: Grand Bahamas

11-02: New Jersey Shore: Cape May Grand Hotel

07-10: Boston, Massachusetts

07-13: Cape May, New Jersey

12-15: Washington DC

1994 - VERMONT: Teresa Joy and I drove up to Vermont in a small car loaded down from NYC with camping equipment. We first camped near Lake George after a day of fishing and swimming in the lake. In the evening, we stopped by the library to hear a musician named Susan Trump. She plays the guitar, banjo, and the mountain dulcimer and is an instructor at the Appalachian State University. She sang "Give Yourself to Love," "Coat of Many Colors" (Dolly Parton),

"Old Lovers," "One Day at a Time" (Willie Nelson), "The First Time I Saw your Face," and "Tree of Life." I was so moved by her music I bought her CD *Tree of Life*. I recommended it to all as SusanTrump. com. The favorite of Teresa Joy and I was "Ole Jack," the song of their family donkey that worked the fields. "He did not look like much, but he was a friend to me!"

WHITEHALL, NY: BIRTH OF U.S. NAVY AND FAMOUS BIGFOOT SIGHTING: On the border of Vermont is Whitehall, NY. It has a sign, saying, "Birthplace of the U.S. Navy," and it has the picture of Bigfoot holding a golf flagpole on the Skene Valley Golfing Club. Unfortunately, smart phones with Internet had not yet been marketed to citizens, so I was left wondering about the navy and Bigfoot in Whitehall, NY.

1975 - BIGFOOT NEAR GOLF COURSE: Cliff Sparks, owner of the golf course at the Skene Valley Country Club in Whitehall, NY, saw a tall, hairy, manlike creature with big red eyes bigger than himself on the golf course. He observed it quietly and then saw it quickly crash through the woods. "Some people think I am crazy. They were not there. I saw it!"

BEN AND JERRY'S ICE CREAMERY: In Vermont, after we stopped by Ben & Jerry's for some Cherry Garcia, I noticed a nice smell wafting into the car as we drove through the farmland of Vermont; and it smelled like Kentucky Fried Chicken. I pulled over, and the trunk was so loaded down. The rubber bumper was setting on the blistering hot tailpipe, giving off the smell of the colonel's famous cooking. Yum! We were on our way up to see Gumby on Lake Bomoseen.

As we were driving around the lake, the sun was setting. I said, "I need to do some fishing. This is the best time!" Teresa said, "Watch out for the bats. They can get caught in your hair." I gave her a look like "Are you kidding me?" As soon as I threw out my first cast, I hooked a nice bass. Just before my second cast, a bat flew down and bounced off the top of my hatless head. "Okay, we're done fishing for now." We met with Gumby, and he made a nice crab dinner and played his guitar, and we went fishing the next day on his buddies' pontoon boat and hooked into a bunch of lunkers. It was the vacation I needed from NYC.

SUMMER OF 1995 - LAKE SWAN TRIP IN ADIRONDACKS: Teresa and I decided to take a trip in Upstate NY with Julie and Rob Davis. Julie's maiden name is Hall, and Teresa used to live with Julie, Danielle Neiswanger, Laurel Jarrett, and Sherry Laing, who became Sherry Jarrett when she married Laurel's brother. They lived in a home in West Nyack by the Clarkstown Reformed Church on 107 Strawtown Road and behind the playing fields of the Clarkstown High School. It was in a secluded area and had woods behind them and the church. One of the girls bought a husky dog, and I built a doghouse for it. The dog was always getting away.

Julie and Rob live in Pinecliff Lake in West Milford, NJ, and we drove from Queens to visit them. *I love the area they live in.* I made a mental point to myself that if I was to continue working in NYC, this was the area I would not mind moving to. Rob works for WMCA radio, the Christian station in the NYC metropolitan area. Rob and Julie attend the Brooklyn Gospel Tabernacle, and both are in the world-famous choir. Rob and Julie have never been camping and wanted to go on a trip with Teresa Joy and I. We decided to go up to the Adirondacks for the Fourth of July weekend but ended up missing our exit to our campground and drove 218 miles to exit 27 of the NY Thruway in the Adirondacks.

On our drive up to go camping, we talked about church, Nyack College, the Alliance Seminary, New Life Fellowship, the Brooklyn Tabernacle Church, and a book that came out in 1992 called *Four Views on Hell* by four authors with differing views. Dr. William Crockett, my former professor, is one of the authors. One author takes a literal view, another a metaphorical position, and another the annihilation of the souls of the wicked.

As we pulled up to a campground, it said, "Word of Life" Campground on Lake Schroon. We laughed because one author of the book was from the Word of Life Institute and believed hell was literal fire with all the suffering included. Rob and I walked into register, and the host behind the desk asked if we are married to the ladies. We said yes. Then he asked if we were saved, and I said, "I am a pastor in NYC, and this guy is in the Brooklyn Tabernacle Choir and works for a Christian radio station." The host looked at me with all seriousness and said, "That does not get you into heaven." Well, he was right in a literal sense.

It had been a long, hot drive; but the camp pool closed at 5:00 p.m. on Saturday, so no swimming for us. We found a very pretty spot to set up our tent next to a pond with a nice mountain view in the background. During dinner, I said, "Look, there is a forest fire over there!" It must be at least ten miles away, but I was a bit nervous that night, afraid if the winds picked up, we could be in the midst of a forest fire. I told Rob, Julie, and Teresa, "If that fire spreads, we all go out into the pond to keep safe." It was ironic we were at a fundamentalist camp that believed hell was a place of literal fire, and our campground could be destroyed by literal fire.

The next day, we drove out of the campground and fond a public area to go swimming in Lake Schroon. Now I am a pale guy, and Teresa is half Irish and half Canadian, and Rob and Julie are pretty pale as well. We sunbathed, and I urged Rob and Julie to use our suntanning lotion. They said, "No, it's not too sunny out." I asked them one more time, and they said, "We are okay!" After four hours, they were red. We went home for our last night at Camp Fundamentalist World. In the middle of the night, my spouse and I were frisky. The other couple was on the other side of the ten-person tent and out of it. My wife and I did the horizontal mambo without waking them up and laughed and laughed that we pulled it off. On the way home the next day, Rob and Julie were red as cooked lobsters; and every time I hit a bump when driving, they made an "ow" noise that told me they were in pain. Hey, I practically begged them to put on sunscreen. I also told them before we got back to West Milford to drop them off my wife and I made whoopee in the tent while they were sleeping. They both said, "Ewwwww!"

WINTER OF 1996 - DOGSLEDDING: Teresa and I went to Grand Marais, Minnesota, to go dogsledding. Teresa had gotten to know John and Kathy Patten through the Africa Inland Mission in Pearl River, NY. He completed the All Alaska Sweepstakes dog race (400 miles) in 1983. He is the founder of the John Beargrease dog race in Minnesota in 1980, the longest dog race in the lower forty-eight states. John won the John Beargrease dog race in 1984 (400 miles) along the shore of Lake Superior. He also placed eighteenth in the Iditarod (1,158 miles), the Super Bowl of dog racing, in 1988, winning $2,400. In 1994, John was hired by Walt Disney to act as a consultant for the dogsledding scenes in the movie *Iron Will*. He was even in the movie, for they used him as a stuntman in one of the wipeout scenes.

He also was part of goodwill trip to Russia with a dogsledding trip in 1990, right after the Mikhail Gorbachev and his Perestroika Party pushed for glasnost (openness in government). I wish John would write an article about his trip. On the trip, he was asked to eat with a group of people, and it was whale blubber or who knows what, and it made John sick. During the trip, a moose attacked and killed one of his dogs. There was a whiteout, and he and his guide got separated. At night, his sled team almost got run over by a huge plow. He was lost, and he saw some lights. He and the dogs headed to the lights. It turned out to be a military base, and they suspected John was a spy, and they imprisoned him. His goodwill trip turned out to be a nightmare. There was more, but this was all I can remember. I did write it up and send it to *Guidepost* magazine with John's contact information. They wrote back and said it was an incredible story, but they did not believe it. They could have verified it if they wanted the story. Oh well.

The John Beargrease race is a qualifier to get into the Ididarod race. Its racers must travel through the rugged Sawtooth Mountains of the North Shore of Minnesota. John Beargrease was an Anishinabe Indian born in 1858. His family survived by hunting, fishing, and trapping. John and his brothers picked up the job of delivering mail between Two Harbors and Grand Marais. They made the trip weekly using canoes, horses, and large boats. In the winter, he used a dogsled. The year 1899 is the last year he delivered mail. The route he traveled became a road and was traveled now by horse and buggy. He last trip to Grand Marais was on April 26, 1899.

The huskies that pull the sleds weigh between 40–45 pounds and are friendly and full of high energy and ambition. During the Iditarod, the dogs run 125 miles a day and are checked out by veterinarians at every stop on the ten-day trip. The trip can sometimes last two weeks; and about one-third of the dogs (1,500 dogs) are flown home because they are sick, injured, or exhausted, and at least one-third of the dogs die on the trip.

On the day we went sledding, John set up sled for himself, Teresa, and myself. For himself and Teresa, he had eight dogs; for me, he set up ten dogs. He told us, "Don't worry about steering. I will be the front person. The other sled dogs will follow behind me." There was a rope with a snow anchor on it. It looked like a giant double letter *C*, and as soon as you pulled the anchor out, the dogs were off. Before the ride, they pulled every ten to fifteen seconds to see if the anchor was free, and the dogs were all barking like crazy.

We all got on the sleds, and John said, "Let's go!" He was in front, Teresa Joy was second, and I was behind both of them. As soon as we took off, there was a path through the woods we went to. It immediately got quieter. The dogs stopped barking, and I can hear the swish of the sled blades flying across the snow. There was a nice breeze blowing in our faces. The dogs were happy. When they were thirsty, they took bites out of the snow as they ran along. It was funny to hear the dogs farting, and when they had to evacuate or urinate, they just went when they were running. I didn't know what John fed the dogs, but the dog farts were pretty bad. At the beginning of the trip, we went down a hill approximately six hundred feet long or the length of two football fields. At the bottom of the hill, we had to make a right-hand turn with the sleds. John stuck his right foot out as he leaned his sled to the left and cleared the turn, and Teresa almost fell over but with her athleticism was able to use her balance to stay up. I, being the biggest guy, ended up going straight and flying in the air toward the tree line as I watched my sled of dogs chasing after Teresa.

John stopped his dogs and put his anchor in the ground, laughing up a storm. My jacket was full of snow as I took a dive in it. He stopped my sled, and I got back on, and we started again. During the trip, Teresa fell but hung unto the handlebar with her feet being dragged. She pulled herself up like an Olympian gymnast on the parallel bars. At another point, John stopped us to check on his one dog. He said, "She is not running right." He checked her and said, "Oh, you are pregnant. Okay, lady, you get to sit in the sled basket the rest of the trip." And she did and seemed to enjoy the other dogs pulling her along.

We sled through the woods, and we went over a frozen lake, and to be sledding in a vast open space was surreal. I am so happy to have the opportunity to be dogsledding with a guy who is an expert musher, has won the John Beargrease race and finished eighteenth in the Iditarod, and is a movie consultant. I am being blessed as a result of Teresa acting as a guide for them when they took a missions trip to Kenya, Africa, with AIM. This will always be in my top 10 trips in my lifetime. Thank you, John and Kathy Patten for such a memorable trip. Apparently, they have moved from Grand Marais, Minnesota, and now live in Anchorage, Alaska, where he serves as a men's pastor at Cornerstone Church, a full Pentecostal church.

1999 - NOVA SCOTIA, CANADA (SHAG HARBOR UFO STORY): Teresa and I went up to Nova Scotia with Jim Carlese and Dianne Thomas from New Life Fellowship Church. We went golfing, riding our bikes, eating, and playing some board games on a rainy day. On the day we went for a bike ride, we stopped by a place; and it had a sign, saying, "Sight of the Famous UFO Encounter," but it had no explanation as to what happened. I thought, *I wish I knew the story on this*. A few years later, when I watched a program about UFOs, I learned about the famous Shag Harbor sighting in Nova Scotia.

On October 4, 1967, at 11:20 p.m., eleven people saw a low-flying lit object making a whistling noise and hen a whoosh and a bang as it hit the water. The object was then seen floating approximately eight hundred to one thousand feet away. Observers called the police, saying they believed an airliner had crashed into the harbor and the Rescue Coordination Center in Halifax. Constable Pounds said the object was sixty feet long. The object began to sink. Within a half hour, fishing boats showed up to look for survivors; but no survivors, bodies, or debris were found. After one hour, a Canadian Coast Guard and rescue cutter searched the harbor. Constable O'Brien and Cpl. Victor Werbieki said they saw a yellow object moving on the water and left a yellowish foam that also was confirmed by sailors on the Coast Guard Cutter.

It was turned over to the Royal Canadian Air Force, which investigates UFO sightings. The final report said no object was found, but new information surfaced in 1993. Several in the military went off the record for fear of losing their pensions but told this story. There were two of the divers in Granby who said the object was spotted on sonar and moved for twenty-five miles to a place called Government Point. A few days later, a second UFO joined the first underwater. The belief was to render aid to the craft. After a week, the navy was told to "investigate a possible Russian submarine," and the two objects broke the surface of the water and flew into the skies. There was little doubt something of unknown origins crashed into Shag Harbor.

CHAPTER 9

Minister of Peace and Justice at NLF 1997–1998 (31–32)

8-28-93 - THIRTIETH ANNIVERSARY MARCH ON WASHINGTON FOR JOBS AND FREEDOM: As a seminary student, I wanted to take a bus trip to the DC Trip to honor the work of Dr. Martin Luther King for civil rights, jobs, and freedoms. I have much respect for the man despite his infidelities as recorded by Hoover's FBI. I believe what got MLK killed was not this civil rights work but his speaking out against the Vietnam War and for starting to organize the Poor People's Campaign. It was not just blacks who had a monopoly on poverty but also people of all colors—white, brown, black, and yellow—and children. I am sure the chamber of commerce, which Uncle Tom says is just another kind of union, did not like the idea of children and the poor having a lobbying group in Washington DC, for it tends to cut down on corporate welfare when corporate welfare has to be shared with actual people in poverty. The military industrial complex and the 1 percent who profit from the defense industry also would not like the threat of having to have their budget reduced. The poor can have help in getting a boost, to get living wage jobs, or to be able to start their own businesses to help other people.

In 1963, Dr. Martin Luther King gave his famous "I Have a Dream" speech on August 27, 1963, to civil rights, labor, and religious organizations. It was estimated 250,000 people showed up for the march and helped pass the Civil Rights Act of 1964. On the day I went, I would guess 100 to 150,000 were there on this 104-degree day. They had sprinklers set up for the marchers to walk through. I was wearing a sign "Keep the Dream Alive and No to NAFTA" to show my support for union blue-collar workers. It was the United Automobile Workers union that funded MLK and the civil rights movement. President Clinton, Hillary, and Chelsea were on vacation at Martha's Vineyard; but he sent word from a taped broadcast to keep the dream alive. Unfortunately, Clinton the Democrat was pushing for NAFTA.

I protested NAFTA or the North American Free Trade Agreement. Clinton signed NAFTA on December 8, 1993, and it became law on January 1, 1994. Presidential candidate Ross Perot predicted if it passed, "Americans will hear a sucking sound of American jobs fleeing to Mexico."

RESULTS OF NAFTA: Between 2001 and 2011, 2.7 million jobs were lost or displaced with the closing of 60,000 manufacturing facilities. GE, Chrysler, and Caterpillar fired U.S. workers and moved to Mexico. NAFTA destroyed American auto and parts manufacturing jobs and entire regions in the United States. It drove down wages and eroded the tax base. Despite gains in American productivity, 2012 wages dropped to 1979 levels. It had not increased Mexican wages, most still made 30 percent of what American workers made. Real wages in Mexico had fallen significantly below pre-NAFTA levels, dislocating millions of Mexican workers, doubling the numbers of those who fled into the United States as undocumented workers flooding the U.S. labor market. For the United States, it created a 2.5 billion deficit with Mexico and a 29.1 billion deficit with Canada. The U.S. agricultural deficit with Mexico was 800 million. The food imported into the United States did not meet our safety standards. There were 53 percent of Americans who believed NAFTA should leave or renegotiate NAFTA; only 15 percent believed we should continue to be a member. Congressman Bernie Sanders of Vermont voted no to HR3450, which passed the House by 234–200. NAFTA was used in the justification of taking from "We the People" and giving to "A Few People," a power grab by the investing class. 1) NAFTA needs to be repealed. 2) Rewrite NAFTA to give ordinary citizens rights and labor protections at least equal to the current privileges of corporate investors.

1996 SUMMER OLYMPICS (GOLD): Michael Johnson (running), Carl Lewis (long jump), men's basketball team, women's basketball team, Kerri Strug, Shannon Miller, Dominique Dawes, Jaycie Phelps, Amanda Borden, Amy Chow and Dominique Moceanu (women's combined gymnastics), women's softball team, synchronized swimming, Amy Van Dyke (swimming), Andre Agassi and Lindsay Davenport (singles tennis), and Gigi Fernandez and Mary Joe Fernandez (doubles tennis)

Pres. Bill Clinton (1993–2000)

Domestic

Presided over the longest peacetime economic expansion	Passed welfare reform
Twenty-two million jobs created	**Lowest unemployment in thirty years**

Connected 95 percent of schools to the Internet

Lowest crime in twenty-two years

1994 Omnibus Crime Bill

1993 Brady Bill (five-day waiting period for gun)

Paid of 360 billion of the national debt

Lowest government spending in thirty years

Impeached on perjury charges

Most diverse cabinet in history

*Hired one hundred thousand more police

State Children's Health Insurance Program

Fought for universal health care (GOP-no!)

Converted largest deficit to largest surplus

Lowest tax burden for middle class in thirty-five years

Foreign

Signed NAFTA

Deactivated more than 1,700 nuclear warheads in former Soviet Union

Operation Storm against the Serbs for two weeks plus NATO's air campaign

Dayton Accords: Holbrooke worked out framework and was signed in Paris

*He did not respond to genocide in Rwanda or in Sudan.

GOP PREDICTIONS ON CLINTON TAX RAISE ON THE 1 PERCENT: In 1993, President Clinton wanted to raise taxes on the top 1 percent from 35 percent to 39.6 percent.

"This will lead to a recession." —Newt Gingrich (Georgia)

"Raising taxes will put people out of work." —Sen. Phil Gramm (Texas)

"This plan will not work. If it was to work than I'd have to become a Democrat and believe in more taxes and bigger government." —Rep. John Kasich (Ohio)

It led to one of the greatest times in U.S.history of economic growth, and led to a 5 trillion dollar surplus for the next incoming president.

1995 - CCDA CONVENTION - DENVER, COLORADO: CCDA stands for the Christian Community Development Association. It pushes the three *R*'s: 1) relocation, 2) reconciliation, and 3) redistribution. In other words, we can't just meet the spiritual needs of people without addressing their physical needs as well. Dr. John M. Perkins is one of my favorite people, and the convention offered all kinds of presentations to attendees in addition to the plenary sessions. One lady who made an impression on me was Dr. Lorraine Monroe. It was here I also had the chance to meet Ms. Alexie Torres of the Youth Ministries for Peace and Justice in the Bronx. *Sojourners* magazine had written about her activism in the Bronx, and she would go on to serve on the White House Advisory Council on Faith-Based and Neighborhood Partnerships.

PRINCIPAL DR. LORRAINE MONROE: She is the founder of the Frederick Douglas Academy in Harlem, NY. I had seen *60 Minutes* do a piece on her, and she was all about education and tough love. What I remember her saying as a principal was "My mantra is I love you, but I will kill you." She has written a book *Nothing's Impossible* (1999), saying, "The most worthy of work is that which changes lives profoundly—in mind, body, and spirit." At the end of each chapter, she has quotes on things like attitude, perseverance, competence and idealism, high expectations, and leadership.

FEBRUARY 1999 - JOHN M. PERKINS: He was the one who wrote *With Justice For All* about growing up in Jackson Mississippi, and how his brother was killed at age seventeen by the sheriff's department. As a pastor, John was involved in the civil rights struggle in Mississippi, probably the most racist state in the union. John, as a pastor, had been imprisoned by the sheriff's office and beaten so badly; one-third of his stomach had to be removed. His book talks about how to bring about racial and economic justice by churches by using the three *R*'s: relocation, reconciliation, and redistribution. For those who are interested, you can go to Christian Community Development Association website at www. ccda.org.

FEBRUARY 1999 - BLIZZARD: Dr. Perkins came and spoke at my church in Queens several times and, in February of 1999, was to stay at my apartment for one night but ended up staying for three days, thanks to the blizzard of 1999. It was an honor and privilege for me to be able to pick his brain, ask questions from his books, and listen to him share stories with me. A song called "The John Perkins Blues," which has a good tune and has a video as well, was written by the group Switchfoot in 2010 to honor the life of Dr. Perkins. Seattle Pacific University has the John M. Perkins Center that trains people for leadership and for community development.

I was looking out the window, and a guy was walking down the street and hit an icy spot. He started sliding and spun around with arms flying and managed to keep his balance. It was really impressive he did not fall on his bum. He looked around to check if anyone saw him. He thought, *No one saw me. I can keep my dignity.* But I saw him, and he never knew it. Lol.

JANUARY 1996 - CMA CHALLENGED ON WHITENESS: I sent a letter to Dr. David Rambo, president of the Christian and Missionary Alliance, and Harold Mangham, VP of Church Ministries, to inform them about the Christian Community Development Association and challenge the CMA in regard to making more of an effort on racial reconciliation. At the next annual CMA convention, a committee is set up to look into this. In hindsight, the CMA, for the most part, is a rural demonization with a scattering of churches in major cities. I also believe that different cultures have different styles of worship. Dr. Martin Luther King said, "The most segregated hours in America are on Sunday morning when we worship." I do not have an answer, except to respect people, allow for equal energy among all, and speak up for the poor and oppressed as Jesus did. If you look at the CMA overseas, we are very culturally diverse with the intention of turning over church leadership to the locals, and that is a good and righteous thing.

2-21-96 - PROMISE KEEPERS EVENT IN ATLANTA FOR PASTORS: Promise Keepers is a growing national movement started in 1990 by Coach Bill McCartney, football coach at Colorado State. His concern was about men abdicating responsibilities and using churches to encourage them to follow the seven promises of the movement. It calls for following Christ, biblical principles, being a good husband, and reaching out beyond racial and denominational barriers. Many of the leaders from New Life Fellowship in Queens flew to Atlanta to join the forty thousand others in worship. My concern about this group is its ties to James Dobson of Focus on the Family and its connections to the political right. While it is not supposed to be a political group, every movement has political consequences.

While we were in Atlanta, a guy walked up to me with an empty gas can and said, "I am around the block and ran out of gas. I forgot my wallet. Can you loan me $5 to $10?" I laughed and told the guy I am from NYC. The scammer looked at me, knowing I was unto him, and laughed to scam his next mark.

1987 - WALL STREET MOVIE: The ruthless hedge fund manager Gordon Gekko said to Bud Foxx, a blue-collar kid whose dad works on airplanes at Blue Star Airlines, "The richest one percent of this country owns half our country's wealth, $5 trillion. One third from hard work, two thirds from inheritance, interest on interest and stocks and real estate speculation. You have 90% of the American public with little or no net worth. I create nothing; I own. We make the rules pal. The news, war, peace, famine, upheaval, the price of a paper clip. We pick the rabbit out of the hat while everyone else wonders how we did it. You are not naive enough to think we live in a democracy, are you buddy?"

AMERICA, WHAT WENT WRONG?: The book _America, What Went Wrong_ by Barlett and Steele back in 1981 talks about the dismantling of the middle class 1) Tax policies made the top 4% as wealthy as the bottom half of American workers (ix). In 1981, there were 20.2 million factory jobs; and by 1991, 1.8 million manufacturing jobs went overseas. Between 2000 and 2015, we lost another 5 million manufacturing jobs, over a million, because of NAFTA. In the 1980's Americans making 20,000–50,000, their wages went up 4 percent a year; those making 200,000 to 1 million went up 69 percent a year; and those making over 1 million went up 218 percent. Why? Reagan was the president from 1980 to 1988; and it was done with deregulation of laws, busting unions, 1,800 plants moving to Mexico, shifting the tax burden from the rich to the working classes, and the lobbying of the chamber of commerce, corporations to Congress.

WINNER-TAKE-ALL POLITICS: The book _Winner-Take-All Politics_ by Hacker and Pierson (2010) is about how our economy has drifted from a mixed-economy cluster to a capitalist oligarchy through deregulation and tax policies favoring the rich. From 1983 to 2004, only 10 percent of all wealth gains went to the bottom 80 percent. Democracy is supposed to be good at responding to the problems of the vast majorities, but this has not been the case since 1980. 1) The Government is doing less to reduce inequality through taxes, but is passing laws to benefit the very top of the income ladder. 2) Government also has the power to affect distribution of market income with laws governing unions, the minimum wage, regulations on corporate governance rules, rules for financial markets (45). *Public policy really matters!*

TAX RATES ON THE RICH: The *Wall Street Journal* likes to say the rich pay "larger share" of income taxes, but that does not mean they are paying higher rates. Tax rates on the rich have fallen dramatically. Taxes on the rich have stayed the same for the most part since 1970 (49). During the Great Depression, 35 percent of Americans said should redistribute wealth by heavy taxes on the rich. In 1998, that went up to 45 percent; and by 2007, it was up to 56 percent. The biggest barrier to changing tax rates to a more fair, progressive tax is changes in the senate filibuster. Insisting on sixty votes to cut off debate has allowed relatively small minorities to block action on issue of concern to the large majorities (53).

CEO PAY: In 1965, CEOs made twenty-four times what a worker made. In 2007, CEOs made three hundred times what their workers made. American CEOs, averaging twelve million a year, are making twice as much in average as other rich nations (62–63).

JULY 17, 1996 - FLIGHT TWA 800 CRASH: On July 17, 1996, TWA Flight 800 took off from JFK headed to Paris. Just twelve minutes later, it exploded over the shores of Long Island, killing 230 on board. The government spent four years and millions of dollars to investigate. The FBI interviewed 755 witnesses; 258 claimed to have seen a streak, rocket, or missile; and of the 258, 100 saw it go from Earth to the plane. One said it looked like an upside-down Nike swoosh logo that followed the plane before hitting a wing. Another said it "zigzagged" until it made an arch motion, hitting the plane. The National Transportation Board found probable cause to be a spark in the center fuel tank. Many thought it was either a bomb on the plane or a shoulder-mounted, surface-to-air missile. The U.S. Navy was doing wartime exercises in the area, and some believed it was a wartime exercise gone awry. Popular mechanics said there were too many people watching radar that night for a warship and missile to not be reported.

TERRORIST-RELATED EVENTS AROUND THE CRASH OF TWA 800: America was on a high state of alert with the following events happening:

1. 12-21-88: Pan Am Flight 103 exploded over Scotland; a Libyan was found guilty in 2000
2. 2-26-93: Twin tower bombing
3. 4-19-95: Alfred Murrah Building bombing in Oklahoma City
4. 4-29-96: Yosef went to trial for the twin tower bombing
5. 6-25-96: Nineteen U.S. soldiers killed by truck bomb near Eastern Saudi Arabia
6. 7-17-96: TWA Flight 800 exploded (at least 258 saw streak shoot up to plane)
7. 7-27-96: Olympic Games bombing in Atlanta, killing one and injuring over one hundred

ACTIVISM OF JAMES GEIST, MINISTER OF PEACE AND JUSTICE AT NLF: I had made the decision I no longer wanted to be a parish pastor, but I felt a prophetic calling to speak out on justice issues. The church elders at New Life Fellowship gave me the title "pastor of peace and justice," and, thus, backing to get involved in speaking out against child labor, sweatshops, persecution of Christians in Islamic and Communist countries, and genocide in Sudan and modern-day slavery.

I am grateful for Pastor Pete Scazzero's support in this. I was not paid to do this, but I was given authority to minister in the church's name.

9-13-96 - CALL TO RENEWAL IN WASHINGTON DC: Rev. Jim Wallis of the Sojourners Community held a national forum on faith and politics, a politics transcending the left and right and speaking out on behalf of the poor in the United States. At this meeting, Sen. Bill Bradley addressed the audience on "rebuilding a civil society."

9-17-96 - CALL TO RENEWAL IN HARLEM, NY (ST. MARK'S CURCH): Rev. Jim Wallis and Rev. Dr. Calvin Butts spoke after I recruited him to speak with us. I got the chance to speak about the campaign for the Haitian Disney workers. It was a good evening, and when I went home on that rainy night, there was no one on the subway train I was on, except for one fellow who was white. A few weeks later when I organized a demo at the Disney Store on Fifth Avenue and on the trip home on the packed subway, I looked around and saw a guy who looked familiar to me. It was the same guy who was on the train after my message at St. Mark's Church in Harlem.

7/25–28/96 - CROSSROADS CONFERENCE ON FAITH AND PUBLIC POLICY -EVANGELICALS FOR SOCIAL ACTION: I attended a conference at Eastern College in St. Davids, Pennsylvania, on a progressive response to global warming, welfare, immigration, community policing, health care, income inequality, human rights, and interest group politics and how to respond to the Christina coalition. I got to hear Ron Sider, author of _Christians in an Age of Hunger_; Rev. Dean Trulear; Rev. Eugene Rivers; Dwight Ozard; and Tony Campolo.

BOOKS THAT HAVE INFLUENCE ON ME: _Books That Changed the World_ by Robert Downs says books have had an immense power for good and evil in the course of human history because ideas in print can have tremendous power on human development. Every movement begins as an idea. The influential books and authors are The Bible, *The Odyssey* by Homer, Plato and Aristotle, poetry, Hippocrates, Fathers of the Church, Copernicus, Machiavelli, Newton, Adam Smith, Marry Wollstonecraft, Malthus, Harriet Beecher Stowe, Darwin, Marx, Mahan, Freud, Hitler, Rachel Carson, and so forth.

> The Bible by many humans inspired by God
> *Tuesdays with Morrie* by Mitch Albom
> *Malcolm X Speaks* by George Breitman
> *The Essential Gandhi* edited by Louis Fischer
> *Romero: A Life* by James Brockman (Orbis-Maryknoll)
> *Martin & Malcolm & America* by James Cone (Orbis)
> *Dorothy Day: Friend of the Forgotten* by Deborah Kent
> *A Theology of Liberation* by Gustavo Gutierrez (Orbis)
> *In Her Own Words* by Mother Teresa
> *The Road Less Traveled* by M. Scott Peck
> *In the Name of Jesus* by Henri Nouwen
> *New Seeds of Contemplation* by Thomas Merton
> *Breathing Underwater* by Fr. Richard Rohr
> *The Soul of Politics* by Jim Wallis
> *The Power of Mythology* by Joseph Campbell
> *Affluenza* by De Graff, Wann, and Naylor
> *Imperial America* by Gore Vidal
> *Rich Christians in an Age of Hunger* by Ron Sider
> *With Justice for All* by John M. Perkins
> *Learning About Theology from the Third World* by William Dyrness
> *Contemporary American Theologies* by Deane William Ferm
> *Bring Forth Justice* by Waldron Scott

THREE KINGS: David of the Old Testament was the young son of a shepherd. When the king visited his family, the king announced David will be king one day. King Saul became jealous of David's youth and tried to break his spirit. David ignored the poor treatment and refused to return it. In fact, when Saul threw a spear at David, he duck the spear and did not throw it back. When Saul ordered David killed by his soldiers, David was forced to hide and live in caves. To get king training, one sometimes has to duck spears and live in cold, dark, and damp caves and go through to the school of brokenness. When David became king, he had a son. Absalom thought he can run the kingdom better than David. David chose to do nothing about it, and Absalom took over and ran the kingdom for four years until he was killed by David's commander in chief. David said he would have rather died than have his son killed.

You cannot tell who is the Lord's anointed. No one knows the answer by God, and He never tells (20). David the sheepherder could have grown into Saul II, except God cut away the Saul in his heart. The operation took years, was brutal, and almost killed the patient. God used the outer Saul to cut out the inner Saul of David's heart (22). David said, "Better Saul kill me than I learn his ways. I will not avenge, I will not allow hatred to grow in my heart (35). The Sauls of this world can never see David: they can only see Absalom. The Absaloms of this world can never see David: they can only see Saul" (82). David's philosophy was to do nothing. "The throne is not mine. Not to have, not to take, not to protect and not to keep" (97).

NEW YORK LABOR-RELIGION COALITION: The NY Labor Union in NYC is started by Sam Hirsh, a union organizer, and Fr. Robert Kennedy. It is also built with the help of Rev. Howard Moody of Judson Church and Prof. Bill Webber of the NY Theological Seminary. The NY Labor-Religion Coalition is a network of people of faith and faith institutions across New York uniting with community and labor allies to fight for and to win social and economic justice in New York state. Its core belief is to promote economic and social justice, and it believes faith and conscience must be linked with action. The group believes in a living wage, access to education, jobs, housing, healthcare, and a safe living environment and believes in ending disproportionate influence of corporations on the political process. Some in the labor movement understand how important and powerful an image it is to have "some collar" or "men/women of the cloth" show up at a labor rally.

Mayor Ed Koch said, "Sam Hirsh was one of the best union organizers I ever saw." Sam was part of the committee that helped organize the Robert Kennedy car ride through Brooklyn with the famous film image of RFK throwing the football with kids from the neighborhoods from his car, standing on the backseat with passengers holding on his legs so he does not fall over. I was informed Sam passed in 1998–2000. In 1998, the coalition was looking to hire a NYC director, and Sam told me it was between me and another person. Sam was rooting for me, but it was not meant to be. I loved Sam's laugh and twinkle in his eye and that he was a great union man. I am glad I got to work with him for several years in my life.

WALT DISNEY SWEATSHOPS IN HAITI: As a member of the NY Labor-Religion Coalition, I was able to meet the movers and shakers on social justice issues. It was here I met the Disney/Haiti Justice Campaign and the National Labor Committee, the group that made Kathy Lee Gifford cry over the child laborers making Kathy Lee clothing. The Disney workers in Haiti were making 28 cents an hour producing Mickey Mouse and Pocahontas pajamas. The Haitian workers were making $2.25 a day. Each worker was making a profit of $10,000 a day for Disney and helping pay Disney CEO Michael Eisner $97,600 per hour in 1993. All the workers were asking for was 58 cents an hour so they could afford rent, food, and tuition to send their children to school.

I organized a rally in Forest Hills, Queens, in August of 1996 and in front of the Disney Store in Manhattan on Fifth Ave. near Central Park and at the Disney Store in the Nanuet Mall in Rockland County, NY. In the Manhattan rally, I was joined by several who were members of the Catholic Movement. One was Carmen Trotta, and the other was Jeremy Scahill. Scahill said, "We should go in the store and do some chanting." I said, "I am not getting arrested, but I am not stopping anyone who wants to go in the store to do that." We handed all the flyers to passersby about what Walt Disney was doing in Haiti because in Haiti, Mickey Mouse really is a rat.

JEREMY SCAHILL THE CATHOLIC WORKER AND HIS WRITINGS: He was born in 1974 and raised by activist parents who are both nurses in a suburb of Milwaukee. He moved to the East Coast to work with homeless shelters and worked with the Catholic Workers in Manhattan. This was how I met him when he worked with the Catholic Workers, which was started by Dorothy Day and Peter Maurin. The Catholic Workers is committed to nonviolence, prayer, voluntary poverty, and hospitality for the homeless, exiled, hungry, and forsaken. The Catholic Workers continue to protest injustice, war, racism, and violence in all forms. Scahill was the influence of radical anti-Vietnam War priest Daniel Berrigan and Dorothy Day of the Catholic Worker she started.

After his stint with the Catholic Worker, he began working as a reporter for WBAI Radio (99.5 AM) in NYC for *Democracy Now!* with Amy Goodman. In 2000, he was a producer for a Michael Moore TV series on Bravo called *The Awful Truth*. He covered the Kosovo War in 1999 and Bagdad from 2001 to 2003 for the Iraq War and has reported from Afghanistan, Somalia, and Yemen. His first book was published in 2008 called *Blackwater: Rise of the Most Powerful Mercenary Army*, which is a *NY Times* best seller and won a Polk Award. He also wrote *Dirty Wars: The World Is a Battlefield* in 2013 about President Obama's missiles and drone strikes. In 2013, he began working with Glen Greenwald and Laura Poitras with a digital magazine called *The Intercept*. He had been interviewed by Charlie Rose and was a frequent guest on the Bill Maher Show on HBO. Good work, Jeremy Scahill!

REV. DAVID DYSON OF THE LAFAYATTE AVE. PRESBYTERIAN CHURCH IN BROOKLYN: Reverend Dyson prefers to be called Dave. He graduated from Pittsburgh Theological Seminary in 1972 and became the boycott coordinator for the United Farm Workers in California and even served as a body guard for Cesar Chavez. It was the Rev. Dr. Martin Luther King Jr. who inspired Reverend Dyson to enter ministry. His preaching colleagues who focused on sin, sin, sin were only reading half the book since Jesus talked about justice for the poor three times more than personal sin. From 1978 to 1990, he served as the director of the Union Label Department of the Amalgamated Clothing and Textile Workers Union (ACTWU). Once in the South, he had to leave a motel for threat of it being blown up for his progressive cause.

1965–1970 - THE DELANO GRAPE STRIKE AND BOYCOTT: On September 8, 1965, Filipino American grape pickers walked out on strike against Delano to protest the poor pay and working conditions. They asked **Cesar Chavez** and the National Farm Workers Association to join their strike. The mostly Latino farmworkers joined the Filipino workers, and they shared the same picket lines, strike kitchens, and union hall. The strike drew unprecedented support from other unions, churches, activists, students, Latinos, and civil rights groups.

Cesar led a three-hundred-mile march from Delano to Sacramento. He also started a hunger strike in February 1968 to rededicate the movement to nonviolence. He fasted for twenty-five days, only drinking water. He lost thirty-five pounds in twenty-five days and ended his hunger strike. MLK sent a letter of support, and Robert Kennedy attended the mass that ended the hunger strike. Chavez read about Gandhi's boycott of salt in 1930 and about Dr. King's Montgomery bus boycott in the mid-1950s. For one hundred years, the farmworkers failed to organize a union. He was able to organize the United Farm Workers because he reached out to the American people. A field strike would not be enough to convince the growers to change since they controlled all the levers of power politically in the local sphere. By convincing ordinary Americans to sacrifice by not eating grapes, they could help the poorest of the poor.

PEOPLE OF FAITH: The church he worked at was founded by abolitionists, and "Dave" started a People of Faith Network in 1995 of people who were activists against anti-sweatshop and anti-child labor. It also provided a list of activists for demonstrations against such activities. Dyson told David Gonzalez the type of work Pastor Geist had been doing was like guerrilla warfare. He was making copies of literature at night and organizing those who would oppress workers.

Dave was the first executive director of the National Labor Committee, which was run by Charlie Kernighan and Barbara Briggs, who joined in 1988. Charlie became the director in 1991. The NLC has now moved from NYC and became the Global Labor and Human Rights Institute in 2011 and is currently in Pittsburgh, Pennsylvania. The purpose of the NLC or the GLHR is to address sweatshops and child labor happening around the world. The NLC is known as the human rights group that made Kathy Lee cry.

CARlLA HORTON AND DYSON - J. P. STEVENS CAMPAIGN: In 1974, seven textile mills in North Carolina owned by the J. P. Stevens Company refused to sign a contract with the Amalgamated Clothing Workers of America. Dave and CarlLa met at Gimbels in NYC with approximately twenty-five other people who walked around the store and then took off their shirts to reveal the hidden T-shirts that said "Boycott J. P. Stevens!" Gimbels had their own police and had jail cells to lock people up until the police showed up. It was mostly men who showed up to protest, so the majority was put in a large cell room, and CarlLa was placed in a very small cell, where she began to experience major claustrophobia. Thank you, agitators, for being willing to fight for living wages, job security, and safe working conditions.

The union began a campaign from 1976 to 1980 to get J. P. Stevens to recognize the union. The national boycott was recognized by religious groups, labor unions, municipal governments, women's organizations, and many others. Activists publicized the boycott with marches and rallies and by distributing literature.

NORMA RAE: The 1979 film *Norma Rae* was released starring Sally Fields, which was loosely based on the life of Crystal Lee Sutton, a textile worker who helped organize the union at the Roanoke Rapids plants. Stevens met with the union secretly and eventually entered into a contract that included retroactive pay and seniority protection for workers and a check-off provision to allow union dues to be deducted.

The ACTWU agreed to end the boycott and corporate campaign. Crystal Lee Sutton was cut from the same mold as Mother Jones, Fannie Lou Hammer, Rosa Parks, and Delores Huerta. She lost her battle with cancer on September 11, 2009.

9-7-96 - DAVID GONZALEZ OF THE *NY TIMES: TAKING A STAND AGAINST DISNEY*: Charlie Kernighan of the National Labor Committee spoke to the NY Labor-Religion Coalition, and I met his assistant, Maggie. I told her I will work with their campaign on fighting Disney's sweatshops in Haiti. I was encouraged to reach out to Rev. Dave Dyson of the Lafayette Ave. Church in Brooklyn since he was one of the founders of the NLC and had a group called People of Faith. I got literature and some video's from the NLC and plan some demonstrations in front of Disney Stores in Manhattan; Forest Hills, Queens; and the Nanuet Mall in Rockland County.

For some reason, I was in midtown in August of 1997, and I saw Walt Disney was filming some commercial there. I took the subway to Queens, grabbed some literature, and took the subway back to Manhattan to hand out the literature to the press people. I saw Michael Eisner, the CEO of Disney, and he gave me the hairy eyeball. The press people all worked for Disney. They will not accept any of my literature. A guy with brown hair and sunglasses and looked like our family friend Skeeter Tidabock asked what I was doing. I handed him the literature and explained, and he shook my hand and said, "My name is David Gonzalez, and I write a weekly piece for the *NY Times*. Here is my card." I told him about Rev. David Dyson, and he set up a time to meet us at Dave's church in Brooklyn. The desk Dave sat behind was the desk where Abraham Lincoln signed the Emancipation Proclamation on. Gonzalez interviewed us, and he rubbed his hands together and laughed like an evil scientist knowing how much this was going to upset the Disney Corporation.

One thing I noticed after the article came out was whenever I spoke on the phone and mentioned the word "Disney" or "Nike," my phone started a slight clicking noise, meaning my calls were being recorded. I know the NYC Police kept tabs of new groups that demonstrated. Plain-clothes police recorded our events. I was followed on the train twice by the same guy from two different events, and this was pre-9/11 attacks. It could have been the NYC police, maybe Pinkerton Investigator types for Walt Disney.

Articles Generated on Disney Sweatshops in Haiti

10-4-96:   "Seminarians Hear of Plight of Sweatshop Workers" —*Rockland News*

9-7-96:   "Taking a Stand Against Disney" —*NY Times* - David Gonzalez

10-17-96:   "Protest at Disney Store" —*Forest Hills Times* - Howard Girsky

10-17-96:   "Haitian Exploitation Inspire Protest at Disney Store" —*Queens Chronicle* - Betty Cooney

12-11-97:   "Protestors Blast Disney Workers Plight" —*Rockland News* - Dave Barry

2-11-97 - COLUMN - "PERSECUTING THE CHRISTIANS" BY A. M. ROSENTHAL OF THE *NY TIMES*: I read the piece that said, "Millions of American Christians pray in their churches each week oblivious to the fact that Christians in many part of the world suffer brutal torture, arrest, imprisonment and even death—their homes and communities laid waste—for no other reason than they are Christian. The shocking untold story of our time is more Christians have been killed this century simply for being Christian than the first nineteen centuries after the birth of Christ. They have been persecuted and martyred before an unknowingly, indifferent world and largely silent Christian community." I was so moved by this piece I prayed and said, "God, use me any way you can on behalf of my brothers and sisters who are suffering. I formed the Interfaith Alliance of Christian Human Rights. Over a few months, we have members from every major world religion, atheists, labor union members, Democrats, Republicans, Socialists, Protestants, Catholics, Main Liners, Evangelicals, and other human rights activists. We met to strategize as to best help the suffering.

MARCH OF 1997 - INTERFAITH ALLIANCE FOR CHRISTIAN HUMAN RIGHTS: I created a mission statement and flyer; and the data of what was happening in China, North Korea, Saudi Arabia, Egypt, Lebanon, Pakistan, Sudan, and so forth was based on research and data from Christian Solidarity International, The Coalition for the Defense of Human Rights under Islamization, National Association of Evangelicals, The Puebla Program of Freedom House, World Evangelical Fellowship, and Voice of the Martyrs. I began reaching out to different organizations, and this was a sampling of the groups that joined in NYC. There was another group called the Interfaith Alliance, and they wanted me to change our name, but I told them no, because the name of our group was exactly what we did.

MEMBERS OF THE ALLIANCE: American Academic Alliance for Israel, American Baptist churches in NYC, American Coptic Union, Africa Action Study Group of St. Ferrer and St. James churches, Africa Fund, American Committee for Africa, Bangladesh Christian Association, Bangladeshi-Am. Christian Solidarity, Brooklyn Council of Churches, NYC Council of Churches, Committee for a Free Lebanon, Chinese Catholic Info Center, Church of the Intercession, The Catholic League, Freedom Now (media), Free Middle East International, Jewish

Action Alliance, Manhattan Central Baptist, Manhattan Christian Coalition, Manhattan Council of Churches, Intercommunity Center for Justice and Peace, International Peace Forum, National Council of Churches, Laogai Foundation (Dr. Harry Wu of China), New Yorkers for Constitutional Freedoms (Long Island), World Lebanese Organization

11-16-77 - INTERNATIONAL DAY OF PRAYER FOR THE PERSECUTED CHURCH: It is a special day to remember the persecuted throughout the world. The first organizing meeting for the event took place on January 23, 1996, and was convened by Nina Shea, the director of the Center for Religious Freedom (then at Freedom House but now at The Hudson Institute in Washington DC). It consisted of Faith McDonnell, the director of Religious Liberty at the Institute on Religion and Democracy; Michael Horowitz; the late Chuck Colson of Prison Fellowship, the National Association of Evangelicals; and Dwight Gibson of World Evangelical Fellowship (now the World Evangelical Alliance). The website was originally www.PersecutedChurch.org but then became www.idop.org. In 1996, it started out with

The NCC or National Council of Churches did not join because they felt the focus should not just be on Christians. I do not understand why the NCC would be educating people and praying for the persecuted church. The Jews have the American Jewish Committee, the Muslims have the Council on Arab and Islamic Relations (that does not address modern slavery or genocide in Sudan), the Hindus have the Hindu American Foundation, and Tibet has Students for a Free Tibet, so why is it wrong to advocate for one cause?

NYC INTERNATIONAL DAY OF PRAYER: Once I found out about the persecution of Christians via the A. M. Rosenthal op-ed piece in the *NY Times*, I prayed and said, "God, I am willing to do whatever I can. Guide me." I received the materials for the IDOP (International

Day of Prayer) and ended up becoming the NYC director of IDOP from 1997 to 1999 and on several occasions had the chance to work with Steve Haas, the national director of IDOP. In August of 2016, Steve informed me since IDOP had completed its mission of "shattering the silence" on the persecuted church, the organization closed down roughly five to six years ago (2009 or 2010). There is no IDOP staff or organization anymore, but the work has been picked up by the World Evangelical Fellowship.

The ministries that work on this issue are called Open Doors USA and a group called Voice of the Martyrs. In 1996, the first year, fifteen thousand American churches participated; in 1997, sixty thousand churches prayed; and by 1998, over one hundred thousand churches participated. **The Day of Prayer for the Persecuted Church is always the second Sunday in November.**

<u>11-10-96</u>	11-10-02	11-11-07	11-11-12
11-16-97	<u>11-09-03</u>	11-10-08	11-10-13
11-15-98	11-14-04	11-09-09	11-09-14
11-14-99	11-13-05	<u>11-08-10</u>	<u>11-08-15</u>
11-11-01	11-12-06	11-13-11	11-13-16

BUDDY PASTOR BROGNA AND IDOP: The *Lodi News-Sentinel* paper in Lodi, California (11-14-98), did a story called "Day of Prayer for Religion's Oppressed." It interviewed Pastor Mike Brogna of Calvary Church in Lodi. Pastor Mike was quoted as saying, "More than one hundred thousand churches are expected to take part in Sunday's observance. We're going to pray that God is powerful enough to change the oppressors hearts." Pastor Mike's service will use the story of Saul, who persecuted Christians until his conversion to Christianity. Saul then became Paul, and his Epistles became part of the New Testament.

FIRST MEETING OF IACHR: At the first meeting several groups showed up including theCoptic Christians from Jersey City, NJ. A man got on his knee and started kissing my hand and cried. He said, "Thank you, Pastor Geist, for speaking on this issue!" This gentleman had been a Sunday school teacher in Egypt and was kidnapped by the authorities, chained to a metal bed frame, and electrocuted. I will never forget this moment, and it fired me up to fight for my fellow Christian brothers and sisters suffering for their faith in Islamic and Communist countries.

THE INTERFAITH ALLIANCE FOR CHRISTIAN HUMAN RIGHTS

1. **Demonstrations**

   7-8-97: **Egyptian Consulate** in NYC; 7-28-97: **Sudanese Consulate** in NYC

2. **Media Coverage**

   Radio

   6-18-97: WMCA 570 AM Christian Talk with Andy Anderson (China)

   6-22-97: WABC 770 AM *Religion on the Line* (oldest radio program in the United States)

   6-26-97: Andy Anderson Show

   7-8-07: Steve Malzberg on WABC Radio

   7-29-97: WOR 710 AM *The Bob Grant Show*

   10-18-97: *The Steve Malzberg Show*

   10-21-97: Oliver North's radio program

   Curtis (Sliwa) and (Ron) Kuby Morning Show WABC

Newspaper

NY Times; *Queens Chronicle*; *Catholic New Yorker*; *National Catholic Reporter*; *NYC Council of Churches Courier*; the Allentown, Pennsylvania *Morning Call*; *Episcopal NY*; and the *Rockland Journal News*

Television

October '97: "Point of View" program - Telecare Cable in Long Island

January '98: *The John Tomicki Show* - North and Central Jersey

3. **Political Influence**

    1) **Congresswoman Velazquez:** met with her staff, and she became a cosponsor of the Spector/Wolfe Religious Freedom Act of 1997.

    2) **NYC council speaker Peter Vallone:** We sent a delegation to meet with the speaker on November 7, 1997. He promised to hold hearings for NYC to divest in the fifteen countries persecuting Christians. The hearing was to take place in March or April of 1998.

    3) **Congressman Thomas Manton:** We set up a meeting on behalf of Pastor Noor Alam's family in Pakistan. Pastor Alam's church was destroyed on December 6 by Muslims. On January 27, 1998, Pastor Alam was stabbed to death in front of his family.

    4) **Egyptian Delegation Trip:** As a result of our demonstration and media coverage, Egypt invited "religious leaders" from the NYC Council of Churches to visit the country on a public relations tour in March of 1998. Rev. Calvin Butts was the president of the COC at the time.

5) I met with the **Rev. Calvin Butts of Abyssinian Church** before he went to Egypt and about Christian persecution and modern-day slavery.

6) **Mayor Ed Koch** and I spoke by phone on March 8, 1998.

7) **A. M. Rosenthal of the *NY Times*; Bill Shulz of Amnesty International**

8) **Religious persecution summit hosted by Michael Horowitz (Hudson Institute):**
   2-4-98: sponsored by the Southern Baptist Ethics Committee

4. **International Day of Prayer:** In 1996, fifteen thousand American churches prayed for the persecuted church. On November 1997, sixty thousand churches participated. If each of the sixty thousand churches recruited three churches, then half of America's churches will be participating in 1998. By 1998, over one hundred thousand churches prayed for their persecuted brothers and sisters around the world.

5. **Speaking Forums:** We were invited to speak to ecumenical groups, churches, synagogues, and college campuses in NY, New Jersey, and Pennsylvania to educate people about the persecution.

6. **Solidarity Events:** We demonstrated with and/or showed support for Students for a Free Tibet, Committee for Democracy in Hong Kong, Coalition for a Free Democracy in China, the Laogai Research Foundation (Dr. Harry Woo), and the East Timor Action Network.

7. **Inspire a Grassroots Movement in Lehigh and Berks County, Pennsylvania:** John Noska of Albertus, Pennsylvania, organized a group. On March 17, thirty churches gathered one thousand blankets to send to Sudan.

WABC RADIO: Beth Gilinski of Jewish Action Alliance (JAA) is friends with Steve Malzberg of WABC Radio. She said, "We need to get you on WABC Radio! I can get you on Steve Malzberg's program, and I will get you on *Religion on the Line* on Sunday mornings. I will call Rabbi Joe Potaznik." She did, and she got me on the programs. Over a two-year period, I was on the programs approximately five to six times. At a meeting held at the Interchurch Faith Center next to Union Seminary, I was sitting next to Beth, and I said to her, "On the Christian persecution issue, you are more of a Christian than most Christian leaders." She smiled and said thank you.

9-2-98 - UNITY BREAKFAST WITH JEWISH ACTION ALLIANCE AT SYLVIA'S RESTAURANT TO DENOUNCE LEADER OF THE MILLION YOUTH MARCH BY KHALID MUHAMMAD AND THE NATION OF ISLAM'S BIGOTRY AGAINST JEWS, CATHOLICS, WHITES, WOMEN, HOMOSEXUAL AMONG OTHERS: I was invited to join the peace breakfast with thirty-five others from the NYC community to condemn bigotry. I gave a press release to Beth Gilinsky of JAA with a quote from Malcolm X (5-10-64) where he said, "The Koran compels the Muslim world to take a stand on the side of those whose human rights are being violated, no matter what the religious persuasion of the victim is. Islam is a religion which concerns itself with the human rights of all mankind, despite race, color or creed. It recognizes everyone as part of one human family."

Beth Gilinsky - Founder of Jewish Action Alliance

Contributions to the Jewish Cause

1) 8-19-91: She, JAA, and the Guardian Angels went to Crown Heights in Brooklyn during the riots using trucks to move people out of the riot zone.

2) Organized a yearly press conference in 1997 and 1998 to denounce Khalid Muhammad's bigotry. K. M. is the Million Youth March organizer for the nation of Islam (he died at age fifty-three on 2-16-01).

3) July 1997: condemned Yassar Arafat and the PLO for handcuffing the Russian Orthodox Church monks and nuns, beating them and throwing them out of their monastery

4) November 1997: called upon Congress to impose sanctions against Russia until it stopped supporting development of nuclear weapons in Iran

Contributions for Persecuted Christians

1) She was the first to attend my first meeting with the Interfaith Alliance for Christian Human Rights.

2) She helped recruit different groups to join the movement.

3) She came to the demonstrations in front of the Egyptian and Sudanese consulates in NYC.

4) She helped our group by sharing her contacts in the media world.

5) She came to our meetings with NYC politicians (NYC comptroller Alan Hevesi and NYC council speaker Peter Vallone).

SIR MOSHE BARR-NEA OF THE *JEWISH POST* OF NY:
Moshe Barr-Nea was an interesting character. He was a holocaust survivor of Auschwitz and five other camps, and I will never forget when at one of our meetings, he showed me his ID number tattoo courtesy of the Nazis. He helped the Jews to emigrate from the USSR to the United States and helped push for Jews to adopt Jewish families from 1970 through 1986. He started an organization called Free Middle East International and had been involved in speaking out for the rights of Jews and Christians for decades. To me, he looked like an older Jewish version of David Crosby of Crosby, Stills, and Nash with his white Bernie Sanders-like hair and mustache. He was knighted by the Knights of Malta, thus his first name of "Sir." He was also a journalist for the *Jewish Post* of NY, and Moshe always had great ideas and was always full of energy and had a great laugh. The last I spoke to him was in 2002, and at the writing of this book in 2016, I am sure he has passed. He was a vital component to bringing in many people into the Interfaith Alliance for Christian Human Rights.

Jewish Population in Arab Countries

(American Jewish Committee 1-30-0)

	1948	2001	
Algeria	130,000	0	Jewish cemeteries, hospitals, schools,
Egypt	75,000	200	and synagogues were expropriated or destroyed.
Iraq	90,000	100	700,000 Jews were forced to flee.
Libya	30,000	0	Arab states from 1948 have turned their backs on
Morocco	286,000	5,800	Palestinians. Only Jordan allowed citizenship for

Syria	20,000	100	Palestinians.
Tunisia	70,000	1,500	
Yemen	53,000	200	All other Arab states have turned
TOTAL	**754,000**	**7,900**	their backs on the

Palestinians, creating two refugee populations.

DR. HARRY WU (1937–2016) ANN NOONAN AND THE LAOGAI FOUNDATION: One of my favorite persons is Anne Noonan, a good Catholic and the director of the Laogai Research Foundation. She was the contact person for Dr. Harry Wu in the United States. Harry Wu's family lost all its properties in the 1949 Mau Communist Revolution and was arrested in 1960 and spent nineteen years in a Chinese labor camp called the Laogai. He was from a well-to-do Shanghai family. He came to the United States in 1982 to publicize the systematic human rights abuses there. The foundation documented American company ties to the Chinese labor camps, for exporting Laogai products was illegal in the United States, Germany, and Italy. Harry went into the camps disguised as a prison guard with a hidden camera to document conditions for the CBS program *60 Minutes*. In 2008, the Laogai Research Foundation opened a museum in Washington DC at the foundation's headquarters in Dupont Circle. He died on April 16, 2016, while on a cruise with his family near Honduras.

9-18-97 - JAA AWARD: The Jewish Action Alliance gave me an Interfaith Outreach Award on September 18, 1997. It read,

In deep appreciation of his dedication, persistence and boundless energy in bringing together people of goodwill of

all backgrounds, to make a better world for all. Job 14:19
"Water wears the stones."

Very nice. Thank you, Beth and Jewish Action
Alliance.

11-18-97 - NYC COUNCIL OF CHURCHES AWARD: A
certificate of appreciation as a distinguished lecturer for the citywide
clergy convocation at the interchurch center. Thank you, Rev. John
Hiemstra and Rev. Michael Kendall and Rev. Robert Foley.

**RELIGION ON THE LINE (770 AM) - YOU CAN'T SAY
THAT!** The hosts of the Sunday morning program in 1996 were Rabbi
Postaznik, Seif Ashmawy, Reverend Schafer, and Father Keenan. They
took turns hosting the show once a month, and one week a month,
they were all on together. The asked me to speak about the fight for
International Religious Freedom Act and the slavery issue in Sudan.
When I asked if I can speak about the Disney sweatshops, Reverend
Schafer said to me on the phone, "Pastor Geist, WABC Radio is owned
by Disney. If you say anything about that, you will never be allowed on
WABC Radio again." I lost the battle on Disney but continued on in
the war on slavery and Christian persecution. When corporations own
TV and radio, free speech does get limited.

IMAN SEIF ASHMAWY: Seif was from Egypt, and when I
mentioned Christians got persecuted there, he went nuts. Luckily,
Reverend Schafer backed me up on what was happening there. Seif
died in a car crash on an icy highway entryway on January 23, 1998,
at age sixty. Seif started a newspaper called *The Voice of Peace* and, as
a moderate Muslim, called out Islamic groups that were extremist or
had ties with terrorism. He would speak in churches, synagogues, and
school classes. Seif had confronted Omar Abdul Rahman before the

1993 bombing of the World Trade Center (WTC). He also said that CAIR, the Council on Arab and Islamic Relations, had extremist views that did not represent Islam. Omar Ashmawy was asked to speak to the congressional hearing in 1998 about Islamic extremism and the moderate Muslim voice five years after the bombing of the towers. In his talk, he gave ten excellent suggestions on how to confront extremism in Islam. Omar served eight years in the air force as a war crimes prosecutor in Guantanamo Bay. He currently serves as the chief council for the Office of Congressional Ethics.

Articles Generated

10-22-97: "The Politics of Battling Persecution" —*NY Times* - David Gonzalez

11-13-97: "Elmhurst Minister Heads Queens International Day of Prayer Effort" —*Queens Chronicle* 1997 - Betty Cooney

9-29-97: "Pulpit and a Platform: A Pastor Goes Beyond Preaching . . ." —*Morning Call* - Tim Blangger

10-2-97: "Jewish Action Alliance Honors Two for Outstanding Peace Efforts" —*Queens Chronicle* - Betty Cooney

11-13-97: "Vallone Promises a Bill on Persecuted Christians" — *Catholic NY* - John Burger

7-30-98: "Nigerian Pastor Fleeing Persecution Denied Political Freedom" —*Queens Chronicle* - Felicia Persuad

3-15-98: "Interfaith Group Cites Attacks on Christians" —*Daily News* - Joyce Shelby

2-13-98: "Minorities Feel Persecuted in Islamic Pakistan" — *India Times* - Haider Rizvi

6-18-98:   "Fellow Soldiers Sound Alarm for Persecuted Christians"
             —*Morning Call* - Kirk Jackson

2-25-99:   "AASG Opens Chapter in Queens" —*Queens Tribune* -
             Gary McClendon

3-10-99:   "Gospel Witness to Muslims in Queens" —*Alliance
             Life* 12–13

             -Pastor Geist introduced Rev. Peter Sayed to Rev.
             George Reitz of the NYC CMA.

4-99:   "Geist Named NYC Chairman of the A.A.S.G." —*Tri-
             State Voice*

4-99:   www.anti-slavery.org —*Tri-State Voice* - Tom Campisi

4-5-99:   "Fight Against Slavery" —*Daily News* - Albert Ruiz

4-15-99:   "Nyack College Turns Spotlight on Sudan Civil War"
             —*Rockland News* - John Barry

4-13-99:   "Local Abolitionists Say Stop Slavery in North Africa"
             —*Queens Chronicle* - Fel. P.

5-99:   "NY Pastor Asks Why Is the West Silent on African
             Slaves?" —*Tri-State Voice*

9-9-99:   "Hunger Strike by Pastor Urges Vallone to Keep
             Promise" —*Queens Chronicle* - Betty Cooney

9-16-99:   "Elmhurst Pastor Ends Hunger Strike" —*Queens
             Chronicle* - Betty Cooney

9-22-99:   "Elmhurst Pastor Prevails in Dispute with Vallone" —
             Queens Courier - Howard Girsky

10-99:   "Pastor Ends 12 Day Hunger Strike: Christina Life
             Times" —*L.I.* - Regina Willis

10-14-99: "Elmhurst Minister Heads Religious Persecution Hearings Before (NYC) Council" — *Queens Chronicle* - Betty Cooney

12-22-99: "Still Enslaved: Sudanese & Mauritanians" —*NY Voice* - Felicia Persuad

9-16-99: "Sudan's Suffering Taking Center Stage" —*Religion Today*

12-99: "NY Pastor Protests Sudan's Slave Trade" —*Charisma Magazine*, p. 21

12-21-97 - *NY TIMES* MAGAZINE FRONT COVER: "THE RAGE OVER CHRISTIAN PERSECUTION: A CONSERVATIVE-LED WASHINGTON COALITION TRIES TO REMORALIZE AMERICAN FOREIGN POLICY." The article talks about A. M. Rosenthal, Nina Shea of Freedom House (started by Eleanor Roosevelt), Michael Horowitz of the Hudson Institute, and Gary Bauer of the Family Research Council.

Sept. 1997 - A. M. ROSENTHAL - EDITOR OF THE *NY TIMES* AND STEVE HAAS OF THE INTERNATIONAL DAY OF PRAYER FOR THE PERSECUTED CHURCH: I was the NYC director of the IDOP for two years in 1997 and 1998. It was my job to recruit as many churches as possible for the Day of Prayer in November. Steven Haas is the founder and national director for the IDOP. On the trip, we met with the NYC Council of Churches and with Bill Schultz, the director of Amnesty International. Schlutz said it was nice to see Evangelicals getting more involved in speaking out on human rights abuses. We also met with A. M. Rosenthal, the editor of the *NY Times*.

Rosenthal had to step down in 1986 because of mandatory retirement but wrote two columns a week for the *NY Times*. He was a journalistic juggernaut, and on his watch, the *Times* published the "Pentagon Papers" about America's secret involvement in the Vietnam War. He started working at the *Times* in 1946. His devotion to quality journalism was impeccable, and he instantly grasped the essence of any story. He was not always a nice man to work with, but it fell in line with his maxim: "keep the story straight." On July 9, he was awarded the Presidential Medal of Freedom by President Bush for his significant contribution to the passage of the International Religious Freedom Act of 1998. Abe died on May 10, 2006, at age eighty-four.

We got off the subway and walked to the *NY Times* building. Steve Haas told the front desk we were there to see Mr. Rosenthal. We got the okay and took the elevator way up the building. He had a large office with couches and a large bathroom and a shower in it. Abe was on the phone and said, "I am sorry, Henry. I will talk with you later. I have two important people here." Mr. Rosenthal was wearing a coat and bow tie. He reached out his hand and said, "That was Kissinger. Welcome, welcome!" We sat and chatted about how the movement had been growing. He said, "I hope a movement does grow because we must confront terrible things like genocide and religious persecution." **The website use to be www.idop.org.** It is now organized yearly by the Open Doors Ministy.

THE EVANGELICAL BLIND SPOT: It points out the whole in the mind that labor is not seen as a moral-ethical issue worthy to support in most Evangelical circles. Homosexuality, bad; abortion, bad; exploiting working-class laborers, blind eye. When I read the gospels, I saw a God who took the side of the poor and oppressed. If a modern prophet were to speak to the Evangelicals today, one of the criticisms would be "You have become friends with the rich and powerful and, thus, are afraid to address the issues of the oppressed." Most Evangelicals support Republicans who are "pro-life" but are also anti-union. I have never heard a sermon in all my life, even on Labor Day weekend, about how God loves working people, something not un-noticed by my blue collar working father.

CHRISTOLOGY OF JURGEN MOLTMAN: On November 20, 1992, Moravian College awarded Jurgen Moltman the Comenius Medallion. That day was the 400th anniversary of John Amos Comenius and the 250th anniversary of Moravian College in Bethlehem. The college had given this award to Elie Wiezel and also to Pres. Jimmy Carter. In _The Way of Jesus_, Moltman's Christo-praxis calls for a therapeutic Christology that not only gathers proofs for Jesus's messiahship and resurrection but also confronts the misery of this world with salvation Jesus brings, which means religion is not private. If Christianity is to deal only with the human heart and be emancipated from social ties, "then the economic, social and political sins of human beings who have led to this personal isolation and spiritual aloneness are left without the liberating criticism and without the saving hope of the gospel (45)." He further states, "The End-times condition of this world today requires us to see the real misery of the earth. The deadly fear . . . of nuclear catastrophe and the ecological life (59)."

The three questions I ask are the following:

1) Who is Christ for the second- and third-world countries, those in America, Africa, and Asia, which bore the largest share of the human and material costs of European progress?
2) Who is Christ for us today, threatened by nuclear inferno?
3) Who is Christ for our dying nature and ourselves?

Jesus's messianic mission makes it clear that He had a preferential option for the poor. Jesus broke the vicious cycle of discrimination in the system of values set up by "the righteous." How far can the way of Jesus be taken? "Ever since the Reformation, this has been the critical question put out by Anabaptist, Mennonites and Moravians to the Protestant Churches" (118).

10-27-98 - <u>TIMELINE FOR PASSAGE OF THE INTERNATIONAL RELIGIOUS FREEDOM ACT</u>: On October 9 of 1998, the Senate passed the act by a vote of 98–0; and President Clinton signed the legislation on Tuesday, October 27, turning it into law. It was A. M. Rosenthal's piece in the *NY Times* on February 11, 1996, called "Persecuting the Christians" that woke me up. I was part of a movement that consisted of people of different faiths and had the opportunity to learn more about my faith from my Orthodox, Coptic, and Catholic brothers and sisters in the process of advocating for this bill.

2-4-98 - A. M. ROSENTHAL AWARDED - AT RELIGIOUS PERSECUTION SUMMIT (WASHINGTON COURT HOTEL) IN WASHINGTON DC (MY TALK WITH GARY BAUER): All the players involved in getting the religious persecution law were there and the politicians who helped get it passed. I was invited as well. I really enjoyed hobnobbing with the different leaders and seeing Steve Haas and so many others. I ran into Gary Bauer of the Family Research Council. He asked who I was, and then said, "You are the one I read about in the *NY Times*. Good work." I asked him why so many Evangelical groups were anti-labor. He said, "My father was a custodian, so I am familiar with how hard blue-collar workers work." It was a nonanswer. I said, "My dad works at Mack Trucks, and one of the reasons he and so many other workers don't like your organization, the 700 Club and the Moral Majority, is you take the side of the bosses and corporations." He said, "Nice meeting you." He was a short fellow, and the assistant who was with him was an amazingly gorgeous, drop-dead blonde bombshell.

NOTE ON THE SOUTHERN BAPTIST ETHICS COMMITTEE: The Southern Baptists were calling on a boycott of

Walt Disney World as a result of Disney Corp. giving health benefits to gay partners. I called Richard Landis, president of the Southern Baptists, and asked his denomination to address the sweatshops in Haiti run by Disney where the workers were paid starvation wages. He said he did not see this as moral issue. I said, "Starving children is not a moral issue?" President Landis responded, "Starvation is a moral issue, Pastor Geist, but we (the Southern Baptists) are just not going to address Disney's sweatshops in Haiti." Well, what could I expect from the denomination that used to support slavery in this country? Gays, we speak out; Disney was not doing right by its black Haitian workers; not what the Southern Baptist Jesus would do I am guessing.

4-24-1997 - ACTIVISM FOR STRAWBERRY WORKERS: I met Laura Rivera and Sarah Johnson of the United Farm Workers (UFW) in NYC. The union was started by Cesar Chavez and made famous by the 1965–1970 Grape Boycott and Strike Filipino American grape workers. The UFW in NYC wanted Scaturro's Supermarkets, a seven-store chain in NYC, to join 240 other NYC stores in joining the "pledge for strawberry worker rights." The pledge endorses basic improvements in the living and working conditions of California strawberry workers, including clean bathrooms, drinking water in the fields, a living wage, job security, health insurance, and a voice on the job to end sexual harassment and other abuses. By raising the price of a quart of strawberries by five cents, it would double the wages of the workers.

In early January, Sister Mulready, who was on chemotherapy, from the Interfaith Center for Justice and Peace called Mr. Scaturro on behalf of the NY Labor-Religion Coalition. On January 25, a thirty-person coalition led by Pastor Jim Geist went to the store in Corona, Queens, to speak with the manager. In January and February, Mr. Scaturro received at least 15 letters and hundreds of phone calls. On February

20th, Rabbi Bently, Father Bennet and Pastor Geist went to the Scatturo Headquarters in Floral Park. While Mr. Scatturo was not in, the clergy visit lasted for approximately seven minutes. Within the week, Mr. Scatturo agreed to raise the prices by five cents per quart of strawberries to improve the life of strawberry pickers.

9-15-1997 - PASTOR GEIST WAS ASKED TO SPEAK WITH CONGRESSWOMAN NYDIA VELAZQUEZ ON BEHALF OF FIFTY-SEVEN DISABLED DEAF-MUTE MEXICANS FORCED TO SELL TRINKETS ON THE NYC SUBWAYS: On September 15, I was asked to speak at a press conference with Congresswoman Nydia Velazquez about the fifty-seven deaf-mute Mexicans who had been smuggled into NYC and forced to work eighteen-hour days. If they did not earn enough money, they were beaten. They were forced to pay high rent and to eat meager meals. Congresswoman Velazquez said, "Sweatshop operators use immigrants' fear of deportation to abuse their employees . . . These fifty-seven Mexican workers do not know if they will be allowed to stay in the country . . . This week, I will bring legislation to the floor of the House of Representatives that would allow these victims of a terrible crime to remain in the U.S."

My statement to the press was "In Haiti, Walt Disney pays its Haitian workers $2.40 a day to sew eight hundred to one thousand T-shirts. In Indonesia, Nike pays its workers $2.20 a day to make sneakers. In China, they kill prisoners to sell body parts. In Sudan, you can purchase a slave for $15. And in America, you can smuggle deaf-mute Mexicans and for them to sell key chains on the subway and then beat them if they do not meet their quotas. I am here today to support the Congresswoman's legislation."

1998 - RUN INTO MAYOR GIULIANI - ASK HIM TO TALK WITH SANITATION UNION: I do not have an exact date, but I attended a meeting with the People of Faith and the NY Labor-Religion

Coalition in the morning with NYC sanitation workers to show our support for them. The mayor was not willing to meet with them. In the afternoon, after I got home from the meeting, I went to Big Apple Bagels to buy a coffee. Just as I was about to enter, two black SUV unmarked vehicles pulled up to the deli. It looked like the Secret Service coming out of the vehicles, and out came Mayor Giuliani. I reached out my hand and shook his and said, "Hello, Mayor Giuliani. I am Pastor Jim Geist, and I am with the NY Labor-Religion Coalition, and we had a press conference this morning, asking you to meet with the sanitation workers to finalize a contract. The mayor looked at me like I was from Mars and said, "Have a nice day, Pastor." Talk about serendipity.

AUGUST 10, 1998: VISIT LEBANESE CHRISTIANS IN WACKENHUT IMMIGRATION DETENTION FACILITY: The NYC Council of Churches asked Teresa and I to visit Mrs. Shamun and her daughter who were Lebanese Christians in the Wackenhut facility near JFK Airport in Queens. The NYC Council of Churches sent a letter to Jacob Aponinis of the Immigration and Naturalization Service, expressing concern about the dangers that faced the Shamuns if they were sent back to Lebanon.

WACKENHUT DETENTION CENTER: Wackenhut is a detention center for asylum seekers by JFK Airport. The detention center is a two-hundred-bed facility in large dorms with tiny slit window. There is extreme lack of privacy with no barriers separating the toilets and showers from the sleeping and eating areas. It was built by one of the leading building companies, Wackenhut Corrections Corporation, founded by the multimillionaire George Wackenhut. Wackenhut is a former FBI agent who made his fortune in the 1960s by collecting files of progressive people and selling them. In November of 1999, Wackenhut was profiting from 38,600 people behind bars.

1998 WINTER OLYMPICS (GOLD): Eric Bergoust, Jonny Moseley, Nikki Stone (freestyle skiing), Picabo Street (Alpine skiing), Tara Lipinski (figure skating), and U.S. ladies hockey team

(SILVER): Michelle Kwan (figure skating), Gordon Sheer and Chris Thorpe (luge), and Chris Witty (speed skating)

10-27-1997 to 11-2-1997 - CHINESE JIANG ZEMIN'S VISIT TO THE UNITED STATES: Chinese president Jiang Zemin visited the United States and President Clinton for a week. He spent two days in NYC on October 31 and November 1. Governor Pataki and Mayor Giuliani refused to meet and welcome President Zemin to New York. He was met with protests, and I took part in one of the protests and helped lead chants about the abuses in China in NYC next to one of the places the president visited. He visited the NY Stock Exchange and the offices of IBM, AT&T, and Lucent Technologies and had a dinner at the Waldorf Astoria. There were 59 percent of Americans who favor greater support for human rights in China at this time.

2-25-98 - SALUTE TO DEMOCRACY IN CHINATOWN DINNER: From 6:00 to 9:00 pm at the Nice Restaurant in Chinatown, the Coalition for Pro-Democracy in China gave a human rights award to Wei Jingsheng and had Mayor Ed Koch as the guest speaker. Mayor Giuliani and Dr. Harry Wu were also given special recognition in the event. I got to see Ann Noonan of the Laogai Foundation and John Tomicki, who invited me on his cable TV show to speak about the persecution of Christians. I was asked to say a word and opening prayer, which I gladly did. I got my picture taken with Mayor Koch, but the flash did not work, and I never got it, but I did have a picture with Dr. Wu, Ms. Noonan, and Mr. Tomicki.

MARCH OF 1998 - U.S. RELIGIOUS DELEGATION TO CHINA: Rabbi Sneider, Archbishop McCarric, and Don Argue of the National Association of Evangelicals got a tour of China—Beijing,

Shanghai, Nanjing, Hong Kong, and Lhasa Tibet—over an eighteen-day period. They say many of the government leaders realize religious tolerance is an important part of advanced civilization.

1999 - WORLD TIBET DAY: I was asked by John Hocevar of Students of a Free Tibet to help support and participate in World Tibet Day on the weekend of July 10 in 1999. I was asked to inform the groups connected with the Interfaith Alliance for Christian Human Rights in NYC. The event took place in NYC, Chicago, LA, and Boston and in Australia and New Zealand. The purpose was spend a day in prayer in education about restoring religious and cultural freedoms to the endangered people. Since the 1949 Chinese occupation of Tibet by the Chinese military, 1.2 million Tibetans had died, and more than 6,000 monasteries had been destroyed. The website is www. WorldTibetDay.com.

11-23-1999 - PASTOR GEIST ADVOCATES FOR NIGERIAN PASTOR IN A WACKENHUT INS FACILITY NEAR JFK AIRPORT: Pastor Livinus Tobechukwu, a Pentecostal pastor in Nigeria, came to the United States to escape political and religious persecution from the Nigerian regime. On February 15, 1998, while in transit to Canada, he requested political asylum. Pastor Tobechukwu knew firsthand the brutal treatment accorded political prisoners in Nigeria from his prison ministry. At Onistsha, he brought food, clothing, and medicine and otherwise ministering to the prisoner's physical and spiritual needs. There were two fellow ministers from his church who were accused of a plot to overthrow the Abacha government and detained by the SSS and disappeared. Pastor Tobechukwu was afraid this too would be his plight with aggravated persecution by the widespread persecution of Christians by the pro-Muslim government.

Patrice Perillie of the law firm Wilens and Baker said, "The U.S. is the only country in the Western world in which an alien seeking religious asylum cannot be released on bond." She represented dozens of these aliens seeking asylum, many who had been held for over a year. The pastor had been denied reading materials, except for the Bible. The Wackenhut facility's physical plant is poor, built for a three-week stay, and many are held up to a year. In addition, there is no outdoor area for exercise.

Attorney-at-Law Patrice Perillie asked me to write a letter to the district director of the INS, which I was more than happy to do. I was also asked to visit him and to see if I could generate some media attention to help the Nigerian pastor's plight. Felicia Persuad of the *Queens Chronicle* and Howard Girsky of the *Queens Courier* obliged me. With the help of other NYC clergy who spoke out on behalf of Pastor Tobechukwu, he was eventually released and able to get into Canada.

Post note 1:   On January 7, 2015, three hundred gunmen from the Islamic Boko Haram killed two thousand people in over sixteen villages in Nigeria.

Post note 2:   The Wackenhut Detention Center was closed in May of 2005. The detainees were moved to the Elizabeth (NJ) Detention Center, which has one of the lowest release rates in the country.

OCTOBER OF 1999 - HUNGER STRIKE: New York City council speaker Peter Vallone from Astoria, Queens, promised to hold hearing on NYC, declaring sanctions against the countries committing persecution of Christians overseas. He ended up not holding the hearings, so I called his secretary and spoke with her, telling her I would not eat any food until the council speaker set a date for hearings. I went on a hunger strike that ended up lasting twelve days. A press release was sent out to local papers about the strike, but on the seventh day of the hunger strike, it began making news in the local Queens papers, and his office started getting calls from the media. I did not eat any food, but I did drink water during this time, and I lost eleven pounds over the course of twelve days. On day 12, I received a call from Vallone's office, telling me a date had been set and to eat something. I received a phone call from WABC Radio, and I was interviewed by Curtis Sliwa and Ron Kuby of the Curtis and Kuby Show. The interviewed me for five minutes. Kuby asked me what I ate to break my fast, and I told him chicken noodle soup. Ron Kuby also said, "Pastor Geist may be the only person who has ever gotten Curtis and Kuby to agree on an issue." CBS radio also ran a news piece on 1010 WINS AM radio from morning until two o'clock in the afternoon every twenty minutes. I was inspired to do this from the work of Gandhi and Caesar Chavez of the United Farm Workers. I was glad it was not longer than twelve days.

1999 - HUNGER STRIKE DOCUMENTED IN BOOK: In the book _A Public Faith: Evangelicals and Civic Engagement_ edited by Michael Cromartie in 2003, in the article "Evangelicals and International Engagement," Dr. Allen D. Hertzke, professor of political science and religious studies at the University of Oklahoma, wrote about Christian groups speaking out on the atrocities in Sudan. "This material has been picked up by a variety of activists . . . to New York City Pastor Jim Geist who held a well-publicized hunger strike (1999) aimed at pressuring the city to take divestment action similar to that during the South Africa sanctions campaign (228)."

The NYC AMERICAN ANTISLAVERY GROUP: I met Dr. Charles Jacob at a event in Washington D.C. sponsored by the Freedom House. At this event I met Nina Shea and was able to have dinner with Dr. Charles Jacobs and Congressman Fauntroy. Dr. Jacobs started A.A.S.G. up in Boston and in the course of our conversation he said, "Would you like to be part of A.A.S.G. I said I would love to be part of it. Dr. Jacobs said, "Good, I dub you the NYC director of AASG," and that is how it all started for me in 1998.

A.A.S.G.'s POLITICAL INFLUENCE

8-12-99:　　A religious delegation of twenty leaders organized by Pastor Geist met with City Council Speaker Peter Vallone. The speaker promised to introduce a bill in which NYC would divest any monies it held in Laos and Sudan, similar to sanctions on South Africa over the apartheid issue.

9-24-99:　　The NYC Council passed a resolution number 414 condemning Sudan's atrocities.

1-25-00:　　Peter Vallone asked NY attorney general Eliot Spitzer to submit an amicus curiae to appeal the "Massachusetts Burma Law" that Federal Judge Tauro held the law was unconstitutional. That would have prohibited the state and its agents from purchasing goods and services from Burma.

Radio and Television Coverage and Speaking Engagements

4/98:　　Dr. Charles Jacobs knights me the NYC chairperson of the NYC AASG. I worked in conjunction with Maria Sliwa on the issue of modern-day slavery.

1998:　　Dr. Samuel Cotton of NYC wrote _Silent Terror: A Journey into Contemporary African Slavery_ by Harlem River Press. It was dedicated to those fighting slavery in Mauritania.

7-12-98:　　Spoke to the Queensboro Hill Community Church in Flushing, NY

11-11-98: Spoke to the Campaign of Conscience Event (Washington DC) where sixty universities attended, organized by Nina Shea and the Freedom House Center for Religious Freedom

1-24-99: Spoke on WABC's *Religion on the Line* radio show about Sudan

1-28-99: Spoke on the Bob Grant radio program

1-24-99: Spoke to New Life Fellowship Youth Group

1-31-99: Spoke on *Religion on the Line* with Rabbi Potaznik

2-2-99: Barbara Vogels Class in Colorado raised $70,000 to free slaves in Sudan.

2-5-99: UNICEF declared the redemptions intolerable, yet in 1996, they paid money so Indian mothers could buy their children out of bondage.

2-5-99: John Tomicki cable TV show in Northern New Jersey with two youth group kids

2-8-99: Telecare cable: Keeler and Lowe program (*Newsday* newspaper reporters)

2-14-99: Spoke to College Point Queens NLF Church

3-9-99: Speak to Queens College Newman Catholic Center

3-11-99: WMCA Radio - Andy Anderson Show with Michael Horowitz of the Hudson Institute

3-27-99: WABC Radio with Steve Malzberg - Dr. Sam Cotton, escaped slave Moctar Teyeb, and Pastor Geist

3-30-99: WMCA - Andy Anderson interviewed Christian Robb of Freedom House and myself.

4-1-99:   Manhattan cable channel 57: World Prophetic Ministries TV

4-14-99:   Telecare's God Squad (Long Island TV)

4-15-99:   Spoke at Nyack College with Faith McDonnell (thirty-hour fast to raise $ for slave redemp.)

4-24-99:   Hunter College human rights forum

4-26-99:   Telecare's God Squad (Long Island TV)

4-27-99:   Spoke at Dr. Harold Takooshian's psychology class (916) at Fordham University next to Lincoln Center in Manhattan with Maria Sliwa. Curtis Sliwa showed up.

1999:   I worked with Brooklynite Michael Frazier from Tufts University as my intern for his credit in the Peace and Justice Department.

7-5-99:   Letter to Rev. Jesse Jackson and Reverend Sharpton to speak out on modern-day slavery

3-25-99:   Rally against police brutality of Amadou Diallo. I held up a sign "Why are Reverend Jackson and Reverend Sharpton silent on slavery in Sudan?"

9-26-99:   CBS Program *Touched by an Angel* ran a show about slaves in Sudan.

4-8-00:   Rally for Sudan at UN; sixty showed up; Sam Cotton and Curtis Sliwa spoke. Statements of support by Hevesia and Ed Koch. Colleges showed up—Nyack, Marymount, and Fairleigh Dickinson—as well as Students for a Free Tibet and Park West High School students; 201 signatures collected.

Press: BBC, ABC Radio, *Catholic New Yorker*, independent reporter, local Queens papers

5-21-00: Demonstration in front of B. P. Amoco Headquarters (3:00–5:00 p.m.), 525 Madison at Fifty-Fourth St.

9-5-00: Guardian Angels attempted to make an arrest of General Beshir for crimes against humanity at the Sudan Mission at 655 Third Ave.

9-14-00: NYC comptroller Alan Hevesi divested NYC's shares from Talisman's Oil (Sudan).

11-7-00: John Eibner of Christian Solidarity International came and spoke about redeeming slaves to the NYC Council of Churches.

1-19-01: Letter sent to President Bush with over one hundred signatures of religious and civil rights groups and with my name as well about strengthening Sudan policy

2-17-01: The Holocaust Museum in Washington DC opened an exhibit on suffering in Sudan.

4-13-01: Washington DC: Michael Horowitz, Joe Madison, and Rich Cizik were arrested for chaining themselves to the front of the Sudanese Embassy; Ken Starr and Johnny Cochran acted as their attorneys.

2-1 and 2: Presenter at the Greater Metro NY Social Studies Conference (UFT)

3-28-01: Mayor Koch informed me Reverend Sharpton was going to Sudan.

4-25-01: NYC comptroller Carl McCall dumped Canadian Talisman oil company and sold their stock for it operating in Sudan.

5-2-01:   **Rally against slavery at Sudanese consulate in NYC *arrested were Curtis Sliwa, Charles Jacobs, Maria Sliwa, and Roy Vogel of WWDJ Radio**

                -Fr. Daniel Berrigan stated support for the NYC rally

5-10-01:   Johnny Cochran, Kenneth Star, Dick Gregory, and Michael Horowitz spoke out.

5-21-01:   Spoke at Bergan County Academy (NJ) to the operation liberation program

5-28-01:   Secretary of State Colin Powell urged Sudan to halt Civil War.

7-6-01:   Spoke to Prof. Patrick Mull's class at Pace University in Manhattan

9-6-01:   Escaped slave Francis Bok met President Bush to be part of the Rose Garden announcement of John Danworth becoming special envoy to Sudan.

2002:   I worked with Mr. Mark Torres, who was a student at NYU. He spent the year helping the AASG NYC grow. He invited me to his wedding to say a prayer before the wedding reception for him and new wife, Claudia. He became a labor attorney.

October 2004:   I sent a letter to the Holocaust Museum, asking them to hold an exhibit on the genocide in Sudan. I was told the museum just focused on the Jewish Holocaust.

7-24-01:   David Morales of Operation Freedom Muslim Association organized a fund-raiser at the Studio Club in Staten Island.

1-9-02: <u>Victims of Jihad Rally at UN</u>: Fr. Keith Roderick of the Coalition for the Defense of Human Rights and Mary Beth Roderick, Maria Sliwa, Jim Geist; statement from Alan Hevesi and Comptroller Bill Thomson; Rabbi Potaznik, Curtis Sliwa, Dr. Roy Vogel, and speakers from Afghanistan, Nigeria, India, Egypt, the Philippines, Indonesia, Bangladesh, Pakistan, and Sudan

1-27-02: Spoke at Saint Bartholomew's Church in Manhattan with escaped slave Francis Bok, and 125 people attended

3-20-02: "Slavery Is Not History" at the Ben Snow Dining Room of the NYU Bobst Library organized by Mr. Mark Torres

10-20- 04: Mayor Koch supported my idea and wrote to the NYC Holocaust Museum. They had an exhibit for one month.

Press Coverage

4-5-99: "Fight Against Slavery Teacher Wages War on Human Bondage" by Albor Ruiz of the *NY Daily News*

9-16-99: "Queens Pastor Ends Hunger Strike" by Michael Sheridan of the *Queens Chronicle*

10-14-99: "Elmhurst Pastor Heads up Religious Persecution Hearings Before the (NYC) Council" by Betty Cooney of the *Queens Chronicle*

10-20-99: "Sudanese Persecution Dealt Setback by 'determined' LIC Pastor" by Howard Girsky of the *Queens Courier*

Spring 00:   ATS in Action - "Jim Geist 12 Day Hunger Strike Against Genocide & Slavery"

9-14-00:   "Queens Joins Sudan Protest at UN Headquarters" - *Queens Chronicle* - Felicia Persaud

4-13-00:   "Local Abolitionists Rally Against Slavery (UN)" - *NY Trends* - Felicia Persaud

6-27-00:   "Black Slaves Not News in NY" - *Village Voice* - Nat Hentoff

5-3-01:   "Ex-Slave Wonders: Why Do so Few Care?" - *NY Post* - Rod Dreher

2-15-01:   "Former Slave Speaks Out" - *Daily News* - Joyce Shelby -Francis Bok spoke to Rabbi Potaznik's synagogue in Brooklyn Heights.

7-21-01:   "Freedom Fighters: Island Based Muslim Group to Fight Enslavement of Christians" - *Staten Island Advance* - Michael Paquette

10-24-01:   "Rev. Al Has No Bravery on Slavery" - *NY Post* - Andrea Peyser

7-18-02:   "No Silencing This Slavery Foe (Maria Sliwa)" - *Daily News* - A. M. Rosenthal

MARIA SLIWA'S ADVOCACY: Maria is a former NYC police officer and runs a group called Freedom Now. Freedom Now sends out e-mails about human rights abuse of Christians worldwide but especially on the atrocities in Sudan. A. M. Rosenthal of the *Daily News* said, "Maria Sliwa is . . . a stunning example of a one-person cause. No paid researchers, no staff or special equipment, all from her office in New York." Maria is the sister of Curtis Sliwa, who founded the

Guardian Angels in 1979. She had been to Sudan several times, and she was aware that slave masters regularly raped their female slaves. She also learned that many of the boy slaves were also raped by their owners. She was great at helping recruit people and organizations, getting out press releases, and going around and speaking to colleges and radio programs. She is a pit bull for advocating against the persecution of Christians and especially in fight for Sudan. She runs Sliwa Media Relations, and her website is M.Sliwa.com.

4-27-99 - FORDHAM UNIVERSITY AND CURTIS SLIWA: After the event, Curtis Sliwa, founder of the Guardian Angels, walked Maria and myself out to the street. Before we went outside, he took out his phone and made a call, saying "Angel number 1 ready for pick up." Outside the Fordham was a van with two Guardian Angels inside it. Curtis kissed his sister good-bye and asked me if I needed a ride downtown. I didn't think I really needed a ride, but I wanted to hang out with Curtis Sliwa for a bit. I told him I was grateful for his support on speaking out on the persecution of Christians in Islamic and Communist countries and for his support on speaking out against genocide and slavery in Sudan. I asked him to share his story with me when he was shot by the Mafia. He did.

The Guardian Angels started in 1979 with the rise of crime in NYC's subways. Sliwa made a name for himself by starting a volunteer force to patrol the subways. Some police liked it, and many did not. In 1992, Sliwa used to make fun of the Mafia and the John Gotti Family on his radio program. On April 23, Sliwa claimed that three guys with baseball bats tried to assault him, but he got away. Every morning, Sliwa was picked up by a yellow cab to be taken to the radio station for his talk show. On June 20 of 1992, he got in the cab and realized that he cannot open the door. He got shot several times by Joey D'Angelo, a mob associate of Sammy the Bull Gravano. The hit on Sliwa was put out by John Gotti Junior.

Sliwa kicked the glass out of the window and jumped out of the taxi. He was taken to the hospital, where they took out all his intestines to make sure they had gotten all the bullets and had closed up any of the holes caused by the bullet. D'Angelo cooperated with the state and testified four of five trials that all ended in hung juries. Little Joey D'Angelo spent four years in prison. When he finished telling me this story, I noticed Sliwa and the other Angels were very vigilant and always looking around, and I got a little nervous. I said, "Thanks for the story. You guys can drop me off here."

SUMMER 2000 - SHAYKH ABD'ALLAH LATIF ALI OF THE ADMIRAL FAMILY CIRCLE ISLAMIC CIRCLE: I met Shaykh Latif in Harlem at the transatlantic slave trade sculpture celebration. I introduced myself to him and explained what was happening in Sudan. I wanted to know if we can get more imams to speak against modern-day slavery in Sudan. He took my literature and said, "Pastor Geist, I do not know who you are or if there is any dirt in your life, but if there is, we will find it." I said, "I am sad to hear you are more concerned about my personal life than about being part of a coalition to speak about against the genocide and slavery being committed by the National Islamic Front." I also spoke to some men in bow ties in the subway who were part of the Nation of Islam and told them I believe Muhammad Ali and Malcom X would speak out against this issue.

MARCH 1999 - UNICEF VS. CHRISTIAN SOLIDARITY INTERNATIONAL: CSI has a program where they raise money and pay slave owners in Sudan to free slaves from $14 to $50 a person. Carol Bellamy of UNICEF denounced the practice, saying it only encouraged the capture of more slaves. Baroness Carolyn Cox, former Parliamentarian, said, "What do you do? Should we look a child in the eye and say sorry, we cannot purchase your freedom because it upsets UNICEF? UNICEF begins to criticize AASG for having helped free 5,942 slaves since 1995 at $50 a piece. It turns out UNICEF used to support a program to help Indian mothers buy their children out of bonded servitude. What is the difference? It is not the cure, but it is a solution until slavery is no longer practiced."

1998–2004 - MAYOR ED KOCH: <u>Religious Persecution</u>: Mayor Ed Koch was great at speaking out against the persecution of Christians in Islamic and Communist countries. He also supported me in putting pressure on NYC council speaker Peter Vallone for NYC to pass a bill similar to the Religious Freedom Act Congressman Frank Wolfe of Virginia was putting together in 1997. He wrote an op-ed in the *Daily News* (3-6-98): "Let's Smite Religious Persecution." The mayor said, "People worldwide ought to be able to worship freely . . . Should we not do for them (persecuted Christians) at least as much as we do for the whales? Governments that persecute, imprison, and kill those who practice their religions must be punished."

<u>Purchasing of Slaves:</u> In his op-ed in the *Daily News* entitled "I'm Ready to Be Arrested Too" (about Mayor Giuliani not being willing to meet with civil leaders over the abuse of Abner Louima and the killing of Amadou Diallo), he condemned UNICEF and Human Rights Watch for not supporting the buying of slaves by AASG. Mayor Koch wrote, "John Brown's body lies a-moldering and a-twisting in his grave."

<u>His Support of</u> AASG: Mayor Koch also gave us statements to read at rallies, showing his support of the work of the American Anti-Slavery Group. He wrote to me on April 6, 2000:

> *Slavery in Sudan and Mauritania must end. That will*
> *not happen unless people of good will, like the Abolitionists of*
> *old, continue to keep the issue before the world's conscience*

and the world's assembly, the United Nations . . . You (Jim Geist) and your colleagues at A.A.S.G. are doing your part in alerting millions of citizens of a host of countries encouraging them to apply pressure to their governments to end one of the greatest of sins—the enslavement of one human being by another.

<u>Mayor Koch Supports Geist's Idea for the NYC Holocaust Museum</u>: In 2004, the genocide and forced starvation of those living in Dafur was finally getting the coverage it deserved. It was just on the cusp of breaking worldwide and then the 9/11 attacks, and it took another three years before it became a hot issue again. In June of 2004, the Holocaust Museum in Washington DC sponsored an event called Bearing Witness for Dafur, in which a Holocaust survivor spoke and a representative from Dafur spoke and someone from the Committee of Conscience spoke. It was to help raise the national conference.

I called the NYC Holocaust Museum and sent a letter to them, asking that they open a display for Sudan and for all other countries suffering from genocide. The lesson from the Holocaust is to be "Never Again." Unfortunately, I was told the Jewish Holocaust was unique and therefore wanted to keep its focus on that. I was disappointed to find out for the NYC Holocaust Museum, "Never Again" apparently only applied to genocide, impacting Jews, and that it ignored Gentile genocide.

I wrote to Mayor Koch about this on October 20 of 2004. Mayor Koch wrote to David Maxwell, the director of the museum, saying,

I received an enclosure from Jim Geist. Since the issue is a legitimate one and there will be more like it, why not consider having an exhibit which talks about current acts

of genocide taking place throughout the world. I doubt it
would be a great expense involved since it would probably
consist of available news articles and photos.

I was told there was an exhibit, and it lasted for approximately one
month. One of the options for educators at the living Museum to the
Holocaust was "contemporary genocides." The website is www.mjhnyc.
org/teach_.htm. This made me happy.

Koch served as a congressman for four years and as NYC mayor for
twelve years. Koch was a "Jewish boy from the Bronx" and died of heart
failure at age eighty-eight on February 1, 2013. To honor Mayor Koch,
NYC named the Fifty-Ninth St. Bridge the Mayor Ed Koch Bridge. He
truly was a man of the people.

**5-9-00 - GETTING INTO THE HOWARD STERN RADIO
PROGRAM GREEN ROOM:** I was listening to Stern in early May,
and he made this statement: "I read there is still slavery happening.
Can you believe it?" There it was, our opportunity to get the word out
about AASG and what people could do to combat modern-day slavery.
I called up the radio station, and I ended up speaking to a guy named
K. C. I told him I can come on the program and talk about modern-day
slavery. K. C. said, "Let me get back to you." Benji called back and said,
"Howard will have you on, but you need to bring an escaped slave on
the program with you." I talked to Moctar Teyeb, escaped slave from
Mauritania. He said he will come on the program, and the date for the
show was set for May 9 after 8:00 a.m.

I was working as a NYC teacher, so I have to take a personal day to
make this happen. I ended up telling family and friends I was going to
be in 92.3 K-Rock in NYC, one of the countries' biggest radio stations.
I faxed about ten pages of information to the Stern show. I got to the
radio station and took the elevator up to the floor Howard was on.

When I got off the elevator, there was some guy with a TV camera, and Benji walked me to the green room. I brought some posters for the crew. They asked me where the slave was. I said, "He said he was coming." When I used the bathroom, Fred and Jackie the Jokeman were in their urinating and said hi to me.

I called Moctar, and he said, "I am not coming in." I said, "What? You realize I took a day off work, and we have the chance to get the message out to twenty million listeners? We have the chance to publicize what is going on, to try to get Howard to support our cause, and maybe even get some celebrity support for our cause. We are supposed to push the National Sudan Day for June 9 of this year!" He said, "No, I am not coming in." Well, I did get to sit in Howard's green room but never got to meet the great Howard Stern, Gary Baba Booey, or his sidekick Robin, who was a huge Muhammad Ali fan. So close . . . so close. I did see Howard a few years later at the off-Broadway show, Blue Man Group.

3-26-99 - REVEREND SHARPTON AND REVEREND JACKSON SILENT ON MODERN-DAY SLAVERY: March 26, 1999, at One Police Plaza, was a rally for <u>Amadou Diallo</u>, aged twenty-two, an unarmed West African immigrant who was shot forty-one times by police. His wallet and beeper lay next to his crumpled body. On July 5, a rally was organized at One Police Plaza to organize a civilian commission with subpoena powers to oversee the police department, something Mayor Giuliani was against. On August 9, 1997, in Flatbush, <u>Abner Louima</u>, a Haitian, was picked up in a club and taken to the police station after mistakenly being identified as a person sucker punching a police officer. NYC's finest beat Louma with their fists, nightsticks, and handheld radios and took him to the bathroom in the station, handcuffed him, kicked him in the testicles, squeezed his testicles with a hand, and anally raped him with a broomstick.

Those who showed up to be arrested were Mayor Dinkins, Representative Rangel, State Comptroller Carl McCall, Susan Sarandan, Reverend Sharpton, and Reverend Jackson. Of the protesters, 219 got arrested for disorderly conduct. The crowds of diverse students, religious leaders, and workers on their lunch breaks began to fill Police Plaza. Protesting police officers read the names of 100 officers slain since 1977 and then rang a bell.

On July 5, 1999, I sent a letter to Reverend Sharpton of the National Action Network and Rev. Jesse Jackson of the Rainbow Coalition to inform them about genocide in Sudan and modern-day slavery. I sent a second letter to Sharpton on July 27 via fax and spoke to his secretary, who informed me he received the letters. On July 31, 2000, Nat Hentoff wrote a piece called "Silent on Slavery: Jesse Jackson Ignores Horrors in Sudan."

I got to the rally at 10:00 a.m. and held up a sign that said, "Why is Jackson and Sharpton silent on Sudanese Slavery?" Many people walked by and looked at the sign in horror. I held my own counterprotest on Sharpton and Jackson, and *no one* was brave enough to come up and speak with me. Finally, one woman came up to me and asked what the sign was about. She said to me I will be meeting with Reverend Jackson later tonight. I will speak with him about it. I thanked her. In March, I wrote to Mayor Ed Koch, and he wrote back on March 28. saying, "I had breakfast with Sharpton this morning, and he is going to Sudan. You may want to get in touch with him. All the best."

4-15-01 - REVEREND SHARPTON GOES TO SUDAN: Reverend Sharpton finally went to Sudan. When I was asked by the reporters and radio hosts why I tried to get Sharpton on board, I said, "Because Sharpton gets more media coverage than I do." On 4-9-01 in the *Daily News*, Sharpton said, "I am going to Sudan he wants to confirm if slavery still exists. It is outrageous that no nationally known civil rights group has gone over to Africa to criticize what is happening there." He went on to say "I hope to shape U.S. policy and the UN Human Rights Commission on this to stimulate debate." The new abolitionist said, "If I don't join the fight, what will happen to the suffering people?" Sharpton and his delegation with Africa Action spoke with slaves and witnessed the sale of slaves. Sharpton said he planned to meet with black leaders like Farrakhan, Jesse Jackson, Secretary of State Colin Powell, and UN Secretary Gen. Kofi Annan. On April 20, pop singer Michael Jackson vowed to join the cause, and on April 23, Jesse Jackson joined the modern abolitionist movement, thanks to Reverend Sharpton.

SEPTEMBER 1999 - RECRUTING REV. MICHEL FAULKNER OF CENTRAL BAPTIST CHURCH IN MANHATTAN: He played defensive lineman for the NY Jets in 1981–1982 but was cut after a leg injury. He was a conservative Republican and, in 2015, announced he was running for mayor of NYC. I called Reverend Faulkner in September of 1999 to ask him what he knew about the genocide and slavery happening in Sudan. He said nothing. I explained it to him and gave me twenty minutes of his time. He was known in the Harlem community, and I thought it would be good to have him on board for recruiting other ministers for the cause.

10-4-99 - PUBLIC HEAR ING TO EXAMINE GENOCIDE AND ENSLAVEMENT AND FORCED STARVATION OF BLACK AFRICANS IN SOUTHERN SUDAN AND APPROPRIATE ACTIONS (NYC COUNCIL CHAMBERS 1:00 P.M. BY COUNCILMAN PETER VALLONE):

Cliff Notes of Jim Geist Testimony: Good afternoon. Thank you, Mr. Chairman, for the opportunity to address the atrocities in Sudan. More people have been killed in Sudan than Bosnia, East Timor, and

Rwanda combined . . . Edmund Burke said, "The only thing necessary for the triumph of evil is for good people to do nothing."

Like the movie *Schindler's List*, I have been haunted with the images of starving people, women being raped, and people enslaved. Why is the American church silent on this issue? A Sudanese student asked me, "Why are Americans more interested in Monica Lewinsky than our plight?"

President Clinton on Genocide in Africa

1993   - Washington DC Holocaust Museum:

"Never again! The U.S. must intercede in times of genocide."

1994   - The Rwandan genocide begins.

1998   - Summer trip to Africa (Rwanda)

"We did not know what was going on. We did not act quick enough."

1998   - (December 10) Fiftieth anniversary of the U.N. Dec. of Human Rights

The president announced the creation of an early warning center to focus American intelligence resources on uncovering potential genocide and an increase in funding to stop child labor.

1999   - (March 24) The eve of the Kosovo bombings

"We learned if you do not stand up to the brutality and the killing of innocent people, then you invite the people who do the killing to do more of it."

1999   - (April 14 - *Washington Post*)

Elie Wiesel	questioning the president
Elie Wiesel:	"Why are we so nobly involved in Kosovo and why were we not in Rwanda? I think we could have prevented the massacre."
President Clinton:	"I will do my best to make sure nothing like this happens again."

I have come to the following conclusion about the United States. When three thousand white people got killed in Kosovo, we intervened. When two hundred thousand brown people got killed in East Timor, we waited six months before intervention; and when two million black people got killed in Sudan (or Rwanda), we did not need to intervene.

We need more church leaders involved. We need more Muslim leaders involved. If Malcolm X were alive, I believe he would be part of our coalition. We need more black leaders involved. Where are Rev. Jesse Jackson and Rev. Al Sharpton?

As the Rev. Dr. Martin Luther King said, "Injustice anywhere is a threat to justice everywhere. We are caught in an inescapable network of mutuality, tied in a single garment of destiny. Whatever affects one directly, affects all indirectly."

4-5-00 - I GET UN AMBASSADOR RICHARD HOLBROOKE TO KEEP SUDAN OF HUMAN RIGHTS COMMISSION: On March 26, 2000, the *NY Times* magazine had a front cover story called "The Ambitions of Richard Holbrooke." Holbrooke was the U.S. ambassador to the United Nations, and on page, it mentioned how he dedicated the month of January to issues in Africa since many of the African nations complained the UN focused too much on Europe and Asia. I was impressed Holbrooke was able to help work out a peace agreement with the Dayton Peace Accords signed on December 14 in

1995. He was able to help broker a peace agreement after three and a half years of a bloody civil war between Bosnia and Herzegovina and the Serb Republic. The Bosnian Serbs could have their own autonomous entity, and the Mosnian Muslims were able to prevent the partition of Bosnia.

I called his office, and he was not in. I spoke with his secretary and told her who I was and about the genocide and slavery happening in Sudan by the National Islamic Front government. She said, "I will speak to Richard about this. He must do something about this!" I also told her Sudan wanted to get on the UN human rights panel. I called Nina Shea of Freedom House in Washington DC and Dr. Charles Jacobs. Freedom Houses sent out a letter on May 2, 2000, to meet with the ambassador. A meeting was set up in May in New York City, and our coalition got U.S. Amb. Richard Holbrooke on board. In October of 2000, Holbrooke and the U.S. lobbied against Sudan and kept them off the human rights panel. With one phone call, I was able to make a difference. The following year in 2001, Sudan and Pakistan got on the Human Rights Commission at the UN. The other countries on the commission were Korea, Armenai, Sierra Leone, Tog, and Uganda.

2000 - SUSAN RICE - U.S. ASSISTANT SECRETARY OF STATE FOR AFRICAN AFFAIRS: Susan Rice had this title from 1997 to 2000. With the passage of the Religious Freedom Act, in which the president of the United States must address the three countries committing the worst violations of religious persecution, a meeting was set up with Susan Rice. Dr. Charles Jacobs and several others reached out to Ambassador Rice about Sudan and were invited to the White House and met with Susan Rice in early 2000. I made it clear I wanted to be part of the coalition. I would love to see the White House and to meet the assistant secretary of state. I was told I will not be part of the coalition, but I found out Rev. Michael Faulkner will be attending. I thought, *I helped start the movement in NYC, starting in 1996, giving my blood, sweat, and tears to this issue, with all the time I spent advocating against human rights abuses, and a guy I got on board for six months and has not really done much for the cause gets to go.* I was hurt and angry about this.

SLAVERY IN SUDAN: Holbrooke said, "No one can openly condone slavery. It still exists and is usually ignored by most people and the media . . . How can we stop it?"

7-31-00 - LAUNCHING OF PERSECUTED CHRISTINAN CONCERN BY STUART WILLET (OF THE HIGLAND CHURCH IN JAMAICA, QUEENS): Those who spoke at the launching were Dr. Charles Jacobs, founder of the American Anti-Slavery Group; Francis Bok, escaped slave from Sudan; Jim Geist; and Stuart Willet. Stuart asked me to share about the history of AASG in NYC for the previous three years and to help people understand fighting for human rights and making changes does not happen overnight. We are reponsible to act; we are not responsible for the result. God asks us to be faithful whether there is seen success. Their website is www. PersecutedChristianConcern.com

STARTING TO FEEL PANGS OF BURNOUT: I am grateful for Maria Sliwa and for Stuart Willet because there are times I have energy to advocate and times I do not. From 1996 to 1999, I left full-time "paid" ministry and began going to school to get my teachers certificate. I was housepainting to help pay bills and working as an advocate for persecuted Christians and against the genocide in Sudan. My marriage was beginning to suffer but not totally for the activism. In October of 1999, I began working full time as a high school social studies teacher, so I did not have as much time to work on activism. I had more time in the summer than the school year. Thank God Stuart came along to pick up the torch on Sudan.

THE ACTIVISM OF STUART WILLET AND PCC:

9-9-00:   New Yorkers gathered at the UN to ask why the UN was silent about slavery and genocide in Sudan.

9-15-00:   12:00–2:00 p.m., Christians will meet at the UN and then will march to two embassies (Saudi Arabia and China).

6-9-01   Rally at City Hall Park at 12:00–2:00 p.m. for the National Sudan Day.

The PCC also encourages calling and writing companies and getting hedge funds to pull out BP, Vanguard to pull out its Talisman stocks, and the American funds to pull out the Talisman stocks and writing to senators and the United Nations about setting up a no-fly zone in Sudan to prevent the North from bombing Southern Sudan.

SUMMER OF 2001 - PUSHING FOR
A SUDAN PEACE ACT:

5-27-01:   Secretary of State Colin Powell urged Sudan to end its civil war. He said, "Sudan is perhaps the greatest tragedy on the face of the earth."

6-13-01:   The Sudan Peace Act passed the House of Representatives by 422–3. The bill urges the president to 1) support peace talks, 2) to deliver humanitarian aid, 3) to appoint a special envoy to Sudan, and 4) the Bacchus Amendment to prevent oil companies in Sudan from raising capital in the United States from trading securities. In September 9, 2002, Nat Hentoff of the Village Voice wrote the senate will support the Act but without the Bacchus Amendment.

8-7-01:   President Bush may endorse tribunals to prosecute atrocities in Sierra Leone, Congo, and Sudan.

9-7-01:   Francis Bok, escaped slave from Sudan, met with President Bush as the president appointed Republican Senator Danforth, age sixty-five, an episcopal minister from Missouri.

9-11-01   **Senate slotted to vote on the Sudan Peace Act . . . but the 9/11 attack took place!

Dr. Charles Jacobs on his Washington DC - 9-11-01 : At 9:00 a.m., Charles stood in the U.S. Capitol Building, awaiting the 9:00 a.m. start of a historic press conference. The Sudan divestment campaign, to stop Western oil companies from fueling slave raids on black Africans, was on the verge of a vote. A remarkable coalition of African American clergy and congressional leaders from both sides of the aisle and human rights activists were uniting to demand rigorous oil sanctions.

Suddenly, the news came about a terrifying attack on the World Trade Center. Minutes later, we were rushed from the Capitol and found ourselves dashing through the streets of Washington DC, looking for cover.

The victims of the "holy war" slave raids in Sudan had become blood brothers and sisters of Americans in NYC, Washington DC, and Pennsylvania, who were murdered by Khartoum's partner, Bin Laden. President Bush must know the fight against terror will fail if we strengthen the Sudanese regime and abandon Southern Sudanese bondage.

1-10-01:   Sudan Special Envoy Danforth went to Sudan on a peace mission.

1-19-01:   Sudan and rebels agreed to a cease-fire (which does not stick).

MARCH 2004 - DAFUR SUDAN: Pro-government Janjawid militias (Arab) began to carry out systematic killing of Africans in Dafur. Over 300,000 got killed in the genocide, and it created 2.5 million refugees, many of whom moved into Chad. In August of 2006, the UN rejected allowing for a UN peacekeeping force, saying it would compromise Sudanese sovereignty. In November 2006, the African Union mandated its peacekeeping force will stay for another six months. In March of 2009, the International Criminal Court ordered the arrest of Al-Bashir for crimes against humanity.

1-11-04 - DR. SAMUEL COTTON (1947–2003) - AUTHOR OF _SILENT TERROR: A JOURNEY INTO CONTEMPORARY AFRICAN SLAVERY_ (1998): Sam was born in 1947 and grew up in Brooklyn. After high school, he spent four years in the air force. He studied at Lehman College and received his masters and a doctorate of philosophy from Columbia. He was an adjunct professor, teaching U.S. social welfare policy, and worked with mentally challenged prisoners. In 199, he published his book _Silent Terror_, and he started a group called CAMAS or the Coalition Against Slavery in Mauritania and Sudan. He testified before Congress in 1996 and appeared on a Dateline program called _Silent Terror_. His life inspired many young people to join the modern abolitionist movement, including mine. I remember seeing him on the Dateline piece before I ever really knew who he was. I got to meet him in 1997–1998. He told me he did not have time to waste, but if I asked him for a favor, he would give his time and willingness to speak to different events. The second-last time I saw Sam, as I got into his car, I noticed he had shaved his head; and I told him I liked his new "Shaft" look. He just laughed. The last time I saw him was at a fund-raiser in

Staten Island for AASG. Then I heard about his death in December of 2003. He died of brain cancer, and he never told me he was sick.

ANDY ANDERSEN OF WMCA RADIO (570 AM) (d. 11-30-02): It was just like Andy Andersen of the "Andy Andersen Show" on WMCA radio; he never told me he was sick with cancer either. I am grateful that Andy Anderson used his program to educate people about the International Day of Prayer for the persecuted church and about AASG. He even let me do his program for two hours one time. He passed six months later.

2003 - GEORGE CLOONEY JOINS THE CAUSE: In 2001, Perry Farrell of Jane's Addiction joined in a rescue mission with Christian Solidarity International to free 2,300 slaves. In 2003, actor George Clooney got on board. In 2006, Mia Farrow joined the cause. In 2007, actor Don Cheadle, who starred in the movie *Hotel Rwanda*, joined the movement. As you know, in the United States, most Americans don't pay attention until Hollywood actors speak out. Thank God for George Clooney and the others.

DR. CHARLES JACOBS AND THE NYC DIRECTOR: I gave four years of my life to AASG. I did not make any money; it was all voluntary. One day in the teachers' cafeteria at Park West, I talked about modern slavery and AASG. One lady said, "I think my synagogue is giving an award in Manhattan to someone from AASG." It turned out to be Dr. Charles Jacobs, who never told me he was going to be in NYC for his award. On a second occasion, after I was not able to go on the Howard Stern radio program when the escaped slave chose to not show up and not tell me beforehand, Dr. Jacobs went on the show with another person who escaped slavery. He never told me when he was going to be on. When I heard Dr. Jacobs was going to the White House to meet with Susan Rice, I said I want to be part of the coalition, at least as a thank-you for all the time, effort, and money to the effort. He told me there was not enough room, but there was room for Reverend Faulkner, the Harlem minister I recruited to the cause. This was the third time I felt slighted by AASG founder Dr. Charles Jacobs. I was saddened, hurt, and angered by the way he had treated the "NYC director he appointed." He took all the contacts I put together and all the politicians I helped recruit for the cause and had my name taken off the official AASG speakers list.

THE MALCOLM X OF AASG: The final betrayal took place the day after the March 20, 2002, NYU event, "Slavery Is Not History," organized by asstant for 2002, Mr. Mark Torres. I was asked to speak, and on that night, NYC was beaming two huge lights from where the towers came down just six months earlier. I was still very upset by what had taken place, and in my speech, I said, "I hope that whoever brought these towers down, that we get those cockroaches overseas." The next day, Dr. Jacobs told me I was no longer an official representative of AASG. He said, "You are too much of a bomb thrower, and you are going to cost us money." Wow . . . So that was it. I had become the Malcolm X of AASG, just as when Malcolm X was kicked out of Nation of Islam by Elijah Muhammad. I am glad Malcolm X came back a different person after his trip to Mecca.

In Mecca, Malcolm X saw people of all ethnicities, including Anglo, worshipping and fellowshipping together, and said, "We were truly all the same because of our belief in one God had removed the white from their minds and behavior and attitudes . . . I could see from this that perhaps if white Americans could accept the Oneness of God, then perhaps they could also accept the Oneness of Man."

IRONY OF HUMAN RIGHTS LEADERS: In the course of meeting so many wonderful people organizing, sacrificing, and fighting for human rights and just causes, I also came to hear stories of leaders of many of these groups who did not treat their workers or volunteers with the same consideration. In fact, too many leaders treated workers and volunteers in unkind ways.

I forgive Dr. Jacobs. I am grateful for the work he has done, for helping create AASG and helping educate Americans about modern-day slavery. I am grateful for the four years I was able to be the NYC director. Perhaps it was best for me to step down. It was tough being a full-time teacher and trying to organize events and to try to salvage a marriage that in the end broke apart. I have to let it go and move on. It took me a few years to let it go and for the hurt to leave. Life has other opportunities ahead.

2004 - SERENDIPITY IN WEST MILFORD, NJ: It was a Saturday morning in March of 2004, and I stopped by the local Quik Mart to pick up a cup of coffee. While standing at the cashier counter, I saw a gentleman wearing a Nyack College sweatshirt. I yukked it up with him and told him I graduated in 1988. He told me he was a professor at the Nyack College MBA program in NYC. He asked me to come and speak to his class of eight at the Park Central Hotel on Thursday, March 25. The class was a mixed class—it was not all Christians—but I was given the chance to talk about sweatshops, modern-day slavery, immigration, the persecution of Christians, and what would be the "utilitarian way" to address such issues. Who knew there was a Nyack College professor in West Milford, NJ, and I also was able to inform him of the Living Word CMA Church in the West Milford area.

CHAPTER 10

Becoming a Teacher in NYC
1999–2000 (33–34)

1998 - SUBBING SIX MONTHS IN QUEENS: I subbed in Queens for six months. The AP (assistant principal) there was very gay but nice to me. That school in Astoria kept me working five days a week. What was my experience like subbing at the junior high school level in Queens? Let me say I walked out of school every day with my jaw on the ground. The children were hyper, loud, and extremely disrespectful.

BECOME A TEACHER! My father used to tell my sister and me to consider becoming teachers for a livelihood. The hours are good, from 8:00 a.m. to 3:00 p.m., especially if you are raising a family. It is a professional job that comes with some respect. You get two months off in the summer, so you can travel, work a summer job to make more money, or spend time working on your home and property. He also said, "Teachers always have the most groomed homes!"

After leaving ministry, it took me three years to get to the place where I could get a NYC Department of Education job. I had hoped that I would be able to get a job in the human rights field with Amnesty International, Human Rights Watch, any organization at The

Interchurch Center by Union Seminary, the National Labor Committee, the NY Labor-Religion Coalition, Jobs With Justice, or even the Red Cross. It is very tough to get a job in the business world as a "religion major" with a seminary degree. I did not want to go back into ministry. I was not a fan of doing weddings or funerals or waiting for people who wanted counseling but would not show up. Ironically, I heard too many stories of leaders of human rights groups who mistreated those who work under them. Strange.

1997–1998 - EDUCATION CLASSES: I ended up taking classes in education and two classes in history to be eligible for a NYC teaching license. I had to also take two state tests to measure reading and writing skills and teaching abilities at the Jacob Javits Center by the Department of Education. At the time I took these tests, I had not taken any education classes, and I passed the test.

I only needed a college degree to be able to sub, so as I was going to school and housepainting to help pay the bills, I was also working as a sub. . Think back to when you were in school and were dreading the subject at hand or were supposed to hand in a project or a test, you enter the room and see a sub sitting at the teacher's desk. There were cheering, hysteria, and near rioting! As a result of working as sub almost every day for six months, I have a soft spot for substitute teachers today.

1997 - LACK OF AUTHORITY AND RESEPCT FOR SUBSTITUTE TEACHERS: The substitute teacher really has no power. If you don't know the students' names, you don't have power. If you do not have students' phone numbers, you do not have any power. If you do not give the students their grades, you do not have power. If the students feel entitled to a free party period when the teacher is out, the sub is in store for five to six periods of noise that at times can be ear-piercing. A trick some students like to pull is to skip a class they are supposed to attend and instead choose to sit in your room because it has friends of theirs in it. The way students could speak to you, respond to you, or treat you with lack of respect can be humiliating and can wear on you mentally, physically, and spiritually, even when I did my best to not take it personally. Love, hate, and apathy are energies and powerful.

I believe a teacher who does not leave a lesson plan with copies of work for the kids should be charged a low-level criminal charge of negligence. To be a sub without any work for the students can and often does lead to horseplay, loudness, and unnecessary horseplay. Horse play often leads to fights.

A friend from church, Russ Nitchman, invited me to sub in Elmhurst, Queens. He was a science teacher, and we had gone deer hunting together the winter before in Upstate NY. While we stopped by a Wendy's on the way up there, an African American gentleman hunter also came in. It was the first time I had ever seen this. Good for him!

What you have to understand is substitute teachers are at the bottom of the Department of Education food chain. We are the chum of the shark tank. I would walk into the school, and they would hand you a schedule of the classes you are to cover. They usually give you copies of lessons for the class. The teacher assignment was written out 50% of the time.. If you are lucky, you get a bathroom key. You are even luckier if they give you a list of phone extensions to call if you have any problems in your classroom. You have hit the jackpot if the school gives you a sheet with school regulations so you can know what is proper and unprofessional behavior.

SUB SCHOOL #2 – FEBRUARY OF 1998: It was the last period of the day. Many of the students had completed their work early. Then fifteen minutes before class ended, a student asked if he can leave early. I looked at his work, and I was not sure. I said, "Sure, why not? Good work should have some reward. Why should you have to sit here for an extra fifteen minutes?" I then let five to six other students do the same.

The next day, as I was awaiting my assignment in the principal's office, the secretary said, "Sorry, Mr. Geist, we no longer need your services." When I inquired why, she said, "I don't know." I asked to see the principal for an explanation to understand why. She said he was busy. I said, "I am not busy, so I can sit in the waiting room until 3:00 p.m. until he gets two to three free minutes to talk with me." She said, "You need to leave." I said, "I am not leaving." After fifteen uneasy minutes, a chapter leader for the union (teacher) came in and told me why I was being let go. He said, "You cannot let students out early. If a student gets hurt or injured before 3:00 p.m., the school can be held liable." I felt terrible. I asked him if can ask the principal to give me another chance. The UFT representative said the principal will not. "It is best if you leave for future subbing jobs."

SUB SCHOOL #3 - MAY 1998:

My friend from church, William, was a science teacher at another school in Long Island City, next to Astoria. He told the principal about me, and there was a chance for me to get a full-time job there the next fall. I worked there for two months. I was given a work schedule with times and classroom numbers and sometimes work to hand out to the kids, who will ignore the work anyway, talk, and play games for the "free period." I did not have a phone list for the principal's office, the AP's office, the dean's office, or for security.

After subbing at my second junior high school in Astoria for four months, I switched to a junior high school in Long Island City, Queens, a bit closer to me. I liked this principal who was Italian and full of pep and cool as a cucumber. He was organized and smooth and had purpose in his steps. I came into the school because a mutual church friend worked there. After being there a few months, I was in a seventh-grade class, where a young boy started taunting a young lady. The next thing I knew he was on top of her and starting to beat the tar out of her. They were both African Americans. Before the punches had flown, I ran in the hallway to find a security agent or dean. There was no one in the long hallway. I did not have a phone list to call a dean, security, or the principal's office for help. I ran over as he started hitting her, grabbing him by the neck with my right hand and his left arm with my left hand, and pulled him off her. I dragged him over to the hallway and shut the door and locked it so he cannot get in again.

I asked a student to go get a dean or security agent; a student volunteered. A young lady ran out of the class, saying, "Oohhhh, I am going to report you for beating up a student!" *Great*, I thought. This happened in the first class of the day. In my last class, an announcement was made over the loudspeaker. "Mr. Geist, report to the principal's office." I was expecting the principal to shake my hand and thank me for helping prevent a young lady from getting injured. Instead, he said, "Mr. Geist, we no longer be needing your services." "For what?" "I was not there in the room and cannot afford to have students getting hurt in class." "So are you saying I should have let them fight until security or a dean showed up? If I was the daughter's parents, I am sure they would be grateful for what I did for her today. I also kept the young man from getting into more trouble than he could have gotten into."

The event had happened in the middle of the week. Mayor Giuliani used to have a radio program on WABC Radio (770 AM) on Fridays from noon till one o'clock. I called in and explained what happened. He said he would look into it. I said I wanted my job back. The principal called me and was appalled I called attention to his school via the mayor's office and that I would never work for him.

FINALLY: Shortly after this experience, I received a call from Park West High School. They wanted to interview me for a social studies position. I remember meeting with AP Richard Shevlin and with Principal Frank Brancato. The interview went fairly well, considering I had not done many job interviews before, and I was very happy when I received the call I was hired. My full-time teaching career began in October of 1999.

OCTOBER OF 1999 - PARK WEST HIGH SCHOOL: I got a call telling me to report to Park West High School at Fiftieth Street and Tenth Avenue in Manhattan. I reported to the job and filled out paperwork for the school—emergency info, health insurance forms, a 1040, and the United Federation of Teachers. The next thing I asked for was the TDA form, the Teachers Deferment Annuity. Over thirteen years, I put in 5 percent to 8 percent of money, depending on how tight my yearly budget is. As a Jewish teacher said to me, "Jesus saves, but Moses invests. Make sure you sign up for the TDA."

The AP was three years from retirement, had a bad back, and was tired. He did not have time for me or care to help train me. I ended up learning everything I needed to learn from the elder teachers in the teachers' lunchroom or at Druid's Bar on Fridays after school. I really liked our UFT union representative Bob McCue. The UFT chapter at our school had a real sense of solidarity. We looked out for one another and helped support one another.

At the end of my first semester, I received a pink slip. Luckily, the principal liked me, and with the help of the chapter, Harvey Rosenberg stepped down as dean. With only three classes for me to teach, having two periods to working as a dean will save my job. It was a great opportunity to get to meet kids, to learn discipline codes, and to build relationships with security agents.

JULY OF 1998 - APARTMENT BREAK-IN: Teresa Joy and I went away for a week, and someone must have seen us loading our suitcases into the car and waited until we left. I locked the door handle lock, but I did not lock the dead bolt lock. Probably some kids broke in using a crowbar. When we got back to the apartment after driving ten hours from Maine and found a parking spot and carried up our suitcases, I saw our apartment door open. I was sick to my stomach. When we walked in, things had been ruffled through, drawers were opened, and things were on the floor. In the end, the thing that bothered me most was someone found my Coleco Football handheld video game, which my grandparents had given me when I was in sixth grade.

We cleaned up the apartment, called the police, and filed a report; and I called a locksmith to come and fix the door since it would not close and lock properly. I think it cost $150 to $200. The next day, I called my landlord and told him what happened and wanted the cost of the locksmith deducted from our rent. He would not agree with that. I ended up going to some event, and seated at my table was the honorable NY Supreme Court judge Richard Braun. He was a nice guy. I told him my story, and he said I had a winning case, and the landlord should deduct the charges. I called my landlord to give him the news, and he said, "Okay, Geist, you win the battle this time." It was weird since I lived there for five years, and we paid the rent on time every month and never gave him any problems; and if it had gone to small claims, we would have won the case anyway.

MY NIGGA! As Dean Geist, I walked the halls and moved kids to where they were supposed to go. If a kid was harassing a teacher, I may take the kid to my office to the detention office. Many kids who got me as a teacher said, "Oh boy, I have Dean Geist." After a few weeks, they said, "Mr. Geist, I thought you were mean, but you are a funny and nice guy." One day I walked down the hallway, and two kids were in front of me. They did not see me, and one kid said, "I hate Dean Geist!" And the other kid said, "What? No way. Mr. Geist is my nigga!"

ON GRADING STUDENTS: I graded fairly. My policy was 50 percent for test grades, 20 percent for classwork, 20 percent for homework, and 10 percent on class participation. This way, if you were a poor student but showed effort, you could pass; and if you were intellectually smart, you could not breeze by without having done your work. For me, grades were a tool that helped me know who needed extra help and an idea as to why some had behavior issues out of frustration and as to what students who excelled in a class could help me mentor and help struggling students.

DO GRADES MEASURE INTELLIGENCE?: It depends on your definition of intelligence. For me, the grades showed me whether a student was mastering a topic or struggling. Some say grades don't measure intelligence, and age does not define maturity. I always understood a kid was more than a grade. I also understood there are many qualities not measured by tests, such as creativity, critical thinking, resilience, motivation, humor, reliability, self-awareness, empathy, leadership, resourcefulness, spontaneity, and humility. The most important for me is being able to take what you have learned and to be able to use it as responsiveness to change. As Darwin said, "It is not the strongest or the most intelligent of species who survives, but the ones most responsive to change."

POINTING AT STUDENTS: Sometimes in the middle of class, I would start pointing at students and not say a word. Inevitably, someone would ask, "Why were you pointing your finger at certain students?" I would say, "I have just pointed at students who I believe are good students, but I would never hire if I run a business." This would lead to a discussion about how I thought some of the smarter students can be lazy and were not working as hard as they could. Other times, I would just point at certain kids, and they asked what I was doing, and I said, "These are the *B* and *C* students I would hire at my business because I see them being resilient, motivated, and hard workers. There is more to being smart in this world to be successful."

WORLD LEADER GRADES? Those who probably would have gotten *A*'s are Mussolini in psychology, Hitler in speech, Kaczynski in mechanical engineering, Madoff in economics, and most politicians in acting. Those who would have failed are Picasso in art, Jobs in business, Dylan in music, Gandhi in foreign policy, and Oakland A's Billy Beane in stats.

DRUID'S BAR - TEACHING CENTER (15th STREET AND 10th AVENUE): The assistant principal Richie S. seemed nice enough, but he was close to retirement and having back problems and was not really interested in helping me or coaching me. The most frequent answer I got from him was "Are you not licensed to teach social studies in New York City?" The first year was the toughest, learning names of students, fellow teachers, school rules, union rules, about managing classroom discipline, parent-teacher conferences, how to grade, etc. The key to classroom management is to have a good lesson plan and always have more than less on the plan to keep the students busy. If you don't keep the students busy, they will keep you busy.

Where I learned most about teaching was by going to the teachers' cafeteria and on Fridays going to Druid's Bar across the street. It was here I can bring up particular students or situations or any questions I had about pedagogy that got answered happily by the elder teachers. Park West High School was a real sense of brotherhood and sisterhood of being union brothers and sisters. We had one another's backs. I love being a member of the United Federation of Teachers and have no problem paying my biweekly union dues. The rumor was Bruce Willis used to bartend there. Another story was Bruce Coker of "Find a Little Help from a Friend" 1969 Woodstock fame, who walked into Druid's, sat at the piano, and then stood and said, "I don't feel like playing today."

I learned to not expect many thank-yous. The thank you get from the NYC Department of Education comes in the form of a paycheck every two weeks. It will take me three and a half years to earn tenure, and since I did not have student teaching experience, my first year of teaching will count as my student teaching. The UFT has a teacher center that offers classes on teaching, so I do feel supported by my fellow teachers and union, not by my AP. I must say I did like and respect our new principal, Frank Brancato. He was a good guy, a good Catholic, and met with the union reps regularly too in the process of making our school the most successful it could be.

The first thing I did on my first day there was to go to Rene H. of payroll and ask for a TDA form or Teachers Deferment Annuity. In my years teaching in NYC, I tried to put 5 percent to 8 percent of my income into it as a way to help build up my nest egg. The money I had accrued over the years would come in handy thirteen to fifteen years later when times got tough. With $100,000 in the TDA and with approximately 6 percent to 8 percent of interest per year on my earnings, I was able to withdraw money to help pay my mortgage and pay the bills.

1999 - AGE 33 - FIRST YEAR TEACHING: The first year of teaching was draining. There was so much to learn and lessons to write every night and often having kids test you to see if you are the real deal and going to stick it out. In one of my classes in my first year, I had a Puerto Rican girl who was the leader of the class. If she was peaceful, the class was peaceful. If she was in a testy mood, she could make the class go ballistic. I pulled her in the hallway to have a talk with her to make peace with her. It did not work. A few days later, I pulled her out of class and said, "Did you know I served in the Persian Gulf War in 1991? Did you know I have six confirmed kills, and I also shot and killed at least a dozen camels?" Her eyes widened, and she said, "Yo, mister, you are crazy!" From there on in, she never gave me any problems. How about that, a former pastor having to make up lies in order to get control of a class?

In another class, in the middle of the year, this really tall African American kid came into class. I pulled him to the side and asked him why he had transferred so late in the year. He told me, "I just got out of Spafford." I asked my union rep about this and found out Spafford was a detention center in the Bronx for youth. I asked the Spafford student why he was in Spafford in the first place, and he told me, "I punched my last teacher in the face." I said, "Oh, welcome to my class." He sat in the back row and never gave me any problems.

THE LOVE BOAT: The school was originally built in the shape of a cruise ship. The original vision was to train kids for jobs in the food and hospitality business, including culinary. A principal by the name of Budias, to impress the NYC Department of Education, told them the school can handle more. A school that can manage two thousand students now had three thousand kids in it. It became a chaotic school, a student fired a gun into the hallway ceiling, and there was a day when an all-out riot broke out in the school that ended up with a student getting a butcher knife in the head. The union rep tried to locate the principal so they can create a plan to handle the chaos, and he found the principal in his office, hiding under the desk. The *NY Post* newspaper calls nicknamed the school The Wild West High School. As a new teacher, I was placed in a center room with no windows. I had a metal bucket I filled with water to clean my board. Then one day I grabbed the bucket, but it had a smell. I found out the fattest security agent sometimes napped in my room and used the metal bucket as a pee bucket.

Principal Brancato liked me, and the teachers liked me, but I was going to be "excessed" in second semester. I will not have five classes to teach, but if I can get a "comp" job, such as deaning, I can stay on by teaching three classes and deaning the rest of the day. I was surprised they asked me to be dean since I was new to the school, and it was because they thought I was a good teacher, and they wanted to keep me. I was grateful that one dean stepped down so I can keep a paycheck coming. I got my first tastes of union solidarity, and I liked it. One day I can pay it forward. I got my tenure in 2003.

STUDENT'S FAMILY TO BE EVICTED: One of my Dominican students came up and asked if she can speak to me after class. I said, "Sure, what's up?" She told me her father had been a superintendent of a building for sixteen years and that the landlord wanted them to move out at the end of the month. She said, "Mr. Geist, you teach government, and you were involved in politics as a pastor. Can you help us?" I said, "I am not sure, but we can call your NYC Council person, and they will have a staffer to help you." We looked up the information on the computer and contacted the office, and I gave her the staffer's name. Her family met with the staffer and found out they cannot be kicked out at the end of the month. Legally, they can stay there for one year before moving, and the landlord must pay the superintendent a month's wages for every year her father worked there, so the family at the end of the year will get a check worth equal to seventeen months of wages. This is what is meant by "knowledge is power." I was glad I could steer her to the right place that could help her family.

A **STUDENT DIES:** I had a sophomore student named Regalio (pronounced Ra-hay-lee-o). He was Dominican, full of life, passionate, could argue well for his beliefs, always laughing, and part of a swimming club. It was the Wednesday before Thanksgiving, and my room was on the first floor by the stairs. The day before, I had the kids act out machines they had created in our studies of the Industrial Revolution. Regalio was pushing a student around in a chair, laughing. On this day, he looked terrible. I said, "Regalio, you look terrible. You should see a doctor." He had his head down, and he said, "Mr. Geist, I am seeing one on Saturday." I said, "Great. I hope you have a great Thanksgiving weekend!"

I came back on Monday, and I saw several students crying. I asked one student what was wrong. He said, "You did not hear? Regalio went to swimming practice on Friday, and his heart exploded, and he died." I said, "Don't tell me that. That is nothing funny to joke about." My union rep confirmed it was true, and here was a kid on the swimming team looking healthy as a horse a week earlier, and now he was gone. He was a pleasure to have as a student.

2000 SUMMER OLYPICS (GOLD): Michael Johnson (running), baseball team, basketball team, women's basketball team, women's softball team, women's soccer team, Laura Wilkinson (diving), Brooke Bennett (swimming), Venus Williams (singles tennis), and Venus and Serna Williams (doubles tennis). From 2002 on, I lost interest in the Olympics; but starting in 2016, I began to feel the urge to start watching them again, maybe as a result of doing research for the book.

SHAME ON PARKING POLICE OFFICER O'CONNOR: It was the wintertime, and we had lost much parking because of construction on Forty-First Street. NYC gets its water from the Adirondack Mountains from a pipe that you drive a Mack Truck through. It then broke down to smaller pipes to deliver the water to all the boroughs in NYC. Thanks to the construction and a snowstorm, a small cul-de-sac had been created on Thirty-Third Ave. on Forty-First Street. People parked in the makeshift cul-de-sac because of the loss of parking. On a Saturday night, a parking police officer by the name of Mary O'Conner sneaked around like a snake in the grass and gave at least a dozen cars parking tickets. I was not one of the people ticketed, but I made a note of it in my mind. The following summer, when you have to move your car by 11:00 a.m., there was Officer O'Conner waiting to give out tickets. I went on the roof with some eggs and waited for her to pull up by my apartment building. As she wrote up a car in front of my apartment, I toss an egg, and it hit the front hood. I took another egg and did the same and went two for two from the third floor. I ran down the roof stairs into my apartment and looked out the small opening of my curtains, and there were civilians pointing to the top of my apartment roof like the Kennedy assassination. I kept laughing to myself the rest of the day out of nervousness and from the stress of having waited five months for this perfect occasion.

2000 RIGGED ELECTION: On November 8, the Florida Division of Elections reported that Bush had beat Gore with 48.8 percent of the vote and a margin of 1,784 votes. With it being less than .05 percent, there was a recount, and Bush's margin decreased to 327 votes. On December 8, the Florida Supreme Court by a 4–3 vote ordered a statewide manual recount. On December 9, the U.S. Supreme Court voted to stay the Florida recount, and Bush would be credited with winning by 537 votes. Justice Scalia said, "The counting of votes . . . threaten irreparable harm to petitioner Bush." In other words, if there was a recount, Bush could lose the election. The Supreme Court dissenters said, "Preventing the recount from being completed will inevitably cast a cloud on the legitimacy of the election." In 2013, retired justice Sandra Day O'Connor, who voted with the majority, said the court should have declined to hear the case that "gave the Court a less-than-perfect reputation":

1. Florida secretary of state in charge of elections paid $4 million to Database Technologies, a company with Republican ties, to remove anyone suspected of being a felon to be thrown off the voter registration rolls. She did so with the blessing of Gov.

Jeb Bush of Florida. As a result, 173,000 registered voters in Florida were wiped off voter rolls. There were 54 percent of those deleted who were black, and in Florida, 90 percent of blacks voted Democratic. Thousands of blacks who had never committed a crime were denied the right to vote.

2. There were 680 votes of the 2,490 overseas military ballots that were considered flawed but not thrown out in Florida. There were 4/5 votes that went to Bush, meaning 544 votes should have been thrown out, dropping Bush's 537 vote to -7.

3. The butterfly ballot: *The Palm Beach Post* estimated three thousand voters, mostly elderly and Jewish, who ended up punching the wrong whole for Pat Buchanan. Even Buchanan went on TV to declare that no way in hell did those Jewish voters vote for him. Buchanan explained, "My name next to Al Gore cost him thousands of votes—and the presidency" (from "A Very American Coup" in _Stupid White Men_, pp. 5–13).

4. In Volusia County, a Diebold-made electronic ballot voting computer showed the Socialist candidate getting nine thousand votes and Al Gore getting minus nineteen thousand. Had it not been for this computer error, CBS News would not have called Bush the winner at 2:17:52 a.m.

QUEENS LAUNDROMAT SHIRT ROBBERY: The laundromat was down the street. If I found a parking spot the night before where I would not need to move the car because of alternate side of the street parking, it made doing the laundry so much easier. I bought $150 of new school clothing for school, dress shirts, and pants. I took them to the laundromat, washed them, and threw them in the dryer. I went home to do some work on the computer, went back, and picked all my clothes. I went home and folded my clothes, but something did not feel

right. I realized all my dress shirts had been stolen. For the next week, I
kept my eyes open, looking for a man who may be wearing my clothes,
but to no avail. I went back to Old Navy and bought new shirts. Many
of the ladies in the laundromat spoke Spanish. My neighbors had two
young boys, and they were out of control. When the mother took them
to the laundromat, they talked trash about the kids and mother in
Spanish. Grace was white but knew Spanish. She said good-bye to the
gossipers in Spanish and told them she hoped they had a great day and
that she grew up in Costa Rica. Oops.

2000 - FILING FOR DIVORCE: After courting for five years and
being married for nine years, I felt there was too much criticism of who
I was, and I could never live up to what the wife wanted as a husband. I
will admit, I am obsessive, and codependent, and gave much of my time
to social justice causes. It is not fair to say I was never around when my
spouse would go to work and then come home and teach aerobics and
then go out with girlfriends. When I left the church in 1996, it took
two and a half years for me to find a full-time job. I always paid half
the bills with my apartment painting, but I also had to go to school
to earn education credits to become a teacher and was involved in my
social justice ministry.

DID YOU DO THE LAUNDRY TODAY?: For the most part
during this period, I was Mr. Mom, doing the food shopping, cleaning
the apartment, doing the laundry, and often doing the cooking. I became
upset because I felt I was not getting recognition for keeping the "house"
(apartment) going. One day I did the laundry, but I only did my laundry.
When Joy came home, she said, "I thought you did laundry today?"
I said, "I did do laundry, my laundry." The following week when the
money from our joint account was missing, I knew it was over.

What did she want to make the marriage work? "I want you to go
to the gym." I did. "I want you to go to ballroom dancing with me." I

did. "I want you to go to counseling with me." I did. In our last session, the counselor asked the bride what she needed for the marriage to work. She started listing the things she wanted me to do. "I want Jim to do A, B, C; and D, E, F; and G, H, I; and J, K, L; and M, N, O; and P and Q"; and I yelled, "Stop! I cannot live up to these expectations! She listed seventeen things and still had more changes she wanted me to make. What? Why can't you accept me for who I am? I have an announcement. I want a divorce!" I got an attorney through the union. We each paid $750 to the attorney divided up the stuff, and she moved out a month later, just two weeks before the 9/11 attack.

Pres. George W. Bush (2001–2008)

Domestic

Enacted Medicare Part D

*Energy Policy Act of 2005 - extending daylight savings by four weeks, three weeks earlier on the second Sunday in March and one week later on the first Sunday in November, saving one hundred thousand barrels <u>of oil a day by turning lights on later and more time to enjoy outdoor activities.</u>

Foreign

Signed the U.S. civil nuclear agreement	Committed $15 to combat AIDS over five years in Africa

<u>Short List of Dirty Tricks and Bad Legislation</u>

Presided over the 2008 Great Recession	Added five trillion (really eight) to national debt

Poor response to Hurricane Katrina

Falsified justification for Iraq War

False reporting on Pat Tillman and Jessica Lynch

Subprime mortgage bubble

Tax cuts to rich, increasing the national debt

USA Patriot Act: Suspension of habeas corpus

Faith-based initiatives

Failure to capture Bin Laden

Ignoring warnings of 9/11 attack

EPA gag rule on climate change

Outing CIA Agent Valerie Plame

Gutted the Clean Air Act

NSA wiretapping of citizens

Black sites and rendition

K Street lobbying - Abramoff-Reed

War by contractors cronies

Appointing Roberts and Alito to SC

Rigged elections 2000 and 2004

Stopped funding stem cell research

Increased balance of trade deficit

Bankruptcy bill favored creditors

Trying to privatize Social Security

Against net neutrality

Labor Department ground gutted by McConnel's wife

Bush's ties to Enron

Cheney opting fracking out of Clean Air Water Act

Fraud to suppress minority voting

Swift boating of John Kerry

White House e-mails on RNC servers	Twenty-two million White House e-mails disappeared
Talon: Pentagon spying on citizens	Using torture and Guantanamo
Auditor of no bid KBR Iraq contract demoted	Six nuclear cruise missels flown over the United States
White House logs declared state secrets	Soaring oil and gas prices
Drilling in Bristol Bay, Alaska	SEC blind eye to Wall St. violations
Unsafe helmets, bad ammo	Department of Defense cannot account for billions.
Dumping of mining debris in rivers okayed	Lax oversight led to bank failures

Labor Department pulled rug under corporate whistleblowers

Taken more vacation days than any president

Delayed implementation of 9/11 Commission recommendations

MSNBC, JOHN STEWART, STEVEN COLBERT, AL FRANKEN, AND MICHAEL MOORE BUOY ME: I was depressed during the Bush (W)-Cheney administration. What helped me keep my sense of humor and a compass as to the assault on civil rights and our Constitution were the the writings of Al Franken, Michael Moore, and James Carville. I really enjoyed watching the following on MSNBC: Phil Donahue, Keith Olberman, Ed Schultz, Martin Bashir, and Melissa Harris Perry. What do they all have in common? All of them were fired by MSNBC. When I hear my conservative friends talk about how liberal MSNBC is, I have to say "Not so much" when you see all the people they have fired over the course of a decade from 2005 to 2015. I found Olberman, Stewart, and Colbert to be extremely intelligent and served as soothsayers to me, to explain what was happening in our country. While I knew all the things listed as dirty tricks and bad legislation, at least by watching the listed commentators, I was able to get some humor from them to help lessen the pain. The only survivor I am aware of since the founding of Air America Radio and MSNBC is Dr. Rachel Maddow.

JIM GEIST DIARY (September 11, 2001)

"The Day My Mayoral Primary Vote Did Not Count."

Queens: Tuesday, September 11: At 6:30 a.m., I went to the polls to vote for Alan Hevesi to become NYC's next mayor. I thought about how when I got home I will be watching the television to find out what was happening with the polls. I went to the Steinway subway stop to catch the *R* train to go to Park West High School at Fiftieth Street and Tenth Avenue. I got there twenty-five minutes later because the trains were running slow; I had no classes until period 4. It was a beautiful fall day in the seventies with a blue, blue, blue sky.

Manhattan, 9:00 a.m.: After period 1 scanning (metal detectors checking for guns or knives), I made my way to a period 2 coverage when I heard on the dean walkie-talkie: "Two planes have hit the twin towers." After I proceeded to the principal's office to drop off the collected cell phones and beepers, Mr. Wallach, the music teacher grabbed me and said, "Did you know there is a twenty-minute difference between the planes hitting the towers? The Pentagon has also been hit with a plane!"

Feelings: It sank in, a terrorist attack. Is this the beginning of WWIII? How many have been killed or injured? I got a sick feeling in my stomach. Principal Brancato called for all security and deans to report to his office. The secretaries were standing by the TV and screamed as they saw the second plane fly into the towers and then saw the first building collapse. I felt tears welling in my eyes but kept my composure until all the kids were taken care of.

The principal placed security officers at every door to keep kids from leaving. The deans were told to not teach any classes but to roam the hallways to keep moving kids back into classrooms. We were under attack and not too far from the Empire State Building and had no idea what will happen next.

The word started spreading throughout the student body. Most kids will not really understand what was happening until they see the TV images. With the classes that I had, I briefed them about the towers, the Pentagon, the plane downed in Western Pennsylvania, and reports of a bombing in the Capitol Building and State Department (which turned out to be false). Is this our generation's Pearl Harbor? How does one fight a war on terrorism?

The principal made an announcement over the intercom as to what was happening. First, there was shock and then silence; but slowly, student panic built up, and the energy was ready to burst. By 1:00 p.m., the students were running through the hallways, trying to get out of the school. The principal told the staff to not use the phones; half the phone lines were down anyway. I tried to call my soon-to-be ex-wife; I just filed a divorce three weeks earlier. I cannot reach her, but I was able to leave a message on my apartment phone.

The bridges and tunnels had been closed. The subways were not running, and I was not sure about buses. If you lived outside Manhattan, they were saying you may have to stay in Manhattan overnight. I hoped

I would not get stuck in the building with hundreds of panicking students.

Tears began as teachers and students began to realize they had family and friends who had worked in the towers or in that area of Manhattan. Anxiousness was setting in, and we were holding our breath, waiting to hear from the schools chancellor what the next move was. Teachers had been working without a contract for nine months. The hell with Mayor Giuliani's insolence with teachers, duty calls. Teachers did not go into teaching for the money but to help kids out.

10:30 a.m.: Announcements were being made every ten minutes to report to the principal's office. Parents were coming in to get their kids, everyone to get access to the phone landlines. There was a line of seventy-five kids at the pay phones. I sneaked into my private little office frequently to get the latest information off the radio.

12:30 p.m.: The NYC mayoral primary was canceled until further notice.

2:00 p.m.: The announcement was made that students will be excused starting at 2:10 p.m., followed by "Please listen to the TV or radio if there is school on Wednesday." The kids in my class in room 419 left and said, "Good-bye, Mr. Geist." As the students left, I hoped I would see them again.

2:30 p.m., Faculty Conference: The teachers met for a briefing. The principal was staying in case any students were not able to get home tonight. I offered my apartment for any teachers who may not be able to get home as well.

3:00 p.m.: I went to O'Doyles Bar in midtown before trying to get on a train. The TV was on, and people at the bar were sharing stories about people they knew who worked in the towers. It hit me. I was supposed to meet with one of my best friends, Edward Nanno. He worked for the Bank of New York and was doing some business in the area of the twin towers. All I thought was *I hope Ed is okay. Please, God, be with Ed!*

4:00 p.m.: I took the *E* subway train home. Everyone on the train was in shock. I had never heard it quiet on the trains before. I got home and watched TV until I fell asleep.

Every hour I tried to call my parents and sister. The phone lines were down. The sky was quiet, except for the jet fighters that screeched by every half hour. When the first one flew by, I yelled, "Where the hell were you seven to eight hours ago?" The Star Wars flying by sound brought some comfort knowing we had a chance of stopping any other planes trying to crash into buildings.

4:30 p.m.: The announcement was made that NYC schools had been canceled on Wednesday.

7:00 p.m.: My sister Jody called by cell phone, panicked to find out if I was okay. I told her I was fine. She called my parents and friend Mike Brogna to inform them as well. I later found out Dad had a headache all day until he found out I was okay.

7:30 p.m.: I went to the top of my roof with a radio, camera, and a Budweiser beer to look at the sunset skyline of Manhattan with the plume of death smoke signal rising from the towers. I was ten miles away on my Queens apartment, and I wished I was watching a *Twilight*

Zone episode, but this was reality. As I sat there, I can read in the smoke signal: "America's way of life will never be the same again."

The streets around my apartment neighborhood on Forty-First Street and Thirty-Fourth Ave. were quiet. At night, you can see the glimmer of all the TV screens through everyone's apartment windows. Neighbors were on the streets, sharing stories. I sat on my front porch with a candle burning, and strangers walked over to share stories with me. I felt anger. "The bastards must pay!" American flags were popping up everywhere in the neighborhood.

Wednesday, September 12:

A.M.: I woke up and went to Big Apple Deli on Steinway Street to get my scrabbled egg on a roll with ketchup, salt, and pepper with a copy of the *NY Times*, the *Post*, and the *Daily News* under my arm. As I walked out of my apartment, two things hit me: 1) I smelled smoke. I looked up and down the street to see if any apartments were on fire. Nope. It was not until I got to the Deli that I heard on the news the same smoke from the tower pits can be smelled all the way out to the tip of Long Island. I gasped, realizing I was breathing in death. I saw many police officers on Steinway Street. Was this to prevent rioting? Was this to protect businesses owned by Indian and Arab business owners? Again, it was another beautiful day of blue skies and in the seventies. There were people strolling everywhere. Many had off because they worked in lower Manhattan. Mayor Giuliani had requested people to stay out of Manhattan and to only come in if it was necessary.

I felt like I needed to do something. I wrote some letters to President Bush, NY senators Schumer and Clinton, and Rep. Joseph Crowley of Queens. It helped me vent some of my anger. President Bush was upsetting me. He looked like he was shitting his pants. I wanted my president to be strong and as mad as hell. He better gets some backbone soon or step down and let Uncle Dick take over. I would feel safer if "Poppy George Walker Bush" was in charge or even Pres. Bill Clinton, who cleaned out some clocks over in Kosovo.

P.M.: <u>A Bangladeshi pastor I knew who spoke Arabic</u> told me that the Islamic community just six blocks from me was laughing and saying to one another in Arabic, "What a great day for Islam!" He had heard the local imam (mosque leader) preaching hatred against Americans. We must get these cockroaches responsible for this terrorism. How can we let such people be able to stay in our country on visas for ten to fifteen years? I was infuriated. The pastor said he believed some of them knew about the attack before it happened and wanted to speak with the FBI in Queens. I looked up the number for him and gave it to him. I sat out on the steps again that night with my candle. People were walking around, sharing stories with one another again. **I made the decision to throw an antiterrorism party at my apartment to divert people's attention from this horror for at least four to six hours.**

STORIES I HEAR:

<u>My building superintendent</u> Mike's wife, Deirdre, worked in a doctor's office by the twin towers. On Tuesday morning, she was on her way to work when she realized she forgot to make lunch for her kids. She went back home to make lunch, and as she went to the school to drop it off, she found out about the attack. The dust cloud and debris landed on her boss's office.

At O'Doyles Bar in midtown, an African American <u>woman</u> told me she worked at the Marriott Hotel by the twin towers. Tuesday was her day off. My <u>neighbor Yolanda</u> who worked as a maid near the twin towers said in the evacuation panic, she was pushed down the stairs; and while her leg was not broken, it was badly hurt.

My friend <u>Andre Flax</u> was leading a business meeting where he had a grand view of the towers. People noticed smoke coming from the tower. He said he was able to keep the meeting running until the second plane hit, something all the meeting goers were able to witness, and they all ran out of the room. The meeting was canceled.

My college and graduate school buddy and who was in my wedding party, <u>Edward Nanno</u>, a Syracuse, NY, resident would be in Lower Manhattan from September 10 through 15 for some business as a representative of the Bank of New York. He called to inform me he was okay on Thursday, September 15, with an incredible story.

On Tuesday morning as he was getting off the *A* train on Chamber Street, he heard a loud noise. It sounded to him like a front loader had dropped a metal plate on the street. Half a block later, a woman running down the street yelled, "Run like hell! There has been a bombing!" As Ed walked around the corner, he can see the sky full of papers flying around the twin towers.

He and his workmate turned around and started running for five blocks. They got to a spot where there was a crowd to watch the smoke bellow out of one of the towers. They watched the paper and debris circling around. It did not take long to recognize some of the things coming out of the building were workers jumping from the heat of the building into the coolness of the outside air to plummet to their deaths. He and his friend went into St. Peter's Church to pray. After five minutes, the whole church rattled and shook, and windows shattered as from the sound wave of the impact of the second plane hitting the other tower. Ed said it was as if someone grabbed his head and pushed it between his legs. He suffered whiplash as a result and lost a significant amount of hearing from the crash explosion. As of Sunday, September 16, Ed had not been able to sleep.

Thursday and Friday (9-13 and 9-14): At Park West High School, only a third of the students had shown up for classes. Many Islamic parents kept their children home.

Since 1998, I had been the NYC director of the American Anti-Slavery Group, (www.iAbolish.org) speaking to people about modern-day slavery and genocide in Sudan. Many now understood how fundamentalist religion killed. My ex-wife once accused me of adultery and called my mistress human rights. She now called me to say "I never understood your passion for human rights and for your speaking out for persecuted Christians in Islamic countries. Now I do. Tell me what I can do."

I cannot watch television anymore. Since the attack, I only got two stations, CBS and ABC. They had become the twenty-four-hour antiterrorist network. I did not have cable, but thank God I recorded two weeks' worth of the Simpson episodes. Homer, Marge, Bart, Lisa, Maggie, and Santa's Little Helper had been my salvation in regard to diverting my attention from all the shock, pain, and anger.

P.M.: I cleaned the apartment and went to Pathmark to buy all the supplies for the Saturday Party. Keeping busy was good during this time.

Friday, 9:00 p.m.: I felt President Bush had redeemed himself by giving a speech of a lifetime. I was moved and ready to follow his leadership in getting the terrorists responsible for the attack.

Saturday, September 15:

I spent the morning getting ready for the Uplift America Party. At noon, I went to the United Nations where Highland Church (in Jamaica, Queens) was planning on holding a prayer meeting for Christians being persecuted in Communist and Islamic countries. The previous year, 2000, showed up for the rally.

A friend of mine was the founder of Fellow Soldiers, a group of activists in the Lehigh Valley addressing the present-day persecution. When we got to the UN, we found dump trucks full of sand, concrete, and metal blockades. The police had pulled the permit, and the event had been canceled.

There were six other Christians who showed up, and we spent twenty minutes in prayer for our persecuted brothers and sisters. One of the believers was Indonesian, and his name was Karl. He told us that for the last six months on the island of Melaka, nine thousand Christians had had their throats slit by Muslims. The fundamentalist Muslims in Melaka had been inspired by Osama bin Laden and had declared jihad there. I am so angry with fundamentalist Islam persecuting Christians, violating female rights, using terrorism, attacking the United States on 9/11, and then having the nerve to celebrate it in the United States.

8:00 p.m.: The party started, and twelve people showed up. There were Mexican salad, "freedom" hot dogs, wine, music, and a game of salad bowl (charades). The party went on until 1:30 a.m. and was a success. I felt the objective had been met. We got together and were able to live in the present and get our minds off the horror for four to five hours. *Victory!*

At the party, I had a rubber band gun with two spinning targets. I pasted pictures of Saddam Hussein on one and bin Laden on the other.

Throughout the evening, people came over and shoot rubber bands at the bastards. We did have one party casualty, and that was Matt the science teacher from Park West. I last spotted him from my third floor window, blowing his cookies next to someone's passenger side back tire. He did show up to work on Monday I am glad to report.

Sunday, September 16: My buddy from Pennsylvania stayed overnight on the living room couch. We hung out all day before as he helped me prepare for the party. I slept horribly this night, only two and a half hours. There was too much on my mind—terrorism, nine thousand Christians killed on the island of Melaka, Muslims near my neighborhood reported to be celebrating the 9/11 attack, my divorce getting finalized, and knowing people who survived and others who had lost loved ones. I felt I had been beaten worse than Reginald Denny.

4:00 a.m.: I went to a local diner and ordered pancakes and coffee. I can only eat two bites. I bought the Sunday papers. I got in my car and started driving home. I pulled over and cried for five minutes.

7:00 a.m.: John Noska drove me to my church in Manhattan as he headed back home to the Lehigh Valley. I walked to St. Bartholomew's Episcopal Church (Fiftieth St. and Park Ave.). This was the church where they filmed the wedding scene in the movie *Arthur* with Dudley Moore. Next to the church was a police station and a fire station. There were pictures of missing people, the dead, flowers, candles, and notes posted everywhere. There were TV cameras, international reporters, and the saddest faces I had ever seen. These were NYC's "finest" and "bravest" who had served and made the ultimate sacrifice in serving humanity.

I needed to go to church today like I never had before. As Gandhi said, "I must deal with my demons before I deal with the demons of others." I went to church to pray the hatred I was feeling. I wanted to join a vigilante group and confront those who had allegedly celebrated the death of Americans in Queens. I knew it was not very Christian, but this was how I felt. The service was not moving for me. I was too raw, angry, and numb. I was tired and needed to get some sleep. I needed to clean up from the party as well.

Thursday, September 20: I heard on the radio this morning that three Arab men had been arrested in Astoria at the candy store on Steinway Street and Twenty-Fifth Avenue. I passed this store every time I went to cross the Triborough Bridge (now the JFK Bridge).

Perhaps my friend, the Rev. Peter Sayed, was correct. My Bangladeshi friend and converted Christian minister from Islam who spoke Arabic, this was what he reported to me, and I wondered if his phone call was the one that tipped off the police. He was a good man and Christian. For those who are Arabic and/or Islamic who love America and religious tolerance, welcome to the our melting pot. If not, you have to go back to your country of origin. May God give us courage, wisdom, mercy, and grace in these difficult days.

Saturday, September 22: My <u>neighbor Jim</u> who worked as a custodian down near the towers told me how janitors were finding fingers and teeth on top of their buildings. A woman strapped in an airplane seat was also found. My other <u>neighbor Jeff</u> who was a stock broker told me how he had lost twenty to thirty friends who were stock brokers.

Post note: After three weeks, I was at the corner bodega when Jill, Jim's wife, walked in. It was about 5:00 p.m., and I said, "Hi, Jill." She looked terrible. I went on to say "Say hi to Jim for me!" She looked at me in disbelief and said, "You haven't heard? Jim died of a heart attack last week." I said I was so sorry to hear this and gave her a hug. Imagine that, you survived a 9/11 attack only to die from natural causes two weeks later.

PSS: My sponsor told me a story related to 9/11 in 2008. He used to work in Manhattan, and one day he was down at the towers a month before the attack. My sponsor was Jewish, and he noticed an Islamic person standing between the buildings and taking pictures. My sponsor said when he walked by the guy, he gave him a dirty look. In his gut, my sponsor felt this man was up to no good and went to the FBI in NYC to report what he had witnessed. After the attack, when they showed pictures of the nineteen terrorists, he recognized one of the pictures of the guy he saw at the towers the month before the attack, casing the area.

Tuesday, September 25: I went to the polls a second time (two weeks after the 9/11 attack) to vote a second time for Alan Hevesi for mayor. He used to be the comptroller of NYC and met with myself and several others to discuss how NYN could hold Sudan accountable for the slavery and genocide happening over there. Alan Hevesi also hated cigarette companies for all the people they killed and made sick. He ended up losing the Democratic primary election to Mark Green. Michael Bloomberg would go on to beat Green to become NYC's next mayor.

DR. ED NANNO'S ARTICLE: My buddy Edward Nanno had an article in the Alliance Life (November 2001) entitled "A Mighty Fortress" about his business trip to the twin towers on the morning of September 11, 2001.

NAZI SUBS OUTSIDE NYC: September 25 is my Grandpa Short's birthday. During WWII, he served as a navigator for the Merchant Marines, taking U.S. troops and supplies to and from the war theater. Grandpa Short said the day before he was given his ship, the Nazis sank a U.S. ship just outside the NY Harbor. I hope our generation will rise to the occasion as his generation did after the Pearl Harbor attack.

Terrorism Attacks Since 1988

12/21/88:   Pan Am Flight 103 (London to NYC) - 259 killed; Libya responsible

              Note: Three weeks before Nyack College came home from London Winterum

02/89:   Soviet forces pulled out of Afghanistan.

12/89:   Muslim conference in Oklahoma City (future U.S. Embassy bomber and ninety-three WTC bombers met)

11/90:   Authorities discovered bomb manuals and photographs of the World Trade Center and Empire State Building found in a radical Muslim apartment in Brooklyn, NY.

1992–1996: Al-Qaeda reached out to Iran and Hezbollah to take part in a war against the United States.

02/26/93:   WTC bombing - six killed and hundreds injured

1998:   U.S. Embassy in Kenya and Tanzania bombed - 224 killed, eight years after U.S.-Kuwait war

10/12/00:   U.S. Ship *Cole* explosion - seventeen U.S. sailors killed

01/01:   FAA warned of hijackings

01/25/01:   Terrorist Czar Richard Clarke warned of sleeper cells in the United States.

02/01:   Suspicious flight school student in Arizona; poor English and limited flying skills

06/2001:   Intelligence wars of an imminent attack, and the FBI withdrew from Yemen.

06/28/01:   National Security Advisor Condoleezza Rice warned that Al-Qaeda attack was highly likely.

9/11/01:   <u>Twin towers and the Pentagon</u> were hit by airliners; three thousand were killed.

2002:   Bali, Indonesia, bombing - 202 killed

10/02:   Washington <u>DC Beltway sniper attack</u>: John Muhammad killed ten with son in three weeks.

03/02/06:   Nine students injured at UNC in Chapel Hill, North Carolina, by Muslim driving a Jeep into them.

07/28/06:   Seattle Jewish Center shooting - one killed

06/01/09:   Little Rock, Arkansas, military recruiting center - one soldier killed

11/05/09:   Fort Hood, Texas, shooting: Muslim major psychiatrist killed thirteen and injured thirty.

2009:   Jarkarta, Indonesia, bombing - eight killed, fifty injured

05/01/10:   Attempted Times Square bombing

11/26/10:   Portland, Oregon, attempted Christmas tree lighting bombing

04/15/13:   <u>Boston Marathon bombing</u> - three killed, two hundred injured

09/24/14:   Moore, Oklahoma, Vaughan Foods beheading

10/23/14:   Queens, New York, hatchet attack

12/20/14:   Slaying of two NYPD officers

05/03/15:	First Annual Muhammad Art Exhibit in Moore, Texas, a security agent was shot.
07/16/15:	Chattanooga, Tennessee, recruiting center shooting - five killed
11/13/15:	Paris, France - gunmen killed 129
06/12/16:	Orlando, Florida, gay nightclub shooting - forty-nine killed and fifty-three injured
7/14/16:	Nice, France - eighty-four killed by a lorry (tractor-trailer)

Attacks Deadlier Than France in 2015

-01/07/15:	Nigeria - 300 gunmen from Boko Haram killed 2,000 in 16 villages.
-10/31/15:	Sinnai Peninsula, Egypt - 224 killed
-04/01/15:	Garissa, Kenya - 146 killed
-09/20/15:	Maiduguri, Nigeria - 145 killed
-03/20/15:	Yemen - 137 killed
-11/13/15:	Paris, France - 129 killed

NOVEMBER 12, 2001: FLIGHT 587 CRASHES IN QUEENS:
I was in Lancaster, Pennsylvania, with my father, who was buying me a new hunting jacket for my Christmas gift. The radio was playing when it was announced an airplane had gone down in a Queens's neighborhood near the airport, and it was believed there were no survivors. I was upset when I heard this because I lived just ten minutes from La Guardia Airport, and I was hoping the crash had not been near my apartment. Americans were raw and angry from the recent attacks, and many were suspecting this was the result of a terrorist attack. When we got back to Danielsville, I felt I need to get back to Queens to check out if all was

okay. I later found out Flight 587, a weekly flight to Santo Domingo, Dominican Republic, flew out of JFK on the southern part of Queens. There were 587 who ran into the wake turbulence of the Japanese Airlines Boeing 747, and the pilot used aggressive rudder inputs to left to right for twenty seconds until the stabilizer snapped off. Structure failure and incorrect pilot training were to blame. There were 260 who died on the plane, and 5 were killed on the ground when it crashed into Belle Harbor homes.

BUDDY JOHN FIORI: One of the best things about living in Queens is I got the chance to make friends with John Fiori and with Ivan and Janet Valle. They were in my New Life Fellowship "parish" and wonderful people. John was a Queens's boy, who lost his father to murder as a young kid. He went to a school that was mostly black and was an excellent basketball player. Teresa and I had done some marriage counseling with John and his pretty Latina wife, Bobbi, before Teresa and I filed for divorce. They could not make it work, and John ended up moving to Long Island. He was working as a boiler engineer and custodian at a junior high school in the neighborhood but ended up getting a job near JFK Airport. He was taking classes to get his electricians license in the city, and after Teresa moved out, John would crash at my place two to three nights a week. I enjoyed the company. When John came to the apartment, he could sit on the couch with a beer and watch ESPN. He would look at me and laugh because he thought I had Attention Deficit Disorder (maybe I do). I could not sit still. I would get up and do dishes and sit, get up and go on Match.com on the computer and sit, get up and vacuum and sit, and get up and make some calls and sit. It was very tough for me to just be.

John worked out and was an excellent softball player. He and Ivan Valle often worked out together. The three of us got together for a beer and to talk. John took a trip to California and played some hoops out there. Someone called a foul on John, and he said, "Foul? Look, pal, I am from Queens. If there is no blood, it is not a foul. Get back to playing hoops or go home." When I started dating Vanessa, John said to her, "What does it feel like to be Mrs. Ex-Geist number 3?" Thanks, John.

SMALL WORLD: One of the deans I worked with at Park West High dated a woman named Tina. They broke up, and he talked about her all the time. John started dating someone, and her name was Tina. She was nice, and when she found out I worked at Park West, she asked if I know Alex R. I said yes. She said, "That is the guy I used to date." Weird. Alex would try to get info from me about her, and I said, "Dude, you are married, and secondly, it is none of your business, and lastly, I don't want to get in the middle of craziness between friends." Alex finally got the message.

WORKING OUT WITH JOEY ZAZA'S "VITO" AT ASTORIA SPORTS COMPLEX: During this time, I went to the gym two to four times a week. It was just two blocks away, and I didn't have a house to take care of, so I have the time and convenience of getting there. I was working out one day, and some guy said to me, "Do you know who that guy is over there?" I said no, and he said, "That is Vito Antuofermo. He boxed Marvin Hagler, and he was in *Godfather III*. HEY, VITO, YOU BEAT THE MOOLIE!" Vito said in a quite voice, "Don't say that. You shouldn't use that word." Moolie came from the Italian word *mulignan* or eggplant, which is a racial slur in reference to you as dark as the skin of an eggplant.

This Antuofermo fan was referring to the second fight Antuofermo had with Hagler, which came to a draw, but many said Antuofermo won by 1 point. The fight ended before the fifteenth round when Hagler head-butted Antuofermon. Antuofermo was born in Italy in 1953 and came to NYC at age seventeen and learned how to fight on the streets.

Vito drove trucks, fixed trucks, pulled weeds, and stuffed sausages to make money. He got into boxing but always worked a job while a boxer and won the golden gloves at the 147-pound division. In the 1980s, he worked for Coca-Cola while living in his home in Howard Beach section of Queens. His weakness in boxing was that he bled easily around his eyes.

He played a bodyguard for Joey Zsa-Zsa in *The Godfather Part III* and had a role in *The Sopranos*. Vito was the undisputed heavyweight champion at one point and had a record of fifty wins, seven losses, and two draws. It was estimated he earned over one million in his career, but he always kept working even while being a professional boxer. Today he owned a successful landscaping company in Long Island, NY.

SATURDAY 9-24-05 - WASHINGTON DC PROTEST AGAINST THE WAR IN IRAQ: The bus trip was organized by Dr. Arlene and Stuart Hutchison of William Paterson University. We met at 5:00 a.m. and were to be in Washington DC by 10:00 a.m. The all-day peace and justice rally started on the Washington Monument grounds on the National Mall. On the trip down, about an hour outside of Washington DC, there were plenty of cars that were passing our bus; yet our bus was pulled over for speeding by the police. The officer clearly saw we were a group of protesters going to protest the President Bush's war in Iraq. We took a donation of all the people on the bus to pay for the driver's ticket, but he was going to be stuck with the points. What a lousy thing to do and truly an abuse of power by the Republican officer, I am sure.

At 11:30 a.m. was a rally at the Ellipse across the street from the White House, and the march began at 12:00 p.m. The rally was to close at 3:00 p.m., and music was provided by Joan Baez; and there was a special speaker, Cindy Sheehan, antiwar activist whose son, U.S. Army Specialist Casey Sheehan, was killed in Iraq. She gained media attention when she built a makeshift camp outside President Bush's Texas ranch. At one point in the march were at least fifteen photographers taking pictures of all the protesters walking by. I wondered who was taking the pictures, assuming it was the FBI for intelligence purposes.

2-27-06 - IKE SAW IT COMING: In the documentary *Why We Fight* directed by Eugene Jarecki, the central character is Dwight Eisenhower, the Republican president who had been the Supreme Allied Commander in Europe in World War II, who warned us about the profound danger inherent in the rise of the military industrial complex. Bob Herbert told us, "He warned us, but we did not listen." Eisenhower said, "The potential for the disastrous rise of misplaced powers exist and will persist. We must never let the weight of this combination endanger our liberties or democratic processes." Bush and Cheney in a deceptive maneuver took the eye of our real enemy in Afghanistan and launched a pointless war in Iraq. At the end of the movie, Mr. Sekzer, a NYC police officer who lost a son on September 11, said, "The government exploited my feelings of patriotism for a deep revenge for what happened to my son. I was so insane with wanting to get even, I was willing to believe anything."

HIGHLANDS PEACE ACTION: The main movers of the group are Clint Hebard, Ken Veroli, Ann Benedito, Alice Courage, Judith B., Renee Allesio, and Tim Dalton. We protested the war in West Milford next to Town Hall, and West Milford being mostly Republican and "patriotic," we got many dirty looks and comments. It was rewarding when we got thumbs-up from eight to ten people, and it was good to know we were not alone in the insanity of this war in Iraq. I also invited speakers from The Manhattan Neighbors for Peace and Justice, which sent two Vietnam War vets to speak to my classes in Washington Heights about "What Military Recruits Don't Want You to Know."

9-14-01: PASTOR MIKE BROGNA VISITS LODI, CALIFORNIA, MOSQUE: After the Friday service, many of the Islamic worshippers hang out in the park near the mosque. Pastor Mike Brogna, my buddy from Allentown, Pennsylvania, went to talk with the Islamic community the Friday after the 9/11 attack. Mike was a pastor at Calvary Bible Church in Lodi, which had 2,500 Pakistanis living there. Mike talked with some members, and they said they would like for him to meet the iman of the mosque. The mosque had a Pakistani flag flying but no American flag flying. There were three police cars parked in front of the mosque. Mike walked into the room with about a dozen men with the iman at the head of the table. There was also a local reporter sitting at the table. It was clear from the daggers the iman was sending Mike he was not really happy he was there to visit. Mike offered a Bible as a gift, which the Islamic elders refused to take; however, they offered Mike a Koran, and he graciously accepted the Islamic holy book. "I did not feel welcomed by many in that room," Mike said.

JUNE 5, 2005 - FIVE MEN ARRESTED BY FBI AT LODI MOSQUE: Of the five arrested, 1) Iman Shabbir Ahmed of the Lodi mosque for urging followers to back Bin Laden and to kill Americans. He was also accused of having links to a terrorist group in Pakistan. 2) The other Lodi iman linked to Ahmed was deported back to Pakistan. Before 9/11, terrorist mastermind Ayman Al-Zawahiri, a close friend of Bin Laden and number 2 leader in Al-Qaeda, attended the mosque. Several of the men arrested came over on R1 religious worker visas through the San Francisco Airport. Intelligence knew of Ahmed from November of 2001 but had not passed on the information to the State Department consular officers, one of the problems noted in the *9/11 Commission Report* of agencies not communicating well with one another. Since 1990, more than 145,000 religious workers had entered the United States and, approximately 2004–2005, did law enforcement agencies begin investigating Muslim clerics. 3) On <u>April 25, 2006</u>, a jury convicted Hamid Hayat from the Lodi mosque was sentenced to twenty-four years of providing support and resources to terrorists in addition to spending two years at an Al-Qaeda training camp in Pakistan. 4) In <u>March of 2014</u>, the FBI charged Nicolas Teausant, a twenty-year-old National Guard reservist, for planning to blow up the Los Angeles subway. He was found to be in possession of "lone wolf" terror manuals wowing how to build and detonate bombs. Mike said, "When I saw the men arrested, I said to my wife, 'Those are the guys I spoke with!'" Mike said he was surprised but again was not surprised.

11-20-06 - EAGLES' DEFENSIVE BACK ANDRE WATERS COMMITS SUICIDE: Andre Waters, aged forty-four and former defensive back for the Philadelphia Eagles, died of a self-inflicted gun wound on November 20, 2006, in Tampa, Florida. Forensic pathologist Dr. Bennet Omalu of the University of Pittsburg He played 156 games, played from 1984 to 1993 for the Eagles, and was known for his hard-hitting tackling game. He led the Eagles in tackles in 1986, 1987, 1988, and 1991. Dr. Omalu determined that Waters's brain tissue had degenerated into that of an eighty-five-year-old man hasted by numerous concussions and would have been incapacitated within ten years. During his career, when asked how many concussions he suffered, Waters replied, "I don't know. I stopped counting after fifteen."

2007 - DR. BENNET OMALU MOVES TO LODI, CALIFORNIA: Dr. Omalu, a neuropathologist, performed the first autopsy on Hall of Fame center Mike Webster while working for the Allegheny County Coroner's Office. Webster died at age fifty, experiencing dementia and depression, and Omalu found in his brain tangles of tau protein consistent with CTE (chronic traumatic encephalopathy) and found in "punch drunk" boxers. It was the first of eighty-seven deceased ex-NFLers diagnosed with CTE. He believed

90 percent of NFL players will develop CTE. He moved to Lodi, California, where my NFL—Philadelphia Eagles, Herschel Walker, Walter Payton—loving buddy, Pastor Mike Brogna, lives.

2015 - MOVIE *CONCUSSION*: *Concussion* came out at Christmas in 2015 starring Will Smith as Dr. Omalu. This was written about in the book *League of Denial* by Steve Fainaru and Mark Fainaru-Wada and in the subsequent PBS Frontline special in 2013. HBO's Real Sports hosted by Bryant Gumbel ran a piece on concussions in the NFL in August of 2007 and on CTE in September of 2014. The NFL Players Union said, "We are encouraging players to see it as a teaching tool about not-so-ancient history." The NFL agreed on $765 million to settle a lawsuit brought on by 4,500 players. Omalu, not a football fan, was first stonewalled by the NFL with his scientific finding on CTE. A coworker told him, "You are going to war with a corporation that owns one day of the week."

FORMER PLAYERS CONFIRMED
WITH CTE POSTMORTEM

Dave Duerson	Mike Webster	Tyler Sash - 27	- NY Giants
Ray Easterling	Frank Gifford	Terry Long	
Earl Morrall	Junior Seau	Ken Stabler	
Bubba Smith	Justin Strzelczyk	Andre Waters	O. J. Simpson?

SYMPTOMS OF CTE: The symptoms of CTE include cognitive impairment like memory and multitasking, mood problems like depression and apathy, behavior changes like aggression and mood control, and, most rarely, motor problems like body tremors or difficulty making facial expressions.

LIVING FORMER NFL PLAYERS WITH
CTE OR ALS SYMPTOMS

Brent Boyd	Tony Dorsett	Bernie Kosar	Leonard Marshall
O. J. Brigance	Mark Duper	Fulton Kuykendall	Ricardo McDonald
Harry Carson	Brett Favre	Dorsey Levens	Jim McMahon
Wayne Clark	Andrew Glover	Jamal Lewis	Bob Meeks
Joe DeLamielleure	Steve Gleason	Dwight Harris	

AGE 36-45 2001-2011

Part IV. Midlife Crisis: Entering The Cave

West Milford, Teaching, Politics, Courtrooms, Heartbreak, Recovery

CHAPTER 11

West Milford and Teaching at Wild West High School 2001–2005 (35–39)

7-1-02 - WEST MILFORD, NEW JERSEY, JULY 1, 2002, FROM QUEENS (36): It was nine months after the 9/11 attack in NYC and nine months and three weeks since my soon-to-be divorced wife, Teresa, had moved out. I had packed up all my stuff and had five people help me load the rental truck, and two guys plus myself helped me unload the truck and drove it back to Queens. I had my own parking spot on a long driveway, a deck where I had twenty-six acres of woods behind me, a garage, a shed, a deck with a bar where I can cook food on a grill, and a campfire area. My first couple nights were tough to adjust. The peeper frogs were so loud at night. I had a home just ten feet from me, but no one will live here for three years.

PHIL RIZZUTO: I met a neighbor one day, an older gentleman; and he told me he was from Canarsie, Brooklyn; was a munitions guy in WWII; and that he worked in sanitation in NYC all his life. When Mayor Lindsey will not meet with the garbagemen, a warehouse in Queens, Manhattan, and the Bronx blew up. Lindsey met with the sanitation union; they came up with a contract. I told the gentleman

I had been keeping watch of his property, mowing the back lawn, and keeping it clean of tree limbs. He threw me $40 and thanked me. He told me his family used to come up to the summer home; and the Phil Rizzuto of the Yankees, the "holy cow" announcer for the Yanks, was a relative and used to come up for picnics. The reason the homes were so close together was because after the first cabin was built (my place), an aunt wanted another home built. That was why the homes were so close. It will be three years before I got neighbor, Kenny, who moved in.

POOR MAN'S LAKE: Upper Greenwood Lake is a manmade lake a mile long and one-third of a mile wide. On Warwick Turnpike is a deli on the north side of the northwestern side of the lake that is called the Lakeside Deli but used to be "Fred's Landing," a place where Norton and Ralph Cramden of the TV show *The Honeymooners* supposedly went fishing in one episode. The area is owned by a newspaper man, who uses the trees to print newspapers; and then in the area where the trees have been cut down fills it up with water; and in his paper sells affordable lots to blue-collar guys who want a place to get away in the summer. As the NYC metropolitan area grows, more people move out to west and north in New Jersey, and most of the summer homes are now insulated and year-round homes for many who commute by taking the 196 Express Bus into NYC.

SHORT HISTORY OF WEST MILFORD, NEW JERSEY - (A BICENTENNIAL OF WEST MILFORD BY INAS OTTEN AND ELEANOR WESKERNA, 1976): West Milford has four major glaciers move through it, the last being the Wisconsin glacier that receded fourteen thousand years ago. It is eighty square miles with the Bear Fort Mountains and Pequannock River on the west and southern borders, with Greenwood Lake to the north border, and with the Wanaque Reservoir and Ramapo Mountains on the Bloomingdale border. It has forests of hemlocks, oaks, and maple interspersed with white pine. It is full of game and fish, minerals in the mountains, and waterpower to turn mill wheels. It was said a squirrel could walk along the tree lines from the Hudson to the Delaware River without touching the ground.

John Heckewelder, a Moravian missionary, said in 1876 that the red man and white man lived in peace . . . until they began to believe they (whites) wanted all their country." Trappers and traders made their way to Greenwood Lake (then called Long Pond) in the mid to late 1600s. Within a hundred years of the founding of New Amsterdam (New York City) by the Dutch, English, French, and Dutch settlers pushed their way up to Pequannock and Wanaque valleys. The Lenape Indians were known as peaceful until maltreatment led to reprisals. By the mid-1770s, there were Irish and free blacks also working in the iron industries.

In 1763, Perter Hansenclever came from Germany to set up an iron ore in the mountains. Within a year, 535 German families said the smoke from the furnace filled the atmosphere for miles and produced twenty to twenty-five tons of pig iron. In 1853, Abram S. Hewitt bought the iron ore for $100,000. In 1869, 120 people were employed by the Long Pond Iron Works. Hewitt was a Democrat and did not always agree with Lincoln but contributed to the union by manufacturing gun barrel iron for the government at production cost.

ABRAM S. HEWITT (RingwoodManor.com): Hewitt graduated from Columbia in 1842 in the study of law. He taught grammar school at age thirteen. He traveled to Europe and befriended Peter Cooper, one of the richest men in America who started Cooper Union College; and they survived a shipwreck on the voyage home, which strengthened their friendships. Hewitt married Cooper's only daughter and had six children. Starting in 1874, Hewitt served as a congressman for ten years. He also became the chairman of the Democratic National Committee.

In 1886, Hewitt was elected as a NYC mayor and lost the next election because he was critical of immigrant loyalty and refused to attend the Saint Patrick's Day parades. He enforced a law closing saloons on Sundays and supported building small parks in crowded areas of NYC. He epitomized Victorian America and was honest to the point of bluntness. He was a pillar of righteousness in the political world of Tammany Hall favoritism, demanding compromise and pragmatism.

OTHER INDUSTRIES IN WEST MILFORD: In addition to the iron ore industry was the growth of lumber mills, cedar shingles, barrel hoops, tanneries for shoes and leather products, a knife factory, and icehouses where the lake water ice had to be at least ten inches deep. Single-room schoolhouses appeared to educate children and churches of various denominations—Methodist, Presbyterian, Catholic, and Episcopal eon (really the Anglican or Church of England) and later on a Baptist, Lutheran, and Assembly of God Church. With the emergence of a stage coach line in 1857 from Paterson to Newfoundland and the rise of the New Jersey Midland Railroad in 1869 came the emergence of the Greenwood Lake Casino, Brown's Hotel, and the Montclair Steamboat of 1900 on the lake. In 1845, Newark took over much of the water in West Milford to supply fire hydrants and cisterns; and in 1860, the state legislature created the Newark Aqueduct Board.

PROPERTY WORKAHOLIC: I was so happy to be out of NYC. I loved sitting on the deck in the morning indisbelief and feeling some culture shock from having lived on a city street with thousands of residents and to have twenty-six acres of land behind my home with deer, bear, and beautiful gold finches coming to the feeder that look like bright-yellow canaries. It was so quiet, and I had all of July and August to myself. I felt so emotionally drained and suffering from such evangelical guilt for getting divorced I worked from sun up to sun down on my property. I started with the inside of the house and then the outside of the house, staining the home and deck. Toward the last few weeks, I spent my energies on the yard and the woods around my property. I was keeping busy to not sit with my feelings or do the proper grieving I should be doing over such a loss as this. I will pay in the near future for having stuffed my feelings all my life when I hit the age forty-two.

2002 - HELLO, GOOD-BYE!: Over the years in West Milford, I had had my run-in with bears. I moved to West Milford, New Jersey on July 1 of 2002. I spent the summer working on my home and property. I stained the house, the shed, and the back deck. I worked on the shrubbery on my property, cleaned up the campfire area behind my home, and went into the woods behind my place and cleaned that up as well. There were some dead trees and downfalls behind my home. Behind the house were wetlands, and to the side of my property were woods where the campfire area was. There were twenty-seven acres of wetlands and woods behind my place.

I had an electric chainsaw Grandpa Short gave me. It was about ten o'clock in the late August summer morning as I was cutting away at some downfall. The hair on the back of my neck stood up, and I strongly felt eyes were on me. Bears can move quietly, and if you have a chainsaw going, you can hear no foot steps on the forest floor. I turned around to see a massive 450–500-pound bear sitting 50 feet from me. I put the chainsaw down slowly and started talking to the bear.

"Hi, bear. I did not see you. I am in your neighborhood, and I am leaving now." As I was speaking, I was slowly backing away from the bear, who was watching me with curiosity. There was a little hill up to my property; and as soon as I got to the bottom of it, now one hundred feet from the bear, I ran away like a nest of stirred up hornets was chasing me up to my deck. The bear stayed in his seated position for another ten minutes and then moved on. My first New Jersey bear experience.

ANIMALS I HAVE SEEN IN MY BACKYARD

Deer	Raccoons	Opossum	Owl	Blue bird
Bear	Dogs	Hawk	Chickadees	Warbler
Foxes	Cats	Crows	Gold finches	Woodpeckers
Squirrels	Turkeys	Scarlett taniger	Turkey vultures	Blue jays
Squirrels	Garter snake	Chipmunks	Humming birds	Groundhogs
Blue birds	Orieles	Coyote/ Coydog	Red taningers	Two boas

NEIGHBOR WELCOMING: Actually, no one welcomed me to the neighborhood. The first weekend I was in my new home, the people across the street from me were playing that crazy rock-and-roll music all day late into the evening. With my windows opened on these hot summer evenings, it carried right through my screen windows and kept me up. I will have a talk with the neighbors the next day. On Monday morning, I introduced myself to Ron and Lynn. He was a disabled police officer, and she worked for the West Milford Board of Education. After the niceties, I asked if they can play their music lower in the evenings. Officer Ron said, "Jim, I am really sorry. That was my son. We were away over the weekend, and I will talk with him. Thank you so much for not calling the police on him." They had a pool in the backyard and, as of 2016, had never invited me over for a dip or a glass of vino. We have neighborly chats from time to time, and I did invite them over for a campfire, which Lynn came over for. I introduced myself to the other neighbors, and they never said hi to me in the fourteen years I have lived here.

WINNING FRIENDS, INFLUENCING PEOPLE: I did not know a soul in West Milford so to meet people, I went to the Living Word Alliance Church pastored by Rev. Tim Barnes meeting at the high school on Sundays. The church eventually bought the old synagogue on Upper Greenwood Lake. I also attended the Warwick (NY) United Methodist Church pastored by Pastor Chris Yount, a graduate of the Alliance Seminary and basketball player at Nyack College. I also joined the West Milford Democratic Club and, in time, made some very good friends.

2002 - BOAT DOCK: At the end of the summer, I went down to the lake, 250 yards from my home, and looked around at the boat docks in Croton Cove. There was a pontoon boat with a burly guy on it and a huge German shepherd named Hunter barking at me like it wanted a piece of me. I spoke with Scott Kessler, and he told me I needed to go to the Upper Greenwood Lake Clubhouse to file for a boat dock. I did so and eventually heard from the boat dock committee chairperson months later. When we talked on the phone, I asked him if I needed to grease his palm to get a dock, and he said, " No, no, no, no!" I was not sure because there seemed to be a lot of Italians up here, and I heard about the body found on the island that was the result of a hit. The following summer, I bought a boat that had a motor and built my boat dock.

U.S. History 2000s

1980:	MTV (Music Television Videos) started
	Ronald Reagan elected president (defeated Dukakis)
	- age of Reaganomics and the New Right
1981:	Space Shuttle Columbia
	- personal computers introduced
1985:	Live Aid (helped Ethiopian famine)
1986:	Chernobyl Ukraine nuclear reactor disaster
	- Iraq-Iran war ended (one million killed)
1988:	**George Herbert Walker Bush** elected president (defeated Michael Dukakis)
1989:	Fall of the Berlin Wall

Inventions of the 2000s

2000:	Segway Human Transporter, GPS
2001:	Artificial heart and liver, fuel cell bike, iPod portable music digital player
2002:	Braille glove, phone tooth, nanotechnology wearable fabrics, birth control patch, camera chip, date rape drug spotter, virtual keyboard
2003:	Hybrid car, robotic cat and roving robo raptor, infrared fever screening
2004:	Translucent concrete: optical glass fibers transmit light and color,
	SonoPrep: delivering medication by sound waves rather than injection
2005:	YouTube

2006:   Facebook, Nintendo

2007:   iPhone

2008:   iKindle e-books

2009:   3D cameras

Cars of the 2000s

Camaro '02 (last of the Camaros), Pontiac Azteck, Chrysler PT Cruiser, Toyota Prius, Hummer 2, Hyundai Genesis, and Tesla Electric (2003)

Music of the 2000s

2000:	Papa Roach: "Last Resort"	Incubus: "Drive"
	Destiny's Child: "Say My Name"	Creed: "With Arms Wide Open"
	Comedy: Lewis Black	
2001:	Train: "Drops of Jupiter"	Godsmack: "Awake"
	Mary Blige: "Family Affair"	Alicia Keyes: "Fallin'"
	Comedy: Zach Galifianakus	
2002:	Nelly: "Getting Hot in Here"	Comedy: Lewis Black
2003:	Jane's Addiction: "Just Because"	Nickelback: "Someday"
	Beyonce and Jay-Z: "Crazy in Love"	Comedy: Dave Attell

2004:   Green Day: "American Idiot"   U2: "Vertigo"

          Velvet Revolver: "Fall to   Comedy: Bill Burr
          Pieces"

2005:   Fall Out Boy   The Killers   Papa Roach

          Audioslave   The Strokes   The Bravery

          Comedy: Dane Cook

2006:   Foo Fighters: "Best of You"   Incubus: "Anna Molly"

          Comedy: Jim Gaffigan

2007:   Linkin Park   Muse

          Modest Mouse   Comedy: Kathy Griffin

2008:   Paramore   Comedy: George Lopez

2009:   Lady Gaga: "Just Dance"   Black Eyed Peas: "Union"

          Stone Temple Pilots: Alice in Chains
          "Between the Lines"

          Kings of Leon   The Killers   Comedy: Nick Swardson

Television Shows of the 2000s

Boston Public (2000–2004)	*Boston Legal* (2004–2008)
Countdown with Keith Olbermann (2007–2011)	*Nip/Tuck* (2003–2010)
The Chris Isaak Show (2001–2004)	*The Colbert Report* (2005–2013)

The Office (2005–2013)

Queer Eye for the Straight Guy (2003–2007)

The Shield (2004–2008)

House (2004–2012)

Chappelle's Show (2003–2006)

Curb Your Enthusiasm (2000–2011)

Dirty Jobs (2005–2012)

Mad Men (2007–2015)

Mind of Mencia (2005–2008)

Rescue Me (2004–2011)

The Osbournes (2002–2005)

UFO Hunters (2008–2009)

Insomniac with Dave Attell (2001–2004)

The Chelsea Handler Show (2006)

Deadwood (2004)

The Ellen DeGeneres Show (2003–present)

Malcolm in the Middle (2000–2006)

The West Wing (1999–2000)

Movies of the 2000s

34-2000:   (PWHS): *Snatch, Gladiator, American Psycho, Castaway, Ali*

35-2001:   *Planet of the Apes, Blow, Ocean's Eleven, A Beautiful Mind*

36-2002:   *Spider Man, Barbershop, My Big Fat Greek Wedding*

37-2003:   *Finding Nemo, Pirates of the Caribbean, Mystic River, Old School*

38-2004:   *The Incredibles, Mean Girls, Crash, Napoleon Dynamite, Million Dollar Baby*

39-2005:   *V for Vendetta, Brokeback Mountain, War of the Worlds, Cinderella Man*

40-2006:   (HSHCS) *The Departed, 300, Invincible, The Good Shepherd, Little Miss Sunshine*

41-2007:   *Superbad, No Country for Old Men, Juno, Zodiac, Into the Wild, There Will Be Blood*

42-2008:   *The Dark Knight, Slumdog Millionaire, Milk, Grand Torino*

43-2009:   *Inglorious Bastards, Avatar, The Blind Side, Precious, The Hangover*

Board/Video Games of the 2000s

Rock Band	The Sims	Grand Theft Auto
Who Wants to Be a Millionaire?	Call of Duty	Tomb Raiders

LETTERS TO THE EDITOR OVER THE YEARS by Jim Geist of Hewitt, New Jersey

7-23-03:   "Hunting Does Not Equal Anti-Wildlife" —*Suburban Trends*

2-14-03:   "I Support the NJ Bear Hunt" —*The Record*

8-25-04:   "Time to Send in Peace Troops into Sudan"

3-25-05:   "NJN Must Run 'Bears: Too Close for Comfort'"

9-25-05:   "A Massacre (Opposing the War in Iraq)" —WM *AIM*

9-30-05:   "Let the Poor Sacrifice" - letter by W

10-8-05:   "War in Afghanistan: W Is a Corrupt and Incompetent Leader"

10-13-05: "Losing Faith in Bush" —*NJ Star-Ledger*

10-14-05: "Bush Says He Is Not Concerned About Bin Laden"
—*WM Messenger*

10-28-05: "Does the U.S. Need 6,000 New Immigrants a Day?"

1-28-06: "Skirmishes with the Mexican Cartel Along the Border"

2-7-06: "Jack Abramoff Uses $100k to Bribe the GOP"

2-8-06: "The Romans Exploited Slaves (As the Rich Exploit the Undocumented)"

2-17-06: "Time to Start Impeachment Hearings for Bush-Cheney"

2-24-06: "Leave No Student Unrecruited (By the Military)" www. LeaveMyChildAlone.org

3-26-06: "Illegal Immigration Hurts Unskilled American Workers"

4-2-06: "Lower the Immigration Numbers" —*NJ Record*

6-13-07: "Time for WM to Go Back to Non-Partisan Gov't." — *Suburban Trends*

6-22-07: "Time for Universal Health Care" —*WM Messenger*

6-22-07: "Time for WM to Go to Nonpartisan Government Again"

10-3-08: "How Can the WM GOP Vets Honor Rep. Garrett?"

10-5-08: "Irony of Deregulation Republicans Now Asking for Regulation for 2008 Banks"

3-11-09: "Medical Marijuana (NJ) Needs Support"

9-28-09: "We Need Universal Single-Payer Health Care"

10-2-09: "Out of Afghanistan NOW"

4-5-10: "Speaking Out on Priest Molestation in Catholic Church" —*NJ Record*

4-7-10:   "Nelson Mandela Not a Terrorist Thug"

4-25-10:   "A Democrat for Many Reasons" —*Suburban Trends*

11-7-10:   "Tea Partiers Are Whiny Adolescents on Taxes"

11-3-10:   "Why Does Mass Murderer Columbus Get a Federal Holiday?"

11-13-10:   "Obama Could Learn from Clinton on Fixing the Economy"

11-26-10:   "Highlands Pipeline Could Be a Big Fracking Deal"

12-22-10:   "Waiting for Superman Is Anti-Teacher Union Propaganda"

4-30-10:   "Bottle Redemptions in School, Automakers Should Recycle Cars and a Unicameral System in NJ to Save Money"

5-21-10:   "I'd Love to See Christie Teach My Class for a Week"

6-23-10:   "Memorial Day: Why So Many Wars, USA?"

8-8-10:   "WM Dems and GOP Should Work for Tax Relief By Getting $ from Newark for H2O"

1-23-10:   "Tiger Woods and Sex Addiction"

9-22-10:   "So Many Cops in West Milford It Resembles a Police State"

10-7-10:   "How Can Someone on the Zoning Board Get Work Done Without a Permit?"

10-28-10:   "Columbus Not Worthy of a Holiday" —*New York Teacher*

4-15-11:   "Columbine: Is Happiness the Barrel of a Warm Gun?"

4-15-11:   "A Few Ways to Improve Schools"

4-27-11:   "High Gas Prices Demand Action"

4-4-12:   "Oil Speculators Cost $40 on a $100 of an Oil Barrel"

5-6-11:   "Goldman Sachs Branch of the White House?" —*NJ Record*

5-6-12:   "Campaign Finance Reform Is Needed"

10-8-15:   "Shame on GOP and NRA for Not Supporting Background Checks"

10-24-15:   "75 Ways You Are a Socialist"

2-18-16:   "Gov. Christie Is wrong on Medical Marijuana and Driver Licenses for Illegals"

2004 ELECTION - BUSH VS. KERRY: No Republican has ever won the White House without Ohio. Ohio became the Florida of the 2004 presidential election. As Stalin said, "It's not who votes that counts. It's who counts the votes." If you think the ruling class would leave it up to voters to decide who gets elected, think again. In 2002, with the HAVA Act or the Help America Vote Act, Bush signed a law for 3.9 million to replace voting equipment—Sequoia, Diebold, and EE&S—which began as Data Mark. Walden O'Dell, CEO of Diebold and top fund-raiser for George W. Bush, made a public promise to "deliver: Ohio's electoral votes to Bush."

2004 - RIGGED ELECTRONIC VOTING MACHINES - AGAIN! In Montgomery and Cuyahoga counties in Ohio in the 2000 election, the Democratic precincts had an under vote of 25 percent when it was usually 2 percent. In Miami County, a reported 19,000 additional votes went to Bush after 100 percent of the precincts had reported on election day. In Franklin County, 4,258 votes went to Bush and 260 to Kerry in a precinct where there were only 800 registered voters. In Mahoning County, there was "vote hopping," meaning you vote for one candidate, but the machine records the opposing candidate.

In Butler County, Kerry-Edwards received 5,000 less votes than the Democratic court justices contrasted to the GOP that has 40,000 less votes for Republican judges than for Governor Bush (his last truly elected office).

Ballot box fraud is egregious, but with corporate-owned software, one programmer can shift thousands, if not millions, of votes with the stroke of a key. Victoria Collier said it was the equivalent of an electoral drone strike. Clint Curtis, an attorney and computer programmer for and ex-employee of NASA and ExxonMobil, testified in 2006 before the U.S. judiciary members in Ohio. Curtis claimed he was hired by Florida congressman to build software to rig elections using electronic voting machines. Curtis could rig the machines in such a way to determine a 51–49 splint in favor of the person he wanted to win.

WHY WE NEED PAPER BALLOTS: We want paper ballots, not vapor ballots. Bev Harris, author of _Black Voting Box_, has documented fifty-six cases where voting machines got it wrong. As of 2003, these machines were used in thirty-seven states. In 2002, in Clay County, Kansas, Jerry Mayo lost his race for county commissioner; but when there was a hand count, he won by 76 percent of the vote. f. Black box voting = blind faith voting. What if when you voted, the electronic voting machine said, "Your vote has been corrupted. Better luck next year"? In Ohio, State Sen. Teresa Fedder proposed a bill for a "voter verified audit trail." New Jersey congressman Rush Holt pushed for a similar measure in Washington DC. No paper, no proof.

2005 - BOAT ENGINE STOLEN: I love the boat; I love going fishing. I was in heaven compared to when I lived at 34-09 Forty-First St. Apt. 3c in Queens. I sat in the boat, smoked my cigar, and looked at the sky and mountains and the cabins on the lake, and I wanted to pinch myself. I usually took my engine off the boat every time I leave the lake, but I thought, _No one will take it_. I left it there for three days, and when I went back to go fishing, the engine was gone even though I had a lock on it. I called the police to file a report. Here is the lesson I learned from this: The next time my boat, motor, or boat and engine are stolen, I will report it was taken off my property. This way, the home insurance will cover it. Since I reported it being stolen off the lake, my home insurance, which I have paid $500 for over fourteen years ($7,000), would not pay to replace a $1,500 boat motor. Ouch. In time, I went out less and less to go fishing, and I sold my boat and motor to a nice polish plumber for $1,200, and I tore down the dock that cost me $500 in materials and burned it in my campfire.

2002 - DO YOU HUNT BEARS?: When I first moved to West Milford, I used to see bumper stickers that said, "The NJ Bear Group." One day someone asked me how I felt about the NJ bear hunt. I said, "What do you mean? Are you asking me if I support hunting or not? I am a deer hunter." The person said, "In Northern NJ, we love our bears, and the NJ Bear Group is against the hunt in NJ for bears." "Oh," I said, "I have grown up deer and turkey hunting in Pennsylvania, and I have gone hunting in New York State. I have never heard anyone in those states say they were against bear hunting." The bear lover asked, "Are you going to go bear hunting in NJ?" I answered, "Um, I will definitely go deer and turkey hunting. I probably won't go on the bear hunt."

6-22-03 - COUNTERPROTEST: In time, too many from this group annoyed me about being a hunter. I wrote a letter to the editor of our local weekly free paper, *The AIM*. In the letter, I talked about the contributions hunters had made to conservation of wild areas and had brought back populations like the wild turkey and were the first to point out where pollution was affecting the environment. I wrote about how the polar bear was in danger of extinction, how many remained silent in the midst of the genocide happening to human beings in Sudan, and how the bear hunting in Pennsylvania and NY State had not exterminated black bears. I said, "Let the NJ biologists and scientists tell us if there are too many black bears, and when that is the case, then allow the hunt."

The NJ Bear Group had a rally on Route 23 June 23 in 2003 against New Jersey's first bear hunt, and Pierre Sevweenie and I with Eric Bunk from Ted Nugent's United Sportsmen of America showed up to counterprotest, and some in the group got really upset about it, mostly because he and I got quoted with pro-hunting arguments. One of the Bear Group ladies yelled at us, saying, "Why don't you organize your own event?" and called us alcoholics and white trash. One guy in his Lincoln car with leather seats yelled, "Hunting is bad!" Another car drove by and said, "Move out of West Milford!" We get thirty thumbs-up from people driving by. Oh, the first amendment, let freedom ring!

BEAR STORIES: In Sparta, New Jersey, a man was taking a nap in his hammock. He felt something tickling his feet, and it was a black bear licking his feet. I woke up one morning and opened up the blinds on my window to see a bear sitting on the edge railings of my deck, trying to reach the bird feeder. I opened the door, and he took off. Another time in August of 2016, I opened the blinds, and there was a bear in the tree at eye level with me, trying to get my bird feeder hanging twenty feet in the air by a wash line. He was chewing on the clothesline, trying to pull it down with his claws. I yelled at him, but he looked at me with the look "Naw, I will balance my two hundred pounds on the bend of this tree for as long as I want." I grabbed my BB gun and gave him a shot to the butt. The BB bounced off his thick bear skin but did the job. He shimmied down the tree and took off into the woods.

GARBAGE: My garbage gets picked up on Monday mornings, but you cannot take your garbage out on Sunday night, or it will be ripped up by raccoons or dragged into the woods by a bear. I keep my garbage bags in the shed outside till my door is almost ripped off the hinges, and there is ripped wood where the lock is connected to both doors. I can no longer keep birdseed or garbage in the shed.

One day I was sitting on my deck and watching a young bear, maybe one hundred pounds, walk down a path in the woods into the small creek behind my home. There was a tree that had fallen a year earlier, and the young bear can smell ants or grubs inside the fallen trunk. He took his claws, found a small opening, and with three pulls ripped the tree open and ate his snack. These animals are amazingly strong. On another occasion, my neighbor Richie came home from ShopRite and took two bags of groceries up his deck into the kitchen, walked back to his truck, and saw wet bear prints next to his truck door. Good thing he shut his door or his other bag of groceries would have ended up in the woods with the bear.

One morning in the summer of 2005, my then wife Kelly woke me to say "I just heard growling outside the bedroom window." I laughed and brushed it off and fell asleep again. The next morning, the flagpole on a forty-five degree hanging just below the window had been bent toward the ground, and the flag had claw marks and teeth marks in it. I guess she was right. In mid-July of 2016, Helen and I were sitting on the deck, drinking our coffee, and I saw a black blob one hundred feet high in a pine tree. I got the binoculars and sure enough was a bear up there, taking a nap. He hung up there for over an hour.

9-21-14 - FIRST HUMAN KILLED IN NEW JERSEY BY BLACK BEAR: There were five students of East Indian descent from Rutgers University who went for a hike in West Milford's Apshawa Preserve. As they walked in, a male and female hiker warned them about a large bear in there that started following them. They young men went in to explore, and when they saw the bear three hundred feet away, they began taking pictures of the three-hundred-pound bear. When it was one hundred feet away, they took pictures. The bear began to follow them until it was fifteen feet away, and they all ran away, and then the bear attacked Darsh Patel, twenty-two years old, and had taken six pictures of the bear before being mauled to death. The other boys called the police when they cannot find their friend. After two hours, they found the body with the bear nearby, and the West Milford police shoot and killed the bear. Human remains were found in the bear's stomach, and it left teeth mark on his cell phone. He was the first person ever in New Jersey who was killed by a black bear. There were sixty such fatal attacks that had happened in North America over the century. I now carry bear spray with me when I go hiking in northern NJ.

BIRD FEEDERS: THE YANKEE FLIPPER: When I first moved to West Milford and put out the bird feeders, the squirrels crawled out on the wash line and sat on the feeders all day, eating the birdseed. I heard about a feeder called the Yankee Flipper. It is a long plastic tube with a motorized wheel on the bottom, which will not spin with the weight of a bird but will with a squirrel. Watching the squirrels, which are the king of the bird feeders, try to get food the first two to three times is hilarious. They first have to slide down the long tube, but then the wheel starts spinning. They grab on the wheel with their front feet and spin around and around until they let go and go flying. When they hit the ground, they look up as if thinking, *What the heck just happened?* They soon stop trying to eat the birdseed out of the feeder. If you want to see something funny, go to YouTube and type in Yankee Flipper.

2003 - MARIAH CAREY'S SISTER: I hate being alone. It makes me feel sad and that I am missing out on something. I don't really know many people up in West Milford, I keep busy by working on my home. During the school year, I am pretty good, because I keep busy with all my teacher work. I went on the eHarmony website and went out on some dates. I love meeting new people. I met a woman who looked like Mariah Carey's sister. She was a graduate of Nyack College like me, and she looked Spanish to me, but I found out she was a biracial. Her father was black, an excellent piano player, and worked at Walmart. Her mother was Anglo and worked at a local municipal legal department as a secretary. We dated for a while. She was pretty, spiritual, and funny and worked as an adolescent counselor. After dating for a year, we got engaged and, six months later, got married.

2001–2004 - WORKING NIGHT SCHOOL: I worked night school at Park West High School on Tuesday and Thursday nights. Night school went from five-thirty to eight-fifty. At 4:30 p.m., Pierre Sevweenie and I would go to a Chinese restaurant for dinner. For an appetizer, we ordered the tripe that was covered in hot sauce. It was excellent, but when you went to the bathroom, it made your sphincter muscle burn. Each class was an hour and a half with a ten-minute break in between. While I was grateful for the extra clams I made during those years, there was a price to pay for it. The way to teach night school was to break the class up into thirds. The first third was reading, lecturing, and notetaking; the second third was individual work; and the last third was kids doing group work. I thought, *Will I ever work with a teacher in the future who used to be my student?*

PLEASE DON'T TALK TO ME: In 2004, I told Kelly, "Please do not try to speak with me on Tuesday or Thursday nights. I am so exhausted, and my voice is so strained from teaching four to six classes a day. I need to take a shower and go to bed on those nights to survive." Of course, had she worked, it would have made things a bit easier for me because I would not have had to work night school.

LARGE NIGHT SCHOOL CLASSES: If you failed a class, no problem. You go to summer school or to night school to make up the credits. How did this impact day school? Negatively in my opinion. We had kids who did not care if they passed, especially those with terrible classroom manners. If there was no night school or summer school, then more kids would improve behavior and attitudes to get passing grades. Night school and summer school helped encourage "slacking." In the first week of night school, the classroom would be packed. If you wanted to get rid of the less serious students, then you announce to the class, "To pass this class, you will have to write a fifteen to twenty type-written paper." This would easily help you wean out ten to fifteen kids. Then you would later tell the class, "I changed my mind on you having to write a paper."

BLOW OUT MY CAR ENGINE: I used to have a Dodge Aries K car. It was a good car. I loved the green color since green is my favorite color. I used to drive forty-two miles one way to NYC or eighty-four miles round trip. I drove my car only on Tuesdays and Thursdays and took the 196 Express Bus to work the rest of the week. I like the bus because I could sleep, listen to music, or read on the way home from work. On the way home after passing the George Washington Bridge on Route 4, just before you hit Route 208 North in Glen Rock, New Jersey, is a huge Nabisco factory. I would pass the factory about 9:30 p.m., and I would roll down my windows and take in large whiffs of smell because it smelled like fresh Vanilla Wafers. That was one of my favorite parts of the trip. One night coming home, I noticed some smoke coming behind my vehicle but only because I had blown my engine. I loved my Aries car, and it served me well. I guessed I worked night school in 2004, so I could buy my next vehicle, which turned out to be a 1996 Jeep Dad found me from cousin Karen Geist for $3,000. It had only forty thousand miles on it, and it felt like a new truck to me. Having the four-wheel drive made parking a breeze in NYC, especially on the snow high side of the street, depending which way the plows had come down.

AP CRUISIN' ON EMPTY: I got my tenure in 2003. I also got a new assistant principal, Jose Cruz. He had a hearing aid, so he had trouble listening. He was Dominican and had a shaved head. He looked like Geoffrey Holder, the actor from the 7-Up commercials, "The Uncola," and then gave the "Ahhhh-ah-ahhhh" laugh at the end of the 1970's commericals. Many of the teachers in the department thought he was nice or harmless. I didn't think he was. Time would tell.

BACK TO WORK: FEBRUARY 2002 - AP RECOMMENDATIONS: Social studies assistant principal Jose Cruz of Park West High School came to my room to observe me and made several recommendations. It was easy to make suggestions without modeling the way he/she wanted it done. A leader will sit with you, suggest what they want, model it for you, or send you to a professional development or to a teacher who does it well. Cruz asked me to observe him, and I wrote up a one-page report of what I witnessed, listing four positive aspects of his lesson with three recommendations. He had no aim written down, which was a major no-no. It took him ten minutes to cover the Do Now, which was only to take four to five minutes to give the teacher time to take the attendance. Lastly, two students were reading sports magazines in the back row, and a girl was playing a handheld Nintendo game, which he did not address for fifteen minutes. See how easy it is to find things to criticize?

On February 24, I received a letter from the principal saying the purpose of my visit was to contribute to my professional development, not for me to write an evaluation of my boss's teaching skills. At the meeting, I said I misunderstood the expectations of my observation of my boss, and I would not do it in the future. When I walked out of the room, I noticed the principal and union representative looked at each other and laughed.

NOVEMBER 23, 2002 - BOOK DEPOSIT LETTER: It upsets me when I see a kid throw books or kick them across the floor or mistreat them in general or not return their homework books at the end of the year. I sent a letter to NY governor Pataki, Mayor Bloomberg, and the NYC comptroller William C. Thompson, suggesting we charge $3–$5 per book, and you will get all your books back at the end of the school year. The communications liaison from the State Education Department said, "According to section 701 of the Education Law, textbooks must give out textbooks for free." I was told I have to convince the state assembly, the Senate, and the governor to agree with this for it to pass. The NYC comptroller's office told me it was a worthwhile suggestion that could save the city and the state millions of tax dollars and forwarded my letter to the NYC chancellor. And that was the end of that idea to help save NYC tax payers millions of dollars.

APRIL 2003: BOOK ROOM INCIDENT: I was teaching in three different rooms, and I needed a set of books for my world history classes. AP Cruz had the keys to the book room, which was full of books for the U.S., world history, economics, sociology, and psychology. Mr. Cruise was giving me the stiff arm for a class set of books. In the room outside his office by the book room was a bookshelf with books from the floor to the wall. These books were not the newest and covered in dust. I waited until AP Cruz was teaching his one and only class, and I "liberated" the books from the book racks. The next day, AP Cruz came to my room to ask if I knew where the "stolen books" were. I said, "You mean these books over there?" He said yes. I said, I needed a set of books, so I took the books for the kids their parents paid for in taxes. I was called to the principal's office with my AP Cruz and my union rep. When I inquired as to what the problem was, the AP said, "Someone needed those books!" I asked which teacher. Cruz said, "Ahhhhh . . I needed those books!" I said, "AP Cruz, you have access to the book room. Why would you want to use a set of dated books?" The principal looked at the AP with an annoyed look and said, "Mr. Geist, you are excused."

I WAS RIGHT ABOUT MCCRUISING: Years later as I was sitting in my own "rubber room," doing research in preparation for my arbitration case, I got reminiscing about my second AP, Jose Cruz. I typed in his name and found out he had now become a principal in Queens. Prinicipal was spelled with a "pal" on the end instead of "ple" because principals are supposed to be your "pal." I found an article in the *Daily News* (1-11-11).

DAILY NEWS - NEW BULLY PRINCIPAL IN QUEENS: AP Cruz was at Park West from 2002 until 2009. In 2010, he was an AP at Murray Bertraum High School, a school under the Brooklyn Bridge with 2,445 students. The principal of the school locked the bathrooms, and as a result, students began texting one another to cause a disturbance during period 5 on Thursday, December 10. Many students did not go to school the next day out of fear of the riot that had broken out.

When I googled AP Jose Cruz and I found a headline in the *NY Daily News*: "PARENTS, TEACHERS SAY CAMBRIA HEIGHTS HIGH SCHOOL PRINCIPAL'S A BULLY." It turned out to be the former Park West AP Jose Cruz, who many thought was nice, quiet, and harmless. He was called little Napoleon at his new post by the teachers there.

Teachers said Principal Cruz "routinely threatens to give them poor reviews." In one meeting, he said he wished he could replace all the teachers, and he threatened one teacher "to give her an unsatisfactory evaluation at the end of the school year if she didn't bring test scores up." Several teachers of mathematics, science research, and Technology Magnet School said, "They have had enough of the autocratic rule."

Science teacher Jachan Watkis said, "Cruz does not have the capacity to lead. Cruz is incapable of motivating his staff." Over seven teachers requested transfers to other schools since workloads had gone up, U ratings of teachers had gone up, and teachers were having 3020a charges filed against them. Principal Jose Cruz made teacher hunting season a full-time art. He was being called Principal Napoleon by some as he terrorized the people trying to help the students.

One teacher speaking under anonymity said, "He told us to bring up test scores without any guidance, or he would give unsatisfactory ratings." In 2013, the school was under a twenty-month DOE investigation for extremely lenient scoring of the NY Regents Exams. Many believed the AP of history was only doing what the principal told him to do. In 2010, the U.S. history exam had a passing rate of 54 percent; and in 2011, it jumped up to 88 percent. One parent, Darlen Newell, said, "I don't like the way he treats kids or talks to teachers. He has a Rikers Island mentality." See, I was always right about this guy ten years ahead of the *Daily News*.

DEANING AT PARK WEST HIGH SCHOOL: Our mix of students was about 47.5 percent African American and 47.5 percent Dominican and led to many fights. Part of my job was to walk the hallways, contact parents when teachers had concerns, and fill out paperworks if one of my students was suspended.

What I found interesting was practicing something called active listening. Active listening is where I listened to what the kids were saying, would repeat back what they were saying to help them process their feelings, and show a little empathy when it was called for it; and when they left my office, without me really giving them advice, they would say, "Thanks, Dean Geist, for helping!"

MENACING: As a delegate of the UFT and as a dean of the school, I used to sit in principal meetings almost every two weeks. We had a kid in our school dealing drugs, and he was always stirring up trouble in school One day I went outside to get a slice of pizza for lunch and ran into the kid. He said to me, "You are not so tough out here by yourself without your walkie-talkie and connection to the security and the principal's office, are you?" The kid was right, but you never let them see you sweat. I said to the kid, "I have a job to do, that's all. It's business, nothing personal, as they say in *The Godfather* movie." The kid said, "I should kick your ass right now." I said, "Think about it, hitting a teacher is a federal offense, and you will go away for a year." I spoke with Principal Brancato, and he was thrilled. I was asked to go to security, to call in the NYPD, and to file a menacing charge against him. I called the kid's apartment and left a message. The next day, I got a call from an attorney from Child Protective Services, and she asked what happened and what the next step was. I said, "Ms. Attorney, if your client comes to school tomorrow, the metal detector scanner will go off when he slides his card. He will be escorted to the security office, and I will call the NYPD who will arrest him, and he will be tried in court. If he never comes back to Park West, I don't see any charges being filed." That was the last we saw of that kid, and the principal shook my hand for getting rid of his number 1 problem that year.

ON A LIGHER NOTE - SEX TOYS: I was in my office and got a call from a female security agent. She said, "Dean Geist, I have a situation you must handle." I said, "Bring the ladies down." The security agent said, "I found these two ladies in the bathroom, and they were using this," and she unwrapped a purple dildo from the newspaper. I said, "Wrap that thing back up, and please take this to the principal's office." On another occasion, a boy was picking on a girl, and he began horseplay by trying to slap her. She told him to stop; he did not; and the young lady who had been going to a boxing gym for over two years bobbed, wove, ducked down, and threw a left and a right; and the boy was on the floor, holding his stomach because she had knocked the wind out of him. The boy got called into a fellow dean's office, and he was advised to transfer to another school; otherwise, he will live the rest of his high school days as the kid who got his butt whopped by a girl. My last story had to do with a nice kid named Osama. After 9/11, I called him over and said, "Osama, two things. Firstly, when you turn eighteen, you may want to change your name if you continue living in the United States. Secondly, we need people who speak Arabic to work for the FBI. Think about it."

TRACKING BLOOD ON THE SECOND FLOOR - LIKE DEER HUNTING: It was the last period of the day, and I was walking down the hallway with Bob McCue, my union representative. I looked on the floor and saw a droplet of blood and another one about every two to three feet. I said, "Bob, look at the blood!" Like a bloodhound, my hunting skills kicked in like I was tracking a deer in the woods that had been shot. We followed the very tiny blood drops every 4-5 feet down the hallway, down the stairs, to the right, and into the boys' bathroom, where you can see blood all over the bathroom sink; but no one was in the bathroom. I backtracked the blood with Bob, and we found the broken window of a swinging door, and it had chicken wire in it. We later found out who it was, and luckily, they went to the nurse to have it wrapped up and to the emergency room to get it stitched up.

MAYOR OF NYC 1994–2002: Mayor Rudolf Giuliani defeated Democrat David Dinkins, NYC's first black mayor. Mayor Giuliani would not meet with the United Federation of Teachers (UFT) for over five years to negotiate a new contract. He wanted the teachers to work an extra twenty minutes a day. The fear was for teachers teaching five classes; it was setting us up to teach six classes a day, which would cause many to leave the profession because of the extra stresses and drain of such a thing. The UFT had a rally in front of city hall. He was involved in an infidelity with a woman named Judy. I made up a placard that read, "Forget about Rudy's infidelity. He is screwing 78,000 NYC teachers!" I received over three hundred thumbs-up at the rally by very smart and appreciative brothers and sisters.

SOME NAMES FROM GEIST CLASSES 1999–2016

Kemberlin	Shytifee	Aldo	Marino	Shailz
Marlin	Tyshawn	Sherlin	Noeliz	Amarillys
Xavier	Coreon	Princess	Venus	Shasean
Miloagros	Adonnys	Ivy	Caesar	Achman
Sol	Jada	Yadira	Shamela	Merisha
Marlenyes	Finan	Wilfredo	Chiquita	Saquan
Nariele	Malida	Seetreeon	Lanea	Aurys
Yaribel	Zaki	Quincy	Ephriam	Esmeiry
Yordy	Thatiana	Damaine	Xheehan	Shifat
Vianfy	Rosinell	Iasia	Ivory	Isamar
Eladio	Abualghaith	Khaliah	Kennis	Breslin
Jensabeth	Ronaldo	Liana	Keron	Sheridan
Eleuterio	Matou	Donise	Thameshwai	Flora
Mayrobi	Jameka	Clorina	Bernaldo	Rawan
Zeary	Edison	Maximo	Amit	Madochen
Ambar	Arisleidy	Marwan	Socrates	Wallies
Marbelly	Omar	Osama	Mahatma	Radelkys
Yonauri	Anelkis	Latoya	Eulises	Darri
Jameel	Omar	Kendall	Cintaya	Onny

Milkeya	Imani	Gerard	Kemesha	Lilibeth
Raimarie	Sinelly	Vladimir	Gamel	Disaky
Lisabony	Hennesy	Navrous	Equan	Brias
Brynner	Hackerson	Shem	Jatono	Mauro
Tamkia	Gia	Magdelina	Nekita	Milvio
Fernelys	Sharina	Elether	Cheivas	Arsenio
Yanilza	Djouba	Haresh	Sherman	Elvis
Fardod	Ilana	Shasta	Salvador	Tajanae
Jallame	Akmall	Bibi	Tempest	Naje
Shalinie	Raisel	Thamen	Ameesha	Abdo
Jesus	Tenise	Zena	Dayvonne	Noah
Mabiolene	Nakesa	Ivory	Zullymar	Senthia
Dariel	Rakeem	Asia	Rodhamer	Jazmin
Jonralist	Rahmeen	Nalah	Cornelius	Ju'Dayah
Dayanara	Kaleeah	Jameel	Junelsy	Niyah
Adajah	Destiny	Al Tariq	Anaise	Kei
Natai	Ka'Asia	Javonte	Sharabia	Amir
Latrina	Saeed	Ijustice	Nemesy	Kwadjo
Muhammad	Dakell	Rodolfo	Genesis	Ja'Juan
DiQue	Fahim	Deaniphis	Rayquer	Orisa
Noreem	Ladasia	Kareem	Ty-Jamier	Tia
Tyleeh	Shidaia	Lawanna	Brensy	Aaliyah
Tyquan	Taleb	Ticeson	Yeredin	Shakia
Nacir	Fabienne	Lakeith	Abdias	Zarriyah
Shavaugn	Kervin	Quinn	Jada	Ta'Zai

2002 - PARK WEST HIGH SCHOOL - VICTIM OF THE SMALL SCHOOL MOVEMENT - BILL GATES:

In 2001, NYC mayor Mike Bloomberg appointed Joel Klein to become the chancellor of NYC schools. Why? Because mayors like to appoint education chancellors with no experience in education. In 2002, Klein began to create two hundred "small schools" in NYC. What he did was take large high schools and then break them down into smaller schools.At Park West, he would phase out our school over a four-year period, and a new school was added each year until year 4, when there were four new schools. Something called Leadership Academy was created to produce principals in a one-year period, whom most had no experience in education. Under the old system, you had to work as a teacher and then assistant principal before you could become a principal. The idea came from the prick Jack Welch, CEO of General Electric. He was a hard-nosed antiunion businessman who believed you just fire the bottom 10 percent when you start.

Leadership Academy, received $95 million under Bloomberg. Of course, many of these principals with no education experience were respected by teachers or by assistant principals. Ironically, the Bill and Melinda Gates Foundations donated $51.2 million to help create these schools. The $29.9 million went to "New Visions Schools." What was being sold to the public as small schools was the salvation of NYC schools; but it had been experimented, already tried in NYC, and had failed. This was really about trying to bust the NYC teachers' union. What was ironic about this alliance with Klein and Gates was that in June of 2001, Bill Gates's Microsoft was charged with violating the Anti-Trust Act (creating a monopoly) by the federal government with Joel Klein as the lead prosecutor.

2005 - PARK WEST HIGH SCHOOL PHASED OUT:

Park West began to be phased out in 2005. The first school came in

September of 2004, and by September of 2008, it had four new schools in the building. It was interesting to see the teachers from the new school come in. They were young. They were not friendly to us and probably thought the UFT teachers were lazy with their contract and all. We jumped two feet every day, while they jumped two and a half feet a day for their classes with the extra things they were required to do. By the end of the year, the cohort of young new teachers looked worn out. Teaching for a career is not a sprint; it is a marathon; and while you give your best, you need boundaries so you can teach for thirty years to collect a pension.

EVERYWHERE ARE SIGNS: About two months before the Kelly wedding, I saw some warning signs, and I called my soon-to-be mother-in-law to tell her I was getting cold feet. Carol told me, "We have spent a lot of money on this wedding, and many of our friends have already purchased plane tickets, and so much work has been done already, and we will lose for canceling reservations that have been made, and you will break my daughter's heart if you do so." I can honestly say, as a result of my codependency, I was more concerned about the needs of other people than saying, "I am really sorry, but I have to trust my gut instinct. I have to take care of myself first, and if our marriage were not to work out, then I am saving your daughter the heartbreak of a divorce."

The wedding was up at Alton Bay in New Hampshire at a Christian conference center. The area is absolutely beautiful. I must say the wedding was fun, and it was good to see family and friends and college buddies gathered for the rehearsal dinner and for the wedding and reception afterward. This would be the second wedding for the following groomsmen: Mike Brogna, Ed Nanno, and my father.

CREEPER PEEPERS: There was a neighbor gentleman who lived next to Carol's cabin. Ed my groomsman told me that one late night when he was in his motel room on the Alton Bay Christian Conference Center, he saw the neighbor peeping in between his curtains. It was absolutely creepy and disappointing to hear this, especially since I was going to be sleeping in this guy's cabin the night before the wedding. I should have stayed in Mike's room or Ed's room. The guy let me sleep in the bedroom that had a king-size bed. I fell asleep, and at about two o'clock in the morning, I heard wood boards making that wood board cracking noise. I could hear the "shhhh" of feet across the floor, and it was coming toward me until my hair stood, and I could feel someone standing over me, looking at me. I quickly rolled around and made a loud pirate "arrrr" sound, and he ran out of the room. He did not come back in the room, but it was a truly uncomfortable experience to have the night sleeping in the home of "Mr. Creepy" before a wedding. I told my folks, Carol and Kelly, and their other neighbor June that their neighbor had some issues.

10-30-91 - THE PERFECT STORM: Hurricane Grace started near Bermuda on October 27 and on October 30, the "Halloween Storm." There were forty- to eighty-foot waves that hit the Atlantic, causing coastal flooding in Massachusetts and Nova Scotia on October 31. The *Andrea Gail* fishing boat went missing with six souls on board. It was reported another boat was in the hurricane. In Alton Bay was an old salt who was in the navy his whole life and was out in the hurricane. I looked forward to hearing a great story from the old man. I asked him about what it was like being out in the perfect storm. He said, "Big waves, big waves."

TROUBLE IN PARADISE II: On our honeymoon in the Bahamas, Kelly told me, "Guess what. I will no longer be working! I quit my job before the wedding!" I said, "What?" I started thinking, *Oh no, I married someone who wants a sugar daddy.* I said back, "Really? I quit my job too. I guess we will have to move into a tent behind the house and live off the love and roots and berries and, in the wintertime, cuddle really close so we don't freeze to death." I felt betrayed and angry, especially when we got back home, and she started talking about "I want a new floor," and "I want a new couch," and "I want to go away for vacation next summer!" I said, "Kelly, I am a teacher. I am not a doctor or attorney. I can't afford to buy all this stuff you want. I can pay the bills, put a roof over your head, feed you, and take you out occasionally for dinner and a movie. If you want all this stuff, then you need to work."

I used to give her $25 a week for gas money. She said, "My parents say you should give me more money!" I told her, "My parents said you should work at least a part-time job somewhere." Kelly would call her mom when we had heated discussions. It was like "I have to talk to Mom to know what I am thinking, and you keep paying the bills." Kelly one time called the police on her father before we married. I always had this fear it could happen to me one day. She took medication, and 95 percent of the time she was mellow, but that 5 percent of the time, watch out! The one night we were discussing something, fighting about something, she picked up the phone and hit 911. I jumped over the bed, knocked the phone out of her hands, and said, "Are you crazy? If I get arrested, I could lose my job. How will we survive if I lose my teaching job of the last nine years?"

HONEYMOONERS - ALICE, TO THE MOON!: A few weeks later, there was an argument over something, and she took a broom and hit me with the handle end. I called her father to say "Hey, things are not working here. I think it is best if your daughter moves back with you." He said to me, "Don't change your locks on the house. You married her. She can live upstairs, and you can live downstairs. She is not moving back to my place.." The following week, she got upset with me and said, "I should take your deer rifle and shoot you." I pretended not to hear her. The next day, I went directly to the courthouse in Paterson to file an order of protection and to get her out of the house.

When I walked into the room of the courthouse for domestic abuse cases, it was all women sitting there. I was the only guy, and I am a big guy. All the women looked, thinking, *What is he doing here?* I knew what they were thinking, and I said, "You know, ladies, no matter how big you are, when you are sleeping, it can hurt when your partner decides to hit you with a hammer or baseball bat." They nodded and said, "Uh-huh!" The judge listened to me and said, "Mr. Geist, I find your testimony of terroristic threats to be credible. You will get your order." That night, the West Milford Police showed up and told Kelly, "You have twenty minutes to pack up, and you must vacate the premises. You may not come back for ten days or contact your husband for the next ten days." I stayed out of the home, and she stole my alarm clock, which would make it difficult for me to get up for work the next day.

SAFE HOUSE: When I came home, I wanted to feel safe. It was tough being an urban teacher. Then I felt like I was a daddy instead of a husband. Kelly had asthma, so she did not do laundry or clean or cook because it could set off the asthma. In addition to working and keeping the house running, I was now the cook and maid while working evening school. I was tired and feeling used and feeling resentful and feeling angry at myself for not listening to my inner ding when it was telling me to cancel the wedding. I only had myself to blame. The worst part after getting hit by her was I did not feel safe in my own home.

HINDSIGHT: I do not hate Kelly, and I wish her the best. I made the mistake of confusing "rescuing" with love. It is not my job to rescue another. I will love you and encourage you in your growth (spiritually, mentally, emotionally, or physically), but it is not my job to raise another. How did I get into a situation where I am a two-time divorcée? Am I not good at choosing a partner? What do I need to focus on? I have the God connection, but something is missing in my person detector, and I don't know how to fix it at this point in my life.

WEST MILFORD, NEW JERSEY, ABDUCTION ATTEMPT STORY: I was glad to move from Queens, NY, to woods of West Milford, New Jersey. I did not miss the noise, the graffiti, the crammed parking, the car alarms, the people, and the crime. The movie named *The Village* by M. Knight Shamalan, is about a group of people who moved to live together in a rural setting, and they live like it is in the 1800s. The shock is it really is in the twenty-first century, and all the couples have had a loved one murdered and want to live in a Utopian society, only to find you can take humans out of the twentieth century, but you cannot take out the human flaws or character defects. My cousin Cheryl played an extra in the movie.

As the characters in the movie *The Village,* I thought I had moved into a safe community. It was a summer day in West Milford and as I was driving home, I decided to stop by 3 Roads Deli. It intersects at Union Valley, Warwick Turnpike, and White Road. They have pretty good fried chicken and macaroni and cheese. I picked up a chocolate milk and a newspaper. As I was shopping in the tiny store, I heard a kid, a three-year-old with a Mohawk haircut crying. As I looked, there was a middle-aged man and a middle-aged woman who each were holding a hand of the kid and walking him out the store pulling him out. Someone yelled, and before I knew it, the couple had disappeared. All I could think was, *Who would give their three-year-old a Mohawk haircut?*

I was new to the West Milford, New Jersey, area; so the two ways I was going to get to know people in the area were to attend a local church and to join the Democratic Club. I saw an advertisement for the church on the local diner mats and read about the West Milford Dems in the local paper. The Dems met monthly.

The next day, I was sitting in the Alliance Living Word Church, which at this time was meeting in the auditorium of the WM High School. In the middle of the service before the prayer time, Pastor Tim Barnes said, "Does anyone have anything they would like to testify to or rejoice about?" A man took the microphone and said, "Yesterday I was at a local deli with my son, and as I turned to the counter to pay my bill, a couple tried to grab my son and kidnap him. Praise the Lord they did not get him." As I looked and saw him pick his son, it was the kid with the Mohawk haircut I witnessed the day before.

After he finished, I walked over to the father and asked him if he had reported the incident to the West Milford Police. He looked at me and said no. I said, "You realize some pedophiles tried to kidnap your son and are in our area, and the local and county police have no idea of what happened yesterday. You need to go to the police station immediately and report it. What did they look like? Did you see the car? Did you see the car license?" I followed up with him about it the next week, and he did go to the police. The incident was not reported in the papers until a month later. I guess the police did not want to give the potential kidnappers a heads-up the cops were unto them.

It made me sick to my stomach when I realized I was in a small country store, where I overheard an attempted kidnapping of a child. I knew a couple from the church in Queens who had a daughter killed, and they never caught the murderer. About one in three murders in the United States goes unsolved. How did the father from our church find out about his daughter's murder? He was riding on the Long Island train into NYC to work when he opened the *Daily News*, and there was the story of her murder with her name in the story. As a result of his families' activism with other families of murdered family members, they lobbied the NY Legislature to make it illegal to print a murdered person's name in the paper until the family had been informed first by the authorities.

I moved out of the NYC to the country but not from human nature.

MARCH 2, 2003: MISTY MOUNTAIN BATHROOM BREAK: I had just celebrated my birthday and my sister's birthday in Allentown, Pennsylvania. It was a Sunday; and Kelly, my fiancée, and I drove back to Tuxedo, NY, so I can drop her off at her folks. As I dropped her off, I felt the need to urinate but thought I can hold it a half hour till I got to Hewitt. I drove down to the bus stop by 17A, next to the mountains of Sterling Forest. It was roughly 8:00 p.m., so I pulled over and took a wiz in the woods. I started to pull out of the bus stop parking lot, and a car made a U-turn right behind me with his headlights on. *That is strange,* I thought, and then the red and blue police lights came on. I pulled over, and a young officer walked up to my car.

I put the inside light on. I put my hands on the wheel. He asked me what I was doing at the bus stop. I told him the truth, and he went into convulsion, saying, "That is a violation of code *XYZ*, section ABC, and I can take you to the judge right now if I want." I said, "Officer, first, it is my birthday today. Look at the presents in my car and look at my birthdate on my license. Second, where do you think the animals and hunters go to the bathroom on this mountain? I hunt this mountain in December." The youngster said, "Oh, we have a wise guy here. I will be right back." I thought, *Great. If he gives me a ticket, I will have to tell my principal and call the superintendent's office to tell them I was arrested for public urination.* The officer came back and said, "I have an emergency I have to respond to. You are lucky today sir. Next time, use a gas station bathroom." I said, "You got it, Officer!" And I almost felt like he had given me a birthday present, but really, his supervisor most likely told him, "You are not arresting someone for public urination."

AUGUST 2005: SYRACUSE, MUSHROOMS, AND HURRICANE KATRINA: On Thursday, August 24, my boat engine wass stolen; and on Friday, my paddle boat on the lake was gone. It turned out someone took it for a joyride. The Upper Greenwood Lake security found it. I filed a police report and, at 10:00 a.m., left for Syracuse to visit my buddy John Paxton. It was a gorgeous drive up Route 17, Route I-84, and Route I-81, full of mountains and valleys and farmland. I enjoyed the three-and-a-half-hour ride every time.

Paxton's home is a multifamily home with a family living below him and paid rent. We sat in his screened-in porch with a couch and several lawn chairs, plants on a table, and a green designed carpet. Ed loved music, so he had his music playing; and we were eating steak, roasted garlic, and bananas. I am not really an illegal drug taker. When my students asked me if I do drugs, I told them, "My name is Mr. Geist, and I am an addict. I am addicted to coffee and caffeine." They responded, "No, no, no, that's not what we mean." I responded back, "Coffee is definitely a drug. When I don't have my cup of coffee, I get a headache, and I become grumpy and tired."

CANNIBUS AND PROSTITUTION: I am not a pot smoker, but I think cannabis should be legalized. There are five hundred thousand people who die a year from alcohol or from tobacco, legal drugs. How many have died from cannabis? I am a Libertarian when it comes to legalizing cannabis and prostitution. As adults, people should be given these freedoms. The nineteenth prohibition amendment experiment failed. All it did was give control and profits to the gangsters and deplete money from the tax coffers. People are going to drink, smoke, and use hookers, so why not legalize it and tax it? Sex workers could unionize and get health benefits and vacation, and those struggling with addiction could go to rehab.

PARTY LEGENDS: At 5:00 p.m., Paxton pulled out a plastic bag, and it looked like dried mushrooms. I said, "Is that mushrooms?" He said yes. I asked, "They make you laugh, right?" He answered, "Oh, you will definitely be laughing! Just make sure you drink a lot of water." I took some; he took some. We sat in the room and listened to music. He was playing "Yellow Submarine" by the Beatles, "Break on Through to the Other Side" by the Doors, Bob Dylan, and "Find the River" by REM. In the evening, he broke out the Pink Floyd. On Viceland Channel was a program called *Party Legends*, stories told by actors of absurd party stories, often involving drugs, and were animated as they narrate their party experiences.. This is the Jim Geist version of *Party Legends*.

BREAK ON THROUGH TO THE OTHER SIDE: Why did I try it? It was a friend suggesting it, it was summertime, and I had never done mushrooms and wanted to get the experience of it. As we were talking, every five minutes, Paxton said, "Look at the carpet! See anything?" "Nope," I said. He asked me this every five minutes. My stomach felt upset a bit, which I did not like. At 5:25 p.m., Paxton asked me again. I looked at the carpeting that was mostly green with white-and-black lines and said, "Holy crap! The carpet lines are fluorescent green and moving like the lights in amusement park rides." I knew in my head how the carpet was supposed to look, but it did not look that way anymore. Ed laughed and now had become my mushroom trip shaman. He said, "Look at the trees." I looked at the trees, and I can see the leaves pulsating, moving in and out breathing, like the ribs of a sleeping animal. I looked at my feet and can see the blood moving through my veins. I looked at my toes, and they began twitching like the head of the monster Tim Robbins kept seeing in the movie *Jacob's Ladder*, which was about the Vietnam soldiers the government tested drugs on without their consent. He said, "Let's go to the living room and look at the pictures." He had drawings of Chinese countryside on his wall, and when I looked, the pictures became alive. The characters on in the landscapes become moving cartoons. In my intellect, I knew these were not moving, and yet they were moving. The clouds on the pictures were swirling beautifully.

Shaman Paxton said, "Let's go outside. Take your shoes off." The grass felt amazing. My sensations of smell, feel, and sight were heightened. When we went outside, I looked at the woodpile, and it made a mean face. I turned to look at the tall scrubs about eight feet high, and they looked like five knights giving me the hairy eyeball, but when I gave it back and took control, they cowered. Paxton said, "Let's go to the river." As we walked there, I saw a muskrat running to the river, but it kept running and running like it was on a gerbil wheel and never made it there. It was like the scene in Monty Python's *The Holy Grail* where the men were charging the castle, but it took forever for them to reach it. I also saw a black squirrel in the tree.

SQUIRRELS: In Pennsylvannia and New Jersey, I have only ever seen gray squirrels. In 2015, my Filipina fiance worked as a nanny in the Scarsdale in Westchester County, NY, and I witnessed gray squirrels, red squirrels and black squirrels. Helen even saw an albino squirrel there one day. Gray, black, and red squirrels can be found inWestchester County, NY, but not on western side of the Tappan Zee Bridge in Rockland County. I would think some of the red and black squirrels would have crossed over via the TZ Bridge or the Bear Mountain Bridge in Orange County or even swam across the river. I learned there was the Great Squirrel Migration of 1968 on East Coast, from Vermont to Florida, as a result of an abundance of acorns that grew in 1967. It led to low winter mortality and increased reproductive success. The squirrels moved in their search to store their food, thus the migration. Ironically, in August of 2016, Helen and I drove up to Dad's hunting camp; and just outside of Renovo, Pennsylvania, a black squirrel ran in front of my car. One month later, a black squirrel runs in front of my car in West Milford. The squirrel world is becoming more integrated lately.

TAKE ME TO THE RIVER: We watched the river, but it just looked like a river. Paxton kept saying, "Think happy thoughts." My Syracuse mushroom guide kept saying, "Think happy thoughts." The renter mother and kids came out and rode on the swinging horse. The horse kept changing colors on me. Paxton's brother-in-law came over, and it freaked me out a bit. Did he know Paxton and I were on mushrooms? He kept looking at me with a goofy smile, and I don't like it because I am feeling judged. We sat on the front concrete steps as the day was starting to cool off. The sky was blue, and I saw a *V* formation, like geese made in their fall migration; however, this is a V formation of air turbulence. Then I saw a fly swoosh by in slow motion. I just saw the wind turbulence caused by a fly, and I was astonished. His brother-in-law was looking at me, and I said, "Am I here to amuse you?"

We went upstairs, and Paxton said, "What do you smell?" I smelled fresh lemons! I walked into the bathroom and looked in the mirror. As I looked at myself, my forehead was a field, and my hair was a forest, and just as I was about to go hunting on my head, Paxton walked in and said, "Looking into mirror is not a safe thing to do." We went to the front porch on the second floor and drank beer and smoked cigars and listened to music from 6:00 p.m. to 9:00 p.m. Pink Floyd was playing, and I heard, "Have a cigar, you're gonna go far." *Yes, I am,* I thought. As I looked at the beer, my hand was melting into and out of the can, my feet were also melting in and out of the floor.

RUSH AND MY NEIL PERT DRUM SET: Paxton is a huge Rush fan. In the course of the afternoon, I slowly built up a drum set to play to while we were listening to music. There was a barrage of plant pots of different sizes, some made out of clay, others plastic, and one brass. I was surrounded by a potting soil bag, flower seed packets, a pillow, and glass bottles. I had created a Neil Pert drum set that I used my two long plant sticks on. Paxton's Dad came over and laughed when he saw the homemade drum set.

By 8:00 p.m., the psilocybin mushroom hallucinogen was wearing off. At 9:00 p.m., we went to a bar until 1:00 a.m. We got home and slept until 9:30 am on Saturday. The trip can last from three to eight hours and altered time and connected the brain with parts usually not connected. Many found it to be a spiritual experience.

BARMAID KATRINA: At 9:00 p.m., we went to the corner bar, and the maid's name was Katrina. I went with Paxton and his cousin Eddy, who worked with the United Automobile Workers. Eddy asked for a sandwich, and she said she did not make sandwiches. Eddy said, "You might want to expand your job skills since most people also like to order sandwiches at bars." The barmaid was cute, and I only remember her name because the next day was when Hurricane Katrina hit the shores of Alabama, Mississippi, and Louisana.

8-28-05 - HURRICANE KATRINA: I left Paxton's place and on Route 81 South on my drive home on Sunday afternoon through Upstate NY. The clouds were getting darker, and the winds were picking up as the rain came down with Hurricane Katrina hitting Alabama, Mississippi, and Louisiana. Katrina was one of the deadliest hurricanes to hit the United States. It was estimated 1,833 people died in the hurricane, causing $108 billion in damage, and millions were left homeless along the Gulf Coast. What started out as a tropical depression on August 23 turned into a raging hurricane 5 by August 28. The surge exposed engineering mistakes in the levees and flood walls. 20% of the levee had not been completed, because President Bush too the money earmarked for the levee completion, and spent it on a War in Iraq, that had nothing to do with the 9/11 attack in America. Eighty percent of New Orleans and large portions of the parishes that were flooded and did not recede for weeks.

The National Guard, about a third in Iraq, looking for weapons of mass destruction not there, were called in to help with the evacuations. Thousands seeked refuge in the New Orleans Dome, which was overwhelmed. It became one of the largest displacements of population since the Great Depression according to the NOAA. Governor Bush flew in to tell Mr. Brown of Fema he was "doing a heck of a job." Brown's training in emergency management came from his business raising Arabian horses and donating a large amount to Bush.

2-26-04 - NEW ORLEANS, USA, VS. TSUNAMI HIT JAKARTA, INDONESIA: For days, I watched on the television screen people on their roofs, waving flags and signs spray painted with the word "HELP!" I thought, *This is the USA. By day 3, they will have a system in place to help these people, mostly black Americans who are mostly Democrats.* On December 26, 2004, eight months earlier when the tsunami hit Indonesia, the United States sent over a navy carrier, the *Abraham Lincoln*, which provided a base for daily helicopter flights of food and water to the victims. At the Banda Aceh Airport, there were cargo planes and helicopters packed on the tarmac. The U.S. military flew more than 2,800 relief missions, treating 2,200 patients. The soldiers delivered food and purified water, removed rubble, and tended to the wounded. The soldiers guarded the relocation camps, and George H. Bush and Bill Clinton led a delegation to the tsunami-struck countries. You would think our government under the George W. Bush would have done as much, if not more, for his own citizens; but most of our forces must are looking for weapons of mass destruction in Iraq that did not exist in the first place. I was sick to my stomach and had lost the belief that America can rise to any situation. How could we do for Indonesia that our government did not do for her own people? Why did the navy carrier *Abraham Lincoln* not do the same for the victims of Katrina?

SUMMER OF 2006 -VISITING PAXTON: I went to Paxton's, and we spent several days painting three rooms in his apartment, staining his swing set and shed. For dinner, we went to the Dinosaur Bar-B-Q house. We went to the NY State Fair in Syracuse, and we saw many men with missing hands and arms, lost in the farming equipment. Farming is an extremely dangerous job. We took a walk along the canal and listened to some band that played Grateful Dead music. A couple of lady friends from his job place met us there, and we hung out for some time. I ended up with a terrible hangover. I drink too much when I hang with Paxton.

Patxon did not ever wash his car or clean his apartment. Either his mother cleaned the apartment or a girlfriend did so for him. I found the bathroom so grody, the tub and sink so full of grime I had to clean it, for I was afraid to step in the tub to shower or to brush my teeth in the sink. Paxton said, "You don't have to clean it." I said, "I am cleaning it for me, not you."

11-28-14 - ALLEN HIGH THIRTIETH YEAR REUNION: The reunion will be held at Samuel Owens Restaurant in Coplay, Pennsylvania. The week before I met with Lainie Lambert and William Lui, I brough my yearbook from 1984. I had not lived in the area for a long time, and we started looking at our classmates (over seven hundred of them). They were pointing at people, saying, "This one is dead, this one a drug addict, this one is in jail, this one is an alcoholic, this one is a prostitute, this one killed someone." I was in shock. Wow.

DOMESTIC VIOLENCE: As of 2016, at least three of my former classmates were in jail for homicide, all males who killed their girlfriends. Darrell Dunst (1996) used a gun, Willie Ward (2011) chopped up his girlfriend into pieces, and Mike Horvath, who had been charged in October 13, 2016, murdered his girlfriend, who had gone missing. The cause of death had not been announced yet.

CHAPTER 12

Running for Office - Throw My Hat in the Ring! (46-47)

2002 - WEST MILFORD DEMOCRATIC CLUB: When I moved to West Milford, New Jersey, I only knew one person. To get to know people, I attended the Living Word Alliance Church in town and started attending the monthly Democratic Club meetings. The group was started by Ms. CarlLa Horton (notice small *l* then capitalized *L* in her name) and her boyfriend, George, in 1996. She grew tired of the town being run mostly by Republicans and thought it was important to get the Democrat view on issues for healthy discussion, debate, and solutions.

2006 - CANDIDATE FOR TOWN COUNCIL: In March of 2006, the West Milford Democrats had only one candidate running for town council. We could not get another to run. I had a few people bend my ear, and I remembered when I was not sure if I should run for student government president at Nyack College, and it turned out to be a great experience. This opportunity for town council could also be a great experience, if I only knew ahead of time what was to come.

I ran with James Rauth who was a police sergeant who worked in Trenton. I enjoyed the campaign meetings with Democratic councilmen James Warden and Bob Nolan and the other committee members. We worked on slogans, what the signs would look like, fund-raising ideas, letters to the editor, and what our platform would look like and practicing for debates. I spent most of my time from September, October, and until November 8, the Election Day, going door to door after school and on Saturday and Sundays standing in front of A&P or the ShopRite to meet voters. What you have to understand is in West Milford, it is approximately 42 percent Republican, 33 percent Democratic, and 25 percent "independent." On Friday, April 8, the *West Milford Messenger* paper announced the Democratic candidates running for the West Milford council seats. There are six seats, and every year two seats open up. The length of a term for council is for three years.

NEW JERSEY STATE AFL-CIO LABOR CANDIDATE'S SCHOOL AT RUTGERS: I went to the Labor Candidates School at the Eagleton Institute at Rutgers from August 4 through August 6. It was run by John Shea, the COPE (Committee on Political Education) director for the AFL-CIO. Over the weekend, we learned about campaign planning, message development, voter contact, public speaking, media relations, self-research, opponent research, and volunteering. As of the first weekend in August, we had ninety-one days and thirteen weekends until the upcoming election. New Jersey is the only state to have a Union Candidate School. There were 74 percent of graduates who went on to win their elections and helped elect 385 school graduates. Businesses had money and outspent unions 9 to 1, but unions had the organization. There were 92 percent of politicians who were attorneys, and we needed to get more union members elected to office.

One candidate winner told us the following: 1) "Keep to your message," 2) "Pace yourself," 3) "Target the undeclared," and 4) "On the last three days, get the vote out by phone or door to door." Congressman Pallone told us the following: 1) "Have a plan," 2) "Be decisive," 3) "Try not to use notes," 4) "Use value language" (integrity, civility, honesty, fairness), and 5) "Make it personal by using stories." When it comes to fund-raising, 30 percent to 50 percent comes by phone, 50 percent to 70 percent by person, 20 percent to 30 percent by events, and 20 percent from mailings.

The NRA expends a significant amount of time and resources in recruiting, training, and mobilizing volunteers for legislative and political campaigns. The NRA likes to hunt where the ducks are, meaning they find their resources at gunshops, gun and hunting clubs, shooting ranges, and gun shows. Recruit and put volunteers info into a database. Find out what they can do, sign them up, and find out network of contacts they are connected to. Train them and give them titles. Always bring with you generous amounts of signs, stickers, literature, and a sign-up list for volunteers. Some volunteers had called the week before an election to find no voice mail to leave a message.

For a town council position, they said you need at least six responsible people and make a plan that is small, measurable, and deliverable. A good plan prioritizes priorities, allocates resources wisely, and had deadlines. The part of the weekend I enjoyed most was getting to hang out with Congressman Pallone, and when we practiced our door-to-door campaigning. This is an excellent idea, and I wish every state in the United States had a Union Candidate School like this.

2006 - WHO DONATED TO MY CAMPAIGN: Town council is not like dealing with national issues as a congressperson or senator. These are local issues. The following donated to me, many of whom were not Democrats. I am grateful for the financial and emotional support all gave. One from Nyack whom I served on student government with, whom I had known for four years and went on a date with one time, said, "I cannot give you a donation because you are a Democrat." Even in West Milford, I thought having a pro-life background and being evangelical would have gotten me elected, but being a Democrat was too much to swallow for many of the West Milford Republicans.

DEMOCRATS DEMS REPUBLICANS NOT SURE

DEMOCRATS	DEMS	REPUBLICANS	NOT SURE
Mom and Dad	Jack C.	Dr. Crockett	Becky and Charlie
Vera J.	Tom Shea	Timmy S.	Furlongs
Bob and Alice	Ann B.	Lori and John	Stuart W.
Joe P.	Tom and Adele	John A.	Liddle
John S. Sr.	Mike T.	Drew M.	Jim U.
Elliott V.	Sam H.	John S.	Moshe B.
Dan F.	John G	Chas G.	Darryl R.
Dale and Sandy	Peter S.	Karen	Tommy B.
Carol and Bart	Dr. John		Dr. Joseph M. Walter G.

AUGUST 2006 - DOMINICAN PRINCESS - LIFE IS GOOD!:

I love being a teacher. I love my new home. I love living in the woods. I love having a gorgeous girlfriend who is Dominican. I knew Vanessa for thirteen years from New Life Fellowship. She was a single mom who worked and went to college and became a physician's assistant at Montefiore Hospital in the Bronx. Her daughter was in college in the time, and she had divorced from her husband early in the marriage because he had been physically abusive. I called her Pocahontas. She looked like Dominican actress Alexandra Cheron. After I filed for a divorce from Kelly after the death threat, I called up Vanessa and asked her how she was doing and what her status was. Is she engaged, married, or has a boyfriend? She said no. I asked her if she was free that night and if she would like to go out. She said yes, and I picked her up in the Bronx.

Long story short, we began dating, and I was ecstatic about the relationship. I got her apartment key, and I stayed over one to two times a week. She lived in Riverdale, NY, which is a nice section of the Bronx, and her apartment flat had an outside deck with some trees lining the other side of the street. We had dinner, watched a movie, and drank wine, and life was good. She had a blue SUV Mercedes and, when she was able, came up to my place. With all the craziness of being involved in a campaign, I thought, *Even if I lose the election, I have Vanessa.* When we drove around West Milford, there were campaign signs around town, saying, "Vote for Geist & Rauth." I asked her if she was attracted to me because power is an aphrodisiac. She just laughed. She was a quiet person, a good cook, smart, knew how to handle finances, and had family in the Dominican Republic and Miami. I looked forward to visiting these places.

THE WEST MILFORD DEMOCRATIC PLATFORM: Our website was www.WMBest.com. Our Slogan was Vote for the Best! B = Bipartisan Balance, E = Environmental and Ethical Integrity, S = Sensible Ideas, and T = Tax Stabilization and Relief. West Milford is approximately twenty-seven thousand people living over eighty square miles of land, and about a third of the land is covered by water. Most of the water are in reservoirs, and the water goes to the city of Newark, New Jersey.

WHY DEVELOPMENT IN WEST MILFORD, NEW JERSEY, IS BAD:

1) <u>Not enough water</u>: The township had conducted four water studies, and based on our soil type, we are pulling more water out of the ground than can be recharged.

2) <u>Development *always* raises taxes. *Always*</u>: If you pay $6,000 in taxes in West Milford, one-third goes to the town, and two-thirds goes to pay for schools. Schools are 98 percent full right now. For every new home built, taxes go up by $9,000. Eagle Ridge will add 280 new students and Valley Ridge; taxes will go up by $342 per taxpayer. A new school will cost $30 million coming to another increase of $216 per taxpayer for a total of taxes going up by $558!

3) <u>COAH</u>: For every ten new homes built, one additional home must be built for a low-income family. Moreover, those in Trenton who thought of COAH never thought about well and septic.

4) <u>The myth of the ratables chase</u>: When you try to lower taxes by development, you *always lose*. In 1993, the town did a study that was initiated by Mayor Carl Richko and found to save taxpayers $200 and ratable would need to be increased by $73 million or the equivalent of six ShopRites, six A&Ps, and two more banks to the tax rolls.

PUSHING FOR A SEWER SYSTEM IN ALL OF WEST MILFORD: If you allowed for a sewer system to be built in West Milford, it would be the end of our rural town. Sewers equal development. In addition, every home that hooked up to the sewer system would be forced to pay $30,000, in addition to paying the water company monthly for water, which now was being provided for free by Mother Nature for those with septic systems and electric water pumps.

HIGHLANDS ACT: In 2004, the NJ Legislature enacted the Highlands Water Protection and Planning Act. The highlands provides drinking water for 65 percent of the state. The plan is designed to protect families, farmers, and businesses against water shortages, dry wells, and costly water treatment systems. Incentives are put in place for municipalities to voluntarily conform. The plan protects water quantity and quality; promotes sustainable communities, agricultural viability, existing homeowners, and preservation funding; and assists towns through grants and lawsuit protections.

PARTISAN VS. NONPARTISAN GOVERNMENT: West Milford used to have a nonpartisan form of government, where your council person represented an area and the concerns of his/her constituents. Unfortunately, the Republicans held a referendum in the early 2000s, and the town voted on a referendum for a partisan form. So instead of representing constituents, it seems it is more about party politics. That is too bad. Many in West Milford feel the town council is more effective and less partisan under the nonpartisan form of government.

LOWERING TAXES - NEWARK WATERSHED: The Newark Watershed supplies the city of Newark with its water and sells water to surrounding communities and is managed by the Newark Watershed Conservation and Development Corporation. The watershed provides water to 50 percent of New Jersey. It was in 2003 when the West Milford Democrats suggested the town seek greater compensation for the water taken from the watershed since its property covers 32 percent of West Milford. When the idea was brought forth in council, the Republicans laughed out loud and mocked the idea. As Gandhi said, "First they ignore you, then they laugh at you, then they fight you, then you win." By 2006, when I was running, the GOP candidates were trying to claim the idea as their own. By 2010, the parties were working together for the sake of the people. In 2014, West Milford won a $500,000 appeal on the watershed tax, bringing up revenue from $845,000 to $1.41 million in 2014.

Mayor Bettina Bieri (Democrat) said, "For years and years, West Milford's elected officials and staff have been working hard for tax relief, specifically as it relates to the watershed lands and taxation of them. Between development restrictions and loss of revenues on existing retables, it's been a hard hit for West Milford. It's a never-ending battle with Newark." In August of 2015, West Milford and several other towns hired a lobbyist to seek compensation for the water. The passage of a bill into law would establish an appraisal method for the taxation of watershed lands. Water is a precious commodity and a public policy issue. It is unreasonable and unjust to expect the host watershed communities to bear the burden associated with those protections.

POLITICS GETS DIRTY: Party operatives for the WM GOP were writing letters to the editor, full of some truth, half-truths, lies, and spin. To run for office, you need to have a thick skin, but I was not prepared the dirty tricks and sharp elbows of this full-contact sport. I was running for town council, not for a state assembly person or congressman. I lived in the most conservative district north of the Mason-Dixon line, and conservative congressman Scott Garrett had been in office since 2002 in Northern Passaic County (fourteen years as of 2016).

CAR TIRE SLASHED, TRUCK WINDOW BROKEN: In addition to political signs getting stolen, being charged with bribery, someone posting on a local website as "Jim Geist" when it was not me, and the weight I was feeling of campaigning, learning the issues, and raising money for the campaign, I came out to my car on one Sunday to find a flat tire. I took the tire in to get fixed. Someone used utility knife to make a small incision. I got the tire plugged only to find there was another cut in the same tire. A week later, I came out to see a crack in my car windshield.

#1 COUPON-GATE: BRIBERY CHARGE AGAINST RAUTH AND GEIST: On October 23, 2006, the West Milford GOP slapped the Democrats with four counts of bribery. James Rauth was friends with the owner of Miller's Tires. Millers Tires paid for a door hanger, it said, "Sorry we missed you" and asked for the homeowners' vote. At the bottom of the door hanger, it said, "$25 of any repair from Miller's Town Tire and Automotive." The state made it clear that candidates cannot give voters money or things of monetary value or any incentive to gain votes. The local papers dubbed it Coupon-Gate or Tire-Gate.

The West Milford GOP claimed in the papers to go to the police, the superintendent of elections, the assistant attorney general's office, and the county prosecutor to file bribery charges. The papers reported Republican candidates Mike Ramaglia and Joe Smolinski signed the complaints of bribery charges against Geist, Rauth, and the WM Democratic treasurer Bob Nolan. Ramaglia said political candidates "are not even supposed to give away as much as a cookie." What he forgot was the previous year, the Republicans handed out candies and trinkets while campaigning. The Democrats will have to answer for this on November 21 in Superior Court.

KIDS SENT TO MY HOME ON HALLOWEEN: On Halloween, one group of kids who stopped by my home asked for the coupons. I pulled some out and asked, "Do you mean these?" and a girl grabbed the coupons out of my hand and ran away. There were two people who started posting on the www.nj.com/forums/westmilford site that Geist was handing out coupons with his trick-or-treat candy. It was a sad and pitful to use children for political purposes.

THE TRUTH: The truth was that Candidate Ramaglia hired a Republican attorney, Joseph Afflitto, to act as a prosecutor. The case was transferred from the West Milford courts to the Pompton Lakes Municipal Court. On Tuesday, May 15, 2007, Mike Ramaglia, under pressure from his attorney and Pompton Lakes judge Frank Santoro, withdrew his complaint from the West Milford Democrats 2006. Camille Abate, who ran for Congress against Scott Garrett and lost, represented Geist and Rauth. She said, "From the beginning, the charge lacked merit, and this appeared to be a way of maneuvering and manipulating the local election. The West Milford Democrats may well have a case against Ramaglia for a violation of section 11 of the Federal Voting Act."

The West Milford Democrats put out a press release following Ramaglia's withdraw of the complaint, stating, "There was no way that the advertisement by Miller could be viewed as anything but an advertisement. The summons was not reviewed by the police or the prosecutor's office but was solely the creation of the Republican brain trust to gain an unfair advantage in this election by attempting to smear the Democrats a taint of 'corruption.' This piece of chicanery could fall under the federal law or false reports to law enforcement authorities under New Jersey Penal Code." For almost eight months, I had to live with this charge over my head. It caused me much stress, sleepless nights, and many gray hairs.

WEST MILFORD'S GOP KARL ROVE SPIN DOCTOR: President Bush called the GOP's Karl Rove Turd Blossom or Genius Boy. His name was Frank Hannon, and his contribution was writing weekly "guest columns" for the GOP entitled "Frankly Speaking." On August 25, 2006, he wrote, "Jim Geist Is a GGIT, a Gotcha Guy in Training." I wrote a response where I called Mr. Hannon Mr. RAIL (Regularly Accusing Inaccurate Lowdown). I could have also called him

Mr. LIAR (Leveling Inaccurate Accusations Regularly) but did not. I sent a letter to Frank's home and told Mr. Hannon I thought he was better at spinning that Lance Armstrong, or ice-skater Dorothy Hamill doing her flying camel move or better than the Spinners' busting dance moves.

I sent him a second letter, saying,

> *During my quiet time with the Lord this morning, these two thoughts popped into my head. 1) We are inclined to see things not as they are, but as we are. 2) Keeping old scores, getting even and one-upping make you less the person who you are. When I write a letter to the editor, I ask myself, am I addressing the issue or attacking the person? If Jesus was to edit my letter, what changes would he make?*

Mr. Hannon never responded to me, and the following year, he seemed to fall off the face of the earth. I never saw another letter written in the paper by Mr. Hannon.

FROM THE DESK OF GOD ABOUT POLITICS (BY ANDY BOROWITZ)

Dear West Milford GOP Club,

> *As the King of the Universe, I don't usually get involved in the rough-and-tumble of a political campaign, but this year is different because so much is at stake. Now you are probably saying to yourself, "God, are you kidding?" If you*

want Ramaglia and Smolinski to win, could you not just
smite their Democratic foes of Geist and Rauth?

The fact of the matter is, even if I want to smite every
Democrat, the simple truth is the federal election laws
prohibit me from doing so. Here's the great news, though,
the way to smite your Democratic foes here on Earth is
called negative campaign ads. That's why it's important
you send me money today.

One final thing, many of you keep asking when the
world is coming to an end. When it comes to the end of
the world, I can think of no one who would be better at
helping me do it than the Republicans.

Yours in Heaven,
God

WM GOP OPERATIVE SENDS ARTICLES TO GEIST AND RAUTH BOSSES: Principals and assistant principals keep files on teachers. I asked to review my file in June of 2007 and found a letter about the Coupon-Gate trial with Jim Geist being charged with bribery. I was able to pull out any letters that were three years or older that were not discipline-related or that were deemed unjustified. I met with Principal Harris and my UFT union rep and was able to get the letter pulled from my file. James Rauth, the police sergeant, was called in to see his supervisor on three different occasions because of the articles. His colleagues at work used to call him Jimmy Coupon. Imagine trying to steal a person's livelihood because they ran against your candidate.

WHO WAS THE DIRTY OPERATIVE? It was Pierre Sevweenie. We had worked together at Park West wherewe both worked as deans . We commuted to work together, we went hunting and fishing together, and I visited his home so much his kids thought I was Uncle Jim. One day I did not bring his check home. There were fifteen people in line, and I just wanted to get to the bus and get home, and I would loan him some money until Monday. As a result, after I ran for office, he became the president of the WM Dems. He was the one who had the tires slashed and I believe broke the window. Unfortunately, he allowed his politics to impact the friendship. Every day I had to hear him spew like a ditto head the "entertainment" baloney Rush Limbaugh had been spouting the day before. I never pushed my Democratic views on him, but he felt it was okay for him to dump his views on me. As the saying goes, some people are not loyal to you, they are loyal to their need of you; and once their needs change, so does their loyalty.

2006–2007: SPY VS. SPY: In *Mad* mmgazine, they had Spy vs. Spy. This is what happened between Pierre and I over the next one and a half years. He thought it was funny to go after me by writing to my bosses. Pierre was Italian, and his nickname was Moussa because he loved Mussolini. He also said in the Italian world, those whose names end in *I* are at the top, those with *A* are in the middle, and those that end in *O* are on the bottom. He had a Napoleon complex and was a fascist. This was the time the HBO show *The Sopranos* was on, and he thought he was Tony Soprano, always making quotes from *The Godfather* movie. When I got a new vehicle, the Jeep, I parked in his spot for a week. When I found an orange NYC parking ticket on the street, I placed it under his car windshield. Someone dumped acid or painted on my back deck and left a footprint on the deck. The following weekend, I re-stained the deck in a half hour, and it looked brand new.

As a dean, he did not have to teach five periods a day, which gave him free time to post political stuff on NJ.com. I just made copies of all the material he posted at all times of the workday; it was not just during his lunch period. I sent it to the superintendent's office, and Sevweenie was put under investigation. In New Jersey, to get a deer archery license, you have to go through a six-hour course. He ended up getting one without taking the course. I reported him to the New Jersey Game Commission, and he was put under investigation by the NJGC. They guy was bald, so I did not see any gray hairs grow, but it was not so funny for him when the shoe was on the other foot. It was okay to have the GOP file charges of bribery. It was okay for people to pose as Jim Geist on the West Milford website. The beach sign for the he was president of, disappeared I was told. You see, when you pull "mafia-like" moves on another, the table can be turned, and the same thing be done to you.

When I realized partisan operative was getting divorced, I posted on NJ.com, saying, "Well, Pierre, good luck with future ex-wife number 3. With your second, you will have to pay alimony and child support for your two kids. Of course, she will also get half your pension in addition to the two college educations you have to pay for and for the two future weddings you have to pay for. ShopRite is having a sale on tomato soup this week, ten cans for $5. Remember, when you play with the bull, you are bound to get gored." I stopped posting on NJ.com because the only way for it to stop is for one to stop, me. It had made my life much more peaceful, and I stopped looking at the sight. As a former reporter Martin O'Shea told me, "The best way to get under the skin of Sevweenie is to ignore him. When you respond, he gets a kick out it. When you ignore him, it annoys him and gives him no pleasure." Tit for tat is immature, exhausting, and stressful.

2012 - FIRE COMPANY RESPONDS TO FALSE ALARM TO MY CAMPFIRE: One of the things I love most about my property is the twenty-six acres of woods behind my home and the campfire area next to my home. I had had probably one hundred campfires with friends over the fourteen years I had lived here (as of 2016). To have a campfire in West Milford, you need to get a fire permit from the

Forest Fire Service. It does not cost anything, and the permit is good for a month. The only requirement is you call the police department beforehand, give them your permit number and phone number, and when you will be having your campfire. If it is too dry out, they tell you no campfire that night.

My neighbor Richie came over about 6:00 p.m. in late August. He worked at FedEx and usually went to bed between eight o'clock and eight thirty at night because he got up so early. I had a campfire permit, but I did not call up the police. As we were sitting, talking, and having a beer, someone drove by, Pierre Sevweenie, and yelled, "Hope you have a permit!" After ten minutes, as I was talking with Richie, we heard sirens coming up the street. They pulled up next to the woods, and I went out to meet the fire chief.

These guys were volunteers. They were home barbecuing with their families, or watching a football game, or doing work around their property when they received a false alarm call because the West Milford GOP president wanted to get a former friend who was a Democrat in trouble. I apologized to the chief and told him what happened. I told him, "If you want to file a complaint for someone calling in a false alarm, here is his name." The chief said, "People who call the fire department are protected by anonymity, but if you want, you could file charges with the police." I chose not to. I had more important things to do in my life.

12-18-12 - SEVWEENIE ACTS AS A LIVE SHOOTER HOAX ON HANDICAPPED STUDENT SCHOOL IN NYC:

On December 18, 2012, just four days after twelve girls, eight boys, and six adults were killed at the Sandy Hook Elementary School in Newtown, Connecticut, according to Horan Watch and www.zmLongBeach website, Mr. Sevweeni impersonated a gunman at PS 79 under the guidance of the principal at Horan School in East Harlem unannounced to the teachers, students, or parents of the three hundred mentally and physically handicapped students. It was an unannounced "active shooter" drill. The drill started approximately at 10:00 a.m. The lockdown started at 10:00 a.m. with a woman's voice, saying over the loudspeaker, "Shooter, intruder, lockdown, get out!"

It was planned in secrecy without warning or notice to any of the victims. Desperate students and staff were traumatized and struggle today with the aftermath. Hundreds of stories had emerged of teachers holding doors down to save their students while calling loved one to say good-bye and staff falling on the floor in prayer with dozens of acts of protection and heroism. The three hundred disabled students who had worked all their lives to overcome emotional hardships were terrorized by Mr. Sevweenie's live gunman drill. Imagine a person pushing through your door, only to see a smirking face from a school manager.

A petition was put out by Horan Watch, demanding a full investigation of Principal Greer Philips, VP Jason Sands, VP Mildred Rodriquez, and Dean Pierre Sevweenie. There were no press conferences and no denouncements from the NYC mayor or any council persons to condemn the actions of the school leadership or to scrutinize the rationale behind the drills. I am sure if this mock drill had been committed in city hall, every action possible that could have been take would have been taken. For information, it can be found in the *NY Times*, the Daily Kos, and Horan Watch.

GUN DEATHS STATS FROM THE CDC

Of the 32,000 killed by gun in the United States: 60% are suicide - 19,200

4% are justified - 1,280   33% are homocides - 10,560

3% are accidents - 960   80% of homocides are gang-related.

Your chances of being killed by a gun are less than 1 percent if you don't hang out in gang-controlled area. Do not commit a crime with a gun or plan on committing suicide. For me, it is still too many.

5-11-07 - HARRY CLARK ARRESTED FOR IMPERSONATING GEIST ON THE INTERNET: Harry Clark, aged forty-seven, was arrested for alleged identity theft by the Passaic County's Internet Fraud Division, who monitored the website over a two-month period. Clark had been posting on NJ.com as "Jim Geist" before and after 2006 election in West Milford, New Jersey. Clark, a member of the WM Republicans and elected to the county Republican committee, was charged in his West Milford home at 1:00 p.m. on Thursday; and a Pompton Lakes judge released him on his own recognizance. Jim Geist, the complainant, said, "The messages defamed and ridiculed others without my consent." Clark also posted as Jimbo Warden for James Warden was a Democratic Councilman for West Milford at the time. Clark offered to sell the screen name after someone on the message board complained it was an impersonation of Democratic Councilman Jim Warden. Barbara Williams of the *NJ Record* paper said, "Clark will most likely face fines and could be given jail time" (in addition to legal costs).

5-06-08 - CHARGES AGAINST CLARK ARE DISMISSED: Judge Santoro dismissed the charges, claiming Geist and Passaic sheriff detective Juan Passsano did not provide full discovery to the defense.

The judge claimed Geist and Passano violated Clark's Fourth and Fifth Amendment rights and prejudiced Clark's ability to defend himself. Clark also claimed he suffered personal harm as the result of his arrest and was forced to resign as Cub Scout Leader at Our Lady Queen of Peace Church in Hewitt, New Jersey. When *AIM* reporter Bryan LaPlaca asked Clark why he posted under Geist's name, Clark said, "I was just pointing out funny things that happened in West Milford." Clark went on to say "I believe my attorney is going to be filing against some actors in this event." Clark said, "These people used the process, the criminal justice system, in the most perverted way possible. This should not happen to someone in the U.S." (after being cleared from harassment charges for two years).

WHY DID I FILE THE CHARGES? I have always felt in order to make on postings on a community web-site, the poster should legally have to post their true identity should post his or her real name and where you live to hold the poster accountable for any libelous language. I also felt I was being bullied by some unnamed person using "Jim Geist" on the West Milford NJ.com website. There is only one Jim Geist, and that is me. The only way to deal with a bully is to punch him in the nose, and I used the law to do so. I may have lost the case on some technicality, but Clark had to spend tens of thousands of dollars, so as they say, "If you mess with the bull, you are going to get gored." Since my case in 2008, dozens of states had made it illegal to use another person's name to post on the Internet.

OCTOBER 4, 2009 - SUBURBAN TRENDS EDITORIAL BOARD: The *NJ Trends* board of editors said they "believed Geist abused power by trying to silence posters through intimidation and law enforcement officials . . . We think Clark should sue the Passaic County's sheriff's office." Then on behalf of Geist they said, "But we also hated the goading nature of Clark's bullying tone of the others on the forum during that time. The postings did nothing but ratchet up the vitriol between the parties. Clark's victory for free speech could be a loser for the West Milford public . . . and most of the public is sick of it."

MY RESPONSE TO THE TRENDS: I filed a complaint at the sheriff's office to protect people from impersonating them on a website; it is wrong and cowardly to post without using your real name. I went to court five times, but my representation was never given the opportunity to present our evidence. Clark's attorney never requested any discovery (information) from me. In September of 2007, I sent a letter to Mr. Clark to let him know I did not intend to file a civil suit against him because I did not want his family to suffer for his poor choices and hoped my letter would bring his family some peace. The problems brought unto Mr. Clark by posting as "Jim Geist" on NJ.com were brought on by his decision to do so. The mere fact that the case was not heard does not necessarily make Mr. Clark a victim, and it certainly does not make him innocent. While Mr. Clark considers it "goofing around," a mature person takes responsibility for his actions. I have been honorable in my actions and continue to believe its wrong to impersonate others and to assume identities on Internet sites."

***N.J. STAR-LEDGER* COLUMNIST PAUL MULSHINE:** In October 9, 2009, columnist Paul Mulshine said, "When I spoke to sheriff's spokesman Bill Maer on the phone, he said Speziale stands by the prosecution. We maintain that our investigators found that the manner in which Clark did this by saying there was someone else setting up a fictitious name and saying there was someone else is illegal." Mulshine went on to say "Only Clark had his name dragged through the mud and spent tens of thousands of dollars in legal fees." Mulshine closed by saying the sheriff's office should read the Constitution, especially the First Amendment. He also said he will be keeping track of this case and writing more after Clark's civil case against the sheriff's office and Geist.

WHAT A BIRDIE FROM THE SHERIFF'S OFFICE TOLD ME: 1) This case should have been handled on the county level, not the local level. Clark's attorney kept moving the case until he found a "friendly" judge. 2) Superior Judge Falcone sent this case to the municipal level for harassment. Falcone could have dismissed your case on "lack of disclosure," but he did not. 3) The state prosecutor looked in the case before giving it to the sheriff's office. The state, the sheriff's office, and the prosecutor's office thought the case had merit. 4) There was no police misconduct; it was hand on the merit of the case. 5) Why didn't Clark's attorney sue the prosecutor's office or Judge Falcone? This was the first Internet case we had lost. My sense is they wanted this case to disappear.

California, Washington, Texas, and New York have laws that would punish anyone who creates a social or website account in someone else's name without their consent that has purpose to "harm, defraud, intimidate or threaten." Violators can face a combination of misdemeanors brought against them.

2009 - JUDGE SANTORO ORDERS GAG ORDER: I sent a letter to Public Defender Judith Accardi on April 20, 2009. They made it clear no one was to talk about the case until a decision was made by him. On April 13, between noon and one o'clock in the afternoon, Harry Clark stopped by the offices of the *Suburban Trends* to talk with the *AIM* editor Jai Agnish and *Trends* editor Matt Fagan. My source was my girlfriend at the time, who worked at the *Trends* and witnessed this taking place. Harry wanted to make sure the papers were at the trial happening at 3:00 p.m. that day because I was testifying. Clark said, "This should be an interesting trial today." Clark spoke about the case, and nothing came of it.

10-22-10 - CASE #3: CLARK VS. SHERIFF'S DEPARTMENT AND JAMES GEIST: I was making dinner when I heard a car pull in my driveway, and someone knocked on my back door. I opened the door. "Are you Jim Geist?" "Yup." The man said, "You have been served." I called my home insurance and found out I will be represented by Raina Johnson of Methfessel and Werbel. We met at a diner on Route 17 in Ramsey. I told her the story and had over all the evidence I had in December of 2010. After two years on December 27, 2012, I received a letter from Methfessel and Werbal, saying, "Mr. Geist, we are pleased to have dismissed Mr. Clark's lawsuit against you with prejudice. It was a pleasure working with you. Best of luck in the future." Signed by Raina (Johnson) Pitts. "With prejudice" means the case is dismissed permanently and cannot be brought up to court again. I sent an e-mail to columnist Paul Mulshine to inform him of the court's decision and looked forward to his follow-up of the case. Mulshine never wrote a follow up piece in his weekly column.

INTEVIEWED BY CHANNEL 11 NEWS: I received a phone call from Vanessa Tyler of Channel 11 News in NYC. She told me she had heard about the case from a cameraman from West Milford who worked there. She was empathetic to the situation and asked me to explain how my name was used, why it was used, how I addressed it, and what the result was. In this case, it was about intimidating people from another political party. It was not about "free speech."

WEST MILFORD NEIGHBOR KID: Across the street from me on Bayonne Drive is a retired police officer. On the corner of Bayonne and Jenkins, the West Milford Public Works Mower came by two summer earlier and, with the blade on a tractor, cut down the shrubbery on the corner for safety purposes so cars could see better when wanting to make a left or right onto Bayonne Drive. This summer, the shrubbery had grown up; and on a summer morning, when they were not home, I trimmed the bush. The next day, Ron called me over and asked if I had seen what happened. I should have said, "The town came through with the tractor again to cut the roadside shrubbery," or I should have said, "No, Ron, I don't know what happened." What I should not have said was "I know what happened. I cut the bush on the corner. It was getting high and was causing a safety issue on the corner." He said, "Should you not have asked me first?" I said, "Probably, but you might have said no. I figured since the town cut it last year, it would not be a problem." The next day, on a tree along the road was a sign posted, saying, "Trespassers will be shot, and survivors will be shot again."

That night, I had a few beers and was upset with the sign. When the sun went down, I went over with a flashlight and tried to take the sign down. Ron came out with a flashlight with his wife, Lynn. "Hey, what the hell is going on?" I said, "Really, you would shoot me and then shoot me again if I survived?" To his wife, I said, "If your husband had a heart attack or stroke, don't you think I would help you get him to the hospital?" The other neighbors came out and said, "Is everything okay, Ron?"

Mind you, when I moved into this neighborhood in 2002, not one neighbor came over and welcomed me to the neighborhood. No one said, "Hi. If you have any questions about needing a service, we would be more than happy to advise you." It was such culture shock moving from Forty-First St. and Thirty-Fourth Avenue in Queens with yelling, car alarms, and jets flying overhead as they were on their way to landing at La Guardia Airport. I went from constant noise to the noise of peeper frogs giving mating calls and a sense of solitude and loneliness living in West Milford, New Jersey.

The other neighbors on Bayonne and Jenkins never said boo to me; however, they lived uphill from me and liked to use their leaf blower to blow leaves into the street, which led to my driveway and yard, and were the wind current pushed the leaves into my yard. I had to clean up my leaves and then do the double duty of cleaning the leaves of my unconscious noncop neighbors. They had two boys. The one who lived on the second floor was a pretty good guitar player. I liked hearing him play in the late afternoons. They had a basketball court in the backyard, where the young kid shot hoops with the dog running around him.

The older boy used to shoot firecrackers and fireworks from the backyard, and the rockets often landed in the woods behind my home. When it rained or the woods were wet, the fireworks did not bother me. When it was dry out, I had a real problem with it. I did not move to West Milford and took care of my home and property so some ignorant teenager who knew everything and drove like Formula 1 driver Dale Evans would set the woods on fire and burn down my home I loved so much.

So I said to the other neighbors, "This is none of your business. This is between Ron and myself." The cocky eleventh-grader got in my face and started talking trash. I pushed him out of my face and said, "Do you know that I have collected over a dozen firecracker rockets you have shot into the woods? Do you know why? So if and when you start a fire in the woods and may or may not burn down homes, including mine, along Bayonne Drive, I have proof of the knuckleheaded kid who shot them into the woods. Then I can sue your parents, take your home, sell it, and rebuild my home!" His parents said, "Let's go home. This is not our business." We all parted ways, and the following weekend, I bought Ron and Lynn a pallet of flowers and placed it by their door on their back porch. After two days, I saw the flowers planted around their home.

NIGHTTIME GARDEN VANDALIZER: I have a garden I plant every summer, about fifteen by twenty feet, mostly tomatoes and some herbs like cilantro and basil. One evening I thought I heard some commotion outside. I went outside and heard something running, and all of a sudden, I heard "oooommmmfff!" as something ran into the fence between the woods and edge of my property in front of my house. It was too dark to see. I waited until the morning to see what had happened.

In the morning, I saw one of my tomato plants had been pulled out; and down where the heavy metal livestock fencing was in place, I can see an indenture. I put two and two together and realized it was the sixteen-year-old punk across the street from me who had done this. He pulled the plant from my garden, heard me come to the front door, and took off, only to run into the livestock fencing when I heard the "oomf" grunting noise. Lol. That had to smart.

The young tomato puller, with a checkered scratch-marked face, got his driver's license shortly thereafter and drove up and down our small street like a maniac. He even drove on neighbor Richie's lawn one day to avoid hitting another car with his reckless driving. The following summer, on Union Valley Road, his car swerved off the road on a curve, hitting a tree; and I will never need to worry again about plants being pulled or the woods being set on fire by firecrackers because the neighbor kid killed himself from the impact of hitting a tree. I still had the three bottle rockets in a drawer in my shed. It must be a terrible thing to go through losing a young son.

The next summer, the town came and cut down the shrub like it did two summers earlier. The summer after the town cleared the shrubs, Ron and Lynn cleared out the scrubby area and had the corner landscaped professionally. We still wave and talk to one another to this day.

CLINTON ROAD: NEW JERSEY'S MOST HAUNTED ROAD: According to *Weird New Jersey* magazine, Clinton Road in West Milford is the most haunted road in New Jersey. A body was found off Clinton Road in 1983 with ice crystal marking found on the heart, which was deposited there by one of the best hit men ever called the Ice Man. Richard Kuklinski was a Polish from Bayonne, New Jersey, and was never going to be made in any of the mafia outfits in the metropolitan area; but he was such an excellent contract killer. He worked for all the families in the NYC area. He often kept bodies in freezers or packed in ice. He was arrested in 1986, claimed to have killed over one hundred people over twenty years and was convicted of killing five, and died under suspicious circumstances in jail in 2006. Clinton Road is a wooded road tenn miles long and next to Clinton Reservoir. There have been reports of blue-and-white lights or occasional UFO activity on the reservoir. There is the legend of a ghost boy who walks the road at night, and there is suspected KKK activity in that area in the past. There is a famous Big Foot sighting they call "Red Eyes" in Newfoundland, New Jersey, in the 1970s and in 2008, which is very close to the Clinton Road area. In Ringwood off Skyline Drive on the Ramapo Mountains, there was a Bigfoot sighting in 2004 by a bow hunter and 1979 by a New Jersey woman.

MY CLINTON ROAD EXPERIENCES: There had been two times over the years coming home late on the dark roads of Clinton Road I had passed an old woman walking the road, and it was strange because it was so late at night, and she did not carry a flashlight. Another time, late at night, I passed a man who was dressed in a Union soldier's outfit carrying a lantern. West Milford does have Long Iron Pond and a Union soldier camping reenactment yearly, so maybe one of the men was trying to freak some drivers out. On this road, I had seen deer, bear, rattle snakes, and twice I saw a coyote.

APRIL 1, 2013, FROG CROSSING: I was driving home on Clinton Road on April 1st. I drove up Van Orden Road past the horse farms, past the gun club, and past the power line and made a right at the stop sign on the dark, long, and curvy road of Clinton Road. As I came up to the other end of the power line, I could see what looked like at least a dozen high-powered flashlights on the road. The first thought was, *I hope these are not aliens because I do not want to get anally probed and end up on the TV program Hunting UFOs.* I was actually feeling a little scared because I do believe there is another life in the universe when something in black and with the skull face from the movie *Scream* runs out in front of me. What a stupid high school kid! I literally had to swerve to not hit him, maybe even killing him. I drove for a quarter mile, and there was a police car with running lights. I slowed down and told the West Milford police officer, "If you turn your lights off and drive down the road one-fourth mile, you will be able to arrest the *Scream* guy when he runs in front of your car."

It literally looked like the scene out of *Close Encounters* when the scientists and military were on the road with flashlights. As I got closer, I saw a large yellow sign on a fluorescent orange road cone that said,"Beware, Frog Crossing." Well, it was April Fool's Day. I started laughing and thought, *Wow, these people are really committed to putting on a great April Fool's Day prank.* When I slowed down to congratulate the people with flashlights, they told me, "This is not a prank. This is the mating season for the tree frogs, and they cross this road to get to the swampland for mating." As I drove on, I avoided running over a dozen tiny frogs crossing the road and thanked the volunteers for their service. They do this every year for a few days around April 1.

MY CONTRIBUTION TO WEST MILFORD, NEW JERSEY (CLINTON ROAD SIGH): I love to turn up Van Orden Road, pass the horse farm and the small windy road passing a gun club on the right and a small farm on the left, and pass the power line up the hill to get to Clinton Road. If you are not familiar with the road, as soon as you reach the top of the hill, Clinton Road is approximately twenty feet away; and if you are speeding or drunk or driving at night, you can easily get in an accident or drive into the woods by the Clinton Road Reservoir. It is definitely a spot for potential accidents. I wrote a letter to Mayor Bettina Bieri about my concerns, who forwarded the letter to the county since it is a county road; and two months later, they put up a sign with six yellow reflecting arrows, three pointing to the right and three to the left. Every time I pass the sign, I call it my sign.

GREENWOOD LAKE OF NY AND NEW JERSEY: Greenwood Lake is three miles south of Upper Greenwood Lake and is three times larger, three miles long, and one mile wide. This lake is a natural lake, and half is in New Jersey, and half is in NY. The lake is surrounded by mountains and was a popular spot for many to come up to visit before the invention of air-conditioning.

BABE RUTH, JOE LOUIS, AND DERRICK JETER: Babe Ruth used to frequent Northern New Jersey in the 1920s and 1930s to relax, hunt, fish, golf, gamble, and drink. The Bambino enjoyed many years happy hours visiting the lakeside hotel, the New Continental, and always stayed in room 3. He kept his boat at a marina located off 7 Waterstone Road. There is a great picture of Ruth sitting on the ground next to the Greenwood Lake, drinking a beer with a large pot with ice and three beers next to him and a line of twenty-two trout on a string in front of him. World champion boxer Joe Louis had a training camp in Pompton Lakes, New Jersey, for many years. He held an exhibition match and helped raise $2,620 to help the town purchase a new Packard ambulance. The champ moved his training camp to a property one mile west of the New Continental Hotel at Greenwood Lake in 1944 before his fight with Billy Conn. There is a picture of Louis sitting in a boat on Greenwood Lake and an old-time movie reel of him running by the lake. Derrick Jeter's grandparents lived next to Greenwood Lake and, when he retired from the NY Yankees, had a stone mansion built next to the lake, which as of 2016 is still being worked on. Some in West Milford want a road named Jeter Way since Jeter attends a WM Catholic church. Some say there are more important people to honor than baseball players. The New Continental Hotel is in business where you can stay in the summer or stop by for lunch or dinner by the lake.

BABE RUTH VS. HANK AARON: Who was better, Babe Ruth or Hank Aaron? Hammering Hank had 755 home runs to Babe Ruth's 714, but Aaron had 3,965 more at bats to Babe's 8,399 at bats. One fan guessed if Ruth had that many more at bats, he would have had hit 1,051 home runs.

BABE RUTH VS. BARRY BONDS: Barry Bonds had 847 more at bats than Babe Ruth and hit 764 home runs to Ruth's 714. Barry Bond faced 228 pitchers who were 6'3" or taller to Ruth facing 20 pitchers who were 6'3" or taller. Bonds was one of the best left fielders ever and won three MVPs before the doping scandal charges. Others say that Ruth's charisma helped rescue professional baseball in the aftermath of the Black Sox scandal. When Babe Ruth died, they let his body lie in state at Yankee Stadium, where over 77,000 fans paid their respects.

STATS TO USE?: There are many stats you can use, from hits to on-base percent, to slugging percent to OPS or on base plus slugging percent, to home runs, and to runs batted in. The top 10 runs batted in are Ty Cobb, Barry Bonds, Hank Aaron, Babe Ruth, Pete Rose, Willie Mays, Cap Anson, Stan Musial, and Alex Rodriguez. How can you argue against these great ball players?

SLUGGING AVERAGES: In Babe Ruth's first season, he had 172 hits, and this is how the slugging average is calculated: $(73 \times 1) + (36 \times 2) + (9 \times 3) + (54 \times 4) = 388$ slugging average. The lifetime slugging average of the following are:

-Bonds: 863 -Ruth: 847 -Aaron: 554 -Mike Schimdt: 523 -Jeter: 440

The top slugging averages are Babe Ruth, Ted Williams, Lou Gerhig, Jimmie Fox, Barry Bonds, and Manny Ramirez at 584, who attended George Washington High School where I taught. I did not say he graduated, but he did attend there.

8-12-04 - NEW JERSEY GOV. JIM MCGREEVY STEPS DOWN: I was watching TV, and it kept being reported Governor McGreevy had an important announcement to make. McGreevy walked up to the podium and said, "At a point in every person's life, one has to look deeply in the mirror of one's soul and decide one's unique truth in the world, not as we may want to see it or hope to see it but as it is. My truth is that I am a gay American." The Democrat admitted to having an affair with a man and asked his family's forgiveness. "I was wrong, foolish, and inexcusable." His resignation took place on November 15th, 2004.

In 2006, he wrote about the duality of his gay life before coming out and began attending St. Bartholomew's Episcopal Church in Manhattan. In 2007, he was accepted to the Episcopalian General Theological Seminary. In 2009, he started volunteering with Exodus Ministries, where he performed service to former prisoners seeking rehabilitation. HBO did a program on Reverend McGreevy in *Fall from Grace* on HBO.

WEST MILFORD NEIGHBORS: On my first three years at 57 Bayonne Dr., I lived next to an empty home. In the third summer there, a new septic system was put in at 53 Bayonne, a new roof was put on, and a back porch was added to the home and a for sale sign went up.

There were two guys who moved into the home. I rarely saw them. In the winter, I put insulation in the window of my garage windows and in the bathroom of the house to keep the cold out. With a marker, I put "garage" and "bathroom" on the pieces so I knew which windows to place the insulationpieces in. In the spring, when I took them down,

I noticed the neighbors, only ten feet away, had a sign on their window that said "kitchen." I thought nothing of it, only to find out one of them felt offended by my sign and thought that I thought my neighbors were Peeping Toms, and they thought wrong. The goofier guy moved out, and then I finally met Kenny.

2005 – KENNY G.: Kenny had grown up in Ringwood, and his parents still lived there. He worked for some clock company; and he was skinny, organized, and kept his property taken care of. We got to meet and became good buddies. He went to church, liked to have a beer with me, and was always the first to come over whenever I had a campfire. He had been through a divorce and was picking up the pieces, grateful he was finally at a place financially to own his own home. He was always working on something on his property.

2006 – JULIE AND TODD: A nice young couple from Pompton Lakes moved to the home next to Kenny. I saw the moving truck as they carried in their stuff into their blue-colored home. The following weekend, I welcomed them into the neighborhood, like I never was. In time, we became friends, and they came to campfires, and they invited me over for their annual Halloween party. Julie looked like actress Kate Blanchett to me with shining blue eyes. Todd worked for a defense contractor and was part of a heavy metal band as the drummer. I went to see his band several times. Of all the pictures Julie had of him, he was always making funny, silly faces as he drummed. The band was good, but they did a little too much blow for me. Julie was always wanting to do home improvements, and Todd just wanted to relax on the weekends and watch the Yankees. They met neighbor Kenny at my campfire, and Kenny started doing work at their home. Hey, if someone wants to come to my place and fix things up, come on over.

VOLUNTEER ADA ERIK PICKS UP CHAINSAW ACCIDENT VICTIM: I was invited to a party of a fellow West Milford Democrat.

It was when I was running for office for the Democratic Club for town council. Today was the annual West Milford Clean Up Day, when volunteers went out and walked the roads and cleaned up the trash accumulated from political signs to tires, to bottles, etc. Piles of garbage were made for the town trucks to pick up on Monday and Tuesday. Ada Erik was at the party, and she owned a horse farm and was a commonsense moderate Republican. She drove up in an ambulance and was a volunteer EMS worker.She volunteered much of her time to the township. While at the late afternoon barbecue, we were sitting around chatting when she got a call that there had been a life-threatening accident with a chainsaw, and she must pick up a person and then transfer them to a local baseball field where an emergency helicopter will transfer this person to the Rutgers Hospital in Newark to the major trauma unit. I didn't even want to imagine what had happened and said a prayer for this poor soul.

2008 - SUNDAY BLOODY SUNDAY: Julie and Todd moved to another home in West Milford by "flipping" their property. She moved into her grandmother's place after granny passed. The property had trees that needed trimming. Kenny had metal tree climbing stirrups he used to climb up and down the trees. He climbed the trees to cut down some of the branches. Kenny was up high on the tree and reached all the way around to cut a branch. Todd was on the ground, holding the rope connected to Kenny, and on a with blue skies said, "Hey, is it raining?" Yeah, raining blood drops all over his face. Kenny yelled, "I am hurt bad! Call an ambulance!" As he climbed down the tree with his good arm, the other arm from the middle of the forearm was dangling from the connected skin. As he lay on the ground, he turned gray from losing so much blood. Julie and Todd wrapped Kenny's arm with a towel and duct tape. Kenny was also diabetic. He was driven to the baseball field by Ada Erik and transferred to the hospital by the helicopter. Kenny not only kept his life, thanks to the Rutgers trauma surgeons, but his arm was also saved; and he was able to use his hand and fingers on the formally severed arm. Amazing!

2010 - THE PLUMBER NEIGHBOR: Ken's job was moving to Chicago, and he could transfer if he wanted to and get half his pay. Our campfire friend Scott Kessler offered him a job working for his auto parts company that was growing in New Jersey, but Ken decided to move to a town on the ocean and worked in a warehouse with Mexicans. Ken's rented his home to a plumber My plumber neighbor and his girlfriend were sitting on their front porch of screened windows literally ten feet away from my bedroom, which also had the screened windows open. Teresa Sarne and I had some afternoon delight, and as we went to nap off, the neighbors made sounds of passion noises in a joking way, and I laughed and thought, *Eat your hearts out, oh jealous ones.*

2011 - NEW JERSEY TROOPER SHAUNA NEIGHBOR: He rented out his home to a New Jersey state trooper named Shauna . She had a golden lab, and she liked to jump out of airplanes. She was divorced and cute. Shauna looked like actress Emma Rossum or Fiona Gallagher in the TV show *Shameless*. She was a wallflower in high school and joined the marines because her sister said she could never make it there. She even gave me some home baked cookies for Christmas.

TOYS FOR TOTS: I was filling up my car at a Luk Gas at a Riverdale, New Jersey, station; and they had a poster of a female marine for their Toys for Tots Christmas Campaign. I looked at the picture and thought, *That is a pretty, cute-looking marine. I wonder if she is a model, or is she really a marine?* I said to myself, "I would like to know the answer to this question at the gas station." The following year, I talked to my neighbor Shauna; and as we were talking, she said, "Let me show you something." It was the Toys for Tots poster, and I got my question answered. It was my neighbor, the marine, in the poster. We hiked one time. She gave me a marine haircut one time and homemade cookies for Christmas.

HEROIN IN THE NEIGHBORHOOD: I was sealing my driveway, all covered in sealer, and a car pulled over. It was a woman, and she said, "Did you know there have been burglaries in the neighborhood in the last few weeks? It is probably the kid four houses up from us who is doing heroin." I told her. "Thanks for the news." I did find a syringe and needle in the woods behind my house the week before. Yikes. Now when I went to work, every time I came home, I thought, *Is today the day I get robbed?* I informed neighbor Shauna, the New Jersey trooper, about this. When on duty, she drove by the home to scan things out. One day someone ran up to her trooper vehicle to tell her some kid just robbed their house, and she ended up catching and arresting him. He went away for a few years, and now I don't worry about him robbing my home.

SUMMER OF 2007 - VISITING PAXTON: I went up to Syracuse and brought my friend CarlLa Horton with me to hang out for a few days. The highlight of the trip was going to a pasta festival and the NY State Fair. On a walk around the neighborhood, we ran into an old-timer, and he said to Paxton, "I knew your grandfather. He drank more than anyone I knew." Paxton's dad was a major drinker and drug abuser as well. His dad used to live in Florida and was a cocaine cowboy, flying in cocaine from South America into Florida. Paxton's dad had a conversion experience and today lives a sober life and is part of the elders at his church.

We later went to a bar up the street, and I can see from across the street a little red laser was being shot into the bar. It was strange, and I wondered if the police were listening in and what kind of illegal activity was happening in this bar. I told Paxton, "Let's get out of here." We walked to a different bar. I was concerned about my friend's drinking. When we had breakfast in the morning, I can see his hands shaking. I also noticed that when he got drunk, he took his left hand and placed it above his left hip on his back and twisted his hand and index finger in swirls when he drinks. It was the Dr. Jekyll and Mr. Hyde situation where Jekyll was a kind person, but his alter ego of Mr. Hyde was a homicidal maniac. Paxton was a kind person, and I loved it when he was sober, but his Mr. Hyde Addict was a condescending and mean drunk. I was worried about the health of my friend.

9-16-08 - THE GREAT RECESSION: Bear Sterns, Lehman Brothers, and AIG collapsed. In a week, Merrill Lynch fell to the bottom with Lehman after six years of reckless gambling. The Ponzi scheme of subprime (predatory) lending and gambling with stock market "derivatives" imploded the economy. In 2004, Lehman, Morgan Stanley, Merrill Lynch, Goldman Sachs, and Bear Sterns got the net capital rule of $12 for every $1 they upped the debt-to-equity ratio from 20:1 to 40:1 with the help of Hank Paulson, head of Goldman Sachs, at the time. With credit default swaps, allowed insurance companies protection without having actual money to pay the insurance.

The repeal of Glass-Steagall by Bob Rubin, secretary of the treasury under Bill Clinton, prevented mergers of investment and commercial banking and the 2000 law deregulating derivatives. As Matt Taibbi in *Griftopia* said, "There is the grafter class (Wall Street) and everyone else. The government is the slavish lapdog (and tool) that the financial companies use to make money" (30).

"In early February 2008, almost a decade after the creation of derivatives, the Securities and Exchange Commission admitted they did not really know what was going on in their multi-billion dollar securities market" (*Plunder* by Danny Schechter, p. 2).

<u>BROOKSLEY BORN AND ELIZABETH WARREN</u>: Brooksley Born warned Wall Street six years before the collapse as the chair of the Commodity Futures Trading Commission in the Clinton administration warned that "derivatives must be regulated" but was bullied by Robert Rubin, Larry Sommers, and Fed Chair Alan Greenspan. In the end, Wall Street had its way, and she resigned. <u>Elizabeth Warren</u>, a law professor, pushed for and created the Consumer Financial Protection Bureau, whose purpose is to make markets for consumer financial products and services work for Americans whether applying for a mortgage, credit cards, or other financial products.

<u>TARP</u>: Following the 2008 crisis, was put on the panel for TARP (Troubled Asset Relief Program). TARP was originally for $700 billion, but under Frank Dodd, it was cut to $475 billion. As of August 4, 2016, according to ProPublica, our government has realized a $68.8 billion profit among refunds, dividends, interest, stock warrants and fees, and sales of equity or assets.

<u>GOLDMAN SACHS</u>: He had hurt the U.S. economy by pushing for derivatives, creating the housing bubble, artificially raising gas to $4 with speculation when it really should be $2.50 a gallon, pushing for profit colleges, and repealing the Glass-Steagall. There is such a revolving door of people working at the treasury department from Goldman. It is called Treasury Goldman Sach. Bernie Sanders, a presidential candidate in 2016, said the revolving door between Wall Street and Washington Government Jobs must stop.

<u>ROSS PEROT CIRCA 1992</u>: Ross Perot said the main reason America had a $4 trillion debt in 1992, which would grow to $8 trillion by 2000, was because of the "cost of elections." Representatives spend one-half of their time raising money instead of "representing the people," so the rich get to influence legislation that favors them. For example, the savings and loan crisis of 1984 was a $20–$30 billion problem, but lobbying money pushed the issue under the rug until it became a $405 billion problem that cost taxpayers $135 billion dollars.

SAVINGS AND LOAN CRISIS OF 1984: The book _The Best Way to Rob a Bank Is to Own One_ by William K. Black, who was a banking regulator, said the Securities and Exchange Commission (as of 2005) has not taken fraud seriously. When the Association of Certified Fraud examiners offered free materials to business schools, only a few accepted. The University of Texas had launched a new institute for fraud studies to bring about reforms. Former bank regulator Black said (as of 2005) the U.S. Department of Justice does not keep records of white-collar crimes (xiii). Black said "control fraud" causes massive losses from property crimes, and the S&L crisis started out of systematic controlled fraud.

ROSS PEROT PROPOSALS: 1) Term limits for Congress and the Senate, 2) restrict campaign contributions to $1,000, curb PAC money, 3) make elections for five months and have voting on a Saturday and Sunday, 4) release no polling data until polls are closed, 5) cut military spending, and 6) no corporate welfare.

2005–2006 CITIBANK PLUTONOMY MEMO: In Michael Moore's documentary _Love of Capitalism_, he showed the Citibank memo to its richest clients, saying, "The world is dividing into two blocs—the plutonomy where economic growth is powered by and largely consumed by the wealthy few." He went on to say "A risk to the plutonomy is political pressure to end the increase in income and wealth inequality, and political enfranchisement—one person, one vote—is likely to fight back against rising profits share of the rich."

9-17-11 - OCCUPY WALL STREET MOVEMENT: Inspired by the anti-austerity protests in Spain coming from the 15-M movement, protesters moved into Zuccotti Park in Wall Street. The OWS (Occupy Wall Street) slogan was "We are the 99%," referring to the inequality and wealth distribution in the United States between the 1 percent and the 99 percent. The protesters were eventually pushed out by the police on November 15, so the movement began their focus on occupying banks, corporate headquarters, board meetings, foreclosed homes, and university campuses. Naomi Wolf of *The Guardian* turned up documents, showing how the FBI and Department of Homeland Security monitored these events through surveillance and infiltration. The movement grew into at least 125 Occupyrelated groups posted on Facebook. It was in the tradition of Coxey's Army in 1894, the Bonus Marchers in 1932, and the May Day Protests of 1971. The Wall Street movement gave rise to the Occupy movement in the United States. I took over one hundred pictures of the protest and the 99 percent Zuccotti Park Camp.

My father's criticism is that you need to run people for office. The Tea Party movement grew because they ran people for office. How will Washington be influenced unless a progressive runs and speaks the message for the working class? Presidential candidate Mitt Romney, or Mitch as David Letterman called him, said the movement was about envy and class warfare. The goals of the movement were more balanced distribution of income, raising minimum wages, the rich paying a higher share in income and corporate taxes, more and better jobs, relief for indebted students, and alleviation of home foreclosures among other things. Nicholas Kristoff of the *NY Times* said, "The movement is not about the overthrow of capitalism, it highlights the need to restore basic principle like accountability."

10-4-11 - UNIONS JOIN THE PROTEST: The AFL-CIO, Transit Workers Union, Service Employees International, United Federation of Teachers, and United Automobile Workers joined the protest of marching from Foley Square in NYC to Zuccotti Park. The Square was full of people, and I even saw actor Tim Robbins (of *The*

Shawshank Redemption, Bull Durham and *Jacob's Ladder*) riding around on his mountain bicycle with a big smile on his face. The unions held a protest the year before in October in Washington DC, and one hundred thousand showed up, and it hardly got any news coverage. The 99 Percent Movement was the children of many union workers, and the parents were joining in because their message aligned with the union message.

I had a sign I carried that said, "What happened to GLASS-STEAGALL?" This was the act that allowed the economy to collapse in late 2008. I got many thumbs-up for my sign. The movement spread to over 190 cities across the country. The rally had a carnival atmosphere, and many people were talking and sharing thoughts, personal stories, and ideas with one another. There was a feeling of hope that there can be change against the rigged system.

VERMONT DEMOCRATIC SOCIALIST SEN. BERNIE SANDERS ENTERS PRESIDENTIAL RACE IN 2015:: He did not win the Democratic primary in August of 2016 but was able to get the Democratic Party to accept 95 percent of the 99 Percent Movement's issues in the platform.

CONFESSIONS: AUGUSTINE OF HIPPO (ALGERIA, AFRICA): Augustine is an early Christian theologian and philosopher whose writings influenced Western Christiainity. When the Western Roman Empire was beginning to disintegrate, he developed the concept of the church as a spiritual city of God, distinct from the material earthly city. In the Catholic and Anglican, Augustine is considered a saint and doctor of the church. Many Protestants consider him to be one of the theological fathers of the Protestant Reformation.

Augustine was born in 354 and died in 430, aged seventy-five. As a youth, he lived a hedonistic lifestyle and, to gain acceptance among the young boys, made up stories of his sexual experiences. It was during this time he uttered the prayer, "Grant me chastity and continence, but not yet." At age nineteen, he began a fifteen-year affair with a young woman in Carthage and gave birth to his son. In 385, he ended the relationship to marry a ten-year-old heiress. He could not marry her legally until she became age twelve.

There are thirteen books in Confessions. The first nine are autobigraphical, and the last four are commentary. In book 6, he talked about a girlfriend breaking up with him, and his heart was wounded. He found another girl, but it was only for bodily pleasure; and in the end, all it did was make him miserable. Augustine experienced heartbreak, suffering with the break up of the woman he loved. There is even a twelve-step fellowship named after him, The Augustinian Fellowship or SSLA (Sex and Love Addicts Anonymous).

AUGUSTINE FELLOWSHIP: It is a twelve-step program for people recovering from sex addiction and/or love addiction. It was founded in Boston in 1976 by a member of AA, who repeatedly acted out and was serially unfaithful to his wife. Many practicing the SLAA recovery program developed the ability to engage in a healthy, committed relationship. SLAA also helps in recovery from sexual anorexia, emotional anorexia, and social anorexia.

HEARTBREAK: Vanessa broke up with me in February of 2007. She left me for another guy. I walked into her apartment one evening to surprise her and she was drinking wine with another guy. Surprise! In the end, she chose him over me. Seeing her was my escape from the pressures of running for office, charges of bribery, someone criminally impersonating me on NJ.com, and dealing with an incompetent assistant principal. My life raft, my escape, and my drug had been snatched from me. I could get her out of my mind. I was a wreck, and I was in terrible pain, and it felt like I was dying. The truth of the matter is God was not central in my life at that time. I was too busy working, running for office, and running to my drug of choice. Pascal said, "There is a void in every person's heart until it is filled with God." Okay, I had had connection with God since tenth grade, from age fifteen to thirty-five, yet I still felt something was missing. It made me feel frustrated and angry at God. Why is this hole in my soul not getting filled? When I first made a commitment to God, there was much joy; and now as I was in the fidelity faith phase of trusting when I was having doubts, I felt a hole again. I prayed, "God, I am in trouble. Please guide me for the healing and hope I need in my life."

I felt angry and betrayed by Vanessa, but in the end, I learned the only person I can control was myself, my thoughts and actions. I have no power to control another person. It was just like the movie *Bruce Almighty* when the NY *Buffalo News* reporter, played by Jim Carrey, tried to win back his girlfriend. God, played by Morgan Freeman, said, "I told you, Bruce, you had almighty powers, but you cannot impact human will." So true, unfortunately. I also learned in the future when I focus on another, I have more grieving work to do. When I focus on the other, it means I have more work to do on me. My ego needed problems to survive, and the death I was feeling was the death of ego, of the false self. It is the kernel that must die before it can become a living plant Jesus talks about. What was being birthed was my true self.

I eventually learned I must constantly let go, and I frequently prayed, "God, I do not own Vanessa. She is yours. I release her to you. I want the best for her even if it means a future not including me." I prayed this and the "Serenity Prayer" probably ten to twenty-five times a day for over a year. In time, I can go a day without thinking about her. In time, I can go days without thinking about her as long as I do not see a trigger like a woman looking like her or the vehicle she drove or see her apartment building from the shool I worked at.

Going up to Syracuse may give me some respite. It was painful, tiring, draining, to be so obsessive. It also brought up shame and embarrassment I could not stop. It kept me from enjoying life and living in the present. It was a terrible affliction. My mind was in such a fog, I forgot I told my parents I was going to Allentown that weekend but ended up going to Syracuse. My Mother called the West Milford Police to check on my home to see if I was okay. On Sunday, it crossed my mind, and I called to tell my parents to apologize. Dad was upset and told me if I needed help, I should get it. He told me guys he knew from Macks who had their wives leave them either became alcholics, went crazy, or killed themselves. I found a book called *Love Addiction* by Susan Peabody, and it talked about a twelve-step group called the Augustine Fellowship. I decided I should give it a try. I also decided to find a therapist in my area on my healthcare network.

MACHO HELL: Poet Charles Bukowski in a poem wrote, "I can forgive all the women . . . who left me. I now realize I am dull . . . back then it was difficult for me to forgive or understand; I remember the nights of macho hell . . . there was my precious ego, never able to understand how you could prefer someone else to me . . . hoping for some kind of cheap vengeance, instead of having accepted gracefully . . . I understand that I never would have met any of you if had not left me for someone else for me or been dicarded by someone else—so here's to all the good nights along with the bad."

FIRST MEETING IN NORTHERN NEW JERSEY: It was a Thursday night, and there were only two guys sitting in a room. I dragged myself into the "Augustinian Fellowship" room, feeling like I had crawled in. They introduced themselves and asked me why I was there. I told them I was heartbroken and could not stop obsessing my ex-girlfriend. They told me their stories that were very similar. Hearing the characteristics and the promises of the program gave me hope. They told me the pain will stop one day. Keep coming back to meetings, read *The Big Book*, find a sponsor, work the steps, and you will begin enjoying life at a deeper level than you can ever imagine. The worst part was going through the withdrawl stage where you commit to not contacting the other person and learning to sit with your feelings, sitting with your pain, doing your grieveing work, listening to the inner critic, healing inner shame, and changing those thoughts as well as learning the difference between the *true self* and the false self and learning how to love myself.

ADDICTION: Addiction is a brain disease characterized by compulsive engagment in rewarding stimuli despite adverse consequences. Addiction is a disease and has symptoms, a course, and an outcome predictable in a medical sense. Without treatment, it can be disabling and/or fatal. Some of the symptoms of addiction are lying, manipulating, being angry, projecting, blaming, euphoric recalling, denying, stealing, emotional thinking, immaturity loss of standards, and loss of spirituality.

COMMON ADDICTIONS

Alcohol	Gambling	Sexual abuse	Dependency
Caffine	Nicotine	Love addiction	Sex
Competition	Overeating	Television	Sugar
Drugs	Pain	Work	Video games

MOVIES ABOUT LOVE AND/OR SEX ADDICTION

Thanks for Sharing	*Choke*	*Fatal Attraction*
500 Days of Summer	*In the Mood* (Woo Woo Kid)	*Love Addict*
Shame	*The Great Gatsby*	*Don Juan*

CHEMICALS RELEASED WHEN FALLING IN LOVE: A Rugter's biological anthropologist made brain scans of people recently broken up. When they saw the pictures of their ex, the parts of the brain that lit up are the same as ones associated with cocaine and nicotine addiction. The chemicals released in love or sex are dopamine, oxytocin, vasopressin, phenethylamine, tyamine, and testosterone and estrogen. These are powerful chemicals indeed. For many, they suffer withdrawal symptoms for the person suffering dependency on the other. When a break up occurs, the body produces cortisol, the very opposite of oxycotin. High levels of cortisol make the body react with flight, flee, or freeze. This is why we often see people suffering heartbreak react so wildly or irrationally.

FAMOUS LOVE AND SEX ADDICTS

Colin Farrell	St. Augustine	Michael Douglas	Amy Winehouse
Lindsay Lohan	Russell Brand	Jessie James	Amber Smith
Tori Spelling	Tiger Woods	Charlie Sheen	Kari Ann Peniche
Halle Berry	Kanye West	David Duchovny	Tom Sizemore

JUNE AND JULY 2008 - RECOVERY WORK BEGINS: In June, I started attending the Augustine Fellowship for love addiction and, in July, I began attending Codependents Anonymous. I also began seeing Dr. Roman in Warwick, NY. Dr. Roman was a Green Beret in Vietnam, a good Catholic, and was a survivor of a stroke and sometimes forgot a word or had trouble pronouncing a word; but I liked him and always know what he was trying to communicate with me. My first year in recovery, I attended seven to eight meetings a week and saw my therapist once a week because I was an emotional wreck.

He also thought I suffered from depression and suggested medication. "How can you know what it feels like to feel good if you have never felt good?" Depression does not have the stigma it used to have, and 10 percent of Americans suffer from it, so I got a prescription. It did lift my mood, but it was not the magic bullet. I must keep doing the work of going to meetings, reading, praying, calling to my sponsor, and doing service work. I learned how to sit with my feelings and pain and to do grieving work if necessary, which for me lasted about one and a half years after stuffing my feelings for forty-two years.

FAMOUS PEOPLE WHO SUFFERED DEPRESSION

Bruce Springsteen	Lorraine Bracco	Ernest Hemingway	Ludwig vAn Beethoven
Edgar Allan Poe	Jackson Pollock	Leonard Cohen	Kurt Cobain
Woody Allen	Virginia Woolf	Ingmar Bergman	Sylvia Plath
Brian Wilson	Vincent van Gogh		

QUOTES ON THERAPY

"The greatest discovery of any generation is that a human being can alter his/her life by altering his/her attitude."

—William James

"Neurosis is always a legitimate substitute for avoiding suffering."

—Carl Jung

"The feeling of being valuable is essential to mental health."

—M. Scott Peck

"The most common cause for depression is when a person is caught between the need to give something up and their will to hold on to it or their anger at having to give it up."

—M. Scott Peck

"Those who go to psychotherapy are the wisest and most courageous among us . . . to submit themselves to self-examination."

—M. Scott Peck

"The desire for pleasure is the desire to escape reality."

—Nathaniel Branden

"We have to crush the grapes before we can drink the wine."

—Fulton Sheen (*The Life of Christ*)

"Nobody can go back and start a new beginning, but anyone can start today to make a new ending."

—Maria Robinson

WHO ARE YOU?: I attended a retreat on codependency, and in the lunch line, the therapist leading the sessions was behind me. She said, "So, Jim, who are you?" I said, "I am a son, brother, teacher, human rights activist, and a former minister." She said, "That is not who you are. Who are you?" I said, "I don't know. I am a person who does not know who he is."

HUMANITY OF JESUS: M. Scott Peck in *Further Along the Road Less Traveled* wrote, "When I read the gospels, the Jesus I discover is continually frustrated . . . frequently sad, sometimes depressed . . . frequently anxious, scared and terribley lonely . . . Jesus did not seem to have much peace of mind (167) . . . Some things seem to be missing. Did he have a sense of humor? What about his sexuality?" (97)

QUOTES ON LOSSES AND LETTING GO

How to Be Your Own Best Friend (Newman and Berkowitz)
"No one can take the risk out of life; in a relationship you are offering yourself and can always be rejected . . . take the chance of being hurt. If you are an adult, if you love yourself, and you lose your lover, you will still have yourself. If you look to someone else to establish your identity, losing that person can make you feel destroyed" (74).

Necessary Losses (Judith Virost)
"Freud observed we are never so helplessly unhappy as when we have lost our beloved object or its love" (121).

Opening Our Hearts: Transforming Our Losses (Al-Anon)
"What I lost is an illusion of what I thought life would be (39) . . . Grieving the loss of a relationship is not unlike grieving a death (75) . . . 'Live and let live' reminds us that we cannot control the actions of or decisions

of other people. If someone chooses to end a relationship with us, that is their right" (81).

Healing the Child Within (Dr. Charles Whitfield)

"All our losses (traumas, common and sublte) produce pain and unhappiness; we call this pain grief. In the grieving process we allow ourselves to feel these feelings . . . we share the grief with safe others and in group or individual therapy. To complete our grief work takes time . . . a major loss can take up to two to four years . . . When we experience loss, it stirs up energy within us that needs to be discharged . . . With no release this chronic distress is stored up within us and can manifest as anxiety, tension, fear, anger, resentment, confustion, guilt, emptiness or shame" (85).

"To break free, you must 1) identify the loss, 2) re-experience the loss and 3) complete the grief work (86) . . . We consume too much energy in avoiding grieving as we would if we went ahead and grieved the loss" (93).

GRIEVING WORK: A huge and tiring part of the work is grieving work. When I felt sad, I sat with it. I cried two to three times a week for ten to fifteen minutes, and this went on for almost a year. At the end of the year, the pain was out. All the repressed pain from stuffing feelings was out. One day I went and sat on the steps behind my shed that led to the campfire area. As I was sitting with my sadness and weeping, I looked up and saw a doe about thirty-five feet away from me. In a five-minute period, she walked up approximately eight feet away from me. It was almost as if she knew I was in pain and wanted to give me comfort. I took it as a sign God was watching over me and that He was with me in this important work.

Further Along the Road Less Traveled (M. Scott Peck)
"<u>Desirability</u>: There is nothing that holds us back more from mental health as a society and from God than a sense that many have of unimportance, unloveliness and undesirability (95) . . . God says, I love you, I want you, you are beautiful . . ." (97).

Facing Love Addiction (Pia Mellody)
"The combination of trauma of being left and re-experiencing childhood trauma can be crushing. It can trigger experiences of depression to feeling suicidal . . . Many people who experience the withdrawal pains of losing a lover get so overwhelmed, they jump into obsession to put them out of touch with the painful feelings by staying obsessed. This means more grieving work is to be done" (30).

Alcoholics Anonymous's *The Big Book*
"Until I accept life completely on life's terms, I cannot be happy. I need to concentrate not so much on what needs to be changed in the world as on what needs to be changed in me and my attitudes" (417).

"<u>Serenity Prayer</u>" (Reinhold Niebuhr)
"God, grant me the serenity to accept the things I cannot change,
The courage to change the things I can,
And the wisdom to know the difference."

SYMPTOMS OF CODEPENDENCY

1) Difficulty identifying feelings

2) Difficulty expressing feelings

3) Fearful of rejection

6) Others' reactions determine how I respond.

7) Esteem bolstered by others

8) Judgeful of everything

4) Trouble with decision-making -Nothing done or said is "good enough."

5) Perfectionist

CODEPENDENCY: I had a talk with my Godfather Joe about what was going on in my life, and he mentioned Codependents Anonymous. I looked it up on the Internet and found I can identify with many of the qualifications. Ernie Larsen defined it as "Those self-defeating learned behaviors or character defects that result in a diminished capacity to initiate or to participate in loving relationships." Melody Beatty said, "Codependency is a way of getting needs met that does not get needs met." Dr. Charles Whitfield in _Codependence: Healing the Human Condition_ said, "Codependence is the most common of all addictions: the addiction of looking elsewhere. We believe something outside ourselves can give us happiness and fulfillment . . . self-neglect is no fun and the payoff in focusing outward is a reduction in painful feelings or a temporary increase in joyful feelings" (4). Robert Burney in _The Dance of the Wounded Souls_ said codependence should be called outer-dependence and really was a disease of the abandonment of self.

VERY GOOD FRIEND - CARlLA: I ended up hanging out with CarlLa Horton for a number of years from 2008 to 2012 and gave her much credit for helping me through my "dark night of the soul" experience. We went to the movies, went to concerts, and hung out to the Bellevale Creamery for the best ice cream in a fifty-mile radius and frequently to Blini's restaurant that had an amazing Politana Pizza. CarlLa was a good Democrat, and Rev. David Dyson said I should hang with her because I could learn much from her about unionism and how to help the poor. She used to work with the Screen Actors Guild in NY circa 1980–1982. When _Tootsie_ was being filmed, Dustin Hoffman hit on her, and she refused. A director offered her a role in a movie if she slept with him, and she said no. That is a person of integrity.

She currently serves as the executive director of Hope's Door in Westchester County, NY, a place to go to if you are a victim of domestic abuse, male or female. It has a twenty-four-hour hotline and provides a danger assessement and safety planning. At least one in three women has been beaten. Every nine seconds, a woman is assualted or beaten, and men who witnessed abuse at home as children are twice as likely to act out violently. Hope's Door also has a Family Justice Center to help victims navigate the court system, children's programs, and programs for teens to identify what healthy love and relationships look like. Hope's Door is also an advocacy center helping victims in securing rights, benefits, and other needed services. After 9/11, much governmental money disappeared, and CarlLa spent a lot of time fund-raising and grant writing. Oprah Winfrey created a show called the "Big Give," and the winner of each program was able to donate to a nonprofit, and one of the contestants donated the money to Door's Hope.

LONELINESS VS. SOLITUDE

Paul Tillich said, "Loneliness expresses the pain of being alone and solitude expresses the glory of being alone." Dietrich Bonhoeffer said, "Let him who cannot be alone be aware of community, and let him cannot be in community be aware of being alone." Carl Jung said, "Communion giveth warth, singleness light." Poet Charles Bukoswki said, "There are worse things than being left alone, but it often takes decades to realize this, and most often when you do, it's too late."

At the fiver year mark of my recovery work, I so learned to love myself and to be comfortable sitting with my feelings and thoughts, not having to run to food, alcohol, tv, finding a relationship, looking for sex, or workaholism, that *now* I must be careful I do not isolate. I so enjoyed my own company today I had to remind myself of the importance of community. I had learned how to become my best friend, so when I lost a relationship, instead of going into crippling, devastating depression, I can let go and still have myself as a friend. I finally learned to become comfortable in my own skin. There is no magic bullet, it is hard work, but I am worth it.

THE ANONYMOUS PEOPLE: It is estimated eighty million Americans are related to someone who is chemically dependent or in a relatinship with one. If there are three hundred million people in America, almost one-third Americans are connected with addiction in some way. This is the name of a 2013 documentary about twenty-three million people struggling with alcohol and drug addiction. Part of being in a twelve-step program is to keep your anonymity and to respect other people's anonymity so the meetings can remain a safe place. The documentary talks about how more funding is needed from the government to deal with this national epidemic but that there is no lobbying group for addicts because most want to maintain their anonymity. Many are beginning to speak out, saying, "I am an addict. I am also an activist or lobbyist for more funding for recovery. I am an advocate of including recovery services in health care and dealing with addiction as a health issue as opposed to a criminal issue."

ALCHOLICS ANONYMOUS: Thank God for Bill W. who started Alcoholics Anonymous on June 10, 1935. I am not in AA, but it is the mother ship of twelve-step groups for all other addictions. It took awhile before society saw the importance and value of this group, and many who are involved in SLAA are especially fearful of their anonymity being exposed. There is much shame and fear associated with this addiciton, and while it started in 1976, the group is forty years old compared with AA, which is over eight years old.

TIGER WOODS: In February of 2010, the famous golfer went to sex addiction rehab, and many made fun of him, saying, "Hey, that's just being a guy." Sex addiction and love addiction is forty years behind AA but is slowly gaining acceptance by general society and fully accepted by those involved in recovery work and those who are members of the fellowship. In the *Sex and Love Step Recovery Booklet* by Transeed Publishing, it said, "There are tragic and costly symptons of a society weighed down with active sex and love addicition. Sex and love addiction is a major factor in domestic abuse, homicide, depression, sexism, divorce, and suicide" (11).

BLUE BIRD BY CHARLES BUKOWSKI: "There's a blue bird in my heart that wants to get out. I am too tough for him. I say, stay in there, I am not going to let anyone see you. I pour whiskey on him and inhale cigerettes . . . and I say, stay down, do you want to mess me up? I only let him out at night sometimes and I say, I know you are in there, don't be sad. Then I put him back and he sings a little in there. I haven't quite let him die . . . and with our secret pact it's nice enough to make a man weep, but I don't weep, do you?" For me, I believe the blue bird for Bukowski equals the *true self* trying to emerge from the false self, whether he had awaresness of such a concept but may have since mystic Thomas Merton was fairly popular during Bukowski's life.

GOD BOX: In my kitchen, I kept my God Box. It was a small wooden box that I stained and put the word "God Box" on. I kept 3 x 5 inch index cards in there, and when I had a prayer request, I wrote down the date and the request. I had done this from 2006 throught 2013, and I was amazed at the answers I had received. I did not always get a yes or what I thought I should get, but I always got what I need. My needs were always met. When I needed money, it showed up. When I needed a job, it showed up. When I needed guidance or an answer, it showed up. What it did was help give me faith, to trust God to meet my needs.

At times I felt down, I broke out the God Box and went through all my prayer requests, and I was amazed at the miracles I saw in my life.

ANGRY YOUNG MAN: I can identify with Billy Joel's song "Angry Young Man" my life of activism and recovery work. The "Piano Man" sings, "There's a place in the world for an angry young man, with his working class ties and his radical plans . . . and he's proud of his scars . . . and he bleeds as he hangs on the cross . . . he's been stabbed in the back, he's been misunderstood, it's a comfort to know his intentions are good."

The Long Island singer, who sang about my hometown "Allentown," went on to point out why there was pain for the angry young man. "And he's never been able to learn from his mistakes, so he can't understand why his heart always breaks . . ." And then the song came from the perspective of an older man looking back on his life, saying, "I believe I've passed the age of consciousness and righteous rage, <u>I found just surviving was a noble fight</u> . . . and life went on no matter who was wrong or right."

LEARN TO LET GO: My sponsor told me I was having trouble letting go of the idea of my relationship being over. He suggested I go to an Al-Anon meeting. Al-Anon is for family and friends of alcoholics. One of the main concepts Al-Anon teaches is a concept called detachment. Detachment means you take care of your business and allow the qualifier (your alcoholic or addict) to live his/her life and to suffer the consequences of their decisions, to not rescue or help enable their addictive behavior. I cannot control anyone except me. I cannot control others, but I can control how I respond. I always have choices.

In the meeting, a person shared and said, "My son is an alcoholic, and sometimes I think it would be better if he were dead." Another shared, saying, "My child is an alcoholic and disappeared ten years ago." I almost fell out of my chair. Here were people who were going through very tough situations, yet there was laugher in the meeting, and people were focused on taking care of their business, their lives. It was a group of people living lives of reasonable happiness, accepting reality, and having lives filled with much serenity. The group had so much wisdom, and courage, and recovery in it I was inspired to live a better life.

2009 - JIM'S FIFTH STEP: Step 4 of any twelve-step program is doing a searching and fearless moral inventory of one's life. Step 5 is admitting to God, to ourselves, and to another human being the exact nature of our wrongs. The thing that struck me most meeting with a recovery brother was when he asked why I had a vindictive streak in me. I said, "I am not sure, but it is not something I am proud of." My recovery brother said, "It is your lack of faith in God. If you believe your Higher Power has all power, then you should be able to let go and trust God will work in the other person's life. Maybe you need to let the other person hit their bottom so they can reach out for the help they need." I felt like I had been hit in the head with a 2 x 4 wooden board. A second truth that has been important in my life is "the greater my acceptance (of life), the greater my serenity." Today I asked myself, "Do I want to be right, or do I want to keep my peace?" These simple truths had added much peace to my life. The twelve-step program had deepened my faith and given me practical tools for living.

THE JOURNEY OF MANY ADDICTS: In the rooms, I got to meet people who were in recovery for all kind of things. What often happened to the person who put down the drink or drugs in time figured out they were not good at relationships and joined SLAA or Codependents Anonymous. Then many realized they were not good at handling money and joined a twelve-step group called Debtors Anonymous. The twelve-step groups are a way to give tools to people who find they are stuck in an area and need help. It takes courage to admit life is not working in one area and that one needs help. Kudos to them!

HOW RECOVERY WORKS - JONAH IN THE BELLY OF THE GREAT FISH: Fr. Richard Rohr talked about "The Sign of Jonah" in Matthew 12:38–42. Why is the symbol of Christianity the fish? Many Christian tombs in the first and second century have the fish of Jonah on their tombs. It is not until the third century when the cross begins to appear on Christian tombs. The sign of Jonah is metaphor for transformation and has many similarities to recovery work.

When you are in the belly of a great fish, there is nothing you can do until you are spit out. You cannot control it, fix it, understand it, use a formula, predict the outcome, or change it. What you can do is wait in darkness, weep, and feel all your pain until you have learned its lessons. It is like hanging on the cross, between heaven and earth. It is called the cauldron of transformation. It is called the dark night of the soul. This is where God gets you, and you will learn about trusting and believing. You know you are a sinner, you know you screwed up, and all you can do is wait and be present until you are spit out, transformed. God never lets anyone down who puts their trust in Him.

As Joseph Campbell said, "The cave you fear to enter holds your treasure." For me, the thing I was fearing was sitting with my pain and grief of unfelt feelings for forty-two years. When I sat with it, I cried for two to three times a week for almost a year . . . and then the pain was gone, and I had been able to stay present and keep current with my feelings. The greater my acceptance of reality, the greater my serenity.

True self vs. **False self:**

Codependence: Healing the Human Condition, Dr. Charles Whitfield

True Self	false self
Authentic self	Inauthentic self or mask
Genuine	Ungenuine
Expansive, loving	Contracting, unloving
Giving	Withholding
Compassionate	Other-oriented, overly conforming
Accepts self and others	Critical and perfectionist
Needs play and fun	Avoids play and fun
Enjoys being nurtured	Avoids being nurtured
Nondefensive	Defensive
Connected to God	Believes he/she is the Higher Power
Open to the unconscious	Blocks unconscious material
Feels feelings	Hides feelings - does not feel
Assertive	Aggressive or passive
Loves unconditionally	Loves conditionally
Boundaries	No boundaries
Connected to inner child	Overdeveloped parent/adult scripts
Feels "connectedness"	Feels separated

2013 - RECOVERY SUMMER PARTY: I threw a party, and it was open to all recovery people and their family and friends. Approximately twenty-five to thirty showed up. In the workroom, I set up tables for the plates, cups, utensils, food, and drink. I had a badmitten and horseshoes set up outside. There were four to five who were muscians and set up their guitars and bass to the speakers and provided music. It started to get cloudy and started an afternoon shower. Everyone moved inside. I set small carpets all over the TV room, and people were seated everywhere in the room and on the stairs while the band continued playing inside but now accoustically. The five-gallon bucket drummer was banging a little too loudly, but it was fun.

NEEDLE IN THE HAYSTACK: The next day, early on Sunday morning, I got a call from a woman who said her friend lost a small red piece of expensive jade from her ring and to see if I could look for it. How am I going to find a small piece of jade? I took out a blue piece of canvas and dumped all the garbage from the party all over it and began to look. I looked all around the house. I looked all over my driveway. What a pain in the butt this was turning out to be. I took all the small carpets I rolled up from the evening before and shook them out on a drop cloth. Lo and behold, on the first carpet I shook, I saw what looked like a small piece of red glass shimmering on the drop cloth. Voilà, I had found it. I mailed it to the mistraught backup singer of the clangy drummer guy. Thank you, God!

SUMMER OF 2008 - VISITING PAXTON: Each year I had gone up to Paxton's, I had noticed him drinking more beer and starting to drink earlier each summer trip. In 2005, we would have a drink after dinner; in 2006, it was by four o'clock in the afternoon; in 2007, it was by three o'clock in the afternpon; and in 2008, it was by two o'clock in the afternoon. The back stairwell was full of boxes of empty beer cans. There must have been over twenty boxes of cans back there. When I got to his house about 6:00 p.m., he broke out a joint and said, "Try this." I am not really a pot smoker. The stuff I tried in high school was pretty weak. I took two to three hits of it, and it made me sleepy. I fell asleep on the couch. The 2008 stuff was much stronger than the 1982 stuff from twenty-six years earlier.

We went out to a bar, and he drank and drank and drank. I could not keep up, nor do I feel I have to. There were four to six women dancing on the dance floor. He said, "I am going out dancing." I was sitting with some guys, and one of them said, "Hey, look at the idiot dancing with our wives." I said, "I got this, gentlemen." I grabbed Paxton and said, "We have to go *now*!" I grabbed him and pulled him out of the bar. When we got home, he callede up some coworker, and they ended up having sex in the front porch. His kids were at his ex-wives' place, and I slept on a twin bed with Spider Man bedsheets, while Paxton slept in his room. At about 3:00 a.m., he walked in the kid's room and pissed all over me, thinking he was in the bathroom. I took a shower and slept in the other bed. What is it about drunks liking to pee on me?

The next morning, I asked him if he remembered what happened. He did not. He was extremely apologetic and embarrassed. He later told me he was dating someone and she was really pretty, but he thought she might be doing heroin. I was shocked and saddened to hear this. I don't hate my best friend, but I do hate the disease of alcoholism. I told him I was uncomfortable around him when he drinks. I told him he was like Jekyll and Hyde, and I missed the old Paxton. I didn't like Drunk Paxton. He told me he did not have a problem. By 2:00 p.m., he was drunk and was being impatient and nasty. As I cleaned up the apartment from beer cans, he walked in the kitchen and saw me pouring out about one-third of a beer, and he glared at me and said, "You never pour beer down the sink."

The reason I love Paxton is his brilliance.. We talked about everything from life to music, to women, to theology, to philosophy, to current news, to economics, and to scientific inventions. He had no need to talk about politics, and I really appreciated that. We came from different parties, but he was so intelligent we talked about everything except politics.

His father stopped by later that night, and I expressed my concerns to him. His dad said, "Paxton will not change until he hits bottom. You are a good friend to my son." When I came back home, I called up Paxton's home to speak with his mother because I knew how much influence she had on his life. She never picked up. I sent her literature from Al-Anon and sent Paxton *The Big Book* from AA. He sent me an e-mail to tell me his mother hated me and thought I was a bad influence on her son. Paxton also told me, "Don't ever send me anything from AA again."

8-13-2008 - MICKEY MANTLE DIES: He had two young boys, and I thought of Yankee Mickey Mantle who died in August of 2008. In 1995, after recuperating from a liver transplant, the Mick said from the Baylor University Medical Center, "I owe much to my family, God, America and my fans." He said, "I am no role model. I squandered my life because of alcohol." He died at age fifty-eight and lamented, "I regret a wasted life."

Unfortunately, that was the last trip where I saw my friend in person. He had chosen his drug of choice over friendship. I miss him. But I had worked so hard on my recovery by attending twelve-step meetings at Codependents Anonymous and Al-Anon for two years I was not willing to jeopardize my peace, serenity, and sobriety. My friend ended up moving to Texas in 2014, and we were still friends on Facebook. Friends come into my life for a day, a season, or a lifetime. I am grateful for the many great times I had with Paxton and only wish him the best.

As I look back, I should have handled it differently. For that, I have amends to make, and the way I do so is to respect my friend's wishes to no longer be best friends with me.

AGE 46-50 2012-2016

Mid-Life Crisis Resolution – The Best Years

<u>IF YOU WERE BRAVE ENOUGH TO ENTER THE CAVE</u>

CHAPTER 13

High School of Health Careers and Sciences 2006-2011 (40–45)

2005 - TRASFER TO THE HIGH SCHOOL OF HEALTH CAREERS AND SCIENCES AT THE GEORGE WASHINGTON CAMPUS AT 192ND STREET AND AUDUBON AVENUE: My first day I reported in September of 2005, I was told by the AP John Cosenza to report to the George Washington High School Campus. I took the train up to 192nd Street and walked into the principal's office and said, "Hello. My name is Jim Geist. I teach social studies, and I was told to report to this school." Principal Harris said, "What? No one told me about this!" I said, "Call the Department of Ed. I am only doing what they told me to do." And that was my welcome to the new school. I was never made to feel welcome by the principal or by the assistant principal of social studies Campgreenblatt. She interviewed me in the afternoon and seemed content with it. I was not shown anything, where the copy room was, the library, or the room I will be teaching in. I was told, "Hang around the building."

I didn't know anyone. I didn't know what I will be teaching or where I will be teaching. I saw the dean's office, and there were three people there, and I saw a free desk. I sat at the desk and took out a book and started reading. One dean, Ms. Eboh, said to me, "Who are you?" I told them who I was and if it was okay for me to sit at the desk. She said, "This room is really just for deans." I said, "Oh, well, I don't know the building. I don't have an assigned room, and I was told to stay on the floor, so I will just sit here for today."

BACK INTO THE SWING OF THINGS: Over the course of the year, I got to know the students and teachers. I enjoyed preparing students for the New York Regents Exams for U.S. history and global history. I got to know my fellow teachers and staff. I enjoyed working and hanging out with Jose Soriano, Matt Stern, and Dan Flanagan.

THE NEW ASSISTANT PRINCIPAL: AP Campgreenblatt was a new assistant principal. She used to teach English, and she observed me. The first observation was satisfactory, but she wrote up a four-page observation single-spaced that was usually two pages or less and used the words always and never. I took umbrage with this because that was the first official observation, and it was unprofessional to use those words, and observation reports were generally two pages long, not three-and-a-half pages long. It was much more critical than pointing out the positive aspects, and there was a way to write suggestions without being so critical. Tell me what you want, model it for me, and I will make the changes.

SEPTEMBER 1ˢᵗ ADMINISTRATION MEETINGS: We had monthly faculty meetings with the administration on the first Monday of the month from 2:50 p.m. to 3:45 p.m. and departmental meetings on the second Mondays of the month. We also had four to five staff development days a year in addition to the first couple days of school where we met with the administration in the morning and, if we were lucky, got a hour or two to prepare our rooms for the kids (preparing books and posters, setting up the desks, cleaning the desks and boards, and making sure we have supplies). Thist double or triples your work loadif you teach in two or three rooms. There was so much talk about the children and administrative rules they forgot teachers needed time to prepare for the classes, which we needed to prepare for in one to two days.

CONSTANT CHANGES: For a seasoned teacher, you know what needs to be done. We are considered "professionals." Unfortunately, with bosses, their goals for the teachers and school change almost every semester or every year. Just when you become comfortable with a new system, they change it on you. The excuse always used is "This is all for the children." Maybe all the changes are really for the administration. If you stuck with a plan that worked and you did not make changes every semester, perhaps fewer administrators would be needed to check up on everyone implementing the new program. It gets to the point when a new focus is introduced. I would laugh knowing it would no longer be used in the next four and a half or nine months. Were the constant changes about helping students and teachers, or was it about keeping and maintaining administrative positions or even adding new ones? With the small school movement and money to hire corporate teaching coaches, now we had even more people we had to listen to. Sometimes I was not sure if my priority was following the principal, AP, or the Kaplan teaching coaches. It was frustrating and confusing, maybe the way they wanted it. If no administrators show up, can school run? Yes. If no teachers show up, can you have school? No.

10-16-05 - JAMES GEIST IS WEST MILFORD'S "MR. 5,000!": On October 16, West Milford received its five thousand pint of donated blood. The New Jersey Red Cross said in many parts of the state donations had been down, but in West Milford, under the leadership of Jim Gilligan, they kept increasing. Donor number 5,000 was Jim Geist, resident of Hewitt, New Jersey, and teacher at the High

School of Health Careers and Sciences on the George Washington Campus in New York City. They quoted me as saying, "I am amused and honored to be given the name Mr. 5,000. It says a lot of good things about our community to be able to reach such a plateau in such a short amount of time." Remember, give more than thanks, give blood!

AUGUST 9, 2005 - PHILADELPHIA, PENNSYLVANIA: JODY GEIST SMITH IN FRONT OF THE NATIONAL LABOR RELATIONS BOARD (JUDGE RICHARD SCULLY):

My sister Jody worked at Valley Central Emergency Veterinary Hospital in Whitehall, Pennsylvania. They hired a new manager, Bart Ueberroth, whom employees complained had cut vacation time, given measly pay raises, and given tardy reviews. It took Jody two years to get her ninety-day review. The main arguments according to Jody Geist Smith was not about money but about the management. The workers lawfully organized a union and were then penalized for it. It led to a strike in December of 2004, which led to an employee lockout. Jody was out of work for five months. NLRB Judge Richard Scully found Valley Vet. Hospital guilty of unfair labor practices. They were found guilty of every charge Ms. Geist Smith said. On December 14, 2005, Judge Scully issues files his decision in favor of the employee and union in "a landmark decision." You can google DVM, February 1, 2006, "Union Prevails in Landmark Decision," by Jennifer Fiala.

11-9-07 - NYC COUNCILMAN MARTINEZ: I invited NYC councilman Miguel Martinez to come and speak with my government classes. I told him it would be nice for him to meet his constituent's kids and students who would become voters in a few years. He ignored the e-mail I sent to him. It came to graduation, and who was on the stage but the councilman. As soon as he was done talking about the importance of education and loving the Washington Heights and his constituents, he quickly exited the stage for his next appointment. I waited for him at the door.

When he walked by, I reached out my hand, grabbed his, and didn't let go. I said, "Hi. I am Mr. Geist." He said, "Oh yeah, you sent me an e-mail. Sorry I did not get back to you." I said to Councilman Martinez, "Let me tell you, if you do not visit my kids, I will make sure you do not speak at graduation next year." He looked at me like "Who is this guy?"

The following year, I called the councilman's office and, again, did not hear back from him. I told the students about this and put down his office phone number on the blackboard. "Do you want to see how democracy and advocating work? Keep calling this number until we get him to commit to a day." After about a week, his staff person called me and said, "Please tell your students not to call our office anymore. We can stop by on *XYZ* date. Is that good?" I said yes. I invited the administration to come to class, and the principal acted like he cannot be bothered.

2007 - HSHCS GIVEN A PLAQUE OF RECOGNITION BY NYC: The councilman came to the school to meet with my classes in November of 2007 and had a great time. They asked him why he got involved in politics and what he had done for the community and even had some suggestions for him. It turned out to be a great experience. A month later, I saw the principal and AP Camp-Greenblatt all dressed up and getting ready to leave. I asked, "So where are you two going?" "Oh, our school is getting an award of recognition from Councilman Martinez." I said, "Really? May I get my jacket and come along?" "No," he said incredulously. I said, "Do you think we would have gotten this award had I not invited him to meet our kids? Why, I invited you, and you did not even show up." The award hung next to the entrance of the principal's door to this day. Does it cost anything to say thank you or to give some credit in a faculty meeting? Why can't it be a victory for the school instead of being so competitive?

12-15-09 - COUNCILMAN GOES TO THE BIG HOUSE: On Tuesday, December 15, 2009, Martinez went to prison for five years for the theft of $106,000. He misappropriated $55,000 that was to go to two nonprofits, The Washington Heights Art Center and the Council for Assisting Neighbors. Martinez said, "If I could change time, I would do things differently." Judge Crotty said the ex-councilman betrayed his oath to office and did so over a prolonged period. He pleaded guilty to mail fraud and conspiracy to money launder. He should have been nicer to my kids; he might have gotten more Christmas cards in prison.

FELLOW COMMUTERS: The contracters for the NY Public Schools were working on the steps behind our school, and we lost parking spots. Our school had a very small parking lot, and all the administrators got spots, and roughly eight to ten teachers got rotating parking spots there. There was an area in the front of the school where only those with Department of Education passes can park and spots behind the school if you have a George Washington High School pass. If you don't get in one of those parking spaces as a commuting teacher, good luck. I had three commuters I met in Teaneck, New Jersey, and we drove back and forth, to cross the GW Bridge. It saved all of us approximately $1,200 a year ($133 a month for nine months), which was nothing to sneeze at. The carpool consisted of Lissette Parra, Jason Hull, and Nate Masuica. Ms. Parra taught English as a second language, Hull taught English, and Masuica taught Math. With all the changes happening in the school, it was nice to have a sounding board to try to know how to play our cards right while keeping our sense of humor.

PARKING AT SCHOOL THREE BLOCKS AWAY: There was an elementary school three blocks away from our school. I left at five thirty-five in the morning and met my commuters at six thirty. We usually pulled in front of the school after crossing the GW Bridge at six forty-five. My one commuter had a Board of Ed. pass, so on the days I cannot find a spot, I parked by the elementary school that had "Board of Ed Pass" parking only. I was able to do this for four to five times. The one morning I parked the Jeep, a woman ran up to me and said, "You cannot park here!" I assumed she was a teacher at the elementary school. I said, "Hi. My name is Jim. Are you a member of the United Federation of Teachers?" She said yes. I went on. "See the street sign? It says 'Department of Ed Parking.' See my pass? It says Department of Ed. I can park anywhere in NYC with this pass, and as a union sister, you be supporting your brothers and sisters in the union." She scowled and said, "Parking here is only for our elementary teachers, and I will have you towed next time you park here." I found out from my friend's wife who worked at the school that cars had been towed if they didn't work at the school. Parking in NYC is a bitch. Too many rats in the cage make them nasty. As I walked away from the miserable woman, I said, "You would call a tow on a union brother? Where is your solidarity? Solidarity forever, sister!" Too many rats in the cage make the rats turn nasty.

MY SISTER (IN THE LORD WHO HAPPENS TO BE PUERTO RICAN): There was no teachers' cafeteria at GW High, but next to the school was Isabella's. Isabella's was an assisted living complex in a huge apartment building, and it had an open cafeteria. It was open to the public, so the workers and residents of the building can mingle with GW teachers and neighbors. I saw a lovely Latina lady with long, dark hair dressed classy, wearing glasses and reading a paper. I asked if I can sit with her, and she said yes. In time, we became best buddies. Her name was Liz Serrano, and she lived in the Bronx, was divorced, and had two daughters. She worked as an accountant at Isabella's and attended a Pentecostal church. We shared family stories and what was happening in our lives and encouraged each other with Christian encouragement.

Her father once rented a camper, and they drove from the Bronx to the Grand Canyon. Her brother adopted and helped a neighbor who had a litter of puppies, and as a gift, he can have one. He chose the one with no back legs, named it Igor, and built a makeshift doggie wheelchair so the dog can run around. They had two dogs, a golden Lab and a pit bull. The one dog was named Lazarus, and her daughter liked to say "Come forth, Lazarus." Liz's commitment to God was strong, and I got invited to a birthday party and the younger daughter's sweet sixteen party. I was grateful to meet such a lovely family. My daily lunches with her made the bosses' snubbing, incompetence, and antagonism more manageable by focusing on the positive. Ms. Silver, our art teacher who used to model, said, "Mr. Geist, I don't know how you do it. The bosses go after you every week, and you show up with a smile and stay positive."

Her church group had a secret sister Christmas exchange. The person who Liz had as a secret sister said, "All I want is a trip to the Caribbean." Liz said to herself, "No, maybe certificate and trip to the spa or to Target. The Caribbean? What are you, a *loca*?"

OCTOBER 4, 2006: I WANT CLASS-SIZE REDUCTION; THEY SEND ME FOR A MEDICAL EXAM: Principal: "What the f——k did you say to the psychiatrist yesterday?"

Me: "I told her as a seminary student, I had taken some counseling classes, and you usually wait until a person finishes answering before you ask the next question."

Principal: "You are not allowed back in the school until you are cleared by her. You need to get a physical and eval from your therapist and a final interview with the NYC Dept. of Ed. psychiatrist before you can return to work!"

The day before I was ordered to see a NYC Dept. of Ed. psychiatrist in Brooklyn, because the High School of Health Careers and Sciences administration claimed I made a suicide threat. What? I was asked by the principal, the AP of the organization, and my department AP why I sometimes fell asleep in the faculty meetings from 2:50 p.m. to 3:45 p.m. I told them because I got up at 5:00 a.m. every day, commuted for an hour, got into school by 6:30 a.m., and then worked until 2:50 p.m.; so when we met from 3:00 p.m. to 4:00 p.m. for a faculty meeting, my body shut down. I told them I was so tired "because they have so many students in my four of my five classes—thirty-three, thirty, twenty-nine, and thirty." I asked why some teachers only had twenty kids in a class, but most of my classes were stuffed. As Dad says, "The horses that work hardest get whipped hardest."

I said I was sometimes so I tired I almost fell asleep at the wheel on the way home (true), and if you ever go to my funeral in the future, it will probably because of this. And so the admin deemed me a suicide risk. Any teacher worth his or her salt knows good teaching is exhausting mentally.

The NYC Dept. of Ed. psychiatrist asked how I was doing. I told her I was doing well. Before I finished, she asked me if I like being a teacher. I said yes for many reasons, but before I finished, she asked me another question. "Have you been under stress lately?" I said, "Not excessively, but being a teacher in NYC has its stressful moments—" and before I can finished, she cut me off. I asked her, "Is this the best way to act as a counselor with someone?" She wrote variously on her NYC Dept. of Ed. pad with her NYC Dept. of Ed. pen at her NYC Dept. of Ed. desk. I was told to get a physical from my doctor and an evaluation from my therapist and go back to the Department of Ed. psychiatrist. The next time we met, I told I had too much to live for— my faith, my home, my family, my girlfriend, and my teaching job. On

October 3, they told me I was "not fit" and, on October 16, I was "fit" again to teach. It was like being in Communist Russia, where if you ask questions the leaders don't like, they can send you to an insane asylum to silence your voice.

Students made me laugh so hard sometimes. When I came back to work after my hiatus (two weeks of classes), as I entered the room, my classes gave me standing ovations. Most said they were so happy to have me back. I actually teared up every time it happened. It was one of my favorite teaching memories. Many of the kids gave me hugs at the end of class. I asked the students to guess why I had been out for nine days, and here were some of the responses: "Mr. Geist was suspended," "He quit," "Family emergency," "Anger management," "Fired," "Hunting," "Court," "Rehab," and "He was arrested by the program *To Catch a Predator*." Nice kids I teach.

11-12-08 - MY DESK CHAIR IS STOLEN: With teaching, it is important to have comfortable shoes, for there is much standing on the job. I prefer to buy Rockport's, very comfortable and made in the United States, but they started making them in China starting in 2008. I also did a lot of sitting on the job writing lessons, reading, and correcting papers; so I needed a comfortable chair. I was usually the first person in our school, so I stole a nice swiveling chair from the teachers' lounge and then wrote GEIST in large letters in permanent marker. I came on November 12, 2008, and saw my chair was missing. I went around from room to room, looking for my chair, and found it an assistant principal's office. Just as I was about to sneakily get my chair back, the AP walked in the room and said, "Why are you taking that chair from the community table?" I lifted the chair and showed him my name and wheeled the chair back to my room.

1-15-09 - MIRACLE ON THE HUDSON: On this day, I took the 196 Bus from West Milford, New Jersey to the Port Authority and caught the A Train uptown to 168th Street and transferred to the number 1 train up to 192nd to get to school. I got to the bus station by 4:00 p.m. and caught the 4:20 p.m. out of the terminal back home. I did not have a cell phone, but I heard people talking about a plane going down in the Hudson, and no one was hurt. I thought, *Great, I will catch it on the news at six thirty tonight.* The bus exited the city through the Lincoln Tunnel and made a large U-turn to catch Route 3. As you make this turn and look behind you, there is a great view of the Hudson River. There is also a great view of the airliner floating on the Hudson next to the *Intrepid* ship by Fiftieth Street, next to my old school Park West High.

Capt. Chelsey Sullenberger and First Officer Jeffrey Skiles safely glided the plane into the Hudson flying out of JFK when both engines were hit by multiple birds at 3:27 p.m. After three minutes, all 155 passengers on A-320 airbus on the way to Charolette, North Carolina, lived to tell the tale. The movie *Sully* played by Tom Hanks showed how the National Transporation Safety Board wanted to crucify both Sully and Skiles for not attempting to land the plane in La Guardia or in Teterboro, New Jersey. At the time of the hearings, they had no proof the second engine had been knocked out by birds, thus the computer simulation said they could have saved the plane. When the second engine was found in the Hudson, it was clear it had been damaged by birds. Sully was invited to speak to Congress (House aviation subcommittee) in February of 2009 so they could honor a hero but were less than enthusiastic when Captain Sully began to talk about pilot pay and benefits being cut by 40 percent, and pilots and families were put in untenable financial situations. Sully said, "No pilot is telling their children to follow in his or her footsteps. Without experienced pilots, we will see negative consequences to the flying public."

In the movie *Sully*, Captain Sully said during the investigation, "I have flown safely for over 40 years, and my aviation legacy is going to based on 200 seconds in my career. I don't care what your computer simulation tells you. My 40 years of experience told me that we had lost the second engine. We also saved the lives of 155 souls, and this was the first successful water ditching in aviation history."

1-25-10 - REQUEST FOR PSYCH EVALS FOR FIVE STUDENTS: I had five students whom I believed needed help. They were making the teaching of class extremely exhausting and frustrating, and maybe they can get some help if neededI also had two classes of freshman that were hyper and ten students in each of the classes who talked nonstop. I wrote up a memo to the administration, asking for help. Most teachers, including myself, were often afraid to ask for help because the administration can use it against us, saying that our "management skills are lacking" and can use it to give us an unsatisfactory rating at the end of the year. I listed the names of the students, and I had called all the parents. I asked if they can remove two to three students to make it more manageable. I got no response from my principal or assistant principal.

11-2-10 - SECOND MEMO FOR HELP: The principal responded in writing, saying, "It is the teacher's responsibility to manage his class. You should notify guidance after you have asked for help from your AP." Well, my memo was sent to my AP, and I got no response from her on October 29, 2010. It was clear my bosses didn't care or may even want me to suffer, trying to get me to quit or transfer. If that was the case, call me in, help me transfer, and I will gladly do so, hoping to get supportive bosses.

CHANCELLOR'S REGULATION A-443 ON DISRUPTIVE CHILDREN: In the chancellor's regulations is the Student Removal Form. If the principal does not help, you are to contact your chapter leader to file a grievance under Article 9 and Appendix B. The disruptive student is to be removed for one to four days. The administration is to provide a space to move the disruptive student for that period. The **SAVE ACT** is covered under state law and stands for Safe Schools Against Violence in Education Act. The student is to receive instruction in an alternative setting for that period. Our school did not have a SAVE room, which was a violation against the chancellor's regulations, UFT contract, and NY State law. The administration is not happy to get a call from the UFT headquarters about this.

4-5-11 - GUN SHOOTING THREAT: In my 2010–2011 year, I had two classes of extremely immature and obnoxious and disrespectful freshman classes. By this, I meant one out of three students met those requirements. I felt so bad for the kids who really wanted to learn and for the teachers who had to work with this cohort. I made many calls to parents, and it made some improvement. I had a really quiet kid who sat in front of my desk. On April 4, he said, "I am bringing a gun to school and shooting up this class." I pretended not to hear him and, at the end of class, asked him to stay in the room. I said, "Alex, when you said you want to shoot up the class, you were speaking metaphorically, you were just sharing your frustration about the disrespectful students who constantly talk during class, right?" Alex said, "No, Mr. Geist, I am bringing in an actual gun and shooting up those assholes!" Of course, I had to report this to the counselor, who brought in the mother and talked the kid down. This showed how bad my freshmen were to have a student want to kill some of their fellow students.

ASSISTANT PRINCIPAL CAMPGREENBLATT'S
POOR DECISIONS

2007: She pulled a special education kid off a desk, and he almost fell to the ground; there was no consequence for her. It was swept under the rug.

Fall 2008: She had student mentors work with us to make teachers' lives easier. The students who were expected to teach a a 50 minute class usually finished in five to ten minutes. The lessons the AP was to provide the students were handed out last minute and sometimes not at all.

1-29-08: The social studies department was called into the principal's office and asked to come up with ten ideas to improve our grades and Regent scores. We were to meet the following week at the same time to discuss the ideas. I wrote up then ideas, and then we never met to discuss them, A.P. Campgreenblatt canceled the meeting.

03-09: I was told to put up a word after the secretary put up new paper on the bulletin boards. This did not happen, and I got scolded for no bulletin board. I put one up, the AP came in the next day, and told me to move it to the other wall. I did. The next day, she came in and asked me why I moved it.

4-09: I filed a complaint against AP Campgreenblatt with the Office of Equal Opportunity (a Department of Ed. entity) for harassment and dropped the case as a sign of good will.

09-10: The department was told to create an assessment test for our students. We took time to create one, we gave the test, we collected the test, and we turned them into the AP, who was then supposed to give us data or feedback. At the end of the semester when I asked for the results of the assessment, AP Campgreenblatt said,

"There was just too much data, and we did not have time to compile it."

2010: My AP frequently came in the room, walked around, and wrote in her notebook. There were two of my best students, Katherine and Krisagel, who said, "What is that lady's problem with you? She is always coming in here to check up on you. What a bitch she is!"

9-12-11: I was told by the AP to rewrite a test. I rewrote the test and made copies for the next day. She looked at the revised test and told me to redo it. When I told her I didn't have time to redo the test and make copies for the next day, she wrote me up.

2011: The administration started giving the U.S. History Regents to the freshman. Our scores of the junior passing rate in 2010 was 61 percent, but our scores with the freshman dropped to 27 percent passing in 2011 and 49 percent passing in 2012.

9-11: The administration told us there will be a new grading policy. It was not introduced until a year later in September of 2012.

9-12: We were told to create another assessment test, give a test, and hand the data to her. When I asked why we did not get any results, she said, "Hurricane Sandy is what happened!"

1-12: The administration told us they will be judging us based on the Kim Marshall rubric. In June, they told us they will now be using the Danielson rubric.

2-7-12: I asked her to come observe me again, to tell me what she wanted me to do for a satisfactory rating. She never came back or met with me.

Mid-June: Mr. Geist was voted teacher of the year by his peers. AP Campgreenblatt was heard to say "That is ridiculous!" by the UFT representative of our school.

Dec. 2012: I filed with the EOE again about possible "institutional racism" and harassment. The principal and AP were Jewish, and they hired two mentors who were Jewish, a curriculum mapping consultant who was Jewish and a PLC/SQR consultant who was Jewish. Our students were mostly Dominican, and there were rumblings in the staff about who got hired for jobs. I was not saying my bosses were racist, but just hiring your own may be and was definitely not best practices, for it bred resentment, hurt morale, and disincentive for good service. I was told just because they hired five people of their same faith did not necessarily make it institutional racism. Kangaroo courts everywhere in the DOE.

CANUNDRUM WITH UNION SENIORITY: I knew that AP Campgreenblatt was going to screw me in April when she would not meet with me for a pre-observation. Before the last contract, if you had troubles with a supervisor, you could put in for a transfer to three other schools. This way, you had a win-win of a teacher keeping their job and a supervisor happy to get you out of his or her department. Under the new contract, the teachers voted to give away seniority right to get a little more money. I never thought this would impact me, but it did. I voted for a new contract twice, but on the next one, I voted no. Principal had more power in the hiring process, and Bloomberg changed the budgets of schools that encouraged principals to hire newer teachers to save money for their school. This combination hurt me in finding another job as a NYC teacher.

2007–2008 - <u>RENTER DONNA</u>: I met Donna through eHarmony dating website. We met and took a long hike in Harriman Park and got a drink at a local dive bar. She lived in Fairlawn with another girl, but the lease was about to go out. I told her, "I have a spare bedroom, and I would charge you $500 to stay there." She said, "No, I have two other places I can move into." After three weeks, I got a call from her, and she was speaking very nicely to me, so I knew she needed a place, and I was right.

Donna worked as an IT person (computers) for Toys "R" Us. She was nice and clean and paid rent on time. She was Italian and had dark hair and, for the most part, was rarely home. On the weekends, she got up early and disappeared. The extra money was nice. It was easier than working night school and working as a housepainter on the weekends.

She liked to read and was into holistic stuff. She burned sage in the house every week. She left burn mark in my blue kitchen carpet. I can show you. She liked to doodle, and she made several doodles I still had today. The bear got a hold of my Yankee Flipper bird feeder and put some teeth marks in it. She drew a picture of a bear, saying "Thanks for the Bird Feed Candy Jar." I collected wood for my campfires and made a couple piles of wood. She drew a picture of a beaver looking at me, saying "I wish I made dams as nice as that." One was of a heart in a jar that said, "Jim's Jar," and it had a heart inside it that said, "Self-Love" since I was attending twelve-step meetings for codependency and Al-Anon meetings.

She voluntarily started paying me an extra $50 a month since gas and home oil prices had more than double under Pres. George W. Bush and VP Dick Cheney. She also used to work for AIG (American International Group), and she told me she got out of there because she saw some stuff going on and did not want to be there when the house of cards fell. Smart lady. On September 17 of 2008, the government loaned $85 billion to keep AIG afloat. She was very independent, and in the two years, I thought we only went out to eat once and watched one to two movies together. She was diagnosed with breast cancer and moved out, and I had not heard from her since.

RENTER: <u>JIM THE GARBAGEMAN</u>: I got a call from George the carpenter. George was in his seventies, and he liked to work half days and to go hiking in the afternoons. He had a wood shop up in Warwick, NY, and he was full of stories. I hired him to do some work on my roof, to put up a patio porch on my deck, and eventually to tear down my garage door and put in a wall with two windows and frames out my workroom, which I insulated and put up drywall to help me warm up my cold cabin.

George knew Donna and asked me if I was interested in another renter when she moved out. His friend's name was Jim, and he was a garbageman. Jim and his wife were having problems and needed a place to live in for three to six months until things cooled down. Jim was a decent guy and paid his rent on time. He stopped by the Country Roads Deli to pick up fried chicken and macaroni at least once a week. He liked to drink, and I did not like talking politics with renters. The one day on the back deck, he pointed his finger at me and said in a growl, "You are one of those people who support Obama." I got up and went downstairs to be by myself.

11-08-08: MY SUSPENDED NY DRIVER'S LICENSE: It was early in the morning, and I was driving through Warwick up to Pine Island. I got pulled over by an officer. He told a headlight was out. I gave him my driver's license, and he told me, "Your driver's license in NY is suspended." I said, "I do not understand, Officer. I live in New Jersey and have a New Jersey license." "He said, "You cannot drive this vehicle. You must leave it here, and I must get it towed. Unless this auto service station lets you park here, then you can." The auto owner let me park there and used his phone. I called Valerie and George DeLaura from the Democratic Club, and they picked me up.

I got to court and paid $235 for a surcharge and fine for the light. I then had to go to Orange County DMV and paid the $435 for the suspended license to get my name cleared. When I moved from Queens to New Jersey, I was sent a ticket and never received it. When I asked the judge why they did not send it to my New Jersey address, she said, "We do not do that." I told her, "With today's technology, you don't think they could find me, Your Honor?" She said, "That is not our job." Of course, if they found me, my fine would have been much lower, and I would not have to pay the court fee.

In the Greenwood Lake news under the "police report for November 8, it said, "James C. Geist, 42, was arrested and charged with aggravated unlicensed operation third following an incident on Route 1. He was released and ordered to appear in court." I was not aware I had been arrested. I thought when handcuffs were put on you, you were arrested. In NYC, if you are arrested, you have to inform your principal and the superintendent's office for protocol. I did so on November 25, the day after I saw the notice in the paper. I filled out some paperwork and sent it to the OPI office, and that was that.

2008 WORLD CHAMPION PHILLIES: The Phillies defeated the Dodgers to win the National League Pennant and the Tampa Bay Devils in the World Series. The starters for the Phillies were Carlos Ruiz C, 1B Ryan Howard, 2B Chase Utley, Jimmy Rollins SS, Pedro Feliz 3B, Pat Burrell LF, Shane Victorino CF, and Jayson Werth RF. The pitchers were Cole Hamels, Jamie Moyer, and Joe Blanton.

GAS AND OIL PRICES - CLINTON VS. BUSH/CHENEY:

Gasoline: Gasoline prices under Pres. Bill Clinton averaged $1.15 a gallon. Under the Bush-Cheney administration, it doubled the price to an average of $2.65. With adjusted inflation, the gas prices were as follows: Reagan to be $2.49, George H. Bush to be $2.87, Bill Clinton to be $1.70, George W. Bush to be $2.51, and Barack Obama to be $3.03. In Bush's last year, gas was $3.24, and in 2016, gas under Obama was $2. The actual price of gasoline in New Jersey was in the $1.80-to-$2.30 range in Obama's last two years in office.

HEATING OIL: With heating oil, I spent on average $636 more under President W. Bush than I did under President Obama. Since Cheney was an energy guy having been CEO of Haliburton and the Bush family having connections with oil companies, I believed the $600 Bush stimulus per person (or $1,200 per married couple) was a way to ensure their buddies got paid. The stimulus money I received went right to my heating oil company in 2008, the highest I ever saw oil reach and when I stopped using oil and switched over to a wood pellet stove.

MY EXPERIENCE WITH HEATING OIL: W. BUSH VS. OBAMA

JAMES GEIST Oil, Propane, and Wood Pellets

	Propane	Oil	Wood Pellets	TOTAL
March of 2003	$1,794	$440		$2,234 Pres. Bush
March of 2004	$1,387	$886		$2,273 W
March of 2005	$1,611	$1,156		$2,767 W
March of 2006	$1,888	$886		$2,774 W
March of 2007	$1,946	$744		$2,690 W
March of 2008	$1,593	$1,597		$3,170 *Bush Stimulus $600*
March of 2009	$1,281	$1,355		$2,636 Pres. Obama

| March of 2010 | $2,338 | $3,086 | $470 (2) | $3,556 Obama |

*I bought a wood pellet stove

| March of 2011 | $1,790 | | $490 | $2,280 Obama |
| March of 2012 | $1,288 | | $515 | $1,803 Obama |

*I switched from Burnwell Propane to SOS Propane (2012)

March of 2013	$1,640		$525	$2,169 Obama
March of 2014	$1,610		$543	$2,153 Obama
March of 2015	$1,314		$803 (3)	$2,117 Obam

Bush Propane Average:	1,703	Bush Total:	3,023
Obama Propane Average:	1,608	Obama Total:	2,387
Obama yearly savings	**$95**	**Obama ave. yearly savings**	**$636**

CARPENTER GEORGE: George had grown up in this area. He had done carpentry all his life. He told me a story that he was putting in a boardwalk in a natural area next to the Macopin Junior High School. When he turned around, a bear was watching him from ten feet away. George rolled backward and slowly walked away. Another time, he was doing work on someone's deck when he heard a thump, and there was a bobcat on the deck who jumped off as quickly as he had jumped on. But his story about the coyote was the best.

WHAT HAPPENED TO FIDO? George was working at Greenwood Lake on a roof with an employee. Outside in the metal-gated yard was the lady of the house sunbathing with one of those little fluffy dogs. She went inside the house, and George's hired help said, "Look at the German shepherd coming down the hill." The coyote jumped over the fence, grabbed the fluffy dog, and jumped back over the fence up the mountain with its lunch. The lady came out and started sunbathing and then a half hour later called for the dog, which was now missing. George did not want to tell the lady what he saw, so he kept his mouth closed.

The woman was hysterical and called her husband at work. He came home, and George called the guy over and told him what happened. George told the husband, "I did not want to be the one to tell her. I am telling you, and you can decide what you want to tell your wife."

Pres. Barack Obama (2009–2016)
Domestic

***Avoided scandal

Stopped a Bush depression

American Recovery and Reinvestment Act

Created more jobs in 2010 than all W's eight years

Fifty-five months of jobs growth (ten million jobs)

Budget deficit of 9.8 percent (W) to 2.9 percent of GDP

Fraud Enforcement Act (in financial world)

Helping Families Save Their Homes Act

Reduced speculator power in oil market

Closed offshore tax loopholes

Passed health care reform

Recapitalized the banks

Wall St. Reform - Dodd-Frank Bill

Increased support for veterans

Passed credit card reform

Appointed Sotomayor and Kagan to SC

Passed Fair Sentencing Act

Invested in renewable technology

Improved school nutrition

Claimed resolution (black and Nat. Am. Farmers)

Pushed for more broadband coverage

Dismantled the Minerals Management System

Paycheck Fairness Act (women)

Inflation at its lowest rate in fifty years

4.6 billion expansion in mental health for vets

Turned around the U.S. auto industry

Began closing dirtiest power plants

Tripled AmeriCorps

Expanded wilderness and water protection

Let the space shuttle die

Cracked down on bad for profit colleges

Expanded stem cell research

Killed the F-22 ($358 million apiece)

Improved food safety (more inspections)

Matthew Shepard Hate Crimes Preven. Act

Janet Yellen as chair of the Federal Reserve

Drop in prison population (first in thirty-two years)

Vacation days (in 5 years) 125 days vs. W's 407 days

Closed loopholes to companies sending U.S. jobs overseas

Brokered agreement for speedy compensation of the BP Gulf oil spill

*Deportations: 2.5 million - more than the previous
nineteen presidents combined

Foreign

Ended Iraq War (12-18-11)	Toppled Moammar Gaddafi
Reversed Bush Torture	Improved America's image abroad
Achieved a New START (treaty)	Trimmed and reoriented missile defense
Helped South Sudan declare independence	Killed Bin Laden
Opened diplomatic relations with Cuba	Iran Sanctions Act - to give up nuclear program
Beefed up border security	Got Syria to dismantle its chemical weapons

Killed the Somalian pirate kidnappers

<u>Poor Policies</u>

Race to the Top education reforms	Pushing for the Trans-Pacific Partnership (TPP)

1-20-09 - PRES. BARACK OBAMA: President Obama was elected and after President Bush won on two crooked elections in 2000 and 2004, having taken us into war in Iraq based on a lie when the majority of hijackers on 9/11 were from Saudi Arabia.

Bush's Last Year vs. President Obama 2016

	Bush	Obama
Unemployment	7.2%	5.1%
Cost of gas	$3.24	$1.91
Uninsured rate	15%	9.2%
Oil barrels imported	11 mill.	4.5 mill.
Teen pregnancy	40.2k	26.5k
Iran's centerfuges	19,000	6,000
GDP growth	-0.03%	+3.7%
Dow Jones	10,355	16,275

TTP CIRCA 2016: In 2015, President Obama said the Trans-Pacific Partnership (TPP) said the deal "will put American workers first." The document, which was one thousand pages long, was full of incomprehensible legalize that was hard to understand and will be used to help the investor class, leaving American workers behind. Under NAFTA, 62.5 percent of the value of cars and 60 percent of auto parts were to be made in NAFTA countries. Under the TPP, 45 percent of cars and 30 percent of parts needed be made in TPP countries. The language saying non-TPP countries really meant "made in China."

New Balance had been trying to continue to make shoes in the United States, and this removal of tariffs by the TPP was likely to force them to give up staying in business against Nike. The U.S. steelworkers said TPP will result in the loss of hundreds of thousands of jobs. The union said TPP provided incentives for U.S. companies to outsource production and to send jobs overseas. The same arguments for TPP were the arguments that had been used for NAFTA, which allowed for

The first option was the Congress will need to ensure that the Fast Track was permanently dust-binned, and the NAFTA model was not expanded through TPP. President Obama supported it. Presidential candidate Hillary Clinton said in July of 2016 she did not support TPP. Time will tell.

2007 - LAURIE: I met Laurie with blond hair and blue eyes on eHarmony. She looked like actress Laurie Holden in the movie *The Majestic* with Jim Carrey. Laurie and I talked, and it turned out she grew up in Baldwin, NY, in the town I use to be a youth pastor. She had a condo next to Mount Vernon Ski Lodge in Vernon New Jersey, just undereath the ski lodge with a beautiful view of the mountain and the ski paths. The condo resort had a restaurant, a gymnasium with a basketball court, and a spa area. She worked in Long Island, and she was a mortgage broker. She felt good about helping people to get into homes.

She stayed in Baldwin a few nights a week and traveled home on Tuesdays and Fridays for the weekend. She talked on her bluetooth phone while driving home, and I asked her questions from *The Questions Book*, which had some funny and thought-provoking questions. The first time we met, we met at the bar. She seemed a little tipsy and invited me to her apartment. She went in the bedroom, pushed me on the bed, jumped on me, and started to take her shirt off. I said, "Stop. I need to get to know you. You don't have to do this." She lay next to me and then rolled off the bed in a drunken stupor and hit her head on the wooden floor.

She told me her ex-husband was the youngest judge appointed to federal court by Bill Clinton but went to jail because of an association with a restaurant connected with the mob. Her son was a heroin addict in jail, and her other daughter was a cutter. She told me she only drinks on the weekend, but she drinks almost every time I went there. I saw her for three months.

On my last visit to Laurie's, it had snowed, and there was a guy shoveling snow, and he was young and having a conversation with himself, out loud. I talked with him, and it was clear he suffered mental illness or was high on some drug. I went in the apartment and told Laurie about this guy. I told her, "Whatever you do, don't invite this guy in the house." We went for a walk. On the way back, she talked to the kid and invited him in for coffee or tea. We sat at the table, and as we were talking, he fell asleep at the table. Laurie clapped her hands and told him to wake up. Turned out the shovel boy was on heroin. I pulled her into a side room and told her to be careful on what she shared with him. She walked out and told him she worked in Long Island and only came home one to two times a week. She then offered the kid a job to feed her dog and to take it for walks and gave him a key to the apartment. All I can imagine was her coming home and seeing all her stuff stolen because the kid needed money for heroin. The kid looked at me and said, "For an ex-pastor, you sure give me judging looks!" I apologized and said I had never seen a person nod off asleep in the middle of a conversaton before. That was the last time I saw Laurie.

2007 - KAREN N.: I met Karen on eHarmony. She had blond hair and looked like actress Laura Linney. We met at a bar in Butler, New Jersey, called Jiggs McAllister's. It had excellent food at reasonable prices, and they usually had live music on Thursday through Saturday nights. She worked with a health insurance company and lived in Morristown, New Jersey. We dated for approximately six weeks. We watched the Grammys in 2007 when the Foo Fighters won the best rock album with *Echoes, Silence, Patience and Grace.*

I took her to Allentown to meet the folks and Uncle Tom and Aunt Adele. When we went to the Meyers, cousin Laurie was also there. After batting the breeze for about an hour, Uncle Tom said, "You know, Karen, nephew Jamesy has not been doing a good job of picking women in his life, so is it okay if my family makes a judgment on you, say from 1 to 10 like they do for diving or gymnastics?" Karen looked nervous but bravely agreed. They all talked with one another, and all had their papers; and Laurie turned over her paper, and it said 10; and Aunt Adele turned her paper over, and it said 10; and Uncle Tom turned his paper over, and it said 10. Karen said, "I like your family!"

2010 - THE AFFORDABLE CARE HEALTH ACT (OBAMACARE): In the end, we did not work out. She was a Republican, and I was a single-payer universal health care guy, and this made Karen nervous because she did not know how it would affect her job.

The GOP says the sky will fall if it passes! Ted Cruz said it would send us into a recession. Scott Walker said it would hamper our economy. Bobby Jindal said expanding Medicaid would cause employers to dump insurance plans. Lindsey Graham said millions of employers would reduce work hours to not pay for health insurance.

The Big Five Insurance Companies: Since 2009, WellCare's stock had risen to 1,410 percent, thanks entirely to federal and state customers. United Health, Aetna, Cigna, Humana, and Anthem had all outperformed the broader stock market by a wide margin since Obamacare was signed into law in 2010.

Benefits of Obamacare (WhiteHouse.gov - benefits of ACA 2-2-15):

1) A decline in uninsured - 16.4 million now have access.
2) The CEA (Council of Economic Advisers) estimated it had created 130,000 jobs in the health sector.
3) The slowest growth of health care cost in fifty years on record: 2011, 2012, 2013.
4) 50,0000 deaths avoided (2010–2013), and 150,000 readmissions avoided (2012–2013).

5) The average family in employer-based coverage was $1,800 lower in 2014 than since 2010 had matched the 200-10 average.

6) Sixty months of continuous job growth

7) Unemployment decreased by 1.2 percent (2012–2013)

8) 101 percent of overall increase in employment had been in full-time jobs.

9) Part-time employment had decreased slightly.

10) The CBO (Congressional Budget Office) said this law will decrease the deficit by generating a savings of more than one trillion over two decades.

2007–2010 - TERESA S.: It was 2007. I was sitting in the gallery of a West Milford, New Jersey, council meeting. I always brought schoolwork with me, newspapers, and a book in case the meeting was excessively boring. As I was pursuing the audience to see who the usual suspects were, usually pasty-looking white people from the township, just to the left two aisles ahead of me was a woman who looked to be Hawaiian or Polynesian. She had great cheekbones, a tan color, brown eyes, and long curly hair like many Dominicans had. She had bright white teeth with her tan skin and a nice smile. To me, Teresa S. looked like actress Tia Carrere, Hawaiian, who was in the movie *Wayne's World*.

Before the meeting started, I sneaked up to introduce myself. After some small talk, I gave her my phone number and told her I would love to take her out for dinner. After two days, I received a phone call from Ms. Teresa S. Her father was African American, and her mom was a Filipina, which explained the curly hair. We decided to meet at a diner in Ringwood, New Jersey. We hit it off. She was a newspaper person, and research was a big part of her job. She told me, "You know, I did some research on you, and it is quite impressive. You have done a lot. You were a pastor and an activist, and you ran for a West Milford council seat in 2006. You are kind of famous." "I don't know about that, but thanks for the compliment!"

She lived in Hackensack with her mother. Her mom was a librarian at the Hackensack New Jersey Library. Teresa's father had passed when she was in elementary school. Mr. Sarne grew up in Texas, and I was sure had to deal with much racism. He ws the one who gave Teresa her love of reading. Teresa was an only child who learned how to entertain herself, and no one ever had to tell her to do her homework. I loved her laugh, and she liked to laugh a lot, and the more the better with me.

Teresa was a single mother of a six-year-old girl. Teresa met the father at Farleigh Dickinson University, where they dated, and Teresa became pregnant. Davonne was the person who cheated on her and, on several occasions, was physically violent. When I used the bathroom in the small apartment for the grandmother, mother, and child, I wondered why there was a baseball bat in the bathroom. It was then I learned about the behavior of the ex. The daughter, Natalia, liked to talk about her stepsister, Nike, but never knew the particulars of her father's cheating leading to having a stepsister.

Teresa worked for a small newspaper called the *Suburban Trends*. She was paid peanuts—twenty thousand a year for writing six stories a week for the paper that came out on Sundays and Wednesdays. She was the Ringwood, New Jersey, beat reporter who covered the council meetings and any other big stories or human interest stories. She was a writer, she was smart, she liked to write poetry, and she was in the process of writing a book. I love dating smart people. Pretty is nice, but intelligence can make the relationship deeper and last longer. One of the best memories I had being with Teresa was our trip to Boston for a weekend.

PLEASE PULL THE CAR SEAT OUT. THANK YOU!: Teresa S. was short, about five feet three inches; and whenever she borrowed my car or we switched cars, when I would try to sit, I would get squeezed in between the seat and steering wheel. It made me feel like André the Giant trying to get in the front of a Volkswagen. It was like a midget or leprechaun purposely moved the seat to torture me.

CAMBODIAN MAIL-ORDER BRIDE: My students asked me how I met my girlfriend. I told them she was a Cambodian mail-order bride. I said her English was terrible, but we communicated by hand signals. When I was hungry, I pointed to my mouth. When the house needed cleaning, I took my hand back and forth like I was vacuuming. When I want kissy face, I puckered up my lips. The best part was I didn't get any lip back. My students would believe anything I said, but in the end, I told them the truth.

CHRISTOPHER COLUMBUS AND THE GAMBINO FAMILY: I sent a letter to the editor in October, questioning if Columbus Day should be a federal holiday. The Spanish introduced the *encomienda* system, which categorized people by the color of their skin; and the lighter the skin, the higher up you were in the social strata. I always felt the Spanish conquistadors introduced exceptional racism into the New World. Columbus's men landed on Quisqueya and changed the island's name to Hispaniola to make it sound Spanish. We knew that place as the Dominican Republic and Haiti today. It was said that Columbus's men killed over three million Taino people on the island. When we talked about mass murderers—Jeffrey Dahmer, Charles Manson, or the Columbine School Shooters—I said Columbus was one of the best at it. If this was the case, why does our country celebrate a mass murderer? Teresa called me to tell me the *Suburban Trends* had received a phone call from a person very offended by this letter going after someone of Italian heritage. This person turned out to be connected to the Gambino family.

MY NEMESIS: After dating for two years, I asked her and Natalia to move in with me in 2009. I knew that Teresa and I would be able to live together, but I wanted to find out if the daughter was going to bond with me because I did not want to live with a daughter who would treat me in a resentful way for the next eight to twelve years. I took Natalia out to the movies, to eat, on errands, and to a girl's softball game and prayed with her. One day as I put up shelves for her in her newly painted pink room, with a dresser painted in three shades of pink, I saw the birthday card I gave her; and it had my name crossed out with the word "nemesis" written underneath. I made the decision this child will not accept me as stepfather, and I called off our relationship.

A positive role I believed I played in Teresa's life was sharing with her about my codependence recovery. I shared how I got there and how much my life had improved since attending the twelve-step group Codependents Anonymous. Through it, I had learned how to love myself and how to be comfortable being alone, being less perfectionist, and being kinder to myself and learned how to become my own best friend. It taught me how to sit with feelings and to not run from them or to cover them with alcohol, food, sex, TV, workaholism, or any other way. For forty years, I had stuck my feelings into a freezer. I now had pulled them out and had done much grieving work to let out the pain I did not want to sit with. As a result, I thought by me living my life and sharing with her, she was able to do much recovery work on herself.

10-29-10 - HURRICANE SANDY: Hurricane Sandy hit New Jersey pretty badly. Many trees around West Milford were felled by the wind, and many power lines were knocked down. Power crews from the north and south of New Jersey came into our area to restore electricity. It took eleven days before my home got electricity. Teresa moved back to her mom's with Natalia in Hackensack for heat and electricity, and

I moved into my folks place my folks' place in Pennsylvania for three days.

I had a propane stove but no heat or water without electricity. I had a pellet stove, but it ran on electricity. Maybe I needed to get a woodstove in case we get hit with another hurricane like Sandy. NYC schools were closed for a week, but New Jersey was declared a state of emergency, and the roads in my area had trees on them and, in some cases, power lines on them. The UFT fought so that teachers were not penalized for losing two days in a time of state of emergency. It showed me how dependent society was on electricity and how dependent I was on it. I hope to buy a wood stove in the near future to have heat for the next emergency.

2011 - TIFFANY: I don't handle breakups well, it stirs up feelings of abandonment for me. At this point, I was four years into recovery work . . . but the truth is, as much as I don't want to be codependent, I tend to do better when I am in a relationship. I can focus on me instead of "the hunt" for a significant other.

Her profile made it clear she was a human rights advocate, which meant she was probably a Democrat. She was blond, working, had a dog, lived in Nyack, was an advocate, actor . . . and an atheist. What to do, what to do? Hey, it's just a date. We spoke by phone, where I learned her name. I shared with my friend Ms. CarlLa Horton from WM about my upcoming date. Based on what I told her, she said, "I may know this person." I said her name was Ms. Tiffany Blah-blah. "Yup, I did a radio interview with her in Warwick, NY, about women's issues." Small world.

Tiffany and I agreed to meet at a place in Sloatsburg at the Rhodes Tavern. It was a hot summer day, and she showed up wearing a miniskirt, showing a lot of leg. She was also quite endowed with pretty blue eyes and a big contagious smile. We walked up the stairs to our table and began to share our stories. I had the wild card of us both knew a mutual friend who could vouch I was a good guy and would not rape her and bury her in the woods behind my home. After dinner, she followed me to Ringwood, New Jersey, to park her car in a baseball field lot and came home with me. We sat on back deck of my home and conversed for hours. She looked like actress Kim Basinger with her long blond hair and long legs. I drove her back to her car so she could get back to Nyack. Long story short, we became a thing for almost a year. The best part about love for me is falling in love. When it comes to long-term relationships, I am told we should "sacrifice for the sake of the relationship," not just for the other.

CIRCA 1990 - I SEE A BLONDE ON A FOX NEWS STORY: It was summertime, and some Budweiser girls were in town. Fox News Live did a story about, and they interviewed a blonde in what looked like a "summer-ized" version of the St. Pauli beer girl in October Fest gear but with red, white, and blue colors. There were three or four ladies there, and the interviewer threw out a question to the lady smoking a cigar. I don't remember the question, but what I do remember was I could see the woman think about the question and then give a great response back. I thought, *Wow. Good answer. I would love to meet that woman.* Tiffany told me a story about how she used to be a Budweiser dirl, how she was asked a question by a reporter from Fox News, and how she came up with a totally bogus answer that actually came out very intelligently. I not only got to meet her but also dated her for a year.

Tiffany and I had things in common, except for the recovery work part and the God part. Tiffany was usually not degrading about religion or those who were religious. Her philosophy was live and let live. If it worked for you, good for you. She was a huge advocate of equal energy in a relationship.

She had been in a "polyamorous" relationship before me. What that means is a couple is open to seeing other people but is able to do so without getting jealous. Hats off to them. I would have a tough time with someone of the opposite sex spending time and having sex with someone I wanted to do the same with. If you can do that, you are a bigger person than me. She dated a married guy in Washington DC and would see him every other weekend. The husband's wife had a male friend on the side and practiced the same thing. Eventually, the wife got tired of this, and the husband had to choose who he wanted to be with.

Tiffany had a Boston Terrier named Ellie, short for Eleanor Roosevelt. When I met the dog, it was a bit older, and the love of this dog's life was chasing tennis balls. Tiffany was working for Planned Parenthood, and there was a chance she might be losing her job based on the fact she had been put on probation for three months and also depending if enough funding came through for her to continue as the Hudson Valley Planned Parenthood communications director. I told her, "No problem. If you lose your job and lose your apartment, you can move into my place until you get your next job." I threw out the safety net for her, for which she was grateful. In the end, she ended up getting a job working as the communications person for the NY Assembly Woman of the area.

It was a great summer. We went to the Elks Lodge to listen to a band. A woman walked up to Tiffany and said, "You're beautiful!" The drunk woman looked at me and said, "You're okay." Tiffany worked from my home using my landline or her cell phone and laptop. She would hang out for three to five days in a row. It was fine with me. I usually liked playing ball with the dog. I am not a huge NYC Broadway kind of guy, but I attended a play with her and ate at a French restaurant before the show, costing me $300. I also thought it was great she was involved with the Nyack Playhouse but did not make it to the show because of snow. My mother, sister, and aunt Sandy were planning on coming up for the show with me. She never forgave me for missing her show.

I began to go to Nyack more to her apartment. Tiffers was not the most clean or organized person. Her roommate was even messier. I felt a bit like I was imposing when her roommate was home. One night I showed up, I tied up the garbage and put in a new garbage bag in the kitchen plastic container in the corner. There were dirty dishes in the sink, so I cleaned up the dishes. There was a great show on at the time called *Orange Is the New Black*, a show about a middle-class woman going to jail and all she had to do to get by. As I was on the couch next to the blonde bombshell, I moved the computer six inches so my neck will not crink up as we watched the show. I can feel her burning a hole through me.

"Is there a problem?"

"You just moved the computer without asking me."

"This bothers you?"

"Yeah, and washed the dishes and took out the garbage! You are taking over my apartment!"

Silence.

I said, "You are kidding, right?"

"NO!"

"Well, anyone is welcome to come to my home, do the dishes, take out the garage, wash my car, and I will kiss him/her on the lips!"

There was a not-so-fun-awkward kind of silence the rest of the night.

She was planning on moving to a new place and wanted to do some painting. It became clear to me she did not want me helping her move or helping her paint the new pad. It was pretty clear she no longer wanted me. During this time, I lost my arbitration and my NYC teaching job. I signed up for unemployment and became very focused on finding another teaching job. Somewhere at the three-month period of my search, she made a comment to the affect, "You know, when a person loses his/her job, it changes a relationship." I thought that was a strange comment to make and was not really sure what she was getting at. When I spoke to neighbor Richie, he said, "When she needed help, you threw her a lifeline. You need help, and she is willing to let you sink. I knew she was too good to be true. How does a smoking hot chick go so long without being in a long-term relationship? See, now you know why."

F——K WEST MILFORD!: Being vindictive can be one my character flaws. I am not proud of it, and I am aware it comes from the fact I do not have enough faith in God (or karma) to handle the situation. I could feel Tiffany pulling away from me. It upset me that she never broke up with me. She just kept pulling further and further away. It clearly began to happen the night we were on my deck drinking wine, and she was drunk. She looked me right in the eye and said, "I f——ing hate West Milford, and I hate the f——ing twelve-step program!" *Wow. WOW,* I thought.

She had no problem hanging out at my place for most of the summer and up until the cold weather began to kick in and when her play practices for *Les Misérables* at the Nyack Playhouse began. I made a comment that it was not nice, and I was not proud of. I liked her body, which had some extra pounds on it, but so do I, so who am I to criticize? She struggled with body issues with herself. I said to her, "You were willing to drive to Washington DC to have sex with a married guy, but you can't make time to drive fifty minutes from Nyack to my place. I am sure you will have no problem attracting some chubby chaser." The cost is when you say something, it cannot be taken back. I have never stayed friend with any exes, nor have I ever wanted to, so that is that.

She did not deserve that, I apologized, but I said it, and it will not be forgotten, I am sure.

I have good memories of us playing many games of tennis and of going to music events in Sugar Loaf, NY, in the summertime and when I took her to see an Elton John concert at the Madison Square Garden. I am grateful for things she taught me and for the time I had with her. She was able to speak in a kind and professional way when things got heated, something I wish I did better. She was a good Democrat and was an amazing human who advocated for the poor.

U.S. History 2010s

2010:	House approved the ACA (Affordable Care Act) or Obamacare.
	-Horizon Deepwater oil leakage in the Gulf of Mexico (Haliburton)
2011:	Occupy Wall St. Movement
	-Osama bin Laden killed
2012:	President Obama defeated Mitt Romney
	-Sandy Hook School shooting (twenty children and seven staff members killed)
2013:	Ebola virus outbreak
	-Pope Francis elected
2015:	Cuba and United States reestablished full diplomatic ties
	-Same-sex marriage legalized
	-Virus treatment being used to kill cancer cells
	-E-cigarettes

Inventions of the 2010s

2010:	iPad, GPS
2011:	Siri virtual assistant on iPhones, Trekker scooter
2012:	Wingsuits, self-inflating tires
2013:	Wingsuit racing, self-inflating tires
2014:	Hoverboards
2015:	Apple watches

Cars of the 2010s

Dodge Challenger, Chevy HHR, Ram 1500 Trucks, Chevy Volt, Ford Focus Electric, Ford Fusion Hybrid

Music of the 2010s

Bruno Mars: "Just the Way You Are"

2011

Red Hot Chili Peppers: "The Adventures of Rain Dance Maggie"

Bush: "The Sound of Winter"

Adele: "Rolling in the Deep"

2012

Mumford & Sons: "I Will Wait"

2013

Robin Thicke: "Blurred Lines"

2014

Pharrell: "Happy"

Television Shows of the 2010s

Boardwalk Empire (2010–2014)	*American Horror Story* (2011–present)
Better Call Saul (2015–present)	*Penny Dreadful* (2014–present)
Game of Thrones (2011–present)	*Halt and Catch Fire* (2014–present)
True Detective (2014–present)	*Finding Bigfoot* (2012–2015)

Movies of the 2010s

44-2010: *Wall Street, The Social Network, The King's Speech, True Grit*

45-2011: *The Help, Girl with the Dragon Tattoo, Ides of March*

46-2012: (HSHCS) *Django Unchained, Argo, Silver Linings Playbook, Flight, Lincoln*

47-2013: *Dallas Buyers Club, 12 Years a Slave, American Hustle, The Great Gatsby, Rush*

48-2014: (HSHCS) *Selma, Citizenfour, American Sniper, Foxcatcher, The Imitation Game, The Theory of Everything*

48-2015: (NLA) *The Revenant, Spotlight, The Big Short, Joy, The Hateful Eight*

49-2016 (MPCS) *Elvis & Nixon, Money Monster, Everybody Wants Some, Eddie the Eagle*

CHANCE MEETINGS WITH BILL MAHER GUESTS: On January 21, 2010, David Stockman was a guest on the Bill Mahr program. He was Ronald Reagan's budget director, who said Republicans have talked about cutting taxes and government programs, but for the last thirty years, they had cut taxes and increased spending and the national debt. I walked into David Stockman two weeks later in midtown Manhattan, thanked him for speaking out on the insanity of cutting taxes and raising spending, and we shook hands.

In April of 2011, Dr. Michio Kaku, a physicist, futurist, and populizer of science, appeared on the Bill Mahr show to talk about the impact of the leakage of radiation from the Fukushima nuclear plant caused by the March 12, 2011, earthquake in Japan. One week later, I was on the number 6 train uptown and saw what looked like to be him. I asked him, and he shakes his head yes. He was working on some formula, probaly to save the planet, so I did not want to waste his time but thanked him for his service and contribution to science and speaking out on climate change. I would run into Dr. Kaku and his wife on Broadway Street in 2014 and then again ran into Dr. Kaku and his wife at the mall in Nanuet, NY, in 2016. Maybe I will remember to take a selfie with Dr. Kaku if I run into him again. He often appeared on the History Channel, the Discovery Channel, and the Science Channel and did a weekly program on WBAI Radio. He had written several books on subjects, such as the theory of the universe, parallel universes, time warps, scientific revolutionalizing of the twenty-first century, and the future of the mind. He believed we will be able to upload our minds to computers neuron per neuron, take smart pills enhance our congintion, and push the very limits of immortality.

THE INCREDIBLE POWER OF CHANCE EVENTS IN NYC: I had my run-in with Mayor Giuliani, Dr. Kaku, and David Stockman. Psychology estimates each person know 300 people. NYC has 8.2 million people, which comes to 26,402 per square mile or 733.4139 per linear mile. If all 300 of your friends are in NYC on a particular day, you have a 12.7 percent chance of running into them.

MONDAY, SEPTEMBER 9, 2013 - BRIDGATE: I picked up my fellow commuters in Teaneck, and there was major congestion on the George Washington Bridge. There were two of the lanes that were closed down. Why? It was this way on Monday, Tuesday, Wednesday, and Thursday, causing major conjestion for the city of Fort Lee, New Jersey. I was stuck in traffic, thanks to NJ governor's bully cronies dishing out retrobution "Tony Soprano" style. Finally, on Friday, the two lanes were opened up, ending the unnessary morning congestion into NYC.

After an investigation, blonde, forty-one-year-old Bridget Anne Kelly, deputy chief of staff for NJ governor Christie, was fired for orchestrating the GW Bridge traffic scam as retribution against Fort Lee's mayor Mrak Sokolich (D) for not endorsing Christie in the 2013 gubernatorial elections. Federal charges were brought up in 2015 aginst Bill Baroni and David Wildstein, Christie's appointees to the Port Authority. Wildsten pleaded guilty, and Kelly said Wildstein was lying. As a result, it was estimated four died of EMTs not being able to move quicker; and hundreds of thousands of commuters, workers, teachers, and students were delayed from a half hour to one hour extra to get to work. Governor Christie claimed he had no prior knowledge of this. As of 2016, the case was still under investigation by the U.S. attorney general for New Jersey, Paul Fishman.

8-2-12 - GEIST REPTILE ZOO – TWO PYTHONS IN THREE DAYS: The afternoon summer torrential downpour had stopped. It was 5:00 p.m., and I went on the deck with a book to read. As I was sitting with my feet up and my class of coffee next to me, I happened to look in the woods about one hundred just on the edge of the wetlands and the dead leaves on the ground by two large rocks. I saw something that looked long and white. It must be a large branch that fell in the rainstorm. I went back to reading, and lifted my head again to look at the branch. Something did not seem right. I went inside, grabbed my binoculars, and took another look when the branch lifted its head; and I realized it was a long albino snake. It turned out to be a sixtee-foot-long female albino Burmese python.

I called the police, and I stood outside to wait for him. When he drove up, I said over here, and he said, "If it was up to me, I would shoot it. I am picking up some snake handlers." He came back with two guys, and they were more afraid of black bears than python snakes. I grabbed my camera and took some picture to document the strange occurance. I read about how in Florida, a family lived over a pet store, and a large python escaped and ended up constricting and suffocating their young twin boys. What if I had been sunbathing and the thing came up and did the same to me? The one python wrangler wrapped the snake over his shoulders and carried it from the woods to put into a sack and hauled it away. Good riddance!

After two days, at nine o'clock, I was making breakfast, an omelette on the stove. I had three Adirondack chairs I rescued from the garbage and painted white and then the backseat boards red, white, and blue. The chairs were on my lawn next to my shed, and what did I see but a ten-foot caramel Burmese python in my yard. Yikes! I called the police to tell them I had a python in the yard, and the dispatcher asked, "Is this 57 Bayonne Drive?" I said yes. She said, "Your yard is a magnet for pythons." It was lying there, sunbathing in its creepy kinda way. I called my neighbor Richie over, and he can't believe it, and he took pictures with his cell phone.

The cop showed up, and he called animal control. Some older woman pulled up and said, "Do you have any bags I could use?" I gave her a pillowcase, and I thought, *There is no way this woman is going to bag this thing. She must live in an assisted living home. How did she get this job?* The snake started to move, and before it can get under the shed, the police officer grabbed it by the tail and held onto it until the snake handlers showed up again. The albino snake ended up in the local pet store. The snake handlers took the ten-footer. I was creeped out and, for the rest of the summer, always scanned the yard before going outside.

I wrote up mini press release for the local weekly paper and to the *NJ Record* to alert the neighbors in the community to look out for pythons in case there were any others out there. This way, they can keep an eye on their pets or little children. The release got picked up by worldwide media. I had four TV crews show up to my home—local channel 12 NJ news, NBC, ABC, and another crew that all the other stations used like Fox, Telemundo, etc. You can see the piece if you google West Milford NJ pythons and nbc local (or abc local). I had students who saw the piece in Puerto Rico and in the Dominican Republic.

HUMMING BIRDS: I had a hummingbird feeder I put out every spring. They are as big as a thumb and the only bird that can fly backward. They are competive and mean to each other. If there are two or more hummingbirds, they dive bomb each other when one goes in to feed. In the spring, I was on the deck reading, but I had not put the feeder out yet. As I was reading, I can hear a *bzzz, bzzz, bzzz* going back and forth in front of my head. It was a ruby-throated hummingbird, and it was as if he was saying, "Hey, where is the feeder, buddy?" I immediately filled up the feeder and put it out. They and the gold finches are my favorite birds.

CHAPTER 14

Arbitration, Unemployment, Renters 2012–2013 (46–47)

10-17-12 - OFFICE OF APPEALS (2012 UNSATISFACTORY RATING): On October 12, 2012, I reported to the Department of Education in Brooklyn with a UFT representative, Al Sarasohn. The hearing was recorded. I handed my evidence to my rep, and he began to question my bosses. The administrators were allowed to give their side and to ask me questions. After they asked me question, my UFT representative was allowed to ask my bosses questions. He was an excellent advocate.

To start, Principal Harry and AP Campgreenblatt put all their evidence of documents on the table. The chairperson for the hearing said, "What is this?" They responded, "Our evidence." As I look at the chairperson, I realize he is my first A.P. of the school I subbed at in Astoria Queens fourteen years earlier. I am sure he did not recognize me.The chairman asksed if they e-mailed the documents to him twenty-four hours in advance. My bosses claimed they never received an e-mail from the chairman. The chairman pulled out a document and said, "These are your e-mail addresses, and this is the letter I e-mailed you about getting your evidence to me. You may not use any of your documents on the table."

AP Campgreenblatt used the 2011 end-of-the-year report to point areas of improvement, but the union rep pointed out, "Mr. Geist was given a satisfactory rating for 2011." In fact, I have eleven satisfactory ratings in a row. Of my two observations in 2012, I was never given a pre-observation meeting or a post-observation meeting even though I sent an e-mail requesting these meetings with the bosses. To make a long story short, here is how they did not follow proper protocol:

1) I was never given a formal warning I was in danger of a U rating for 2012.

2) The UFT contract stated teachers in danger of a U are to be given pre- and post-observations (2009 collective bargaining).

3) I was to be given a written plan of action and to be monitored; AP Campgreenblatt did not provide a plan or monitor me.

4) She observed me twice in 2011–2012 and never came back after February 7, 2012.

5) There was to be a log of assistance showing how an administrator had attempted to help a teacher in danger of receiving a U. She had no log of assistance.

6) AP CampGreenblatt testified she was not aware of these procedures.

7) She claimed she did not know in February if Mr. Geist was in danger of getting a U, but the principal said he knew.

8) AP Campgreenblatt testified the SQRR team (teams that rate NYC schools) mentioned my name in their report. Principal Harry said that was not true.

When the meeting finished, UFT rep Mr. Saransohn said to me, "In all my years as an appeals representative, these two bosses are the most incompetent I have ever seen." When AP Campgreenblatt walked out, she yelled at me, "I HOPE YOU ARE DONE WITH YOUR INSUBORDINATION, MR. GEIST!" The chairman looked at me like *"What is wrong with her?"* and the principal said, "Let me talk to her." I received a letter dated November 29, 2012, from the senior deputy chancellor Shael Suransky, saying, "The 2012 said rating has been sustained as a consequence of failure to implement the directions and recomendations made by the Administration which negatively impacted his classroom instruction."

I learned the NYC Dept. of Ed. appeals review was a kangaroo court. On **February 14, 2013**, I received a letter from the Office of Appeals, stating, "Due to procedural errors at your original appeal hearing, a new hearing has been set for March 1st, 2013." But by this time, they had filed a 3020a charge against me, and the appeal hearing would have been moot, plus, I was sure I would have lost again after all the contractual breeches by the administration. The Department of Ed. was going to do what it wanted to do.

4-18-13 - HSHCS - MR. GEIST, I PRESUME? YOU HAVE BEEN SERVED: I just finished my mini-lesson, and I was about to turn the class into "group work" when knock, knock on the door. I opened and a grim-faced principal said, "Someone wants to talk with you." He slinked away in an extra slinky with a frown on his face. At the door was an African American or a Caribbean American male in his mid-fifties, and he looked utterly familiar to me, not as a parent or grandparent but as someone I recognized on TV. Oh yeah, the show *Working Life*, and this was the guy who served subpoenas.

I thought, *Well, there are no cameras. Darn it.* I could probably sue for filming me without my permission, and he asked, "Are you Mr. James Geist?" Oh shoot, I was being served a subpoena. For what? I asked if I can introduce him to the class. He said sure. As he walked in, two to three of the kids' eyes opened up and said, "That guy is on TV."

The whole class got excited. I said to the class, "Guess what, I was just served a subpoena from the NYC Dept. of Ed. I think I am about to be fired soon." The whole class looked in disbelief and said, "What?"

When the famous TV subpoena server asked, "What's up?" I answered, "This is about a personality conflict with my boss. I was just voted teacher of the year by my teaching peers." And with his Caribbean accent, he said, "Oh . . . this is personal. I am sorry to hear that. Good luck!"

It had been a stressful four years at the job; a hostile boss can make it eminently so. I had asked for help, for AP meetings, so I could get concrete suggestions, but she will not meet with me. She had given me a "coach" who was making suggestions I felt the suggestions work better at the elementary level. I was also being coached at the end of the year when the focus for the social studies department was preparing the students for the NY State exams called the Regents.

RUBBER ROOM: When you get charged with a 3020a for insubordination, you are sent to a place where other teachers had been 3020ed. You can be in a "rubber-room" for anywhere from two to three years or longer before your case gets to arbitration. For more information on its craziness, you can google it. Betsy Combs of ATR Connect had a good site for it. Fortunately for me, it was changed by a judge that teachers had to be kept in their own schools. I used to report to the empty art room; but when they saw me reading, bringing in DVDs to watch, and working on the computer, they moved me to an AP's room. I ended up sitting in my personal rubber room from April 19, 2013, until the end of June and then from September 2013 through November 21 until I got my decision from the arbitrator, which added up to six months of my life.

ARBITRATION: The Department of Ed. paid half the cost of an arbitrator, and the UFT paid the other half. I hired my own attorney instead of going with a union attorney. We met over the course of five different days from June 5 through June 27, and Arb. Mark Winters sent out his decision on November 21, 2013.

I was happy with my representation. I went through the docments and sent suggested arguments and questions for the upcoming witnesses. I had arguments, documents, pictures, testimony of others, and an award that said, "Teacher of the Year." I will shorten this part by listing the arguments my supervisor introduced and then the response by three students and a co-teacher.

Complaints by AP Campgreenblatt: "I did not see Mr. Geist post an agenda on the board or a word wall, or use group work, or use the Smart Board, or have a class library and that his students were not learning. Therefore, he is insubordinate." Unfortunately, I was not able to bring in the testimony of a former student who was in the special ed program whom she pushed off a desk to show her temperament. I did not find out until after the arbitration she did not even observe senior teachers. She asked them for a lesson and made up observation reports.

Student Testimony: Those who testified were Claudia, Amina, Aldo. and Mr. Miller. All testified that I put up a daily agenda, had a word wall, had a class library, used the Smart Board, employed group work, prepared the students well for the Regents Exam, and made the class fun and that I had excellent classroom management skills and that they learned in class. Mr. Miller also testified the same.

Decision of the Arbitrator: "Mark Winters called for your immediate resignation. You are terminated on November 21, 2013. You will be removed from the Department of Ed.'s payroll and placed on the ineligible list." Wow, four years of college, three years of graduate school, and one and a half years taking education classes and taking tests to get my NYC teachers license. What does this mean? I can teach in NY State and in New Jersey but no longer in NYC. I can file an appeal to the Supreme Court and to the appelate level if I lose the Supreme Court case. With all the evidence and testimony, I had lost.

My father told me as a union rep himself he had sat in dozens of arbitration cases, and it came down to who the arbitrator believed. He had seen cases his workers should have won, lost, and vice versa. He saw guys who should have lost but were great liars, and the arbitrator believed them.

What Have I Learned?

1) Even if you are not guilty, an insubordination charge is tough to beat. You have a 10 percent chance of winning so take the plea if one is given.
2) Losing a job is scary.
3) Fighting to keep a house and pay bills and food takes courage, perseverance, and faith.
4) My AP wanted to be liked, and I would not give that to her. I should have played the game better, and I did not.
5) I gave my power over to another, the arbitrator. I should have gone with the sure thing, admitted guilt, and kept my job by paying a $4,000 fine.
6) Bosses and management have the upper hand in legal cases.
7) Looking at how I contributed to the problem and make appropriate changes.
8) I can choose to be right, or I can have my peace. Let stuff go more easily.

"Grant me the serenity to accept the things I cannot change,
And the courage to change the things I can,
And the wisdom to know the difference."

20/20 HINDSIGHT ON THE ARBITRATION CASE: I wish I had not followed the advice of Betsy Combs of ATR Connect website. She made $1,500 off me whether I won the case. She told me, "1) Do not settle with the city, and 2) based on my experience, if you go with a UFT-NYSUT attorney, you will lose your arbitration." I lost my case, and in the end, I was the one who made the decision to pursue the arbitration. If I had admitted guilt to the alleged **charges of insubordination, I would have paid a $4,000 fine with a three month suspension from the classroom,** and then got my job back as a NYC teacher. I was informed by Ms. Combs I had a strong case, and my ego believed her. When I told her I wished I had not followed her advice, she posted the arbitration decision on her internet site, making it tough for me to find a job in NY or NJ since most employers do an internet search of potential employees. You would think that would be a breach of client-"paralegal" privilege, but she is not officially a member of the court, and uses her web-site to punish those would question her services.

TITLE OF MY NEXT BOOK ON TEACHING: _The Savage Inequality for Teachers: Administrators sucking the passion from pedagogues stifling by creativity like their hair is on fire and making the classroom boring at the expense of dumbing down young people to become spokes in America's economic wheel, training students in a subconscious way to never question those in authority for the purpose of students only knowing just enough to run machines and shuffle paper for the corporations._ All I can say is to understand what is happening in education today and how it will not improve. Google the three-minute YouTube video of George Carlin riffing in a segment called "The American Dream."

KARMA: Principal Harry was removed from the school in December because the superintedent had received anonymous letters with concerns about his mental state. When you tell teachers and administrators you think your mother needs more oral sex to be happy, you may need some help and need to be moved out of your leadership role. A new principal came in named Principal Trejo. He was a big guy who looked like Rosey Grier, NFL football player for the Rams. Trejo was a former marine and talked most of faculty meetings not giving teachers much time for questions. As a few months went by, it was clear he was not happy with AP Campgreenblatt. She burned bridges with Trejo, thinking she had a job elsewhere, but it fell through. She had to work with Trejo for the whole year in 2013–2014, and he took away her office, put her in the hallway, and gave her classroom sub-coverages. She ended up crying in the hallways about how tough her life was, and I wondered if she even cared about destroying the life a teacher who had lost a license because of her manipulation and deceitful ways. I found out after the arbitration she had not even observed out two most senior teachers for years, just asking for copy of their lesson plan. She had written up false observation reports with satisfactory ratings, but when I had asked for help, she had let me flounder and then pulled the hangman's noose on my career in NYC. Karma, I say. She was transferred out of the High School for Health Careers and Scienes by the new principal for the 2015–2016 year.

2013 - UNEMPLOYMENT: I had lost my job; and I was in disbelief, anger, and fear week. I signed up for unemployment. New York State pays $450, and New Jersey State pays $650. I lived in New Jersey, but I worked in New York, so I collected the lesser amount minus the 10 percent that will go to taxes. I was mowing my lawn and worried and trying to figure out how to make ends meet until I find my next job. I had an extra room. I can take in a renter. If I moved downstairs, that opened up two rooms. I can take in two renters. Among the unemployment, rent and side jobs, and money I was taking out of my pension, which will take two months to receive, I should be able to get by.

I went to the Social Service Office for Passaic County in Wannaque and signed up for food stamps and ended up getting $400 to help pay for heating oil for the upcoming winter. Thank God for Pres. Franklin D. Roosevelt, or I could easily have lost my home and would be living back at home or in a tent. I had visions of the poor traveling to California during the Great Depression in the movie *Grapes of Wrath*. I thought of the the HBO Series *Mildred Pierce* about the woman who got divorced from a drunk husband, and all her struggles in the Great Depression, and how she opened up a restauarant in her home serving baked chicken, potatoes and peas, and a slice of her famous pie. She ended up opening three restaurants in California called Mildred's.

I ate much pasta and frozen vegetables and only bought things on sale, trying to stretch my dollar the best of my ability. While I felt fear, I tried to place my faith in God that my needs will be met. I must testify, each time I needed money, a job, or food, it showed up. I even tried dandelion salad but found the stalks to be extremely bitter even after soaking them in vinegar to kill the bitterness. Unemployment used to be for two years, and then the GOP cut it down to one year, and now it was only good for six months. As long as the GOP holds the majority in the House and/or the Senate, the unemployed are screwed.

9-20-12 - UNCLE DALE JAMES GEIST PASSES (61): Uncle Dale was a few years younger than Dad and the youngest of Fred and Edith Geist's brood. He had cancer, and he looked good at the Geist family summer picnic at Mom and Dad's, but one never knows with this terrible disease. I have heard it is better to send flowers to someone when they are alive than to their funeral. I wrote up a letter of memories of times he and Aunt Sandy included me in their lives and characteristics and sent the letter on July 21.

Uncle Dale was laid-back, laughed a lot, and love the outdoors, hunting and fishing. He and Sandy owned a beautiful farmhouse in Northampton County, Pennsylvania. They raised chickens and pigs and had horses on the farm. They grew vegetables and every year made up a funny-looking scarecrow. Geist summer picnics were held there, and one time Bill Furler got on a pony to ride it and got bucked off. At the picnic, a sixteen-foot aluminum ladder fell on Jody's head; and she was fine until she touched her head, saw blood, and started crying bloody murder. He also put on a great fireworks show at the Geist summer picnics.

Uncle Dale worked at Mack Trucks, was a good union man, and was the first baseman for the Roaches softball team. He loved dogs and had an incredible wife and two children, Jesse and Daniel. He was left-handed, a lefty they called them. He was skinny growing up, and Uncle Tom used to call him The Skin. He loved all the Philadelphia professional sports teams and for the Iron Pigs baseball team. He and Sandy took me skiing at Doe Mountain when I was seven or eight. Sandy and Dale came back from the Montreal Olympics in 1976 and brought me back an autograph of boxing gold medalist Sugar Ray Leonard.

He was an excellent deer hunter, forgetting his hunting boots and using his loafers one time and still got a deer. One time he brought up two left hip boots, and it looked funny to see him walk in circles. Dad and I used to go up to his place for the first day of fishing, and I always enjoyed the Dunkin' Donuts. Dale and Sandy, and the Strohls, and the Lohrmans used to go fishing up in Canada. We went up when I was very young one time. Dale went out night fishing, and he reached in the cooler and pulled out what he thought was a Yoo-hoo, and it turned out to be a bottle of motor oil.

His middle name was my first name, and we both shared the same last name, and we both celebrated our birthdays on March 2. He and his family always listened to my NYC and teaching stories and laughed at them. He had an amazing spirit, and I miss him terribly, and I am glad I was able to share with him what he meant to me before he passed into the next world.

2012 - NEW NEIGHBOR RICHIE: When Kenny moved, I was concerned I might get an obnoxious neighbor. Richie worked for FedEx, took care of his property, and liked to go fishing in his boat. We will sit on the deck, talk, and drink beers. He had a good sense of humor, and after having gone through a divorce, he was finally at a place where he can get his own home. We sat on the deck and said, "See that tree? That's my tree! See that rock? That's my rock." He lived in Paterson with his folks after the divorce and had to fight for parking. He loved having his own driveway. He was so tight with money at one time. If he bought a coffee and bagel, he was over budget. Richie said, "I survived on eggs and macaroni for three years! You have to fill the hole somehow." He now enjoyed his life riding his motorcycle, shooting his BB gun, and often out fishing on the lake on his boat with his fishing buddy. He went to the bar every Thursday night with friends and played darts.

RENTERS - <u>MICHAEL</u>: I made up three ROOM FOR RENT signs and posted them in strategic spots in town. I received a call from Michael. A half hour later, I got a call from Dominick. I set up times to meet them separately. Michael showed up with a friend Kenny. They pulled up in a fairly new pickup truck. Mike said he was a short-order cook, and I asked him my list of questions. I did not ask for a deposit, just pay me $650 a month. I felt good about this tenant, but it was not until later I realized Mike did not have a car. It was his buddy Kenny who drove him to the interview. Mike got the bigger room since I interviewed him before Dominick.

Michael was orignally from Bayonne, New Jersey; was divorced; and had three kids. He was not a drinker. He was in the program. He was a good car mechanic, and he liked to go catfish fishing on Upper Greenwood Lake at nights. He did smoke, and he did love to drink Red Bulls. He was working down at Pennings Farm as a short-order chef, and it was approximately four miles from where I lived. Pennings had been around for thirty years and had apple orchards popular in the fall, a pub and grill, ice cream stand, animal petting zoo. and a beer garden that frequently had bands playing on the weekends.

Mike usually started work about 1:00 p.m. and liked to sleep in. He did not like to be interuppted when sleeping, and Mondays were his day off. When he got up, he coughed and hacked and made all kinds of ungodly noises in the morning. He was Irish and loved to tell stories, and he was a funny guy. After about a year, Mike started working for the Pioneer Bar in Upper Greenwood Lake.

He was not the neatest guy, and his strong odor came out of the room from his dirty laundry, and there were clothing all around his room. He paid his rent for the first six moths, but then I started hearing excuses. When I asked him how much his cigarettes cost, he said $8 a pack coming to 8 x 30 = $240. I asked about his Red Bull, and he said he spent twice as much on Red Bull than on cigerettes. $480 + $240 = $700 a month or $8,400. Imagine if he spent half of that, paid my full rent, and put one-fourth into savings and sent one-fourth of that for child support; but I guess that was not my business. The point was, he had money to pay me but made choices for himself.

Mike usually worked from 1:00 p.m. to 9:00 p.m. as a chef. On two weekends, he picked up a girl from upstate. She had blond hair and was a big girl. They met on the Internet. He picked her up and stayed overnight Friday and hung out at the house all day until Mike got home. He did this for two weekends in a row. Then on Sunday morning, he drove her home. She was nice but one of the neediest people I had ever met.

DOMINICK: When time came to interview Dominick an hour after Mike, I saw two guys walk up the deck. One looked like a twenty-two-year-old college kid; and the other guy looked like a mix of Gene Simmons of the rock band Kiss and Lyle Alzado, defensive end for the Oakland Raiders, and a mix of a pirate with his long curly hair and handlebar mustache. The older guy turned out to be Dominick. He was Italian, a Northern New Jersey officer on disabilty, and he got a monthly check for $2,300 a month. He was funny, loud, and a big guy. Dom also did construction work on the side as a handyman. He was going to Passaic Community College with Jonathon, and they lived together on Northern Long Shore Drive with a landlord they were having trouble with.

Jonathon did modeling and got paid good money for shoots and got to travel to different parts of the world. He also brought gorgeous people to the apartment or to parties who were also models. He worked with Dom at times on construction jobs. They both lived on Northern Lakeshore Drive with another landlord who turned out to be a lech. Dominique and Jonathon fixed the holes in the wall, painted the bathroom and living room, and even put in some fixtures in the bathroom. When it came time to collect the rental deposit, the landlord claimed they damaged the rooms, and he will not give it back to them. Long story short, when they first moved in, they took before and after videos and pictures of the place; and the judge told the landlord he was a terrible person for not giving back the deposit, and he should be grateful for how his former tenants fixed it up.

Dom, or the Big D, was a police officer on disabilty. After fourteen years in, he got T-boned in his police cruiser and was given two-thirds pay with no taxes. Apparently in New Jersey, as a fireman or police officer, you may never work as a cop or fireman if you are on disability, but you can work another job if you are physically able. He worked construction odd and end jobs, painting, roofing, building decks, cuttting down trees, and so forth. He also got a cadillac health insurance plan and went in two to three times a year to get work done on his shoulders, knees, hips, and so forth. He put up a punching bag hanging from the back deck and lifted weights three to four times a week.

Dom hated his ex-wife. He came home one day to find her in bed with another guy. They shared two daughters, and the wife said she wanted a divorce and the house. Dom hired an attorney and said, "Do whatever you have to do, write letters, set up meetings, but I want so much money spent on legal services. There is no house for her to live in. She and her home-breaking boyfriend are not getting my home that I worked so hard for. I worked double shifts, worked security jobs, worked construction on the side for what? For someone to steal the house. We could have sold it and split the money, but I did not even want her to get half the value of the house." When he told this story, his blood pressure went from 1 to 10 quickly.

Dom had a big heart. He used to be a boxing coach at the PAL in North Bergen, working with poor and disadvantaged kids. He had a sister and two brothers, and he grew up in the projects with his parents. His dad worked, and his mom kept the house and was short but ruled with her wooden spoon. She was the tough one, and Dad was the nice guy. Growing up, Dom stayed away from drugs and alcohol. Sports were his salvation. Most of the buddies he grew up with were dead or in jail. He had a cousin who kept telling Dom to sign up with the police force, and he finally did and, to this day, still thanked his cousin for the great life advice.

CAMPFIRES: I love campfires, and so does Dom. When on a construction site, he loaded up his scrap trailer with wood and dumped it behind my shed, and I always had firewood as long as he lived here. I always liked to invite people over, and I preferred we stay away from politics. Dom claimed to be a moderate, but he watched Fox News all the time, hated President Obama, loved Donald Trump, and thought capitalism in its present form in the United States was the greatest thing ever. He was a funny guy; and as long as he stayed on life stories, cop stories, history, culture, or music, then it was a good time; but when I had two people tell me they will no longer come to campfires with Dom there, I had to have a talk with him.

POLICE STORIES: Officer Dom requested a driving partner who did not smoke. The captain refused his request as he was sitting there, smoking behind his desk. The captain said, "Do you want to speak with the lieutenant?" Dom said yes, and he made the same request to the lieutenant, who was also behind a desk smoking a cigerette. "What is the problem, rookie? No, you take your smoking patrol car partner, or you walk a beat by yourself." Dom got his beat, and in one night wrote over fifty tickets. The next day, the captain and lieutenant got a dozen phone calls from complaining civilians. Dom was given a patrol car partner who did not smoke.

Where do confiscated alcohol and fireworks go? To your buddies on the department, that's where. On Dom's first day on the job, he was assigned to an old-timer, and they walked in a local park. The older officer called a kid over and talked with him. The kid made a wise crack, and the older cop took his nightstick and whacked the kid across the shin. He turned to Officer Dom and said, "Let's get some coffee."

Officer Dom was called to the site of a motorcycle accident. The driver was decapitated, and he and a female officer were looking for the head at night along high grassy area along the road with a captain.

Dom said, "Captain, is this what we are looking for?" as he lifted the head by the hair. The female officer threw up.

On a fall Sunday, a small airplane had crashed near some power lines. Dom answered the call to check it out. He got there and saw all the debris lying around. He put his arms on his hips and said, "That poor bastard did not have a chance." He heard someone behind him, and the guy said hello. It turned out to be the lone pilot who had survived the crash and was not hurt. Officer Dom was then told to park his car next to the crash to keep cars from moving in the area of a downed power line. Dom put his head back and fell asleep to hear a knocking on his window. Dom said, "Aren't you Lawrence Taylor?" LT said, "Yeah, Officer, can I get back to those apartments? I have to see my girlfriend." Dom said, "Aren't you married, LT?" LT said, "Ahh, you know how it goes." On his way back, he knocked on Dom's window again to get out, and Dom said, "Good luck in your playoff game today!"

THE GREAT CAPITALIST VS. DEMOCRATIC SOCIALIST DEBATE: I was a landlord, and I didn't want to talk about politics with my renters. I just wanted to have a cordial relationship and collect the check on the first of the month. Dom asked me who I was voting for in the summer of 2015. I said, "I am a Bernie Sanders fan." He went nuts and said, "But he is a socialist! Socialism can never work. We are a capitalist nation!" He also said, "Taxes are stealing." Well, I had taught history for fifteen years, and I had taught economics for at least five of those years.

Regarding taxes, taxes are the price paid for civilization. Taxes are not stealing as long as you 1) get represenation, and 2) you get services for said tax money. He complained about taxes but had a job where his pay came from taxes and where his healthcare came from taxes and where his disability came from taxes. He collects $2400 a month for his Socialist lifestyle and free healthcare and paying no taxes on his disability payments. Is a person legally allowed to work on the side if you collect disability? I don't know the law for N.J. cops disability. If you benefit from taxes, you should not be complaining about paying them. Regarding Democratic socialism:

1) We live in a mixed economy (socialism and capitalism).
2) Under true capitalism, no welfare would be given to corporations.
3) If you would support free college tuition and universal health care as the modern European countries do, then you are a socialist.
4) Socialism saved the banks and Wall Street after the Great Depression and the Great Recession in 2008.
5) Google seventy-five ways America is Socialist. Why, if you have a Social Security card, you are a card-carrying socialist.
6) Bill Gates and Steven Hawking predicted a Socialist future for the United States and world as more and more jobs are taken by machines and computers.

To the Editor,   Summer 2015

You are likely a socialist and don't even know it. Socialism is taxpayer funds used collectively to benefit society as a whole despite income, contribution, or ability. Here are seenty-five ways America is Socialist:

The military, Pentagon, wars, Homeland Security, veterans' health care (VA), CIA, FBI, prison system, Customs and Border Control, Secret Service, court system, corporate/business subsidies, IRS, farm subsidies, police, fire dept., Postal Service, public schools, bridges, roads, garbage collection, public landfills, public libraries, museums, Social Security, public parks, sewer Systems . . .

And Medicare, Medicaid, GI Bill, Hoover Dam, state/city zoos, town/state parks, disability insurance, state construction, unemployment insurance, Metro buses, WIC, state snow removal, Amtrak, state and national monuments, food stamps, free lunch program, FDA, health care for 9/11 workers . . .

And bird flu vaccine, swine flu vaccine, Centers for Disease Control, welfare, FEMA, public defenders, PBS, NPR, OSHA, USDA, government scholarships, Census Bureau, government officials, Congressional Health Care, EPA, Dept. of Health and Human Services, Dept. of Energy, Dept. of Education, Dept. of Justice, peace corps, National Weather Service, the White House, government, law, and civilization.

Democratic socialism embraces capitalism. Socialism without capitalism is the command economy of communism. Capitalism without socialism is fascism; pretty easy to understand. Now if voters understood America is really a plutocracy, a country run by 1 percent, and voted for SEN. BERNIE SANDERS, we could begin changing the "rigged system" that keeps the majority in poverty wages without benefits or a pension.

Jim Geist Hewitt, New Jersey

FENCE JOB WITH DOM IN SOUTHERN NEW JERSEY:
Dom told me he had an easy fence job in Southern New Jersey for some friends, and we will need to stay there for two nights. I needed

the money and said sure. The couple was gay and going to marry in the spring. They had two dogs and a pool in the fenced-in area. Home Depot had dropped off the new wooden fencing, which was heavy. We cut down the old fencing and placed the new fencing on the old posts. We got it down to a system.

On the second night, I went to the story with the macho guy, and we bought some food and picked up some liquior. We ate Tony Romo ribs that night, and it made me a little sick. In the evening, I went on Match.com to see if I have had any hits. The effeminate partner was drunk and came in the room and played this techno music and started dancing next to me. He then leaned over to plant a kiss on me. I put out my hand and said, "Sorry, pal!" He went in the other room, fell off the couch, and slept on the floor that night. In the morning, I asked Dom for some chalk 'cause I want to draw a chalk police line around the dead body. I was glad when the job was over. Mr. Roboto creeped me out.

On the way back, Dom told me before he got drunk, he told Dom he wanted to show him something. He pulled down his pants, and his left leg was all bruised. Apparently, the butch fiancé kept kicking him in the leg. Maybe this is a peron not to marry, but I have enough of my own issue I need to focus on.

WORKING WITH DOM: I had been a housepainter thirty summers. Dom got a job staining a deck and asked me if I wanted work. I said sure, and I was grateful. We worked together and listened to the radio, and when we finished, we cleaned up, and I got paid. I also helped him stain another deck, and it went well. He asked me later in the summer if I wanted work in Warwick staining a deck. He tolld me it was a big job, and he will be hiring two other people. I said fine.

He asked me to drive his car over, and he drove his truck over. I would really like to have my car. This way, if I want to leave for whatever reason, I can. The day started out fine with Dom staining with myself and the two youngsters. He then said, "I have to pick up supplies" and left. He came back an hour later, stained for fifteen minutes, and said, "I have to take a dump. I am going home to dump." I said, "We have hand towels here, and you can go in the woods over there." "Oh, no, I have to use a toilet." He left. He came back an hour later and said, "Hey, you guys want something to drink?" He left and came back with some Gatorades. He said, "What do you want for lunch?" He left and came back with some salads. Now it was nice he bought lunch, but then again, we three were doing the work, and he was acting like a lazy asshole boss. I saw a greedy, lazy side of a friend I had never seen before. After lunch, he was gone for one and a half hours supposedly on some estimates.

I was really pissed because I thought he was going to work with us. In the afternoon, the sun was hot, and we were not in shade anymore. I was tired, and I was upset and feeling used. It was his job, and I had no problem with him making a profit, but I had a problem when I felt I was being used as a working stiff dupe. I told him I needed the keys to the car because I needed to get something. At 3:00 p.m., I got in the car and headed home. At 3:30 p.m., I got a call. "Where are you? You need to come back because I have my driver's license in the car." I didn't pick up.

When he came back to the house, he asked, "What happened?" I said, "Your greedy, lazy side of yourself happened!" I told him I didn't need the money so badly that I can be treated like a college summer worker. He went into the "This is America. This is capitalism. This is my business. I can do what I want" speech. I said, "Yeah, it is America, so I left because that is called freedom. I don't care about your job. You can hire a Mexican, for all I care. Pay me what you owe me, and that's that."

I then remember I gave an estimate on a job and told him we could go 50/50 on the job. I said, "You know the job I got on Lebanon Ave?

Remember how I was going to go 50/50 with you? You have inspired me with your capitalist profit-making speech. You have changed my mind. I am going to pay you $12.50 an hour and keep the rest of the profits. How do you feel about that?" He looked at me, amazed and stunned. "Ahhhh, well, umm, yeah, you can do that. You would be the boss." The pregnant pause was eight and a half months long.

In the end, we came to an understanding. The next job he asked me to help on, he said, "You want a job? I promise not to leave the job site!" I said thanks and didn't work with him again. I will just collect my monthly rent from him as he waxed eloquently how he will be in the 1 percent in ten years. Since he did not have intertie wealth as the Rockefellers and the Du Ponts, he will never enter the 1 percent, but he could become a millionaire and good for him if he did so. I don't begrudge the rich as long as they pay their fair share in taxes and pay living wages and treat people with dignity, not just as a means to an end for higher profits and stock increases.

BROTHERS IN ARMS: I am grateful for Dom. He fixed the showerhead pipe by re-tapping it to put on a new showerhead. He took two and a half days to build steps from my property down to the firepit area. When a vehicle needed to go to the garage, we gave each other rides there. We loaned money to each other. We made meals for each other. He said I was the best brother he had. I am grateful for the other renters as well. When I first got them, I was concerned about privacy and safety issues; but in the end, it was like gaining brothers. It became a family where we help each other out, and when we sat on the deck and talked, we shared our life stories and interesting and funny conversatioins for the most part.

Dom was loud and liked to talk to his TV and rant about politics. His steroid use contributed to his anger, but for the most part, his last three months, he did really well staying away from bringing up politics, and I appreciated him repecting those boundaires. He cleaned the bathroom weekly, paid his rent on time, and was always willing to give a helping hand if I needed one.

LIMA: After living at my place for one year, Mick asked if his nephew can move in with him. This way, I got my $700, and Mick can split the rent with his nephew. His nephew Lima was also a smoker and ended up getting a job at Pennings. Mick was the short-order chef, and Lima was in charge of the donuts and working in the fields helping trim the apple trees. He was a young man at age twenty-three. Lima needed a car to get to work, and there was a car for $700 he wanted to buy. I wrote up a contract with him dated November 18, 2014, and loaned him $700, and he moved out three weeks later, and I heard he had blown the money on marijuana. He moved to Florida with his dad until he was kicked out, moved to Jersey City with his mom, and then moved out to Pennsylvannia to stay with family friends. I contacted him on Facebook, asking when can I get some money, around $100 a month. He said he did not have the money even though I knew he was working at the Giant Food Store in Pen Argyl.

I called the Heanies who the kid was living with, and Mr. Heanie agreed Wilson should pay me $100 a month. After six weeks, it was clear the kid (twenty-three) was not going to pay me. I called my father, and he said I should take the kid to court. I had to hire a detective for $100 to find the correct address of the Heanies. I then wrote up a complaint to the magistrate's office in Pen Argyl, Pennsylvania to be served by a constable. I paid $140 for filing and constable service charges. If he was not home, he cannot be served.

On March 1, 2016, I was told by Judge Schelgel that the defendant can refuse a certified letter, and he did not have to accept a subpoena. I said to the judge, "Why even have a magistrate's court if you have no power?" The judges said, "Mr. Geist, you are right, the perpetrator has more rights than the victim. This case has bothered me more than most. Mr. Calihan does not have the same values as you or I."

GEIST BOARDING HOME LIKE A CATHOLIC WORKER HOME: I must admit I did not like the idea of people moving into my home. What if they turn out to be truly annoying or loud or messy or inconsiderate? In the end, the guys turned out to be like brothers, except for Wilson. It was nice having company and sharing stories and supporting one another. Dom could do work on the house, Mike was good at fixing cars, and we could each give one another a lift when a car needed to be taken to a mechanic and so forth. The two bedrooms upstairs were occupied, and I moved all my stuff down to the first floor. It made living quarters tight, having to move stuff from the upstairs rooms to the the attic, shed, workroom, and my new bedroom downstairs, but one does what needs to be done to survive. I even liked Wilson, but I thought he was touched in the head, and I learned lessons from the experience.

DEBTORS ANONYMOUS: What I learned most from this program was one does not need a lot of money to be prosperous. You can be wealthy moneywise but unprosperous in your heart and view of life. I also learned my ultimate security comes from knowing God provides, and whenever I needed work or money, it showed up. Truly amazing. As long as I have my health, family, and friends, I am prosperous.

4-17-16 - JUDGE SHERWOOD GRIGGS IS OLD AND GRUMPY: COMMONWEALTH OF PA (HEANIES) VS. JIM GEIST FOR HARRASSMENT: I received a notice from the magistrate's office in Bangor, Pennsylvania, from Clarissa Haverland claiming I had harassed her by sending notices of *Geist vs. William O'Brien* at her workplace and home address and that a detective came to their home to confirm their address. I was amazed that sending a legal notice to residence of defendant can be considered harrassment. I spoke with an attorney in New Jersey. He told me I did nothing wrong and that I should use the "reasonable defense":

1) It was reasonable for me to send a legal notice to the defendant's home.
2) I may send a notice to the defendant according to Pennsylvania Code 403 Service by mail.
3) It was not my intent to harass:
   a) It was to inform defendant of a court date.
   b) I was within the law.

JUDGE MUPPETS WALDORF: The judge reminded me of the two old "hecker" guy who sat in the upper box seats and heckled people. This was exactly what Griggs did to me. He served as a magistrate for twenty-nine years from 1969 to 1999, just six months shy of getting a full pension. When asked if he would work another six months to go from 70 percent to 100 percent pension, he said, "I told the voters I would not run again . . . and it is a stressful job and tough on the family." He was fifty-five in 1999, which would make him seventy-two in 2016. He came back to serve after Judge Todd Strohe died in March of 2015 at age fifty-five. Griggs replaced Strohe, and then Griggs was replaced by Bangor, Pennsylvania attorney Alicia Rose Zito, daughter of Judge Leonard Zito. She will serve the seat until the next election in 2017. Each term is six years long.

I went to the magistrate's office with my wife, Helen, and my father showed up for moral support. Judge Griggs was old and cranky and a Democrat to boot. The judge asked me if I was harassing these people. I said no. He said, "Look at the letters you sent to them." He gave me a chance to defend myself. I had ten different files with documents to prove my case, and into my third sentence, he cut me off. "You don't think you harassed them, do you?" I said, "Is it harrassment if the magistrate's office sends a legal document to the defendant?" The judge did not answer. I asked if it was harassment to hire a detective to get a correct address. The judge said, "Are you trying to tell me the law? See this Pennsylvannia legal book? I helped write this. You think I don't know the law? You did all this over $600? You needed to find another way to send the information to your defendant!" I asked, "How, Your Honor, would I do that?" Judge Griggs said, "I could could charge you with forty counts of harrassment. Did you know that?" Dad was behind me and kicked my chair. I knew the case was over. I had no fair hearing in presenting my case. The judge called me up to his bench, and I told him I had to take a day off work to come for the trial. He said, "If you had not shown up, my $600 fine would have been much, much higher."

GETTING "HOMETOWNED" BY THE LOCAL JUDGE: When the case was over, Helen had tears in her eyes. The judge charged me $300 times two for two counts of harrassment. She said, "The judge would not let you speak." Dad looked at Helen who was in the midst of getting her green card and said, "Do you still want to be a citizen?" He looked at me and said, "You were guilty of being from New Jersey ." I called my New Jersey attorney friend to tell him what happened, and he said, "You were hometowned, my friend."

I filed an appeal, and my court date was set for Wednesday, August 24, 2016. My attorney said he had had problems like this before with this judge. So much for justice in the courts of land. I never wanted to set foot in courtroom or arbitration room ever. Dad asked me if I learned anything. I said, "You cannot expect justice in the courts." What I wanna say was "Yeah, I should not have taken your advice to take this to court!" He recommended it to me four months earlier. Sometimes you win, sometimes you get "hometowned!"

I went to Danielsville the weekend of Father's Day 2016. Helen and I went out with my folks to celebrate Father's Day at a local diner for breakfast. Who sat next to us but Judge Grigg, and I assumed to be his daughter. They sat, and there was no converstation between them. It made me feel sad for him or her or both of them. I recognized him right away. He looked at me several times and said nothing. He was trying to place who I was or where he had seen me before. As we left, I told Mom and Dad, "That was Griggs next to us." Dad said, "That guy is a miserable prick!" I said, "Now, now, Dad, he is a fellow Democratic brother."

APPEALING JUDGE CURMDGEON'S DECISION: I hired Atty. Glen Goodge and appealed the decision, and the date for the hearing at the Norhampton County Court in Pennsylvania was set for October 26, 2016.

LETTER TO THE MAGISTRATE'S OFFICE

Dear Bangor, Pennsylvania, Magistrate's Office 8-30-16

I started working on my book, *Modern Augustinian Confession*, in April of 2016. As of today, I will be sending my manuscript to the editor and publisher of the book.

While there is not much I can do after being "hometowned" by Judge Grigg, I can appeal, and thanks to the First Amendment of the United States, I have now included the injustice of his decision in Haverland vs. Geist in my book. I want my family, friends, and general public to know how justice in Bangor, Pennsylvania, with Judge Griggs works when you are an "out-of-stater." I am confident I will win my appeal.

I did grow up in Allentown, Pennsylvania, and lived in the Valley from 1966 to 1990. I am also a Democrat as Judge Grigg is.

The book should be out on Amazon in November of 2016, and I hope many in your office purchase it ($24). It includes many funny stories about ministry, human rights, teaching, recovery work, and injustice in your court system.

My appeal is taking place in mid-December in the Northampton County Court, and I will be represented by Matthew Goodge, esq.

Jim Geist
Hewitt, New Jersey

MIKE MOVES OUT: In the comedy movie *History of the World* by Mel Brooks, when King Louis the sixteenth had to pee, he called for "the piss boy," a boy who had a bucket for him to pee in. Harvey Keitel played the king, and as the boy started to walk away, he says, "Wait for the shake!" Because I was now living downstairs and did not want to wake my renters by walking up the stairs to the bathroom, like *Little House on the Prairie*, I had a pee bucket in the workroom.

One day at approximately three o'clock in the morning, I went in workroom to do my business. My Venetian blinds were down, but apparently, as Mike walked by the workroom on his way up the back deck stairs this ungodly hour, he could see my backside as I was whizzing. The next morning, Mike said, "I have to talk with you. I am moving out because you freaked me out last night. I don't know how to say this, but I saw you playing with yourself last night." I explained to Mike about my pee bucket, but he did not believe me. In the end it does not matter because of J.A.D.E. I never have to justify, argue, defend or explain myself, unless I want to.

I believed Mike did not have enough money to pay his rent and was gas-lighting me. That is when a person manipulates you to get you to question your sanity. I said, "You are a big boy, and if you need to move, go ahead. I don't have to defend myself for urinating in my own home." He moved out three days after and never paid me the balance of his rent. Before he moved, I made a sign and hung it outside my workroom window that saids, "Beware of the Mad Pisser." Mike did not find it amusing, but Dom and Helen laughed at the sign.

THE BLUE VOLKSWAGON: Mike made plans to move to Las Vegas or to California. He was never clear about where he moved and never left an address. I did have his phone number, which was something. He moved to another place in West Milford for cheaper rent and, before moving out West, wanted to know if he can park his blue Volkswagon in my yard until the buddy he sold it to picked it up. The short story is the buddy did not show up. The car was parked next to my garden through winter into the spring. I filled out information for New Jersey to find out who owned the car so I can legally get it towed. It turned out New Jersey said the car belonged to the owner of the Pioneer Bar on top of the mountain.

PHIL: Mike and Will moved out, and I got a call from Phil. He came over for an interview, and we had a mutual friend from Living World Alliance Church in Upper Greenwood Lake. He worked as a general laborer at West Point, and he was in the military for four to five years and did a tour in Iraq, serving as a security officer at one of the bases. He was estranged from his wife, and they had two kids together.

He told me he cannot pay the $650 I was asking for, so I told him I will charge him $500 rent. He had an old station wagon with the wooden panels, and it was old and rusted, but he kept it running. Phil was also a decent guitar player, but again, I had a rent not paying his full freight.

He will sometimes go to the bar, and he really wanted his marriage to work, but he had a girlfriend named Jessie who worked at a bar. He will hang out with her cigarettes and buy her drinks, but not just beer; she wanted the $10 shots. He told me he had paid her money to stay overnight with her, but they did not have sex. Jessie lived with her mother and had a boyfriend, and it was not Phil. He said, "Jessie is a dancer, not a hooker." So I had a guy spending money at the bar and on his "girlfriend who is a dancer, not a hooker."

I can tell when Phil was home because there was a glass in the bathroom where he placed his removable partial dentures. When he was a kid, he wiped out on his bike and smashed his mouth on the curb. When I saw his teeth, he was in his room, and when I didn't see them in the glass above the toiliet, I knew he was not home.

Phil's parents had passed, and he had inherited $30,000. He bought a nice blue 2007 Mustang. He told me about how he had loaned money to a coworker and how he wanted to pay the bail for Jesse who was in jail. I said, "Phil, you do realize that you never fully paid for your rent. Everytime you come here to visit and tell me these stories, I feel like you are slapping me in the face. Please don't tell me about loaning people money unless you want to throw some presidents my way."

NEW JERSEY GOVERNOR CHRISTIE AND NEWARK MAYOR CORY BOOKER AND CHARTER SCHOOLS: Even though Newark mayor Cory Booker was a Democrat, he wanted to make Newark the charter school capital of america. Booker and Governor Christie worked with the $100 million donated by Facebook founder Mark Zuckerberg. To read about it, google the article in *The Atlantic*, "Schooled," by Dale Russakoff (May 19, 2014) about it. Booker became senator of New Jersey in August of 2013. Zuckerberg did believe teachers are one of the most important jobs in urban centers when it comes to helping lift kids out of poverty.

MAY 2016 - The philosophy of the Newark Leadership Academy leadership is "Don't call us unless there is a gun, knife or blood on the floor." Our school was the last chance high school for our kids. Most had been kicked out of other Newark High Schools for behavioral issues. The year before, a teacher had his car stolen. I guess he should not have left his keys on the floor. Another teacher, our gym teacher, was assaulted by a student the year before; however, he should have known better because he got into more trouble for protecting himself than the kid who attacked him.

I had my cell phone stolen the month before. I left it on my desk and locked my door, but the door had not fully shut. The kid sneaked around every day during lunch to check class doors. He found my phone, took it to the library, hid it in a secret place, and at the end of the day had a $700 Samsung Galaxy 5 phone to sell on the streets. Luckily, security caught him on camera, and I got the phone back. Good thing because I sold it on eBay and used Paypal to collect money from the customer named Wang from San Francisco, only to realize, I was scammed by someone, had mailed the phone overnight via UPS, and now only had to pay another $500 for my stolen phone for the next five months.

HELEN AND DOMINICK VISIT NEWARK LEADERSHIP ACADEMY: I asked Dominick to speak to the kids about being a police officer. He told them about growing up in the projects, and most of his friends were in prison or dead. He talked about how he never was attracted to alcohol or drugs but loved sports. He talked about being a police officer and how he trained kids to box at the PAL program. Jason saw Dominick and said, "You are a killer!" On the way home, Helen said she cannot believe how rude and disrespectful so many of the students were. Dominick said he will pray a Novita prayer for me every day because of the populations I worked with.

Teachers had free time from 3:00 p.m. to 4:00 p.m. For me, it was an opportunity to straighten out the desks, clean up the room, work on lessons, and/or correct classwork. It had been a tough year. When you have no deans, no discipline, no detentions, the students knew they can get away with almost anything.

Getting cursed at was a daily experience and considering I just had a student slap me in the stomach twice in the course of five minutes with no punishment for him or any meeting with the admin and myself to hear the story and to give me any empathy. In addition, I had taken the hat of an insubordinate student a few days earlier and tossed it down the hallway because he refused to take his foot out of the doorway for me to close the door. He was unwilling to get a pass from where he came from. I had to speak the language only a thug could understand. He said, "I should hit you!" I say, "Please, that would be a felony, and then I would not have to see you for one year."

It had been a quiet few weeks, quiet in regard to not seeing or hearing from administrators over the last few weeks. I had sent e-mails asking for feedback, but the response was deafening and unsettling. I enjoyed the quiet and thought, *It is nice to be trusted and treated like a professional.* I guess they must trust me, or perhaps it is the quiet before the storm.

MOVIE - *MCFARLAND, USA*: It was 3:30 p.m., and AP Gonzalez ha just asked me to meet with him in his office. The evening before, Helen and I went to see the movie *McFarland* in which Kevin Costner played Coach Jim White, cross-country coach of a California High School, working with mostly Mexican American kids of field workers. In the summer, most of the kids would rise at 4:00 a.m. to go to the fields, putting in twelve hours of backbreaking work and then at 6:00 p.m. would join the Coach White for cross-country practice. White always told the guys to do their best and helped inspire the kids to reach for personal and career goals they would not have otherwise. At the end of the movie, Helen looked over and said, "Jim, why do you have tears?" I said, "Because this is what teaching is about—hope, encouragement, and inspiration. That is why I love being a teacher." In twenty years of coaching, Coach White helped the team win nine California state championships.

AP Gonzalez asked me to go to his office. "Sure thing, boss," I said. He was the Spanish version of actor Matt Dillon. He was a handsome man but with a hair too slick for me. It was tough for me to trust someone who rarely laughed. I said, "Sure, no problem." As we walked to his room, I asked him when he will be having his knee operation and how long the recovery will take place. As he was answering, and I walked in the room, and there at his long desk was the principal and a security agent. I thought, *Ahhhh, this is not good.* "Mr. Geist, this is the toughest part of my job as principal."

The principal was a good-looking Jew with Communist parents who were both professors at Ivy League schools. He was a good man with a good heart who cared for the poor. He looked like actor Dennis Boutsikaras, a former resident of Nyack, NY, whose home I painted back in the summer of 1992. I too have a good heart and care for the poor. What is going on here?

"We have to let you go."

"Why?"

"I cannot legally tell you."

"Does this have anything to do with Jason or Raheem?"

"I cannot legally say."

"So you guys are serious, don't contact us unless there is a gun, knife, or blood on the floor?"

Silence.

"So I have no right to hear from my accuser's?"

"Why don't you ask your union rep?"

"I don't have a union rep."

"Exactly."

"That's it?"

"We have three to four boxes for you to pack up. We will give you a month's severance package with your health care and pay to give you time to find another job."

"I understand. I will pack up."

"What does he mean this is the toughest part of his job?" M. Scott Peck said that employers are never 100 percent sure when they fire someone. Judge Owens said, "My decisions are not final because I am always right, I am right because I am final." I guess it is the same at a workplace, especially if the workers don't have a union rep on sight or if you are a Newark teacher without tenure, which takes four years. I called the Newark Teachers Union, and they told me, "Mr. Geist, before you get tenure, they can blame you for the rain and fire you as a result."

I hope I have had enough time working in New Jersey to be able to collect unemployment, and it turned out I had. Thank God for Pres. FDR and for unemployment insurance. I would have surely lost my home had it not been for that. I must sign up for unemployment, update my résumé, and start looking for another job. Working can be hard, searching for employment is harder. My new job is to find a job.

I had been through this before. I signed up for unemployment, lived one day at a time, kept doing the next right thing, sent out résumés, and in time, I found another job at Merit Prep Charter School across the street from the Newark City Hall.

Part VI: Mellowing (Friends And Privacy Important)

<u>Do I want to be right, or do I want my serenity?</u>

CHAPTER 15

Merit Prep Charter School Newark, New Jersey Age 49 2015–2016

GETTING RE-REMARRIED: On January 11, 2016, I married Helen Estrella Pagaduan. On January 12, I started my new teaching job at a different charter school in Newark, New Jersey.

HELEN ESTRELLA PAGADUAN - FILIPINO: She grew up in the province an hour outside of Manila in the Philippines. She was petite, four feet eleven inches, and weighed 114 pounds. Her family were farmers who planted and picked rice mostly but also grew other vegetables. The rice field was coverd in water, and they worked in their bare feet. They lived outside of their local village where the school was. It was a tough life, and they lived in what was called a nipa hut, and it was near the local road. She had one brother and three sisters. All six of them lived in the small hut, and sometimes the roof leaked when it rained. They did not eat much meat, but they ate a frequent diet of fish; and when they cannot afford fish, the picked and ate vegetables with their rice. They used their right hand for eating. To get water, they had to take a bucket to the water pump.

FOOD: Sometimes they added sugar, or soy sauce, or ketchup with salt onto the rice if there was nothing else to eat. There was something called stinky fish or dried fish. You take it and soak it in water like you would with lentils until it gets soft. Dogs over there were not seen as pets. They just ran around the villages as they did in Africa. I asked her if she had ever eaten dog, and she said no. Of course, on the Lewis and Clark expedition across the West, they always bought as many dogs as they could from the American Indians because they thought it was the best meat they could get ahold of. They liked to capture frogs and eat the legs, and they also did the same with grasshoppers. Fried grasshopper and frog legs was living.

SCHOOL: The Philippines is very Catholic, part of the influence of the Spanish that took the Philippines over in their conquests. It is illegal to get a divorce in the Philippines even today. The school is a Catholic school, and you have to pay to go, and you have to bring your own supplies, and you need to wear the school uniform. There is much respect shown for elders, teachers, and the priests. A sign of respect is called *mano*, where you take the person you respect by the hand, and you take it to touch your forehead. The teachers are tough. They used sticks to hit the kids, and if you give a wrong answer, they will grab you by the skin of your belly or side and pinch it or hit you. When Helen was not able to bring a lunch to school, she was given porridge to eat.

CHURCH AND MARKET: Her mother went to church every Sunday and brought all the kids. She would go to market after church to buy food. Helen and her sister usually helped with buying food for the family. It was a half hour away, so they took a jeep taxi or a tricycle to the village. Helen liked church, the singing, looking at the glass windows, hearing the stories, the smell of incense, and the sound of the priests ringing bells.

HOME LIFE: Her father did not go to church. He liked to drink and smoke cigarettes. Many of the men drink and smoke in the Philippines. Sometimes her dad would get mean and would hit the mother or the kids. For fun, the kids liked to climb coconut trees, mango trees, and banana trees. Helen had marks on her legs from all her tree-climbing days. She and her friends sat in the tree and ate their fruit and sometimes made monkey noises to one another. For Christmas, they had a small exchange of gifts, usually corn or banana chips. It was tough to get grapes or apples in the Philippines for some reason. Sometimes they had no gifts to exchange, but the family went to church and then had a nice Christmas meal afterward. She and her sisters liked to pinch one another, to goad one another, but supposedly in love.

HELEN'S EX-HUSBAND: Helen married Monico, and they had three children, two boys and a girl. In 2016, the daughter and eldest son were in college in the Philipines. Her youngest should start college in 2018. Her husband at the time liked to drink and did not make enough money for the family to survive. There were times there was not enough food for them to eat. There were times her husband got drunk and hit her and sometimes the kids. The only way for her family to survive was for one of them to go to another country to work. The husband was not willing to be the one to sacrifice, and Helen was forced to find work in another country, working as a nanny.

HONG KONG - THE WEBBERS: Helen got her work visa and worked with a rich family that was American, and the husband worked with a hedge fund that was based in New York City, London, and Hong Kong. She started working with the family in Hong Kong, and they had three kids—a newborn, a two-year-old, and a ten-year-old. They lived on a yacht down at the boat docks for five years. She watched their young son and daughter. They took Helen on vacations so she can babysit their kids while they lived the high life. She was able to get back to the Philippines twice a year for seven days each trip, and it was tough for her to be away from the her three kids; but the only way they can afford to live in a home, have food, and go to school was for her to sacrifice. The family eventually moved to NYC at 13 Gay Street in Greenich Village, and this was how Helen got her visa into the United States, and she worked her sixth year with them. They paid Helen the equivalent of $400 a week for sixty hours or $6.66 an hour from 2005 to 2010.

RICHIE-RICHES MOVE TO NYC: The Webbers gave her a cell phone and told her she can use it to keep in contact with her family in the Philippines. At the end of the year, they told Helen she owed them $20,000 for use of the phone, and she will have to work for the family for free for the next year. They never said Helen had to pay to use the phone. If they expected that, 1) they should have told her up front, and 2) they should have expected her to pay monthly. Helen was hurt, saddened, and angered her bosses would try to exploit her like this. She began to look for another job and found one in Livingston, New Jersey.

LIVINGSTON, NEW JERSEY - THE BAYGULLS: Helen found a job from Mila, a Filipino friend. She raised a two-year-old boy and a newborn girl. This family had their own business, they owned two dogs, and they were very messy. In addition to raising children, Helen washed and folded their clothing, cleaned the house, and had to let the dogs out to do their business. They paid her $500 a week for sixty hours of work coming to $8.33. She worked with the Baygulls for four years. Helen got one day off a week, and she took the bus to NYC to get out of Livingston. The family she lived with was Jewish, and in the four years Helen worked with them, they only gave her one week off for vacation.

PULLED OVER BY COPS TWICE IN TEN MINUTES: I had a date with a hot Filipina in NYC. I drove down the mountain and came to the cross drive of Marshall Hill Road and Greenwood Lake Turnpike where ABC Paintball was. There was a big dump truck ahead of me. He pulled out, and I passed him, but I did not see the West Milford policeman. I drove over a double line to pass the truck and started speeding toward Ringwood. After thirty seconds, I saw the patrol car behind me; the red lights went on. He asks, "What's the hurry?" I said, "I have a hot date in NYC, and I did not want to follow that slow truck for the next two to three miles until I got the chance to pass him." The officer said, "Wow, you are honest." I showed him my PBA card that Officer Renter Dom had given me, and then the officer gave me a break. I was lucky, speeding a crossing over a double line.

I got one mile a way and started speeding again next to the Monksville Resovoir. Before I can slow down, I saw a Ringwood officer hiding on a hill between some pine trees. He pulled out and put his lights on. I pulled over. I told him the story I told the West Milford officer, and he said, "I understand. I will give you a ticket for not having your seat belt on. That is $25 and no points. Drive safely and have fun on your date." I met Helen at the Port Authority in NYC. It was worth it.

HELEN'S BOSSES - WE DON'T LIKE JIM: At this point, Helen told her husband she wanted a divorce and met me on a dating website. I was not allowed to pick her up at their home. I must meet her at the Starbucks in town. After dating for about a month in November, I got a call on my way to work to Newark Leadership Academy on a very cold December morning. It was Elyse on the phone, and she said, "You better come over and pick up your girlfriend. We fired her, and she was on the sidewalk in front of the house." I said, "What? Listen, I cannot pick her up until after school. If you have thrown her out, at least take her to the mall or Starbucks or the police stations so she can stay warm." Then the nutcase went on, "We love Helen. She is like family." I said, "You have a strange way of showing love to your family by throwing them out in the cold and by giving them only one week vacation in four years."

Her husband, Adam, took the phone, and I heard his voice, and he said, "Jim, don't come over to our place to pick Helen up. If you do, I will have you arrested for trespassing!" I said, "Make sure there a lot of police there because I will have you two arrested for kidnapping and enslavement!" Click. He hung up the phone. I ended up picking her up on a Friday afternoon after school at the police station with her luggage bags and garbage bags full of clothing and personal items. She had nowhere to go, so I took her home with all her stuff.

It was a blessing to have a happy person in my life who enjoyed simple things and was able to enteratain herself. She can live in the present and was not an empty well. In fact, she often showed love and appreciation and public displays of affection, and I liked that.

DECEMBER 2015 - MS. UNIVERSE: Steve Harvey was the announcer for the Ms. Universe constest, and it came down to Ariadna Gutiérrez, Ms. Colombia, who looked like actress Sofia Vergara of *Modern Family*, and Ms. Pia Alonzo Wurtzbach of the Philippines. I was watching the program with my wife, and it was 10:55 p.m. Harvey announced the winner as Ms. Colombia! Ms. Colombia was crowned, the place went crazy, she did her victory lap, and embraced her victory for four minutes until out Mr. Harvey, in his white tuxedo with his head down, walked back on the stage, and he said, "I have made a mistake. It is Ms. Philippines who has won." Ms. Colombia looked shocked.

Ms. Philippines looked shocked and had the $30,000 topaz crown placed on her head, and she looked in the camera with a puzzled look as Steve Harvey apologized again, and the show ended and went to commercial, and I wondered if what we saw really happened. Then I thought, *This was staged to get the public talking about the event and to get more people to watch the program the following year.* It was so surreal it had to be faked. I called Helen, my Filipina fiancée Ms. Universe for a few weeks after this incident.

On January 15, Harvey invited both ladies on his program to apologize; and to me, it was clear by how broken up he was. He did make an honest mistake. He invited both ladies on the program to get closure. He did not want to do any interviews until he made things right with both ladies. At least Ms. Colombia got more recognition than the second place winners in the past. Harvey really honored her by running a nice tape of where she came from, about her family history, and about the different causes she was involved in. Ms. Colombia gave Harvey a hug as he tear up. Ms. Philippines said to Harvey, "It's time to move on. Don't beat yourself up. Be happy."

MERIT PREP CHARTER SCHOOL

Sixth-Graders

OWLS (ninety minutes)

Casey playing with Pokémon cards	Ayanah and Jordan sitting in the wrong seats
Kiara speaking loudly	Tajanae eating fried chicken
Karasma playing music loudly	Obajie, Jonathon playing video games
Groups of girls talking	Groups of boys talking
Patrice jumping over chairs and tables	Arvin trying to start a fight with someone
Spec. ed. Jasmine and Bryce play fighting	Joseph was tattling on someone
Noah sitting in the wrong seat	Kamora was singing

Noah talking back

Patrice screeched a high-pitched girl scream

Kimberly squeaking her sneakers on the floor

Someone playing music loudly on computer

Kamora, sweet . . . all of sudden became witchy

Ameesha sweet and quiet, smiled

Obajie goes "huuuh!" loudly

Deyanna, Sam, and Jon were doing their work

Carlene and Taneja were playing on cell phones

Trezer is e-mailing Laura

Bryce is making a low humming noise "hhhhmmmmmmm."

TIGERS (ninety minutes)

Kayla and Aalyiah were out of their seats, talking and not following directives.

Several came up to the teacher to told him what he should be doing and how to do it.

Nicholas was talking, and talking, and talking for the whole period every day.

Dayvonne was dancing and dabbing.

Juwanza and Earl were playing video games.

Ty-jamire was out of his seat walking around.

Cidney wass working in a corner quietly.

Rashod made annoying whistling noises.

Janise and Taicha were talking.

Neals and Kwadjo were listening to music.

Osa was in the corner working by himself quietly.

Blessing was doing her work.

Taicha was out of her seat and not doing work.

Mabi and Judayah were talking loudly.

Sania was working but talked loudly.

Kwadjo, and Brandon were working.

Mabi was working on Taicha's hair.

Jaheim was dancing around.

GATORS (ninety minutes)

Justin was out of his seat at least five to six times a day and asked the teacher questions.

Kervin will play video games, walk around, and not listen to teacher directives.

Razere will get out of his seat three to four times and come up to the teacher to ask questions.

Kyra and Shavaugh will be sweet but in a second can become witchy and will rat you to admin.

Tyrese, Junior, and Kervin were in the corner playing video games.

Junior was in his wrong seat and sneaked out it three times during the period.

Jesse worked alone quietly.

Stacey was talking and doing no work.

Yolanda and Yolanda were talking and not working.	Joseph was picking his nose.
Taniah was sitting on the floor instead of her seat.	Zariah had just cursed someone out loudly.

*Students will run to the principal's office to complain about you.

*Students will send e-mails to the principal complaining about a teacher.

*Talking level was to be a 1 (whispering). It was often at level 2 (talking normally) or often level 3 (talking loudly or screaming) for most of the period.

*Sadly, if you let the kids play video games, play their music, and don't stress them about doing class work, they will not complain to the administration about you.

To Principal Harvey and AP Miller of Merit Prep Charter in Newark

Date: Monday 4-11-16   From: Jim Geist

Re: GEIST Response About Two Days Without Pay Suspension Decision

In our meeting, Principal Harvey said he chose to discipline me for speaking inappropriately (telling a student on the seventh time) he had to move his arse to a sixth-grade student. I agree 100 percent with Principal Harvey. Regardless of how frustrated a teacher or administrator gets, he or she must remain a role model for students. It is never appropriate for an adult to address misbehaviors publicly in ways that might embarrass a student. It also is never appropriate for a teacher to use sarcasm or name-calling when it comes to reprimanding a student. I guess it would have helped if they had informed of who the special education kids were, and of the code of discipline used by the school. I wish the administration informed me I could call a dean to have a student removed for level 2 behavior. The second time the student refused to move, I could have called in a dean,

IMPACT OF POVERTY ON LEARNING

The "The Impact of Poverty on Teaching and Learning" by Partners in Learning from Miami University said the following:

"Poverty can impede children's ability to learn . . . children raise in poverty are more likely to display a) acting out behaviors, b) impatience and impulsivity, c) gaps in politeness and social graces, and d) inappropriate emotional responses . . . The most common risk factors of children raised in poverty are: a) emotional and social challenges, b) acute and chronic stress, (P.T.S.D.), c) Cognitive Delays and d) Health Issues."

STUDENT DISSENT OVER AN EDUCATOR

Professor Goodboy of Bloomberg University's communication studies said when it comes to student complaints of a class or teacher, it is important to understand the kinds of dissent that are out there. Not all student dissent is about disrupting the learning process. <u>Rhetorical dissent</u> is communicated by frustrated students trying to meet their classroom needs. However, there is <u>vengeful dissent,</u> which is purely an effort from the students stemming from anger or frustration at an instructor.

A SUCCESSFUL TEACHER IN AN URBAN SETTING

As educators, reflection is a key to becoming a better educator and knowing your strengths and growth areas.

1. Every weakness can be turned into a strength.
2. Knowing your growth areas can make you more successful.
3. Don't be too hard on yourself; spending time wondering why you are not perfect is a wasted of time and energy.

A Princeton paper about successful teachers in urban settings do the following:

1) Continually need to cope, adjust, and change.
2) Believe all children can learn, and environment is not an excuse to lower expectations.
3) Maintaining high expectations for urban poor kids is critical.

Muhammad Ali, one of my all-time favorite human beings, said, "I hated every minute of training, but I said to myself, you cannot quit. Suffer now and live the rest of your life like a champion." Since I had tried to maintain high expectations and pushed my students to do their best, there had been some pushback. I believe some of the complaints have come out of my high expectations for all my students.

SOME STUDENT COMPLAINTS IN LATE JANUARY 2016

In the cases late January (six weeks ago) brought up against me by Gabby, Arisha Wheeler, and Rasha, I am sure most of them would say they have grown to like me as a teacher. In the case brought up by Kiara, it turned out she misheard what I had to say.

As I stated in my meeting with AP Miller and Principal Harvey in late January or early February, I said, "I have never taught sixth-graders before. I have learned my lesson to not joke around with them because many of them do not understand the concept of irony." I agreed, I followed your advice, and I had complied.

In addition to not joking with the kids anymore, finding out who my kids with IEP's (special ed) had helped to cut down on conflict and, moreover, getting the training with Mr. Lewis amd Dean Harris on school culture, merits, and demerits and on how to handle level 2 offenses had made the job more manageable.

Last Thursday, April 7, I was asked to cover Ms. Primus's class for the day. The next day, Tiaja said to me, "Mr. Geist, I cannot believe I am about to say this, but I missed you yesterday." Gabby, in her February 5 apology letter to me, stated "You are the best teacher because you make social studies fun . . . You are really nice and funny . . I want you stay the whole year at our school."

<u>Re: The alleged incident with Jesse W.. He is one of my best students, a scholar, and a gentleman; and if all my students were like him, teaching would be very easy. What is alleged to have been said I never said to Jesse W.</u>

COMPLIANCE AND GROWTH OF MR. GEIST AT MPCS

All I ask is you speak to Coach Laurence to Mr. Lewis and to Mr. Harris and ask them if they have seen me grow in pedagogically in blended learning and in employing the tools we have to make my class a place of joy and hope and civility as a place of learning.

SCHOOL LEADERSHIP

Steven Covey on <u>healthy leadership</u> said, "When you show empathy towards others, their defensive energy goes down, and positive energy replaces it. That's when you can get more creative in solving problems." "When you really listen to another person from their point of view, and reflect back to them that understanding, it's like giving them emotional oxygen."

Covey also said, "The <u>proactive approach</u> to a mistake is to acknowledge it instantly, correct and learn from it."

Mr. Covey also said, "Pay attention to those <u>employees who respectfully ask why</u>. They are demonstrating an interest in their jobs and exhibiting a curiosity that could eventually lead to leadership ability."

When you hired me in December of last year, I told you I had never taught sixth-grade, or blended learning, but as long as you coached me and gave me guidance, I would do everything I could do make the leadership and the school a more successful institution.

While it had been rough, and as the kids tested Ms. Little when she first started, it had taken two months, but I had won over most of them, learned about the Merit Culture, and had progressed in using the Dashboard-Spark Method of gaining standards.

Please don't give up on me. Please believe in me as I believe in our kids and teaching model.

Try to see all the positive and good I have accomplished and how far I have come since January 12. I am grateful for the opportunity you have given me. You still have my 100 percent commitment to growing in the MPCS way.

Thanks for listening.
Jim Geist
Social Studies (Room 208)

END-OF-THE-YEAR REFLECTION OF MY EXPERIENCE AT MPCS (REQUESTED BY MPCS LEADERSHIP ON JUNE 21, 2016): What I wrote to Principal Harvey was even though he plays the role of of the peppy and happy leader, always clapping his hands, and laughing all the time, and pushing for teachers to be "high energy" all the time. the truth is, charter schools are about making profit. This means in the end, students have more power than the teachers, thus bosses turn a blind eye to students playing video games and listening to music on their lap top computers, because it is all about M.O.N.E.Y.

All the students at Merit Prep had laptops, and many of them were playing computer games, watching videos, or listening to music for most of the period. I put pressure on the kids to learn and often called parents when they did so. What happened was students began sending e-mails to the principal or going to his office complaining they did not like the new teacher Mr. Geist.

In my end-of-the-year evaluation, my teaching coach said, "Mr. Geist, you were a professional, you know your content, you implemented the majority of suggestions I made." And then the principal said, "Yeah, but many of the students complained about you. We are going to have to let you go."

I asked the principal if he was responsible for helping create a chaotic room experience by not informing me of the merit-demerit and deaning system my first six weeks at work. Harvey said no. I asked if the administration helped create a chaotic room experience by not informing me of who the "special education" students were in my three classes. Harvey said no. I had three 90 minute classes in a row, with not breaks. Principal Ron Harvey's response was "You are an experienced teacher, you should have handled it better."

BEHAVIOR AND IEPs: The principal who taught special education just could not agree that special educationstudents sometimes have behaviorial problems in class. When I asked him, "Do special education students ever have behaviorial issues?" and he responded no. How can you reason with a person like that? No wonder he was always smiling and clapping his hands, he no longer had to be in the classroom dealing with all the behavioral issues. The day I witnessed Principal walking up to my students in the hallway waiting to get into class, he walked up and yelled "Shut-up!" loudly thre to four times to three or four individual students.

In the e-mail I sent him asking if that was a professional way to address my students in the hallway, I never received a response from him.

TALK OF RACISM IN CLASS: 1) I had several students call me Cracker or Mr. Cracker. Almost every day, I would have at least one student say to me, "Oh, that is a racist statement!" 2) When I used the bathroom using a urinal, someone took and animal cracker and whipped it and hit me in the head. 3) In January when I first started teaching, and challenged the students to do classwork instead of playing video games or listening to music on their head phones, they would run to the principal or e-mail the principal, saying they did not like the new teacher Mr. Geist. 4) One girl named Aliah said to me, "I know why you don't like me. It is because I am not light enough." I said, "Why would you say that?" She answered, "Because a student said you called your students your 'black students.'" When I asked for the student's name, she would not tell me. In an atmosphere like this, I never really had a chance as a white male teacher, even as a former pastor, teacher in NYC for thirteen years, and activist against modern-day slavery.

RON HARVEY - BLACK MAFIA, MUSLIM MAFIA OR MUSLIM MOB: In _Black Brothers Inc._ written by Sean Patrick Griffen, it chronicles the Philadelphia-based African American orgranized crime syndicate. The organization was involved in drug trafficking, burglary, armed robbery, extortion, racketeering, number running, illegal gambling, and prostitution. It was formed in 1968 by former Black Panther Samuel Christian, who adopted the name Suleiman Bey under the Nation of Isalm. The most famous crime is called the Hanafi Murders in 1973.

HANAFI MURDERS AT KAREEM ABUL JABBERS HOME: Hamaas Abdul Khaalis of the Hanafi Muslims wrote a letter saying Eligh Muhammad of Nation of Islam was a false prophet and certain members of the NOI were gangsters. On January 18, 1973, several members of the Black Mafia, including Ron Harvey, went to Jabbar's home in Washington

DC and killed seven Hanafi members, two adults and five children. The adults and one child were shot, the other four children were drowned. Harvey, one of the founders of the Black Mafia, was convicted of murder with several others and died in federal prison in 1977. When I asked Principal Harvey is lives in Philadelphia if he relation to Black Mafia Ron Harvey, he said, "No, but I have read *Black Brothers Inc.*"

CHARTERS VS. PUBLIC SCHOOLS: Back in the mid-2000s was a study that showed only 23 percent of charters were better than public schools, meaning 77 percent of charters are worse than public schools. The goal of charter schools had been about busting teacher unions in our country, and it was working unfortunately until parents began to wake up and see the charter school emperor had no clothes on.

GRADING RUBRIC AT MCPS: The grading rubric at Merit Prep Charter School in Newark was A = 75–100, B = 60–74, C = 45–59, D = 30–44, F = 29 and below. In other words, these grade are automatically padded with extra points to help show that charter schools are have better grades than public schools. They also claim having longer days help improve grades, but what you may not know is they have the same amount of time in class as those in public school, and the extra forty-five minutes of schooling is used for club time, which is not dedicated to studies. If there was no club time, the charter school day would be the same amount of time as a public school.

LETTER TO SEN. CORY BOOKER - FORMER MAYOR OF NEWARK

Dear Senator Booker, 8-25-16

> *I was a pastor in NYC for five years, grew up in a UAW and 1199 union home, and was a UFT member for thirteen years and worked two years in Newark.*

Thank you for your work on prison reform in our country, and I hope you work on making medical marijuana legal and recreational to cut down on the prison population and as a way to raise tax money.

CHARTER SCHOOLS:

In the Atlantic *magazine, it is reported you said as Newark mayor you wanted to make Newark the charter capital of the world.*

I worked at **Newark Leadership Academy** *on 301 West Kinney St., and THERE WAS NO DISCIPLINE CONSEQUENCES. Students knew they would get a meeting with a counselor with no real consequences. I ended up getting assaulted there. The motto of Principal Gabe and AP Gonzalez was "Don't call us unless there is a knife, gun, or blood on the floor."*

The following year, I worked at **Merit Prep Charter** *across the city hall at 909 Broadway. The deans were excellent, but like the other school, the students have more power than the teachers. Every student has a laptop, and many were playing video games and listening to music during most of my class. I held the kids accountable to do their work, so they just sent messages to the principal they did not like me as a teacher. My contract was not renewed.*

At my end-of-the-year review. my teaching coach said, "Mr. Geist, you are a professional, you know your content, and you implemented my suggestions." Principal Ron Harvey said, "Yeaaaaaa, but the kids did not like you. We have to let you go."

My experience with charters is they are not better than the NYC public schools I worked for, and in fact, they were experiments in keeping kids busy while using grade rubrics that are a joke. At Merit Prep, a 75 was an A, and anything above a 30 was passing. This is helping prepare kids for college?

CHARTERS ARE ABOUT UNION BUSTING:

I read a study in 2001 that said only 23 percent of charters do better than public schools.
Other studies show the best schools in the country have unions.

Question: Is you position on charters still the same?

Question 2: Whatever happened to the money given to Newark by the famous skateboarding guy to build a new park in Newark that was never built?

Sincerely,
Jim Geist
Hewitt NJ
Former president of the Dem. Club in West Milford, New Jersey (two years)

I never received a response from the Senator, or the Mayor of Newark. I even sent a second letter to both, and they still did not respond to the second letter They must get campaign money from the charter school lobby to be so blind to ineffective charter schools.

PTSD AMONG URBAN TEACHERS: According to Stop Iraq and Afgan Vet Suicides, a veteran who has returned home commits suicide every 80 minutes or 22 per day. Multiply that by 365 days comes to 8,030 suicides per year.It is an anxiety disorder that is shown in the movie *Sniper* and happens when your life is threatened or injury is threatened on a frequent basis. Many suffer flashbacks, go numb, are hypervigilant, and have trouble sleeping. What many Americans may not know is that twice as many children living in violent urban neighborhoods have twice the rate as troops returning home as many as one-third.

The Centers for Disease Control and Prevention factsheet lists a range of symptoms associated with PTSD from panic attacks, depresson, suicidal thoughts and feelings, drug abuse, feelings of being isolated, to not able to complete daily tasks. According to clinical social worker Stephen Rosenbaum speaking about teachers in Chicago, "Depression, anxiety disorders and PTSD are reaching epidemic proportions among teachers . . . and we need to do a better job supporting these students and teachers."

2015: DEMOCRATIC SOCIALIST BERNIE SANDERS RUN FOR PRESIDENT:

I am a Bernie man! I feel the Bern! Vermont senator and Democratic Socialist Bernie Sanders ran for president carrying the message of the 99 Percent Movement. Unfortunately, he lost in the Democratic primaries to Hillary Clinton, but he had succeeded in getting the Democrats to accept 95 percent of the 99 percent's platform. Hillary Clinton won 2,842 delegates to Bernie's 1,865 delegates. She won 34 states to his 23. She won the popular vote 16,912,000 to Bernie's 13,205,000 votes. Before the Democratic Convention was over in Philadelphia in August of 2016, Bernie told his supporters to support Hillary and to vote for her.

THE 2016 REPUBLICAN CONVENTION: Many prominent Republicans did not show up, including the Bush Family—Jeb, W & H, Bob Dole, Mitt Romney, John Kasich, Lindsey Graham, and eighteen other senators. Wife Melania Trump's speech turned out to be plagiarized from a Michelle Obama's speech. When Sen. Ted Cruz spoke, he told the delegates to vote their conscience. One anti-Trump delegate said, "40 are pro-Trump, 30% are relunctant adopters and 30% want nothing to do with him." There were chants of "Lock her (Hillary) up" frequently during the convention. Many times the hall looked only one-half full. The *Daily Beast* said, "Donald Trump is arguably the worst presidential candidate in recent history . . . He hates babies, is racist, mocks the disabled and parents of fallen veterans. And yet here we are" (8-4-16).

THE DEMOCRATIC CONVENTION: Michelle Obama gave an incredible speech. Bernie Sanders was able to get most of his delegates to support Hillary Clinton and bowed out in a class act. Khizr Khan and his wife had lost a son in the War in Afghanistan, and Mr. Khan said, "Mr. Trump, I don't you have ever sacrificed a thing or anybody. I doubt you have read the U.S. Constitution. If you would like to, you may have my copy." This is the highlight of the 2016 convention for the Democrats. The Dems actually did a better job of looking like the Party of Patriots and the military versus the milk-toast GOP convention.

TRUMP - WAGES ARE TOO HIGH!: There were fifty senior U.S. Republican national security official who have said Donald Trump would be the most reckless president in American history. Some of the names were Michael Hayden, former director of the CIA; John Negroponte, former director for national intelligence; and Tom Ridge and Michael Chertoff, former Homeland Security secretaries (August 8, 2016). On July 20, the polls showed Clinton at 43–42 over Trump. On August 10, she was up 47.9 to Trump's 40.2. I hope Trump does not win. The Democratic Party would have done better with Bernie Sanders because he has intregity and less baggage and flip-flopping than Hillary Clinton. If he wins, you can bet C.E.O. wages won's go down. In fact, C.E.O. wages go up as worker wages decrease.

PEOPLE OF THE LIE: In this book by M. Scott Peck, he said those who are evil have the following two characteristics: they do not feel shame about lying, and they can never admit you are wrong. Based on psychiatrist Peck's diagnosis, Donald Trump is evil. When Trump said in one of the earliest Republican debates, "Wages are too high," was when I knew he was a terrible choice for the poor and working class in the United States.

UNLUCKY WITH CELL PHONES: Helen loved her Galaxy 6 Samsung Notebook smartphone. It was not a cell phone; it was a small computer in your hand. This was her connection to her family in the Philippines and the world. I also owned a notebook phone for three months. In that time, it was stolen at my Newark School, I got it back, and sold it on eBay, only to get scammed by a Chinese person. The person used a fake Paypal account, and I sent the phone to San Francisco to get scammed out of $550. I called Verizon to cancel my cell phone number but kept Helen on. After six months, Helen pointed out Verizon has been charging us for two numbers instead of one. I called, but I was told they can only refund me for for months; $120 of the $240 they had stolen from me. I saw my attorney to update my will and told him what happened. He told me, "Call them. Tell them you are taking them to small claims court in Paterson, and it will cost Verizon at least $3,000 for their attorney, or they could just refund your $240." I listened, and it worked.

6-1-16 - VERIZON STRIKE: On June 1, the CWA and IBEW technicians who had been on strike for forty-five days, returned to work with a new contract. On my way to work in Newark, I honked and flashed my headlights for the striking workers. I even gave a small donation for their strike fund while I worked at a charter school with no union representation and needed one badly. Verizon is making 1.8 billion in profits a month and want the workers to pay 200 million more for health care. The battle was won on the picket lines from Massachusetts to Virgina with daily pickets outside Verizon Wireless stores and hounded scabs and company executives wherever they went. The unions won a 10.5 percent increase over four years. One worker said, "I will never forget what this company put my family through. It was only like this because of their greed!

2016 SUMMER OLYMPICS (GOLD): Simone Biles, Gabby Douglas, Laurie Hernandez, Madison Kocian, Aly Raisman (all-around gymnastics), Michael Phelps and Katie Ladecky (swimming) U.S. men and women (swimming relay), Venus Williams and Rajeev Ram (doubles tennis), Kristan Armstrong (cycling), Womens (rowing), Kayla Harrison (judo), Michelle Carter (shot put).

HISTORY SETS THE CONTEXT FOR THE PRESENT MOMENT: In *The Tempest*, Shakespeare wrote, "The past is prologue." Vice Pres. Joe Biden quoted this to Sarah Palin in the vice presidential debates on October 2, 2008. It means that history sets the context for the present moment.

Thanks for your time reading my book: I started in the middle of April of 2016 and finished writing in mid-October. I sent it off to the publisher to be edited, and I am proud of myself of setting this goal and completing my book. I hope you have been able to identify with some of my stories and that some of it had made you chuckle. I close with some ideas that have helped me live a life of reasonable happiness since my recovery work started at age forty-two. The writer must earn the right to be read and to keep the interest of the reader. I hope I have done this.

CLOSING THOUGHTS: The biggest pain I had felt as a codependent had been the pain of being me. Codpendents Anonymous had helped me unmask and heal the pain. The journey had not been easy but had been worth it (Codependent's Guide to the 12 Steps, Melody Beattie, p. 197). I approached recovery with love, acceptance, compassion. and care for myself and others. I remembered that love and codependence cannot exist together.

I was always good at loving everyone else but not good at loving me. Al-Anon had taught me about detachment. Letting go with another person's behavior helped me live a happier and manageable life. Detachment is neither cruel nor unkind; it does not imply judgment of a person or situation that we are detatchng. I mean, we separate ourselves from the adverse affects of another's addiction.

I am whole in or out of a relationship.

As my acceptance of life increases, so does my serenity.

I am loving, loved, and lovable.

Progress, not perfection.

As I continue to live out a life in the principles of the twelve steps, connected to God and to myself (true self), I know I am engaged in a great adventure of discovering true freedom of the human spirit. I continue to receive blessing I would not previously known what to ask for. Step 12 of the Saint Augustine Fellowship Big Book closes by saying, "Life is open ended and wonderful. New chapters of well-being await us" (103).

INDEX

N

O

P

T

Y